Professional Apache Tomcat

Amit Bakore
Debashish Bhattacharjee
Sandip Bhattacharjee
Vivek Chopra
Chad Fowler
Ben Galbraith
Romin Irani
Sing Li
Chanoch Wiggers

Wrox Press Ltd. ®

Professional Apache Tomcat

Reprinted December, 2002

Published by Wrox Press Ltd,
Arden House, 1102 Warwick Road, Acocks Green,
Birmingham, B27 6BH, UK
Printed in the United States
ISBN 1-86100-773-6

Trademark Acknowledgements

Credits

Authors
Amit Bakore
Debashish Bhattacharjee
Sandip Bhattacharjee
Vivek Chopra
Chad Fowler
Ben Galbraith
Romin Irani
Sing Li
Chanoch Wiggers

Additional Material
Matthew Moodie
Peter Wainwright

Technical Reviewers
Subrahmanyam Allamaraja
Kapil Apshankar
Steve Baker
Yogesh Bhandarkar
Vivek Chopra
Kris Dahl
Richard Huss
Romin Irani
Meeraj Kunnumpurath
Massimo Nardone
Neil Matthew
Richard Stones
Sameer Tyagi
Keith Wannamaker

Commissioning Editors
Paul Cooper
Ranjeet Wadhwani

Technical Editors
Kedar Kamat
Unnati Kulkarni
Matthew Moodie
Nilesh Parmer

Author Agents
Shivanand Nadkarni
Safiulla Shakir

Indexers
Bill Johncocks

Proof Reader
Agnes Wiggers

Production Coordinators
Rachel Taylor
Pip Wonson

Illustrations
Santosh Haware
Manjiri Karande

Cover
Dawn Chellingworth

About the Authors

Amit Bakore

Amit is a Sun Certified Java Programmer with a couple of other certifications. Currently based in Pune (India), he works as a System Analyst for Sansui Software. He has been working mainly on J2EE and XML on Linux. Before landing in the world of software, he graduated from Pune University, with Electronics as a major, with first class.

I humbly dedicate this work to 'HIM' and his parents, Dr.Ramkrishna & Sau. Vaijayanti. I sincerely thank all my friends, colleagues, and wellwishers for their extensive support and guidance.

Debashish Bhattacharjee

Debashish Bhattacharjee is a Principal Consultant with the Management Consulting Services unit of PriceWaterhouseCoopers. He has 10 years of experience implementing projects for Fortune 500 clients in the United States and Canada. His areas of expertise are systems integration and project management. He has served as chief architect and led technical teams tasked with the implementation of e-commerce applications, portal implementations, web infrastructure, ERP, and client-server applications.

In his role as consultant, Debashish is often responsible for advising clients on best practices and the adoption of technology. He is the published author of several industry articles.

Sandip Bhattacharjee

Sandip is an open source enthusiast and an active participant in various open source communities in India, especially his local LUG – Indian Linux Users Group, Delhi (ILUGD), http://www.linux-delhi.org/. He has been programming right from his school days in 1991, and carries an engineering degree in Textile technology and an MBA in marketing.

He has been professionally involved in open source technologies for the past three years. He is currently a freelance programmer and advises businesses on ways to use the open source revolution to their advantage.

Vivek Chopra

Vivek has eight years of experience in software design and development, the last two years of which have been in web services and various XML technologies. He is the co-author of *Professional ebXML Foundations* (*ISBN 186100-590-3*) and *Professional XML Web Services* (*ISBN 1-86100-509-1*) both from Wrox Press. He is also a committer for UDDI4J, an open source Java API for UDDI. His other areas of experience and interest include compilers, middleware, clustering, GNU/Linux, and mobile computing. He is currently consulting in the domain area of web services.

Vivek holds a Bachelor's degree in Electronics and a Master's in Computer Science, both from Pune University, India. He lives and works in the beautiful San Francisco Bay Area, and can be reached at vivek@soaprpc.com.

Chad Fowler

Chad Fowler is CTO of GE Appliances Bangalore, India office. For the past four years, he has been an active advocate of open source Java technologies in the enterprise, revolving around the Enhydra suite of software. Driven into software development by a less-than-healthy addiction to the video game Doom, he dropped his professional music career and never looked back. His current interests focus on the Ruby programming language, learning the Hindi (spoken/written – not programming) language, and Agile Software Development methodologies.

Ben Galbraith

Before graduating from High School, Ben Galbraith was hired by a major Silicon Valley computer manufacturer to develop Windows-based client-server applications with international deployments and hundreds of users. In 1995, he began developing for the Web and fell in love with Unix, `vi`, and Perl. After building countless web applications with Perl, Ben discovered server-side Java in 1999 and his relationship with Perl has since become somewhat estranged.

He is presently a consultant in Provo, Utah. He regularly lectures, evangelizes, and gives classes on Java technology. Ben has no college degree but if he had the time he would study both ancient and modern history.

Romin Irani

Romin Irani is a Senior Software Engineer with InSync Information Systems, Inc in Fremont, California. He graduated with a Bachelors degree in Computer Engineering from University of Bombay, India. He has around seven years of experience, starting out in the Microsoft world but now fully immersed into Java technologies. He welcomes your comments at romin@rocketmail.com.

I am most thankful to my wife Devayani, whose cooperation and love made this possible. And of course due credits to my parents, Khushru and Gulrukh for all that they have taught me in life.

Sing Li

First bitten by the computer bug in 1978, Sing has grown up with the microprocessor and the Internet revolution. His first PC was a $99 do-it-yourself COSMIC ELF computer with 256 bytes of memory and a 1 bit LED display. For two decades, Sing has been an active author, consultant, instructor, entrepreneur, and speaker. His wide-ranging experience spans distributed architectures, web services, multi-tiered server systems, computer telephony, universal messaging, and embedded systems.

Sing has been credited with writing the very first article on the Internet Global Phone, delivering voice over IP long before it became a common reality. Sing has participated in several Wrox projects in the past, has been working with (and writing about) Java, Jini, and JXTA since their very first available releases, and is an active evangelist for the unlimited potential of P2P technology.

Chanoch Wiggers

Chanoch is a Java Programmer working with JSP and Servlets who until recently worked at Wrox Press as a Technical Architect (writing this stuff is even more fun than writing about this stuff). Chanoch would like to thank the reviewers and the guys at Wrox Press, especially Shivanand Nadkarni.

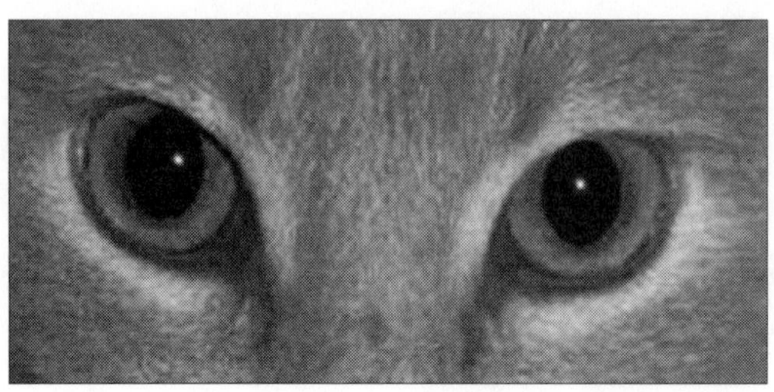

Table of Contents

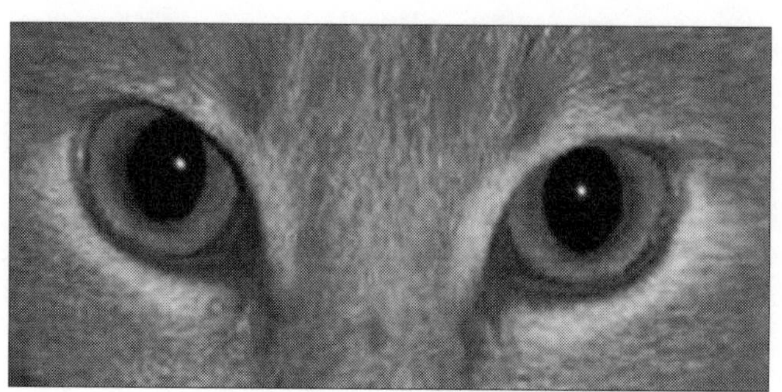

1

Apache and Jakarta Tomcat

If you've written any Java servlets or JavaServer Pages (JSPs), chances are that you've downloaded Tomcat. That's because Tomcat is a free, feature-complete servlet container that servlet and JSP developers can use to test their code. Tomcat is also Sun's reference implementation of a servlet container, which means that Tomcat's first goal is to be 100% complaint with the versions of the Servlet and JSP specification that it supports.

However, Tomcat is more than just a test server: many individuals and corporations are using Tomcat in production environments because it has proven to be quite stable. Indeed, Tomcat is considered by many to be a worthy addition to the excellent Apache suite of products.

Despite Tomcat's popularity, it suffers from a common shortcoming among open source projects: lack of complete documentation. There is some documentation distributed with Tomcat (mirrored at http://jakarta.apache.org/tomcat/tomcat-4.0-doc/) and there's even an open source effort to write a Tomcat book (http://tomcatbook.sourceforge.net/). Even with these resources, however, there is much room for additional material.

We've created this book to fill in some of the documentation holes and use the combined experience of the authors to help Java developers and system administrators make the most of the Tomcat product. Whether you're looking to learn enough to just get started developing servlets or trying to understand the more arcane aspects of Tomcat configuration, you should find what you're looking for within these pages.

The first two chapters are designed to provide newcomers with some basic background information that will become prerequisite learning for future chapters. If you're a system administrator with no previous Java experience, you are advised to read them; likewise if you're a Java developer who is new to Tomcat. Finally, if you're well informed about Tomcat and Java, you'll probably want to jump straight ahead to Chapter 3, although skimming this chapter and its successor is likely to yield some additions to your present understanding.

We will cover the following points in this chapter:

- The origins of the Tomcat server
- The terms of Tomcat's license and how it compares to other open source licenses
- How Tomcat fits into the Java big picture
- How Tomcat can be integrated with Apache and other web servers

Humble Beginnings: The Apache Project

One of the earliest web servers was developed by Rob McCool at the National Center for Supercomputer Applications, University of Illinois, Urbana-Champaign, referred to colloquially as the NCSA project, or NCSA for short. In 1995, the NCSA server was quite popular, but its future was uncertain as Rob left NCSA in 1994. A group of developers got together and compiled all the NCSA bug fixes and enhancements they had found and patched them into the NCSA code base. The developers released this new version in April 1995, and called it Apache, which was a sort of acronym for "A PAtCHy Web Server".

Apache was readily accepted by the web-serving community from its earliest days, and less than a year after its release it unseated NCSA to become the most used web server in the world (measured by the total number of servers running Apache), a distinction that it has held ever since (according to Apache's web site). Incidentally, during the same period that Apache's use spread, NCSA's popularity plummeted and by 1999 was officially discontinued by its maintainers.

> *For more information on the history of Apache and its developers, see* *http://httpd.apache.org/ABOUT_APACHE.html.*

Today the Apache web server is available on pretty much any major operating system – as of this writing, downloads are available for 29 different operating systems. Apache can be found running on the some of the largest server farms in the world as well as on some of the smallest devices (including the Linux-based Sharp Zaurus hand-held). In Unix data centers, Apache is as ubiquitous as air conditioning and UPS systems.

While Apache was originally a somewhat mangy collection of miscellaneous patches, today's versions are state-of-the-art, incorporating rock-solid stability with bleeding edge features. The only real competitor to Apache in terms of market share and feature set is Microsoft's Internet Information Services (IIS), which is bundled free with certain versions of the Windows operating system. At the time of writing, Apache's market share was estimated at around 56%, with IIS at a distant 32% (statistics courtesy of http://www.netcraft.com/survey/, June 2002).

It is also worth nothing that Apache has a reputation of being much more secure than Microsoft IIS. When new vulnerabilities are discovered in either server, the Apache developers fix Apache far faster than Microsoft fixes IIS.

The Apache Software Foundation

In 1999, the same folks who wrote the Apache server formed the Apache Software Foundation (ASF). The ASF is a non-profit organization created to facilitate the development of open source software projects. According to their web site, the ASF accomplishes this goal by:

- Providing a **foundation** for open, collaborative software development projects by supplying hardware, communication, and business infrastructure
- Creating an independent legal entity to which companies and individuals can **donate resources** and be assured that those resources will be used for the public benefit
- Providing a means for individual volunteers to be sheltered from **legal suits** directed at the Foundation's projects
- Protecting the Apache **brand**, as applied to its software products, from being abused by other organizations

In practice, the ASF does indeed sponsor a great many open source projects. While the best known of these projects is likely the aforementioned Apache web server, the ASF hosts many other well-respected and widely used projects.

Apache Projects

The following is a listing of the current Apache projects, all of which can be found at http://www.apache.org/:

Project Name	Description
HTTP (Web) Server	The famous Apache web server.
Apache Portable Runtime (APR)	A library of platform-independent C code that forms a portability layer for compiling applications on multiple platforms, such as Linux, Windows, BeOS, and OS/2.
Jakarta	Apache's Java-related efforts; described in detail later in this chapter.
Perl	Umbrella for Apache's well-known `mod_perl` project, as well as other Apache-specific Perl modules. `mod_perl` enables highly efficient integration with Apache and Perl programs.
PHP	PHP is a *very* popular scripting language for dynamically creating HTML or performing business logic in HTML pages. Like `mod_perl`, PHP can be efficiently integrated with Apache.
TCL	Umbrella for Apache's efforts to tightly integrate TCL with the Apache web server (like `mod_perl`).
XML	Umbrella for Apache's cross-platform XML projects, such as the Xerces and Crimson XML parsers and the AXIS SOAP engine.

The Jakarta Project

Of most relevance to this book is Apache's **Jakarta** project, of which the Tomcat server is a subproject. The Jakarta project is the umbrella under which the ASF sponsors the development of Java subprojects. At the time of writing, there is an impressive array of more than twenty of these. They are divided into three different categories: "Libraries, Tools, and APIs", "Frameworks and Engines", and "Server Applications". We will highlight two projects from the first category (Ant and Log4J), one from the framework category (Struts), and, of course, Tomcat.

Tomcat

The Jakarta Tomcat project has its origins in the earliest days of Java's servlet technology. Servlets plug into special web servers, called servlet containers (originally called servlet engines). Sun created the first servlet container, called the Java Web Server, which demonstrated the technology but wasn't terribly robust. Meanwhile, the ASF folks created the JServ product, which was a servlet engine that integrated with the Apache web server.

In 1999, Sun donated their servlet container code to the ASF, and the two projects were merged to create the Tomcat server. Today, Tomcat serves as Sun's official reference implementation (RI), which means that Tomcat's first priority is to be fully compliant with the Servlet and JSP specifications published by Sun. JSP pages are simply an alternative, HTML-like way to write servlets. We will discuss all this in more detail in the next chapter.

A reference implementation also has the side benefit of honing the specification. As developers seek to put in code that has been defined in the specifications, problems in implementation requirements and conflicts within the specifications are highlighted.

A reference implementation is in principal completely specification-compliant and therefore can be very valuable, especially for people who are using very advanced parts of the specification. The reference implementation is available at the same time as the public release of the specifications, which means that Tomcat is usually the first server out there that provides the enhanced specification features when a new specification version is completed.

The first version of Tomcat was the 3.x series, and it served as the reference implementation of the Servlet 2.2 and JSP 1.1 specifications. The Tomcat 3.x series was descended from the original code that Sun provided to the ASF in 1999.

In 2001, Tomcat 4.0 (codenamed Catalina) was released, and was a complete redesign of the Tomcat architecture and had a new code base. The Tomcat 4.x series, which is current as of this writing, is the reference implementation of the Servlet 2.3 and JSP 1.2 specifications.

At the time of writing, the latest stable version is 4.0.4. Hints of Tomcat 5.0 are on the horizon, as the new Servlet 2.4 and JSP 2.0 specifications are nearing release and Tomcat 5.0 will need to implement those specifications.

Ant

Ant is a tool to automate building and deploying applications that range from the very simple to the extremely complex. If you're familiar with Unix, you might think this sounds like the ubiquitous `make` tool. In fact, Ant was created by a group of people who wanted to create a replacement for `make`. You can read about their comments on the subject at http://jakarta.apache.org/ant/.

Ant can be used for building applications in any language, and it can be used on any platform that has a Java 1.1 virtual machine or better. Ant's versatility can also be extended with Java plug-ins. Ant won awards from both the Software Development and Java World magazines in 2002, and it is extremely popular amongst developers.

Log4J

Developers generally use logging for two purposes: debugging during development and monitoring when the system is in production. When developing systems, developers usually prefer logging to be as verbose as possible, and aren't concerned with its impact on the system's overall performance. However, when a system is deployed into production, developers want logging to impact performance as little as possible.

Log4J represents more than five years of work towards creating the ideal logging solution for Java programs, combining the desire for generation of rich data at development time with the need for minimal performance degradation in production environments. If your current logging technique is executing something like `System.out.println()`, you owe it to yourself to investigate this project and see what else is possible with logging.

Log4J Versus JDK 1.4 Logging

Java 1.4 introduced a logging mechanism to Java as part of the standard J2SE platform. Log4J has been in its present form since late 1999, and thus predates the JDK 1.4 logging mechanism by a little more than 2 years (JDK 1.4 went final in early 2002). When it was learned that Java 1.4 would incorporate logging, the Log4J group lobbied to have its product incorporated into Java as the official logging mechanism for the platform. However, that did not happen.

With the release of Java 1.4, Log4J didn't disappear, and doesn't intend to. Log4J provides two advantages over the Java 1.4 logging mechanism: it has more features and it can be used with Java 1.1 or later.

Struts

The current architectural best practice for web applications is the Model View Controller (MVC) design pattern. Under this model, the application is divided into three logical layers (also called tiers): the View, which represents the user interface; the Model, which represents the business logic specific to the application including any persistent data store (for example, a database); and the Controller, which coordinates how the View and the Model interact, and takes care of any other general application behavior (for example, application lifecycle issues). We'll see more on the MVC architecture in the next chapter.

Servlets and JavaServer Pages are the standard Java way to create web applications. They provide an efficient interface to the Web's HTTP protocol. However, developers who wish to create an MVC architecture with servlets and JSP must still do quite a bit of work.

Many third-party frameworks have been created which attempt to relieve developers from the burden of implementing their own MVC architecture, freeing them to instead focus on solving the unique business problems of their organization. Struts is one of these frameworks. Struts has gained an excellent reputation in the development community as being well-designed and very flexible.

Other Jakarta Subprojects

There are many other Jakarta subprojects, including: Lucene, a full-featured search engine; Jetspeed, a portal server; and James, a mail server. See these and others at http://jakarta.apache.org/.

Distributing Tomcat

Tomcat is open source software, and as such is free and freely distributable. However, if you have much experience in dealing with open source software, you're probably aware that the terms of distribution can vary from project to project.

Most open source software is released with an accompanying license that states what may and may not be done to the software. There are at least forty different open source licenses out there, each of which has slightly different terms.

Providing a primer on all of the various open source licenses is beyond the scope of this chapter, but the license governing Tomcat will be discussed here and compared with a few of the more popular open source licenses.

Tomcat is distributed under the Apache License, which can be read from the `$CATALINA_HOME/LICENSE` file. The key points of this license state that:

- The Apache License must be included with any redistributions of Tomcat's sourcecode or binaries
- Any documentation included with a redistribution must give a nod to the ASF
- Products derived from the Tomcat sourcecode can't use the terms "Tomcat", "The Jakarta Project", "Apache", or "Apache Software Foundation" to endorse or promote their software without prior written permission from the ASF
- Tomcat has no warranty of any kind

However, through omission, the license contains these additional implicit permissions:

- Tomcat can be used by any entity, commercial or non-commercial, for free without limitation
- Those who make modifications to Tomcat and distribute their modified version do not have to include the sourcecode of their modifications
- Those who make modifications to Tomcat do not have to donate their modifications back to the ASF

Thus, you're free to deploy Tomcat in your company in any way you see fit. It can be your production web server or your test servlet container used by your developers. You can also redistribute Tomcat with any commercial application that you may be selling, provided that you include the license and give credit to the ASF. You can even use the Tomcat sourcecode as the foundation for your own commercial product

Comparison with Other Licenses

Among the previously mentioned rather large group of other open source licenses, there are two licenses which are particularly popular at the present time: the GNU General Public License (GPL) and the GNU Lesser General Public License (LGPL). Let's take a look at how each of these licenses compare to the Apache License.

GPL

The GNU Project created and actively evangelizes the GPL. The GNU Project is somewhat similar to the ASF, with the exception that the GNU Project would like all of the non-free (that is, closed source or proprietary) software in the world to become free; the ASF has no (stated) desire to do this and simply wants to provide free software.

What Does It Mean to Be Free?

Free software can mean one of two entirely different things: software that doesn't cost anything, and software that can be freely copied, distributed, and modified by anyone (thus the sourcecode is included or available); such software can be distributed either for free or for a fee. A simpler way to explain the difference between these two types of free is "free as in free beer" and "free as in free speech". The GNU Project's goal is to create free software of the latter category. All uses of the phrase "free software" in the remainder of this section will use this definition.

The differences between the Apache License and the GPL thus mirror the distinct philosophies of the two organizations. Specifically, the GPL has these key differences from the Apache License:

- No non-free software may contain GPL-licensed products or use GPL-licensed sourcecode. If non-free software is found to contain GPL-licensed binaries or code, it must remove such elements or become free software itself.
- All modifications made to GPL-licensed products must be released as free software if the modifications are also publicly released.

These two differences have huge implications for commercial enterprises. If Tomcat were licensed under the GPL, any product that contained Tomcat would also have to be free software.

Furthermore, while the Apache License permits an organization to make modifications to Tomcat and sell it under a different name as a closed source product, the GPL would not allow any such act to occur; the new derived product would also have to be released as free software.

LGPL

The LGPL is similar to the GPL, with one major difference: non-free software may contain LGPL-licensed products. The LGPL license is intended primarily for software libraries that are themselves free software but whose authors want them to be available for use by companies who produce non-free software.

If Tomcat were licensed under the LGPL, it could be embedded in non-free software, but Tomcat could not itself be modified and released as a non-free software product.

For more information on the GPL and LGPL licenses, see http://www.gnu.org/.

Other Licenses

Understanding and comparing open source licenses can be a rather complex task. The explanations above are an attempt to simplify the issues. For more detailed information on these and other licenses, there are two specific resources that can help you:

- The Open Source Initiative (OSI) maintains a database of open source licenses. Visit them at http://www.opensource.org/.
- The GNU Project, mentioned above, has an extensive comparison of open source licenses with the GPL license. See it at http://www.gnu.org/licenses/license-list.html.

The Big Picture: J2EE

As a servlet container, Tomcat is a key component of a larger set of standards collectively referred to as the Java 2 Platform, Enterprise Edition (J2EE). J2EE defines a group of Java-based code libraries (called APIs in the Java world) that are suited to creating web applications for the enterprise (that is, a large company). To be sure, companies of any size can take advantage of the J2EE technologies, but J2EE is especially designed to solve the problems associated with the creation of large software systems. Java developers can download all of the J2EE APIs in a single ZIP archive, which comes complete with binaries and documentation.

Distributed Systems

We saw in the previous section that J2EE is designed with the creation of large software systems in mind. You, the reader, may ask, "What is so different about large software systems versus small systems?" The answer lies in the notion of **distributed systems**.

A distributed system is one in which the various components of the system are distributed across multiple different machines. For example, in a given web application, one server might handle receiving and responding to HTTP requests while another server handles all the business logic, and another server handles all the database I/O:

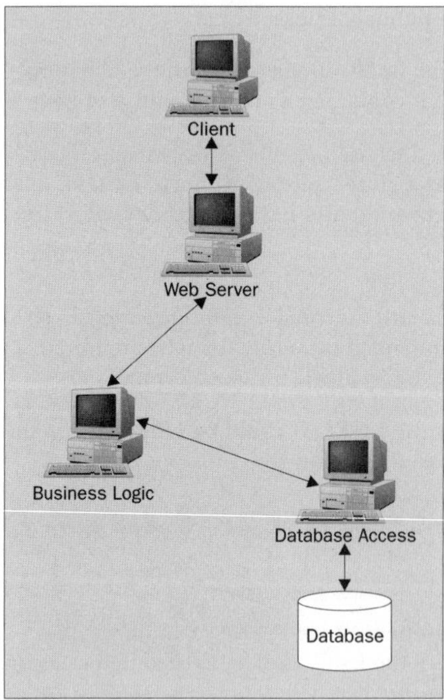

So why create a distributed system? Large web applications and enterprise systems can have enormous demands placed upon them. Frequently, these demands are larger than a single server can meet. While one may be tempted to simply upgrade the server, adding more processors and more memory to it, these upgrades can only stretch the server's capacity so far. Every server, no matter how expandable and efficient it may be, will run up against limitations.

In these situations, where a single server simply cannot meet the needs of a software system, a distributed system is ideal. Multiple servers can work together to meet demands that a single server could not.

But, why bother creating a distributed system? Why not just copy the same application and deploy it on multiple servers? Surely load balancing – splitting up the requests amongst the different servers – can then handle the load?

It turns out that by separating the different logical components of an application, system administrators are free to tune the various components of the distributed system according to their unique needs. For example, the servers that read and write to the database will require different optimizations than those servers which are communicating with web clients via HTTP over TCP.

The J2EE APIs

Creating the distributed systems that we've described in the preceding paragraphs is not an easy task. We mentioned a few paragraphs ago that J2EE is a collection of code libraries called APIs. The J2EE APIs are designed to work together to simplify the creation of robust and efficient distributed systems. Here is a list of some of the key J2EE technologies and a brief description of each:

J2EE API	Description
Enterprise JavaBeans (EJB)	EJB technology provides a simple mechanism for creating distributed business logic components. EJB authors follow a simple pattern to write business logic and the rest of the low-level details relating to lifecycle, distribution, persistence, and so on are handled automatically.
Java Message Service (JMS)	JMS provides asynchronous messaging capability to J2EE applications.
Java Naming and Directory Service (JNDI)	JNDI enables J2EE applications to communicate with registries and directories. A registry/directory is a centralized location for storing business information. JNDI supports the industry standard LDAP protocol and interfaces with many other popular registry standards. JNDI makes it possible to centralize the configuration of a distributed system.
Servlets	As explained earlier in this chapter, servlets work with special servers called servlet containers to process HTTP requests and send HTTP responses. Servlets often work directly with EJBs.
JavaServer Pages (JSP)	JSP technology is an alternative, HTML-like interface for creating servlets. At runtime, the servlet container converts a JSP into a servlet.

Table continued on following page

J2EE API	Description
Java Transaction API (JTA)	JTA enables a web application to gracefully handle failures in one or more of its components by establishing transactions. During a transaction, multiple events can occur, and if any one of them fails, the state of the application can be rolled back to how it was before the transaction began. This technology provides the robustness of relational database transactional technology across an entire distributed application.
CORBA	CORBA technology in Java enables J2EE web applications to communicate with distributed components written in other languages that support the language-independent CORBA standard.
JDBC	JDBC enables Java programs to communicate with relational databases.
Connector	The Connector API enables Java programs to create an abstraction layer for connecting with legacy systems that don't implement other J2EE-supported technologies.
JavaMail	JavaMail provides the ability to send and receive e-mail via the industry standard POP/SMTP/IMAP protocols.
Java XML Parser (JAXP)	JAXP gives J2EE applications the ability to speak XML.

Note that the J2EE APIs are not designed to help developers write their own server software. Rather, they are to designed to work with a special kind of server, called a J2EE **application server** (app server). J2EE app servers are available on many operating systems, including Windows, Linux, Solaris, and Mac OS X. To be considered an official J2EE app server, the app server vendor must show that the app server complies with the J2EE standards and then purchase a J2EE license. Such vendors are referred to as **J2EE licensees**.

Agree On Standards, Compete On Implementation

If developers follow the J2EE standards, they can use a compliant, licensed J2EE app server from any vendor and it is guaranteed to work with their application. This flexibility is intended to help companies avoid vendor lock-in problems, and thus they can enjoy the benefits of a competitive marketplace. The Java slogan along these lines is "Agree on standards, compete on implementation," meaning that the vendors all cooperate on establishing universal J2EE standards and then work hard to create the best app server that supports those standards.

Pick and Choose

However, not all developers want to create the kinds of distributed systems that the entire collection of J2EE APIs are designed to support. Fortunately, it is possible to pick and choose those APIs that are necessary for your projects. For example, if all you need to do is write a GUI LDAP client, the JNDI API is the only J2EE API you'll need to use.

If you want to create a dynamic web site but don't need the additional J2EE APIs, the Servlet and JSP APIs may be all you'll want. As was mentioned earlier in this chapter, a servlet plugs in to a special server called a servlet container (and JSP is an alternative way of writing a servlet). The J2EE app server contains a servlet container, but if all you want to is write servlets/JSP, then you don't need the full app server – you just need a servlet container.

Tomcat is just such a servlet container. As a servlet container, Tomcat is only required to implement the Servlet and JSP APIs, and thus is not considered a J2EE app server. However, as J2EE app servers must themselves contain a servlet container to support the servlet/JSP APIs, J2EE app servers can embed Tomcat into their code to provide support for the Servlet and JSP APIs. One example of just such an application server is the popular open source JBoss J2EE app server (http://www.jboss.org/).

> *For more information on J2EE and its various APIs, visit* http://java.sun.com/j2ee/.

Using Tomcat with the Apache Web Server

Tomcat's purpose is to provide standards-compliant support for servlets and JSP pages. The purpose of servlets and JSP pages is to generate web content such as HTML files or GIF files on demand using changing data. Web content that is generated on demand is said to be dynamic. On the other hand, web content that never changes and is served up as-is is called static. Web applications commonly include a great deal of static content, such as images or Cascading Style Sheets (CSS).

While Tomcat is capable of serving both dynamic and static content, it is not as fast or feature-rich as the Apache web server with regard to static content. While it would be possible for Tomcat to be extended to support the same features that Apache does for serving up static content, it would take a great deal of time; Apache has been under development for many years. Also, because Apache is written entirely in C and takes advantage of platform-specific features, it is unlikely that Tomcat, a 100% Java application, could ever perform well as Apache.

Recognizing that the advantages of Apache would complement the advantages of Tomcat, the earliest versions of Tomcat included a **connector** that enabled Tomcat and Apache to work together. In this arrangement, Apache receives all of the HTTP requests made to the web application. Apache then recognizes which requests are intended for servlets/JSP pages, and passes these requests to Tomcat. Tomcat fulfils the request and passes the response back to Apache, which then returns the response to the requestor.

The Apache connector was initially crucial to the Tomcat 3.x series, because its support for both static content and its implementation of the HTTP protocol were somewhat limited.

The Tomcat 4.x series, however, features a much nicer implementation of HTTP and better support for serving up static content, and should by itself be sufficient for people who aren't looking to max out performance but simply need HTTP standards compliance. However, as mentioned above, Apache will most likely always have superior performance and options when it comes to serving up static content and communicating with clients via HTTP, and, for this reason, anyone who is using Tomcat for high-traffic web applications may want to consider using Apache and Tomcat together.

Apache Connectors

For interfacing with Apache, Tomcat 4.x supports two different types of connectors: AJP and WARP; AJP and WARP refer to two different protocols that govern how the connector communicates with Apache. The Apache JServ Protocol (AJP) dates back to the Apache JServ product that we mentioned earlier in this chapter. The first connector to implement this protocol, called `mod_jserv`, was written for the initial JServ product and continued to function with the Tomcat 3.x series. The newest AJP-based connector is `mod_jk2`.

The WARP protocol was created for the Tomcat 4.x series, and `mod_webapp` is the name of the only connector that currently implements this protocol. The WARP protocol is intended to provide greater flexibility and greater performance than the AJP protocol.

Getting the Apache connectors to work properly can be tricky, and finding helpful documentation is even trickier. However, Chapters 11-13 will help to clarify this sometimes murky subject.

Tomcat and Other Web Servers

The AJP protocol introduced above can also be used to integrate Tomcat with two other web servers: Microsoft's Internet Information Services (IIS) and Netscape Enterprise Server (NES). This topic will be covered in detail in Chapter 14.

If you're not using either Apache, IIS, or NES then don't give up hope entirely. It is still very possible to integrate Tomcat with other web servers, even one that resides on the same machine. All one has to do is set up Tomcat to run on a port other than 80 – the default HTTP port. Note that, by default, Tomcat runs on port 8080. Thus, any normal web requests to a server will go to an HTTP server sitting on port 80, and any requests to port 8080 will go to Tomcat. You can then design your web application's HTML to request its static resources from the web server on port 80. For more information on this topic, see Chapter 5.

Summary

As we draw this chapter to a close, let's review some of the key points that have been covered:

- The Apache Software Foundation (ASF) is a non-profit organization created to provide the world with quality open source software.
- The ASF maintains a whole series of open source projects. The ASF's Java projects are collected under the umbrella of a parent project called Jakarta.
- Tomcat is one of the most popular subprojects in the Jakarta project.
- Tomcat can be freely used in any organization. It can be freely redistributed in any commercial project so long as its license is also included with the redistribution and proper recognition is given.
- J2EE is a series of technologies designed to make the creation of complex, distributed applications easier.
- Tomcat is a fully J2EE-compliant servlet container, and is the official Reference Implementation for the Java Servlet and JavaServer Pages technologies.
- While Tomcat can also function as a web server, it can also be integrated with other web servers.
- Tomcat has special support for integrating with the Apache, IIS, and NES servers.

This chapter has been an overview of Tomcat, but what do Tomcat-served web applications look like? What files comprise them? We've covered that a little bit in this chapter, but in the next chapter we'll go into this subject in detail.

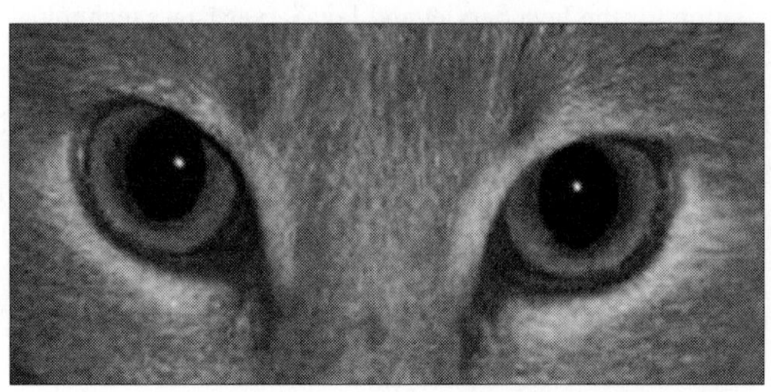

2

JSP and Servlets

In order to understand why Tomcat came about, we will have to delve into the history of JSP and servlets, Tomcat's reason for being. We will look into why there was a need for another type of server (when Apache was already doing such a good job as a web server) and look at the type of services that Tomcat provides for the programmer and the applications that run on it.

From its humble beginnings as a document exchange medium, the Internet has now become a much more complex beast that is the backbone of much of industry and social discourse. It quickly outgrew its beginnings as a document publishing forum when it was obvious that these documents were changing very quickly, and, to avoid it being filled with great amounts of stale information, a system was needed to keep the information up to date, and to isolate information whose usefulness is only over the short-term.

It was also realized that the Internet represented an excellent medium for communications: customers and companies, service providers and clients, and peer groups could all communicate over it. To facilitate this exchange of information and the provision of up-to-date data, additional systems were designed.

First Came CGI...

Well, maybe first was HTML (static content), however as far as dynamic content is concerned, way back when, it was done through the **Common Gateway Interface** (CGI). Executable applications, usually written in Perl or C, were provided with an interface that allowed clients to access them in a standard way across HTTP. This allowed both personalized content and applications for gathering and disseminating information on the Internet to be created.

More specifically, CGI is used for processing client input, storing personal information, creating services, making information available online, and so on. An example of a CGI application is a web site with personalization services, such as content management solutions where a user can store their documents to make them available online, whether for dissemination, shared authorship, or merely as personal storage. Others include commerce sites where purchases can be made online.

> *The World Wide Web Consortium (W3C) has more details on CGI than we can cover in this chapter:* http://www.w3.org/CGI/.

A URL for a CGI program looks something like this:

```
http://www.myserver.com/cgi-bin/MyExecutable.exe?name1=value1&name2=value2
```

The first part of the URL is the protocol name – hyper text transfer protocol in this case – followed by the name of the server. Everything after this and before the question mark is the **context path**.

The /cgi-bin/ part of the URL alerts the server that it should execute the CGI program specified in the next part of the URL. The section after the question mark is known as the **query string** and it allows the client to send information to the CGI program specific to the client. In this way, the program can run with client-specific information affecting the results.

CGI suffers from a number of drawbacks: the languages that applications must be written in are procedural, instability in a CGI program can bring the entire machine down, and, in terms of performance, the way in which CGI applications work requires a new instance of the application to be created for every request, and thus a new thread is created, making scalability difficult. This can cause a significant drain on the server. Each user requires the same amount of resources, and any setup of those resources has to be performed once per user request. It should be noted that improvements in CGI such as the FastCGI extension have meant that CGI suffers less from performance problems than it used to.

One very important point to note is that CGI only describes the contract between the web server and the program – no services are provided that help to implement user-centric systems. These include maintaining the identity of the client, providing access to ways of maintaining a user's information, restricting access to the application to authorized users, and storing runtime information in the application.

Thus it became necessary to provide a framework in which applications that were created for the Web could reside. This framework would provide the services mentioned above, in addition to providing a more mature lifecycle management service so that performance becomes less of an issue.

Then Servlets Were Born...

Servlets are portions of logic written in Java that have a defined form and which are invoked to dynamically generate content and provide a means for deploying an application on the Internet. All servlets implement an interface called `Servlet`, which defines a standard lifecycle – a list of methods that are called in a predictable way. Servlets were created by Sun Microsystems as a result of the problems with CGI that we discussed in the previous section.

Initialization is facilitated through a method called `init()`. Any resources needed by the servlet, along with any initialization that the servlet must do before it can service client requests, is done in this method, which is called just once for each instance of the servlet.

Each servlet may handle many requests from many clients. The `Servlet` interface defines a method called `service()` that is called for each client request. This method controls all the computation of the response that is returned to the client. When a request has been serviced and the response returned to the client, the servlet waits for the next request. In HTTP applications, the `service()` method checks which type of HTTP request was made, whether `GET` or `POST`, and so on, and forwards the request to methods defined for handling these requests.

Finally, a method called `destroy()` is called once before the servlet class is disposed of. This method can be used to free any resources acquired in the `init()` method:

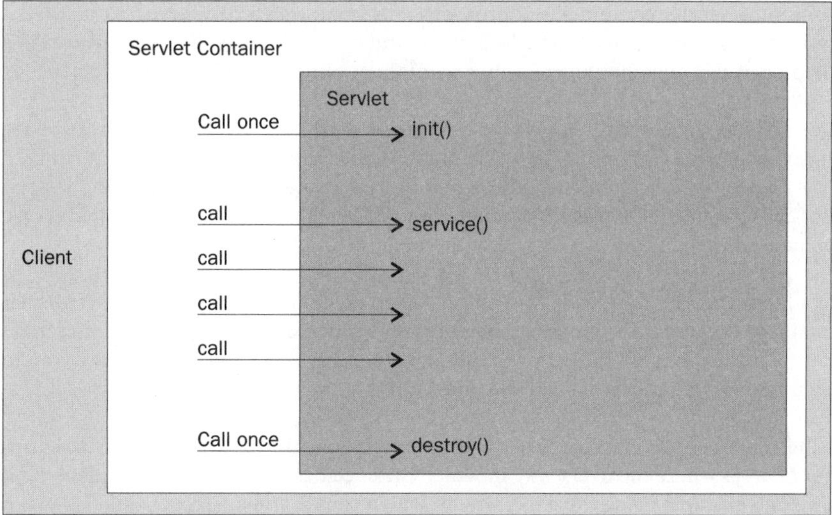

The fact that the lifecycle of the servlet is predetermined means that, firstly, many vendors may implement an execution environment for servlets – known as a **servlet container**; all they need do is make sure that they follow the contract defined for servlets in the Servlet specifications. Therefore, a servlet written according to the specifications should run without modification in any compliant servlet container.

The second point to mention, is that web containers provide services to the servlet in addition to lifecycle management, such as making initialization parameters available, enabling database connections, and allowing the servlet to find and execute other resources in the application. Containers can also maintain a session for the servlet – HTTP by design does not allow a server to track users such that a connection can be said to exist across more than merely the request-response combination. Once the response is returned to the client, there is nothing in HTTP that allows the server to recognize the client when it makes another request.

To circumvent this issue, the container maintains the client's identity through temporary cookies that store a special token referencing the user – this token is known as the user's session. By doing this the container can identify a client to the servlet across multiple requests. This allows for more complex interactions with the client. If cookies are unavailable, the container can also rewrite links in the HTML that is returned to the client, which offer an alternative way to maintain session information.

This means that instead of the application setting cookies in the client browser – and then falling over if cookies are disabled – the container automatically checks if cookies are enabled and uses them, or alternatively uses URL rewriting to maintain the session. The application developer can then create objects that are stored in the user's session and are then available to other servlets in subsequent client requests.

Security, that is, authentication and authorization, is provided through a declarative security framework. This means that restricted resources and authorized users are not hard coded into the application. Instead, a configuration document is used to specify the types of users to whom the resources are available. This means that they can be changed easily according to requirements.

For example, if the standard operating procedure for a given corporate document is that it is available to board members only but if they decide to override this, the application can be reconfigured to give the additional privileges by changing the configuration document.

Tomcat is one such servlet container – it provides an execution environment for servlets, allows them access to system resources, such as the file system, and maintains the clients identity. As we saw in the previous chapter, it has become the reference implementation of the specifications.

Although the Servlets specification allows for other transports besides HTTP, in practice servlets are almost exclusively used to provide application functionality across the Internet, servicing HTTP requests. Like CGI, the Servlet specifications were designed to make a standard for extending web servers beyond static content and creating web-enabled applications. Unlike CGI, the Servlet specifications are confined to the Java language, although this carries with it the benefits of platform-independence.

Like the Java language, the Servlet specifications were created with the purpose of allowing third parties to offer containers that compete on price, performance, and ease of use, and the fact that these containers are standard means that in principle customers of these third parties are free to choose between them and have a relatively painless migration.

In practice, the vendors of servlet containers also compete on extra-specification services. In addition, there are a number of areas where the exact way in which the specifications should be implemented is open to interpretation, one example being the exact way in which class loaders – responsible for making classes available within the container so that they can be used by the application – work within the container.

However migration is usually more a container configuration issue than a matter of reprogramming and recompiling the application. This does however assume that the programmers were not tempted into using non-specification services and programmed the application with cross-container compatibility in mind.

Tomcat, as a result of its reference implementation status does not provide extra-specification features that create application dependencies on it.

One example of a non-specification feature is in JRun 4, which allows the automatic compilation of JSP excerpts into JSP tags – special HTML-like tags that execute a piece of logic (we will talk more about JSP tags later in the chapter). While this is a part of future JSP specifications, currently if an application depends on this functionality, it will require a fair amount of porting to continue to work.

Accessing Servlets

If we consider servlets as program resources, how are these resources accessed? Well, like CGI, the server maps URLs to programmatic resources; however in this case these are servlets. This is done in one of two ways. As part of the application configuration, each servlet is mapped to a servlet name. The name is arbitrary but is often descriptive of the service the servlet provides. The servlet can then be accessed by entering a URL such as the following:

http://www.server.com/Servlet/ServletName

where ServletName is the name given to the servlet in the configuration files. Alternatively, a servlet may be accessed by its fully qualified name as follows:

http://www.server.com/Servlet/com.wrox.db.ServletName

where com.wrox.db.ServletName is the fully qualified name of the servlet. More information on the way in which servlets are named and organized will be provided in Chapter 3.

Alternatively, servlets can be accessed through a logical mapping, which maps context paths to servlets. This is often more obvious in its intention than the straight servlet name, as it is then possible to add information into the path that will give the user a clue as to the intention of the servlet's action. For example, a servlet that loads all available documents to allow administrative procedures may be called `AdminLoaderServlet`, and may be mapped to a context path of:

/admin/LoadDocumentsForAdministration

thus giving the user a better idea of what is occurring at this point in the application.

The container intercepts all requests and looks for patterns in the URL that correspond to a specified servlet and invokes the servlet that matches that pattern. For example, all URLs that end with the `.db` extension may be mapped to the `com.wrox.db.ServletName` servlet from above, probably for providing database functionality. Other possibilities are matching a character sequence to a servlet, and so on.

For example, a system could match all requests that include the character sequence upload to an upload manager servlet that manages the uploading process. Thus, in principle, all of the following URLs would invoke this servlet (a local address has been substituted for the server address in this example):

http://localhost:8080/upload?file=Hello&locationResolver=World
http://localhost:8080/admin/uploadUserDocument/Hello/World/auth
http://localhost:8080/core/Hello.World.upload

Unfortunately, although servlets are an improvement over CGI, especially with respect to performance and server load, they too have a drawback. They are primarily suitable for processing logic. For the creation of content (that is, HTML) they are less usable. Firstly, hard-coding textual output, including HTML tags, in code makes the application less maintainable, since if text in the HTML must be changed, the servlet must be recompiled. If we look at an excerpt of servlet code:

```
out.println("<html>");
out.println("  <head>");
out.println("    <title>Hello World example</title>");
```

```
out.println("  </head>");
out.println("  <body bgcolor=\"white\">");
out.println("    <h1>Hello World</h1>");
out.println("  </body>");
out.println("</html>");
```

the intended effect of this section of code is to output the following HTML:

```
<html>
  <head>
    <title>Hello World example
  </head>
  <body bgcolor="white">
    <h1>Hello World</h1>
  </body>
</html>
```

However, it is a rather cumbersome way of doing so. Secondly, it requires the HTML designer to understand enough about Java to avoid breaking the servlet. More likely, however, the programmer of the application must take the HTML from the designer and then embed it into the application: an error-prone task.

To solve this problem, the **JavaServer Pages** (JSP) technology was created by Sun Microsystems, which we will discuss next.

And On To JSPs...

The first edition of the JavaServer Pages specifications resembled **Active Server Pages** (ASP) – a Microsoft technology. In practice, both have moved on from those early days so much that the resemblance is purely superficial. Specifically, JSP has made a huge leap forward with the introduction of tag libraries.

ASP is a technology for creating dynamic content. The programmer inserts sections of code into the page that carry out conditional logic to insert content dynamically to provide personalization, security, and time-critical information (that is, information whose value expires). The snippets of code are executed by the server (rather than by the browser) and thus the returned content appears to the browser to be just HTML; the insertion of dynamic content is done in a way that is transparent to the user. An ASP page, `HelloWorld.asp`, is shown below:

```
<% @Language = "VBScript" %>
<% Response.buffer = true %>
<html>
  <head>
    <title>Hello World</title>
  </head>
  <body>
    <%
```

```
    Dim HelloMessage
    HelloMessage="Hello World"
    If request.QueryString("message") <> "" Then
      HelloMessage=request.QueryString("message")
    End If

    response.write HelloMessage
    %>
  </body>
</html>
```

This page carries out one of two actions. The default is to show the message Hello World should the URL http://localhost/HelloWorld.asp be called. However, if the URL given is, say, http://localhost/HelloWorld.asp?message=HelloHello, then the message HelloHello will be shown instead.

JSP initially resembled this style very closely. In fact, this same page as a JSP page could look like this:

```
<%@ page language="java" %>
<html>
  <head>
    <title>Hello World</title>
  </head>
  <body>
    <%
    String message = request.getAttribute("message");
    if(message == null || message.equals("")) {
      message = "Hello World";
    }
    %><%=message%>
  </body>
</html>
```

Practically speaking, JSP pages are compiled into servlets, which are then kept in memory or on the filesystem indefinitely, until either the memory is required back, or the server is restarted. The servlet is called for each request, thus making the process far more efficient than ASP since this saves parsing and compiling the document every time a user comes to our site. This means that a developer can write software whose output is easy to verify visually (since the intended result is a visual one), and the result works like a CGI program – a piece of software. In fact, JSP took off greatly as a result of its suitability for creating dynamic visual content at a time when the Internet was growing massively in popularity.

One major practical difference between servlets and JSP pages is that servlets are provided in compiled form and JSP pages are often not (although pre-compilation is possible). What this means for a System Administrator is that servlet files are held in the private resources section of the server, while JSP files are mixed in with static HTML pages, images, and other resources in the public section. We will see later how this can affect maintenance.

In the early days of JSP, the logic of the site, including what content should be shown, was always present in the JSP pages themselves and the user interaction was entirely managed by the JSP pages. This is known as Model 1 architecture. This architecture is actually very suitable for small sites of limited functionality or pages with minimal requirements for expansion. It is quite easy to create sites in this way and therefore productivity is improved when complexity is low. This model is not recommend for larger sites: the cost of this initial productivity is the time lost in debugging complex pages as the complexity and the size of the site increase. The architecture for Model 1 is illustrated below:

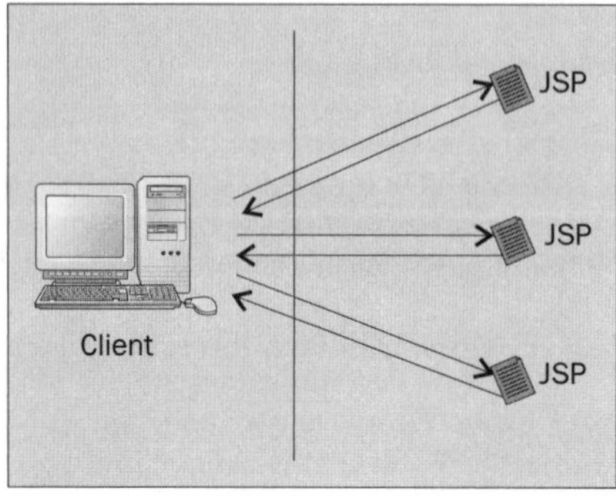

Each JSP page must know where the user should be sent next and where the user has come from. This is embedded in information about how the site should be presented, the color of the fonts, and so on. As such, this approach is quite inflexible.

There are, however, quite severe limitations to implementing large projects using only JSP pages. Mixing code and HTML on the same page means that the designer must be sufficiently proficient with code to avoid breaking the functionality of the page, as well as being able to work with the logic on the page to produce the desired output. At the same time, the developer must do some of the designer's work of laying out the page when the logic is sufficiently convoluted.

In addition, since pieces of logic may be strewn around the page embedded in sections of HTML, it is by no means straightforward to figure out the intended result without a fair amount of inspection. This can cause significant problems with maintenance; the code is mixed with markup. As such, code reusability is very limited, so that sections of code are often repeated across the site and, unlike in traditional code, it is not easy to identify where a section of code is.

The obvious alterative to this is to keep the pages as free from Java as possible, while the processing logic is stored in Java classes.

JSP pages are often used like templates. For example, the header that includes the company logo may be in one page, the main menu for the site may be in another, and a current news table may be defined in a third. When the client makes a request, these separate elements of the page are assembled together and presented to the user as though they were all created as one. The diagram opposite illustrates this:

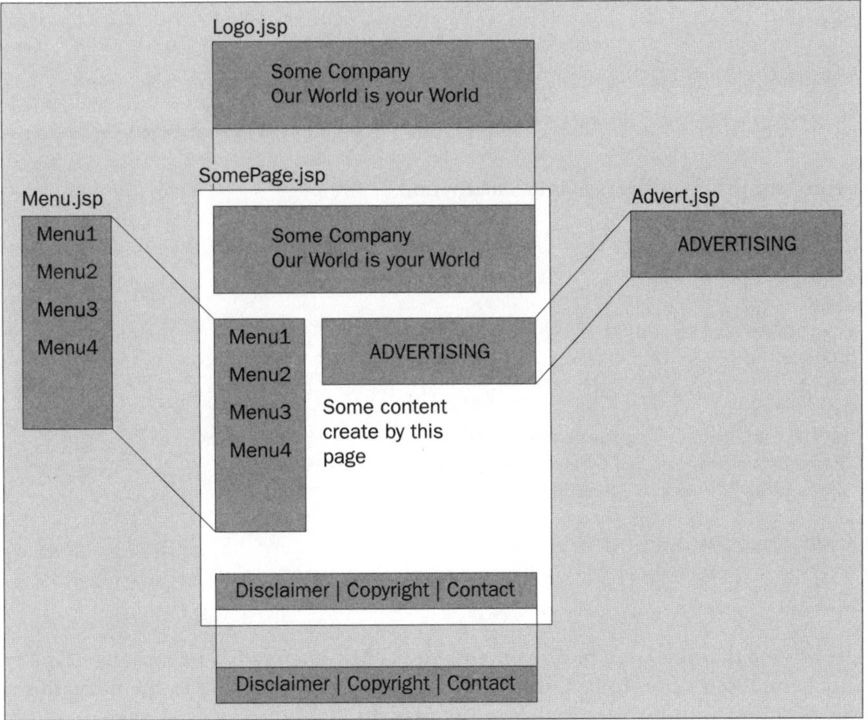

This allows the designer to affect changes globally by updating a single page – the HTML has been centralized. However, code may be spread out according to functionality across the various parts of the site.

Like servlets, JSP pages operate within a container. The JSP container provides the same services as a servlet container, but also supplies the additional JSP to the servlet compilation services before the JSP pages are executed. Tomcat includes both the servlet container that executes servlets and compiled JSP pages (named Catalina) and the compiler service for JSP pages (named Jasper). The combination of a JSP container and a servlet container is known as a **web container** – a container capable of hosting Java web applications.

A web container provides the JSP developer with the services required to create complex interactive, personalized, and secure applications on the Internet.

JSP Tag Libraries

Since the introduction of JSP tag libraries, otherwise known as JSP tag extensions, JSP files look more like the following (where only the changed data from our previous JSP is highlighted):

```
<%@ page language="java" %>
<html>
  <head>
    <title>Hello World</title>
```

```
  </head>
  <body>
    <app:HelloWorld/>
  </body>
</html>
```

When we compare this with the previous incarnation of the page:

```
<%@ page language="java" %>
<html>
  <head>
    <title>Hello World</title>
  </head>
  <body>
    <%
    String message = request.getAttribute("message");
    if(message == null || message.equals("")) {
      message = "Hello World";
    }
    %><%=message%>
  </body>
</html>
```

you can already see that this is an improvement: an HTML-like tag has encapsulated the entire functionality behind our code. In fact, the more complex the application is, the more this replacement of Java code scriptlets with JSP tags improves the readability of the site. The page designer is presented with sections of dynamic content that are far more familiar and, more importantly, the page designer could insert the `HelloWorld` tag without understanding how it works.

Each tag has a corresponding Java class that contains the code that would otherwise appear on the page. The way that this works is that, like servlets, a lifecycle has been defined for these Java classes. Unlike servlets, a tag does not include an initialization method, or a `destroy()` method, but rather works like this: Tags are structured in pairs, with a start tag followed by an end tag with optional content as follows:

```
<i>Something in italics</i>
```

The tag lifecycle includes a method that is called when the start tag is encountered, called `doStartTag()`, a method that is called when the end tag is encountered, called `doEndTag()`, and a method that is called to reset any state (request specific data) in readiness for the next request.

The tag also has power over which parts of the page are parsed by the application. Depending on the behavior of the tag, it can stop the execution of the page, conditionally include its contents, and have its contents evaluated multiple times.

One use is as follows:

```
<app:if cookie="user" value="">
  Please enter your name...
</app:if>
```

The `app:` prefix denotes a group of tags to which this tag belongs. In the previous example, the contents of the `<app:if>` tag are evaluated if the cookie named `user` has an empty string as its value. In this case, the user is prompted for their name.

Here is an example of a JSP page that uses the Struts Framework tags:

```
<%@ page language="java" %>
<%@ taglib uri="struts-bean.tld" prefix="bean" %>
<%@ taglib uri="struts-html.tld" prefix="html" %>

<html:html locale="true">
  <head>
    <title>Intranet Title</title>
    <html:base/>
  </head>
  <body bgcolor="white">

    <html:errors/>

    <html:form action="/ChangePassword" focus="email">
      <table border="0" width="20%">

        <tr>
          <th><bean:message key="prompt.username"/></th>
          <td align="left">
            <html:text property="email" size="20" maxlength="50"/>
            <html:errors property="email"/>
          </td>
        </tr>

        <tr>
          <th><bean:message key="prompt.oldpassword"/></th>
          <td>
            <html:password property="oldPassword"
                           size="16" maxlength="16" redisplay="false"/>
            <html:errors property="oldPassword"/>
          </td>
        </tr>

        <tr>
          <th><bean:message key="prompt.password"/></th>
          <td>
            <html:password property="password"
                           size="16" maxlength="16" redisplay="false"/>
            <html:errors property="password"/>
          </td>
        </tr>

        <tr>
          <th><bean:message key="prompt.confirmpassword"/></th>
          <td>
            <html:password property="password2"
                           size="16" maxlength="16" redisplay="false"/>
```

```
            <html:errors property="password2"/>
          </td>
        </tr>

        <tr>
          <th><html:submit property="submit" value="Submit"/></th>
          <td><html:reset/></td>
        </tr>

      </table>
    </html:form>
  </body>
</html:html>
```

The scripted version of this page runs to several pages, so you will excuse us if we don't include it here. The point is that tags present an elegant way to write pages that create dynamic content.

The encapsulation of code within tags means that, in principle, page designers could use them to construct sites. This does, however, depend on the tags being quite generic so that they can be reused in many situations, and on there being sufficient information in the form of documentation and training for the designer to understand the significance of what they are doing, and to correctly define the tags.

Tags represent the future of JSP and Java-based dynamic content.

Before we wrap this chapter up, we should discuss the typical architectures for web applications written in Java.

Web Application Architecture

The set of all the servlets, JSP pages, and other files that are logically related composes a **web application**. The Servlet specification defines a standard directory hierarchy where all of these files must be placed. It is:

Relative Path	Description
`/`	Web application root: all files that are publicly accessible are placed in this directory. Examples include HTML, JSP, and GIF files.
`/WEB-INF`	All files in this directory and its subdirectories are not publicly accessible. A single file, `web.xml`, called the deployment descriptor, contains configuration options for the web application. The various options for the deployment descriptor are defined by the Servlet API.
`/WEB-INF/classes`	All of the web application's class files are placed here.
`/WEB-INF/lib`	Class files can be archived into a single file, called a JAR file, and placed in this directory.

All servlet containers are required to use this directory hierarchy. What's more, because the location and features of the deployment descriptor (the `web.xml` file mentioned previously) are set by the specification, web applications only need to be defined once and they are compatible with any servlet container. The deployment descriptor defines options such as the order in which servlets are loaded by a servlet container, parameters that can be passed to the servlets on startup, which URL patterns map to which servlets, security restrictions, and so on. The full description of the deployment descriptor is in Chapter 6.

To make distribution easier, all of the files in the directory hierarchy above can be archived in a ZIP file with its extension renamed to WAR (Web ARchive). Server administrators can then place this WAR file into the directory specified by the servlet container and the servlet container takes care of the rest.

This means that a developer need only expend effort creating a web application once. You can then take their WAR file and by simply copying it into the proper location in your servlet container, the web application will be deployed and ready to run. Thus, distributing and deploying web applications is remarkably simple, even if you switch servlet containers at any time.

Deploying web applications and WAR files will be covered in more detail in Chapter 7.

Java Site Architecture

The ideal balance for the majority of sites is, as we have seen above, a mix of servlets and JSP pages. Servlets are ideal for encapsulating the logic of the application, while being somewhat poor at visual representation, and JSP pages conversely are designed for displaying visual material. This suggests that the combination of the two can provide a balance and cover the needs of the majority of sites.

The architecture that aids this separation between logic and presentation is known as Model 2 architecture or **Model View Controller** (MVC) architecture. The **Model** is the logic of the site; the rules that determine what is shown and to whom it is shown. The **View** component of this architecture is naturally the JSP pages that display the content that is created. Finally the **Controller** designates which part of the Model is invoked, and which JSP page is used to render the data – another way to put this is that the Controller defines the structure of the site. A diagram of the MVC architecture is shown below:

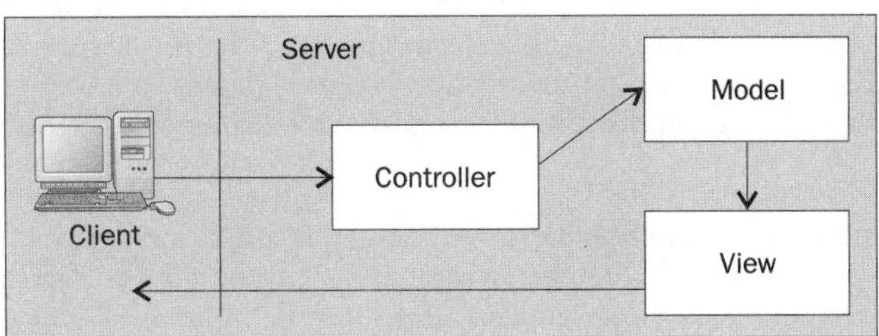

There are two typical types of Model 2 architectures – strict and loose. The strict version designates the role of the Controller to a single servlet, which extracts the information needed to route the query to a piece of logic, executes the logic component, and then forwards the result of the execution to a JSP page.

An example of a strict MVC architecture is the Struts Framework, which we saw in the previous chapter. This framework implements a standard servlet for routing execution. Each piece of functionality is implemented as a special type of Struts component known as an Action. Each Action defines a single method and can place a variety of objects where the JSP that is invoked can use them to render the page. In this type of architecture, the sequence of execution is often very reliable and is of the form:

An expanded example of the MVC strict architecture is shown below:

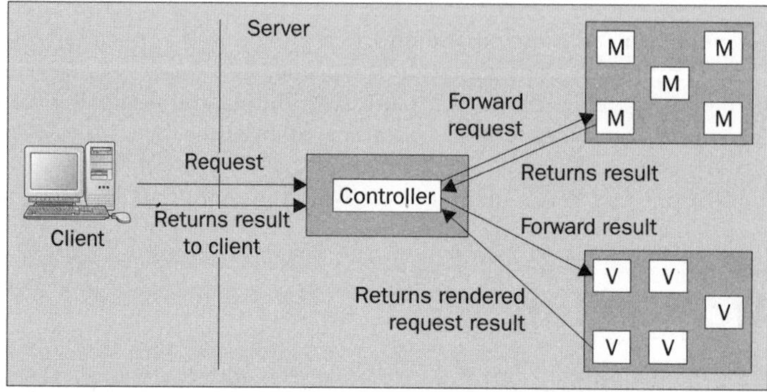

In this diagram, you can see that the single Controller selects the correct logic to execute, and then forwards the result to the View which renders the results for the client.

Small-scale home-grown sites that are not based on a framework are often a looser version; several servlets each take the role of a Controller and part of the Model. In this version of the Model 2 architecture, the JSP pages are still designed so that they contain very little or no logic, and the servlets handle all of the function of the application. This second model can be quite popular because it promotes high productivity in the short term and can be easier to understand than the strict MVC architecture.

In sites that have a pure MVC architecture, the structure of the site is, at least in principle, quite flexible. The site is broken up into units of functionality that can be reused in multiple situations, as well as pages that can be reused. This structure therefore represents the most work for the administrator in often-changed sites. For example, a page that displays contact details in a web site may be used for creating a new contact, updating an old contact, viewing an existing contact, and updating a user's contact details.

A site that allows content management may use the same JSP page and servlet code for uploading a variety of documents each with different needs, such as a report, a tender request, and a procedures manual. As the site expands, these components will need to be integrated with new functionality – the flow control will need to be configured before the various components will work together correctly.

This does, however, represent a very reusable and updateable site: the site can be reconfigured according to business needs and customer requests without rewriting code and can be extended without affecting existing code to any great extent.

Summary

Tomcat came about as a result of a need for complex sites that provide personalization through maintaining client identity, authentication and authorization, and an environment for providing system services to simplify the creation of web applications.

We discussed servlets and JSP pages and compared and contrasted them against alternatives such as CGI and ASP to understand how they came to be. As a wrap up for this section we looked at how all these disparate components are gathered together in a web container.

We also discussed typical architectures for web applications written using servlets and JSP pages.

We will now move on to discuss Tomcat installation in the next chapter.

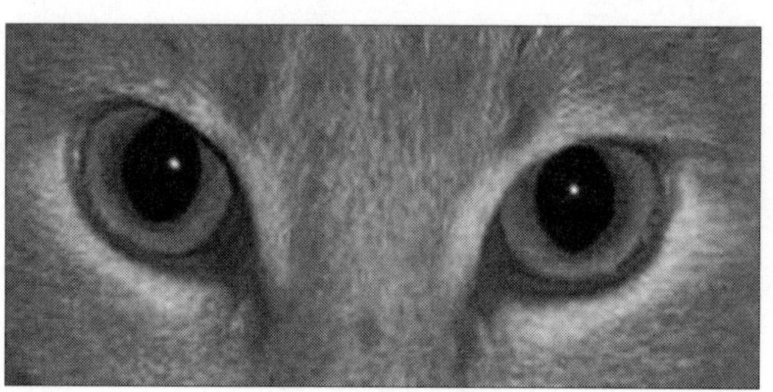

3

Tomcat Installation

Having read a couple of chapters on the history of and reason for Tomcat's existence, you are now probably raring to start with Tomcat. In this chapter we will:

- See how to install Tomcat on both Windows and Linux
- Provide instructions on how to install Java
- Discuss the Tomcat installation directory structure
- Discuss the installation of Ant – a Java-based build tool
- Provide a troubleshooting section that will help you deal with typical problems encountered while installing Tomcat

We will begin by discussing the various decisions to be made over which Java Virtual Machine (JVM) to choose. A JVM is the Java executable needed by Tomcat. Sun Microsystems typically license the specifications for everything concerned with Java out to vendors, who then compete on performance, price, and brand awareness. We will concern ourselves with choosing a JVM for performance in this chapter; if your company uses a specific JVM, no doubt there will be a certain level of support involved. On the whole, installation is quite similar for many JVMs. We will also discuss the other JVMs, notably for Linux.

Installing a JVM

Choosing a JVM is an important decision, in that it can significantly affect the performance of your Tomcat server. The usual argument that free means lower performance does not necessarily hold for JVMs, so it is worth evaluating a few. If you feel somewhat unqualified to make that decision, you can take comfort in two things:

- The next section will provide you with enough information to get you started, and there is also a fair amount of information on this subject on the Internet. You might start at http://java.sun.com/docs/performance/.
- Java makes it very easy to switch JVMs without major reconfiguration, though it will require a restart of Tomcat to take effect. So you are at liberty to change JVMs according to business demands, which usually boil down to performance, cost, and company policies – of which the first two are more malleable.

Tomcat 4.0 requires a JVM with support for Java 2 – which means a 1.2 edition or later. That puts the Microsoft JVM out of the picture at the time of writing. Should Microsoft gain a Java 2 license after 2004, when the current license runs out, it is likely that a future license will require them to be standards-compliant, something that has been lacking to date.

This will also similarly rule out any other JVM with 1.1 compliance, such as the JVM provided for Linux by default in many releases until recently. Luckily, Sun now supports Linux with a 1.4 JDK at the time of writing. In addition, IBM also has recent JDK versions available, and there is also a JDK available from the Blackdown project (http://www.blackdown.org/) – a Linux port of source donated by Sun.

We will also deal with JVM performance tweaking by using the Hotspot JVM (Sun's implementation of the JVM) as an example to get you started on administrating a JVM in a production server.

Choosing a JVM

There are JVMs available for many operating systems including BSD, AIX, HP-UX, OS/2, and VxWorks. We will be limiting ourselves to investigating the Hotspot JVM from Sun for Windows and Solaris, and Blackdown for Linux. IBM also offers very fast JVMs for AIX, Linux, AS/400, and OS/2, not to mention Windows.

Please note that there are also many others available but you should watch out for specialized editions, such as those providing extra high security guarantees (specifically security of in-memory data), real-time VMs, and light VMs for minimum footprints and embedded systems. If you have unusual needs, look around.

Watch out for the level of API supported, which should be as complete as possible. One notable acceptable omission is support for AWT and Swing (the part of the specifications that deals with client windows required for desktop applications), which is rarely necessary in a web server.

Before we discuss installation specifics, it is worth looking at a JVM in a little detail.

Sun Microsystems' JVMs

Unsurprisingly, the Sun JVMs are quite popular. The classic JVM is the original from Sun and was built as a reference implementation to show how the standards for JVMs should be implemented in cases where there was insufficient detail in the specifications. In addition, it was offered so that developers could start writing software immediately, while vendors worked on their JVMs.

Following the classic JVM, a JIT (Just In Time) compiler was offered in one of two forms – the client edition and the server edition. The client edition is optimized for fast boot time, while the server takes longer to load but optimizes the code more strictly and can therefore yield faster running code.

The classic JVM is now no longer offered because the Hotspot JVM, which has JIT compilation, has superseded it. The Hotspot JVM is the one bundled with the JDK that can be found on Sun's Java site at http://java.sun.com/. We will be downloading and installing the 1.3.1 edition, which at the time of writing could be found at http://java.sun.com/j2se/1.3/download.html.

The supported Linux distribution is Red Hat, so from the menu that opens we have the option of downloading the JDK for Windows, Red Hat, and Solaris. Download the JDK appropriate for your platform and follow the instructions below to install.

> **Before we begin, it should be noted that a bug in JDK 1.3 causes the termination of Java-based NT services when the user logs off (and so the server will be shut down unless the machine is permanently logged in). If you are planning to run the server as a service on Windows, consider installing the 1.4 JDK.**

Windows Installation

In the Windows environment, the installer is an executable with easy to follow steps. Simply double-click the download and you will shortly have the JDK installed. The folder where you have chosen to install the JDK is known as `%JAVA_HOME%`. There are a number of subfolders but the only one we are interested in is the `bin` directory where the various executables are stored, including the JVM, the compiler, the debugger, and a packaging utility.

The next step of the installation is to add this folder (`%JAVA_HOME%`) as an environment variable so that Windows can find it when it is invoked. We also need to add the `%JAVA_HOME%\bin` directory to the `Path`. If this is not done, there is a danger that the Microsoft JVM will be picked up as it is in the `Windows` directory (or `WINNT` for Windows 2000 onwards).

To do this, select Start | Settings | Control Panel and choose the System option. Now choose the Advanced tab and select the Environment Variables... button. You can add the executable to the specific user that you are operating as, so that it will only exist when you are logged in as that user, or to the entire system.

To add `JAVA_HOME` for the entire system select the New button in the lower half of the following window:

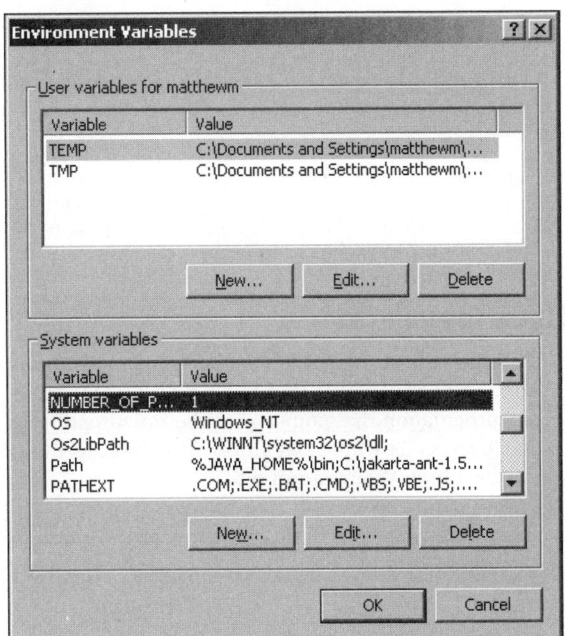

Now enter the following information:

This information may change depending on the specific version of the JVM you have installed and the location of your installation. Next, modify the `Path` variable to include `%JAVA_HOME%\bin`, making sure that it is the first entry in the `Path`, so that it is checked first for the reasons mentioned above:

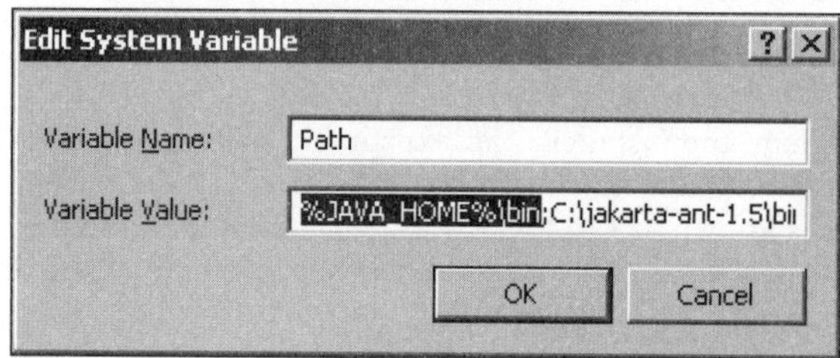

This will make the executables available to the command prompt. To test the installation, open an instance of the command prompt (Start | Programs | Accessories | Command Prompt) and enter the following instruction into the shell window:

```
> javac
```

This should bring up a standard usage message such as the following (source cropped short):

```
Usage: javac <options> <source files>
where possible options include:
  -g                        Generate all debugging info
  -g:none                   Generate no debugging info
  -g:{lines,vars,source}    Generate only some debugging info
```

Linux Installation

First download a suitable distribution from http://java.sun.com/j2se/1.3/download.html. The official supported platform is Red Hat 6.2 and it is very important to have the correct version of `glibc` (the documentation that comes with the download from Sun includes the relevant information). Some testing has been done with other Linux distributions including Mandrake 7.1, Red Hat 7.1, Caldera 2.4, and Turbo Linux Workstation 6.0.

There are two types of download: an RPM package for systems supporting RPMs and a gzipped and tarred shell script.

Shell Script Install

For the shell script the installation process is as follows. You must be running a 2.2.12 kernel or later with a glibc 2.1.2-11 or higher. Common problems exist when the X printing library is not present (as is the case with some older versions of Linux) as the default installation of the JDK depends on it (even if you don't use the windowing API). If you have a recent X11 distribution, libXp should be present in any case. You can test your version of glibc by entering the following command:

```
$ ls /lib/libc-*
```

Any system whose kernel was compiled with the CONFIG_IP_TRANSPARENT_PROXY option, as is the case with Red Hat 6.1, may cause problems with Java running as root. Either don't use Java as root – the preferred option – or upgrade to a system that was not compiled with this option enabled.

For any other problems, you may find solutions at http://java.sun.com/j2se/1.3/install-linux-sdk.html#problems.

The shell script provided is a self-extracting binary file. We will detail how to install the JDK for all users; you should sign in as root using the su command (just remember to use the JDK as another user to avoid any problems). Begin by moving the file into the directory you would like to install the JDK in.

If you are installing the JDK for a specific user, then you must install it into the user's home directory. Alternatively, if you wish to install the JDK for all users (which the Sun installation documentation assumes) then an accepted location is /usr/java/jdk-[version number] where version number is the version number of the JDK being installed.

Now add execute permissions for the file as follows:

```
# chmod o+x j2sdk-1_3_1_03-linux-i386.bin
```

Run the file using the line:

```
# ./j2sdk-1_3_1_03-linux-i386.bin
```

You will be presented with a license agreement before installation commences. Once installation has finished, you should add the environment variable $JAVA_HOME to your system with the location of the JDK, for example if you installed it in /usr/java/j2sdk-1_3_1_03-linux-i386, you should give it this value. This value can be added to the ~/.bashrc file for personal use or to /etc/profile for all users. Alternatively, /etc/profile runs any shell scripts in /etc/profile.d, so the following lines can be added to a file named tomcat.sh:

```
JAVA_HOME=/usr/java/jdk1.4.1/
export JAVA_HOME
PATH=$JAVA_HOME/bin:$PATH
export PATH
```

Note that you may have to log out and log in again for /etc/profile or tomcat.sh to be read by your system.

You should also allow execute permissions for the `$JAVA_HOME/bin` folder for all users or for yourself as owner as appropriate.

To test the installation, type:

```
# javac
```

which should give the following output, cropped for the sake of brevity:

```
Usage: javac <options> <source files>
where possible options include:
  -g                        Generate all debugging info
  -g:none                       Generate no debugging info
  -g:{lines,vars,source}    Generate only some debugging info
```

RPM Install

To install the JDK using the RPM, you must first download the file. The format will be:

```
j2sdk-[version number]-linux-i586-rpm.bin
```

Its executable nature is merely to allow you to agree to the licensing terms – when you have done so, an RPM with the same name as above but with the trailing `.bin` removed is automatically uncompressed. If you wish to install the JDK for all users you must now sign in as root. Set execute permissions for the file:

```
# chmod o+x j2sdk-1_3_1_<version number>-linux-i586-rpm.bin
# ./j2sdk-1_3_1_<version number>-linux-i586-rpm.bin
```

The script will display a binary license agreement, which you will be asked to agree to before installation can proceed. Once you have agreed to the license, the install script will create the file `jdk-1.3.1_<version number>.i386.rpm` in the current directory:

```
# rpm -iv jdk-1.3.1_<version number>.i386.rpm
```

This will install the Java 2 SDK at `/usr/java/jdk1.3.1_<version number>`. You should now follow the instructions above to add execute permissions for the JDK executables and modify the `PATH` to include them. Again, you can test the installation as above.

Tweaking the JVM for Performance

In server applications such as those installed on Tomcat, it is likely that the server JIT compiler will provide better performance compared to the default, at a cost to bootup time. For long-lived applications like servers, this cost to bootup time is of no consequence and the performance improvement is worthwhile. To enable this option, the Java executable must be provided with `-server` as its first command-line argument. We will show how to modify Tomcat's scripts to add this option.

As mentioned previously, the current editions of the Sun JVMs have JIT turned on by default. In this case you do not need to do anything to benefit from the performance improvements available through JIT compilation. In the unlikely event that you wish to turn JIT compilation off (for debugging for example) this can be done by adding a command-line argument to Java:

```
-Xint
```

This will start the JVM in interpreted mode only. You can also choose to use the classic JVM (no JIT) with the following command-line option:

```
-classic
```

or in JDK 1.4 and later:

```
-client
```

Heap Size

The heap size can also be changed to improve performance. The 1.3.1 JDK allows heap sizes of greater than 2Gb. The default heap size is 64Mb, but most server applications will benefit from having this increased. Setting the maximum amount to 256Mb would be done as follows:

```
-Xms256m -Xmx256m
```

To specify memory size in Gb, use the letter `g` instead of `m`. Of course, this does rather assume that the system has somewhere near this amount of memory. The server does not actually have to have as much memory as you assign it, as it will default to virtual memory if there is insufficient to meet demands. However, the amount specified and the amount present on the machine should not differ wildly.

Note that command-line arguments beginning with `-X` are subject to change and may be removed without notice by Sun in future versions of the JDK. The `-Xms` option sets the minimum heap size and `-Xmx` sets the maximum heap size. In this case they are both the same, which minimizes the impact on performance of the JVM's default behavior of starting with the minimum and growing as required. Setting these as the same value will often improve startup time.

The Garbage Collector

If the heap size is too large, there may be strange pauses in the application where nothing appears to happen. Alternatively, this could show as poor performance overall when the server's performance is averaged. This is because the garbage collector (GC) only runs when memory is exhausted and then runs through the entire system. This means that it may have potentially 2Gb of memory to check, which could take some time.

If the heap size is very large, then scanning it for memory reclamation takes longer, hence the pauses. One possible solution is to pass the following command-line option to the Java executable:

```
-Xincgc
```

This makes the GC run in incremental mode, where it runs more often but checks through smaller amounts of memory. However, this option can reduce throughput, and therefore it should be monitored. Alternatively, lowering the size of the heap (or a combination of both) may help. One other possible solution is to use the following options:

```
-Xms256m -Xmx256m -XX:NewSize=128m -XX:MaxNewSize=128m
```

The memory model for the `java` executable differentiates between new objects (the majority of which are typically short-lived and can be reclaimed quickly) and old objects that are long-lived. It contains an algorithm for deciding when to move an object from being tagged as new to being tagged as old. `NewSize` is the initial amount of memory set aside for new objects and `MaxNewSize` is the maximum size the new heap should be allowed to grow to. In the example above, half the memory is set aside for new objects.

The `NewSize` and `MaxNewSize` options can sometimes improve the performance of an application since they set the size of the short-lived object memory to a higher value. This means that objects such as a request (which lives only for the duration of a user request to the server, and is counted in milliseconds) can be collected more efficiently, thus improving performance. If you are particularly performance-conscious, playing around with these figures while looking at performance may be helpful. This is because the balance between the two can be set more precisely to reflect the balance of long-lived versus short-lived objects in your application under typical conditions.

JDKs running on Solaris SPARC boxes also offer options to stop the use of virtual memory and allow double-size paging, among other performance tweaks of the system. More information on this option is available with the documentation for the JDK.

Tomcat Installation

We will begin by showing the installation on Windows, which for the 4.x branch of Tomcat is very easy. We will show both of the most common options starting with the installer.

For each of the following steps, both for Windows, Linux, and Unix systems, you can get the distributions from the same folder on the Jakarta web site. Navigating to http://jakarta.apache.org/builds/ will present a list of the Jakarta projects. Choose the Tomcat version of your choice, which for the purpose of this chapter is Tomcat 4.0.4 (though later versions shouldn't change much from the process we will describe). It can be found in http://jakarta.apache.org/builds/jakarta-tomcat-4.0/release/v4.0.4/bin/ at the time of writing.

In the unlikely event that the files have been moved (Apache are good about this – the main Tomcat project page can be found at http://jakarta.apache.org/tomcat/ if you encounter trouble), it should not prove difficult to navigate to them by following the convention as above.

Navigating to the specific project will present you with a possibility of downloading archives, nightly builds (very likely to be unstable), test builds, and release builds (which is the type we want). As stated previously, we will be using the 4.0.4 version and we will begin with the binary distributions. Compiling Tomcat from scratch will be covered in a separate section later in the chapter.

A final note before we begin: the available distributions of Tomcat are split into J2SDK 1.4 and JDK 1.3 versions. As discussed previously, J2SDK 1.4 includes an XML parser, which Tomcat requires, and to save you 1.2 Mb of download, there is a Tomcat Light Edition available that does not include `xerces.jar` – the XML parser usually bundled with Tomcat. If you already have `xerces.jar` downloaded then you can also download this edition.

The operative point is that, regardless of the JDK type you have installed and the JARs you have on your system, the full download will work and so we will show the installation of Tomcat from the full download. In addition, the JDK version you have does not change the way the server is installed at this time. For this book, we will show how to install Tomcat 4 with JDK 1.3.

> **Please make sure that you read the section on installing Ant, a `make`-like tool written in Java that we will need later in the book for automating administration tasks.**

The Linux installation notes will be self-contained. If you are planning to deploy Tomcat on Linux, you should skip the next section.

Tomcat Windows Installer

Within the bin folder (on the page http://jakarta.apache.org/builds/jakarta-tomcat-4.0/release/v4.0.4/), you will find at least six distributions. The one we want is called `jakarta-tomcat-4.0.4.exe`. Save this file at a convenient location on your machine, and double-click the file to begin installation – you must agree with the general Apache License to continue.

The next window allows you to choose to install the following options:

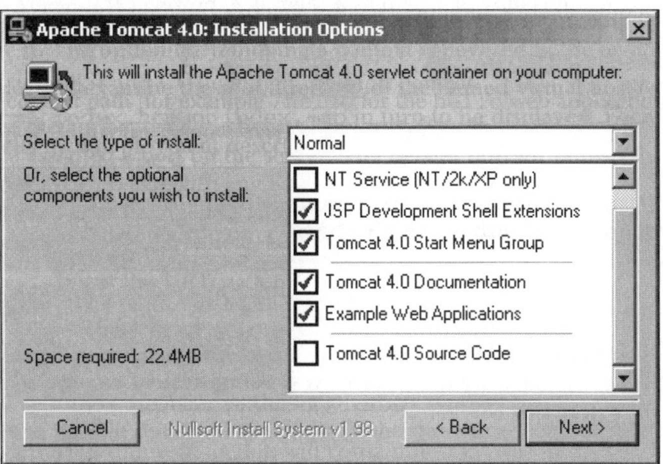

NT Service

Selecting the NT Service option allows you to start, stop, and restart Tomcat in the same way as any other NT service and this option is recommended if you are used to managing your system services in this way.

It is only available for Windows NT, 2000, and XP as Windows 98 is not a server OS. Tomcat will start as soon as the computer is switched on (and so will survive reboots of the machine) and will run in the background even when there is no user logged in. This is clearly the better deployment option, but probably not what you want for development.

> **A bug in JDK 1.3 causes the termination of Java services when the user logs off – this has been fixed in JDK 1.4 and so you may wish to choose this as your JDK as mentioned above.**

This option is not available to Windows 98 users, and they will be required to manually start and stop the server. We will discuss how a daemon-like service can be set up for Windows 98 later in this section.

JSP Development Shell Extensions

In brief, this is a very useful scripting tool and it is recommended that you install the extensions.

Start Menu Group

This option adds shortcuts to the Start menu for starting, stopping, and uninstalling the server, as well as shortcuts to the key configuration files, the installation directory, and the documentation.

Tomcat Documentation

The Tomcat documentation is getting better with time and is certainly worth installing.

Example Web Applications

The example web applications may be useful as a reference, however if they are installed and operational, they represent a certain security risk since they provide a documented and known path into your server that may be used for DoS attack attempts. Choose to install them for now as we will use them to check the installation is working correctly, and we will deal with the possible security implications later in Chapter 16.

> **The latest information, including security issues with Tomcat, is available at http://jakarta.apache.org/tomcat/news.html.**

Source Code

Finally, if you are keen to have the latest sourcecode or want to ensure that Tomcat will compile from source, it is available. As the majority of this process is identical for all platforms and Ant is required, we will cover it at the end of this chapter, after the installation of Ant.

Setting Environment Variables

In most cases, the various scripts provided with Tomcat will be able to guess the setup of your machine in such a way that no further intervention is strictly necessary. However, it is wise to add the following environment variables.

%CATALINA_HOME%

`%CATALINA_HOME%` is the directory where Tomcat is installed. Tomcat needs to know this information to find the resources that are referenced as relative paths to this folder. If you chose the default directory while installing, this will be `C:\Program Files\Apache Tomcat 4.0`.

Catalina, as mentioned in Chapter 1, is the codename of the Tomcat 4 project.

To add the environment variable, navigate to Start | Settings | Control Panel and choose System. Now choose the Advanced tab and select the Environment Variables... button. Now select the New button in the system variables (lower half) section and enter the following values, substituting the path to your installation if it is different to the one shown:

Windows 9x-and ME-Specific Issues

In Windows 9x, setting the environment variables is done by editing the file `c:\autoexec.bat`. Open the file and add the following line:

```
set CATALINA_HOME=c:\jakarta-tomcat-4.0.4
```

Notice that because of file length and spaces in the path issues, it is safer to install Tomcat directly onto `c:\` rather than under `Program Files`. You will also need to increase the default environment space to Tomcat by opening a DOS prompt window, right-clicking on it, choosing Properties, selecting the Memory tab, and setting the initial environment to 4096 bytes (4Kb):

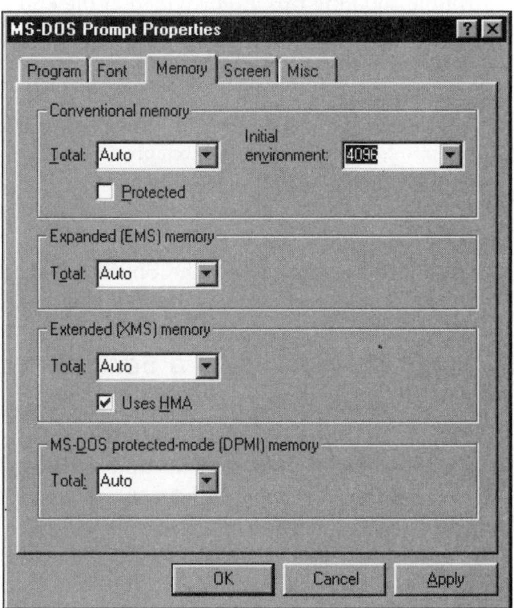

It is also possible to set another variable, called `%CATALINA_BASE%`, that allows multiple instances of the same distribution to be configured independently of each other. This is particularly relevant to hosting providers or other situations where multiple users have access to the same server. This will be discussed in detail in Chapter 19.

Testing the Installation

To test the installation, you must first start the server. We can start the server in two ways – manually or as a service.

Starting the Server Manually

You can do this by going to Start | Programs| Apache Tomcat 4.0 and select the Start Tomcat option – which is probably the easiest for our purposes. The new command prompt window will come up to prove that the server is running.

Alternatively, you can start Tomcat by opening a command prompt window, navigating to `%CATALINA_HOME%\bin`, and typing `startup`:

Note that if the window appears and promptly disappears again, you should check that you have not installed the Light Edition, which has no XML parser and will not work without one. Some further trouble-shooting tips are provided at the end of the chapter in case the server will not start up. You may also get error messages if your `%JAVA_HOME%` variable is not defined, and if the `%JAVA_HOME%\bin` directory within the JDK is not on the `Path`. If this is the case, you will get an error message saying:

```
'java' is not recognized as an internal or external command,
operable program or batch file.
```

You should refer to the instructions earlier in the book if this is the case.

To shut down Tomcat, use the Shutdown shortcut, Start | Programs| Apache Tomcat 4.0 | Stop Tomcat, or type `shutdown` into the command prompt from Tomcat's `bin` directory.

Starting the Server As a Service

If you wish to start the server as a service, and assuming you chose this option when installing the server, you will need to start the service up. In a Windows 2000 installation this is done by choosing the Start | Settings | Control Panel and selecting Administrative Tools from which you can select Services. In the window that opens, there should be an entry for Tomcat as shown opposite:

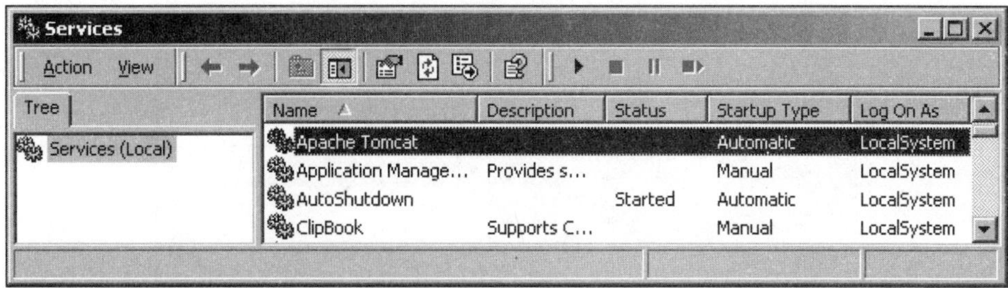

To start the server, right-click on the Tomcat entry and choose Start. No window will be shown as the server is running as a service, also known as a daemon or background thread. Once the server is started, the options for restarting and stopping the server will also be enabled.

Changing NT Service Options

Looking at the last screenshot once more, you can see the Startup Type is set to Automatic, which means that if we were to restart the computer this would also start an instance of Tomcat automatically. From now on, every time Windows is started, Tomcat will automatically start up at boot time and will be available from then on.

We can further customize the service by choosing the Properties option from the context menu. This allows us to change the startup type to manual or entirely disable the service, plus it allows you to choose to automatically restart the service should it crash. This last option is especially useful as it also allows you to run a script should the server fail, as well as rebooting the computer (although consider seriously what you put in this script as it can offer a security hole if the script does something that might be used as a DoS attack).

It also allows you to carry out different actions depending on how many times it has failed (by choosing the Recovery tab), so you can initially request a reboot of the service, then a reboot of the machine, and then any subsequent failures will cause a script to run that perhaps alerts you of the failure.

Remember that when a Java process fails (that is, the JVM exits with an error) it brings the machine down with it, but the server will continue to run as normal. The only possible reason for restarting the machine is if the applications that are running on Tomcat depend on an ordered bootup and no loss of connections between the applications and their various resources. That means that, on the whole, writing a script that flashes a warning or similar is more desirable than rebooting the system.

If you wish to set the recovery options, right-click on the Tomcat service entry in the list and choose Properties. In the window that opens, choose Recovery and you should be presented with the following options:

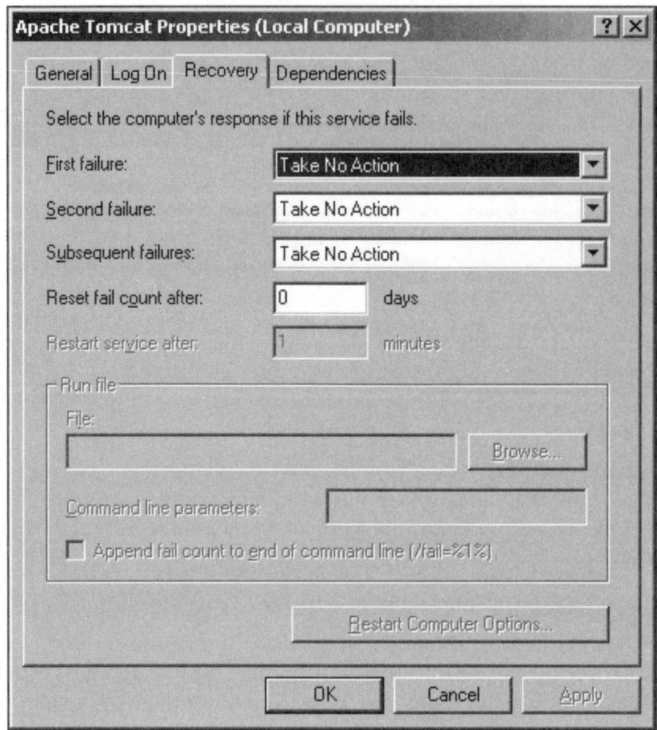

As you can see, the default is for no action to be taken. We are going to change this behavior and restart the server a maximum of twice and then run a script on the third and subsequent failures. Select the First failure drop-down box and choose Restart the Service. Do the same for the second box. We will have 1 minute as the time after the crash that the service should be restarted – this should give any external resources enough time to notice the failure and respond if necessary.

If this is a stable server that rarely fails, set the reset level high, say, to 20 days, which should mean that consistent failures are noticed and dealt with. It may be that it fails only occasionally – you want to know nevertheless. Setting the reset level high maximizes the chance that the third option will be run, thus alerting you to the problem. Remember that the script can easily be responsible for restarting the server so that users feel a minimal downtime, yet you are still notified. In fact, this option may be preferable to having the system automatically restart the server without explicit notification of problems.

If the server fails often, it may be necessary to turn the reset level down so that failures can be noticed.

Now choose Run a File from the Subsequent failures option menu. This will enable the Run file menu where you can choose the file to run (normally a batch file). The fail count is passed to the file as a command-line parameter for the script to report.

For the moment, assuming that you have not specified any other command-line prompts, you can discover the failure count using a file like the following:

```
@echo off
if NOT %1==/fail goto end
echo Number of failures to date is %2 >> T4.fail
:end
cd "c:\Program Files\Apache Tomcat 4.0\bin\"
start startup
```

The above file is the simplest possible reporting script that merely appends the failure count to a file named `T4.fail` each time a failure occurs before restarting the server (but not as a service, rather as a manual start in a new command prompt window). Before we move on, let us quickly explain the file. In the first line we turn off `echo`, the second line checks that the first command-line argument (`%1`) is equal to `/fail` and if so prints out the line:

```
Number of failures to date is %x%
```

where x is the number of failures. Notice the >> `T4.fail` codicil makes sure that `echo` is output to the file `T4.fail` and that the output is appended to, rather than replaces, the existing contents of the file. A single > would replace the file contents.

The result of multiple failures with this file, as set up above to run on the third failure, would be something along the lines of:

```
Number of failures to date is %3%
Number of failures to date is %4%
Number of failures to date is %5%
Number of failures to date is %6%
```

Alternatively, you can run a Java class that extracts the information and perhaps e-mails the failure to you. To do this, simply forward the fail count to your program, calling it as follows:

```
@echo off
if NOT %1==/fail goto end
java ReportTomcatFailure %2
:end
cd "c:\Program Files\Apache Tomcat 4.0\bin\"
start startup
```

The number of failures is now available as `ReportTomcatFailure`'s first command-line argument (accessible as `args[0]`).

In addition to the security risk involved in having the computer automatically reboot itself, it is not entirely necessary. Since Tomcat runs within a JVM, unless you are doing something unusual, a failure of the Tomcat instance is isolated from the rest of the system and a "soft" reboot should suffice for most problems. This puts hardware reboots in the very serious category, and as such, they are something that you probably want to control manually.

Tomcat 4 As a Daemon Thread

If you chose not to run Tomcat as an NT service, or were unable to because you are running Windows 9x/ME, you can still run Tomcat without a command prompt/DOS prompt window being open all the time that Tomcat is running.

To do this, you will need to amend the `catalina.bat` file in `%CATALINA_HOME%\bin`. Search and replace the text:

```
%_RUNJAVA%
```

with:

```
%_RUNJAVAW%
```

Note the added `W` character. This new command calls the window-less version of the `java` executable using `startup.bat`, which is again in the `%CATALINA_HOME%\bin` directory. Tomcat will now start with no attached Tomcat window, although one will appear and disappear.

> **You should create a shortcut to `startup.bat` as the provided shortcuts in the Start menu will not start a daemon process.**

Since the appearing-disappearing window resembles a port contention problem, you should now check that the server is running by attempting to connect to it with a `telnet` session or using a browser. If it is not running, run the `startup.bat` file from the `%CATALINA_HOME%\bin` folder and look at the error message, which should explain the problem.

Viewing the Default Installation

Tomcat, like most servers, comes with a default home page that can be used to check the installation is working. Enter the following address in a browser: http://localhost:8080/.

The following page should come up:

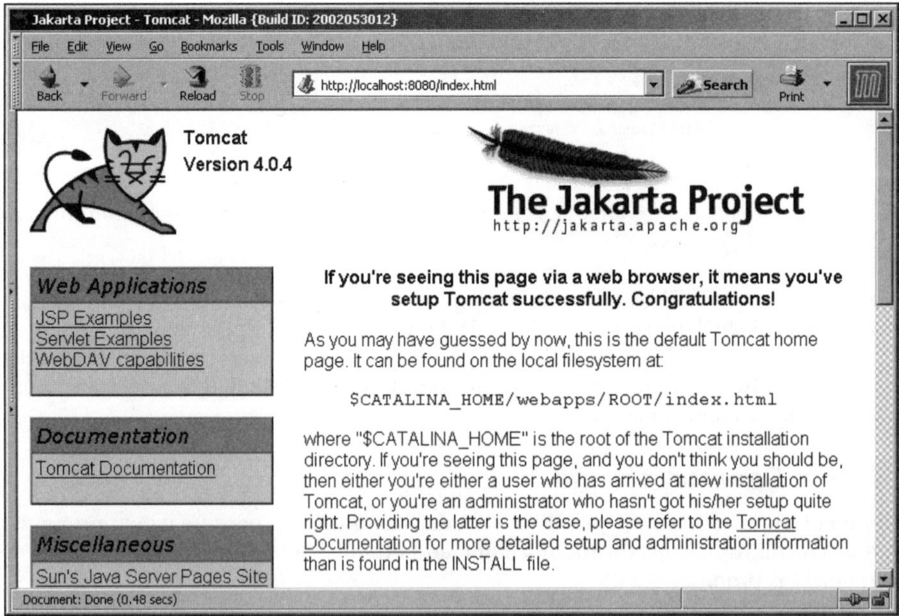

Port Numbers

Note that if you are not used to the port number assignation (the `:8080` section of the address), including it in the address of the server is required in the default installation. Ports are logical addresses in a computer that allow multiple communications with the server and the channeling of different protocols. For example, POP3 traffic is commonly addressed to port 25, while SMTP is addressed to port 110, SSL is addressed to port 21, `telnet` to 23, and so on. Browsers automatically point at port 80 if no port is specified (443 for HTTPS); hence the use of ports is not immediately visible to the average user.

> **As the majority of server hardware already includes a standard web server installation, usually Apache for Linux and IIS for Windows, Tomcat does not attempt to connect to the standard HTTP traffic port, which is 80 by default, but rather to port 8080.**

The configuration file that specifies the port number is called `server.xml` and can be found in the installation folder of Tomcat in the `%CATLINA_HOME%\conf` directory. It's just a text file and somewhere within it you should find the following entry:

```
<!-- Define a non-SSL HTTP/1.1 Connector on port 8080 -->
<Connector className="org.apache.catalina.connector.http.HttpConnector"
           port="8080" minProcessors="5" maxProcessors="75"
           enableLookups="true" redirectPort="8443"
           acceptCount="10" debug="0" connectionTimeout="60000"/>
```

You can find this entry by searching for the string '`port="8080"`'. Changing this to another number will change the Tomcat port number. Changing it to 80 will allow you to connect to Tomcat using the following URL http://localhost/ without the trailing colon and port number.

If you have any problems, refer to the *Troubleshooting and Tips* section at the end of this chapter.

On the other hand, if all has gone well, you are now the proud owner of your own Tomcat instance. Before we finish, we should check Tomcat's ability to serve JSP pages and servlets – there is nothing in the default welcome page that is dynamically generated, so we have not yet tested the JSP and servlet functionality.

To do this, choose the JSP Examples link from the left-hand menu and select some of the examples to run. Check that they all run as they are supposed to without error messages. Do the same for the Servlet Examples link to test this functionality. Let's now take a look at installing Tomcat on Windows using a ZIP file.

Installing Tomcat On Windows Using the ZIP File

Installing Tomcat using the ZIP file is not much different from the process described above. The ZIP file is provided for those concerned with the security implications of downloading and running an executable over the Internet. The ZIP file is significantly bigger than the executable installer but has the same contents.

To install Tomcat using the ZIP, simply unpack the contents of the file, traditionally to C:\Program Files\Jakarta Tomcat 4.0.

Now add the %CATALINA_HOME% environment variable as above. To check your installation, you will need to follow slightly different instructions than before. As the shortcuts for the server will not be create automatically, you will need to call a couple of batch files provided in the %CATALINA_HOME%\bin directory for this purpose.

To start the server, either navigate to %CATALINA_HOME%\bin within the command prompt and type:

```
> cd %CATALINA_HOME%\bin
> startup.bat
```

Alternatively, you can start the server from the command prompt from any directory by adding the path C:\Program Files\Jakarta Tomcat 4.0 to the Path variable before calling the startup file as follows:

```
> set path=%path%;c:\Program Files\Jakarta Tomcat 4.0
> startup
```

A new window will open as with the previous installation method showing that the server has started. To shut down Tomcat type shutdown.

Installing Tomcat from Source

Installing Tomcat from the sourcecode is usually done to benefit from the latest developments after bug fixes or feature releases and sometimes a developer may do this to incorporate bug repairs in the source. In Linux it is far more common for servers to be built for the system, however it is still not strictly necessary with a server such as Tomcat that is written in Java.

Tomcat is conventionally built using the Jakarta Ant utility. Ant is used for automated project building, including compilation and deployment, and benefits from the system independence that Java enjoys as it is written in Java. It uses a variety of configuration files provided with Tomcat to build Tomcat and to deploy it.

In addition to being used to build Tomcat, Ant can also be used to carry out a number of administrative actions on Tomcat with the help of additional files and this is discussed in Chapter 7. A more comprehensive description of Ant is in Chapter 17.

As the procedure for installing Tomcat from source is the same for Linux and Windows, we shall cover it in full after looking at the Linux binary distributions and Ant installation.

Installing Tomcat On Linux

Installing Tomcat on Linux or Unix is easy. Many of the problems that existed with the other branch of Tomcat development, the 3.2.x line, do not exist for Tomcat 4. Download either the ZIP file or gzipped tar file if you have GNU gzip. The files can be found at http://jakarta.apache.org/builds/jakarta-tomcat-4.0/release/v4.0.4/bin/. If you have any problem finding it, try navigating to it from the Tomcat project site http://jakarta.apache.org/tomcat/.

The Light Edition, available as `jakarta-tomcat-4.0.4-LE-jdk14.zip` and `jakarta-tomcat-4.0.4-LE-jdk14.tar.gz` does not contain Xerces, an XML parser required by Tomcat, and is therefore 1.2Mb lighter in download size. This edition is aimed at installations on top of the 1.4 JDK, which has an XML parser included. In addition, the Light Edition does not provide support for JNDI or JavaMail, the JDBC 2 Extensions, or Tyrex (security, transactions, and resource pooling).

If you are using JDK 1.3, then download either `jakarta-tomcat-4.0.4.tar.gz` or `jakarta-tomcat-4.0.4.zip`. Also if you have any stability issues with Tomcat 4 on JDK 1.4 then it may be worth installing the complete binary before going to the trouble of installing 1.3 JDK; since the 1.4 JDK itself is very stable it is likely that it is Tomcat that is the problem.

RPMs are available for installation in the rpms folder if you prefer. Alternatively, the ZIP file has exactly the same contents, and you can then simply unzip the file without compatibility issues.

> **Opera 6.0 occasionally crashes, presumably because it does not recognize the `tar` MIME type. If you have these problems, try another browser or use the ZIP file.**

Unzip (and untar if necessary) the file onto your hard drive to a path such as `/usr/java/jakarta-tomcat-4.0.4`.

Installing the RPM for the full version 4.0.4 was done as follows:

```
# rpm -iv tomcat4-4.0.4-full.2jpp.noarch.rpm
```

`noarch` signifies the package is suitable for all architectures.

You should now export the `$CATALINA_HOME` variable, using the following command (in `bash`):

```
# CATALINA_HOME=/usr/java/jakarta-tomcat-4.04
# export CATALINA_HOME
```

Alternatively, add these commands to `~/.bashrc` or `/etc/profile` as we did for the JDK installation or create a shell file, `tomcat.sh`, and place it in `/etc/profile.d`. It will be run automatically by `/etc/profile` at boot time to make the variable available to all users.

Catalina, as mentioned in Chapter 1, is the codename of the Tomcat 4 project.

You can now start Tomcat by running the following shell command:

```
# $CATALINA_HOME/bin/startup.sh
```

You can shut down Tomcat using `shutdown.sh`. If you want a script for restarting the server, copy and rename `shutdown.sh` as `restart.sh` and add the following line to the end:

```
exec "$PRGDIR"/"$EXECUTABLE" start "$@"
```

or simply write a script that calls shutdown followed by startup.

Viewing the Default Installation

To check that Tomcat is running, point your browser to http://localhost:8080/. You should see the following screenshot:

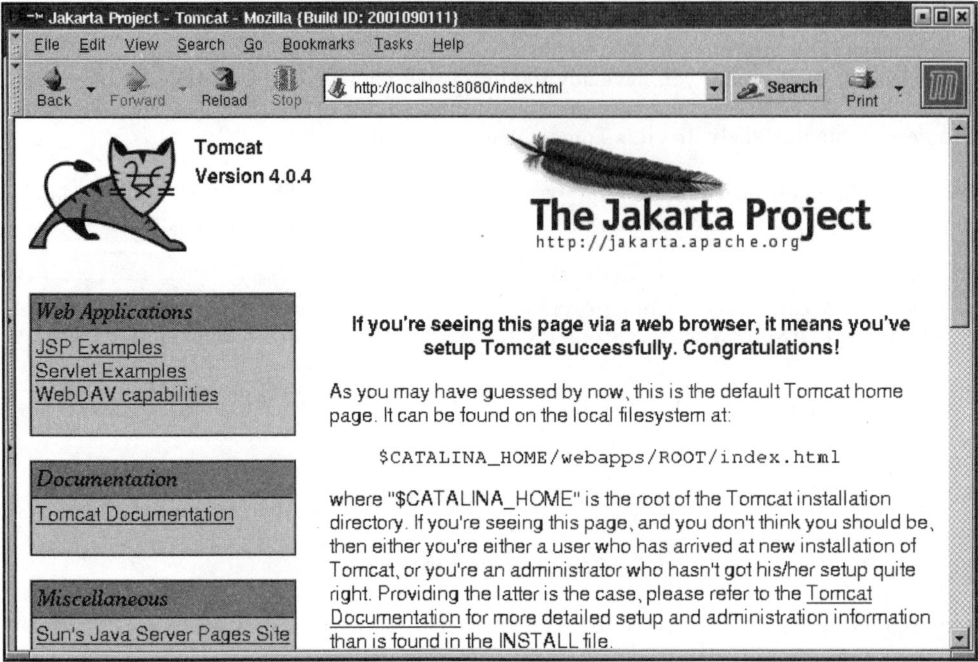

Choose the JSP Examples link from the left-hand side menu and select some of the examples to run. Check that they run without error messages. Do the same for the Servlet Examples to test this functionality.

Port Numbers

Tomcat uses port 8080 by default, as in Linux and Unix systems `root` permission is required to assign port numbers below 1024 to a process. Thus, to make things simple, the port number chosen should be one that is greater than 1024. As the majority of server hardware already includes a standard web server installation, usually Apache, Tomcat does not attempt to connect to the standard HTTP traffic port, 80, by default.

If you wish to use Tomcat as a standalone server without providing the port number in the address bar (by using 80), you will firstly need `root` privileges.

The configuration file that specifies the port number is called `server.xml` and can be found in the `$CATALINA_HOME/conf` directory. Somewhere within it you should find the following entry:

```
<!-- Define a non-SSL HTTP/1.1 Connector on port 8080 -->
<Connector className="org.apache.catalina.connector.http.HttpConnector"
           port="8080" minProcessors="5" maxProcessors="75"
           enableLookups="true" redirectPort="8443"
           acceptCount="10" debug="0" connectionTimeout="60000"/>
```

You can find this entry by grepping for the string 'port="8080"'. Changing this to another number (over 1024 in Linux) will change the Tomcat port number. Changing it to 80 will allow you to connect to Tomcat using the following URL: http://localhost/, providing that the server is started with root permissions.

If you have any problems, refer to the *Troubleshooting and Tips* section at the end of this chapter.

Running Tomcat with the Server Option

Earlier we discussed running the Java executable with the server option, which will increase its efficiency and thus perform better. To run Tomcat with the server option, we will need to modify a number of files in its bin directory. For Windows, we need to edit setclasspath.bat. The last three lines should be changed as follows:

```
set _RUNJAVA="%JAVA_HOME%\bin\java" -server
set _RUNJAVAW="%JAVA_HOME%\bin\javaw" -server
set _RUNJDB="%JAVA_HOME%\bin\jdb" -server
```

Of course this assumes that you are manually starting Tomcat (or that you have copied the shortcut into the Startup folder on Windows 98).

Linux is very similar. This time we modify setclasspath.sh:

```
_RUNJAVA="$JAVA_HOME"/bin/java -server
_RUNJDB="$JAVA_HOME"/bin/jdb -server
```

Alternatively, a simpler option that will work on every platform is to amend the file $JAVA_HOME/jre/lib/jvm.cfg. Usually, the file will look something like this:

```
#
# @(#)jvm.cfg 1.2 99/07/09
#
# Copyright 1999 by Sun Microsystems, Inc.,
# 901 San Antonio Road, Palo Alto, California, 94303, U.S.A.
# All rights reserved.
#
# List of JVMs that can be used as the first option to java, javac, etc.
# Order is important -- first in this list is the default JVM.
#
-hotspot
-server
-classic
```

As you can see the client JVM is the default. To make server the default, change the order of these so that -server comes first in the list.

If the file is somewhat different, with extra settings for native versus green threads, don't worry; the principle is essentially the same. If the file is not present, then the option above is the only one available – Sun have removed it from JDK 1.4.

The Tomcat Installation Directory

The Tomcat installation directory contents are as follows:

```
$CATALINA_HOME/
               bin/
               classes/
               common/
                      classes/
                      lib/
               conf/
               lib/
               logs/
               server/
                      classes/
                      lib/
               src/
               temp/
               webapps/
               work/
```

Note that this structure has changed in the newest beta versions of Tomcat (4.1.3 onwards). `$CATALINA_HOME/classes` and `$CATALINA_HOME/lib` have been moved to `$CATALINA_HOME/shared/classes` and `$CATALINA_HOME/shared/lib` respectively. Also, there is a new `$CATALINA_HOME/server/webapps` directory for server configuration tools. These are covered in Chapter 7 so we won't worry about them just now.

The bin Directory

The `$CATALINA_HOME/bin` directory contains the various shell scripts and batch files for starting Tomcat in various modes. It also includes a pre-compiler for JSP pages that can improve startup time and first time response – the time it takes for the server to respond to a request for a JSP page that has not previously been compiled. Compilation only occurs once (unless the memory is reclaimed by the garbage collector) but it can make the first customer to a site after the server was restarted very dissatisfied because of the long response times.

The classes Directory

The `$CATALINA_HOME/classes` contains Java classes that any web application can have access to. Examples are unpacked libraries dealing with databases, and so on. The standard way to install classes on a server is to use JAR files.

The common Directory

The `$CATALINA_HOME/common` directory is split into two, `classes` and `lib`. The classes in these directories are again available to every web application, with unpacked classes residing in the `classes` directory and JAR files residing in the `lib` directory. The difference between this directory and the `$CATALINA_HOME/classes` and `$CATALINA_HOME/lib` directories is that the classes in this directory are also available to the Catalina engine. For security, it is better to constrain the visibility of classes as tightly as possible, and this approach also allows fine granularity over the visibility of classes in the classpath for each group.

The `lib` directory within this folder includes the Xerces XML parser and the e-mail API for Java, among others. We will also see more information on the internal architecture of Tomcat 4.0 in the next chapter.

The conf Directory

The `$CATALINA_HOME/conf` directory contains the configuration files for Tomcat. These include general server configuration files, a default user list for file-based authentication and security for web applications, and a global configuration file.

The lib Directory

The `$CATALINA_HOME/lib` directory contains packaged libraries of Java classes that are available to every web application but not to the Catalina engine.

The logs Directory

The `$CATALINA_HOME/logs` directory contains the server logs.

The server Directory

Classes that are to be made available to Catalina only are placed within the `classes` and `lib` sub-folders of `$CATALINA_HOME/server` with the same rules as we described for the `common` directory. Libraries for supporting CGI in Tomcat, regular expressions, and the various connectors that allow Tomcat to be used together with HTTP servers are placed here.

The src Directory

If the Tomcat installation includes the sourcecode, it is included in `$CATALINA_HOME/src`. If not, it can be downloaded from http://jakarta.apache.org/builds/jakarta-tomcat-4.0/release/v4.0.4/src/.

The webapps Directory

The web applications provided with Tomcat are contained in `$CATALINA_HOME/webapps`. The web applications provided with Tomcat are as follows:

- `examples`
  A number of example servlets and JSP pages. These are the examples we used earlier to test the Tomcat installation.

- `manager`
  This web application allows remote management of the server including installing and uninstalling web applications. Chapter 7 covers this application in detail.

- `ROOT`
  This is the default web application for Tomcat. The contents of this folder are shown when no subcontext is given in the URL to the server. For example, http://localhost:8080/ will load `index.html`, or `index.jsp` whichever is present, with the latter taking precedence if both exist.

- `tomcat-docs`
  The documentation for Tomcat is available with a default installation. You may wish to remove this directory if you don't wish people to use your server for browsing the Tomcat documentation. Throughout this book we will discuss tightening the Tomcat installation for security and other concerns.
- `webdav`
  WebDAV is a protocol enhancement for HTTP 1.1 that allows distributed authoring and versioning (remote authoring of web content). This web application is read-only by default. If read/write is enabled, it can be set to accept uploads of updated information authenticated through a user/password combination.

The work Directory

The `$CATALINA_HOME/work` directory contains temporary files, precompiled JSP pages, and other intermediate files.

Ant Installation

We will now describe how to install Ant. Ant is a Java-based build tool that has a number of advantages over `make`. It is also used to build and deploy applications, however it benefits from platform independence and is designed to maximize the possibility of providing a single build file for multiple target platforms. There is still some burden on the deployment engineer to write the build files in a way that minimizes dependency on a specific file path (windows paths, for example, will cause problems on Linux and vice versa).

Installing Ant On Windows

A binary distribution of Ant is available from http://jakarta.apache.org/builds/jakarta-ant/release/v1.5/bin/. The latest version of Tomcat requires version 1.4 or greater of Ant, and we will need the following file: `jakarta-ant-1.5-bin.zip`.

Install Ant by unpacking the ZIP file to a suitable location, which for the purpose of this chapter we will assume is `c:\jakarta-ant-1.5`. This directory contains a `lib` folder where extensions can be placed to install them.

Now we must make Ant available in the `Path` so that it can be called from any directory. Follow the instructions given above for creating the `%CATALINA_HOME%` variable to access the system variables and adjust your `Path` variable using the **Edit** button to include the `bin` directory of Ant:

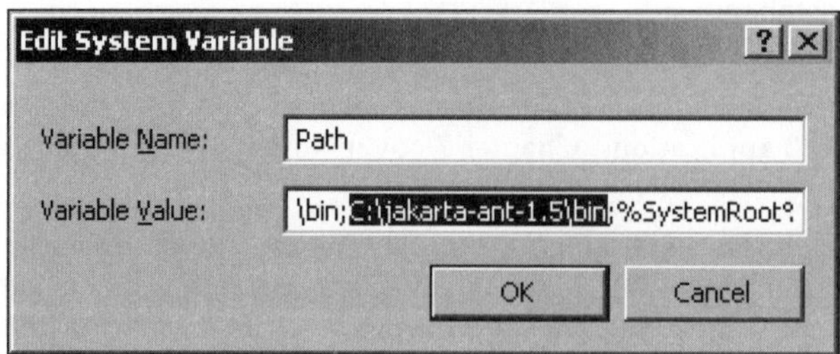

If you have followed the instructions correctly, typing `ant` into the command prompt will now elicit a usage message showing that it is correctly installed. You will note that the Java-related folders are before all the others in the `Path` variable; the existence of the MS `java.exe` executable in the `Path` can interfere with the smooth running of Tomcat.

Installing Ant On Linux

Begin by downloading the zipped, gzipped and tarred, or bz2-compressed binary file from http://jakarta.apache.org/builds/jakarta-ant/release/v1.5/bin/. Alternatively, you can download an RPM from http://jakarta.apache.org/builds/jakarta-ant/release/v1.5/rpms/.

Unzip the file into the folder of your choice, we assume here that it is `/usr/java/ant`. To use the RPM, move the RPM to the desired parent folder of your installation and choose:

```
# rpm -iv ant-1.5-4jpp.noarch.rpm
```

as appropriate.

Now you must define a system variable, `$ANT_HOME`, that points at the installation directory. For the suggested details above, this would be:

```
# ANT_HOME=/usr/local/ant
# export ANT_HOME
```

in `bash`. You can add it permanently as we did for Tomcat and the JDK by setting it in `~/.bashrc` for local effect, `etc/profile`, or a shell script, nominally named `ant.sh`, placed in `etc/profile.d` which will be called by `etc/profile` automatically at bootup.

You must also add `$ANT_HOME/bin` to your `PATH` variable to call Ant with its short name:

```
# ant
```

rather than:

```
# /usr/java/ant/bin/ant
```

You can test your installation by entering:

```
# ant
```

into an open shell window.

Installing Tomcat from Source

Various reasons exist for installing Tomcat from source, including compiling the server without support for unwanted functionality and to benefit from the latest functionality and bug fixes.

The list of required downloads is extensive:

- The Tomcat source distribution: (http://jakarta.apache.org/builds/jakarta-tomcat-4.0/release/v4.0.4/src/).
- Ant must be installed as above: (http://jakarta.apache.org/builds/jakarta-ant/release/v1.5/bin/).
- The Java XML pack: http://java.sun.com/xml/downloads/javaxmlpack.html.
- The Xerces parser from Apache (1.4.3 has been tested on Tomcat): http://xml.apache.org/dist/xerces-j/.
- The Servlet API JAR file from Jakarta Apache – we tested this with the latest nightly build: http://jakarta.apache.org/builds/jakarta-servletapi-4/.
- The JNDI reference implementation and the provider – of which we downloaded `jndi-1_2_1.zip` and `ldap-1_2_4.zip`: http://java.sun.com/products/jndi/. Note that both the LDAP provider and the 1.2.1 release of the RI should be downloaded.

We recommend that you also download the following as they provide useful functionality:

- JavaMail, which allow users to send e-mails from HTML forms. We need version 1.2 or later: http://java.sun.com/products/javamail/index.html.
- The JSSE package which enables SSL and certificates: http://java.sun.com/products/jsse/. Place this file in the `$JAVA_HOME/jre/lib` folder to make sure that security settings are uniform for the whole machine and that you don't have to replicate certificates for each installation. Files placed here are common to the entire machine. It should be noted that this file is also available with the JNDI and LDAP downloads, and that it is also built into J2SDK 1.4.
- The Java Transaction API (JTA) that enables transactional support: http://java.sun.com/products/jta/.
- Tyrex that enables support for object pooling and managed data sources for various resources including JMS, EJBs, and JDBC connections: http://tyrex.exolab.org/download.html.
- JUnit, an automated unit testing framework: http://www.junit.org/.

Note that a number of these come with the binary distribution of Tomcat, so if you have it, many of these downloads can be avoided. The remaining packages are required for a full install:

- JDBC optional package version 2.0 – this download is a JAR file and should not be unpacked, rather copy it into a directory called `jdbc2_0-stdext`: http://java.sun.com/products/jdbc/download.html.
- Java Management eXtensions RI (JMX) version 1.0 or later from (tested with 1.1): http://java.sun.com/products/JavaManagement/download.html.
- Java Activation Framework (JAF) version 1.0.1 or later: http://java.sun.com/products/javabeans/glasgow/jaf.html.

Each of these (including the Tomcat source) should be unpacked into a directory of your own. We suggest `/usr/java` or `c:\java` as appropriate to limit the clutter that this would otherwise create on your drive. In addition, because of the way the build file is set up for Tomcat, it is simpler to build Tomcat if these files are all in a folder of their own within a common parent folder.

The ldap.jar file should be placed in the JNDI directory in the lib folder. The JAXP installation (from the Java XML pack) includes a file called xalan.jar that should be placed in Ant's lib directory. We will configure Ant to recognize the remaining files in the build file for Tomcat.

The Ant Build File

The build file we will use as a starting point is, as recommended by the Tomcat project, the build.properties.sample from the Tomcat source directory. Copy this file and rename it build.properties. Please keep in mind that this next section is very dependent on your personal system setup and so you will need to adapt it according to your environment. In each case, the installation folder of the appropriate API is the only bit that needs to be changed. Everything else is referred to using relative paths and so should survive changes in the location of the API as long as the root folder of each installation has been specified correctly.

The file begins like this:

```
# -----------------------------------------------------------------------------
# build.properties.sample
#
# This is an example "build.properties" file, used to customize
# building Tomcat
# for your local environment.  It defines the location of all external
# modules that Tomcat depends on.  Copy this file to "build.properties"
# in the top-level source directory, and customize it as needed.
#
# $Id: build.properties.sample,v 1.7.2.10 2002/03/24 06:37:10 remm Exp $
# -----------------------------------------------------------------------------

# ----- Compile Control Flags -----
compile.debug=on
compile.deprecation=off
compile.optimize=on

# ----- Build Control Flags
#full.dist=on
#light.dist=on
#build.sysclasspath=ignore
#flags.hide=on
```

The first bit we need to change is the location of the JAR files and various installations.

On Linux:

```
# ----- Default Base Path for Dependent Packages -----
base.path=/usr/java
```

On Windows:

```
# ----- Default Base Path for Dependent Packages -----
base.path=c:\java
```

The next section is unchanged:

```
# ----- Jakarta Tomcat Connectors path -----
jakarta-tomcat-connector.home=../../jakarta-tomcat-connectors

# ----- Tomcat utils -----
tomcat-util.jar=../lib/tomcat-util.jar

# ----- JK 1.3 connector for Tomcat 4.0 -----
tomcat-ajp.jar=../lib/tomcat-ajp.jar

# ----- Coyote connector for Tomcat 4.0 -----
commons-logging.jar=../lib/commons-logging.jar
tomcat-coyote.jar=../lib/tomcat-coyote.jar
tomcat-http11.jar=../lib/tomcat-http11.jar

# ----- Jakarta Regular Expressions Library, version 1.2 -----
regexp.jar=../lib/jakarta-regexp-1.2.jar
```

The following could be left as provided following the download instructions above:

```
# ----- Jakarta Servlet API Classes (Servlet 2.3 / JSP 1.2) -----
servlet.home=${base.path}/jakarta-servletapi-4
servlet.lib=${servlet.home}/lib
servlet.jar=${servlet.lib}/servlet.jar

# ----- Java Activation Framework (JAF), version 1.0.1 or later -----
activation.home=${base.path}/jaf-1.0.1
activation.lib=${activation.home}
activation.jar=${activation.lib}/activation.jar
```

JAXP is now available as part of the XML pack which we downloaded, so the next section needs to be modified somewhat to point to the root of the JAXP folder within the XML pack installation folder. On the summer pack this is:

```
# ----- Java API for XML Processing (JAXP), version 1.1 or later -----
jaxp.home=${base.path}/java_xml_pack-summer-02/jaxp-1.2
jaxp.lib=${jaxp.home}
crimson.jar=${jaxp.lib}/crimson.jar
jaxp.jar=${jaxp.lib}/jaxp.jar
xalan.jar=${jaxp.lib}/xalan.jar
```

The JDBC optional package does not require changes here nor does the JavaMail entry:

```
# ---- Java Database Connectivity (JDBC) Optional Package, version 2.0 -----
jdbc20ext.home=${base.path}/jdbc2_0-stdext
jdbc20ext.lib=${jdbc20ext.home}
jdbc20ext.jar=${jdbc20ext.lib}/jdbc2_0-stdext.jar

# ----- Java Mail, version 1.2 or later -----
mail.home=${base.path}/javamail-1.2
mail.lib=${mail.home}
mail.jar=${mail.lib}/mail.jar
```

The current default downloads for JMX, JNDI, and LDAP require the following line. The remainder can remain as is, except note that the JTA JAR was placed in a folder named `jta-spec1_0_1` and the current release of Xerces is 1.4.4 and not 1.4.3 as is set here:

```
# ----- Java Management Extensions (JMX) RI, version 1.0.1 or later -----
jmx.home=${base.path}/jmx_1.1_ri_bin
jmx.lib=${jmx.home}/lib
jmxri.jar=${jmx.lib}/jmxri.jar

# --- Java Naming and Directory Interface (JNDI), version 1.2 or later -----
jndi.home=${base.path}/jndi
jndi.lib=${jndi.home}/lib
jndi.jar=${jndi.lib}/jndi.jar
ldap.jar=${jndi.lib}/ldap.jar

# ----- Java Secure Sockets Extension (JSSE), version 1.0.2 or later -----
jsse.home=${base.path}/jsse-1.0.2
jsse.lib=${jsse.home}/lib
jcert.jar=${jsse.lib}/jcert.jar
jnet.jar=${jsse.lib}/jnet.jar
jsse.jar=${jsse.lib}/jsse.jar

# ----- Java Transaction API (JTA), version 1.0.1 or later -----
jta.home=${base.path}/jta-spec1_0_1
jta.lib=${jta.home}
jta.jar=${jta.lib}/jta-spec1_0_1.jar

# ----- JUnit Unit Test Suite, version 3.7 or later -----
junit.home=${base.path}/junit3.7
junit.lib=${junit.home}
junit.jar=${junit.lib}/junit.jar

# ----- Tyrex Data Source, version 0.9.7 -----
tyrex.home=${base.path}/tyrex-0.9.7.0
tyrex.lib=${tyrex.home}
tyrex.jar=${tyrex.lib}/tyrex-0.9.7.0.jar

# ----- Xerces XML Parser, version 1.4.3 or later -----
xerces.home=${base.path}/xerces-1_4_4
xerces.lib=${xerces.home}
xerces.jar=${xerces.lib}/xerces.jar
```

Building Tomcat

Assuming that all this information is correct, you should now be able to compile Tomcat using the following line:

```
# ant
```

within the root folder for the Tomcat source directory. The build takes a few minutes and the resultant build is in a subdirectory of the source folder named `build`. To deploy your server, move it out of the source folder and into a folder of its own and set the `$CATALINA_HOME` variable using the instructions given previously.

If there are any problems, they are very likely to be as a result of misconfigured package locations in the file. The error messages you will receive are very clear and it shouldn't be too long before you have a built server.

Troubleshooting and Tips

Finally, before we close this chapter, let's examine the typical problems that may occur with the Tomcat installation. If you have further problems, more material can be found on the Tomcat web site at http://jakarta.apache.org/tomcat/ and at http://java.sun.com/ as well as on various forums. You should also read the release notes available with each download.

Here are a number of problems typically encountered when first installing Tomcat.

The JVM Crashes

This problem is rare and seems to be specific to Linux. Systems using the 2.4 kernel can experience JVM crashes in the 1.2 and 1.3 versions of the Hotspot JVM, usually on startup. IBM's JDK doesn't have this problem, and neither does J2SDK1.4. This can be fixed by limiting the default stack size to 2048 using the following command if you are using a `bash` shell:

```
$ ulimit -s 2048
```

or the following if you are using `tcsh`:

```
$ limit stacksize 2048
```

In addition, if you are also using `glibc` 2.2, you should also export `LD_ASSUME_KERNEL=2.2.5`.

Tomcat Window Disappears

This is particularly difficult to diagnose and applies especially to Windows. Since the problem usually has one of two causes, however, we can start by diagnosing it and then move onto the known solutions.

Diagnosing the Problem

If the Tomcat does not start, it can be run in the current shell or command prompt so we can see what the problem is. Type the following on Linux:

```
$ $CATALINA_HOME/bin/catalina.sh run
```

Or on Windows:

```
> %CATALINA_HOME%/bin/catalina run
```

This will produce the normal startup messages, and any errors will be displayed. These errors also appear in the `stdout.log` file in the `$CATALINA_HOME/logs` subdirectory. The following is a portion of the error message for a missing `xerces.jar` file:

```
java.lang.reflect.InvocationTargetException: java.lang.NoClassDefFoundError:
org/xml/sax/HandlerBase
```

The following means that the port is in use:

```
Catalina.start: LifecycleException:  null.open:  java.net.BindException: Address
in use: JVM_Bind:8080
```

If your error is not one of these, you may need to elicit help from the Apache Jakarta mailing lists or our own lists at http://p2p.wrox.com/.

XML Parser Unavailable

If you have installed the Light Edition, you may have failed to install an XML parser or have a classpath problem: a parser with insufficient support for XML may be loaded before `xerces.jar` (shouldn't really happen in Tomcat 4.0 unless you have installed another parser).

If you suspect that Xerces is missing, check for the existence of `xerces.jar` in `$CATALINA_HOME/common/lib`. If it is not there you will need to download it and place it there.

If you suspect another parser is being loaded in its place, try changing Xerces' name to `_xerces.jar`. Otherwise, the file is loaded late because x occurs late in the alphabet.

The Port Number Is in Use

Tomcat uses port 8080 by default as mentioned previously. You can check if another program is using this port by using `netstat` on both types of platforms. Typing `netstat` (`netstat -ln` on Linux) into your shell/command prompt will list open ports on your system and should show the process that is interfering with Tomcat. You have two options, shut the process down or change Tomcat's port as described earlier.

A common problem is trying to start a new Tomcat instance when there is one still running. This is especially true if it's running as a daemon thread. If you suspect this is the case, you can check it by using `telnet` to connect to the socket as follows:

```
$ telnet localhost 8080
```

and see if you are given a connection. If you are awarded a connection, the screen goes blank rather than giving the error:

```
Connecting To localhost...Could not open a connection to host on port 8080 :
Connect failed
```

When you are connected, type GET / and press return or enter (`echo` is turned off by default on Windows, so it looks a little strange as typing doesn't appear to achieve anything). On Windows, this results in the following output:

```
HTTP/1.0 302 Found
Content-Type: text/html
Location: http://127.0.0.1:8080/
/index.jsp
Content-Length: 167
Servlet-Engine: Tomcat Web Server/3.2.1 (JSP 1.1; Servlet 2.2; Java 1.3.0; Windows
```

```
2000 5.0 x86; java.vendor=Sun Microsystems Inc.)

<head><title>Document moved</title></head>
<body><h1>Document moved</h1>
This document has moved <a href="http://127.0.0.1:8080/
/index.jsp">here</a>.<p>
</body>

Connection to host lost.

>
```

In this case there is an instance of Tomcat 3.2.1 running in the background that is stopping Tomcat 4 from booting up.

Even if you are refused a connection, this indicates that there is a process sitting on that port. If connection fails, then try one of the other possibilities.

A Proxy Is Blocking Access

If you have a proxy set up for all HTTP services, it may be blocking access to the server. You should bypass the proxy for all local addresses. Instructions are provided below.

Opera

In Opera 6.0, Choose File | Preferences, choose the Network option and select the Proxy Servers and click on Do not user proxy on the addresses below. Enter localhost and 127.0.0.1 (separated by commas) in this box and OK all changes.

Netscape

In Netscape 4.7 choose Edit | Preferences choose the Advanced option and choose Proxies. Select the View button of Manual proxy configuration and enter localhost and 127.0.0.1 in the Exceptions box. This may differ between versions of Netscape (and Mozilla), but the principles remain the same.

Internet Explorer

Choose Tools | Internet Options and choose the Connections tab. Select the Lan Settings button and enter your proxy configuration by selecting the Advanced button in the window that opens. Enter localhost and 127.0.0.1 in the Exceptions box. This should work in all versions of IE.

Out of Environment Space Error

This was dealt with previously in the section entitled *Windows 9x-and ME-Specific Issues.*

Summary

We have gone through a great deal of information in the course of this chapter to select and install a JDK, Ant, and Tomcat in a variety of different ways. In the majority of cases, the installation of the server is a very straightforward process as binary versions are available for the common platforms.

If you have any problems, besides the support network at http://p2p.wrox.com/, http://jakarta.apache.org/ also has a number of lists that can be helpful to the beginner. The user list is also archived and you will find that most questions have been asked, and answered, before.

In the next chapter we cover Tomcat's architecture.

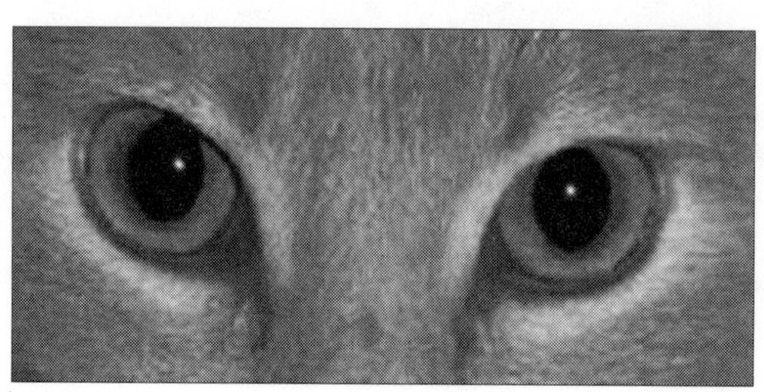

4

Tomcat Installation Directory and Architecture

Tomcat has an elegant architecture and understanding it will stand us in good stead for the remainder of the book. The previous chapter included a brief view of the insides of Tomcat and in this chapter we shall have a more detailed discussion.

Tomcat's internal architecture closely mirrors the way that we administrate it. Each section of the Tomcat architecture is closely associated with a function of the server. It is possible to group administration tasks around these functional components, making administration more intuitive. Thus, to administrate Tomcat effectively, it is necessary for us to know both where to place files within the folder hierarchy of the Tomcat installation and the architecture.

In this chapter we will:

- Gain an understanding of the default Tomcat installation
- Become familiar with the generic web application structure
- Understand Tomcat's architecture

The Installation Directory

The old Tomcat architecture, in versions 3.x and earlier, was found to be somewhat inflexible, and so it was important for those involved in the Tomcat 4 project to start from scratch and learn from previous experience. The result is a simple and flexible architecture. However, this introduces some complexities in the placement of files – there are several locations that have subtle differences.

We will begin by detailing the contents of the `$CATALINA_HOME/bin` directory.

The bin Directory

The `bin` directory contains shell scripts (Unix) and batch files (Windows), from now on referred to as scripts, for starting Tomcat in different modes, as well as a variety of utilities:

Script	Description
`catalina`	This generic script is provided for starting and stopping the server and a number of the other scripts call it. It allows the Tomcat server to be started with or without debugging enabled, with or without a security manager, and in embedded mode to use it as part of a bigger application. Refer to Chapter 16 for a discussion of security managers, a Java language feature that allows fine-grained control over the permissions of an application over the filesystem, access to system variables, and so on.
`cpappend`	Other scripts use this script to create the classpath dynamically before starting the server. The setting provided here could be overridden to allow each user to have personalized configuration files for the same server installation, whether for different instances of the server running at the same time, or for a development environment for non-concurrent users. This means that each user may configure the server without affecting the work of other users.
`digest`	This script creates digested passwords for use with container-managed authentication. Security can be improved by encrypting passwords. While this does not mean that the password cannot be cracked, it certainly makes it more difficult to discover. Container-managed security is a facility by which an application can declare that it wants certain resources secured against unauthorized access and the Tomcat server will take care of checking the identity and permissions of the user. We will cover security in detail in Chapter 16.
`jasper` and `jasc`	Both these scripts refer to the JSP compiler that turns JSP files into servlets. To improve the initial responsiveness of the server, it is possible to precompile JSP files to save doing it when the server is started up. This will save the initial performance hit when the first user visits the site. Also, this means that it is not necessary to include the source JSP files in the deployment environment, which means the size of the deployment file is minimized and it is more difficult to amend the sourcecode of the JSP files.
`startup` and `shutdown`	Both these scripts call the `catalina` script to start up the server and to shut it down. Actually, they are executable files (to which shortcuts can be created in Windows, for example) that can be used to control the server more simply than programming command-line options into the shortcuts. *The shortcuts that are installed as part of Tomcat's installation on Windows in the* Start *menu no longer use these files as they did previously, but rather call the executable JAR file* `bootstrap.jar` *to start the server.*
`tool-wrapper`	This script allows command-line tools to be called in the same environment that Tomcat is run in so that they have a common set of references. For example, command-line analysis tools may need to run within the same environment as Tomcat to identify problems that are specific to Tomcat. If the classpath for the analysis tool is not the same as for the server, then obviously classpath issues cannot be identified, and so on.

The classes, lib, server, and common Directories

Both the `classes` and the `lib` directories contain Java classes that should be available to every web application. The `classes` folder contains unpacked classes while the `lib` directory contains packaged groups of classes in WAR files.

Java classes and packages placed in the `server` directory are internal to the server only and we will not normally need to change the contents of this folder. It is divided into a `lib` directory and a `classes` directory (usually empty).

Files placed in the `common` folder are available both to the server and to web applications. This directory includes utility packages for sending e-mails, accessing databases, using Java naming and directory services, and processing XML rather than custom user classes meant for use by an individual web application.

According to the Tomcat documentation, the `jasper` folder, if present, holds classes specific to Apache's Jasper JSP compiler only. If required and not present, this folder can be created and only JSP pages and Jasper will have access to files placed here. This folder should be used in applications where access to Java files is restricted for maximum security.

The conf Directory

The `conf` directory contains the server configuration files:

File	Description
`catalina.policy`	This file sets up the necessary permissions for Catalina when it is run within the context of a security manager.
`server.xml`	This is the main configuration file for Tomcat and is discussed in detail in the next chapter. We can use it to configure everything from the shutdown command to logging, filtering, connections to the web server such as Apache, the port and host on which the server is running, and the location of each web application's files.

The logs Directory

The `logs` directory is the default location for application log files. The default installation generates time-stamped logs for each connection out of the server, the server itself, and for the `localhost` host (the default home of the server). An access log provides a dump of every request to the server and the standard output stream and standard error streams are redirected here. In addition, the example web application shipped with Tomcat configures its own logging and its files are found here.

It may be necessary to schedule housekeeping tasks to ensure that the size of the `logs` directory does not grow out of hand. Therefore, a regular parsing of the files may be necessary to watch for trends such as attempted breaches in security, failures of the application, application usage patterns, and so on, all of which should be logged in a well-developed application.

The developer of the application may provide parsing utilities, or alternatively some collaboration with the developers may be necessary to understand the format of log messages and the types of events that are recorded.

The webapps Directory

The webapps directory is the default location of the web applications in Tomcat. This location can be changed and it is recommended that you do this, as this separates the application-specific files that change relatively frequently from the server files that don't tend to change much. As a bonus, the installation directory for Tomcat can be kept as read/write for the administrator only, thus maintaining greater security – read/write access for other users need only be provided for the now separate webapps folder.

The web application directory provides an alternative deployment method to editing the configuration file (server.xml) or using the manager web application. Web applications may be placed here, in both packaged and unpackaged formats, and they will be automatically deployed at the next server bootup.

In Tomcat 4.1, it is also possible to place the portions of server.xml that define web applications in this folder and Tomcat will automatically deploy the web application. This latter method allows an alternative to manually editing server.xml when placing the web application within the webapps folder is not desirable and is a very useful addition to Tomcat.

Next we will discuss the web application structure in both packaged and unpackaged formats.

Generic Web Application Structure

Web applications are mapped to URLs in the following manner.

The server, by common agreement, always has one web application that maps to the address of the server with no additional path information, that is:

http://servername:port/

which looks like this in the default installation:

http://localhost:8080/

or:

http://yourintranetname

If DNS has been properly configured, it may also be accessible from a URL such as:

http://www.yourcompanyname.com/

Each web application is known by its name, which in the following example is examples:

http://localhost:8080/examples/

Automatically deployed applications (those placed in the webapps folder) are named after the directory they are in. So the application package (examples.war), would be accessible through the URL shown above and would be known as the examples application. Each application on the server is known by its name and resources are accessed according to the remainder of the URL after the web application's name.

This does mean that the default web application could not have a folder named `examples`, as there would be no easy way of discovering whether the URL is requesting the file `index.jsp` in the `examples` subfolder of the default application or the file `index.jsp` within the `examples` web application:

http://localhost:8080/examples/index.jsp

This possible collision in filenames is rare but is worth considering for unexplainable 404 messages. For example, the file `tryme.jsp` within the `examples` folder of the `ROOT` application would cause a name collision with a `tryme.jsp` file inside an `examples` application:

```
webapps/
        ROOT/
             examples/
                      tryme.jsp
        examples/
                 tryme.jsp
```

This is because they both resolve to:

http://localhost:8080/examples/tryme.jsp

Web applications partition resources into public and private areas. The exceptions to this are JSP page requests that are publicly available only when processed (subject to authorization and access restrictions as defined in the application configuration file, `web.xml`). The private resources are stored in a directory called `WEB-INF` under the root of the web application and may not be accessed directly.

Web applications may be represented in two ways. The first, sometimes known as the expanded web application, is a folder hierarchy on the filesystem with set rules about the location of resources and a number of required files and folders (these requirements are discussed in Chapter 5). This format is convenient for the web application developer as it allows the replacement of individual files while the application is being developed and debugged.

In a deployment environment, it is often more convenient to provide a single file that can be automatically deployed. This reduces the deployment process to placing the file and setting up system resources. Tomcat also allows the automatic expansion of a web application once the server has booted up. The automatic expansion of WAR files is configured in the `server.xml` file as part of the `<Host>` element that configures hosts, discussed later in this chapter. This can be switched on or off at will.

What format your applications will be in, will be highly dependent on the company's procedures.

Tomcat Architecture

Tomcat's architecture was completely revised for version 4. It was rebuilt from the ground up as some felt that the refactoring done in the previous Tomcat release, while improving its performance and flexibility, was always going to lead to a server that was somewhat limited. A hot debate began about whether this was actually the case. This resulted in the 3.2 architecture branching from the main development tree in a continued refactoring effort, leaving the 4.0 version to become the main focus of the project.

Tomcat 4.0 supports the latest Servlet and JSP specifications, versions 2.3 and 1.2 respectively. Tomcat 3.3 continues the work that was started in refactoring the 3.2 line and supports Servlet 2.2 and JSP 1.1.

Tomcat 4 consists of a nested hierarchy of components. Some of these components are called **top-level components** because they exist at the top of the component hierarchy in a rigid relationship with one another. **Containers** are components that can contain a collection of other components. Components that can reside in containers, but cannot themselves contain other components, are called **nested components**. The figure below illustrates the structure of a typical Tomcat 4 configuration:

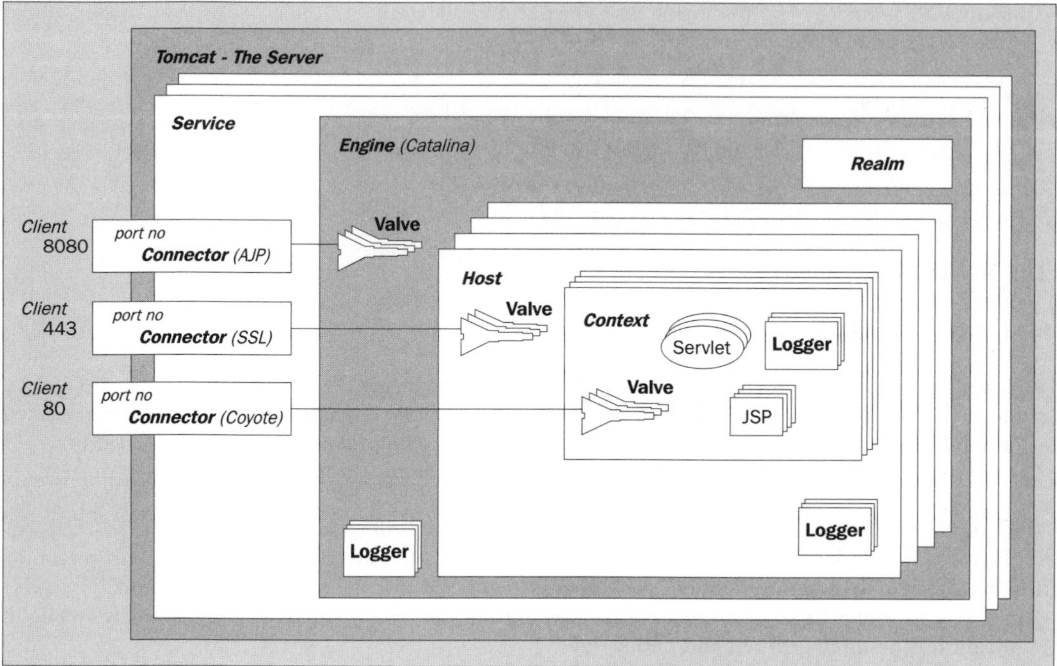

This diagram represents the most complete topology of a server; however, one should be aware that some of these objects may be removed without affecting the server's working. Notably the engine and host may be unnecessary if an external web server, such as Apache, is carrying out the tasks of resolving requests to web applications.

Here, components that can be contained multiple times are denoted by a symbol that has multiple profiles, including logger, valve, host, and context. Connectors are drawn separately to illustrate a point that we will see in just a moment.

In the next couple of sections, we will look into each component in turn and then discuss how to configure them in Chapter 5.

The Server

The server is Tomcat itself – an instance of the web application server – and is a top-level component. It owns a port that is used to shut the server down. Also, the server can be set in debug mode, which instantiates a version of the VM that allows debugging as we discussed in Chapter 3.

Only one instance of the server can be created inside a given JVM.

Separate servers configured to different ports can be set up on a single machine to separate applications so that they can be restarted independently. That is, if we crash a given JVM the other applications will be safe in another server instance. This is sometimes done in hosting environments where each customer has a separate instance of a JVM, so a badly configured/written application will not cause others to crash.

The Service

A service groups a container (usually of type engine) with that container's connectors and is a top-level component.

An engine is a request-processing component that represents the Catalina servlet engine. It examines the HTTP headers to determine which virtual host or context to pass the request to.

Each service represents a grouping of connectors (components that manage the connection between the client and server) and a single container, which accepts requests from the connectors and processes the requests to present them to the appropriate host. Each service is named so that administrators can easily identify log messages sent from each service.

So to say this another way, the container contains the web applications. It is responsible for accepting requests, routing them to the specified web application and specific resource, and returning the result of the processing of the request. Connectors stand between the client making the request and the container and provide additional services such as SSL support.

The Connectors

Connectors connect the applications to clients. They represent the point at which requests are received from clients and are assigned a port on the server. The default port for non-secure HTTP applications is kept as 8080 to avoid interference with any web server running on the standard HTTP port, but there is no reason why this cannot be changed as long as the port is free. Multiple connectors may be set up for a single engine or engine-level component, but they must have unique port numbers.

The default port to which browsers make requests if a port number is not specified is port 80. If Tomcat is run in standalone mode, the port for the primary connector of the web application can be changed to 80 by reconfiguring this component.

The default connector is Coyote, which implements HTTP 1.1 and can be used in both Tomcat 4.0 and 3.3. Alternative connectors are AJP, an SSL connector for secure connections, and an HTTP 1.0 connector. We will discuss each of these as part of Chapters 11-14, which deal with integrating Tomcat with web servers such as Apache and IIS.

The Engine

The next component in the architecture is the top-level container – a container object that cannot be contained by another container. This means that it is guaranteed not to have a parent container. It is at this level that the objects begin to aggregate child components.

Strictly speaking the container does not need to be an engine, it just has to implement the container interface. This interface mandates that the object implementing it is aware of its position in the hierarchy (it knows its parent and its children), that it provides access to logging, that it provides a realm for user authentication and role-based authorization, and that it has access to a number of resources including its session manager and some internally important aspects that we do not need to worry about.

In practice, the container at this level is usually an engine and so it makes sense to discuss it in that role. As mentioned earlier, an engine is a request-processing component that represents the Catalina servlet engine. It examines the HTTP headers to determine which virtual host or context to pass the request to.

When the standalone configuration is used, the engine that is used is the default one. This engine does the checking mentioned above. When Tomcat is configured to provide Java servlet support for a web server, the default class used to serve requests is overridden as the web server has normally determined the correct destination of the request.

The host name of the server to which the engine belongs is set here in multi-homed machines. An engine may contain hosts representing a group of web applications and contexts representing a single web application.

The Realm

The realm for an engine manages user authentication and authorization. As part of the configuration of an application the administrator sets the roles that are allowed for each resource or group of resources and the realm is used to enforce this policy.

Realms can authenticate against text files, database tables, LDAP servers, and the Windows network identity of the user. We shall see more of this in Chapter 16.

A realm applies across the entire engine or top-level container and so applications within a container share user resources for authentication. This means that, for example, a manager for the intranet will have the same rights as the manager of the e-commerce site should both these applications be in the same engine.

By default, a user must still authenticate separately to each web application on the server. We will see how this can be changed in the following chapter, but, in brief, this is implemented as a valve in Tomcat 4.

The Valves

Valves are components that allow Tomcat to intercept a request and pre-process it. However, they aren't part of the JSP or Servlet specifications. Hosts, contexts, and engines may contain valves.

Valves are commonly used to enable single sign-on for all hosts on a server, as well as log request patterns, client IP addresses, and server usage patterns (peak traffic, bandwidth use, mean average requests per time unit, the resources that most requests ask for, and so on). This is known as **request dumping** and a **request dumper valve** records the header information (the request URI, accept languages, source IP, hostname requested, and so on) and any cookies sent with the request. Response dumping logs the response headers and cookies (if set) to a file.

Valves are typically reusable components and so can be added and removed from the request path according to need – their inclusion is transparent to web applications and so their presence or absence should not affect the working of the application (although response time will increase if a valve is added). An application that wishes to intercept requests for pre-processing and responses for post-processing should use the **filters** that are a part of the Servlet specifications.

A valve may intercept a request between an engine and a host/context, between a host and a context, and between a context and a resource within the web application.

The Loggers

Loggers report on the internal state of a component. They can be set for components from top-level containers downwards. Logging behavior is inherited so a logger set at the engine level is assigned to every child object unless overridden by the child. The configuration of loggers at this level can be a convenient way to decide the default logging behavior for the server.

This means that there is a convenient destination for all logging events for those components that are not specially configured to generate their own logs.

The Host

A host mimics the popular Apache virtual host functionality. In Apache this allows multiple servers to be used on the same machine, and be differentiated by their IP address or by their hostname. In Tomcat the virtual hosts are differentiated by a fully qualified host name. Thus we can have http://www.chanoch.com/ and http://www.maimuna.com/ both sitting on the same server, with requests for each routed to different groups of web applications.

Configuring a host includes setting the name of the host. The majority of clients can be depended on to send both the IP address of the server and the host name they used to resolve the IP address. The host name is provided as an HTTP header that an engine inspects to determine which host to pass a request to.

> **If the host is not within an engine, it is possible that it is the top-level container.**

The Context

Finally, we arrive at the web application, also known as a context. Configuration of a web application includes informing the engine/hosts of the location of the root folder of the application. We can also enable dynamic reloading so that any classes that have been changed are reloaded into memory so that the latest changes are reflected in the application. However, this is resource-intensive and is not recommended for deployment scenarios.

The context may also include specific error pages, which allow a system administrator to configure error messages that are consistent with the look and feel of the application, and usability features, such as a search engine, useful links, or a report-creating component that notifies the administrator of errors in the application.

Finally, a context can also be configured with initialization parameters for the application it represents and for access control (authentication and authorization restrictions). More information on these two aspects of web application deployment is available in Chapter 6 and Chapter 16 respectively.

The Remaining Classes in the Tomcat Architecture

Tomcat also defines classes for representing a request, a response, a session that represents a virtual connection between a server and a client, and listeners. These are described in detail in the remainder of the book.

> *Listeners listen for significant events in the component they are configured in. Examples of significant events include the instantiating of the component and its subsequent destruction.*

Summary

We began the chapter by discussing the installation directory for Tomcat, including the `bin` folder where the executable files lie, the various location where classes may reside, the configuration files directory, and the location of the web applications.

We then went on to discuss the architecture for Tomcat 4. We saw that:

- A web application is represented by the context component. It may have loggers that log messages and valves that intercept and process requests and responses. Valves intercept just before and just after the request is processed and a response is generated.
- A context sits within a host that represents a virtual host (an alias assigned to the currently assigned IP address) and many contexts may share a host. The context component may define valves and loggers.
- The host sits in an engine that resolves requests to virtual hosts. It can define valves and loggers too.
- Finally, an engine sits inside a service that groups together the engine with the connectors that connect the engine with clients. The entire object tree lives within the server component that is Tomcat.

Now you should be comfortable with Tomcat's architecture, so in the next chapter we will move on to look at configuring Tomcat.

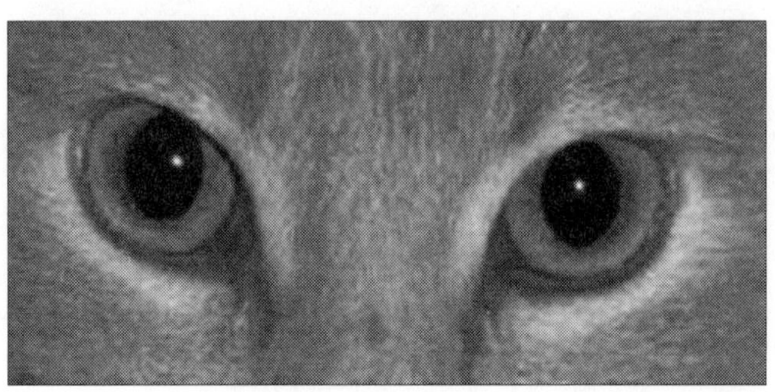

5

Basic Tomcat Configuration

In this chapter, we will focus our attention on the basic configuration of Tomcat 4. We will be examining the files found in the `$CATALINA_HOME/conf` directory of the Tomcat 4 distribution. The default installation of Tomcat 4 will use these files to configure the server when it starts up; therefore, it is of the utmost importance that we understand what the default configuration will do and how we can modify it for our own production environment.

Our journey will take us through a detailed, line-by-line examination of the `server.xml` and other configuration files – `sever.xml` being the primary configuration file for Tomcat 4 servers. To understand the configuration commands, we must first understand the component-based configuration/operation model that underlies Tomcat 4. This model greatly simplifies the configuration of what is inherently a very complex server.

We will examine the top-level components and the hierarchy of containers, as well as nested components that make up Tomcat 4. Their interactions during Tomcat operations, and how their behaviour may be modified by configuration will be discussed. Relevant differences between Tomcat 4.0.x and Tomcat 4.1.x configuration files will be noted wherever applicable.

We will briefly examine advanced topics such as Tomcat realm configuration and configuring fine-grained security policy control over Tomcat 4 server instances – but will leave the detailed exploration of these concepts for later chapters.

By the end of this chapter, you will be comfortable with the basic (default) configuration of the Tomcat 4 server. You will also be able to modify this basic configuration for your own production needs.

Component-Based Configuration

Tomcat 4 has adopted a component-based model for configuration. This model unifies all the configurable parameters of the server and simplifies the relationship and interactions of these parameters. We saw the components that can be configured in the previous chapter.

Reducing Configuration Complexity Via Inheritance

The component-based model considerably simplifies configuration. Any properties that are set on the outer components are automatically inherited by the inner components. For example, a logger that is configured in an engine will be used by a nested host component for logging its error and debug messages.

If there is any need for customization, we can always override the outer configuration by adding components. For example, a context component overrides the logger configured at the engine level and uses its own logger instead. This means that the web applications running within this context will use the newly defined logger instead of the global (outer) one.

All the components in the component-based model are represented by elements in XML files; this makes it very easy to change component nesting relationships and configuration (via a text editor). We can find most of the configuration files in the `$CATALINA_HOME` directory.

Files in $CATALINA_HOME/conf

In the `$CATALINA_HOME/conf` directory of the Tomcat 4 server distribution, you will see five files (as of Tomcat 4.1.3). Here is a brief synopsis of each of these files:

- `server.xml`
  This is the main configuration file for the Tomcat 4 server and is the one that Tomcat actually reads at startup. It contains a configuration that is ready to run on your machine immediately. It contains declarations for many example web applications that come with the Tomcat 4 distribution. Since the example applications take up memory space and consume processing time to load, it is usual practice to remove them for production systems since they are not needed. This is the main reason for a `server-noexamples.xml.config` file (discussed next).

- `server-noexamples.xml.config`
  This file contains a blank template of `server.xml`. This enables you, as the administrator, to easily create your own version of `sever.xml` without having to remove standard Tomat examples definitions from it. In practice, if you need to custom configure your server, it may be easier to start with this file and then rename the resulting file to `server.xml`. There are also detailed comments within this file to assist in understanding the options available when configuring the server.

Both the previous files are server configuration files, only one of which is needed at any time:

- `tomcat-users.xml`
  This is the file that contains user authentication and role mapping information for setting up a memory realm. Tomcat's manager application and graphical Admin application can use it. Memory realm, a feature in Tomcat 4 discussed in Chapter 8, to implement a database of users/passwords/roles for authentication and Container-Managed Security. In Tomcat 4.1.x, an improved and robust implementation of memory realm, called UserDatabase, is available. It will also use this file to set up authentication information by default. Chapter 8 has extensive information on UserDatabse.

- `web.xml`
  This is a default deployment descriptor file for any web applications that are running on this Tomcat server instance. It provides basic servlet definition and MIME mappings for all web applications, and also acts as the deployment descriptor for any web application that does not have its own deployment descriptor.

- `catalina.policy`
  Java 2 has a fine-grained security model that enables the administrator to control in detail the accessibility of system resources. This is the default policy file for running Tomcat 4 in secured mode. We shall cover this in detail later.

Basic Server Configuration

First, let us examine `server-noexamples.xml.config` line-by-line. `server.xml` (and its variants) is created as an XML 1.0 document; it is assumed that the reader is familiar with XML. If you need to brush up on XML, check out *Professional XML 2nd Edition* from *Wrox Press (ISBN 1-86100-505-9).*

Server Configuration Blank Template

Here is the first service defined within the `<Server>` element in the `server-noexamples.xml.config` file, with most of the extensive comments removed to save space and keep the listing concise:

```
<Server port="8005" shutdown="SHUTDOWN" debug="0">
 <!-- Define the Tomcat Stand-Alone Service -->
 <Service name="Tomcat-Standalone">
   <!-- Define a non-SSL HTTP/1.1 Connector on port 8080 -->
   <Connector className="org.apache.catalina.connector.http.HttpConnector"
              port="8080" minProcessors="5" maxProcessors="75"
              enableLookups="true" redirectPort="8443"
              acceptCount="10" debug="0" connectionTimeout="60000"/>

   <!-- Define the top level container in our container hierarchy -->
   <Engine name="Standalone" defaultHost="localhost" debug="0">

     <!-- Global logger unless overridden at lower levels -->
     <Logger className="org.apache.catalina.logger.FileLogger"
             prefix="catalina_log." suffix=".txt"
             timestamp="true"/>
```

```
      <!-- Because this Realm is here, an instance will be shared globally -->

      <Realm className="org.apache.catalina.realm.MemoryRealm" />

      <!-- Define the default virtual host -->
      <Host name="localhost" debug="0" appBase="webapps" unpackWARs="true">

        <Valve className="org.apache.catalina.valves.AccessLogValve"
               directory="logs"  prefix="localhost_access_log."
               suffix=".txt"  pattern="common"/>

        <Logger className="org.apache.catalina.logger.FileLogger"
                directory="logs"  prefix="localhost_log." suffix=".txt"
                timestamp="true"/>

        <!-- Tomcat Manager Context -->
        <Context path="/manager" docBase="manager"
                 debug="0" privileged="true"/>
      </Host>
    </Engine>
  </Service>
```

The <Server> Element

Let's take a closer look at how this first service is defined. The very first active line of the file defines the server component, via the <Server> element. Here is the line from the file:

```
<Server port="8005" shutdown="SHUTDOWN" debug="0">
```

This tells Tomcat to start a server instance (a JVM) listening to port 8005 for a shutdown command. The shutdown command will contain the text "SHUTDOWN". This provides a graceful way for an administrator (or management console software) to shut down this Tomcat server instance. The server instance will not print debugging messages to the log because debug is set to "0". Let us examine the possible attributes of the <Server> element, as well as what sub-elements it may have:

Attribute	Description	Required
className	The Java class for the server to use. This class is required to implement the org.apache.catalina.Server interface. By default, the Tomcat 4-supplied code is used.	No
port	The TCP port to listen to for the command specified by the shutdown attribute before shutting down gracefully. Tomcat will check to make sure that the connection is made from the same physical server machine. Together with a custom shutdown command string that you can specify (discussed next), provides a measure of security against hacker attacks.	Yes
shutdown	The command text string that the server should monitor for, at the TCP port specified by the port attribute, before shutting down gracefully.	Yes

Attribute	Description	Required
`debug`	Controls the amount of debug information logged by the server instance. Setting this to a higher number will provide more debugging details. The range is highly server-and version-dependent.	No

Within the `<Server>` element, we may have only the following sub-element:

Sub-element	Description	How Many?
`<Service>`	A grouping of connectors associated with an engine	1 or more

Readers familiar with XML may wonder if there exists a DTD for validating the `server.xml` file – and if that may be a more concise way to specify what we have described above. It turns out that the attributes of an element can vary greatly depending on the subtype of an element (the type of a valve for instance). Because of this, a DTD will not be suitable for precisely expressing the rules.

The <Service> Element

The next line in the file defines a service component. A service component is needed to group together all the connectors that may be used with the Catalina engine, which is defined by the `<Engine>` element below:

```
<Service name="Tomcat-Standalone">
```

Here, we have defined a service instance with the name "`Tomcat-Standalone`". This name will be visible in logs and error messages, clearly identifying the component. It may also be used by service management software (for example, the Tomcat Admin GUI application covered in Chapter 7) to identify the service instance.

For a `<Service>` element, you can have the following attributes:

Attribute	Description	Required
`className`	The Java class name for the service class to use. By default, the Tomcat 4-supplied Catalina code `org.apache.Catalina.Service` is used. The default is adequate unless you're modifying Tomcat's sourcecode.	No
`name`	A name for the service, used in logging and management. If you have more than one `<Service>` element inside the `<Server>` element, you must make sure their `name` attributes are different.	Yes

The sub-elements that a <Service> element can have are:

Sub-element	Description	How Many?
`Connector`	This is a nested component. Explained in detail in the next section.	1 or more
`Engine`	This is the request-processing component in Tomcat: Catalina. Explained in detail in a later section.	Exactly 1

The <Connector> Element

There are two very different ways of configuring Tomcat 4, they are:

- **Tomcat as an application server**
  We have a front-end web server (Apache, iPlanet, IIS, and so on) serving static content to the end-users while all JSP and servlet requests are routed to the Tomcat server(s) for processing. In addition, Tomcat interfaces to back-end J2EE-compliant services.

- **Tomcat in standalone mode**
  In this case, any static pages and graphic files from our web application are served directly from the Tomcat 4 server. In this mode, an additional front-end web server is not necessary because Tomcat is acting as both the web server and the JSP/servlet container. Again, Tomcat can assist in interfacing to the back-end J2EE services.

In the application server configuration, there needs to be some intelligent piece of software that runs inside the web server and decides on the requests that will be routed to the Tomcat servers for processing. This usually exists in the form of a loadable module or redirector plug-in.

In the case where we are running multiple independent Tomcat servers simultaneously (that is, across a bank of machines for scalability and load balancing), the loadable module or redirector plug-in may also decide which Tomcat server instance to send the request to.

For efficiency, the protocol between the web server and Tomcat is not HTTP. It is typically one of two specially designed protocols: AJP or WARP. Chapter 11-13 will have more detail on these protocols. For now, you only need to appreciate that there must be a corresponding piece of software at the Tomcat server-side that understands this protocol and connection convention.

Therefore, we can appreciate that the connection, protocol, and request/response forwarding logic are significantly different between the following connection points:

- Between the front-end web server and Tomcat
- Between a user web browser, or a front-end client application and Tomcat

Furthermore, the connection in the second bullet above can use a variety of protocols, including HTTP 1.0, HTTP 1.1, HTTPS/SSL, and so on.

One way to handle all of these different connection requirements is to create a customized version of Tomcat for each protocol. This is obviously inefficient and hard to maintain. The Tomcat 4 design factors out this piece of functionality into a component called a connector. A connector adapts an engine (such as Catalina) to the outside world – passing requests into the engine and passing responses back out to the user. The connector knows how to handle the protocol, connection conventions, and so on, so that the engine doesn't have to. This enables the code of the servlet processor (Catalina), to be coded only once, and yet usable to process a servlet regardless of how an incoming request is handled.

More than one connector may be associated with a single engine. For example, we may want the web applications inside our engine accessible through both HTTP and HTTPS (SSL). In this case, we will need to configure both an HTTP connector and an SSL connector with the same engine. The figure below shows how different connectors adapt to different requirements for connecting to the Catalina engine:

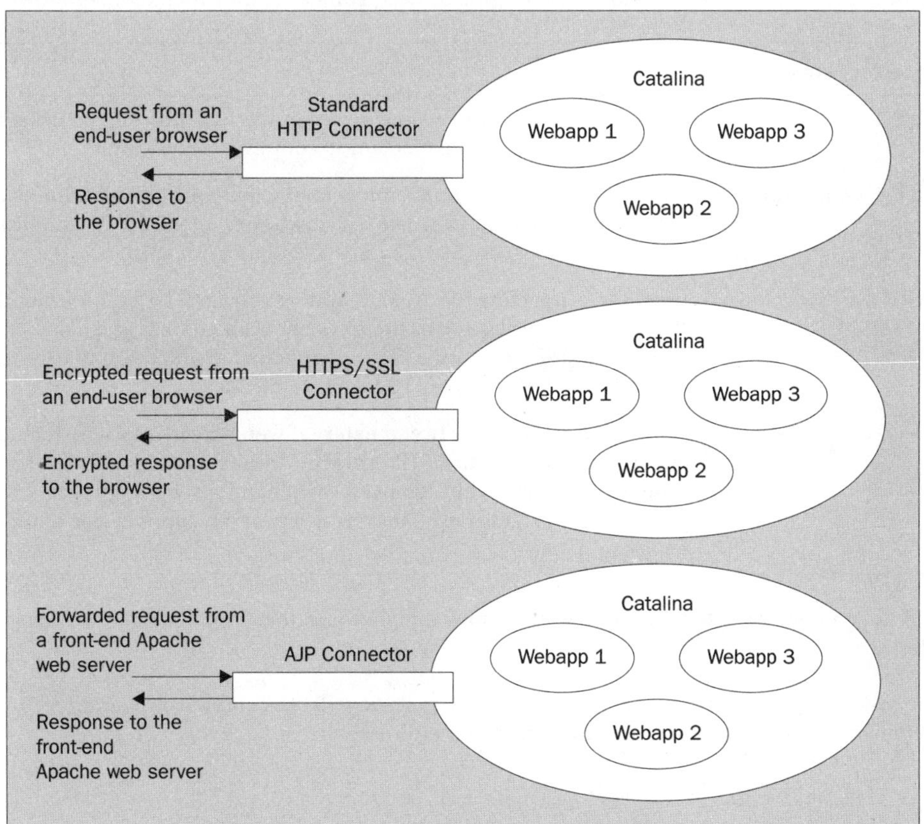

In the above figure, we can see that direct communication to the user's browsers requires an HTTP connector; a secured browser connection requires an HTTPS/SSL connector, and connection to an Apache web server requires a connector that handles the AJP protocol. We will have extensive coverage of how to configure the most commonly used Tomcat 4 connectors in Chapters 11 through 13.

While you can have as many connectors as you need in a service (to handle the different connection requirements for a server), there can only be one engine. The engine component is a container; think of it as Catalina – the servlet/JSP container. An engine executes web applications when processing incoming requests and generating outgoing responses.

In `server-noexamples.xml.config`, we can see that an HTTP 1.1 connector is defined for our `Tomcat-Standalone` service:

```
<Connector className="org.apache.catalina.connector.http.HttpConnector"
           port="8080" minProcessors="5" maxProcessors="75"
           enableLookups="true" redirectPort="8443"
           acceptCount="10" debug="0" connectionTimeout="60000"/>
```

There are several other standard connectors supplied with Tomcat 4; they include the following:

Connector Name	Description
HTTP 1.1	Connecting browser or web services to the Catalina engine using non-secure HTTP 1.1.This connector is configured by default.
HTTP 1.1 with SSL	Essentially the same connector as above, but with the addition of a socket factory added to create a secure, encrypted link to web browsers and/or web services. See Chapter 11 for more details.
WARP	Used for connecting the Apache web server and Tomcat 4 using the WARP protocol. Uses Apache for static web content and Tomcat 4 for servlet and JSP processing. This connection enables you to use Apache's SSL support. See Chapter 12 for more details.
AJP	Used for connecting between external web servers (Apache included) and Tomcat 4 using the AJP protocol. It uses the external web server for static web content while Tomcat 4 will handle servlet and JSP processing – can also use the web server's SSL support. See Chapter 13 for more details.

We will not go into the details of configuring connectors, because they will be covered at length in Chapter 11 to 13.

If we follow along `server-noexamples.xml.config`, we will see sample configurations for all of these connectors – but they are all commented out and therefore not active:

```
<!-- Define an SSL HTTP/1.1 Connector on port 8443 -->
<!--
<Connector className="org.apache.catalina.connector.http.HttpConnector"
           port="8443" minProcessors="5" maxProcessors="75"
           enableLookups="true"
           acceptCount="10" debug="0" scheme="https" secure="true">
  <Factory className="org.apache.catalina.net.SSLServerSocketFactory"
           clientAuth="false" protocol="TLS"/>
</Connector>
-->
```

```
<!-- Define an AJP 1.3 Connector on port 8009 -->
<!--
<Connector className="org.apache.ajp.tomcat4.Ajp13Connector"
           port="8009" minProcessors="5" maxProcessors="75"
           acceptCount="10" debug="0"/>
-->
```

The <Engine> Element

The one and only <Engine> element associated with the service is defined next:

```
  <Engine name="Standalone" defaultHost="localhost" debug="0">
```

An engine is a container, essentially representing a running instance of the servlet processor – Catalina. The name "Standalone" is given to this instance. The defaultHost attribute indicates the virtual host that Tomcat will direct a request to if the request is not destined for one of the hosts configured in the server.xml file. The debug="0" indicates that there will be no engine-specific debug messages written to the log.

The attributes that an <Engine> element can have are:

Attribute	Description	Required
className	The Java class name for the engine code. If not specified, the default Tomcat code, org.apache.catalina.core.StandardEngine is used, and is seldom overridden unless you're modifying Tomcat code.	No
defaultHost	Selects one of the virtual hosts within this engine to field all the incoming requests by default. This is only used if the engine cannot find the host named on the request within this server.xml file.	Yes
jvmRoute	This is an identifier used in clustering Tomcat 4. See Chapter 19 for more information on using this attribute and configuring Tomcat 4 for clustering and load balancing.	No
name	A name given to this engine, which will be used in error logging and by management applications.	Yes
debug	Controls the level of debugging information written by this engine to the log files.	No

As a container, the <Engine> element can have the following sub-elements:

Sub-Element	Description	How Many?
`Host`	Each <Host> element specifies a virtual host handled by the engine. Tomcat 4 can handle multiple virtual hosts per engine/service instance. This mirrors one of the most popular features of the Apache web server.	1 or more
`DefaultContext`	Creates a context (collection of settings for configurable properties/elements) for the web applications that are automatically deployed when Tomcat 4 starts. The properties specified in this default context will also be available to all web applications running within the engine.	0 or 1
`Logger`	Specifies the logging component instance used by this engine for logging messages. Unless overridden by inner containers, this is the default logger instance for any nested components inside the engine.	0 or 1
`Realm`	This realm will be used by default in the declarative security support (see Chapter 8 and 16) to map users into roles; it is used for authentication purposes. Each individual virtual host's <Host> and <Context> elements may have their own realm for this purpose – if they do not define their own, the realm configured at the engine level will be used.	0 or 1
`Valve`	Valves add processing logic into the request- and response-handling pipeline at the engine level. There are standard valves that are used to perform access logging, request filtering, implementing Single Sign-on, and so on. We will cover the configuration of these standard valves in Chapter 8 when we take a look at advanced configuration.	0 or more
`Listener`	This is used to configure lifecycle listeners that monitor the starting and stopping of the engine. Chapter 8 will cover how this optional element is used.	0 or more

The <Logger> Element

The first sub-element inside our <Engine> is a <Logger>, configured as:

```
<!-- Global logger unless overridden at lower levels -->
<Logger className="org.apache.catalina.logger.FileLogger"
        prefix="catalina_log." suffix=".txt"
        timestamp="true"/>
```

A logger is a nested component that collects log information (debug or error messages) from the Tomcat system as well as application programming code and writes it to log files in an efficient manner. Web application programmers can access the configured `Logger` through the servlet context that is passed into their code. These entire log files will be in the `$CATALINA_HOME/logs` directory, by default. This location can be changed by specifying the directory attribute, described later in this section.

You can define an optional default logger at the engine level, as we did here. In this configuration, we use the standard Catalina `FileLogger` class. This configuration will create files in the `$CATALINA_HOME/logs` directory that will be named similar to:

```
catalina_log.2003_11_02.txt
catalina_log.2003_11_03.txt
```

Note how we have specified the filename that the logger will use by specifying the `prefix` and `suffix` attributes.

All `<Logger>` elements can have the following attributes:

Attribute	Description	Required
`className`	The Java class to use for this instance of the logger.	Yes
`verbosity`	Controls what level of logging is performed. Can range from 0 to 4. Default is 1. As a guideline: 0 – Log fatal messages only 1 – Log error messages 2 – Log warning messages 3 – Log information messages 4 – Log debug information The numbers are cumulative (that is, 4 logs all messages, 3 logs everything but debug information, and so on).	No

Unlike other components, the `<Logger>` element must specify a `className` attribute. This will specify your choice of standard logger implementation (all included with Tomcat 4) to be used. The `className` attribute can contain one of the classes shown in the table below:

Java Class Name	Description
`org.apache.catalina.logger.FileLogger`	Log to a file. Most frequently used.
`org.apache.catalina.logger.SystemErrLogger`	Log to the standard error stream. (configurable from most operating systems). Seldom used, maybe for console-based debugging.
`org.apache.catalina.logger.SystemOutLogger`	Log to the standard output stream (configurable from most operating systems).

If we have selected `org.apache.catalina.logger.FileLogger`, then the following optional attributes can also be configured:

Attribute	Description
`directory`	Specifies where to place the log files; relative or absolute paths may be used. "`$CATALINA_HOME/logs`" is the default.
`prefix`	A prefix for all generated log file names. "`catalina.`" is the default.
`suffix`	A postfix for all the generated log file names. "`.log`" is the default.
`timestamp`	Specifies whether the messages in the log files will have a date and time stamp. The default is to have no timestamps. It is recommended that this setting be set to `true` for production systems.

The <Realm> Element

Let's return to `server-noexamples.xml.config`. After the definition of the logger inside the engine, we have a definition for another nested component, a realm:

```
<!-- Because this Realm is here, an instance will be shared globally -->
<Realm className="org.apache.catalina.realm.MemoryRealm" />
```

This configures a memory realm that will allow us to load the `tomcat-users.xml` file into memory for use by example applications. We will cover the attributes for the `<Realm>` element, including how to specify our own XML file for user information, in Chapter 8.

A realm is a security mechanism used to perform authentication and implement container-managed security (see Chapter 16). Essentially, realms are data sources that provide mappings between usernames and passwords (for authentication) and usernames and roles that users play (for container managed security). For example, user `johnf` may have password `xyzzy` (authentication) and a role of `supervisor` (container-managed security). A realm enables access to data sources, external to Tomcat 4, where the user/password/role relationships are stored.

There are many different implementations of realms, differing only in the source from where they retrieve the information. The types of realms that are standard with Tomcat 4 are:

- **Memory**
  Used to access a table in memory that is populated with the user/password/role mappings. Typically, this is read into memory from a file during server startup and stays static throughout the lifetime of the server. For the default implementation that comes with Tomcat, the size of the mappings is seriously constrained by the memory available. This is typically used only in testing and development – and seldom in production.

- **UserDatabase**
  New in the Tomcat 4.1.x series of servers, UserDatabase implements a completely updatable and persistent memory realm. It is backward compatible with Memory realm. Users who are on Tomcat 4.1.x servers should use UserDatabase instead of Memory realm for authenticaton and Container-Managed Security. We will have extensive coverage of UserDatabase in Chapter 16.

- **JDBC**
  Used to access relational database sources for obtaining authentication information. Any other data sources with a JDBC-compatible access interface may also be used (for example, ODBC-compliant sources via the JDBC to ODBC bridge).

- **JNDI**
  JNDI can be used through configuring the JNDI LDAP service provider. It is used to retrieve authentication information directly from any existing directory services and/or authentication systems compatible with the LDAP protocol (for instance, OpenLDAP, Microsoft, or Novell all have LDAP-compatible access drivers). Any other directory service and/or authentication service with a native JNDI service provider may also be used.

We will cover how to configure different realms in Chapter 8 and Chapter 16.

The <Host> Element

After the realm definition, we see that a new container is defined with the `<Host>` element. Each `<Host>` element defined within the enclosing `<Engine>` element represents another virtual host that is handled by this Tomcat 4 server. In our case, the host definition is:

```
<!-- Define the default virtual host -->
<Host name="localhost" debug="0" appBase="webapps" unpackWARs="true">
```

This defines a virtual host named `localhost` matching the `defaultHost` specified in the `<Engine>` outer container. The applications to be deployed for this virtual host are located in the `$CATALINA_HOME/webapps` directory (all the examples from the distribution are installed there). Also, if Tomcat 4 finds any WAR files there, they will be expanded before the web application is executed. If you set `unpackWARS` to `false`, Tomcat will execute the web applications in-place, without unarchiving them – saving space but sacrificing performance.

In Chapter 19, we will discuss the techniques used to support virtual hosting. However, for now, we will explain virtual hosting by examining the following figure:

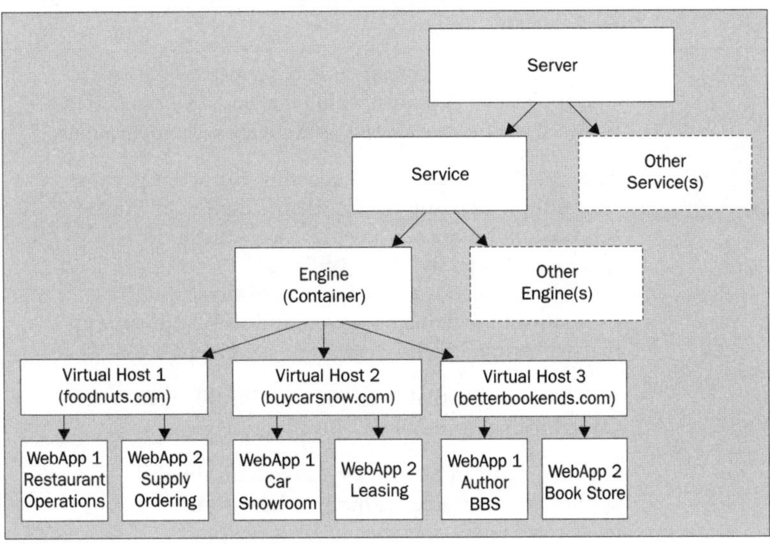

In this figure, we can see a single Catalina engine supporting three different web sites via virtual hosts. The first one is foodnuts.com, the second one is buycarsnow.com, and the third one is betterbookends.com. Each virtual host is running a completely different web application to the others. The engine is responsible for forwarding any incoming request to the corresponding host. If we were to configure the system depicted in the figure, we would have 3 <Host> elements nested within the single <Engine> definition.

A <Host> element is a container. It can have any one of the following attributes:

Attribute	Description	Required
`className`	The Java class that is used to handle requests for the host. The default is the Tomcat-supplied class: `org.apache.catalina.core.StandardHost`, and this almost never needs to be changed.	No
`appBase`	Used to set the default application deployment source directory. Tomcat 4 will look into this directory for applications to be deployed. The path should be specified relative to the installation directory of the Tomcat 4 server.	Yes
`name`	The resolvable name of this virtual host.	Yes
`debug`	Sets the level of debugging information that will be emitted for the log from the virtual host.	No

Note that there must be at least one <Host> entry associated with the <Engine> element. This makes sense since one must be able to reach the engine by at least one name. The `defaultHost` attribute of the <Engine> element must be assigned with one of the <Host> entries defined for this reason.

The sub-elements that can be placed inside a <Host> element are:

Sub-Element	Description	How Many?
`Context`	A <Context> can contain a set of property values for a web application deployed within this host. We can add as many <Context> elements as there are web applications.	0 or more
`DefaultContext`	The <DefaultContext> specifies the set of property values for a web application that is deployed within this host, but does not have its own <Context> specified. Typically, this <DefaultContext> is used for web applications that are part of the standard behavior of the Tomcat server, and web applications that are automatically deployed (see Chapter 8).	0 or 1
`Logger`	A default logger that is configured for this host. Overrides any previously specified logger.	0 or 1
`Realm`	A realm that can be accessed across all the web applications running within this host – unless a lower-level component specifies its own realm.	0 or 1

<Valve> and other Nested Components

In our configuration, the first nested component that is defined within the host named `localhost` is:

```
<Valve className="org.apache.catalina.valves.AccessLogValve"
       directory="logs"  prefix="localhost_access_log." suffix=".txt"
       pattern="common"/>
```

A valve is a Tomcat-specific way to intercept requests and responses. Any requests destined for the host named `localhost` will be passed through the valve defined here. In this case, we are using a standard Tomcat 4-supplied valve called `org.apache.catalina.valves.AccessLogValve`. This valve will create access log files in the same format as Apache's log file. By installing this valve in the host named `localhost`, with the above configuration, access log files, with entries in the "`common`" log format, reside in the `$CATALINA_HOME/logs` directory and are named in a similar way to:

```
localhost_access_log.2003_11_12.txt
localhost_access_log.2003_11_13.txt
```

Valves can also be installed at the engine level. Any valve that is installed at the engine level will have access to every single request handled by this engine – regardless of which connector the request comes through. However, while installing valves at this level, we must make sure that the valve is well tested and does not require a lot of processor time to complete its operation. This is because every request that goes through the Catalina instance will be processed through this valve. The Tomcat-supplied standard valves are designed and tested for efficiency.

> **Note that valves are specific to the Tomcat server – and not part of the Servlet 2.3 standard (http://www.jcp.org/aboutJava/communityprocess/final/jsr053/). Other servlet and JSP containers, such as IBM's WebSphere, Macromedia's JRun, or BEA's WebLogic, may not support Tomcat-style valves. It is possible to get similar interception behaviors portably using a web application component called a filter. A filter is an application programmer-designed component and resides within a web application.**

We will discuss how to configure and use the standard valves in Chapter 8. After defining the valve, the next nested component definition in the configuration file is the `Logger`:

```
<Logger className="org.apache.catalina.logger.FileLogger"
        directory="logs"  prefix="localhost_log." suffix=".txt"
        timestamp="true"/>
```

This defines a logger for this virtual host, and overrides the logger defined at the engine level. Therefore, all web applications inside this host (unless further overridden) will be using this logger. This logger will write files to the `$CATALINA_HOME/logs` directory that has names similar to:

```
localhost_log.2003_11_12.txt
localhost_log.2003_11_12.txt
```

The <Context> Element

Looking back at the `server-noexamples.xml.config` file, the last nested component that is defined in the `<Host>` container is a `<Context>`:

```
        <!-- Tomcat Manager Context -->
        <Context path="/manager" docBase="manager"
         debug="0" privileged="true"/>

      </Host>
    </Engine>
  </Service>
```

This is a context for the Tomcat 4 `manager` web application (covered in detail in Chapter 7). The `manager` is an administrative utility that is hosted in the default host.

> **Note that the Tomcat 4.1.x configuration file does not have this context definition by default.**

A `<Context>` element contains a set of configuration properties that are used by a web application. A `<Context>` element can have the following attributes:

Attribute	Description	Required
`className`	Name of the Java class that implements the context. Default is the Tomcat-supplied class: `org.apache.catalina.core.StandardContext`.	No
`cookies`	Controls how session information is tracked at the client. By default, cookies are enabled. Tomcat will attempt to use cookies on the client to keep track of session token information. If set to `false`, Tomcat will only use URL rewriting (which works on all browsers, but a little less efficient because of long URLs) to keep track of sessions.	No
`crossContext`	Controls whether the programmer can make a call that will dispatch across different web applications running on the same virtual host. For security reasons, this attribute should be set to `false` unless you are certain you can live with the risk involved (that is, all virtual hosts running on the same machines are for the same customer). This is a Tomcat-specific security-bypass attribute that should be used sparingly.	No
`docBase`	The location of the web application associated with this context. It can either point to a WAR file or the directory where the web application is located.	Yes

Attribute	Description	Required
override	Overrides the attributes in <DefaultContext> of the outer <Host> element. Each <Host> can have a <DefaultContext> element that specifies default attributes applicable to all <Context> within the <Host> global settings. This attribute indicates if overriding of these global settings is possible.	No
path	Used to specify the context path for this application. For example, a path of /bookstore will mean that the application can be accessed via the URL http://<host>/bookstore/<resource name>.	Yes
privileged	Allows this context to use container-defined servlets if set to true.	No
reloadable	Tomcat 4 can detect that Java classes in a deployed directory have changed and reload the web application under development. Set this attribute back to false for production systems – this will increase efficiency because Tomcat does not have to check for changes.	No
useNaming	Controls if JNDI support (by supplying a JNDI InitialContext to the application) is enabled for code programmers. This is required for Servlet 2.3 and JSP 1.2 support and is enabled by default.	No
wrapperClass	Specifies the wrapper class used for servlets in this context. The default is the Tomcat-supplied class: org.apache.catalina.Wrapper, which should be adequate.	No

A context is a container and can have the following nested components:

Sub-Element	Description	How Many?
Loader	Change the class loader used to load servlets and support classes. We will have coverage of why we may do this in Chapter 9.	0 or 1
Logger	Specifies a logger to be used with this web application – overriding any logger defined in the enclosing <Host> or <Engine> elements.	0 or 1
Manager	Specifies a custom session manager to handle session persistence for this web application. See Chapter 8 for more details on configuring session managers.	0 or 1
Realm	Specifies a realm to be used within this web application. This will override any previous realm definitions in the outer <Host> or <Engine> definitions.	0 or 1

Table continued on following page

Sub-Element	Description	How Many?
`Resource`	Specifies a custom code module, called a resource manager, for accessing static resources (for serving static web pages, graphics, and so on) within the web application.	0 or 1

This concludes our examination of the first section of the `server-noexamples.xml.config` file. The next section is similar, but configures another service within the same server that will connect via a WARP connector to an external Apache server:

```
<Service name="Tomcat-Apache">
  <Connector className="org.apache.catalina.connector.warp.WarpConnector"
             port="8008" minProcessors="5" maxProcessors="75"
             enableLookups="true"
             acceptCount="10" debug="0"/>

   <!-- Replace "localhost" with what your Apache "ServerName" is set to -->
    <Engine className="org.apache.catalina.connector.warp.WarpEngine"
            name="Apache" defaultHost="localhost" debug="0"
            appBase="webapps">

      <!-- Global logger unless overridden at lower levels -->
      <Logger className="org.apache.catalina.logger.FileLogger"
              prefix="apache_log." suffix=".txt"
              timestamp="true"/>

    <!-- Because this Realm is here, an instance will be shared globally -->
      <Realm className="org.apache.catalina.realm.MemoryRealm" />

    </Engine>

  </Service>

</Server>
```

By now, you should be able to understand the service configuration above. This service is named `Tomcat-Apache`, and is created to communicate with a front-end Apache web server. Note that there is no `<Host>` configuration since virtual hosting is performed by Apache in this case. We'll see this process in Chapters 12 and 13.

In fact, the `<Engine>` definition specifies `org.apache.catalina.connector.WarpEngine` to process the request instead of the default Catalina engine. In this configuration, Tomcat is used to process servlets and JSP requests for the Apache server. Note that two nested components, the logger and memory realm, are configured with the engine in the same way as the `Tomcat-Standalone` service.

This concludes our examination of the `server-noexamples.xml.config` file. We will now take a look at the `server.xml` file and see how it differs from this blank template file.

Comparing the Default server.xml File

The `server.xml` file is identical to the `server-noexamples.xml.config` file that we have examined except for an example context that is added. It is highlighted below:

```
<Server port="8005" shutdown="SHUTDOWN" debug="0">
  <!-- Define the Tomcat Stand-Alone Service -->
  <Service name="Tomcat-Standalone">
    <!-- Define a non-SSL HTTP/1.1 Connector on port 8080 -->
    <Connector className="org.apache.catalina.connector.http.HttpConnector"
               port="8080" minProcessors="5" maxProcessors="75"
               enableLookups="true" redirectPort="8443"
               acceptCount="10" debug="0" connectionTimeout="60000"/>
    <Engine name="Standalone" defaultHost="localhost" debug="0">

      <!-- Global logger unless overridden at lower levels -->
      <Logger className="org.apache.catalina.logger.FileLogger"
              prefix="catalina_log." suffix=".txt"
              timestamp="true"/>

    <!-- Because this Realm is here, an instance will be shared globally -->
      <Realm className="org.apache.catalina.realm.MemoryRealm" />

      <!-- Define the default virtual host -->
      <Host name="localhost" debug="0" appBase="webapps" unpackWARs="true">

        <Valve className="org.apache.catalina.valves.AccessLogValve"
                 directory="logs"  prefix="localhost_access_log."
                 suffix=".txt" pattern="common"/>

        <Logger className="org.apache.catalina.logger.FileLogger"
                 directory="logs"  prefix="localhost_log." suffix=".txt"
                 timestamp="true"/>

        <!-- Tomcat Manager Context -->
        <Context path="/manager" docBase="manager"
                 debug="0" privileged="true"/>

        <!-- Tomcat Examples Context -->
        <Context path="/examples" docBase="examples" debug="0"
                 reloadable="true" crossContext="true">
          <Logger className="org.apache.catalina.logger.FileLogger"
                  prefix="localhost_examples_log." suffix=".txt"
                  timestamp="true"/>

          ...web applications specific properties...

         <Resource name="mail/Session" auth="Container"
                   type="javax.mail.Session"/>
          <ResourceParams name="mail/Session">
            <parameter>
              <name>mail.smtp.host</name>
              <value>localhost</value>
```

```
            </parameter>
          </ResourceParams>
        </Context>
      </Host>
    </Engine>
  </Service>
...the remaining is the same as server-noexamples.xml.config ...
```

We can see that the additional context nested component definition provides support for the various examples that are supplied as part of the Tomcat 4 distribution. In our production environment, this context definition will be replaced with our own web application-specific context properties. The next chapter will provide more information on web applications. Tomcat 4.1.x 's `server.xml` file contains several additional elements:

```
<GlobalNamingResources>
    <!-- Test entry for demonstration purposes -->
    <Environment name="simpleValue" type="java.lang.Integer" value="30"/>
    <!-- Editable user database that can also be used by
     UserDatabaseRealm to authenticate users -->
     <Resource name="UserDatabase" auth="Container"
            type="org.apache.catalina.UserDatabase"
        description="User database that can be updated and saved">
   </Resource>
   <ResourceParams name="UserDatabase">
     <parameter>
        <name>factory</name>
        <value>org.apache.catalina.users.MemoryUserDatabaseFactory</value>
     </parameter>
     <parameter>
       <name>pathname</name>
       <value>conf/tomcat-users.xml</value>
     </parameter>
    </ResourceParams>
</GlobalNamingResources>
```

The `<GlobalNamingResources>` element is new in Tomcat 4.1.x and is defined inside a `<Server>` component, specifying JNDI resources that can be referenced by any web application context running within the server. In this case, a sample test environment entry, and a JNDI resource for the UserDatabase is created. The UserDatabase realm is created later, and the global resource referenced in the realm definition:

```
    <Realm className="org.apache.catalina.realm.UserDatabaseRealm"
             debug="0" resourceName="UserDatabase"/>
```

This sets up the `UserDatabase` realm for Tomcat 4.1.x, in lieu of the more limited memory realm of Tomcat 4.0.x. We will have extensive coverage of JNDI resources setup and the UserDatabase realm in Chapter 8.

Authentication and the tomcat-users.xml File

The `tomcat-users.xml` file is used by Tomcat's memory realm implementation (and also Tomcat 4.1.x's UserDatabase implementation). At startup, either the memory realm or UserDatabase implementation will read the entire file into server memory. Once a memory realm is loaded, no modification to the `tomcat-users.xml` file will be reflected until the next server restart. UserDatabase, on the other hand, allows modification of the loaded data and will properly persist (write back out to the XML file) any changes made to the data. Here is the initial content of the `tomcat-users.xml` file:

```
<tomcat-users>
  <user name="tomcat" password="tomcat" roles="tomcat" />
  <user name="role1"  password="tomcat" roles="role1"  />
  <user name="both"   password="tomcat" roles="tomcat,role1" />
</tomcat-users>
```

Both the `manager` application, and the graphical `admin` application of Tomcat 4.1.x, will use the `tomcat-users.xml` (via either memory realm in 4.0.x or UserDatabase in 4.1.x) for authentication. See Chapter 7 for more information.

> **For security reasons, the `tomcat-users.xml` file is shipped with the access to the `manager` and `admin` web application disabled. To enable access to these applications, you must manually edit the `tomcat-users.xml` file and add the role of `manager` and `admin` to one or more of the user entries.**

After you have added a user with the `manager` and/or `admin` role, you can then use this user to access the `manager` or `admin` application. For example, we can edit the `tomcat` user to add both roles:

```
<user name="tomcat" password="tomcat" roles="tomcat,manager,admin" />
```

The Default Deployment Descriptor – conf/web.xml

According to the Servlet 2.3 specification, every web application must contain a deployment descriptor (`web.xml` file). This file must be placed in the `WEB-INF/` directory of the web application.

There is also a `web.xml` file under the `$CATALINA_HOME/conf` directory. This file is similar to a web application's `web.xml` file – however, this particular `web.xml` file is used to specify the default properties for all web applications that are running within this server instance. We must be careful before making modifications to this file, such as any additions, changes, and security gaps, as this will affect all web applications running on the same server instance. Note also that other application servers may or may not support a global default `web.xml`.

Let us see what default server-wide properties are configured in this `web.xml` file. First, we see the standard XML header, and a reference to a DTD. Unlike `server.xml`, `web.xml` can be formally validated against a corresponding DTD:

```
<?xml version="1.0" encoding="ISO-8859-1"?>

<!DOCTYPE web-app
    PUBLIC "-//Sun Microsystems, Inc.//DTD Web Application 2.3//EN"
    "http://java.sun.com/dtd/web-app_2_3.dtd">
```

Default Servlet Definitions

In the `<servlet>` definition below, a `default` servlet is specified. This `default` servlet is used to serve any static resources (static HTML files, GIF files, and so on) within all web applications (note that we'll go over this in more detail in Chapter 6):

```
<web-app>
  <servlet>
    <servlet-name>default</servlet-name>
    <servlet-class>
       org.apache.catalina.servlets.DefaultServlet
    </servlet-class>
    <init-param>
      <param-name>debug</param-name>
      <param-value>0</param-value>
    </init-param>
    <init-param>
      <param-name>listings</param-name>
      <param-value>true</param-value>
    </init-param>
    <load-on-startup>1</load-on-startup>
  </servlet>
```

The `invoker` servlet can be used to load and execute any servlet directly using a URL similar to the following:

```
http://<host name>/<web app name>/servlet/<servlet name>
```

The invoker servlet is configured next:

```
  <servlet>
    <servlet-name>invoker</servlet-name>
    <servlet-class>
      org.apache.catalina.servlets.InvokerServlet
    </servlet-class>
    <init-param>
      <param-name>debug</param-name>
      <param-value>0</param-value>
    </init-param>
    <load-on-startup>2</load-on-startup>
  </servlet>
```

The `JspServlet` compiles JSP pages to servlets and executes them. This is used to process JSP pages:

```
  <servlet>
    <servlet-name>jsp</servlet-name>
    <servlet-class>org.apache.jasper.servlet.JspServlet</servlet-class>
    <init-param>
```

```
        <param-name>logVerbosityLevel</param-name>
        <param-value>WARNING</param-value>
      </init-param>
      <load-on-startup>3</load-on-startup>
    </servlet>
```

The next set of servlets is commented out. You should uncomment them if you plan to add Apache-style Server Side Include (SSI) features to the standalone Tomcat 4 server.

```
  <!--
    <servlet>
      <servlet-name>ssi</servlet-name>
      <servlet-class>org.apache.catalina.servlets.SsiInvokerServlet</servlet-class>
      <init-param>
        <param-name>buffered</param-name>
        <param-value>1</param-value>
      </init-param>
      <init-param>
        <param-name>debug</param-name>
        <param-value>0</param-value>
      </init-param>
      <init-param>
        <param-name>expires</param-name>
        <param-value>666</param-value>
      </init-param>
      <init-param>
        <param-name>isVirtualWebappRelative</param-name>
        <param-value>0</param-value>
      </init-param>
      <init-param>
        <param-name>ignoreUnsupportedDirective</param-name>
        <param-value>1</param-value>
      </init-param>
      <load-on-startup>4</load-on-startup>
    </servlet>
  -->
```

The next servlet is also used exclusively for configuring the web server aspect of the Tomcat 4 server. If you would like the standalone Tomcat 4 server to process CGI, you will need to uncomment the following section.

```
  <!--
    <servlet>
      <servlet-name>cgi</servlet-name>
      <servlet-class>org.apache.catalina.servlets.CGIServlet</servlet-class>
      <init-param>
        <param-name>clientInputTimeout</param-name>
        <param-value>100</param-value>
      </init-param>
      <init-param>
        <param-name>debug</param-name>
        <param-value>6</param-value>
      </init-param>
      <init-param>
        <param-name>cgiPathPrefix</param-name>
```

```
        <param-value>WEB-INF/cgi</param-value>
      </init-param>
      <load-on-startup>5</load-on-startup>
    </servlet>
-->
```

Matching URLs: Servlet Mappings

A <servlet-mapping> element specifies how incoming requests containing a specific URL pattern are to be handled:

```
<servlet-mapping>
  <servlet-name>default</servlet-name>
  <url-pattern>/</url-pattern>
</servlet-mapping>
```

The rule set up here says:

- When you see a URL request fitting the pattern "/" , route it to the `default` servlet

For example, if our host is www.wrox.com, and we are running a standalone version of the Tomcat 4 server, then the URL:

http://www.wrox.com/

will map to the servlet named `default`.

If we check back to the <servlet> definition earlier in this file, we will see that the `org.apache.catalina.servlets.DefaultServlet` will be handling this request.

The second <servlet-mapping> is:

```
<servlet-mapping>
  <servlet-name>invoker</servlet-name>
  <url-pattern>/servlet/*</url-pattern>
</servlet-mapping>
```

The rule here says:

- When you see a URL request fitting the pattern "`/servlet/*`", route it to the `invoker` servlet

So the following URL request:

http://www.wrox.com/servlet/<name of servlet>

is sent to a servlet called `invoker`.

Looking back, we can see that the `org.apache.catalina.servlets.InvokerServlet` will be used to process the request. This `invoker` servlet will in turn invoke the servlet that is named by examining the incoming URL.

The next `<servlet-mapping>` specifies that all URLs containing `*.jsp` should be passed to the servlet named `jsp` for processing. In the earlier `<server-mapping>`, the `jsp` servlet is specified to be the `org.apache.jasper.servlet.JspServlet` class:

```
<servlet-mapping>
  <servlet-name>jsp</servlet-name>
  <url-pattern>*.jsp</url-pattern>
</servlet-mapping>
```

How server.xml and web.xml Work Together

The figure below illustrates how an incoming URL is parsed by the various components of a Tomcat 4 server, and how a `<servlet-mapping>` with a `<url-pattern>` controls the final mapping of the request to a specific servlet in a web application:

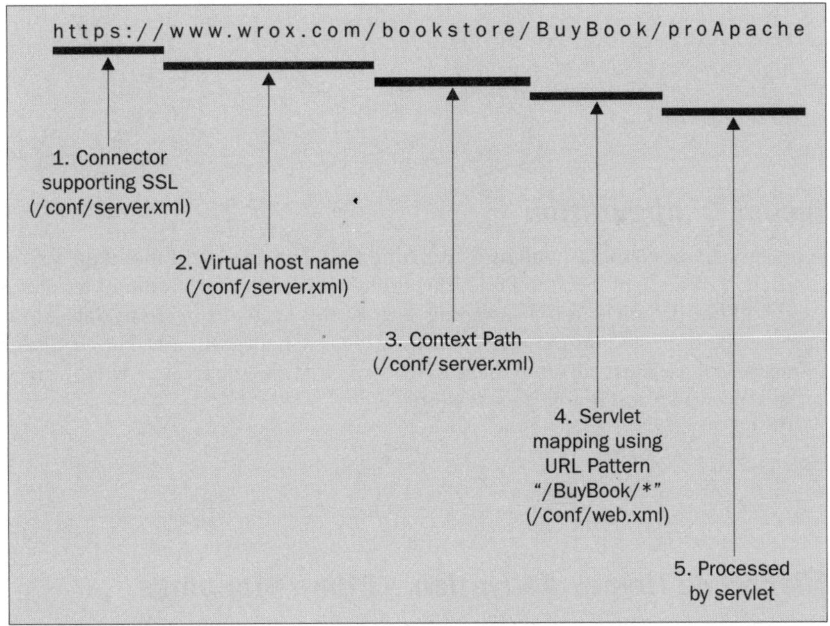

We see in the figure how a URL https://www.wrox.com/bookstore/BuyBook/proApache is parsed through the nested components that make up a Tomcat server. First, the protocol portion (https://) is parsed by the **service** and the SSL connector is selected, and the request passed to the **engine**. Next, the host name (www.wrox.com) is parsed by the **engine** and one of its **hosts** is selected (the one that matches the www.wrox.com hostname).

The **host** then attempts to match the URL against the entire **context** that it contains – the maximum match in this case is "/bookstore" and the `bookstore` web application is selected by the **host** to handle the request. Last but not least, the **context** hosting the web application performs a match against the `<servlet-mapping>` defined in the deployment descriptor, and the URL pattern /BuyBook/* matches the `BookPurchase` servlet. This servlet is finally handed the URL request to process. We can see how the component hierarchy helps in forwarding the request to a single servlet in a web application for processing.

SSI and CGI Mappings

Let us take a look at the next section of the default web.xml file.

The next two default servlet mappings are commented out. They support SSI and CGI on the standalone Tomcat 4 configuration. We will see their usage in Chapter 8:

```
<!--
  <servlet-mapping>
    <servlet-name>ssi</servlet-name>
    <url-pattern>*.shtml</url-pattern>
  </servlet-mapping>
-->

  <!-- The mapping for the CGI Gateway servlet -->
<!--
  <servlet-mapping>
    <servlet-name>cgi</servlet-name>
    <url-pattern>/cgi-bin/*</url-pattern>
  </servlet-mapping>
-->
```

Session Timeout Configuration

The <session-config> element configures the time that Tomcat 4 will maintain a session on the server side on behalf of a client. For example, the client may be in the middle of an online shopping transaction and still has products in the shopping cart. In this case, if the client does not return to the cart for 30 minutes (and no session persistence is used – see Chapter 8), all their cart information will be lost. As administrators, we must carefully balance the <session-timeout> value with the potential of overloading the server with too many stale sessions:

```
  <session-config>
    <session-timeout>30</session-timeout>
  </session-config>
```

Handling Client-Side Helper Activation – Mime Mappings

The next set of elements contains the default <mime-mapping> elements. Tomcat 4 uses these mappings to serve static files with specific extensions to the client. It will generate an HTTP Content-Type header when transmitting the file to the client (typically a browser). Most browsers will use a helper application to process the file being transmitted if it recognizes the Content-Type specified. For example, Microsoft Internet Explorer may start Microsoft MediaPlayer when it detects the video/x-mpeg content type. Note that these are only the default mappings; a web application's own deployment descriptor (web.xml file) can override or add to this list:

```
  <mime-mapping>
    <extension>abs</extension>
    <mime-type>audio/x-mpeg</mime-type>
  </mime-mapping>
  <mime-mapping>
    <extension>ai</extension>
    <mime-type>application/postscript</mime-type>
```

```
    </mime-mapping>
    <mime-mapping>
      <extension>aif</extension>
      <mime-type>audio/x-aiff</mime-type>
    </mime-mapping>
    <mime-mapping>
      <extension>aifc</extension>
      <mime-type>audio/x-aiff</mime-type>
    </mime-mapping>

      ... more mime mappings...

    <mime-mapping>
      <extension>Z</extension>
      <mime-type>application/x-compress</mime-type>
    </mime-mapping>
    <mime-mapping>
      <extension>z</extension>
      <mime-type>application/x-compress</mime-type>
    </mime-mapping>
    <mime-mapping>
      <extension>zip</extension>
      <mime-type>application/zip</mime-type>
    </mime-mapping>
```

Simulating Apache: Welcome File Handling

To be compatible with the default behavior of most modern web servers, including Apache, the `default` servlet will display a welcome file if the incoming URI is terminated in "/". For example:

http://www.wrox.com/

The `default` servlet will examine the root directory of the named virtual host (www.wrox.com) and look for `index.html`, `index.htm`, or `index.jsp` in turn to be displayed. Each web application may override this list in its own deployment descriptor (`web.xml`) file:

```
    <welcome-file-list>
      <welcome-file>index.html</welcome-file>
      <welcome-file>index.htm</welcome-file>
      <welcome-file>index.jsp</welcome-file>
    </welcome-file-list>

  </web-app>
```

Finally, let us examine the file `catlina.policy` in the directory `$CATALINA_HOME/conf`.

Fine-Grained Access Control: catalina.policy

We will have more complete coverage of the role of the Tomcat security manager and its use of this policy file in Chapter 16. For now, we will take a quick browse through the file to understand how it provides fine-grained access control to a Tomcat 4 server administrator.

Tomcat 4 leverages the built-in fine-grained security model of Java 2. When enabled, the basis of the security system is:

Any access to system resources that is not explicitly allowed is prohibited.

This means that we must anticipate all the resources that the Tomcat 4 server will access, and explicitly grant permission for it to do so.

By default, Catalina starts up without security. You will need to start Tomcat with:

```
startup -security
```

for it to run with a security manager. It is only in this secured mode that the following policy file will be read, processed, and enforced. We will provide a glimpse of some of the important sections of the `catalina.policy` file now, but not go into details of the file at this time. Please read Chapter 16 for a more thorough discussion.

The general policy entry is in the form of:

```
grant <security principal> { permission list… };
```

where the `<security principal>` is typically a body of trusted code.

Looking at the `catalina.policy` file, the first set of permissions grant code from the Java compiler directories all access to all resources – this is essentially the Java compiler and runtime system code:

```
// These permissions apply to javac
grant codeBase "file:${java.home}/lib/-" {
        permission java.security.AllPermission;
};

// These permissions apply to all shared system extensions
grant codeBase "file:${java.home}/jre/lib/ext/-" {
        permission java.security.AllPermission;
};

// These permissions apply to javac when ${java.home] points at $JAVA_HOME/jre
grant codeBase "file:${java.home}/../lib/-" {
        permission java.security.AllPermission;
};

// These permissions apply to all shared system extensions when
// ${java.home} points at $JAVA_HOME/jre
grant codeBase "file:${java.home}/lib/ext/-" {
        permission java.security.AllPermission;
};
```

One clear message here is that you must protect these directories using your operating system file protection features.

The next section grants Catalina server code and API libraries access to all resources:

```
// These permissions apply to the server startup code
grant codeBase "file:${catalina.home}/bin/bootstrap.jar" {
        permission java.security.AllPermission;
};

// These permissions apply to the servlet API classes
// and those that are shared across all class loaders
// located in the "common" directory
grant codeBase "file:${catalina.home}/common/-" {
        permission java.security.AllPermission;
};

// These permissions apply to the container's core code, plus any additional
// libraries installed in the "server" directory
grant codeBase "file:${catalina.home}/server/-" {
        permission java.security.AllPermission;
};

// These permissions apply to shared web application libraries
// including the Jasper page compiler in the "lib" directory
grant codeBase "file:${catalina.home}/lib/-" {
        permission java.security.AllPermission;
};

// These permissions apply to shared web application classes
// located in the "classes" directory
grant codeBase "file:${catalina.home}/classes/-" {
        permission java.security.AllPermission;
};
```

Again, in a secure configuration, you must be careful to lock down the above directories, thus avoiding the possibility of an attacker adding malicious code to them. Any class files introduced into these directories will automatically be granted access to all system resources.

The final set contains the permissions given to web applications by default. They are significantly more restrictive; that is, they are never granted the all-powerful permission `java.security.AllPermission`.

The first section enables access to system properties that enable JNDI and JDBC access:

```
grant {
        // Required for JNDI lookup of named JDBC DataSource's and
        // javamail named MimePart DataSource used to send mail
        permission java.util.PropertyPermission "java.home", "read";
        permission java.util.PropertyPermission "java.naming.*", "read";
        permission java.util.PropertyPermission "javax.sql.*", "read";
```

The next section enables read-only access to some operating system description properties: the type of operating system we are running under and what it uses to separate file extensions in a filename:

```
        // OS Specific properties to allow read access
        permission java.util.PropertyPermission "os.name", "read";
        permission java.util.PropertyPermission "os.version", "read";
        permission java.util.PropertyPermission "os.arch", "read";
        permission java.util.PropertyPermission "file.separator", "read";
        permission java.util.PropertyPermission "path.separator", "read";
        permission java.util.PropertyPermission "line.separator", "read";
```

The third section enables read-only access to some JVM-specific properties that are often used in application programming:

```
        // JVM properties to allow read access
        permission java.util.PropertyPermission "java.version", "read";
        permission java.util.PropertyPermission "java.vendor", "read";
        permission java.util.PropertyPermission "java.vendor.url", "read";
    permission java.util.PropertyPermission "java.class.version", "read";
    permission java.util.PropertyPermission "java.specification.version",
                                            "read";
    permission java.util.PropertyPermission "java.specification.vendor",
                                            "read";
    permission java.util.PropertyPermission "java.specification.name",
                                            "read";
    permission java.util.PropertyPermission "java.vm.specification.version",
                                             "read";
    permission java.util.PropertyPermission "java.vm.specification.vendor",
                                            "read";
    permission java.util.PropertyPermission "java.vm.specification.name",
                                            "read";
    permission java.util.PropertyPermission "java.vm.version", "read";
    permission java.util.PropertyPermission "java.vm.vendor", "read";
    permission java.util.PropertyPermission "java.vm.name", "read";
```

The last two sections provide access to BeanInfo and XML parser debug, required frequently during code development (see JavaBean and JAXP specifications for more details on these properties):

```
  // Required for getting BeanInfo
   permission java.lang.RuntimePermission "accessClassInPackage.sun.beans.*";

  // Allow read of JAXP compliant XML parser debug
        permission java.util.PropertyPermission "jaxp.debug", "read";
  };
```

These are minimal permissions that are granted by default to web applications. Typical secured production configuration will require opening up additional access to the web applications such as socket access to a JDBC server or network access to an external authentication system.

Summary

In this chapter, we have examined all the configuration files in the `$CATALINA_HOME/conf` directory of the Tomcat 4 distribution. The files included:

- `server.xml`
- `server-noexamples.xml.config`
- `tomcat-users.xml`
- `web.xml`
- `catalina.policy`

We have seen how `server.xml` is the essential server configuration file for Tomcat 4. `server-noexamples.xml.config` gave us an easy-to-understand and analyze version of `server.xml`; a blank template from which to create our own custom `server.xml` configuration. To understand the model of configuration, we need to understand the concepts of top-level component, container hierarchy, and nested components. In fact, we now understand the function of the following Tomcat components and how to configure them:

- Server
- Service
- Connector
- Engine
- Host
- Context

Furthermore, we have an understanding of how these components relate to each other and work together during normal Tomcat 4 operation.

The `tomcat-users.xml` file is the data supply for a memory realm that is used by the Tomcat `manager` application as well as a sample realm implementation that programmers may use. In a production system, a more robust implementation of a realm – such as a JDBC realm or a JNDI realm – should be used.

The default `web.xml` file in `$CATALINA_HOME/conf` specifies properties that are used in every single web application running on the server. Many of the default servlets configured here provide web server-like features (serving static content, SSI, CGI, and so on) for running web applications.

While Tomcat 4 starts up by default in an unsecured mode, the `catalina.policy` file is vitally important in secured Tomcat 4 installations. It specifies in excruciating detail what can be accessed by whom – and anything else that is not specified cannot be accessed. Tomcat 4 takes advantage of the sophisticated, built-in security infrastructure of Java 2.

In analyzing these configuration files, we have gained an in-depth understanding of the basic configuration features of Tomcat 4. We have also encountered advanced configuration topics such as SSL connector configuration, realm configuration, and detailed security configuration.

In the next chapter, we will see how to administer a web application.

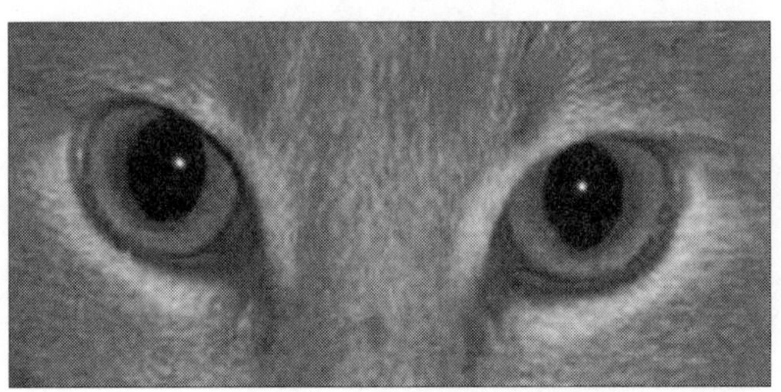

6

Web Application Administration

Most web applications will require a system administrator to maintain them. However, it is fairly common for applications to be quite brittle and inflexible. In other words, much of the code in existence today has hard-coded assumptions about where resources are to be found. This means that most applications will not cope well with the administrator moving files; at least without the developer having to recompile or adjust any code that exists in the JSP pages.

Therefore, there are a number of things that a systems administrator will find useful to know about administering web applications. In this chapter we will cover all the elements and attributes of the main web application configuration file. Before we do that, however, it is worth looking at the makeup of a web application, where files go and what we will usually find in them.

Over the course of this chapter we will cover:

- The contents of a web application
- The `web.xml` configuration file

The Contents of a Web Application

As we discussed previously in Chapter 2, HTML and JSP pages belong to the public resources that a client may request directly. Servlets, JavaBeans, and other resources within the `WEB-INF` directory fall into the category of an application's private resources. The client may use these resources indirectly by mapping a URL to a servlet, or a JSP page might do the same without the client's explicit knowledge. However, private resources cannot be served to the client without some type of intervention.

The majority of Java web resources can be aliased to a URL pattern. `.jsp` extensions are themselves an alias, as all resources ending with `.jsp` are conveyed to a parser and a compiler before the resulting code is executed. Later we shall see that aliasing forms the basis for much of the configuration of a web application.

Here is the typical makeup of a web application required by the Servlet 2.3 specifications. Here, some files are placed arbitrarily and we'll point out when this is the case, soon:

```
webapps/
        wroxexample/
                    contact.htm
                    example.css
                    index.jsp
                    images/
                           photo.jpg
                           graphic.png
                    META-INF/
                    WEB-INF/
                            web.xml
                            classses/
                                     com/
                                         ApplicationResources.properties
                                         wrox/
                                              db/
                                                 DatabaseServlet.java
                            tlds/
                                 app-tags.tld
                            lib/
                                struts.jar
                                webdav.jar
```

The web application is deployed in a folder traditionally named after the web application, and this folder is required. This name is also used to identify the application in a URL (unless it is the `ROOT` application – the application that is available by default when no context path is specified, for example, the URL http://servername:8080/). To describe this more generically, everything after the server and port number is called the **context path** and this part of the URL is used to resolve the location of the resource.

Our imaginary example web application will have a URL like http://localhost:8080/wroxexample/, and is required to contain a folder called `WEB-INF`, which may contain a configuration file named `web.xml`.

URL Mappings

In most cases, there is no intervention from the server or the components of the application and the file is served as is and without modification (that is, parsing the content referred to by the URL for dynamic contents). The one exception to this default behavior is for `.jsp` files, which must never be served without processing unless specifically designed to be so for application-specific reasons. This is because the JSP page contains code that may include business logic or reveal the way that the application works. This is not a good idea as showing source may compromise the application's security by exposing business information.

The code that defines this URL mapping is shown below:

```
<servlet-mapping>
  <servlet-name>jsp</servlet-name>
  <url-pattern>*.jsp</url-pattern>
</servlet-mapping>
```

This specifies that any URL that ends in `.jsp` should be passed to a servlet named `jsp` that is defined elsewhere in the same `$CATALINA_HOME/conf/web.xml` configuration file. The definition for this servlet is shown below:

```
<servlet>
  <servlet-name>jsp</servlet-name>
  <servlet-class>org.apache.jasper.servlet.JspServlet</servlet-class>
  <init-param>
    <param-name>logVerbosityLevel</param-name>
    <param-value>WARNING</param-value>
  </init-param>
  <load-on-startup>3</load-on-startup>
</servlet>
```

As you can see, the fully qualified name of the servlet is `org.apache.jasper.servlet.JspServlet`. The servlet is handed the request, uses the context path to load the JSP page, and passes it to Tomcat's JSP compiler, known as Jasper. The remaining options set the logging level for the JSP compilation and execution process, and ensure that the servlet class is loaded into memory on startup with a priority of 3 (where 1 is most important) to ensure that it is loaded before any JSP pages are requested.

Let's look at the remaining files and explore the features of web applications.

Public Resources

The placement of publicly accessible files (such as JSP and HTML pages, CSS, and images) is arbitrary as far as the specifications for web applications are concerned, and they can be accessed directly by a client.

> *Note, by arbitrary we do not mean that it can be placed anywhere and the server will find it, but rather as long as the files are put within the web application directory, and outside of the `WEB-INF` directory, then the application itself (and its designer) decides where files are placed.*

In our example web application above, `index.jsp` is the traditional default page of a web application. If it cannot be found, then by default `index.html` and `index.htm` will be looked for and served if found. However, this is subject to configuration and can be modified, as we will see later. Thus, the first six entries (within the `wroxexample` folder that our web application lives in) are all public resources.

The META-INF Folder

We have mentioned before that the WEB-INF directory represents the private resources of an application. However, this is not the only directory for private resources; a web application may have a META-INF directory that contains deployment information for tools that create WAR files and resources that applications may rely on. Therefore, a servlet container will refuse to show the contents of the META-INF directory to a client.

There is often only one file inside the META-INF directory named MANIFEST.MF. This file may contain a list of JAR files that an application relies on. The container can then check all the required libraries that are to be made available for the web application.

An entry in this text file should be provided as follows, on a single line:

```
Extension-List: extension1 extension2 extension3
```

Each extension name is separated by a space and is placed as a separate entry in the MANIFEST.MF file. They are named with a prefix followed by the string -Extension-Name, which is an attribute name as shown below:

```
extension1-Extension-Name: com.wrox.extension1
extension1-Specification-Version: 1.0
extension1-Implementation-Version: 0.8
extension1-Implementation-Vendor: WROX Press Ltd
extension1-Implementation-Vendor-Id: com.wrox
extension1-Implementation-URL: http://www.wrox.com/extension1/
```

As you can see, the name of the extension is referenced in each entry. This is suffixed by a specific attribute name describing the extension. The name of the extension in this file is an alias for the extension's name as defined in the JAR file. Thus, the declaration of the extensions alias is done by simply prefixing it to the attribute names; it does not need to be explicitly defined.

The extension's proper name is referred to in the first entry. The server will investigate the contents of each JAR file installed on it and check packages to see if the names match. The specifications and implementation version numbers are self-explanatory as should be the vendor name that is named in the Implementation-Vendor attribute. The vendor should be a globally unique ID; the custom of including the reversed host name is common. In our example this is com.wrox.

Finally, the Implementation-URL should be provided, giving the location of further information and often download instructions. For our purpose, this is the most useful line; if the extension is not installed, the URL should provide enough information to make sure it is made available to the web application by other means.

The JAR files may be placed in the application's lib directory, the web application shared $CATALINA_HOME/shared/lib directory, the system-wide $CATALINA_HOME/server/lib, or alternatively placed on the classpath in some way.

The WEB-INF Folder

The contents of the WEB-INF folder are shown in the diagram earlier in the chapter. As you can see there are three subfolders and the web.xml file. We will discuss these and their relevance next.

The classes Folder

The classes directory contains servlet and utility classes including JavaBeans and may also contain a number of resource files such as key/value message lists which contain error messages and user prompts for the application, and application-specific configuration information.

Each class is stored within a folder hierarchy that matches its **Fully Qualified Name** (FQN). Therefore, com.wrox.db.DatabaseServlet will be stored in the classes/com/wrox/db directory structure. As servlets are merely Java classes that implement a specified interface, they are stored in the classes folder. Previously, it was common to place servlets in an additional directory within the WEB-INF folder named servlets. Classes placed into this directory are no longer on the classpath by default, and they need to be moved into the classes directory.

Ideally, an administrator need not be concerned with the contents of the classes directory; however, it is worth noting that there may be configuration files present in it. The resource files we mentioned earlier may be within this directory and are typically text files that contain configuration information or are used to externalize error messages. This is merely a programming practice and we may have any kind of file here.

For example, there may be an ApplicationResources.properties file (the name is determined by the application developer) that looks like the following:

```
prompt.username=User Name (your email address)
prompt.password=Please enter you password
error.password.mismatch=The password is incorrect. Please try again.
```

This type of list allows an application developer to refer to the text by its name (for example prompt.username) and so allow an administrator to change the values, minimizing the need to touch the sensitive JSP code.

This configuration information might be included within the WEB-INF directory because the specification for Java web applications has a system similar to the classpath, but it allows **any** resource within the web application to be loaded. In this case, it is possible to place the configuration files anywhere within the web application and is therefore a preferred method.

The tlds Folder

Finally, there may be a tlds folder within the WEB-INF directory. The contents of this directory are configuration files for tag libraries.

A tag library is a group of Java classes that define the functionality of dynamic markup tags. For example, we could use a tag that we define such as the following:

```
<date:today/>
```

This would output today's date whenever it is placed in a JSP file. To enable the container to recognize which Java class to invoke when it comes across the tag, we need to provide a configuration file that lists the number of arguments the tag can have (a little like the href argument for the HTML hyperlink), its name (in this case the tag's name is today and the library it belongs to is date). The tag library configuration files have a .tld extension. The configuration of a tag library is the territory of developers and designers so we will not go further on this subject.

The lib Folder

This contains packaged Java libraries that the application requires and that are bundled with the application. JAR files that are placed here are available only to the web application.

We can now go on to discuss what aspects of the web.xml configuration file we can administrate.

The web.xml File

The web.xml file takes the following generalized form:

```
<?xml version="1.0"?>
<!DOCTYPE web-app
    PUBLIC "-//Sun Microsystems, Inc.//DTD Web Application 2.2//EN"
    "http://java.sun.com/j2ee/dtds/web-app_2_2.dtd">
<web-app>
  <icon>
  <display-name>
  <description>
  <distributable>
  <context-param>
  <filter>
  <filter-mapping>
  <listener>
  <servlet>
  <servlet-mapping>
  <session-config>
  <mime-mapping>
  <welcome-file-list>
  <error-page>
  <taglib>
  <resource-env-ref>
  <resource-ref>
  <security-constraint>
  <login-config>
  <security-role>
  <env-entry>
  <ejb-ref>
  <ejb-local-ref>
</web-app>
```

The order of elements inside the <web-app> element must be as shown above, but some elements are optional while others may appear multiple times. The table opposite may be used as a quick reference to the functionality of each element. However, a more detailed explanation is provided later in the chapter:

Element	Description	How Many?
<icon>	Image for an application	0 or 1
<display-name>	Display name for a web application	0 or 1
<description>	Description used for display	0 or 1
<distributable>	A Boolean value to indicate whether an application is distributable across servers	0 or 1
<context-param>	Initialization parameters for the entire application	0 or more
<filter>	Defines a filter valve	0 or more
<filter-mapping>	Defines a URL pattern to which the given filter needs to be applied	0 or more
<listener>	Defines a lifecycle event listener	0 or more
<servlet>	Defines a servlet	0 or more
<servlet-mapping>	Defines a URL patterns to invoke a named servlet	0 or more
<session-config>	Defines session configuration	0 or 1
<mime-mapping>	Defines the MIME type for a given file type	0 or more
<welcome-file-list>	A list of files to be served if no resource is specified explicitly in the URL	0 or 1
<error-page>	Defines a Java exception or an HTTP code-based error page	0 or more
<taglib>	Declares a tag library	0 or more
<resource-env-ref>	Declares a resource administered object	0 or more
<resource-ref>	Declares an external resource	0 or more
<security-constraint>	Restricts access to a resource to a required transport guarantee and by user role.	0 or more
<login-config>	Defines authentication parameters	0 or 1
<security-role>	Declares a security role by name	0 or more
<env-entry>	Defines a web application's environment entry	0 or more
<ejb-ref>	Declares a reference to an EJB's home	0 or more
<ejb-local-ref>	Declares a reference to an EJB's local home	0 or more

We will begin by looking at a minimal `web.xml` file so we can see what must be present.

The XML Header

Every web.xml file complies with the XML specifications that require an XML header in the beginning of the file as below:

```
<?xml version="1.0"?>
```

Optionally, the declaration may also include an encoding type that identifies the character encoding of the document as is standard for XML. For example, if the document is encoded in UTF-8, the declaration may be provided as:

```
<?xml version="1.0" encoding="UTF-8"?>
```

The DTD Declaration

The next tag is a Document Type Declaration (DTD) tag. A DTD is a document that outlines the structure of the web.xml elements, what elements are allowed and in which order, and their content. The inclusion of a standard DTD declaration in our web.xml file looks as follows:

```
<?xml version="1.0"?>
<!DOCTYPE web-app
    PUBLIC "-//Sun Microsystems, Inc.//DTD Web Application 2.3//EN"
    "http://java.sun.com/dtd/web-app_2_3.dtd">
```

Applications that comply with the Servlet specifications prior to 2.3, Tomcat 3 web.xml files for instance, will have the following DTD reference:

```
<!DOCTYPE web-app
    PUBLIC "-//Sun Microsystems, Inc.//DTD Web Application 2.2//EN"
    "http://java.sun.com/j2ee/dtds/web-app_2_2.dtd">
```

Backward compatibility is required as per the Servlet 2.3 specifications and so applications that were written for the Servlet 2.2 specifications will work unaltered on Tomcat 4, except that any dependencies on the exact configuration of the server, such as the location of databases, network authentication, and the name of the server and the host. As the Servlet 2.3 specifications have introduced a number of new tags since 2.2, we will also highlight these tags where appropriate.

<web-app>

The root element of the web.xml is <web-app> and all other XML elements reside inside it:

```
<?xml version="1.0"?>
<!DOCTYPE web-app
    PUBLIC "-//Sun Microsystems, Inc.//DTD Web Application 2.3//EN"
    "http://java.sun.com/dtd/web-app_2_3.dtd">
<web-app>
</web-app>
```

In principle, this is all that is required for the web.xml file to be complete though in many practical cases there will be more. Let's begin by covering elements that describe the application; a number of elements are provided for deployment tools to identify web applications visually and textually.

<icon>

This tag holds the location of the image files within the web application that may be used by a tool to represent the web application visually. The <icon> tag may contain two child elements, <small-icon> and <large-icon> that carry the location of a 16 x 16 pixel image and a 32 x 32 pixel image files respectively:

```
<icon>
  <small-icon>/images/icons/wroxexample_small.gif</small-icon>
  <large-icon>/images/icons/wroxexample_large.gif</large-icon>
</icon>
```

<display-name>

This tag provides a name that can be used for display in a GUI interface. The name need not be unique. For example, the following display name is typical:

```
<display-name>Example Application</display-name>
```

<description>

This tag contains the description of a web application as shown in the example below:

```
<?xml version="1.0"?>
<!DOCTYPE web-app
    PUBLIC "-//Sun Microsystems, Inc.//DTD Web Application 2.3//EN"
    "http://java.sun.com/dtd/web-app_2_3.dtd">
<web-app>
  <icon>
    <small-icon>/images/icons/wroxexample_small.gif</small-icon>
    <large-icon>/images/icons/wroxexample_large.gif</large-icon>
  </icon>

  <display-name>Wrox Example Application</display-name>

  <description>
    The Wrox example application contains a number of simple resources
    for illustrating configuration points.
  </description>
</web-app>
```

These element tags must be listed in the same order as shown earlier in the section (refer to http://java.sun.com/dtd/web-app_2_3.dtd for more information). The actual number of tools for deploying web archives, especially in a drag-and-drop manner as suggested by the use of icon files, is somewhat low, so it is common for these values not to be provided. The web.xml may be heavily commented – XML comments take the same form as HTML ones:

```
<!--
This is a comment
-->
```

<distributable>

This tag describes a web application that is designed to be distributable for load balancing and fail over. By default, the value of this is `false` as the general assumption is that applications are not designed to work being distributed without additional support.

<context-param>

Context parameters are mechanisms used for setting application initialization parameters. For example, we could set the URL to a database here. The example below allows the administrator to change the title and greeting of our example application:

```
<context-param>
  <param-name>title</param-name>
  <param-value>Wrox example application - Chapter 6</param-value>
</context-param>
<context-param>
  <param-name>greeting</param-name>
  <param-value>Welcome to the example application</param-value>
</context-param>
```

There may be any number of context parameters in the application; they are known as **initial parameters**. Each dynamic resource, such as a servlet, a JSP page, or a class with access to the application context is able to look up the value associated with a given parameter name. Typical items provided as a context parameter are the debug status of the application, the verbosity of logging (these two are often interlinked), and as much other externalized configuration as the application developer has allowed.

<filter>

Filters are new to the Servlet 2.3 specifications. Filters are reusable components that intercept the client request and response and apply some type of processing to them. For example, a filter may apply compression to the contents of the response, thus reducing bandwidth usage and improving the performance of the application by minimizing the size of the response packet. This is just an example and to make it work in practical situations would require additional support in the browser.

Filters are intended to be the ultimate reusable web components – they should be virtually independent of the content being created. Examples include the compression filter, a transformation filter that may convert XML to HTML or WML, a filter to provide logging of resource usage, and a filter to restrict access to resources.

A filter, like all web application resources, can be mapped to a URL pattern including the extension of the resource, a section of the site (such as everything within the `images` folder), or even a URL alias such as the `servlet` alias that exists on most default installations of Java web servers.

In addition, filters can have an icon associated with them and can have configuration parameters (initialization parameters). An example configuration is shown opposite:

```
<filter>
  <icon>/images/icons/filter.jpg</icon>
  <filter-name>Compressor</filter-name>
  <display-name>Compression Filter</display-name>
  <description>This filter applies compression</description>
  <filter-class>com.wrox.utils.CompressionFilter</filter-class>
  <init-param>
    <param-name>compression_type</param-name>
    <param-value>gzip</param-value>
  </init-param>
</filter>
```

Once a filter is defined, it can be mapped against any number of URL patterns. Also when many filters are defined for a given URL pattern, they are all applied in the order in which they are defined in the `web.xml` file. In the following example, the compression filter is applied to every URL:

```
<filter-mapping>
  <filter-name>Compressor</filter-name>
  <url-pattern>*</url-pattern>
</filter-mapping>
```

For further information on filter, listener, and servlet configuration refer to Chapter 8.

<listener>

Listeners are designed to respond to events in an application; for example, a JavaBean could send an e-mail when an event requiring administration is recorded:

```
<listener>
  <listener-class>com.wrox.listeners.ExampleListener</listener-class>
</listener>
```

<servlet>

A servlet is declared in the `web.xml` file by assigning it a unique name by referencing its FQN against a shorter, more intuitive name:

```
<servlet>
  <icon>/images/icons/DownloadServlet.jpg</icon>
  <servlet-name>Download</servlet-name>
  <display-name>File Download Servlet</display-name>
  <description>
    This servlet manages file downloads in the application
  </description>
  <servlet-class>com.wrox.servlets.DownloadServlet</servlet-class>
  <!-- require terms and conditions agreement? -->
  <init-param>
    <param-name>require_tc</param-name>
    <param-value>true</param-value>
  </init-param>
```

```
    <load-on-startup>5</load-on-startup>

    <!-- uncomment this if servlet must run in user role
    <run-as>
      <description>
        This servlet does not require authorization to resources
      </description>
      <role-name>admin</role-name>
    </run-as>
    -->
  </servlet>
```

In the example above, our servlet manages the download process, allowing us to decide at run time if a user is required to sign a terms and conditions acceptance form before download commences. The optional <icon>, <display-name>, and <description> elements work in the same way as before. The FQN name of the servlet is specified in the <servlet-class> element.

As JSP pages are ultimately compiled into servlets, an alternative to the servlet class name (<servlet-class> element) is to specify the JSP filename (<jsp-file> element) that these configuration parameters should be applied to, thus making JSP files fully configurable. The reference is a full path, from the root of the application, to the JSP file. An example is given below:

```
<servlet>
  <servlet-name>ExampleJSP</servlet-name>
  <jsp-file>/admin/users/ListAllUsers.jsp</jsp-file>

  <!-- list disabled user accounts -->
  <init-param>
    <param-name>list_disabled_accs</param-name>
    <param-value>false</param-value>
  </init-param>
</servlet>
```

The initialization parameters work in the same way as the application context parameters. However, they are specific to the servlet.

The <load-on-startup> element specifies an integer value indicating that the servlet must be loaded when the Tomcat server boots rather than on a client's request. If this value is not specified or it is negative, the container loads the servlet into memory when the first request comes in.

If the value is zero or a positive integer, the container must load the servlet into memory at startup of the web application: servlets assigned lower integers are loaded before those with higher integers. Servlets with the same <load-on-startup> values are loaded in an arbitrary sequence by the container.

In the Download Servlet example, the <run-as> attribute is not specified as it is commented out, however, if the servlet requires a privileged role, it can be specified here, so that any resource requiring a privileged user will discover it while calling the isUserInRole() method.

<session-config>

Session configuration allows sessions to be configured for every application. The `<session-timeout>` element can be used to set a session timeout value. This value can be calculated by considering typical client usage patterns, along with security requirements. For example, a user may be asked to enter a great deal of information and to avoid information being lost, the session timeout may be set to a larger number.

Alternatively, in low security environments with serializable sessions, it is possible to set sessions to never expire so that the user is always recognized.

The session configuration is defined as follows:

```
<session-config>
  <session-timeout>40</session-timeout>
</session-config>
```

If the value is zero or less, the session is never expired and the application must explicitly remove it as required. If the element is not provided, the default value of 30 is used as specified in the global `web.xml` file within Tomcat's `$CATALINA_HOME/config` directory.

<mime-mapping>

MIME types allow browsers to recognize the file type of the content being returned by the server so that the browser can handle it correctly, whether to display it (HTML, plain text, images) or to pass the content to a plug-in (such as Flash), or to prompt the user to save the file locally.

Tomcat comes pre-configured with the majority of MIME mappings set, which can be seen in the `$CATALINA_HOME/conf/web.xml` file. MIME mappings set in this file will apply for all applications. Additional MIME mappings may be configured on each web application with the `<mime-mapping>` element. This can be especially useful when the developer defines new extensions to suit the application. In addition, this can be useful if you wish to have a certain MIME type treated differently than it is normally. For example, for a content management application, we may want to prevent Internet Explorer from recognizing the MIME type, and thus opening the file in the appropriate application, but rather prompt the user with the File Save dialog box.

Another example may be the automatic generation of Excel files. Excel will accept comma-separated values and convert them to an Excel spreadsheet if the MIME type sent to Internet Explorer is set to the Excel MIME type of `application/x-excel` or `application/ms-excel`. This will make Excel open, although the file is a CSV file. This technique is used in web applications for non-integrated applications where the company administrator wishes to be able to dynamically generate Excel files from the site into their reports since creating Excel sheets on the fly is quite complex.

> **For those interested in creating complex Excel files on the fly, there are a number of Excel file type manipulation APIs including `JExcel`.**

This is a common technique when it is desirable to use an external application to view content from a web application/script. The following shows how the Excel-CVS MIME mapping is done:

```
<mime-mapping>
  <extension>csv</extension>
  <mime-type>application/x-msexcel</mime-type>
</mime-mapping>
...
```

<welcome-file-list>

Sometimes a request is made from a client to an application without a definite resource specified in the URL. For example, the root of the application is requested as follows:

http://localhost:8080/wroxexample/

Whereas a definite resource is requested as shown in the URL:

http://localhost:8080/wroxexample/whatsnew.jsp

In such cases, each web application looks for a file called `index.jsp` in the web application's folder or subfolders and executes this file if it exists. If this file cannot be found, it looks for `index.htm` and `index.html` in turn. This is because the welcome file list defined in `$CATALINA_HOME/conf/web.xml` lists these files by default. If the `web.xml` file in the `WEB-INF` folder of your web application does not mention a welcome file list, the default will be used.

The format for the welcome list is as follows (this will apply to each request that does not specify a resource). This means that each of the subfolders within the application root will also have this rule applied to them. In the example below, `default.jsp` will be loaded instead of `index.jsp`:

```
<welcome-file-list>
  <welcome-file>default.jsp</welcome-file>
  <welcome-file>default.htm</welcome-file>
  <welcome-file>UserWelcome.jsp</welcome-file>
</welcome-file-list>
```

Also note that if all the files in the example list above are not found then depending on the configuration, an error Apache Tomcat/4.0.4 - HTTP status 404 is displayed.

<error-page>

The default behavior for web applications written in JSP is to return a stack trace – a complex view into the internals of the virtual machine that greatly reduces the user-friendliness of the application.

We can configure error pages to provide a user-friendly mechanism for informing the users about the problem and allowing them to continue using the application. The errors are mapped to the HTTP specification error mappings: a code for a resource that cannot be found, the server is malfunctioning, authentication issues, resource issues, and so on.

In addition, since there are no one-to-one correspondences between HTTP errors and Java exceptions, the exception class type may be specified – this allows error pages that are generic and follows good programming practice. Someone without an understanding of the application's internals can configure them. An example is given for the common 404 message and for a `NullPointerException`:

```
<error-page>
  <error-code>404</error-code>
  <location>/errors/oops.jsp</location>
</error-page>
<error-page>
  <exception-type>java.lang.NullPointerException</exception-type>
  <location>/errors/badlycodedpage.jsp</location>
</error-page>
```

Like the JSP page example, `<location>` must be a reference from the root of the application.

These pages often have a message that notifies the user of the problem, and provisionally provides a search box so that the user can locate the resource they need, together with a list of likely links in the site from which they might be helped.

Often the problem is a configuration issue, and the user is best served by being informed that the problem will be fixed and they should return at a later date. The developer may be informed through automated parsing of error logs or through a notification system that may send e-mails to a watched e-mail address or directly to the administrator or the development team.

Should any problem occur in a page, such as missing resources, a bug in the software, or parts of the system being down, a page configured here would be returned. Error pages can also be written so that they display contextual information (one that relates to the specific problem at hand) but this requires an understanding of the inner workings of the system and can only be provided by a developer.

HTTP return codes can be found at http://www.w3c.org/Protocols/HTTP/HTRESP.html. Error pages are configured by associating them with the HTTP return code that covers the error group. Two examples are provided below, one for the HTTP 404 code and one for a NullPointerException – an internal error is often hard to debug in an application and will require a developer's intervention to correct it:

```
<error-page>
  <error-code>404</error-code>
  <location>/errors/ResourceNotFound.htm</location>
</error-page>
<error-page>
  <exception-type>java.lang.NullPointerException</exception-type>
  <location>/errors/ApplicationProblem.jsp</location>
</error-page>
```

<taglib>

Tag libraries, as previously discussed in Chapter 2, are reusable Java components that may be invoked using markup tags in the page. The tag library definition is affected by the application developer and the HTML designers. However, the main configuration of these reusable components is done in a separate file (one with a `.tld` extension), as this entry simply allows aliasing of the location of this configuration document against a URI. The exact location of the configuration file, which is given as a reference to the file from the web application's root folder, can then be referred to by its alias.

This aliasing allows location-independence, that is, the tag library configuration files can be moved around without editing the JSP pages that refer to the tag library configuration file so long as the tag entry points to it. An example entry is shown below:

```
<taglib>
  <taglib-uri>applicationtags.tld</taglib-uri>
  <tablib-location>/WEB-INF/tlds/web-app.tld</taglib-location>
</taglib>
```

In the example above, the tag library configuration file that the web application container needs for resolving references, looking up initialization parameters, and enforcing proper use of the tags is referred to by its alias `applicationtags.tld`. The location of the configuration file is by custom within the `WEB-INF` directory in a folder called `tlds`. If this location is changed we must adjust the `<taglib-location>` entry, but any code referencing it can stay the same.

<resource-ref>

Two elements `<resource-ref>` and `<resource-env-ref>` are provided for configuring resources for a web application environment. These allow two things:

- The management of connections to resources such as a reference to the object pooling resource connection (much like database connection pooling) to make the process more efficient.

  Object pooling allows efficient use of resources by defining a component that manages connections to those resources. In the case of databases, the pool will make a number of connections and when a client requests one, it is handed over to the client to be used. When the client requests the connection to be closed, the pool retrieves the connection but rather than closing it and establishing a new connection, the pool reuses the connection by handing it over to the next client as long as the authority constraints and the type of connection matches.

  As establishing a connection to a database is a resource-intensive process, this can make the application more intensive. A pool can also be configured to refresh the connections periodically and to restore dropped connections so that the application can efficiently recover from database failures.

- A reference to administered objects, which allow the application access to runtime administration of the resource.

Administrated objects allow the application configuration to be changed without restarting the server. They can also be used to monitor the state of the application by interrogating administered objects for their current state.

These are referred to in Chapter 8.

<security-constraint>

Web resources may be associated with some security constraints for authentication and authentication of access to them. The constraints limit access to the resource according to user roles, such as manager, administrator, user, and guest, and by transport guarantee, which can include SSL secure data transmission, guaranteeing delivery and non-interference.

The <security-constraint> element allows a web resource to be defined against an authentication constraint and a user data constraint.

An entry takes the following form:

```
<security-constraint>
  <display-name>Name String</display-name>
  <web-resource-collection>
    <web-resource-name>GETServlet</web-resource-name>
    <description>
      Group together all servlet GET requests on the server using
      /servlet/servletname. We are grouping these requests as (we have
      decided) they require additional security being inherently less secure
      than the POST method and aliased Servlet calls.
    </description
    <url-pattern>/servlet/*</url-pattern>
    <http-method>GET</http-method>
  </web-resource-collection>
  <auth-constraint>
    <description>
      All roles are constrained to secure connection to servlet resource
      via GET calls
    </description>
    <role-name>*</role-name>
  </auth-constraint>
  <user-data-constraint>
    <description>
      Constrain the user data transport for GET Servlet requests to secure
      sockets
    </description>
    <transport-guarantee>INTEGRAL</transport-guarantee>
  </user-data-constraint>
</security-constraint>
```

<web-resource-collection>

The web resource collection identifies a group of resources and methods by which these resources have been requested. So, the example above defines all servlets requested with the HTTP GET method via the classic servlet URL: http://foo.com/servlet/servletname is one of the URLs that is matched against the pattern defined in the GETServlet resource collection above. Any number of URL patterns and valid HTTP methods may be provided to exactly define the resource collection.

<auth-constraint>

The authentication constraint uses user role-based authentication to constrain access to web resources. We can define groups of people to whom this security constraint is applied to using role-based authentication, which will be discussed in detail in Chapter 16. Therefore, placing administrator in the <role-name> tag above would constrain only users who have administrative rights to use secure connections while accessing servlets using GET.

Valid values are as designed by the developer of the application. In the example above, * indicates that all roles should be allowed access. An empty element indicates that no roles should be allowed access to the resource.

This is rather unlikely, as administrators are likely to have higher security rights than the average user. There is no constraint on the number of <role-name> elements required to define security constraints. If none are provided, then the resource is unavailable as no authentication is possible. Making resources unavailable for security reasons might be done by removing all references to <role-name> elements in the web.xml file and then restarting Tomcat.

<user-data-constraint>

The <user-data-constraint> element indicates what guarantees are given about the communication of data from and to the client. A value of NONE indicates that no guarantees are given about the data not being tampered with or intercepted by anyone other than the client and the system (the server). On the other hand, a value of INTEGRAL requires the authenticity of the data to be guaranteed, or that the data has not been interfered with, while CONFIDENTIAL requires guarantees that the data has not been intercepted by a third party. Specifying INTEGRAL or CONFIDENTIAL will mean that SSL will be used by redirecting the client to the SSL port of the server.

This type of configuration is likely to be defined at design time. However, in a well-designed application, it is up to the deployment engineer/system administrator to follow the design architecture to enforce the security constraints defined within it. This allows authentication requirements to be absent from the application code itself thus allowing the application to be very flexible so that it can be configured as business needs dictate.

<login-config>

Login configuration relates to the configuration of login authentication in the application. The <login-config> element contains the authentication method, the realm name and login page, and the authentication error page that should be used if form-based authentication is specified:

```
<login-config>
  <auth-method>FORM</auth-method>
  <realm-name>MemoryRealm</realm-name>
  <form-login-config>
    <form-login-page>login.jsp</form-login-page>
    <form-error-page>notAuthenticated.jsp</form-error-page>
  </form-login-config>
</login-config>
```

Again, this information relates to security, specifically authentication configuration, and we will explain it here in brief. The authentication method breaks down into the HTTP methods available, namely BASIC, DIGEST, FORM, and CLIENT-CERT, which are basic authentication (plain text), digest (base64-encoded response), FORM-based authentication which allows an HTML page with a form prompting the user to log in and returning the username and password, and client certificate-based authentication respectively. For more information on security refer to Chapter 16.

The <realm-name> identifies the realm that the server should use to authenticate the user against – in our example, the realm name alludes to the file-based list of users and passwords provided by the memory realm with Tomcat. In a production environment, using the memory realm is not recommended (although the version in 4.1 includes serialization for updating the data dynamically so that the information is persisted across a server restart). Instead, a JDBC or JDNI realm is far more robust and maintainable. JDBC connectivity is covered in-depth in Chapter 15.

Having chosen form-based authentication, we must specify the login page and also the error page in case a login fails. These elements should not be provided if another type of authentication has been specified and only one of each should be provided. In this case we have specified that `login.jsp` contains the login request and form. Bad authentication requests are redirected to `notAuthenticated.jsp`.

<security-role>

Security roles have been discussed in brief above. The `<security-role>` element allows roles to be defined together with the optional description:

```
<security-role>
  <description>
    Administrator of the application is allowed read/write rights to the
    content
  </description>
  <role-name>administrator</role-name>
</security-role>
```

Further detail is provided in Chapter 16.

<env-entry>

The `<env-entry>` element is used to declare environment entries. These are JNDI value parameters that can be used to configure the application. Unlike context initialization parameters, these values are dynamic; they can be referred to and updated at run time so that the application can be reconfigured dynamically, and resources outside the web application can access them. In particular, they can be administered by non-Java application components, and can be managed as part of the entire enterprise administration system.

This works like all JNDI resources; the parameter is referenced from the JNDI initial context and can be accessed using the `java:comp/env` environment naming context. The entry is defined in this entry as relative to this context.

The environment entry must be typed to a Java data type, such as `String` or `Integer`, so that it can be used within the application and can be used to define environment limits (such as minimum and maximum values). The general structure of an environment entry is as follows:

```
<env-entry>
  <description>Lower limit - minimum allowable value</description>
  <env-entry-name>MinimumValue</env-entry-name>
  <env-entry-value>5</env-entry-value>
  <env-entry-type>java.lang.Integer</env-entry-type>
</env-entry>
```

Environment entries are usually specific to the environment they are operating in: that is, they are application-specific. However, accepted norms for resource naming may be adopted as an attempt to harmonize resource configuration.

The value can then be accessed using code such as the following:

```
// obtain the initial context.
Context initCtx = new InitialContext();
Context envCtx = (Context) initCtx.lookup("java:comp/env");

// Look up environment entry
Integer minValue = (Integer)envCtx.lookup("MinimumValue");
```

EJB Resources

Enterprise JavaBeans (EJBs) are business objects whose administration is independent from their function. This is achieved by externalizing the resource sharing, security, and transaction requirements, thus allowing the developer to concentrate on modeling the business process without consideration for the environment the business rules are going to operate within. To learn more about EJBs, see *Professional EJB* from *Wrox Press (ISBN 1-86100-508-3).*

Summary

In this chapter, we discussed the various elements that make up a web application. Depending on the role of the system administrator, they may be called upon to work with the elements within the `web.xml` file.

Many of the configuration issues will be dependent on access to well-documented and well-designed application specifications, or, if these are not available, working hand-in-hand with a developer. As the age of the application grows, there will tend to be an increasing reliance on the experience of the administrator in the production environment to guide the administration of the application and collaboration between the developers and system administration will increase.

It is very likely that the administration of a web application will mostly concern security configuration. This will also increasingly include the use of filters to given URL patterns, session configuration, error page configuration, the addition of tag libraries, and the administration of application initialization parameters to adapt to the server.

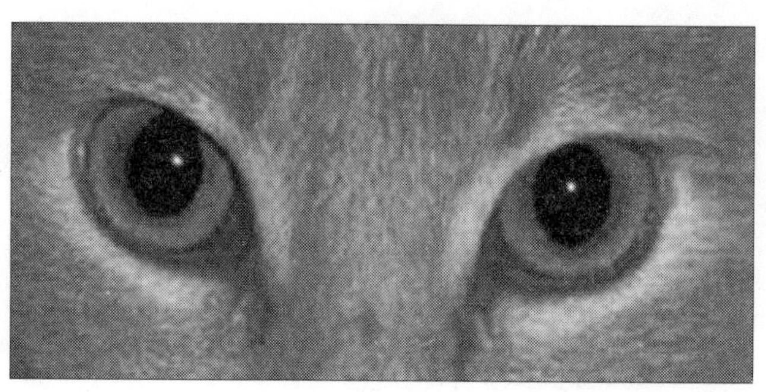

7

Manager Configuration

In this chapter we will go over the management tools available with Tomcat versions 3.x and 4.x. These tools allow administrators to deploy web applications, view deployed applications, and finally undeploy them. While these tasks can also be performed manually by editing Tomcat's configuration files, this method requires Tomcat to be restarted. The `manager` application, however, helps in automating them and also allows them to be performed on a running instance of Tomcat. This way, applications that are already running are left undisturbed.

Sample Web Application

In this chapter, we will use a simple web application for testing the manager commands. This application consists of nothing more than one HTML and one JSP file.

The HTML file (`index.html`) has a form that asks for the user's name and uses HTTP `POST` to send the result to a JSP page:

```
<html>
  <head>
    <title>Hello Web Application</title>
  </head>

  <body>
    <h1>Hello Web Application</h1>
    <form action="/hello/Hello.jsp" method="POST" >
      <table width="75%">
        <tr>
          <td width="48%">What is your name?</td>
          <td width="52%">
```

```
            <input type="text" name="name" />
          </td>
        </tr>
      </table>
      <p>
        <input type="submit" name="Submit" value="Submit name" />
        <input type="reset" name="Reset" value="Reset form" />
      </p>
    </form>
  </body>
</html>
```

The JSP page (`hello.jsp`) then prints a Hello <name> message. The <name> is the name that the user entered in the `index.html` form:

```
<html>
  <head>
    <title>Hello Web Application</title>
  </head>
  <body>
    <h1>Hello Web Application</h1>
    <br/><br/>

    <%
    String name   = request.getParameter("name");
    if (name.trim().length() == 0) {
    %>
      You didn't tell me your name!<br><br><br>
    <%
    } else {
    %>
      Hello <%=name%><br><br><br>
    <%
    }
    %>
    <a href="/hello/index.html">Try again?</a>
  </body>
</html>
```

This web application will be deployed with the `/hello` context path, and therefore http://localhost:8080/hello/index.html would be the URL to access it.

The commands for building the WAR file are:

```
$ cd /path/to/hello
$ jar cvf hello.war .
```

The `/path/to/hello` is the directory where the `index.html` and `hello.jsp` files reside.

Tomcat 3.x Administration Tool

Tomcat 3.x comes with an administration tool for performing simple administration tasks that allows us to list all web application contexts and to remove/install web applications. In this section, we will go over these and also see how permissions for the administration application are enabled. The version of Tomcat used here is 3.3.1.

Enabling Permissions for the Admin Tool

To enable permissions for the Tomcat 3.x admin tool, run tomcat.bat/tomcat.sh with the enableAdmin option, as follows. Here is the command for Linux:

```
$ cd $TOMCAT_HOME/bin
$ ./tomcat.sh enableAdmin
Overriding apps-admin settings
```

This rewrites the <Context> definition of the admin application ($TOMCAT_HOME/conf/apps-admin.xml), changing the trusted attribute to true, and thus allowing it to administer other web applications:

```
<webapps>
  <!-- Special rules for the admin web application -->
  <Context path="/admin"
           docBase="webapps/admin"
           trusted="true">
    <SimpleRealm filename="conf/users/admin-users.xml" />
  </Context>
</webapps>
```

A web application with the trusted attribute switched on can access the internal objects of Tomcat and manipulate them. This feature is used by the Tomcat admin application to perform actions like removing and installing web applications, and examining data from user sessions. The trusted attribute is false by default for security reasons.

After enabling the admin application, its password should be changed from the default "changethis" password. The password is stored in the $TOMCAT_HOME/conf/users/admin-users.xml file (listed below) as cleartext:

```
<tomcat-users>
  <user name="admin" password="changethis"
        roles="tomcat_admin,tomcat,role1" />
</tomcat-users>
```

Leaving the admin application enabled without the password changed from this default password is a security risk.

There is no corresponding disableAdmin command for undoing this step – the administrator will have to edit the $TOMCAT_HOME/conf/apps-admin.xml file, modify the trusted attribute to false and then restart Tomcat.

admin Application Tasks

If Tomcat is running on a local machine, the admin application is accessible via the URL http://localhost:8080/admin/. The host name and port number (localhost, 8080) in the URL should be changed to the appropriate host and port for your installation. If we have just changed the trusted attribute manually, or via the tomcat enableAdmin command, we need to restart Tomcat before we can start using the admin application.

This admin page lists all the admin application tasks (shown overleaf). As mentioned earlier, access to these tasks is restricted via a username/password that is specified in the admin-user.xml file. The screenshot overleaf shows us the admin home page:

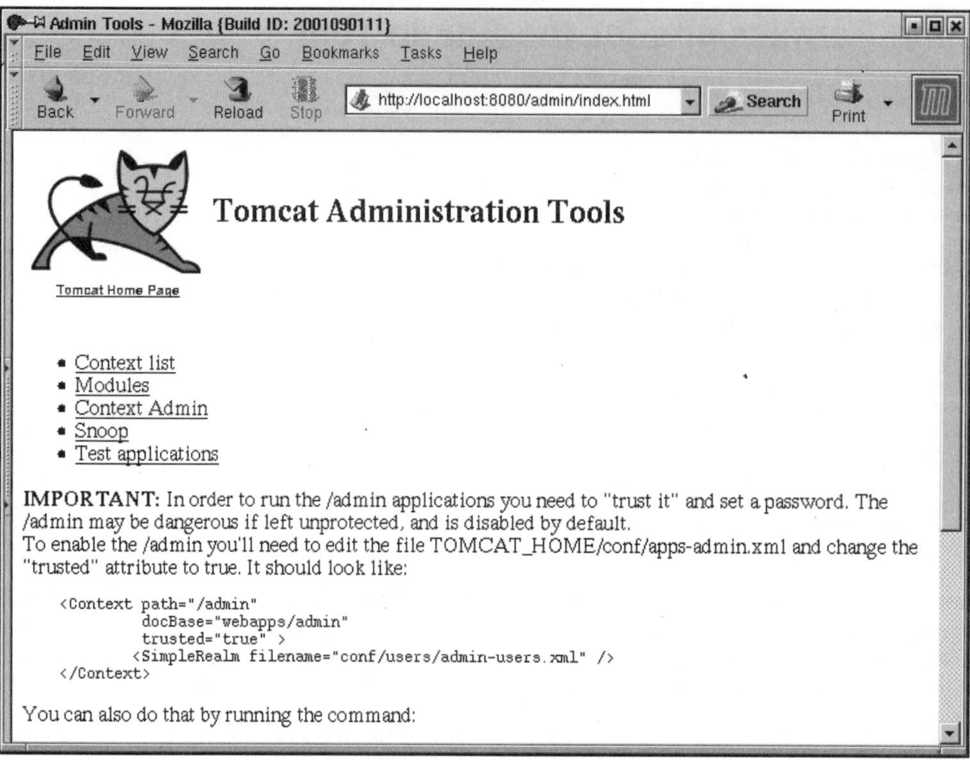

List All Web Application Contexts

The first option of the `admin` application's index page is Context list. This option shows all the deployed contexts (see the screenshot below):

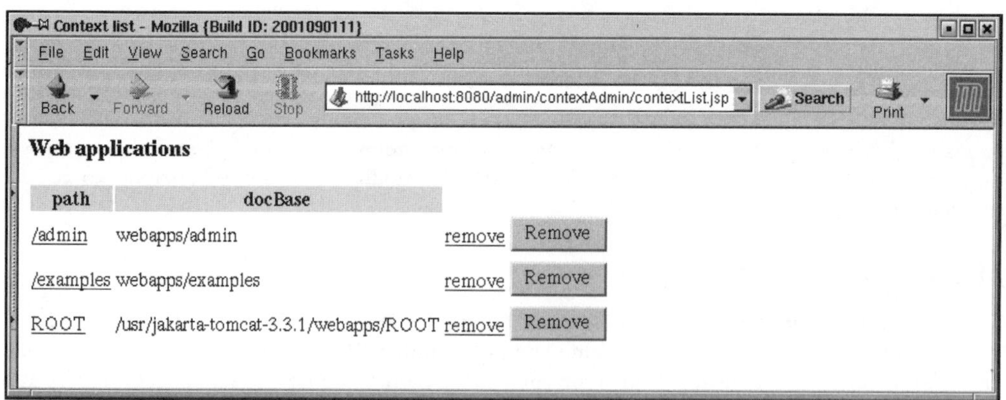

Clicking on any item in the path column, we can see the attributes of the context as configured in the `app-[name].xml` or `server.xml` files. The screenshot opposite shows the context attributes for the `example` web application. We also can see session information (number of active/recycled sessions, default timeout) for each application context via the Session info link:

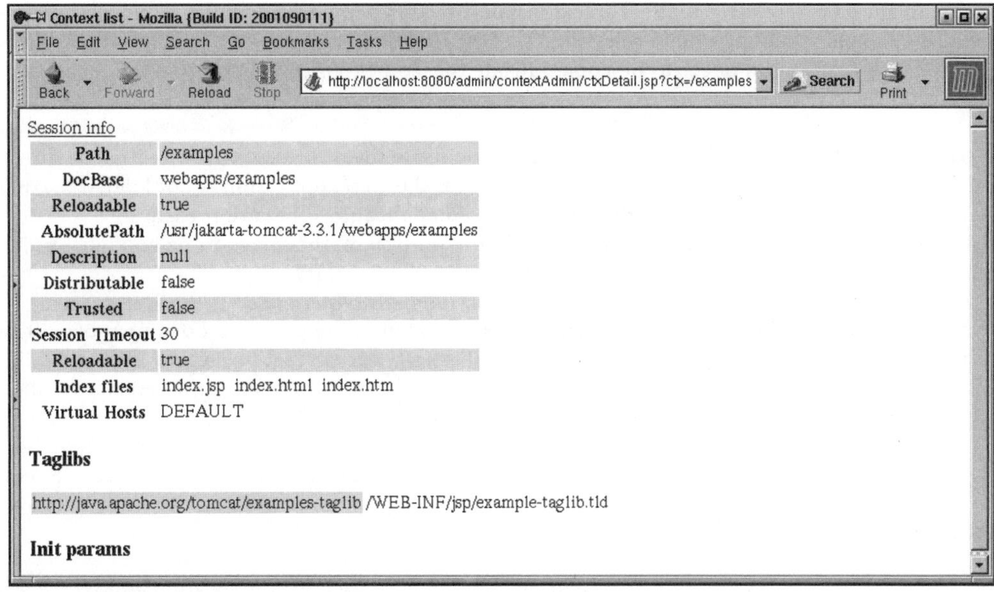

Add Web Application Context

The Context Admin link on the admin home page leads us to the Context Administration page. The Add Context option here adds a web application context to a running instance of Tomcat. This is done by adding a new Context entry to Tomcat's internal runtime representation of application contexts (the `org.apache.tomcat.core.ContextManager` class). Tomcat's configuration files are not modified.

This option is useful for development purposes – Tomcat developers can temporarily add a context, test it, and then remove it. The option for removing a context is covered in the next section.

We can specify the context path (for example `/hello` for the `hello` web application mentioned earlier), and the document base. The web application is then started up without requiring Tomcat to be restarted:

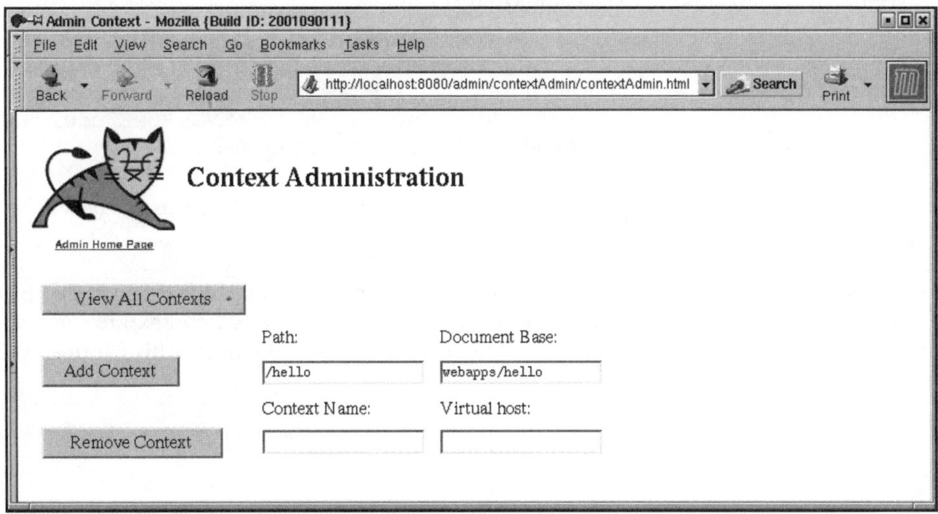

The document base is relative to the Tomcat install directory – therefore, in the screenshot shown previously, the path webapps/hello refers to `$TOMCAT_HOME/webapps/hello`. This means that the expanded web application needs to be copied inside the Tomcat install directory – the recommended place is `$TOMCAT_HOME/webapps`.

We could have placed the web application directory outside the `$TOMCAT_HOME/webapps` directory, for example, under `$TOMCAT_HOME` itself. If we did this, the web application is not loaded if Tomcat is restarted. This is because Tomcat loads only those web applications that are present in `$TOMCAT_HOME/webapps`. If they lie elsewhere in the filesystem, they need to be configured via explicit `<Context>` entries in the `server.xml` file.

The options that we can specify for a new context are limited to the path and document base. The other attributes get assigned defaults – `reloadable` set to `true`, `trusted` set to `false`, and so on. If we want to set an attribute that is not the default, we have to add explicit `<Context>` entries for the application in `server.xml` and restart Tomcat.

If we add an application that already had a `<Context>` entry configured in `server.xml` (for example, if we had removed it earlier, and are adding it again), it still gets default `<Context>` attribute values – the `server.xml` is not read.

The `admin` application does not do any error checking, therefore if we do an Add Context twice, or supply an invalid document base, a success message is still shown in the browser window. Any internal Tomcat errors while adding the context get logged to the standard log files.

Disabling Web Applications

The option to disable a web application context is accessible via the View All Contexts page and the Context Administration page. This option is called Remove or Remove Context, but the name is deceptive. This option:

- Temporarily disables the web application by removing its context from the in-memory representation of the web application contexts. The internal Tomcat class that maintains the list of application contexts is `org.apache.tomcat.core.ContextManager`, and the Remove Context option deletes the context from it.
- Shuts down the web application.
- Doesn't remove the web application from the `$TOMCAT_HOME/webapps` directory, or remove the `apps-[name].xml` configuration file, if any, from the `$TOMCAT_HOME/conf` directory. Hence, if we restart Tomcat, the web application is loaded up again.

As we mentioned in the previous section, the Add and Remove Context options are useful for development purposes.

In the Context Administration page, we need to specify the name of the context (example `/hello` or just `hello` for the `hello` web application or an empty string for the `ROOT` context) to remove that context. The other parameter for this option, Virtual Host, can be left empty. This parameter is ignored by the `admin` application.

The screenshot below shows the hello web application being disabled:

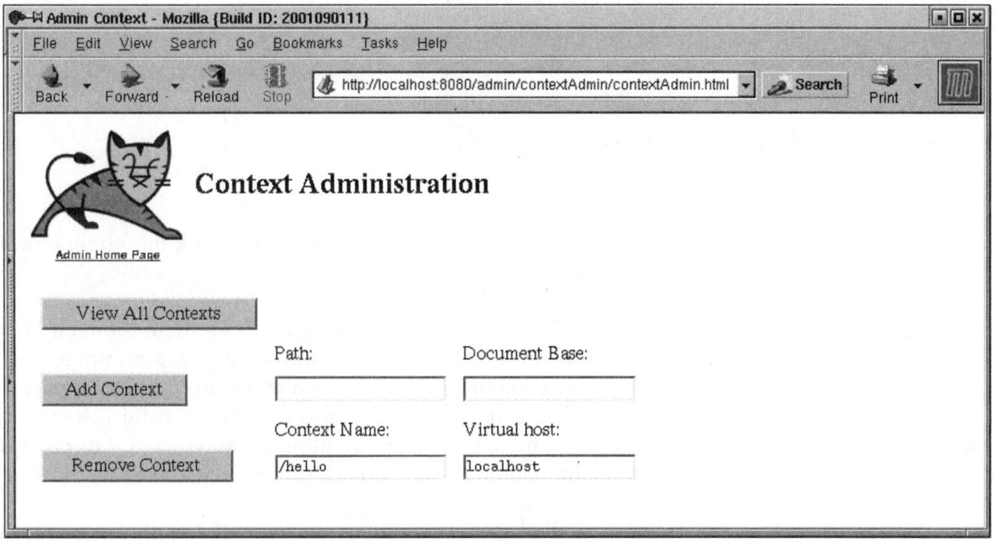

Tomcat 4.x Manager Application

The Tomcat manager application is a web application that allows us to carry out various system administration tasks related to deploying, undeploying, and managing a web application.

Administrators interact with the manager application over HTTP. In Tomcat 4.1, administrators can also run the manager application tasks via Ant scripts. Using the manager application through Ant allows developers to build, deploy, and test web applications easily – we show how this can be done in the *Managing Applications with Ant* section later in the chapter.

Access to the manager application is restricted to authorized users. This prevents unauthorized users from undeploying (or deploying) applications, or performing any other operation that they shouldn't. In the next section, we will see how this access control is configured. We will then examine the other configuration parameters for the manager application. Finally, we will describe all the manager application commands in more detail.

A summary of the tasks that the manager application can do is listed below. Some of these tasks are new features in Tomcat 4.1, and are not available with Tomcat 4.0:

- Deploy a new web application (Tomcat 4.1 only)
- Install a new web application
- List the currently deployed web applications, as well as the sessions that are currently active for those web applications
- Reload an existing web application
- List the available global JNDI resources (Tomcat 4.1 only)

- List the available security roles (Tomcat 4.1 only)
- Remove an installed web application
- Start a stopped application
- Stop an existing application, but do not undeploy it
- Undeploy a web application (Tomcat 4.1 only)
- Display session statistics

In the list above, we use the terms "install" and "deploy". At first glance, these look the same, however, there are differences as far as the Tomcat `manager` application is concerned.

When we deploy a web application, it makes permanent changes to Tomcat's configuration, and hence the web application is available across Tomcat restarts. The install option however, does not make permanent changes to Tomcat's configuration. Thus the `install` command is useful for test purposes. We can build a web application, install it, and then try it out. Once it is sufficiently robust, we can run the `deploy` command to permanently place it into a Tomcat installation. In some ways, `install` and `uninstall` are similar to the **Add Context** and **Remove Context** operations in Tomcat 3.x.

Secondly, the `deploy` command allows us to deploy a web application remotely. With `install`, the web application JAR file (or the extracted web application path) must be on the same machine as that of the Tomcat instance.

The `undeploy` and `uninstall` commands undo the effects of `deploy` and `install` – we shall see these later in the section.

However, to add to our confusion, Tomcat 4.0 has a command called `install` that actually has an effect similar (though not identical) to the `deploy` command in Tomcat 4.1. The Tomcat documentation, to help matters, calls it the command to deploy applications (even though the name of the command is install). We shall shed some light on this later in the section.

Why do we need a special `manager` application to deploy and undeploy applications? We can deploy an application manually too. The ways to do this are:

- Add a `<Context>` entry in Tomcat's `server.xml` configuration file. This allows us to place the web application in a location other than the default `$CATALINA_HOME/webapps` directory.
- Copy the entire application directory into the `$CATALINA_HOME/webapps` directory. The `server.xml` file does not have to be edited in this case.
- Copy the WAR file for the application into the `$CATALINA_HOME/webapps` directory. In this option too, the `server.xml` file does not have to be edited.

However, all these ways of deploying require us to restart Tomcat. When we do this via the `manager` application, Tomcat is not restarted and hence the other running web applications are not affected. Another advantage of using the `manager` application is that we can install remotely. That is, we do not have to transfer the web application directory (or WAR file) via FTP or some other means to the host machine running Tomcat – the `deploy` command takes care of transferring the web application WAR file from our local development machine to the remote machine running the Tomcat server.

> **The latest version of the 4.1.x line (Tomcat 4.1.7 Beta) at the time of writing, added a new web-based user interface on top of the `manager` application. This does not affect the existing application functionality and usage (explained below), but provides a simplified interface. We will be covering this interface later in this chapter.**

Enabling Access To the Manager Application

Before using the `manager` application, we need to configure the server to allow us access. Access to this application is controlled via a security realm (realms were discussed in Chapter 5).

Tomcat comes configured with the memory realm by default. In this case, the usernames and their supporting information are stored in memory and are initialized at startup from an XML configuration file (`$CATALINA_HOME/conf/tomcat-users.xml`) kept on the filesystem.

We need to edit this file to add a user with a role of `manager`. In the entry below, the username and password for this role is `admin` and `secret` respectively.

In Tomcat 4.0:

```
<tomcat-users>
  <user name="admin" password="secret" roles="manager" />
  ...
</tomcat-users>
```

And in Tomcat 4.1:

```
<tomcat-users>
  <role rolename="manager"/>
  ...
  <user username="admin" password="secret" roles="manager" />
  ...
</tomcat-users>
```

We need to restart Tomcat to make it re-read the `tomcat-users.xml` file. We are now ready to use the Tomcat `manager` application. If our setup was successful, the URL http://localhost:8080/manager/list will lead to a prompt for a username and password.

After entering the username and password we should see the applications currently deployed listed in the browser:

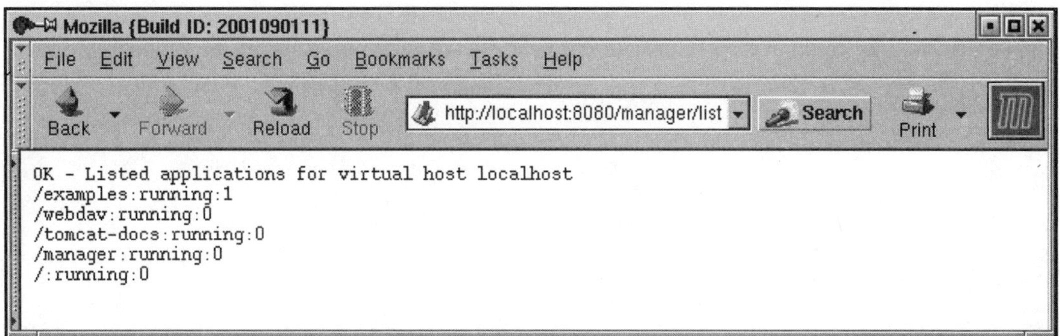

As we can see in the screenshot, the response for a successful command execution begins with an 'OK' string. A missing 'OK' is an indication of failure, and the rest of the response page gives the reasons. We will go over the possible causes of failure for each command later in the chapter. The response page is in the text/plain format, that is, it contains no HTML markup.

The data fields returned in a manager command response are always delimited by the ":" character. In the screenshot for the list command shown previously, each line has the (unique) context path of the web application, the status (running or stopped), and the number of active sessions for the application. In Tomcat 4.1, the document base for the web application is also shown.

These conventions allow for scripts to be written that take the output of the manager command and perform appropriate actions.

Note for Tomcat 4.1 On Windows

During installation of Tomcat 4.1 on Windows, the installer asks the user for the admin username and password. The username and password entered at install time are used to generate entries for the tomcat-users.xml file. Hence, we do not have to do any configuration in this case, except if we need to add another user with manager privileges or need to change the manager password.

Manager Application Configuration

In the previous section, we looked at tomcat-users.xml that defines the username and password for the manager role. The other manager application-related configuration parameters are the manager context entry and the deployment descriptor.

We do not have to make any changes here for the manager application to work – the settings are configured by default. We can, however, modify these to our requirements – for example, change the security constraints for the manager application, the authentication mechanism for users in the manager role, or even change the name of the role from manager to some other name if required.

Manager Application Context Entry

In Tomcat 4.0, the manager context is configured in the same way as the other application contexts. The following is the default configuration for the manager application from the $CATALINA_HOME/conf/server.xml file:

```
<!-- Tomcat Manager Context -->
<Context path="/manager" docBase="manager" debug="0" privileged="true"/>
```

In Tomcat 4.1, the configuration information for the manager application gets picked up from the $CATALINA_HOME/webapps/manager.xml file. The default manager context from the configuration file is listed below:

```
<Context path="/manager" docBase="../server/webapps/manager"
         debug="0" privileged="true">

  <!-- Link to the user database we will get roles from -->
  <ResourceLink name="users" global="UserDatabase"
                type="org.apache.catalina.UserDatabase"/>
</Context>
```

In the context, we specify the context path for the manager application via the path attribute (the manager application can be accessed as http://host:port/manager) and the document base directory for the web application via the docBase attribute ("../server/webapps/manager"). The privileged attribute is set to true – this enables the application to access the container's servlets. This attribute is false for a normal web application deployed in Tomcat. The <ResourceLink> element creates a link to a global JNDI resource database from where the usernames and roles are picked up.

Manager Application Deployment Descriptor

Earlier we looked at the tomcat-users.xml file that defined the username and password for the manager role. We will now see how the security constraints for this role are specified. The deployment descriptor for the Tomcat 4.0 manager application is $CATALINA_HOME/webapps/manager/WEB-INF/web.xml.

In Tomcat 4.1, the web.xml is in $CATALINA_HOME/server/webapps/manager/WEB-INF.

The web.xml defines, among other things, the security constraints on the manager application. The snippet below describes the default security constraint definition for the manager web application (the "/*" URL pattern matches the entire web application). The <role-name> defined below (manager) specifies that only users in the manager role can access the manager web application:

```
<!-- Define a Security Constraint on this Application -->
<security-constraint>
    <web-resource-collection>
      <web-resource-name>Entire Application</web-resource-name>
      <url-pattern>/*</url-pattern>
    </web-resource-collection>
    <auth-constraint>
       <!-- NOTE:  This role is not present in the default users file -->
       <role-name>manager</role-name>
    </auth-constraint>
  </security-constraint>
```

The authentication mechanism for the manager application is also defined here. The default setting is BASIC authentication. Administrators could set up a more rigorous mechanism for manager application authentication, for example a client certificate-based mechanism (<auth-method> set to CLIENT-CERT):

```
<login-config>
    <auth-method>BASIC</auth-method>
    <realm-name>Tomcat Manager Application</realm-name>
  </login-config>
```

The <security-role> lists all the roles that can log in to the manager application. In this case, it is restricted to only one user role – the manager role:

```
<!-- Security roles referenced by this web application -->
<security-role>
  <description>
    The role that is required to log in to the Manager Application
  </description>
  <role-name>manager</role-name>
</security-role>
```

Manager Application Commands

The manager application commands that are issued via the web browser have the following format:

```
http://{hostname}:{portnumber}/manager/{command}?{parameters}
```

In the command above the various parts are:

- hostname
  The host that the Tomcat instance is running on.
- portnumber
  The port that the Tomcat instance is running on.
- command
  The manager command that we wish to run. The allowed values for command are deploy, install, list, reload, remove, resources, roles, sessions, start, stop, and undeploy. We shall be looking at these in more detail later in the chapter.
- parameters
  The parameters passed to the commands listed above. These are command-specific, and are explained in detail along with the specific command below. Many of these parameters contain the context path to the web application (the path parameter) and the URL to the web application file (the war parameter). The context path for the ROOT application is an empty string. For all other web applications, the context path must be preceded by a '/'. The URL to the web application can be in one of the following formats:
  - file:/absolute/path/to/a/directory
    This specifies the absolute path to a directory where a web application is present in an unpackaged form. This entire path is then added as the context path of the web application in Tomcat's configuration.
  - file:/absolute/path/to/a/webapp.war
    This specifies the absolute path to a WAR file. The Tomcat documentation states that this format is not allowed for the install command. However, our tests with Tomcat 4.1.3 indicate that it works fine for install too.
  - jar:file:/absolute/path/to/a/warfile.war!/
    The jar protocol allows for specifying the URL for a WAR file. This is handled by the java.net.JarURLConnection that provides a URL connection to a JAR/WAR file. Here the URL specified is for a file on the local filesytem.
  - jar:http://hostname:port/path/to/a/warfile.war!/
    In this case, the URL points to a WAR file on a remote host that is accessible via HTTP.

The "!/" characters at the end of these URLs allow them to be used in a web browser and not cause the default MIME type action for the .war extension to take effect. For example, if we use the URL shown below to install a web application and leave out the "!/" at the end, we may be prompted to (depending on how the browser MIME settings are configured) save to disk, open the file in the browser, or open the file in an application (for example, Winzip):

http://localhost:8080/manager/install?path=/hello&war=jar:file:/path/to/hello.war!/

There are a number of problems that could occur while working with the manager application. The possible causes of failure are listed in the *Possible Errors* section.

Deploying a New Application (Tomcat 4.1 Only)

The `deploy` command is new in Tomcat 4.1. It allows users to deploy a web application to a running instance of Tomcat. The effect of this command is:

- The WAR file for the web application is uploaded from the client machine to the machine that Tomcat is running on, and copied into the application base directory of the given virtual host. For example, if the virtual host name configured in `server.xml` were `localhost` itself, the WAR file would get copied under `$CATALINA_HOME/work/Standalone/localhost/manager`.
- An entry for the web application's context is added into Tomcat's runtime data structures.
- The web application gets loaded.

The two steps above make the web application available for use right away, but there is a final step in the `deploy` process:

- Tomcat writes out a `<Context>` entry for this web application into the `$CATALINA_HOME/conf/server.xml` file. Due to this, the web application gets loaded each time Tomcat is restarted. If the WAR file contains a `<Context>` element definition (`META-INF/context.xml`), this context entry takes precedence over the default entry that the `manager` application generates.

The general format for the `deploy` command is shown below:

```
http://{hostname}:{portnumber}/manager/deploy?path={context_path}
```

Here `hostname` and `portnumber` are the host and port for the Tomcat instance and `context_path` is the context path for the application. The WAR file to be deployed is passed inside the request data of the HTTP `PUT` request. Therefore, if we were to deploy our `hello` application that we saw at the beginning of the chapter at the context path `/hello`, we would have to do an HTTP `PUT` to the URL `http://{hostname}:{portnumber}/manager/deploy?path=/hello`.

Since the WAR file is passed as the request data, this command cannot be invoked via a web browser. Instead, it should be invoked from a tool (for example, within an Ant script).

Essentially, the tool that sends the `deploy` command will have to build an HTTP request that looks something like that shown below, and execute an HTTP `PUT` command to send it over to the manager servlet:

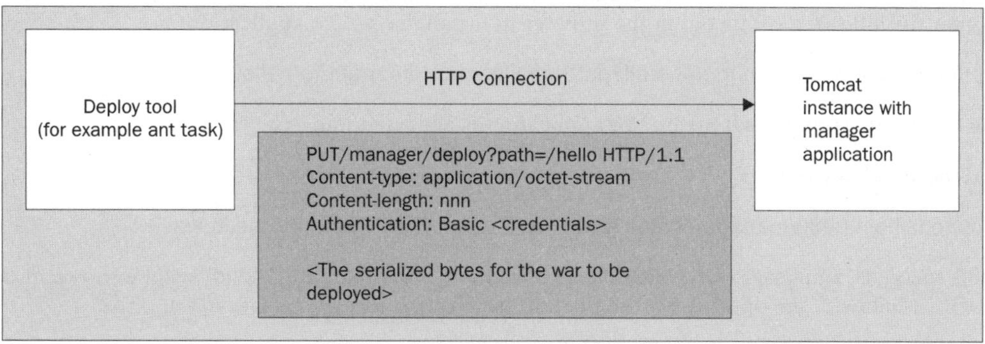

A successful deploy command returns a success message OK – Deployed application at context path {context_path}. If the operation failed, the error message would start with a "FAIL" string, and contain the cause for failure.

Tomcat 4.0 has an install command that it calls a deploy command. This is actually true – the behaviour of the install command is different between 4.0 and 4.1. We shall see this difference in the next section.

Installing a New Application

The Tomcat 4.0 documentation says that the command called install **deploys** an application. This is true, as this command has a permanent effect in Tomcat's configuration. The effect that the Tomcat 4.0 install command has is:

- The web application WAR file (or extracted directory) is copied into the application base directory
- The web application is started
- Tomcat's internal runtime data structures are updated to reflect the new application context

The last two steps ensure that the new web application is available for use right away. The first step (the copying) makes the installation permanent (that is, across Tomcat restarts).

In Tomcat 4.1, the install option just does the last two steps – updates Tomcat's internal runtime data structures and starts the application. Thus, if Tomcat is restarted, the web application is not reloaded. This is the correct behavior for the future, as the install command is meant for developers to test new web applications, and, once they are happy with them, use the deploy command (shown above) to update Tomcat's installation.

The general format for the install command URL (in both Tomcat 4.0 and 4.1) is shown below:

```
http://{hostname}:{portnumber}/manager/install?path={context_path}&war={war_url}
```

To install from a WAR file, we use the command shown below. Here, file:/path/to/hello.war is the URL for the local filesystem location of hello.war:

http://localhost:8080/manager/install?path=/hello&war=jar:file:/path/to/hello.war!/

We can also install the extracted web application from a filesystem path (/path/to/hello). We need to enter the following command in the browser to install the hello application:

http://localhost:8080/manager/install?path=/hello&war=file:/path/to/hello

The command assumes that the hello application is extracted into /path/to/hello:

And the Windows version:

http://localhost:8080/manager/install?path=/hello&war=file:/C:\path\to\hello.war

If this succeeds, a message "OK – Installed application at context path /hello" will be shown in the browser window. If the operation fails, an appropriate error message is displayed.

The screenshot opposite shows the hello application WAR file (hello.war) being installed with the context path /hello:

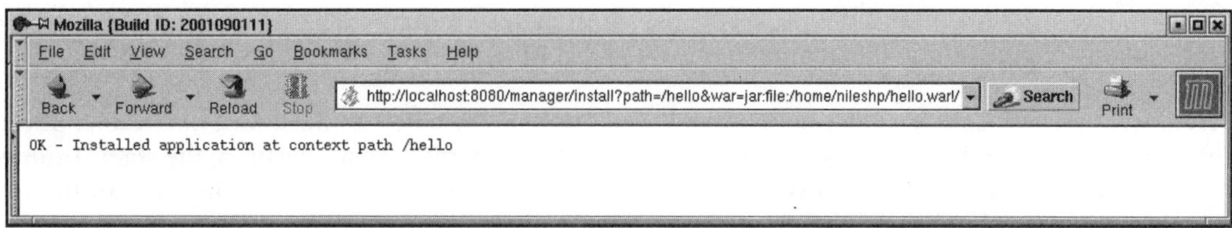

If we try to rerun this command we get the "Application already exists" error message as shown below. The context path for a web application is unique – if we wish to update an already installed application, we would need to either reload it, or remove and install it again. These options are covered later in the chapter:

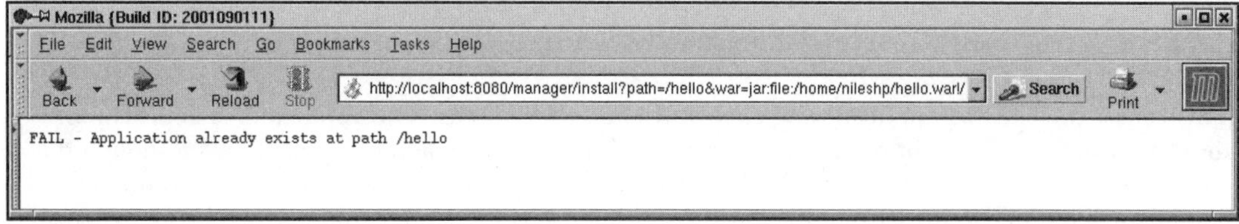

Tomcat 4.1 introduces two new options in the `install` command – unfortunately, these are not listed in the current Tomcat documentation:

```
http://{hostname}:{portnumber}/manager/install?config={config_url}

http://{hostname}:{portnumber}/manager/install?config={config_url}&war={war_url}
```

The `config_url` is the URL for a context configuration file. This file contains the `<Context>` element entry for the web application. The document base in the context is used to point to the location of the WAR file or to the directory where the web application is extracted. The second version of the command allows us to pass the URL to the WAR file (`war_url`). This overrides the document base specified in the context configuration file.

List Installed and Deployed Applications

The format for the `list` command URL that lists all deployed and installed applications is shown below:

```
http://{hostname}:{portnumber}/manager/list
```

The screenshot below shows the `list` command being run:

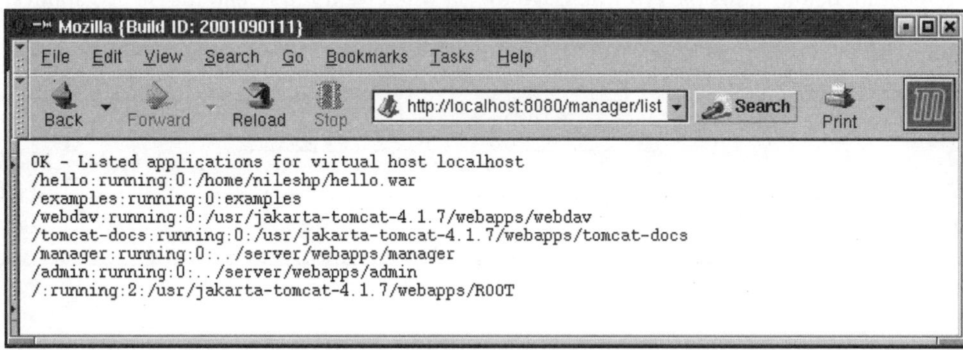

As we can see, the first line of the response message contains a string indicating success ("OK – Listed applications of virtual host {hostname}").

The rest of the response has information on all deployed and installed applications: one web application per line of response. Each line has the (unique) context path of the web application, the status (running or stopped), and the number of active sessions for the application. In Tomcat 4.1, the path for the web application is also shown.

Reload Existing Application

An existing application can be reloaded by accessing the `manager` application via the URL given below:

```
http://{hostname}:{portnumber}/manager/reload?path={context_path}
```

This causes the existing application to shut down and then restart. The application's deployment descriptor (`web.xml`) is not reread (at least not in the current version of Tomcat), even though the Tomcat documentation states that it is. This is a known bug, and it is expected that a future version of Tomcat will fix it. The workaround is to stop and then start the application again. The `server.xml` configuration file is also not reread, but this is by design.

The `reload` command is useful when we have a web application that has not been configured to be reloadable. A web application's `<Context>` entry in the `server.xml` file has a `reloadable` attribute. When this attribute is set to `true`, Tomcat monitors all its classes in `/WEB-INF/classes` and `/WEB-INF/lib` and reloads the web application if a change is detected. This causes a performance hit in production environments, as the class loader keeps comparing the date-time stamps for servlets in memory with those on disk. To avoid this, we can use the `reload` command to make Tomcat reload the web application when we change any of its classes.

The standard Java class loader is designed to load a Java class just once – so how does the `reloadable` attribute work? Tomcat implements its own custom class loader that is used to reload the classes in `/WEB-INF/classes` and `/WEB-INF/lib` if required. Chapter 9 discusses this topic in more detail.

> **The current version of Tomcat (4.1.3 Beta) supports reloading only if a web application has been installed from an unpacked directory. It does not support reloading if the web application has been installed from a WAR file.**

The screenshot below shows the error message we get when we try to reload the `hello` application that we had installed earlier from a WAR file:

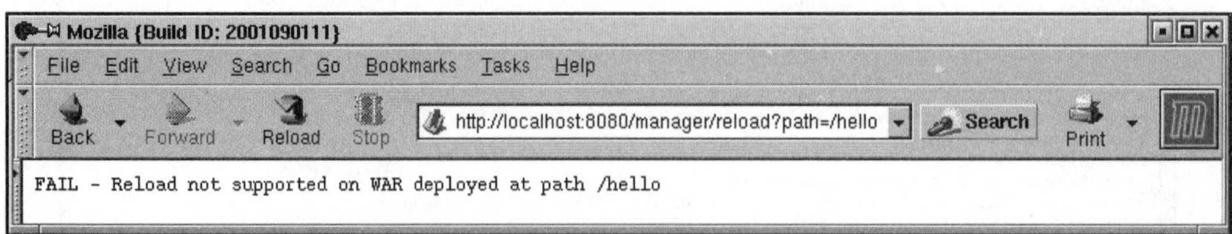

> **There seems to be a bug with Tomcat 4.1.8 (Beta) with the `reload` command. However, it is not a serious one. The message displayed on the browser doesn't show the `context_path` (`/hello` in this case) as in the above screenshot. All other commands give the correct messages.**

The workaround with a WAR file is to either restart Tomcat or `remove` and then `install` the application again.

A successful execution of the `reload` command returns an "OK – Reloaded application at context path {context_path}" message, where {context_path} is the context path for the application.

List Available JNDI Resources (Tomcat 4.1 Only)

The general format of the URL for listing available JNDI resources is:

```
http://{hostname}:{portnumber}/manager/resources[?type={jndi_type}]
```

In the URL above, the `type` argument is optional. When it is not specified, all the available JNDI resources are listed. Otherwise, JNDI resources corresponding to the specified type alone are listed. The `type` field needs to be a fully qualified Java class name. For example, for JDBC data sources, the type needs to be specified as `javax.sql.DataSource`:

http://localhost:8080/manager/resources?type=javax.sql.DataSource

The response to this contains a success string ("OK – Listed global resources of all types" or "OK – Listed global resources of type {jndi_type}") followed by information about the resources – one per line. Each line contains the global resource name and the global resource type. The global resource name is the name of the JNDI resource as specified in the `global` attribute of the `<ResourceLink>` element in Tomcat's configuration. The global resource type is the fully qualified Java class name of this JNDI resource:

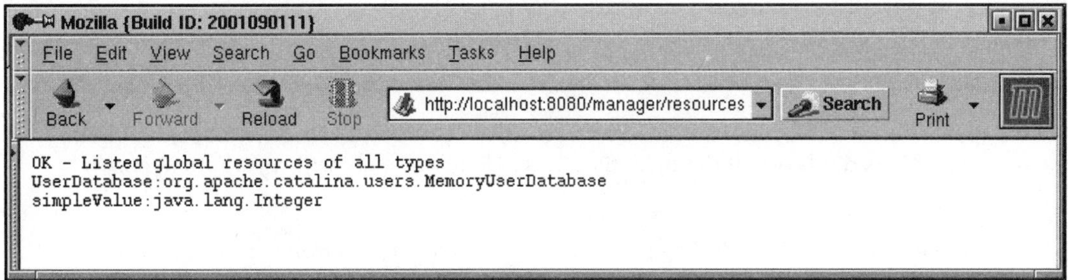

List the Available Security Roles (Tomcat 4.1 Only)

The URL for listing all security role names is:

```
http://{hostname}:{portnumber}/manager/roles
```

On successful execution, the output of this command is an "OK – Listed security roles" message, followed by the security role name and a (optional) description. There is one security role listed per line, and the fields are ":" separated as before:

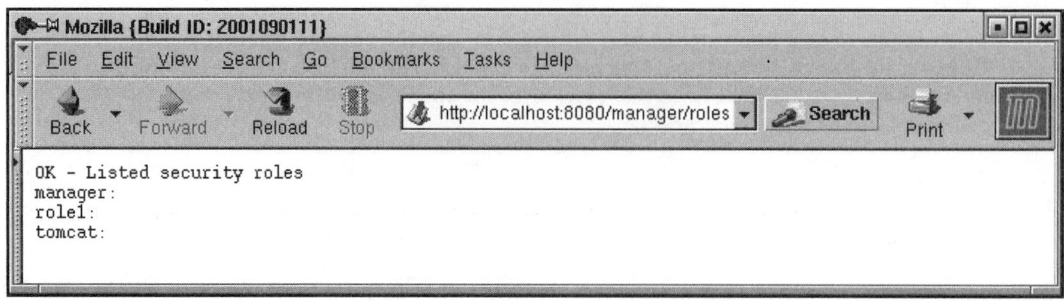

The security roles listed by this command are those that are defined in the user database. The `manager` application's configuration defines the user database resource that should be looked up for the roles in its `<ResourceLink>` section.

Stop an Existing Application

We can use the `manager` application to stop a running application. The URL below shows how this can be done:

```
http://{hostname}:{portnumber}/manager/stop?path={context_path}
```

This command sends a signal to the web application to stop. This application is no longer available to users, though it still remains deployed. If we run the `list` command again, the state of the application would be shown as "stopped":

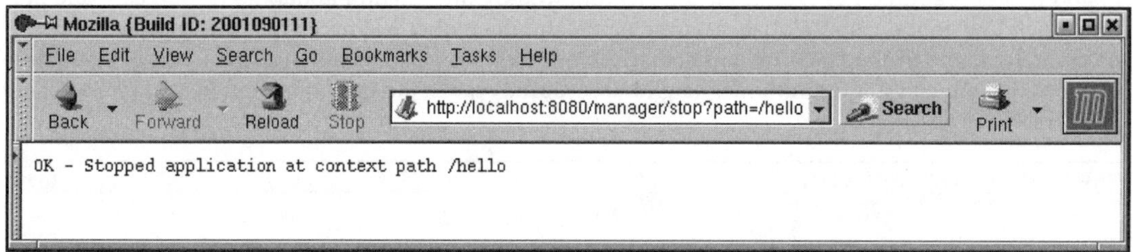

If the application stops successfully, the message "OK – Stopped application at context path {context_path}" is displayed. If the operation fails, a FAIL message with appropriate error information is shown.

The application can be restarted using the `start` command that is shown next.

Start a Stopped Application

We can use the `manager` application to start a stopped application. The URL below shows how this can be done:

```
http://{hostname}:{portnumber}/manager/start?path={context_path}
```

Here `{context_path}` is the context path for the web application (empty string for the `ROOT` application).

If the application starts successfully, the message "OK – Started application at context path {context_path}" is displayed:

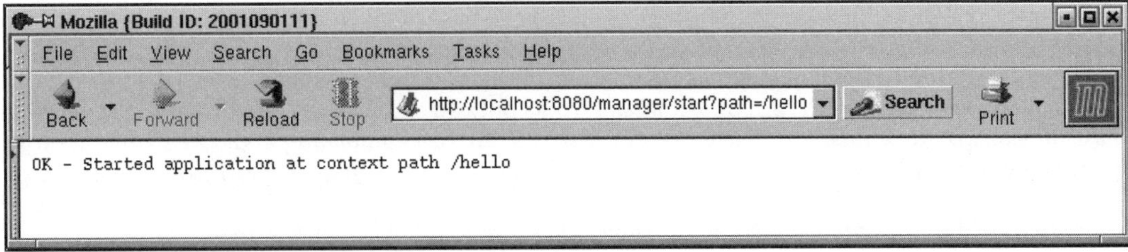

If the operation fails, a FAIL message with appropriate error information is shown.

Remove an Installed Application

The format of the remove command URL is listed below:

```
http://{hostname}:{portnumber}/manager/remove?path={context_path}
```

This command is the opposite of the install command – it signals the web application to shut down gracefully, and then makes the application context available for reuse. This is done by removing the context entry from Tomcat's runtime data structures.

We had seen earlier that the Tomcat 4.0 install command behaves like a deploy command, as it copies the web application over to $CATALINA_HOME/webapps. Does the remove command undo this and remove the web application directory and/or the WAR file? It should, but due to a bug in Tomcat, it does not. We need to manually remove the extracted web application directory:

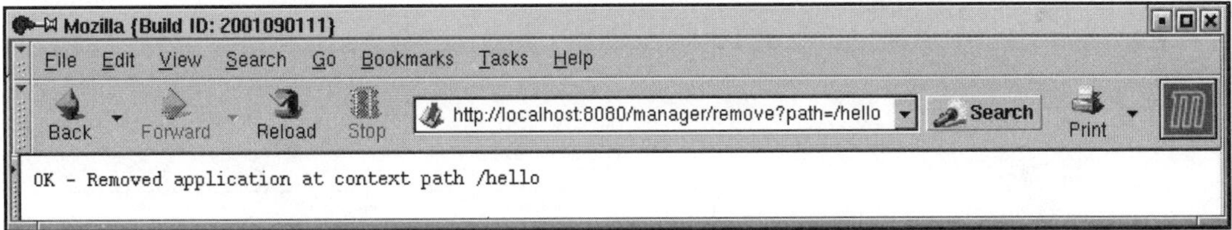

The screenshot above shows the web application running at context path /hello being removed. Its context entry is deleted from Tomcat's internal runtime data structures, hence any attempt to access http://localhost:8080/hello will now fail.

If the application is removed successfully, the message "OK – Removed application at context path {context_path}" is displayed.

Undeploy a Web Application (Tomcat 4.1 Only)

This command should be used with care – it deletes the web application directory that was created when the application was deployed. If we do not want the web application to be removed permanently, but only removed for the current Tomcat lifetime, we would use the remove command.

This command first signals the application to shut down (if it is still running) and then deletes the web application directory and the application WAR file. It then removes the `<Context>` entry for the web application from `$CATALINA_HOME/conf/server.xml`. Tomcat 4.1.3 Beta has a bug due to which the `<Context>` entry does not get removed – users need to manually edit `server.xml`.

In short, the `undeploy` command does the opposite of the `deploy` command that we described earlier in the chapter. However, the `undeploy` command works only on applications installed in the application base directory of the virtual host (the location where the `deploy` command put the web application WAR files) and so cannot be used for applications that were not deployed using the `deploy` command.

The URL for the `undeploy` command is listed below:

```
http://localhost:8080/manager/undeploy?path={context_path}
```

If the application undeploys successfully, the message "OK – Undeployed application at context path {context_path}" is displayed. If the operation fails, a "FAIL" message with appropriate error information is shown.

Display Session Statistics

We can use the `manager` application to get statistics about a particular web application. The statistics shown are the default session timeout and the number of current active sessions.

The URL for accessing this information is:

```
http://localhost:8080/manager/sessions?path={context_path}
```

For example, we can check the statistics for the `hello` application using the command http://localhost:8080/manager/sessions?path=/hello:

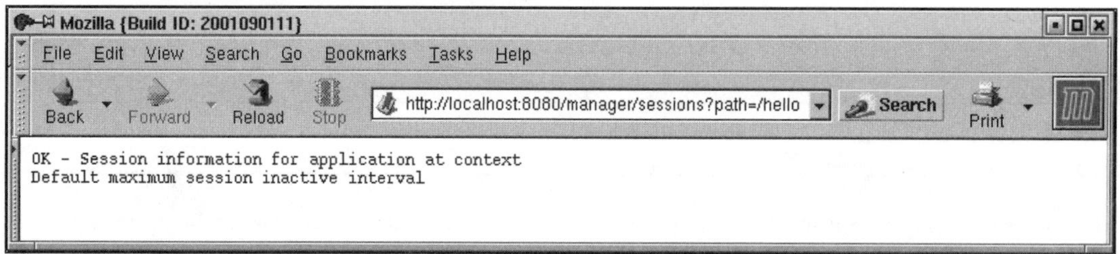

Tomcat Web Application Manager (4.1.7 Beta Only)

As we discussed earlier, the latest version of Tomcat (4.1.7 Beta) introduces a new web interface for the `manager` application. This interface allows us to start, stop, remove, reload, and install web applications without having to type the command URL. It does not allow for the entire `manager` application task though – we cannot deploy/undeploy or view security roles or JNDI resources.

To access the web application manager access http://localhost:8080/ and click on the Tomcat Manager link on the left-hand side on the Tomcat home page as shown in the screenshot opposite:

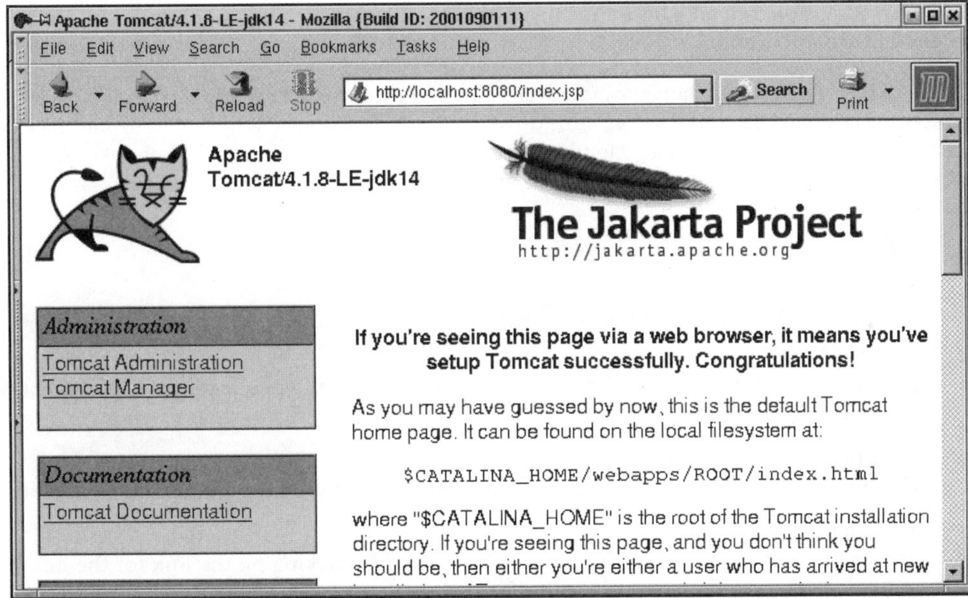

You will then be prompted for a username and password. This will then lead you to the `manager` application home page as shown in the screenshot below:

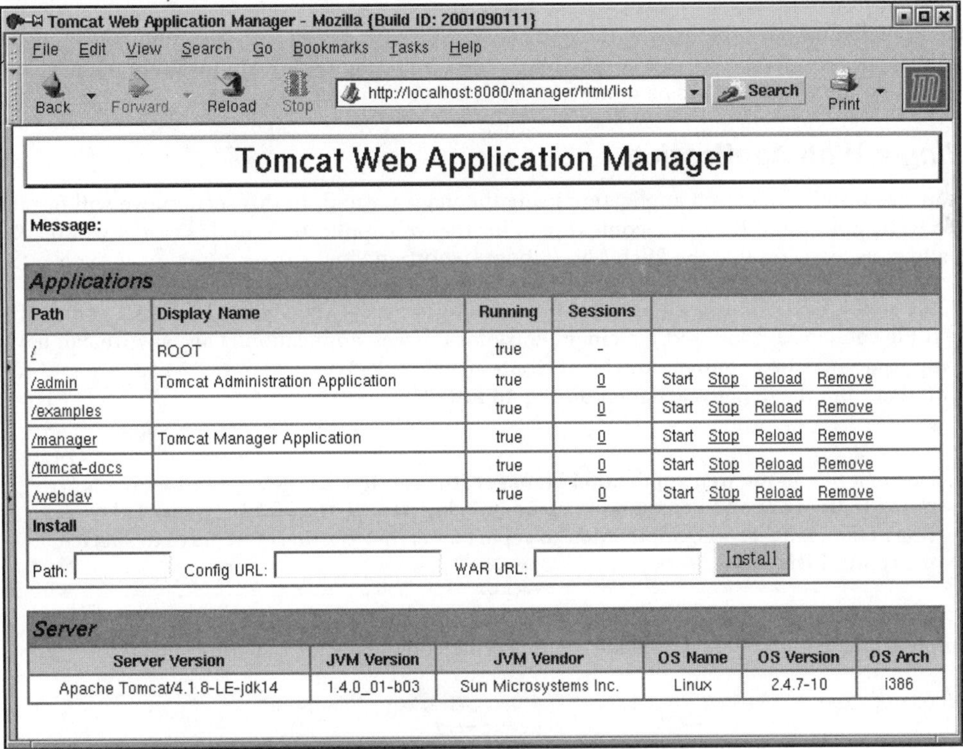

We can then start, stop, reload, and remove web applications by clicking on the relevant links provided at the end of each application.

In Tomcat 4.0 and 4.1.3, the manager tasks were handled by a servlet called the `ManagerServlet` (`org.apache.catalina.servlets.ManagerServlet`). In Tomcat 4.1.7, the new interface is `HTMLManagerServlet`. This class extends the `ManagerServlet` and internally invokes the same commands (`install`, `uninstall`, and so on) that we discussed earlier in the chapter.

The Applications table has five columns:

- **Path**
  This lists the web application path. The path name links to the URL for the web application.
- **Display Name**
  This is picked up from the `<display-name>` element in the application's deployment descriptor (`web.xml`).
- **Running**
  The running status for the application – `true` if the application is running and `false` otherwise.
- **Sessions**
  The number of active session for the web application. Clicking on the link for the number of sessions, we get to the session statistics for that particular web application. This internally invokes the `sessions` command that we saw earlier (repeated below).

```
http://{hostname}:{portnumber}/manager/sessions?path={context_path}
```

- Finally, we have the links to the `start`, `stop`, `reload`, and `remove` commands for the web application. We saw these commands earlier, but using the web application manager saves us from the effort of typing a command URL for performing these tasks.

Installing a Web Application

We can also install a new web application using the manager tool. In this section, we will install the `hello` web application. Enter the context path for the web application; in this case it will be `/hello`. This allows us to access it at the URL http://<host>:<port>/hello.

Next, the config URL – this is an optional field that allows us to specify the URL to a context file. The context file contains a `<Context>` element entry for the web application. This way we can have the web application context configured with attributes (such as `reloadable`, `privileged`, and so on) that are different from the defaults assigned during an install.

> **Due to a bug in the web application manager, the config URL gets passed as an empty string to the `install` command (instead of being passed as a `null` string). This causes the manager web application to report an error. We therefore have to specify the config URL.**

A sample config context file could have the following contents:

```
<Context path="/hello" docBase="/path/to/hello" debug="0"
         reloadable="true" crossContext="true">
</Context>
```

Save this in a file (say `context.xml`) and specify the URL to this file in the context URL field (for example, file:/path/to/context.xml on Unix or file:/c:\path\to\context.xml on Windows). The `docBase` attribute in the `<Context>` element is optional – if we specify one, it overrides the web application WAR file URL (the next attribute).

Finally, a URL to the WAR file or an extracted web application directory should be given. The format for this is the same as discussed in the *Manager Application Commands* section. For example, we could specify this as file://home/wrox/hello.war.

After successfully executing the `install` command by clicking on the Install button, Tomcat adds another row for our application in the list of applications installed/deployed:

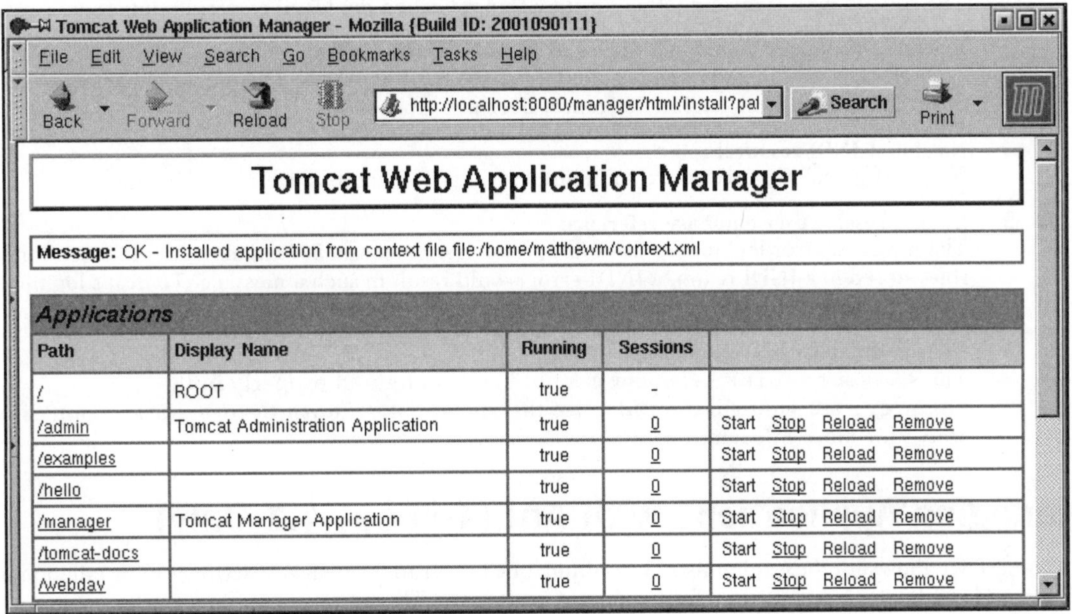

Possible Errors

There are a number of things that could go wrong while working with the `manager` application. The possible causes of failure are listed below:

- **Application already exists at path {context_path}**
  A web application already exists at the path specified. The context path for each web application must be unique. We would get this error if there is another application with the same context path – this can be the same application (that is, we tried to deploy twice) or a different one. To fix this, we have to either `undeploy/remove` the previous application, or choose a different context path.

- **Encountered exception**
  An exception occurred while trying to start the web application. The Tomcat log files will have error messages relating to the specific error. Typical causes of error are missing classes/JAR files while loading the application and invalid commands in the application's `web.xml` file.

- **Invalid context path specified**
  The context path must start with a '/'. The exception to this is when the ROOT web application (that is, at context path '/' itself) is being deployed, in which case the context path must be a zero-length string.

- **No context path specified**
  The context path is mandatory.

- **Document base does not exist or is not a readable directory**
  The value specified for the WAR file path/URL in the war parameter is incorrect. This parameter must point to an expanded web application or an actual WAR file.

- **No context exists for path {context_path}**
  The context path is invalid – there is no web application deployed corresponding to it.

- **Reload not supported on WAR deployed at path {context_path}**
  The web application had been installed from a WAR file, instead of from an unpacked directory. The current version of Tomcat does not support this.

- **No global JNDI resources**
  No JNDI global resources were configured for this Tomcat instance.

- **Cannot resolve user database reference**
  There was an error looking up the appropriate user database. For example, in the case of the roles stored in a JNDI realm, a JNDI error would result in such a message. Tomcat's log files would have more error information.

- **No user database is available**
  The <ResourceLink> element has not been configured properly in the manager.xml configuration file. See the *Manager Application Configuration* section above for more information.

Managing Applications with Ant (Tomcat 4.1 Only)

Tomcat 4.1 allows for these administration commands to be run from an Ant script (Ant installation is covered in Chapter 3 with extra information in Chapter 17). This is convenient for development purposes as the Ant build file could be used to compile, deploy, and even start a web application. The steps for doing this once Ant is installed are:

- Copy the $CATALINA_HOME/server/lib/catalina-ant.jar file into Ant's library directory ($ANT_HOME/lib). This JAR file contains the Tomcat management task definitions for Ant.

- Add $ANT_HOME/bin to your PATH.

- Add a user with the manager role to Tomcat's user database if such a user does not exist.

- Now add <taskdef> elements to your custom build.xml script that call the Tomcat manager commands.

A sample build.xml is shown opposite. This builds and deploys the hello web application that we discussed at the beginning of the chapter. Here is the build.xml script:

```
<project name="HelloApplication" default="compile" basedir=".">

  <!-- Configure the directory into which the web application is built -->
  <property name="src" value="."/>
  <property name="build"    value="${basedir}/build"/>

  <!-- Configure the context path for this application -->
  <property name="path"     value="/hello"/>
```

The <project> tag has attributes for the name of the project and the default target. The default target in this case is called `compile`. Running Ant with no options will invoke the tasks associated with this default target. The `basedir` attribute is the base directory for all path calculations in the Ant build script. This is set to "." (the current directory) and therefore all the paths for the build process are taken to be relative to the directory we run `ant` from. We then define properties for the build, such as the location of the source directory and the target directory where the compiled `.class` files will go.
The properties below specify the access URL and username/password for the `manager` application. We will later see how we can pass the password from the command line too:

```
  <!-- Configure properties to access the Manager application -->
  <property name="url"      value="http://localhost:8080/manager"/>
  <property name="username" value="myusername"/>
  <property name="password" value="mypassword"/>
```

The task definitions for the `manager` application are now specified. Ant allows for custom tasks that extend its functionality. Tomcat implements the custom tasks shown below for executing the `manager` application commands. For example, `org.apache.catalina.ant.DeployTask` executes the `deploy` command against the `manager` application:

```
  <!-- Configure the custom Ant tasks for the Manager application -->
  <taskdef name="deploy"
           classname="org.apache.catalina.ant.DeployTask"/>
  <taskdef name="install"
           classname="org.apache.catalina.ant.InstallTask"/>
  <taskdef name="list"
           classname="org.apache.catalina.ant.ListTask"/>
  <taskdef name="reload"
           classname="org.apache.catalina.ant.ReloadTask"/>
  <taskdef name="remove"
           classname="org.apache.catalina.ant.RemoveTask"/>
  <taskdef name="resources"
           classname="org.apache.catalina.ant.ResourcesTask"/>
  <taskdef name="roles"
           classname="org.apache.catalina.ant.RolesTask"/>
  <taskdef name="start"
           classname="org.apache.catalina.ant.StartTask"/>
  <taskdef name="stop"
           classname="org.apache.catalina.ant.StopTask"/>
  <taskdef name="undeploy"
           classname="org.apache.catalina.ant.UndeployTask"/>
```

Next is the Ant target that does initializations – in this case, create the build directory:

```
<target name="init">
  <!-- Create the build directory structure used by compile -->
  <mkdir dir="${build}"/>
  <mkdir dir="${build}/hello"/>
  <mkdir dir="${build}/hello/Web-INF"/>
  <mkdir dir="${build}/hello/Web-INF/classes"/>
</target>
```

The default `compile` target is shown below. This has Ant instructions to compile all the Java files into class files. Our `hello` application doesn't have any class files, so nothing will be done, but any serious web application will contain Java files. Notice how the `compile` task depends on the `init` task – this ensures that the initializations steps are performed before Ant compiles the Java files:

```
<!-- Executable Targets -->
<target name="compile" description="Compile web application"
        depends="init">
  <javac srcdir="${src}" destdir="${build}"/>
</target>
```

The `build` target builds the application WAR file. It has instructions to move the files to the correct directory format for a web application and build the WAR file:

```
<target name="build" description="Build web application"
        depends="compile">
  <copy file="index.html" toDir="${build}/hello"/>
  <copy file="Hello.jsp" toDir="${build}/hello"/>
  <jar destfile="${build}/hello.war" basedir="${build}/hello"/>
</target>
```

Finally, we have the manager tasks for listing all web applications, and installing/uninstalling and deploying/undeploying web applications:

```
<target name="list" description="List all web applications">
  <list url="${url}" username="${username}" password="${password}"/>
</target>

<target name="install" description="Install web application"
        depends="build">
  <install url="${url}" username="${username}" password="${password}"
          path="${path}" war="file:${build}/hello"/>
</target>

<target name="reload" description="Reload web application"
        depends="build">
  <reload  url="${url}" username="${username}" password="${password}"
          path="${path}"/>
</target>

<target name="remove" description="Remove web application">
  <remove url="${url}" username="${username}" password="${password}"
          path="${path}"/>
</target>

<target name="deploy" description="Deploy web application"
        depends="build">
  <deploy url="${url}" username="${username}" password="${password}"
```

```
              path="${path}" war="file:${build}/hello.war"/>
  </target>

  <target name="undeploy" description="Undeploy web application">
    <undeploy url="${url}" username="${username}" password="${password}"
              path="${path}"/>
  </target>

</project>
```

Before using the Ant script, we must add the `$CATALINA_HOME/server/lib/catalina-ant.jar` to the classpath and the Ant install directory to our system path (we used Ant 1.5 for our testing):

```
$ CLASSPATH=$CLASSPATH:$CATALINA_HOME/server/lib/catalina-ant.jar
$ PATH=$PATH:/path/to/ant1.5/bin
$ export CLASSPATH PATH
```

The `password` property in the Ant script contains the password for the user with manager privileges. This is useful for development environments where we don't want to specify the password each time we build and deploy.

This value can be overridden from the command line, or even omitted from the build file altogether and passed only from the command line. This avoids the security risk of putting the password in a cleartext file:

```
$ ant -Dpassword=secret list
```

The ability to run the manager commands from within Ant files allows for a very integrated develop-deploy-test cycle for web application development. For instance, after developing the HTML pages, servlets, JSP pages, and other Java classes for the web application, the developer would need to compile all the Java code:

```
$ ant build
```

The `build` target in our `build.xml` file compiles all the Java code and puts the class files into the appropriate location (the `/WEB-INF/classes` directory). It then builds the deployable JAR file. Developers may need to fix compilation errors, if any, and then rerun the `ant` command.

Next, they can use the `install` target to install the web application in the Tomcat instance specified in the Ant build file. The `install` target uses the Tomcat `manager` application's `install` command to install the web application:

```
$ ant install
```

This installed application can then be tested, and errors ironed out. During each iteration, developers would fix bugs, recompile, and then restart the web application:

```
$ ant compile reload
```

Once the application is stable, the developers can remove it from the Tomcat installation:

```
$ ant remove
```

This web application can then be packaged as a WAR file and distributed to end users. They can then deploy the application in the production Tomcat installation:

```
$ ant deploy
```

The `reload`, `remove`, and `deploy` Ant targets shown above invoke the `reload`, `remove`, and `deploy` commands of the Tomcat application manager.

Tomcat Administration Tool (Tomcat 4.1 Only)

Tomcat 4.1 introduces a new web-based administration tool. This allows administrators to visually edit the configuration parameters of Tomcat 4.1. These parameters are defined in Tomcat's configuration files (`server.xml`, `tomcat-users.xml`, and so on). Administrators of earlier versions had to manually edit the XML configuration files – a process that was error-prone and painful. For a more detailed description of these parameters and the configuration files, please see Chapter 5.

The `admin` tool can be accessed via the following URL:

```
http://{hostname}:{portname}/admin/index.jsp
```

As before, access to this application is restricted to users with `admin` roles. The screenshot below shows the administration tool:

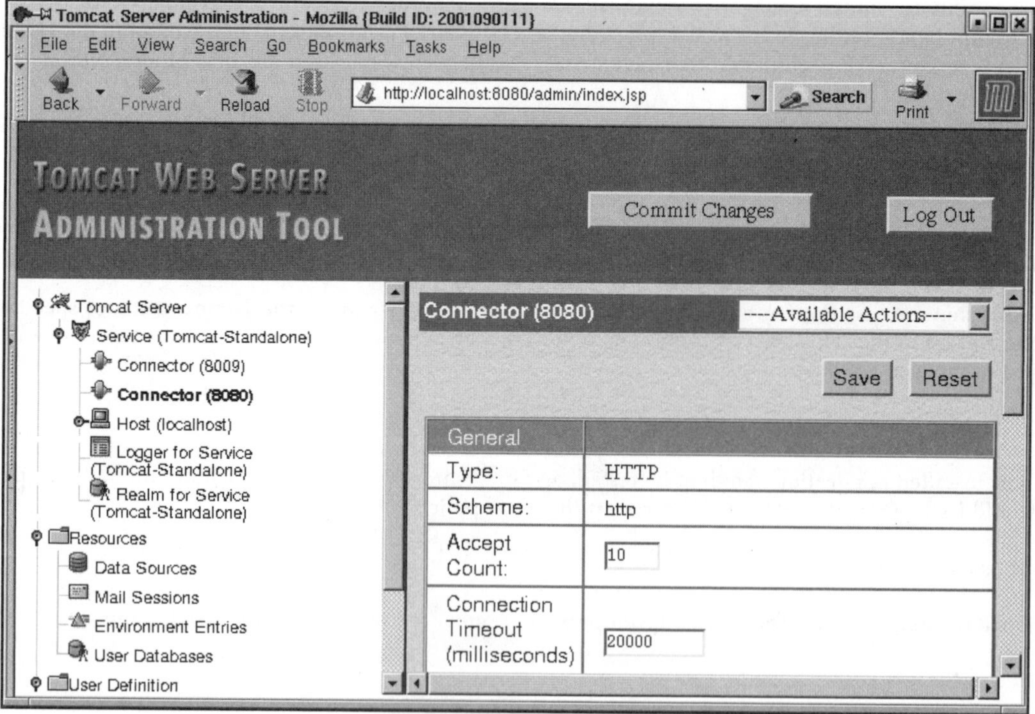

Admin Application Configuration

Access to the Tomcat 4.1 admin application is restricted in a manner similar to the manager application. The following is the memory realm user database file ($CATLINA_HOME/conf/tomcat-users.xml) that defines the admin role and sets the username and password:

```
<tomcat-users>
  <role rolename="admin"/>
  <role rolename="manager"/>

  ...
  <user username="admin" password="admin" roles="admin,manager"/>

</tomcat-users>
```

The configuration for the admin application is specified in the $CATALINA_HOME/webapps/admin.xml configuration file. The default configuration is shown below:

```
<Context path="/admin" docBase="../server/webapps/admin"
         debug="0" privileged="true">

  <Logger className="org.apache.catalina.logger.FileLogger"
          prefix="localhost_admin_log." suffix=".txt"
          timestamp="true"/>

</Context>
```

The other configuration file for the admin application is the deployment descriptor ($CATALINA_HOME/server/webapps/admin/WEB-INF/web.xml). This defines, among other things, the security constraints for the admin application and also the authentication mechanism for admin users.

To illustrate, the following extract from the web.xml file shows that only users with the admin role can access the admin application:

```
<security-constraint>
    <display-name>Tomcat Server Configuration Security Constraint</display-name>
    <web-resource-collection>
      <web-resource-name>Protected Area</web-resource-name>
      <!-- Define the context-relative URL(s) to be protected -->
      <url-pattern>*.jsp</url-pattern>
      <url-pattern>*.do</url-pattern>
      <url-pattern>*.html</url-pattern>
    </web-resource-collection>
    <auth-constraint>
      <!-- Anyone with one of the listed roles may access this area -->
      <role-name>admin</role-name>
    </auth-constraint>
  </security-constraint>
```

The Future

The manager application documentation states that there are plans to add a web service-based interface for Tomcat manager applications. Once this is done, the management tasks can be easily integrated with third-party applications, or triggered from non-Java/non-web-based client programs. However, the proposed feature list for Tomcat 5.0 (the next release) does not include this.

The proposed 5.0 features do mention adding JMX (Java Management Extensions) support to the Coyote connector. The Coyote connector provides both a native HTTP stack for Tomcat (the Coyote HTTP/1.1 connector) as well as allowing Apache and other web servers to tie in to Tomcat (the Coyote JK2 connector). JMX is a new Java technology from Sun for managing and monitoring applications. However, it is still unclear what the JMX support in Tomcat 5.0 will look like.

Summary

In this chapter we saw the administration capabilities of the Tomcat 4.x manager application and the Tomcat 3.x admin commands.

Securing access to the manager application is important. Someone who gains unauthorized access to it can deploy malicious applications, or cause a Denial of Service (DoS) by shutting down running applications. Administrators concerned about security could configure the network to disallow access to the manager application URL from hosts outside the local network, or, if they are paranoid, even disable the manager web application altogether.

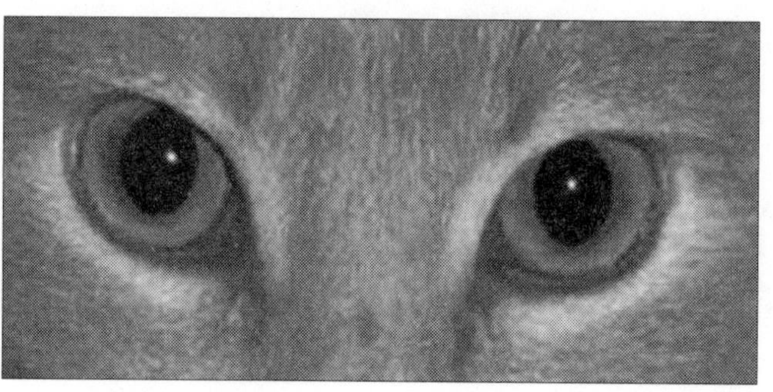

8

Advanced Tomcat Features

Thus far in this book, we have covered the basic configuration of Tomcat 4, how to deploy and administer web applications, and the `manager` web application that helps us do it. In this chapter, we will cover a collection of administration tasks that are advanced features built into standard Tomcat 4.x. As a Tomcat 4.x administrator, you are likely to encounter requests for many of these features from the development team.

More specifically, we will examine:

- Access log administration
- Request filtering
- Single Sign-on across web applications
- Setting up Tomcat JNDI emulation resources for developers' access to external JDBC and JNDI resources
- Installation of a session manager
- Configuration of Realms

This chapter may serve as a "cook book" for these specific tasks. In each case, we will give the background of why a user or a developer may need the feature, followed by the configuration and administrative details. Finally, we will have a practical sample configuration that you can try out. We will also point out any hints, tips, or problems that may apply along the way.

Valves – Interception Tomcat Style

Valves are a filtering mechanism specific to Tomcat that is available since Tomcat 3. As a filter, valves can intercept any incoming request and outgoing response. In Tomcat version 4.1.x, a set of standard valves is delivered with the distribution. They offer value added functionality that includes:

- Access logging
- Single Sign-on for all web applications running under Tomcat
- Requests filtering/blocking by IP address and/or hostname
- Detailed 'requests' dump for debugging purposes

Let us examine this set of standard valves available with Tomcat 4.1.x next.

Standard Valves

Valves are **nested components** in the Tomcat 4.1.x configuration object model (configured using `<Valves>` XML element in the `server.xml` file) that can be placed inside `<Engine>`, `<Host>`, or `<Context>` containers (refer to Chapter 5 for details on containers). The Catalina engine will pass an incoming request and outgoing response through any valve that is incorporated within these containers. This is illustrated in the diagram below:

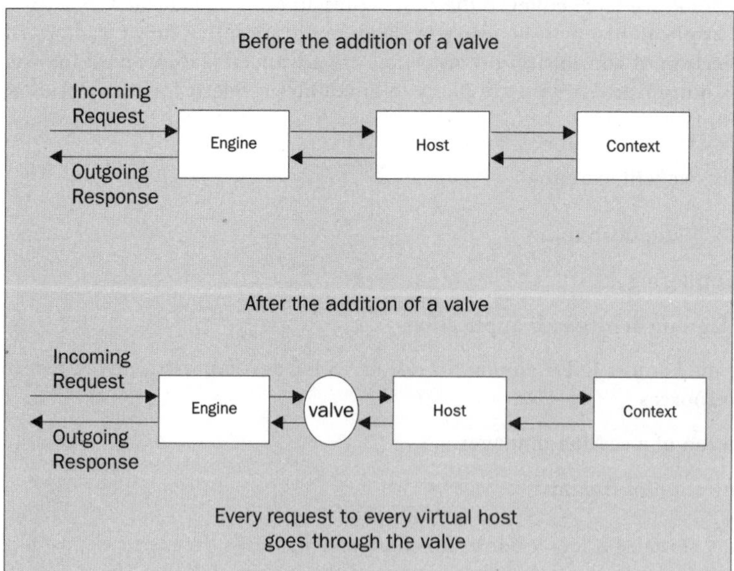

In the figure, we can see that every single incoming request is passed through the added valve. Because of this, we can configure valves to perform work on each request. The Java language programming interface, `org.apache.catalina.Valve`, is well documented, and Java application programmers may create their own valves. For the most common application of valves, however, Tomcat 4 already has basic implementations built in. These standard valves include:

Valve Name	Description
Access Logging	Enable logging of request (the URI of resource requested like: date and time)
Single Sign-on	Enhance the user experience by requesting for password only once, even when user access different web applications on the same host or server
Request Filtering	Enable selective filtering (blocking) of incoming requests based on a list of IP addresses or host names
Request Dump	Prints the headers and cookies of incoming requests and outgoing responses to a log

We will work on the configuration of each of these valves in the section below.

Access Logs Implementation

Logging access to resources is a very common activity for web server administrators. This can include either static resources such as web pages and graphic files, or dynamic resources such as CGI, JSP, and servlets. In Tomcat 4, access logs can be generated by inserting an **Access Log valve**.

Note that this standard valve is completely separate and different from the `<Logger>` nestable component. The `<Logger>` component provides Tomcat – as well as applications running within it – a method to print user-visible status, warning, and error messages. The standard Access Log valve uses its own logic to examine each request for resources and prints only the access request information to its log file.

In case of the `<Logger>` component the format of the log file content is free-formed – it depends on the system or application – whereas the typical format for the standard Access Log valve is a well-known `common` log file format (for more information see W3C link http://www.w3.org/Daemon/User/Config/Logging.html#common-logfile-format). Analysis tools are widely available for the analysis of log files in the `common` log file format.

Scope of Log Files

The scope of logging will depend on where the Access Log valve is inserted. For example, to log all the access within a specific web application, we would place the valve (the `<Valve>` element) in the `<Context>` container in the `$CATALINA_HOME/conf/server.xml` file. To log all the resource access within a virtual host across all web applications, we would place the valve in the `<Host>` container. Finally, if we want to track all access to all resources on a particular instance of the Catalina engine – across all the virtual hosts in that engine and across all the web applications – we would place the valve in the `<Engine>` scope.

If you are using the standard Access Log valve, that is, if the `className` attribute is set to `org.apache.catalina.valves.AccessLogValve`, then you can specify the following attributes:

Attribute	Description	Required?
className	The Java programming language executable class representing the valve, org.apache.catalina.valves.AccessLogValve.	Yes
directory	The directory where the log files will be placed. Usually relative to the $CATALINA_HOME, but can also specify an absolute path instead. The default value is logs.	No
pattern	This attribute specifies the format used in the log. You can custom tailor the format, or you can use the common format or the combined format (common log file entry plus referrer and user-agent logged). The default format is common. To custom tailor the format, you can use any of the following pattern identifiers interspersed with a literal string in this pattern attribute: %a Insert remote IP address. %A Insert local IP address (of URL resource). %b Insert bytes sent count, excluding HTTP headers, will show '-' if zero. %B Insert bytes sent count, excluding HTTP headers. %h Insert remote host name (or IP address if the resolveHosts attribute is set to false). %H Insert the request protocol (HTTP). %l Insert remote logical user name (always '-'). %m	No

Attribute	Description	Required?
	Insert request method such as GET, POST. %p Insert the local TCP port on which this request is received. %q Insert the query string of this request. %r Insert the first line of the request. %s Insert the HTTP status code of the response. %S Insert the user session ID. %t Insert the date and time in common logfile format. %u Insert the remote user that has been authenticated (otherwise it is '-'). %U Insert the URL path of the request. %v Insert the name of the local virtual host from the request.	
resolveHosts	Determines if the log will contain hostnames via a reverse DNS lookup. This can take significant time if enabled. The default is disabled (false).	No
prefix	The prefix added to the name of the log file.	No
suffix	The suffix (extension) added to the name of the log file.	No

The Access Log valve supports rolling logs automatically – a new log file will be created for each day at midnight.

Testing the Access Log Valve

Let's take a look at a practical example for the configuration of access logs. Examine the default `$CATALINA_HOME/conf/server.xml` file, and you will see a commented `<Valve>` entry that specifies the access log. It is placed immediately within the `<Host name="localhost" ...>` entry:

```
<!--
    <Valve className="org.apache.catalina.valves.AccessLogValve"
           directory="logs"
           prefix="localhost_access_log."
           suffix=".txt"
           pattern="common"
           resolveHosts="false"
     />
-->
```

> **If you do not see the commented section detailed above, please type in the `<Valve>` entry manually as shown below. It is possible that you may have modified some Tomcat settings using the GUI Administration Tool. This tool will strip comments when changes are saved.**

Note also that the `resolveHost` attribute may not be available for Tomcat 4.1.x versions prior to Tomcat 4.1.7.

Uncomment this entry and modify the directory and prefix attributes as shown below:

```
    <Valve className="org.apache.catalina.valves.AccessLogValve"
           directory="wroxlogs"
           prefix="wroxtest_localhost_access_log."
           suffix=".txt"
           pattern="common"
           resolveHosts="false"
    />
```

Now, create a `wroxlogs/` directory under the `$CATALINA_HOME` directory (the standard valve will actually create it for you if you forget). Start/restart Tomcat 4, then open a browser and type http://localhost:8080/ .

The default Tomcat 4 welcome page should be displayed. Shut down the Tomcat server and examine the `$CATALINA_HOME/wroxlogs/` directory; you will find the access logs created by the valve.

Note that the log file's prefix is the same as the one we configured in the `<Valve>` element. If you look inside this log file, you will see the access log entries to the home page and the associated GIF files, all in the `common` log file format:

```
127.0.0.1 - - [07/Jul/2003:17:33:14 -0500] "GET / HTTP/1.1" 302 -
127.0.0.1 - - [07/Jul/2003:17:33:21 -0500] "GET /index.jsp HTTP/1.1" 200 -
127.0.0.1 - - [07/Jul/2003:17:33:21 -0500] "GET /tomcat.gif HTTP/1.1" 200 1934
127.0.0.1 - - [07/Jul/2003:17:33:21 -0500] "GET /jakarta-banner.gif HTTP/1.1" 200
8006
127.0.0.1 - - [07/Jul/2003:17:33:21 -0500] "GET /tomcat-power.gif HTTP/1.1" 200
2324
```

You may want to experiment further with other attributes of the standard Access Log valve. This can be done by modifying the `<Valve>` entry above. If you are running multiple virtual hosts, you may want to try configuring the `<Valve>` at the `<Engine>` level as well as the `<Context>` level to control the scope difference. Logging involves disk writes, and will inherently introduce an overhead into the server hosting web applications. For a production site, it is important to discuss and formulate an optimal logging strategy between developers and administrators – based on the application and demand of a server.

Single Sign-On Implementation

Another standard valve that is frequently used is the Single Sign-on valve. Conventionally, whenever a user of a web application reaches a protected page, he/she will be required to sign on. This is required for each web application that may be accessed. Using Single Sign-on, it is possible to eliminate this often-annoying repetition (provided the userid and password are identical for each sign-on; usually authenticated against the same Tomcat realm).

The Single Sign-on valve caches credentials (passwords) on the server side and will invisibly authenticate the user as they traverse between web applications on a host. Without activating this valve, the user will be prompted to authenticate for each and every protected web application – even in case all applications use the same userid and password. The credential is cached against the client session on the server side; this means that a Single Sign-on will be effective throughout a session.

To specify the Single Sign-On valve, set the `className` attribute the value `org.apache.catalina.authenticator.SingleSignOn`. The only additional attribute allowed with this valve is `debug` and this attribute sets the debug level.

Configuring a Single Sign-On Valve

Before we configure the Single Sign-on valve, let's take a look at what the user has to go through without Single Sign-on. To do this, we must enable authentication on two web applications within the same virtual host. We will do this for the following sample web applications:

- The examples web application
- The Tomcat documentation web application

First, to secure the documentation application, edit the `web.xml` file in the `$CATALINA_HOME/webapps/tomcat-docs/WEB-INF` directory by adding the highlighted lines shown below:

```
<?xml version="1.0" encoding="ISO-8859-1"?>

<!DOCTYPE web-app
    PUBLIC "-//Sun Microsystems, Inc.//DTD Web Application 2.3//EN"
    "http://java.sun.com/dtd/web-app_2_3.dtd">

<web-app>
    <security-constraint>
      <display-name>Example Security Constraint</display-name>
      <web-resource-collection>
         <web-resource-name>Protected Area</web-resource-name>
         <url-pattern>/*</url-pattern>
      </web-resource-collection>
      <auth-constraint>
         <role-name>tomcat</role-name>
      </auth-constraint>
    </security-constraint>
 <login-config>
      <auth-method>BASIC</auth-method>
      <realm-name>Single Sign-on Example</realm-name>
 </login-config>
</web-app>
```

This modification will protect all the pages, via the `<url-pattern>/*</url-pattern>`, requiring an authentication for access. Only users belonging to the `tomcat` role can access these pages, as specified by the `<auth-constraint>` element. The `<security-constraint>` and `<login-config>` elements are part of the Servlet 2.2 specification; detailed examinations of these elements can be found in Chapter 6. Note that the `<login-config>` in this case specifies a BASIC authentication. This means the browser's security dialog will be used to obtain authentication information from the user.

Next, we will protect the **examples** web application. In the `$CATALINA_HOME/webapps/examples/WEB-INF/web.xml` file, make the following modifications as highlighted:

```
<security-constraint>
      <display-name>Example Security Constraint</display-name>
      <web-resource-collection>
         <web-resource-name>Protected Area</web-resource-name>
         <!-- Define the context-relative URL(s) to be protected -->
         <url-pattern>/*</url-pattern>
         <!-- If you list http methods, only those methods are protected -->
         <http-method>DELETE</http-method>
         <http-method>GET</http-method>
         <http-method>POST</http-method>
         <http-method>PUT</http-method>
      </web-resource-collection>
      <auth-constraint>
         <!-- Anyone with one of the listed roles may access this area -->
         <role-name>tomcat</role-name>
         <role-name>role1</role-name>
      </auth-constraint>
</security-constraint>
```

```
    <!-- Default login configuration uses form-based authentication -->

<login-config>
   <auth-method>FORM</auth-method>
   <realm-name>Example Form-Based Authentication Area</realm-name>
   <form-login-config>
      <form-login-page>/jsp/security/protected/login.jsp</form-login-page>
      <form-error-page>/jsp/security/protected/error.jsp</form-error-page>
   </form-login-config>
</login-config>
```

Here, we have modified the `<url-pattern>` element to protect all the resources within the example web applications. Note that the `<login-config>` in this case specifies a FORM-based authentication. This means a custom created form will be used obtain authentication information from the user, instead of the browser's security dialog.

Start Tomcat 4, and try to access the `tomcat-docs` web application via the following URL: http://localhost:8080/tomcat-docs/index.html.

Since we have configured BASIC authentication for `tomcat-docs`, the browser will prompt you to enter a username and password as shown below:

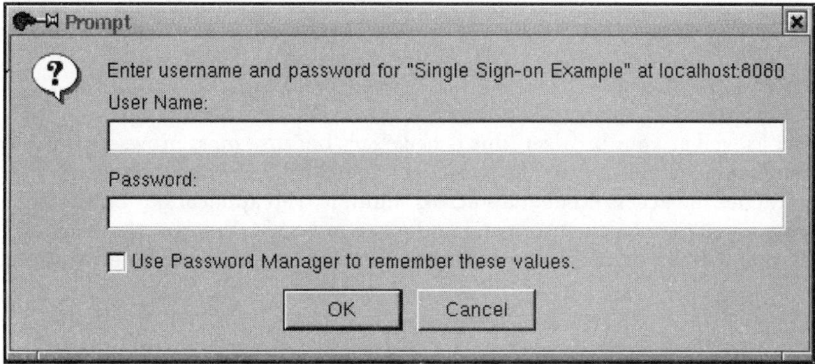

You can use `tomcat` as username, and `tomcat` as password (the password is case-sensitive). This corresponds to one of the password entries in the `$CATALINA_HOME/conf/tomcat-users.xml` (the default location of the XML file to load the Memory realm or UserDatabase). Once you authenticate successfully, you will be able to reach the Tomcat documentation home page. Now, let's switch to another web application on the same virtual host. Try the following URL: http://localhost:8080/examples/jsp/index.html.

Note that you are requested to authenticate again, this time using a custom form that has been created as part of the web application as shown overleaf:

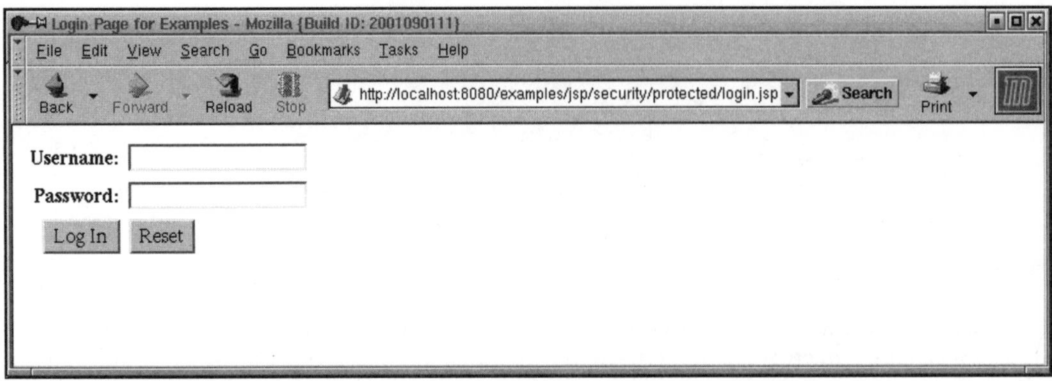

If you enter tomcat for username, and tomcat for password again, you can gain access to the examples pages. In fact, if you have more web applications that require authentication, the user will be prompted again when they first access them unless you enable the Single Sign-on valve.

To enable the Single Sign-on valve, place the <Valve> element as shown below, inside the <Context> element in the $CATALINA_HOME/conf/server.xml file. This is given in detail in the following section:

```
<!--
  <Valve className="org.apache.catalina.authenticator.SingleSignOn"
         debug="0"/>
-->
```

Restart Tomcat as well as your browser (this is necessary because most browsers caches credentials for BASIC authentication). Try accessing the two URLs again, in any order. This time, since the Single Sign-on valve caches the access credentials across multiple web applications on the same virtual host, you will only be asked to enter the username and password once. You can try to access the test again by trying the URLs in a different order after restarting the browser (to create a new session).

Note that we purposely did not use BASIC authentication for both applications because the client browser will typically cache login username and password. This valve is not as useful whenever all the applications use BASIC authentication (because the browser may already cache credentials for BASIC authentication). Therefore, depending on the authentication method used by web applications, your mileage on the Single Sign-on valve may vary.

Restricting Access Via a Request Filter

A very useful valve that enables one to block or filter out specific client's requests is Request Filter valve. This valve is useful in implementing policies that are based on the characteristics of requests passing through it.

Remote Address Filter

If the `className` attribute of the `<Valve>` component has the value `org.apache.catalina.valves.RemoteAddrValve`, then we are creating a **Remote Address Filter**. A Remote Address filter enables us to specify a list of IP addresses (or regular expressions representing IP addresses) from which we will accept or deny requests. Any denied request is not passed through the valve, effectively blocking it. The table below lists the attributes allowed with the Remote Address filter:

Attribute	Description	Required?
`className`	The Java programming language executable class representing the valve	Yes
`allow`	An IP address specified using a regular expression that matches the address of incoming requests	No
`deny`	An IP address specified using a regular expression that matches the address	No

This valve will examine the IP address of the client's request against its `allow/deny` list, and will attempt to match the specified regular expression representing IP addresses – any one that does match the `allow` attribute will be passed through to downstream components. If `allow` is not specified, all IP addresses other that the ones specified in `deny` are allowed.

Remote Host Filter

If the `className` attribute of the `<Valve>` component has the value `org.apache.catalina.valves.RemoteHostValve`, we are creating a **Remote Host Filter**. A Remote Host filter functions like the Remote Address filter, except the filtering performed is based on host names rather than IP. The allowed attributes are `allow` and `deny`, but the regular expression specified is used to match a host name rather than an IP address.

Use of the Remote Host filter requires a reverse DNS lookup; therefore the DNS service must be accessible from the server side. In addition, you must be careful to specify all variants (or use a regular expression) of host names that a particular remote host can assume. For example, if a host just has two names, `printserver.wrox.com` and `charlie.wrox.com`, you should be careful to use `"printserver.wrox.com,charlie.wrox.com"` to match it; `"*.wrox.com"` will also work, but may be too restrictive.

Hands On with Request Filter Valve

Let's look at the details of the configuration of both the Request Filter valves discussed. Before starting Tomcat, add the following line to the `$CATALINA_HOME/conf/server.xml` file inside the `"localhost"` `<Host>` container, then start Tomcat:

```
<Valve className="org.apache.catalina.valves.RemoteAddrValve"
allow="121.121.121.*,111.111.111.*"/>
```

This will setup a Request Filter valve to allow only requests from the two subnets: `121.121.121.*` and `111.111.111.*`.

Now, try accessing the URL: http://localhost:8080/examples/jsp/index.html. The list of allowed IP addresses does not have an entry that matches our IP (`127.0.0.1`), and therefore our request is filtered out. The server returns an HTTP "Forbidden" 403 error and we get a blank page.

> *NOTE: If you need to have a custom page returned when access is denied, you need to use Servlet 2.3 filters within a web application instead. Custom error pages are configurable inside the deployment descriptor.*

Now, edit the above line again to include our IP address:

```
<Valve className="org.apache.catalina.valves.RemoteAddrValve"
       allow="121.121.121.*,127.*.*.*"/>
```

Restart Tomcat, and now we can access the URL again since our IP is explicitly enabled by the allow list.

You can also explicitly deny access by changing the line as shown below:

```
<Valve className="org.apache.catalina.valves.RemoteAddrValve"
       deny="127.0.0.1"/>
```

When you try and access the URL again, a blank page is returned since the request is filtered out again.

The Remote Host filter works identically, but with host names instead. We can try it out by simply editing the above configuration line as:

```
<Valve className="org.apache.catalina.valves.RemoteHostValve"
       allow="*.wrox.com"/>
```

Notice the change in `className` from `org.apache.catalina.valves.RemoteAddrValve` to `org.apache.Catalina.valves.RemoteHostValve`, and that the `deny` list now contains a host name instead of an IP address. Restart Tomcat, and try accessing the URL again.

The access fails and you get a blank page since only hosts from `wrox.com` with names that are DNS resolvable are explicitly allowed.

The Request Filter valve can be quite effective in implementing a security policy, although if filtering on a physical server level is desired, a hardware router-based filtering may be more suitable. Regardless, the Request Filter valve is handy for temporarily removing access to specific remote client(s).

Request Dumper Valve

There is a less known standard valve, useful for debugging web applications that most administrators/users typically overlook, called the **Request Dumper Valve**. This valve dumps the headers and cookies of requests and responses to a log. Request Dumper valve assumes that a `<Logger>` is available and properly configured (see Chapter 18 for more information on logging).

For administrators, it serves two purposes:

- It visually illustrates how the scope of a valve affects the requests that are processed
- It is used to debug the action of other valves (like when a Request Filter valve does not appear to work) or request processing components

To configure a Request Dumper valve, simply add the following to the `<Context>`, `<Host>`, or `<Engine>` elements:

```
<Valve className="org.apache.catalina.valves.RequestDumperValve"/>
```

Please make sure you remove any `RemoteAddrValve` or `RemoteHostValve` before using this valve; otherwise you may not get access to the application at all.

Persistent Sessions

Tomcat 4 features a new **Persistent Session Manager**. At the time of writing, this Session Manager is still a work-in-progress and its features and configuration are still subject to change. It is not configured by default.

The Need for Persistent Sessions

When Tomcat is shut down, typically all session information is lost. Furthermore, sessions that are idle will take up valuable working memory until session timeout – which is typically a long period, since some users may leave their computers.

With Persistent Session Manager, the following features can be enabled:

- Sessions that are inactive can be configured to be **swapped onto disk** thereby releasing the memory consumed by them, making memory available for other active sessions
- When Tomcat is shut down, all the current sessions are **saved to disk**; upon restart the saved sessions are restored
- Sessions lasting beyond a specified threshold period are **automatically backed up** on disk, enabling the system to survive an unexpected crash

The last feature listed above enables continuous reliable execution of the web application despite minor server failure (crash) – and goes a long way to enhancing the availability and robustness of the system. Furthermore, future clustering and session replication solutions may become available that can use the session persistence feature to enable fail-over from one server to another in case some catastrophic failure occurs on a single hardware server.

Configuring a Persistent Session Manager

The Persistent Session Manager is configured through the <Manager> element in the main configuration file: `$CATALINA_HOME/conf/server.xml`. The <Manager> element may be configured at the web application level (that is as a subelement of the <Context> nested component).

The <Manager> Element

Here are the attributes of the <Manager> element that are available for configuration:

Attribute	Description	Required?
`className`	The Java programming language class that implements the Persistence Session manager.	Yes
`debug`	Controls the level of debug messages.	No
`saveOnRestart`	If this is set to `true`. Tomcat will save all the active sessions to the Store upon shutdown, and will reload the session (except the expired ones) from the Store on start-up.	Yes
`maxActiveSessions`	The ceiling on the number of active sessions, before swapping out of session via the Persistence Session manager begins. The value of `-1` allows unlimited number of active sessions.	Yes
`minIdleSwap`	The minimum number of seconds before a session will be considered for swapping.	Yes
`maxIdleSwap`	The maximum number of seconds before a session is swapped out to the Store. Used with `minIdleSwap` also to tune the session persistence mechanism.	Yes
`maxIdleBackup`	The number of seconds a session is active before it is backed up on the Store. This can be used to avert a sudden crash, as the backed up sessions will be restored from the store upon the next start-up. A value of `-1` will disable the backup action altogether.	Yes

The <Manager> element can have only one subelement:

Sub-Element	Description	How Many?
`Store`	Used by the Persistent Session manager to determine how and where to save the session. Currently, the only choices available for a Store implementation are: `org.apache.catalina.session.FileStore` or `org.apache.catalina.session.JDBCStore`.	1

Store uses object serialization to store the session. We will use the FileStore for our hands-on example. By default, the FileStore's serialized session information is placed under the `$CATALINA_HOME/work/<service name>/<host name>/<web-app name>/` directory.

Hands On Configuration with Persistent Manager

To configure the persistent manager, first uncomment the `<Manager>` definition in the file and make the modifications as highlighted below:

```
<Manager className="org.apache.catalina.session.PersistentManager"
         debug="0"
         saveOnRestart="true"
         maxActiveSessions="3"
         minIdleSwap="0"
         maxIdleSwap="60"
         maxIdleBackup="0">
   <Store className="org.apache.catalina.session.FileStore"/>
</Manager>
```

This configures a persistent manager that will allow up to 3 active sessions before activating session swapping. Any session is available for swapping at any time. All idle sessions will be swapped within 60 seconds. An active session is backed up regularly; a value of 0 indicates that they should be backed up immediately after being used.

Start up Tomcat, start a session, and view the session information by going to the URL: http://localhost:8080/examples/servlet/SessionExample. Note down, on a piece of paper, the session ID and the start date of your session.

Now, wait for about 2 minutes for the persistent manager to go to work. At this point, simulate a crash via an ungraceful shutdown. This can be done by a Ctrl-C in the Tomcat window.

Next, start Tomcat again. When Tomcat starts, it will restore all the sessions that were backed up. Try the URL again: http://localhost:8080/examples/servlet/SessionExample.

Note that the session ID and the backed up session information are identical to the ones before the (simulated) crash. In effect, our Tomcat server has survived an unexpected sudden crash. The Persistent Session Manager has already backed up the session by the time we crash Tomcat. Therefore, when we start Tomcat up again, it restores the session from the backed up store – and we resume the previous session.

Note: At the time of writing, under Tomcat 4.1.3 beta, it was necessary to comment out the JMX MBean supporting Listeners for the persistent manager to work. These are the lines that must be commented out in the `server.xml` file:

```
<Listener className="org.apache.catalina.mbeans.ServerLifecycleListener"
debug="0"/>
<Listener
className="org.apache.catalina.mbeans.GlobalResourcesLifecycleListener"
debug="0"/>
```

To see where the persisted sessions are stored, go to the `$CATALINA_HOME/work/Standalone/localhost/examples/` directory, and look for file names with the `.ser` extension.

JNDI Resource Configuration

Within the `server.xml` configuration file we can define JNDI resources that may be accessed in a standard J2EE compliant manner by any web applications. In this section, we examine what JNDI is, how it is used, and the type of administrative requests that developers typically make, as these requests have an impact on the JNDI resources configuration.

What Is JNDI?

JNDI is **Java Naming and Directory Interface**. It is an API used for looking up information pertaining to the network (via naming and directory services). Like JDBC, JNDI is designed to work with any compatible naming and directory service – regardless of its native interface API. Some common information that can be obtained through JNDI includes (but is not restricted to):

- User and password (authentication)
- Access control policy (who can access what)
- Organizational directories
- Servers (e-mail, database, and so on)
- Printers
- Other object or resource

Before the advent of JNDI, we needed to program specifically to a particular network's directory service. On Microsoft-based networks, we needed to program to NT Domains or the Active Directory Service Interface (ADSI). On Solaris/UNIX networks, we needed to program to the Network Information Service (NIS). On Novell networks we needed to program to the Netware Directory Service (NDS). This made the situation even more complex as each of the network directory services above assumes a different convention in naming the resources/information that it stores, and has completely different APIs to search for and locate this information.

The diagram opposite shows how JNDI unifies directory service access across all different networks:

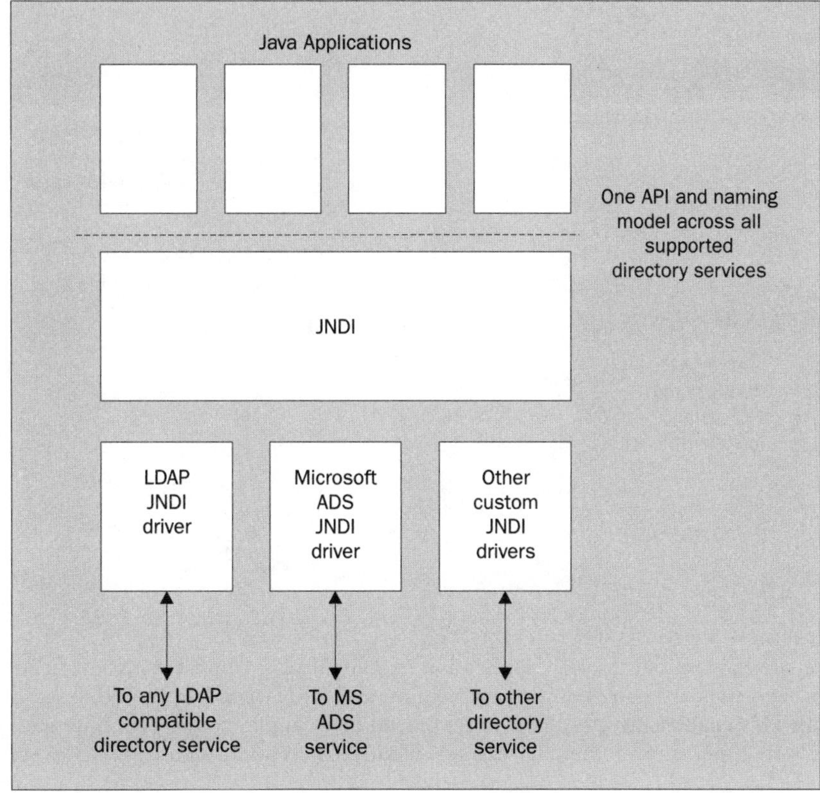

As we can see from the figure, JNDI is the top layer that provides a uniform programming interface to applications – meanwhile translating the API commands to the network-specific operations that are sent out through its plug-in drivers. In fact, many of the modern directory services support the LDAP (Lightweight Directory Access Protocol) protocol. JNDI often gains compatibility with new or legacy directory services through its LDAP driver.

Beyond providing interfaces to existing directory services, JNDI has become a standard way for Java applications (especially in the context of J2EE) to locate network resources. That is, even if there is no physical directory service involved over the network, many of the standard Java APIs have adopted JNDI as the de facto way of obtaining network resources. We will see two such examples in the next section.

Tomcat and JNDI

We now need to understand the role of the Tomcat server with respect to JNDI. In fact, the role of Tomcat in this case is only to provide the facilities. Tomcat as a J2EE-compliant and Servlet 2.3-complaint server will facilitate the use of JNDI by hosted web applications. This is shown in the diagram overleaf:

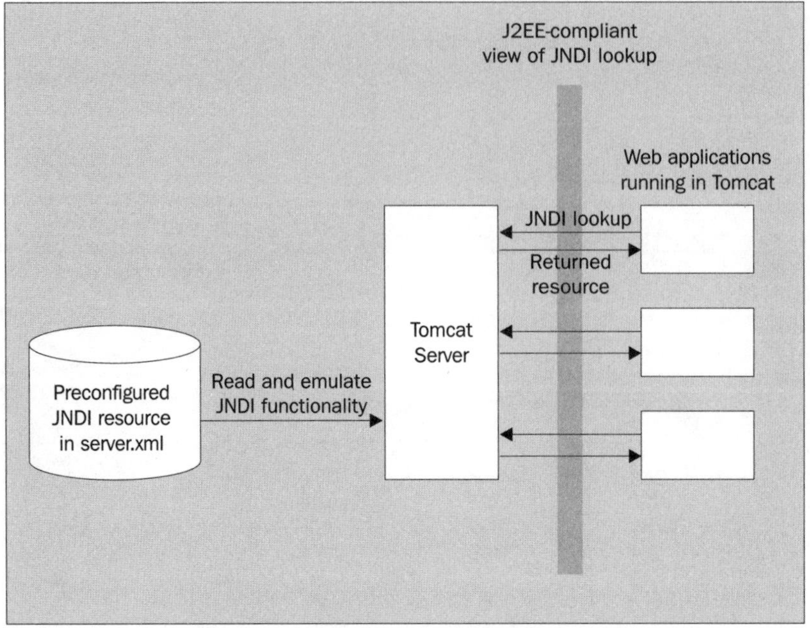

In this figure, we can see that the web application running inside Tomcat is retrieving certain JNDI resources through standard programming convention and APIs (specified by JNDI and Servlet 2.3 specification). This enables these requests to be placed in an application-server independent manner – allowing the web applications to be portable across different vendors' application servers.

The Tomcat container intercepts the standard JNDI requests from the application. To fulfil these JNDI API requests, Tomcat must go to its set of pre-configured resources – in the `server.xml` file – to determine what needs to be passed back to the application. Tomcat essentially provides JNDI emulation service for accessing these resources. It is the responsibility of Tomcat's administrator to configure these resources in the `sever.xml` file.

Typical Tomcat JNDI Resources

Some common resources that are accessed via JNDI requests from web applications include:

- A JDBC DataSource
- A JavaMail Session
- A UserDatabase (Tomcat 4.1 only, used to implement realm)

JDBC is a well-known standard API that enables application programmers to access relational databases (such as MySQL, Oracle, and SQL Server) in a uniform and standard way. To access data from these relational databases, the application must first obtain a `DataSource` object (see Chapter 15 for extensive JDBC coverage. For now, we can view a `DataSource` as a class from which one can obtain connections to a remote database).

JavaMail is another well-known standard API that provides an interface to access e-mail capabilities (that is create and send mails), across different methods of handling e-mail, in a uniform and standard manner. For a web application to access mail servers and send mail, the application must first obtain a JavaMail `Session` object.

The JDBC 2.1 and JavaMail 1.2 specifications are synchronized with the latest J2EE specification. In both cases, it is the responsibility of the container (application server) to provide web applications with JNDI access to these resources. The administrator needs to configure these resources for Tomcat 4 to find them – passing them through to the requesting web application by emulating JNDI action. To learn more about JDBC, see Chapter 15.

Configuring Resources Via JNDI

For JNDI, there are three choices for configuring the resource within the hierarchy of Tomcat configuration components:

- At the server's global `<GlobalNamingResources>` level (only available in Tomcat 4.1 or later), or
- At the virtual host's `<DefaultContext>` level, or
- At the `<Context>` level associated with a single web application

Recall from Chapter 5 that there can be only one `<DefaultContext>` nested component inside a `<Host>` container, and as many `<Context>` nested components as there are web applications. What this means is that any JNDI resource configured at the `<DefaultContext>` level will be available to all web applications running on the same virtual host, while any JNDI resource configured at the `<Context>` level will only be available within the specific application associated with that context.

Resources configured at `<GlobalNamingResources>` are available server-wide (across all services and engines). These resources can then be referred to in subsequent resource configurations via `<ResourceLink>` elements.

We need to add the following nested elements inside the `<Context>` or `<DefaultContext>` to support and configure JNDI Resources:

Sub-Element Name	Description	How Many?
`Environment`	Creates environment entries available from the JNDI `InitialContext` that Tomcat will supply to an application	0 or more
`Resource`	Provides name of datatype of a JNDI resource to the application	0 or more
`ResourceParams`	Specifies the Java programming language class that is used to create the resources, as well as specifying a configuration JavaBean	0 or more
`ResourceLink`	Adds a link to a resource defined in the `<GlobalNamingResource>` element – which is server-wide	0 or more

> **It is also possible for developers to directly embed environment, resource, or resource parameters into their web applications. This is done by defining `<env-entry>`, `<resource-env-entry>`, and `<ResourceParams>` elements inside the `web.xml` descriptor. This will make a resource specific to a web application. However, the `web.xml` deployment descriptor must be changed each time there is a change in the resource information.**

Let us examine each subelement in turn.

The <Environment> Element

The `<Environment>` element is used to pass named data values (like environment variables in a command shell) to the web applications. Web applications can access these values through the JNDI context. These are the attributes that an `<Environment>` element can have:

Attribute	Description	Required?
`name`	The JNDI name for this element.	Yes
`description`	Text description for this element.	No
`override`	Application programmers can use the `<env-entry>` element to override the one defined here. You can disable the override by setting it to `false`.	No
`type`	Java class name of the datatype represented by this element.	Yes
`value`	The actual value of the environment entry.	Yes

For example:

```
<Environment name="maxUsers" type="java.lang.Integer" value="100" />
```

The above will add a JNDI entry named `maxUsers` with a value of `100`.

The <Resource> Element

The `<Resource>` element is used to pass a reference via resource managers (classes that manage and hand out resources – such as JDBC connections) to web applications using a name in simple text. A web application can access the reference to the resource manager through a lookup based on the textual name using the JNDI context. The `<Resource>` element can have the following attributes:

Attribute	Description	Required?
auth	Indicates who does the authentication. If the value is application, then the application itself must sign-on with the resource manager. If the value is container then the container does a sign-on with the resource manager.	No
description	Text description for this element.	No
name	Name of the resource.	Yes
scope	Value can be either Shareable or Unsharable; determine if the resource can be shared.	No
type	Java class name of the datatype represented by this resource.	Yes

For example:

```
<Resource name="myDatabase"
          type="org.apache.catalina.UserDatabase">
</Resource>
```

The above element will add a UserDatabase implementation (for storing authentication and role information on Tomcat 4.1.x – we will cover UserDatabase deployment in detail, later in this chapter), named myDatabase that is available through JNDI lookup.

The <ResourceParams> Element

The <ResourceParams> element associates parameters with the resource manager already configured in a <Resource> element. This element is often used to configure the resource manager. For example, if the <Resource> is a JDBC DataSource, the <ResourceParams> may contain the RDBMS server location, login name and password to use. The <ResourceParams> can contain these attributes:

Attribute	Description	Required?
name	Name of corresponding resource	Yes

Each <ResourceParams> element can contain one or more <nam>/<value> subelements expressed as:

```
<ResourceParams name="jdbc/wroxDatabase">
   <parameter>
      <name>password</name>
      <value>wrox123</value>
   </parameter>
</ResourceParams>
```

The <ResourceLink> Element

The `<ResourceLink>` element refers to a previously configured JNDI resource, typically in the `<GlobalNamingResource>` sub-element associated with a server – making these resources available to all `<Service>`, `<Host>`, and `<Context>`. This allows resources to be defined and shared across servers or globally. A `<ResourceLink>` element can have the following attributes:

Attribute	Description	Required?
global	The name of the resource being linked to	Yes
name	The name of the resource, accessible by web application via JNDI lookup	Yes
type	The Java programming language class name indicating the type of resource returned	Yes

For example, if we have already defined the UserDatabase `<Resource>` element in the server's `<GlobalNamingResource>` subelement (see the `<Resource>` element example earlier), then we can refer to it within a `<Context>` element of a web application using:

```
<ResourceLink name="localDatabase" global="myDatabase"
              type="org.apache.catalina.UserDatabase"/>
```

The above entry will link the previously defined UserDatabase instance (named `myDatabase` in `<GlobalNamingResource>`) to the JNDI addressable resource called `localDatabase`. The web application can perform a JNDI lookup for `localDatabase` and obtain access to the UserDatabase instance.

Let's apply the above elements to configure the JDBC DataSource and JavaMail sessions.

Configuring a JDBC DataSource

JDBC 2.1, including DBCP connections pooling (a Jakarta Commons library for efficient management of JDBC connections), is directly supported by Tomcat. We will discuss JDBC at length in Chapter 15. For now, we will briefly examine how JDBC connections as a JNDI resource can be passed to web applications.

Your JDBC driver should be placed in the `$CATALINA_HOME/common/lib/` directory. This will allow Tomcat to find and access this driver.

Finally, we must configure the JNDI resource factory using `<Resource>` and `<ResourceParams>` elements. In this case, we are configuring the database factory to use the MySQL database, with a virtual host-wide scope. This instance of the database will be shared between all the web applications running within the same virtual host:

```
<Host>
  ...
  <Resource name="jdbc/wroxTC41" auth="Container"
            type="javax.sql.DataSource"/>
```

The above segment configures Tomcat's built-in JDBC DataSource factory. The built-in DataSource factory implementation in Tomcat is `org.apache.naming.factory.DbcpDataSourceFactory`. A DataSource factory is a class from which we can obtain new instances of DataSource objects. Using this factory, the following configuration parameters are possible:

Parameter	Description
`driverClassName`	Java programming language class name of the JDBC driver. This driver should be placed in the `$CATALINA_HOME/common/lib` directory for easy location by the DataSource factory code.
`maxActive`	The maximum number of active connections in this pool.
`maxIdle`	The maximum number of idle connections in this pool.
`maxWait`	In milliseconds, indicates the maximum wait for a connection – by the DataSource factory – before throwing an exception.
`user`	The user ID used to log on to the database.
`password`	The password used to log on to the database.
`url`	The JDBC-compatible URL specifies the database instance to be used.
`validationQuery`	An optional SQL query used to validate a connection. Essentially, the factory will perform this query and ensure that rows are returned before considering the connection valid.

For example, we can parameterize the JDBC resource defined above by using the following `<ResourceParams>` elements:

```
<ResourceParams name="jdbc/WroxTC41">
    <parameter>
        <name>driverClassName</name>
        <value>org.gjt.mm.mysql.Driver</value>
    </parameter>
    <parameter>
        <name>url</name>
        <value>jdbc:mysql://localhost/wroxapache</value>
    </parameter>
    <parameter>
        <name>username</name>
        <value>empro</value>
    </parameter>
    <parameter>
        <name>password</name>
        <value>empass</value>
    </parameter>
```

```
    <parameter>
        <name>maxActive</name>
        <value>20</value>
    </parameter>
    <parameter>
        <name>maxIdle</name>
        <value>30000</value>
    </parameter>
    <parameter>
        <name>maxWait</name>
        <value>100</value>
    </parameter>
</ResourceParams>
```

In addition to the above configuration, the developer must declare the use of the resource in their deployment descriptor (`web.xml`) using a `<resource-ref>` element. For example:

```
<resource-ref>
  <res-ref-name> jdbc/WroxTC41 </res-ref-name>
  <res-type> javax.sql.DataSource </res-type>
  <res-auth> Container </res-auth>
</resource-ref>
```

Within the web applications, the DataSource can be looked up relative to the `java:comp/env` naming context. The code used will be similar to the following:

```
Context myInitialContext = new InitialContext();
Context localContext = (Context) myInitialContext("java:comp/env");
DataSource myDataSource = (DataSource)
  localContext.lookup("jdbc/wroxTC41");

Connection myConn = myDataSource.getConnection();
...
```

At this point, `myConn` contains an instance of a database connection, which can be used to access the MySQL database immediately.

Configuring Mail Sessions

JavaMail is a standard programming API used by J2EE developer to create and send e-mail. Tomcat supports JavaMail by providing the JNDI configuration of the JavaMail session as a resource. Web applications can then use JNDI to look up and use this session.

Support for JavaMail is part of the Tomcat distribution; you can find the support library in the `$CATALINA_HOME/common/lib` directory, called `mail.jar`.

Let us examine how we can go about configuring a mail session. In the `server.xml` file, you will find the following resource definition inside the `examples` context:

```
<Resource name="mail/Session" auth="Container" type="javax.mail.Session"/>
    <ResourceParams name="mail/Session">
           <parameter>
             <name>mail.smtp.host</name>
             <value>localhost</value>
           </parameter>
    </ResourceParams>
</Resource>
```

This will configure the JNDI `mail/Session` context, referring to an SMTP server running on `localhost`. If you are connecting to a remote SMTP server, change the value of `localhost` to the name or IP address of your server. You can also modify the port used (if it is not at the standard port 25) by setting the `mail.smtp.port` parameter.

In the `$CATALINA_HOME/webapps/examples/WEB-INF/web.xml` file, we can see what the application programmer must declare to use the JNDI resource:

```
<resource-ref>
      <res-ref-name>mail/Session</res-ref-name>
      <res-type>javax.mail.Session</res-type>
      <res-auth>Container</res-auth>
</resource-ref>
```

Start Tomcat, and we can try out the example that uses JavaMail to send e-mail. Use the URL http://localhost:8080/examples/jsp/mail/sendmail.jsp.

The screenshot to the right shows what appears on the browser:

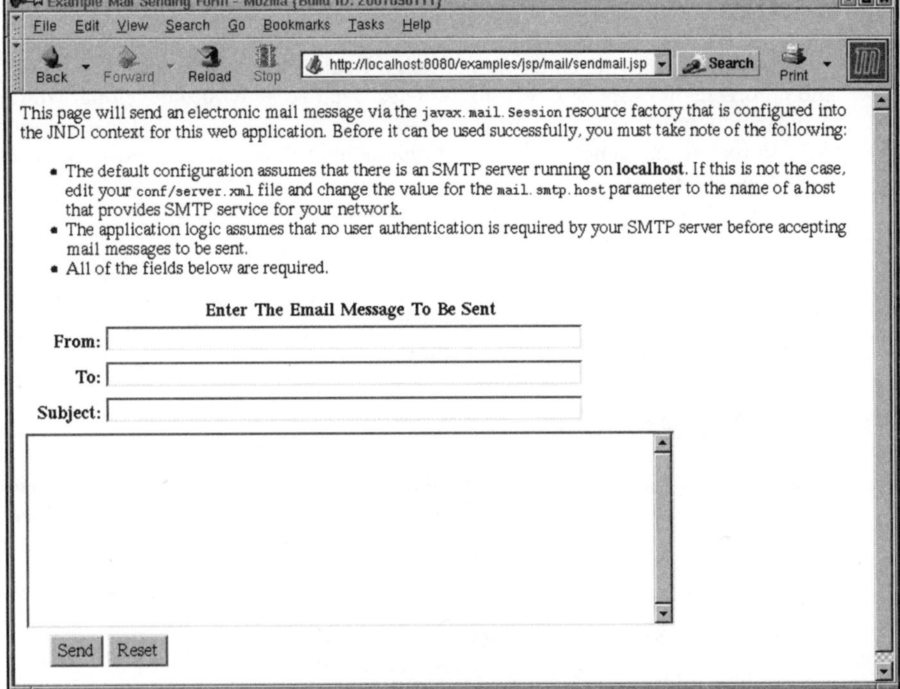

You can fill this form to actually send an e-mail (assuming that you have the SMTP server configured properly).

This JSP collects information for an e-mail from the user, and then submits it to a collaborating servlet for processing and sending. You will find the code of the collaborating servlet, called `SendMailServlet.java`, in the `$CATALINA_HOME/webapps/examples/WEB-INF/classes` directory. The code below shows how an application can look up and utilize the JNDI mail session:

```
    // Acquire our JavaMail session object
       Context initCtx = new InitialContext();
       Context envCtx = (Context) initCtx.lookup("java:comp/env");
       Session session = (Session) envCtx.lookup("mail/Session");
       ...
```

Since our JavaMail session is configured as a JNDI resource with name `mail/Session`, the code above will look up this resource from the JNDI `InitailContext`.

Configuring the UserDatabase

UserDatabase is an in-memory database that is used to maintain tables containing username, password, group, and role information. This database can be accessed and maintained programmatically by web applications, and also be used as a realm in container-managed authentication. We will have more information, including details on configuration of UserDatabase as a JNDI resource, in the following realm section.

Realms

Tomcat 4 introduces the concept of a realm. Realms help web application developers in implementation and enforcement of specific security policies. That is, it enables developers to create web applications that can authenticate the user prior to granting access and control access to certain services or resources. Prior to realms, this functionality was implemented in an ad-hoc, non-standardized manner. A realm itself does not enforce security policies; it is merely a mechanism that greatly facilitates in implementation. Tomcat working in conjunction with the web application sets and enforces application-specific security policies.

Realms enable the implementation of Container Managed Security (also known as Declarative Security) in Tomcat – a requirement for compliancy with Servlet 2.3 specifications. We will examine Container Managed Security in the following section.

What Is a Realm?

Realm is actually a standard programming interface defined in Tomcat for accessing a set of data tables. Realms provide special-purpose database access functionality to the Tomcat server. Unlike a general database, the tables that are maintained by a realm must provide the following information:

- A username
- A password associated with the username
- The roles that are assigned to the user

Tomcat's authentication implementations, including the single sign-on valve that we have covered in the previous section – depend on realms to get its user and password information.

Furthermore, through the web application configuration elements `<security-constraint>`, `<security-role>`, and `<login-config>`, a web application can harness declarative container-managed security that will automatically make use of the data in the realm for container-managed authentication.

Container Managed Security

Container Managed Security defers the implementation of security policies from the development stage to deployment. This is extremely important because it enhances the applicability and reusability of software components, services, and web applications. Web application designers and developers can design and write their security-sensitive code based on roles that users will play (for example, only managers can access employees' salary records). This will enable actual users to be assigned to roles at deployment time and enable the user-to-role mapping to change dynamically without having to change application code.

Let's take an example to clarify what Container Managed Security provides for web application developers and administrators. Imagine a web application that enables employees in a company to view their performance reviews on-line. The very sample application also enables managers to add/modify the reviews. This application must ensure that:

- An employee is authenticated before allowing access to the confidential information
- A manager is authenticated before allowing access to viewing and modification of the employee records

Before using the Container Managed Security, the web application developers must hard-code the authentication routines, and the logic to determine an employee and a manager.

Container Managed Security, often called **Declarative** security, enables the web application developers to work with an indirect mapping called roles. Using Container Managed Security, web application developers only need to ensure that the role `employee` can access the employee's own record and that only the role `manager` can modify the employee record.

The mapping of users or usernames to `employee/manager` can be assigned at deployment time and be maintained in a realm.

As administrators, we can configure and protect access to a web application service based on roles (`employee/manager`). An additional level of indirection can be configured by the developer in the `web.xml` file by adding the `<security-role>` element.

A web application developer can embed a combination of the following elements in implementing the security policy of the application. We will briefly describe only the most frequently used ones here:

Element	Description
`<security-constraint>`	Used to protect a group of web resources (like JSP, servlet, static pages). Also specifies the role required for a user to access it. This is the main mechanism for Container Managed Security.
`<web-resource-collection>`	Used to specify the collection of web resources (that is static pages, servlets, JSPs, and so on) that should be protected. URL pattern using wildcard characters are allowed.
`<user-data-constraint>`	Specifies data transport security constraint, either integral or confidential. Typically used to specify that access be performed over HTTPS only.
`<auth-constraint>`	This is the subelement inside the `<security-constraint>` element that provides an ACL (Access Control List) consisting of the roles that are allowed to access resources.
`<login-config>`	Used to configure the type of authentication that will be performed by the container. The container can use `BASIC` (dialog from browser), `DIGESTED` (slightly more secure because passwords are not transmitted as clear text), custom `FORM` based, or SSL client methods for authentication.
`<security-role>`	Declares the name of the security roles that are used within a web application.

The information maintained by the realm can be changed dynamically while the system is in operation. For example, a user may be an employee who was recently promoted to a `manager` role. Once their role mapping is updated in a JDBC realm (perhaps updating the company's human resource database), they will be granted immediate access to any relevant files. This ability to implement access control policies based on roles at deployment time and dynamically changing the user-in-role assignment are the quintessential reasons for using Container Managed Security.

This eliminates the need to change application code, or even deployment configuration, when these changes take place. This is in contrast to memory realm – in which case the Tomcat server must be restarted to reflect changes.

Configuring JDBC Realms

A JDBC realm is a realm implementation that has tables maintained in a relational database, say MySQL or Oracle. The real appeal of a JDBC realm is the flexibility in addition, update, modification, and deletion that an RDBMS offers us in maintaining the user/role relationship.

Furthermore, sophisticated maintenance and administration tools can be readily created using JDBC to access and maintain the tables within the realm.

Since an RDBMS is dynamic by definition, any changes that are made to the content of the data are immediately reflected in the realm. This is a highly desirable feature of Container Managed Security not just for security, but also for most other applications.

Mapping Columns To the Required View

The JDBC realms implementation in Tomcat 4 has a particular view of how the tables in the realm must be maintained. Fortunately, the configurable parameters of realms enable us to map to any existing schema containing the same data.

More specifically, the JDBC realm implementation expects the following tables – in a standard normalized relation:

Table Name	Description
`Users`	Contains username and password information
`user_roles`	Contains user-to-roles mapping information

The `Users` table is expected to contain the following two columns as a minimum. The users' table has `user_name` as the primary key (indexed):

Column	Type	Length
`user_name`	`varchar not null`	15
`user_pass`	`varchar not null`	15

The `user_roles` table is expected to contain the following two columns as a minimum:

Column	Type	Length
`user_name`	`varchar not null`	15
`role_name`	`varchar not null`	15

Note that the datatype can be any type that results in a character string, and longer length fields will be accommodated.

The compound primary key in this table is `{user_name, role_name}`. This means that a single user can have multiple roles. The `user_name` column in both users and `user_roles` tables can be relationally joined during regular queries.

For maximum flexibility, the above table names and column names are not imposed on the underlying table. Instead, they are mapped during runtime to the underlying table. The mapping is specified in the configuration of the `<Realm>` element.

The JDBC realm implementation, contained in the `org.apache.catalina.realm.JDBCRealm` class, will assume the above configuration while using a JDBC driver to access the data in the realm.

Realm definitions must be configured in a realm element at the level of any container component. Specifically, the JDBC realm implementation may be configured with the following attributes:

Attribute	Description	Required?
`className`	The Java programming language class that implements the JDBC realm. This should be the implementation provided by Tomcat – `org.apache.catalina.realm.JDBCRealm`.	Yes
`connectionName`	The JDBC connection username to be used.	Yes
`connectionPassword`	The JDBC connection password to be used.	Yes
`connectionURL`	The JDBC connection URL used to access the database instance.	Yes
`debug`	Controls the level of debugging information that is printed to the log file.	No
`digest`	Specifies the digest algorithm used when the Container Managed Security uses the digest method of authentication. Takes a value that specifies the digest algorithm such as `SHA`, `MD2`, `MD5`, and so on (for a complete list of current values, consult the JavaDoc `java.security.MessageDigest` class).	No
`driverName`	Name of the JDBC driver, a Java programming language class name.	Yes
`userTable`	The actual name of the table in the database that matches the `Users` table in the required view.	Yes
`userNameCol`	The actual column name of the column in both the `userTable` and `userRoleTable` that matches the `user` column in the required view.	Yes
`userCredCol`	The name of the column in the `userTable` that matches the `password` column in the required view.	Yes
`userRoleTable`	The actual name of the table in the database that matches the `user_roles` table in the required view.	Yes
`roleNameCol`	The name of the column in the `userRoleTable` that matches the `role_name` column in the required view.	Yes

We will see how the combination of the attributes `userTable`, `userNameCol`, `userCredCol`, `userRoleTable`, and `roleNameCol` enables us to map the existing database table and columns containing authentication and role information to the view required by the realm.

If you examine the server.xml file, you will find several JDBC realm definitions that are commented out. They can be readily adapted for configuring your own JDBC realm. For example, the following realm declaration from server.xml specifies a JDBC realm based on MySQL tables:

```
<Realm
        className="org.apache.catalina.realm.JDBCRealm"
        driverName="org.gjt.mm.mysql.Driver"
        connectionURL="jdbc:mysql://localhost/authority"
        connectionName="test"
        connectionPassword="test"
        userTable="users"
        userNameCol="user_name"
        userCredCol="user_pass"
        userRoleTable="user_roles"
        roleNameCol="role_name"
        debug="99"
        digest="SHA"
/>
```

We can see above that the schema in the MySQL table is exactly the required view. Debugging messages is set to the highest level. We are using username test and password test to log on to the MySQL server, and the server can be reached on the local machine via the authority path.

Configuring JNDI Realms

Like JDBC realms, JNDI realms enable us to use existing data in a directory service for a realm. The obvious immediate benefit would be the ability to use an existing directory service (such as SUN's NIS, Microsoft's ADS or NT Domains, Novell's Netware Directory Service) for container-managed authentication as opposed to application-managed authentication, where custom code is written to authenticate a user. Container-managed authentication is often more flexible and more maintainable.

To use a JNDI realm, we must be able to map the various configuration attributes successfully to an existing directory schema. This again is similar to the JDBC table and column name mapping. To better understand how this mapping works, let us examine the configuration attributes that are available with a JNDI realm:

Attribute	Description	Required?
className	Java programming class name of the JNDI realm implementation. Must be set to org.apache.catalina.realm.JNDIRealm.	Yes
connectionName	The username used to authenticate against the directory service via JNDI.	Yes
connectionPassword	The password used to authenticate against the directory service via JNDI.	Yes

Table continued on following page

Attribute	Description	Required?
connectionURL	The URL used to locate the directory service using JNDI.	Yes
contextFactory	Configures the Java programming language class used to create context for the JNDI connection. The default LDAP-based factory is sufficient in all non-custom cases.	No
debug	Controls the level of debugging messages that will be logged.	No
digest	Specifies the digest algorithm used to store a password. By default, passwords are store as plain text.	No
userPassword	Maps the name of the directory attribute from the user element that contains the password information.	Yes
userPattern	Specifies an LDAP pattern for searching the directory for selecting user entry. Use the {0} as a placeholder for the distinguished name.	Yes
roleName	Maps the name of the directory attribute that contains the role name.	Yes
roleSearch	Specifies an LDAP pattern for searching the directory for selecting roles entry. Use the {0} as a placeholder for the distinguished name, or {1} as a placeholder for the username.	Yes
roleBase	Specifies the base element for role searches. The default is the top-level element.	No
roleSubtree	Default is `false`. If set to `true`, a subtree search will be conducted for the role.	No

We can see from the configurable attributes above that the username must map to individual elements at the top-level directory context. Each group of users that are assigned the same role must also map to the individual element at the top-level directory context.

Memory Realm

A memory realm is a very simple implementation of a realm. Tomcat's memory realm implementation can load the user and role information into memory at startup. This information can then become available for read-only access to web applications via the realm programming interface, as well as for Container Managed Security.

The realm element for a memory realm can have the following attributes:

Attribute	Description	Required?
className	The Java programming language class that implements the memory realm. It must be set to org.apache.catalina.realm.MemoryRealm.	Yes
debug	Controls the level of the debugging message that will be sent to the log.	No
digest	The digest algorithm used to store password (like SHA or MD5). By default, passwords are stored in plain text.	No
pathname	Path to the XML file that will be the source of data for the memory realm. By default, the $CATALINA_HOME/conf/tomcat-users.xml file will be used.	No

By default, a memory realm is configured in the server.xml file at the <Engine> container level. The configuration is specified via:

```
<Realm className="org.apache.catalina.realm.MemoryRealm" />
```

This means that a memory realm, with all the information contained in the $CATALINA_HOME/conf/tomcat-users.xml file, will be created. In fact, both the manager web application and the admin web application of Tomcat rely on this default memory realm for authentication. This is why updating tomcat-users.xml with manager and admin roles will enable you to run these web applications.

If you need to specify your own set of users, passwords, and roles for a memory realm, be sure to follow the format of the tomcat-users.xml file similar to the following:

```
<tomcat-users>
  <user>
     <name>.. user name.. </name>
     <fullname> ..full name of user.. </fullname>
     <password>.. user password.. </password>
     <roles> .. roles of the user, separated by commas.. </roles>
  </user>
... more user elements ...
</tomcat-users>
```

However, from Tomcat 4.1 onwards, this memory realm is no longer configured by default. Instead, a greatly improved memory realm implementation called a UserDatabase has superseded this primitive memory realm implementation – although this classic implementation is still available for backward compatibility; that is it is present, but commented out.

UserDatabase as a Realm

UserDatabase is Tomcat 4.1's greatly enhanced implementation of a memory realm. It is improved in many aspects such as:

- It maintains compatibility with the `tomcat-users.xml` file convention. The UserDatabase can take its input, upon start up, from an XML data file. The default file is still the `tomcat-users.xml` file.
- It is no longer a read-only database. The database can be programmatically changed during the lifetime of the engine. This opens up various possibilities for building administrative utilities.
- Most importantly, UserDatabase is persistent. That is, upon modification and shutdown, the UserDatabase can also persist any changes back to `tomcat-users.xml` data file.
- One immediate benefit for using UserDatabase is that username, password, and role mapping can now be easily managed via the `admin` web interface utility.

The intention of UserDatabase goes beyond simply serving as a refined version of a memory realm. It will become an integral part of Tomcat's authentication and programmatic security support moving forward. However, at the time of writing the UserDatabase makes for a handy replacement of the underpowered memory realm.

Configuring UserDatabase

In the default `server.xml`, on Tomcat 4.1.x server distribution, the UserDatabase is already configured in place of the legacy memory realm implementation. The UserDatabase is typically configured in the `<GlobalNamingResources>` as a JNDI Resource. Here is a typical configuration:

```
<Resource name="UserDatabase" auth="Container"
          type="org.apache.catalina.UserDatabase"
          description="memory based user database"/>
<ResourceParams name="UserDatabase">
   <parameter>
      <name>factory</name>
      <value>org.apache.catalina.users.MemoryUserDatabaseFactory</value>
   </parameter>
   <parameter>
      <name>pathname</name>
      <value>conf/tomcat-users.xml</value>
   </parameter>
</ResourceParams>
```

This will make the UserDatabase accessible through application via JNDI lookup, relative to the `java:comp/env` naming context. Furthermore, it also enable us to easily reference it in a later scope. For example, we can use the UserDatabase as a realm at the `<Engine>` container level by adding the following `<Realm>` definition:

```
<Realm className="org.apache.catalina.realm.UserDatabaseRealm"
                 debug="0" resourceName="UserDatabase"/>
```

In fact, this is already done in the default `server.xml` file distributed with Tomcat 4.1.x. This means that both the `manager` application and the `admin` application that we have seen so far actually rely on UserDatabase as the realm for authentication. We have been working with an example of UserDatabase usage all the time.

To see that UserDatabase is a modifiable, updatable realm, we can use the `admin` application to add an entry. Start up Tomcat, then start the admin application via the URL: http://localhost:8080/admin/.

Logon using user ID `tomcat` and password `tomcat`. This is assuming that you have added the role of `admin` to the `tomcat` user in `tomcat-users.xml` prior to starting Tomcat. Note that there is no `admin` role configured by default for security reasons.

Now, click on the users item in the tree view on the left. You should see something similar to the screenshot below:

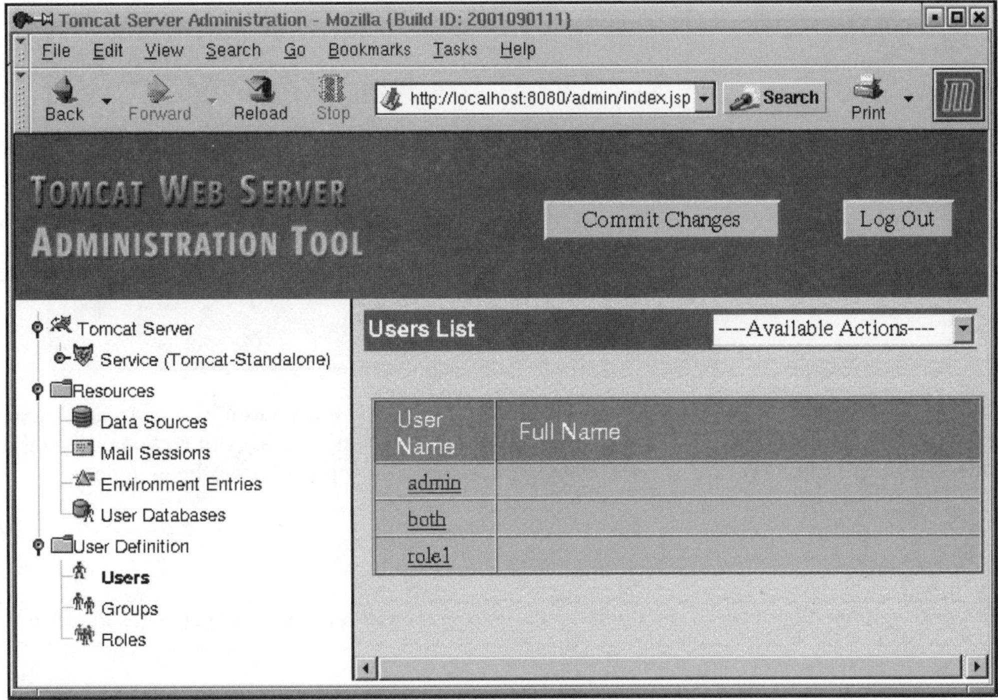

Next, click on the listbox on the right pane –Available Actions– and select Create New User. Fill it in as shown overleaf (password = `joe`):

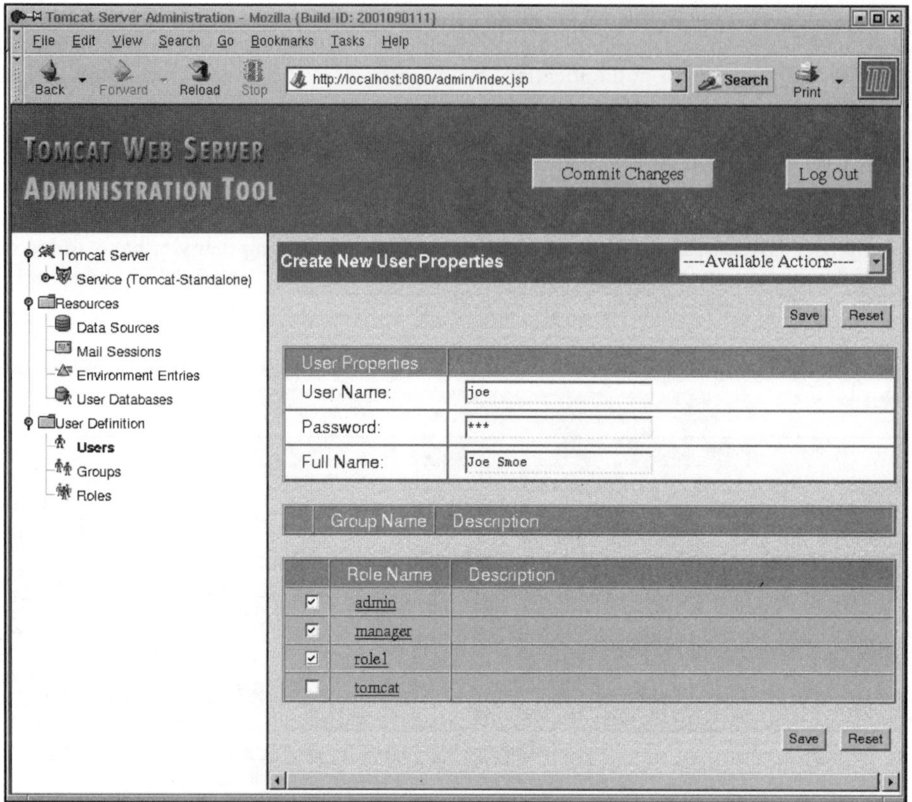

Click the **Save** button. Note that all the user, password, and role information shown in `admin` are accessed through the configured UserDatabase. Now, after clicking **Save**, even without shutting down Tomcat, go to the `tomcat-users.xml` file and check the following entry has been added:

```
<user username="joe" password="joe" fullName="Joe Smoe"
roles="admin,manager,role1"/>
```

The **Save** command has caused the UserDatabase implementation to save the changes made to the database back to the XML persistent representation on disk.

Summary

In this chapter, we have examined Tomcat's configuration topics that are beyond the basic "up-and-running" requirements.

In particular, we have spent significant time exploring the standard valves that are part of the Tomcat distribution. We saw how Access Log valve can enable logging of resource access at the web application, virtual host, or globally across all the virtual hosts. This valve is highly configurable and we can customize the name as well as the actual format of the log entries, although the `common` format is the best known.

The standard single sign-on valve enhances the user experience since users no longer have to type in their username and password every time they switch between web applications running on the same host. This valve caches the credentials and passes them between the applications as required.

The Request Filter valves are easily configured to control all incoming requests that are to be processed or blocked entirely. These valves can block a list of IP addresses or host names.

The less known Request Dumper valve can be used to debug other valves and/or components, and to visualize the effects of scoping.

After the exploration of valves, we turned our attention to the Persistent Session Manager. This component can be used to provide a measure of reliability to Tomcat. It can periodically back up sessions on disk, and also swap out dormant sessions to make room for active sections. Most importantly, it will restore sessions from disk when it starts up. This enables sessions to persist between restarts of the Tomcat server.

Next, we saw how to configure JNDI resources for use within web applications. JNDI provides a uniform interface to different directory services. This makes it possible to write only one set of lookup code across different directory services. JNDI is an integral of many J2EE standard APIs including JDBC and JavaMail. We configured JNDI resources such as JDBC connection factory and JavaMail sessions. We also learned a little about the UserDatabase, Tomcat's built-in store for user, password, and role mapping.

After our JNDI discussions, we examined Realms in Tomcat, and saw how they provide a web application with access to a database for authentication, and also support the Container Managed Security model of Tomcat. Container Managed Security is a requirement to be compliant with J2EE. There are many different types of realm implementations. We discussed the configuration of JDBC realm, JNDI realm, Memory realm, and lastly UserDatabase as a realm.

In the next chapter, we will cover two additional advanced configuration topics that we have not examined in detail here: SSI and CGI configuration for Tomcat.

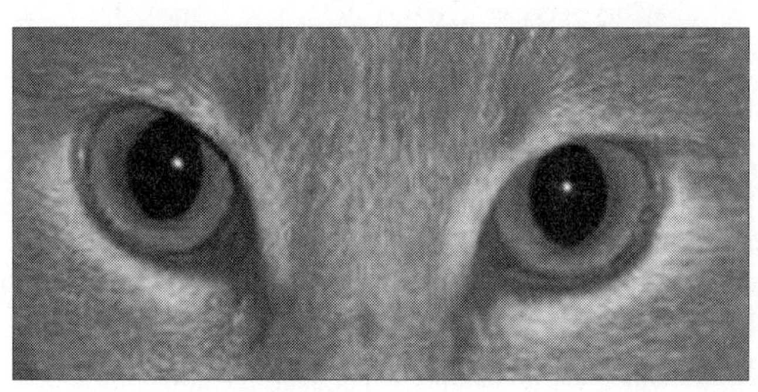

9

Class Loaders

Every Java developer makes extensive use of class loaders, often without knowing about it. This is because each time a given class is instantiated as an object (or referenced statically), that class must be loaded into memory. Thus, even statements as simple as `String greeting = "hello"` or `int maxValue = Integer.MAX_VALUE` make use of a class loader; they require the `String` class and the `Integer` class to be loaded, respectively.

While class loaders are designed to operate fairly transparently from the developer's point of view, there are subtleties to their use that are important to understand. In fact, spending some time to comprehend the issues with class loaders may make your Java experience a much more pleasant one. Not understanding class loaders can banish developers painfully into the abyss of endless classpath problems and `ClassNotFound` exceptions.

So why do we have a class loader primer in a Tomcat book? Well, it turns out that class loaders and their behavior are a big part of Tomcat. Following the Servlet specification, Tomcat is required to allocate a unique class loader to each web application. What does this mean? Why is it so?

We'll address these questions and more in this chapter. After we explain class loaders in general and Tomcat's class loaders in particular, we'll also touch on some common problems related to class loaders. By the end of this chapter, you'll not only be familiar with class loaders in general but also know how they relate specifically to Tomcat. We will cover these points in the chapter:

- An overview of class loaders
- Security issues with class loaders
- Tomcat and class loaders

- Dynamic class reloading
- Common class loader issues

Class Loader Overview

Two important attributes of Java are:

- Java is platform-independent
- Java was built for distributed network architectures

To fulfill both of these goals, Java had to innovate in many key areas. One of these areas is in the basic issue of how to load code libraries. If Java is to be truly platform-independent, it cannot rely on a specific type of filesystem (or even a set of dozens of filesystems) for loading its libraries, as many small so-called embedded computer systems don't even have a filesystem.

Furthermore, because Java was designed to load classes from various sources spread across a network, simply loading classes from a filesystem won't work.

To deal with these issues, the Java architects introduced the notion of a **class loader**. The role of the class loader is to abstract the process of loading classes, making the process completely independent of any type of underlying data store, be it a network or a hard drive.

For example, consider the following simple program:

```
import com.wrox.MyObject;

public class Simple {
    public static void main(String[] args) {
        MyObject myObject = new MyObject();
    }
}
```

When the line `MyObject myObject = new MyObject()` is executed, the Java Virtual Machine (JVM) asks a class loader to find a class named `com.wrox.MyObject` and return it as a `Class` object. The class loader is then free to do whatever it is designed to do to locate the class. Possible actions include searching a file system, checking a ROM chip, or loading a class from a network. Once returned, the `Class` object that represents the `MyObject` class is then used to instantiate the `myObject` instance. The diagram opposite depicts this

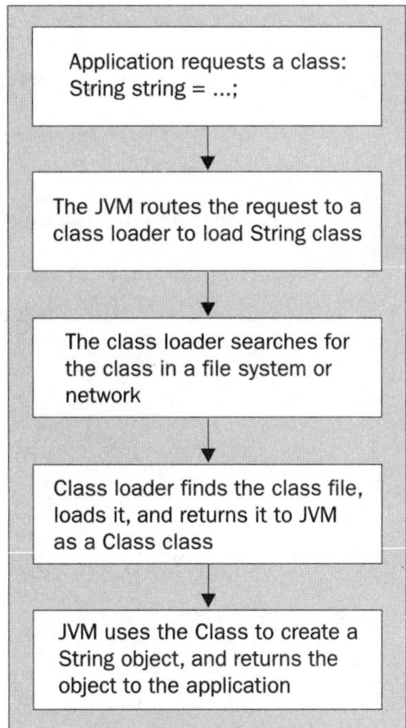

Standard J2SE Class Loaders

We've just talked about how class loaders work in theory; now let's take a look at how the Java 2 Standard Edition handles class loading in practice.

Ever since the J2SE 1.2, the JVM has made use of three distinct class loaders, which we will be discussing next along with their roles:

- Bootstrap class loader
- Extension class loader
- System class loader

These class loaders sit in a hierarchy with the system class loader at the bottom and the bootstrap class loader at the top. The relationships are parent-child, so the parent of the system class loader is the extension class loader. The importance of this relationship shall soon become clear.

Bootstrap Class Loader

As its name implies, the bootstrap class loader is used by the JVM to load those Java classes that are necessary for the JVM to function. Actually, the bootstrap class loader is responsible for loading **all** the core Java classes (such as `java.lang.*` and `java.io.*`).

As class loaders are written in Java, the bootstrap class loader solves a "chicken-and-egg" problem: How can the JVM load a Java-based class loader when the class loader itself must be loaded in? Including the bootstrap class loader in the JVM itself solves this problem and for this reason, the various JVM vendors (including Sun) implement the bootstrap class loader using native code.

For the Curious

We explained that the bootstrap class loader loads the core Java classes, but where exactly does the bootstrap class loader find these classes?

It turns out that the answer to this question varies from vendor to vendor. Sun's JVM 1.3.1 looks in the following locations:

```
jdk/jre/lib/rt.jar
jdk/jre/lib/i18n.jar
jdk/jre/lib/sunrsasign.jar
jdk/jre/classes
```

The paths for Sun's JVM 1.4.0 include a few additional items (highlighted):

```
/java/jdk1.4/jre/lib/rt.jar
/java/jdk1.4/jre/lib/i18n.jar
/java/jdk1.4/jre/lib/sunrsasign.jar
/java/jdk1.4/jre/lib/jsse.jar
/java/jdk1.4/jre/lib/jce.jar
/java/jdk1.4/jre/lib/charsets.jar
/java/jdk1.4/jre/classes
```

On the other hand, Apple's JVM 1.3.1 uses these locations instead:

```
/System/Library/Frameworks/JavaVM.framework/Versions/1.3.1/Classes/ui.jar
/System/Library/Frameworks/JavaVM.framework/Versions/1.3.1/Classes/classes.jar
/System/Library/Frameworks/JavaVM.framework/Versions/1.3.1/Classes/i18n.jar
/System/Library/Frameworks/JavaVM.framework/Versions/1.3.1/Classes/sunrsasign.jar
```

Extension Class Loader

Java 1.2 introduced the standard extension mechanism. Normally, when developers wish to have the JVM look in certain locations for class files, they make use of the `CLASSPATH` environment variable. Sun introduced the standard extension mechanism as an alternative method; we can drop JAR files into a standard extension directory and the JVM will automatically find them.

The extension class loader is responsible for loading all the classes in one or more extension directories. Just as the bootstrap class loader's paths can vary on different JVMs, so can the standard extension paths. On Sun's JVM, the standard extension directory is:

```
/jdk/jre/lib/ext
```

One advantage the standard extension mechanism is that developers don't have to struggle with a huge `CLASSPATH` environment variable as they add more and more libraries to their system. We will consider another advantage a little later in this chapter.

System Class Loader

The system class loader locates its classes in those directories and JAR files specified in the `CLASSPATH` environment variable. The system class loader is also used to load in your application's entry-point class (that is, the one with the `main()` method) and is the default class loader for loading in any other classes not covered by the previous two class loaders.

The Delegation Model

As we've just discussed, J2SE has three different class loaders. If you instantiate a `java.lang.String`, the bootstrap class loader takes care of loading it, and if you instantiate your own class, the system class loader takes care of it. How does the JVM know which class loader to use?

The answer is in the **delegation model**. In every version of Java since JDK 1.2, whenever a class loader receives a request to load a class, it first asks its parent to fulfil the request (in other words, it **delegates** the request to its parent class loader). If the parent succeeds, then the resulting class object is returned, and only if a class loader's parent (and its parent, and so on) fails to load the class, does the original class loader attempt to load the class itself.

Thus, when you reference a class in your Java program, the JVM will automatically route a request to the system class loader load the class necessary. The system class loader will then request that the extension class loader to load the specified class, which in turn will request that the bootstrap class loader load the class. The process stops with the bootstrap class loader, which will then check the core Java libraries for the requested class.

If the class doesn't exist in the core libraries, then the extension class loader will check the standard extensions for the class. If it's still not found, then the system class loader will check the locations specified by the `CLASSPATH` variable for the class. If the class still could not be located, then a `ClassNotFoundException` will be thrown. The following diagram shows this in brief:

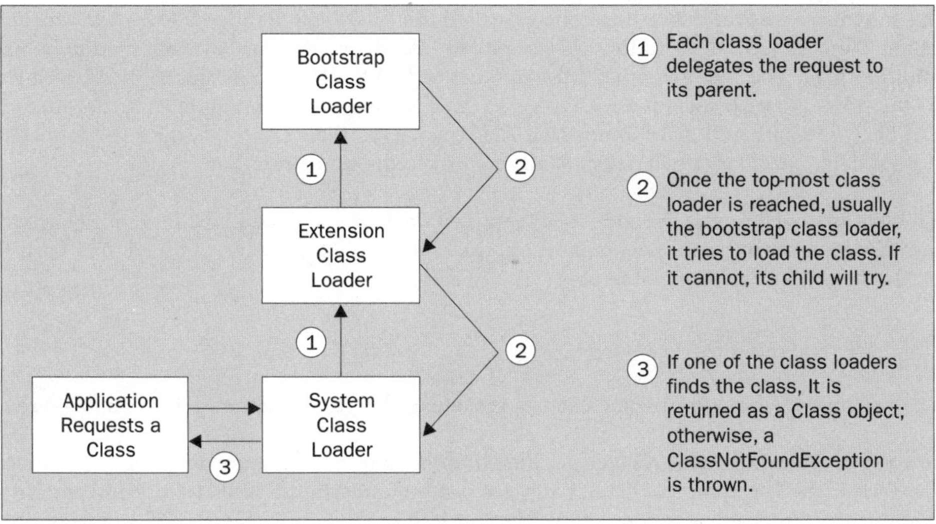

Let's take a look at an example. Consider the following code:

```
import com.wrox.MyObject;

public class Simple {
  public static void main(String[] args) {
    String myString = "test";
    MyObject myObject = new MyObject();
  }
}
```

In this example, when the JVM sees the reference to `java.lang.String` it will request that the system class loader try to load the class. However, before attempting to load the class itself, the system class loader will request that the extension class loader load it, and the extension class loader will pass the request to the bootstrap class loader. Since the bootstrap class loader has no parent, it will check its paths for `java.lang.String`, and it will find it in the `rt.jar` file (at least, on Sun JVMs). The bootstrap class loader will then return the class back down the chain and the `String` class will be returned to the JVM.

The reference to `com.wrox.MyObject` will also trigger the JVM to make the same request to the system class loader, and with the `String` class, the system class loader will delegate this to the extension class loader and the extension class loader to the bootstrap class loader. However, the bootstrap class loader will not find the `com.wrox.MyObject` class, and will return nothing to the extension class loader. The extension class loader will check its paths and it will also not find the class (unless of course the class has been explicitly placed in the extensions directory), and it too will return nothing to the system class loader. The system class loader will search in the `CLASSPATH` locations, and will find the `com.wrox.MyObject` there. The system class loader will then return the class to the JVM.

Endorsed Standard Override Mechanism

Java 1.4 has introduced an interesting concept called the Endorsed Standards Override Mechanism. Over time, the core J2SE distribution has been including more and more of what used to be optional extensions to Java. The best example of this is the new JAXP XML parser that is distributed with J2SE 1.4. As the XML parser is included with the core Java classes, the bootstrap class loader loads it. As a result, if developers try and place alternative XML parsers in their classpath, their version will never be used; the system class loader will delegate all requests to the bootstrap class loader.

The problem is solved by the override mechanism. If developers place JAR files that replace the standard XML parser in some specific location, the bootstrap class loader will load their class files instead. In the J2SE 1.4, this location is:

```
$JAVA_HOME/lib/endorsed
```

Users can change the path for this mechanism by setting the `java.endorsed.dirs` property.

Before you start thinking about replacing a bunch of the core libraries, however, only certain packages can be overridden. The complete list of packages can be found in the J2SE 1.4 documentation (http://java.sun.com/j2se/1.4.1/docs/guide/standards/); in short, only the CORBA classes and the XML parser classes can be overridden with this mechanism.

Class Loader Attributes

Now that we've talked about the standard class loaders that are in the J2SE, as well as the delegation model that governs how these class loaders interact, let's talk more about how class loaders work.

Lazy Loading (Loading Classes On Demand)

None of these three class loaders pre-load all classes in the paths that they search for classes. Instead, they load the classes on demand. Such behavior is said to be lazy because the object waits to load the data until it is requested. While laziness in human beings is generally regard as a negative trait, it is actually quite a positive one for class loaders, for a few reasons. These are:

- **Faster performance**
  At the time of initialization, if each class loader had to load every other class it would potentially take much longer to initialize the JVM.
- **Efficiency**
  More efficient memory usage as loading in all the classes would consume more memory than necessary if loaded early on.
- **Flexibility**
  JAR files and classes can be added to the search paths of all the class loaders even after the class loaders have been initialized.

> **Note that when a class is loaded, all of its parent classes must also be loaded. Thus, if `ClassB` extends `ClassA`, and `ClassB` is loaded, then `ClassA` is also loaded.**

Class Caching

The standard J2SE class loaders look up classes on demand, but once a class is loaded into a class loader, it will stay loaded (cached) for as long as the JVM is running.

Separate Namespaces

Each class loader is assigned its own unique namespace. In other words, if the bootstrap class loader loads a class named `sun.misc.ClassA`, and the system class loader loads in a class named `sun.misc.ClassB`, the two classes will be considered to be in distinct packages and will not have access to each other's package-private members.

Creating a Custom Class Loader

We can even create our own class loaders, which may seem like one of those pointless tasks that only hardcore professional Java academics would ever want to do. However, not only is creating custom class loaders fairly easy, but it could in fact give you flexibility that you never knew you could have in your application.

The key to creating your own class loader is the `java.lang.ClassLoader` class. This abstract class contains all the logic necessary for transforming the bytes of a compiled class file into a class object that can then be used in your applications. It does not, however, provide any mechanism for locating and loading in such files.

The J2SE comes with two concrete implementations of `ClassLoader`: they are `SecureClassLoader` and `URLClassLoader`. The `SecureClassLoader` is a relatively thin wrapper around `ClassLoader` that ties class loading into Java's security model (security issues are covered in the next section). Like `ClassLoader`, it too does not provide a mechanism for loading class files.

`URLClassLoader`, a subclass of `SecureClassLoader`, provides the default Java mechanism for locating class files in directories or JAR files on a filesystem, or across a network. The Extension and system class loaders are both descended from `URLClassLoader`, though they do not directly extend this class. Tomcat uses its own class loaders extensively; we'll talk more about these a little later in this chapter.

So why would you want to create your own class loader? Here are some neat tricks you can perform with your own class loaders:

- Search a database instead of a filesystem for classes
- Load different classes with the same fully-qualified name
- Swap your classes with new versions at runtime
- Load classes before you need them

Additional Class Loader Information

Covering all the details associated with writing your own class loader is an advanced development topic and beyond the scope of this chapter. If this topic intrigues you and you'd like to learn more, here are some excellent resources:

- http://java.sun.com/j2se/1.4/docs/api/java/lang/ClassLoader.html – the `ClassLoader` API JavaDoc file, which is fairly transparent and easy to understand
- www.javageeks.com/Papers/ – has a few white papers related to class loaders, notably Understanding Class.forName() and Using the BootClasspath are recommended reading

Security and Class Loaders

Class loading is at the very center of the Java security model. After all, if a rogue third party were to get your application to load a custom version of `java.lang.String` that had the nasty side-effect of deleting your hard drive whenever it is instantiated, that would be problematic for you and for Sun. Understanding the security features of the class loader architecture will help you understand how Tomcat's class loader system works.

The Java class loader architecture tackles the security problem with the following strategies:

- Class loader delegation
- Core class restriction
- Separate class loader namespaces
- Security manager

Let's talk briefly about each one.

Class Loader Delegation

Recall the class loader delegation model that we talked about earlier in the chapter: each class loader first checks if its parent has the requested class before it attempts to load it.

The delegation model is described by many as a security feature. After all, it seems like it should be: anyone trying to load their own false versions of the core Java classes will fail because the bootstrap class loader has first shot at any class, and it will always find the real copies of the core Java classes.

However, the delegation model on its own is flawed as a security mechanism because class loaders are **not required** to implement it. In other words, if you want to create a class loader that doesn't follow the delegation model, you are free to do so.

Core Class Restriction

So, if a custom class loader doesn't have to delegate requests to the system class loader, what's to stop a custom class loader from loading in its own copy of `java.lang.String`? What would happen?

Fortunately, it's not possible for any class loader written in Java to instantiate a core Java class. The `ClassLoader` abstract class, from which all class loaders must descend, blocks the creation of any class whose fully qualified name begins with `java`. Thus, no false `java.*` classes can be caught hanging around. As the bootstrap class loader is not written in Java and does not descend from `ClassLoader`, it is not subject to this restriction.

By implication, this restriction indicates that all class loaders must at least delegate to the bootstrap class loader; otherwise, when the class is loaded, there is no way for the class loader to load in `java.lang.Object`, from which all objects must descend.

Thus, the delegation model by itself does not provide security. It is the core class restriction mechanism that prevents rogue class loaders from tampering with the core Java libraries (at least at runtime).

Separate Class Loader Namespaces

As we saw earlier, each class loader has its own namespace and so there is a way to load two different classes with the same fully-qualified name. Since every single class loader used has its own completely distinct namespace, class loader A loads a class named `com.wrox.Book`, and class loader B can also load a completely different class also named `com.wrox.Book`.

Having separate namespaces is an important security feature because it prevents custom class loaders from stepping over each other or the system class loader. No matter how hard a renegade class loader may try, it cannot replace a class loaded by a different class loader, nor access the package-private members in classes of a package with the same name that was class loaded from a different location.

Security Manager

If you really want to make sure that no one can damage your program with custom class loaders, you can simply disallow the use of custom class loaders in your program. This can be done through the `SecurityManager` class, which is Java's general mechanism for applying security restrictions in applications.

With a security manager, and its associated policy files, you can disallow (or allow) a large number of tasks. For example, you can prevent a program from opening any socket to some network host, or prevent it from opening any file on the local filesystem, and of course, also prevent an application from loading a class loader. In fact, you have the following options for preventing class loader-related operations:

- Prevent the loading of any class loader
- Prevent a reference to any class loader being obtained (including the system class loader)
- Prevent the context class loader of any thread being changed

There are only two steps:

- Configure a policy file with the permissions you want for a given application
- Turn on the application's security manager

There is a lot more to the security manager than this, but the complexity of the topic means that we've dedicated Chapter 16 to it rather than cover it here. For more information on using policy files and the Security Manager, see the following URLs:

- http://java.sun.com/j2se/1.4/docs/guide/security/PolicyFiles.html
- http://java.sun.com/j2se/1.4/docs/guide/security/permissions.html
- http://java.sun.com/j2se/1.4/docs/guide/security/smPortGuide.html

Tomcat and Class Loaders

After covering how class loaders function in general, we're ready to talk about how Tomcat's class loaders work. Recall the default Java class loader hierarchy:

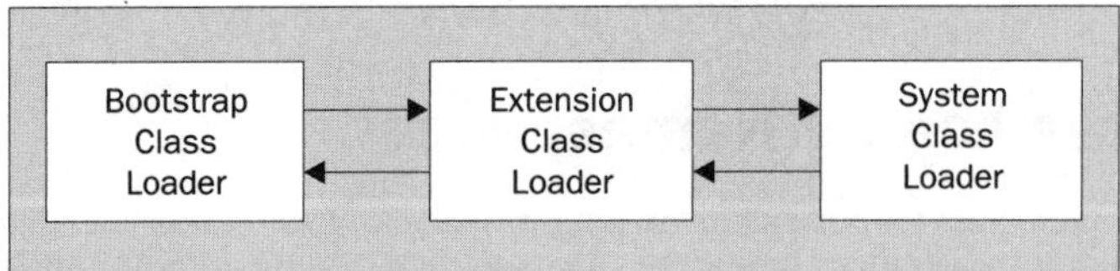

Tomcat builds on these class loaders by adding its own after the system class loader. They are shown in the diagram below starting from the common class loader, Catalina class loader, shared class loader, and web application class loader:

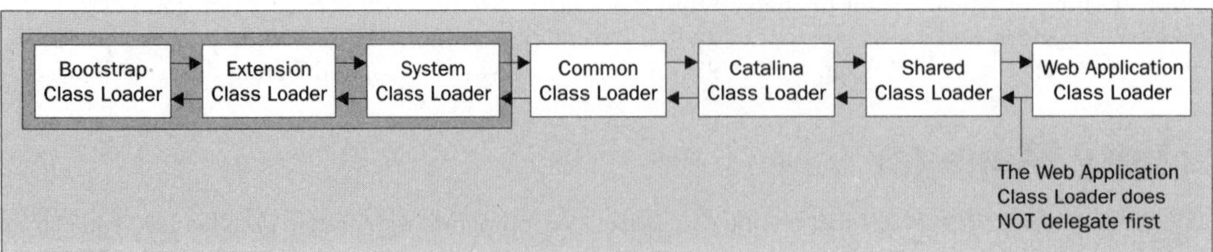

We will talk about each one in detail in the following sections.

System Class Loader

Tomcat uses the default system class loader, but it does something a little different from the default behavior of the JVM. In the Tomcat startup file (`startup.bat` on Win32, `startup.sh` on Unix), the `CLASSPATH` environment variable is cleared. In its place, Tomcat points `CLASSPATH` to two Tomcat files: `bootstrap.jar` and `tools.jar`. You'll recall that the system class loader searches the `CLASSPATH`, but since the `CLASSPATH` is set to these two files, Tomcat nullifies the normal effect of this class loader; whatever you set the `CLASSPATH` to before executing the startup script is thrown away.

The `bootstrap.jar` file contains those classes necessary for Tomcat to start up and the `tools.jar` file contains the `javac` compiler, which is used to compile JSP pages into class files at runtime.

Endorsed Standards Override Mechanism

On startup, Tomcat 4.0.x changes the Endorsed Standards Override Mechanism to point to the following directories, rather than the default ones mentioned earlier:

```
$CATALINA_HOME/bin
$CATALINA_HOME/common/lib
```

Tomcat 4.1.x uses slightly different paths:

```
$CATALINA_HOME/bin
$CATALINA_HOME/common/endorsed
```

The net result is that Tomcat's XML parser is preferred to the one shipped with Java 1.4 (if you're using 1.4 and have not downloaded the Tomcat Light Edition that doesn't include the XML parser).

Common Class Loader

Next in the hierarchy is the common class loader that loads classes that are used by Tomcat and are also publicly available to all web applications. It loads these class files from two different locations:

- `$CATALINA_HOME/common/lib` – for JAR files
- `$CATALINA_HOME/common/classes` – for class files

Tomcat includes a number of JAR files in `$CATALINA_HOME/common/lib`. As the Tomcat 4.0.x series differs from the Tomcat 4.1.x series, we'll include both versions in a side-by-side comparison. As of this writing, Tomcat 4.0.4 is the latest version in the 4.0.x series, and 4.1.8 beta is the latest in the 4.1.x series. In the table below * indicates these files are not included with the "Light Edition" distribution of Tomcat:

JAR File	4.0.4	4.1.8b	Description
`activation.jar`	X*	X*	Java activation framework – used by the JavaMail API

Table continued on following page

JAR File	4.0.4	4.1.8b	Description
`ant.jar`		X	The popular Jakarta Ant
`commons-collections.jar`		X	Another Jakarta project is the Commons library of general-purpose code; the Collections component adds features to the standard J2SE Collections framework
`commons-dbcp.jar`		X*	DBCP provides database and object pooling services
`commons-logging-api.jar`		X	Logging is an abstraction layer for the various logging packages on the market
`commons-pool.jar`		X*	Pool is also an object pooling service
`jasper-compiler.jar`		X	The Jasper compiler, which turns JSP files into servlets
`jasper-runtime.jar`		X	More Jasper files – these are required to execute JSP pages that have compiled into servlets
`jdbc2_0-stdext.jar`	X*	X*	JDBC 2.0 standard extensions
`jndi.jar`	X*	X*	JNDI API – not loaded by the common class loader unless running under JDK 1.2 (JDK 1.3+ includes it)
`jta-spec1_0_1.jar` or `jta.jar`	X*	X*	JTA (Java Transaction API) API
`mail.jar`	X*	X*	JavaMail API
`naming-common.jar`	X	X	JNDI implementation – used to provide the default JNDI naming context
`naming-factory.jar`		X	More JNDI support files – these are object factories exposed via the default JNDI context
`naming-resources.jar`	X	X	JNDI directory context implementation – provides interface for retrieving static resources
`servlet.jar`	X	X	Servlet API
`tyrex-0.9.7.0.jar`	X*		JTA/JTS/OTS transaction manager and a `DataSource` connection pool implementation
`xerces.jar`	X*		The Xerces XML parser and JAXP 1.1 API

While you may reference all of the above listed APIs, you should not place your own classes or JARs in `$CATALINA_HOME/common/lib`. If you want to place classes and JAR files where they are visible to all web applications, you should put them where the shared class loader can see them.

Putting your own classes in the common class loader paths would be bad for at least two reasons, one trivial and one non-trivial:

- The trivial reason is that it's easy to forget which classes/JAR files are yours and which belong to Tomcat. Maintenance would therefore be tricky, especially for others who would not expect user classes to be in those locations.
- The non-trivial reason is that placing your own classes in those paths could conceivably cause compatibility problems with Tomcat. For example, if you placed your own XML parser in this directory, and it wasn't tested with Tomcat, it could introduce very hard-to-fix bugs. The same would be true if you introduced an older version of the Servlet API into these paths.

Catalina Class Loader

The catalina class loader is used to load all of the Tomcat classes that are only specific to Tomcat (that is, not publicly defined APIs, and so on). These classes are not visible to other applications, as mandated by the Servlet specification. They are stored in `$CATALINA_HOME/server/lib` and `$CATALINA_HOME/server/classes`:

JAR File	4.0.4	4.1.8b	Description
`catalina.jar`	X	X	Catalina servlet container classes.
`catalina-ant.jar`		X	Support files that enable easy deployment via Ant.
`commons-beanutils.jar`		X	Jakarta web-site: "BeanUtils provides easy-to-use wrappers around the Java reflection and introspection APIs".
`commons-digester.jar`		X	Jakarta web-site: "Digester is an XML-to-Java-object mapping utility commonly used for parsing XML configuration files".
`commons-logging.jar`	X	X	This is also a wrapper around logging API implementations.
`commons-modeler.jar`		X	Jakarta web site: "Modeler provides mechanisms to create Model MBeans compatible with the Java Management Extensions (JMX) specification".
`jaas.jar`		X	The Java Authentication and Authorization Service API.
`jakarta-regexp-1.2.jar`	X	X	Jakarta's well-known Java regular expression implementation.

Table continued on following page

JAR File	4.0.4	4.1.8b	Description
mx4j-jmx.jar		X	MX4J (http://mx4j.sourceforge.net/) is an open source implementation of the Java Management Extensions (JMX) API; JMX is used for monitoring and management of deployed applications.
servlets-XXX.jar	X	X	Some of Tomcat's basic services are actually provided by servlets, such as SSI, CGI, serving static content, and so on. These JAR files contain such servlets.
tomcat-ajp.jar	X		AJP connector classes.
tomcat-coyote.jar	X	X	Coyote connector classes.
tomcat-http11.jar	X	X	HTTP/1.1 connector classes.
tomcat-jk.jar		X	JK connector classes.
tomcat-jk2.jar		X	JK2 connector classes.
tomcat-util.jar	X	X	Shared classes for the various and sundry Tomcat connectors.
tomcat-warp.jar		X	WARP connector classes.
warp.jar	X		WARP connector classes.

Shared Class Loader

The shared class loader is a bit like the common class loader, except that you can place your own classes and JAR files into the shared class loader directories. Under Tomcat 4.0.x, the shared class loader looks in `$CATALINA_HOME/lib` and `$CATALINA_HOME/classes`. However, Tomcat 4.1.x has changed its location to `$CATALINA_HOME/shared/lib` and `$CATALINA_HOME/shared/classes`. Anytime you have some general classes that you want shared amongst two or more web applications, this is where you should put them.

Despite having the common class loader all to themselves, the Tomcat developers have also placed some of their JAR files in the shared class loader too. They are:

JAR File	4.0.4	4.1.8b	Description
jasper-compiler.jar	X	X	The Jasper compiler, which turns JSP files into servlets
jasper-runtime.jar	X	X	More Jasper files – these are required to execute JSP pages that have compiled into servlets

JAR File	4.0.4	4.1.8b	Description
naming-factory.jar	X		More JNDI support files – these are object factories exposed via the default JNDI context

Web Application Class Loader

Each web application also has its own class loader, which looks in `$CATALINA_HOME/webapps/<webapp>/WEB-INF/lib` and .../`WEB-INF/classes` for JARs and class files. There are two things that make the web application class loader unique. First, each web application has its own instance of this class loader, which means that no two web applications can see each other's class files.

Second, the web application class loader does **not** use the delegation pattern that class loaders are encouraged to use. Instead, it tries to load classes first, before delegating the request to the other class loaders. This behavior makes it easy for web applications to override classes in the shared and common class loaders on a per-web application basis.

Class Loader Order Revisited

To review how these various Tomcat class loaders work together, let's show what happens when an individual application requests a class. The following is a list of class loaders that will look for a class in the order that they attempt to find it:

- The web application class loader looks in `$CATALINA_HOME/webapp/<webapp>/WEB-INF/lib` and `$CATALINA_HOME/webapp/<webapp>/WEB-INF/classes`
- The bootstrap class loader looks in the core Java classes:
- If you're using Java 1.4, the bootstrap class loader will also look in $CATALINA_HOME/bin and $CATALINA_HOME/common/lib ($CATALINA_HOME/common/endorsed on Tomcat 4.1.x) for alternative implementations of CORBA and XML parsing classes
- The system class loader looks in `$CATALINA_HOME/bin/bootstrap.jar` and `$JAVA_HOME/lib/tools.jar`
- The common class loader looks in `$CATALINA_HOME/common/lib` and `$CATALINA_HOME/common/classes`
- The shared class loader looks in `$CATALINA_HOME/lib` and `$CATALINA_HOME/classes` (or `$CATALINA_HOME/shared/lib` and `$CATALINA_HOME/shared/classes` under Tomcat 4.1.x)

Dynamic Class Reloading

As we discussed earlier, once a class loader has loaded a class, it caches the class. This means that future requests for the class always get the cached copy returned to them, and thus if the class in the file-system is changed while the JVM is running, the changed copy will be ignored.

However, because Tomcat uses its own class loader to load each web application, it can accomplish dynamic class reloading simply by halting the web application and then reloading it using a new class loader.

The web application's original class loader is then orphaned and thus garbage collected at the JVM's convenience. This eliminates the need to restart the JVM when new versions of classes are deployed.

There are two mechanisms for instructing Tomcat to reload a web application:

- Configure Tomcat to scan `<webapp>/WEB-INF/classes` and `<webapp>/WEB-INF/lib` for changes
- Explicitly reload the web application with the Tomcat `manager` application

Note that in both cases, Tomcat does not simply direct its class loaders to dump their caches and reload from disk, but rather, when it detects a change or receives an explicit reload instruction, it reloads and restarts the entire web application.

Performing either of the above tasks is fairly simple and is covered in Chapters 5 and 7.

Common Class Loader Pitfalls

There are a couple of common problems that occur when dealing with Tomcat's class loaders. The solutions to these problems are derived from the information we've covered so far.

Packages Split Amongst Different Class Loaders

As each class loader has its own unique namespace, it has a very practical application in Tomcat. If you have multiple classes in the same package (for example, `com.wrox.servlets`), they must be loaded by the same class loader. For example, if you have two classes, `com.wrox.servlets.MyServlet` and `com.wrox.servlets.Constants`, you must place them both in the same class loader directory, such as `/WEB-INF/classes` or `$CATALINA_HOME/classes`. If you split them up, they will no longer have access to each other's `private`, `protected`, or package-private (default) members.

Singletons

A singleton is a class designed so that it can only be instantiated one time in any given JVM. Say you have a singleton class that is an interface to an object pool of some kind. You want to share this singleton amongst multiple web applications, and wish to maintain the contract that only one instance be created in a single JVM.

The singleton class could look something like this:

```
public class ObjectPool {
    private static ObjectPool objectPool = null;

    private ObjectPool {
        // initialize object
```

```
    }

    public synchronized static ObjectPool getInstance() {
        if (objectPool == null) {
            objectPool = new ObjectPool();
        }
        return objectPool;
    }
}
```

So, where do you put this class? Placing this class in the web application class loader path guarantees that each web application will create a new instance of this class. This is because each web application has its own class loader, and class loaders maintain distinct namespaces.

The solution is to place this class in the shared class loader paths, where the singleton will be shared amongst all web applications as they all share the same class loader.

XML Parsers

There have been a lot of different XML parsers created and a lot of different versions of those parsers. The default distributions of Tomcat include the Xerces XML parser. However, if you're using JDK 1.4, it includes its own XML parser. You can use this parser instead of Xerces by downloading the Light Edition of Tomcat. Depending on your architecture, you need to do the following:

- JDK 1.4 + Tomcat Light Edition + your own XML parser
  If you're relying on the JDK 1.4 Endorsed Standards Override Mechanism to introduce your own XML parser, and you're using the Light Edition of Tomcat, **Tomcat will break your configuration**. This is because Tomcat sets the `java.endorsed.dirs` property, and you'll have to make sure you place your XML parser in the shared class loader or web application class loader path.

- JDK 1.4 + Tomcat Normal Edition + your own XML parser
  As Tomcat uses the Endorsed Standards Override Mechanism, your web applications will not be using the JDK 1.4 XML parser. Now, if you want to use your own XML parser instead of Tomcat's Xerces parser, you can place your XML parser in the web application class loader path.

  If you want to share your XML parser among multiple web applications, you could place it in the shared class loader path, but because the common class loader is higher in the delegation chain, Tomcat's Xerces parser will be used first.

  To solve this problem, you could either use the Tomcat Light Edition or move `xerces.jar` from the common class loader path to the system class loader path, which would make it available to Tomcat but invisible to your application.

- Versions before JDK 1.4 + Tomcat + your own XML parser
  The instructions for this configuration are the same as the ones above.

Summary

In this chapter we saw how class loaders abstract the process of loading class files before the first instantiation and make them available for use. Java comes along with class loaders that support loading classes from the local filesystem to the network and also gives developers the facility to create their own custom class loaders. The three basic class loaders we saw were bootstrap, extension, and system class loaders.

Class loaders use the delegation model where every class loader passes the request to its parent until the bootstrap class loader is reached, and then each class loader looks for the class, and if it can't find it, goes back down the chain. Implementing the delegation model is optional, but class loaders are basically useless if they don't delegate to the bootstrap class loader at some point. There are also some advantages of having a unique namespace for each class loader.

The Java security model prevents the misuse of custom class loaders by allowing only the bootstrap class loader to load classes that start with `java.*`. Also by using the Security Manager, an application can forbid the use of custom class loaders.

Lastly we saw that in Tomcat there are four different class loaders: common, Catalina, shared, and web application and, to share classes with all web applications, users should use the shared class loader.

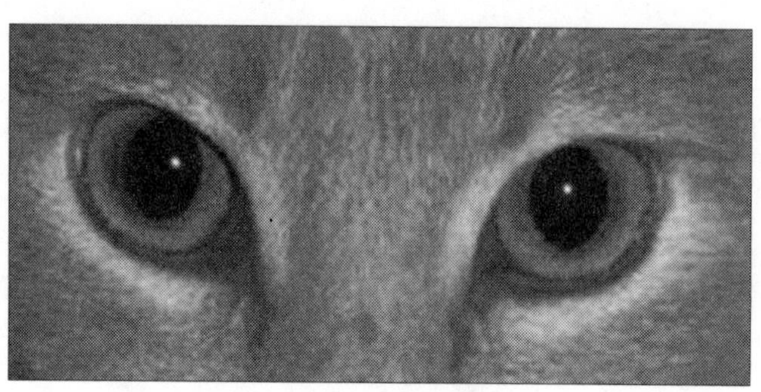

10

HTTP Connectors

When we use Tomcat out of the box to run web applications, it is able to serve HTML pages without any additional configuration. The reason this works is because it comes configured with an HTTP connector that can handle requests from a user's web browser. Because of this connector, Tomcat can function as a standalone web server, and serve static HTML pages in addition to handling servlets and JSP pages.

Tomcat connectors provide the external interface (over HTTP or HTTPS) to Tomcat clients. There are two kinds of connectors – those that implement an HTTP stack of their own (called HTTP connectors) and those that tie Tomcat to an external web server like Apache or IIS (called web server connectors). The next three chapters cover web server connectors.

In this chapter, we will see the configuration of the HTTP connector in Tomcat 3.x (the HTTP/1.0 connector) and Tomcat 4.x (the HTTP/1.1 connector). Later, we will look at the new Coyote HTTP/1.1 connector that makes both these connectors obsolete, and is also backward compatible with both Tomcat 4.x and Tomcat 3.x. The Coyote HTTP connector is the default connector for Tomcat 4.1.

As we mentioned earlier, we do not have to do any additional configuration to get the HTTP connector working. So why do we need this chapter? This chapter is useful if we need to modify the connector configuration.

Note that we will provide a reference to the HTTPS-related configuration here, but will leave the details of SSL setup to the security discussion in Chapter 16.

HTTP Connectors

The HTTP connectors are Java classes that implement the HTTP protocol. Tomcat 3.x's connector class (`org.apache.tomcat.modules.server.Http10Interceptor`) is invoked when there is an HTTP request on the connector port. The port that the connector listens on is specified in the `$TOMCAT_HOME/conf/server.xml` configuration file, and is usually set to 8080. The connector class has code to parse the HTTP request, and take the required action of either serving up static content or passing the request through the Tomcat servlet engine. This connector class implements the HTTP/1.0 protocol.

The corresponding connectors in Tomcat 4.x are the HTTP/1.1 (`org.apache.catalina.connector.http.HttpConnector`) and the Coyote HTTP/1.1 connector (`org.apache.coyote.tomcat4.CoyoteConnector`). Both of these implement the HTTP/1.1 protocol like the Tomcat 3.x connector and listen on the connector port for incoming HTTP requests. We will now go over these three HTTP connectors and their configuration in more detail.

Tomcat 3.x: HTTP/1.0 Connector

The HTTP/1.0 connector handles incoming HTTP requests in Tomcat 3.x. It can also optionally handle HTTPS requests – this configuration is described next.

HTTP/1.0 Configuration

The HTTP connector, like other Tomcat connectors, is configured in the `$TOMCAT_HOME/conf/server.xml` file. The default configuration for this connector is listed below:

```
<Http10Connector port="8080"
                 secure="false"
                 maxThreads="100"
                 maxSpareThreads="50"
                 minSpareThreads="10"/>
```

Note the `port` attribute. This is the only mandatory attribute, and sets up the HTTP connector to listen on port 8080. We can therefore browse over to http://<hostname>:8080/ and view the home page for the web site.

Let us now see what the other configurable attributes of the HTTP connector are:

- `reportedname`
  This attribute specifies the string to be used for the `Server` header that is sent back to the browser. The `Server` header is an optional HTTP header that provides information to the browser about server software. If this attribute is not specified, Tomcat sends back its build version. The sample HTTP header below shows this:

  ```
  HTTP/1.0 200 OK
  Content-Type: text/html

  Server: Tomcat Web Server/3.3.1 Final ( JSP 1.1; Servlet 2.2 )
  ```

- `port`
  This is the port on which Tomcat listens for client requests. The `port` attribute is the only mandatory attribute in the connector. The default connector configured (see above) has the port number set to 8080.

- `address`
  This attribute specifies the IP address on which the Tomcat server binds. The default value is an empty/`null` address, and this makes Tomcat bind to all addresses on the machine (if the host has multiple IP addresses).

- `socketCloseDelay` (Tomcat 3.3.1 and later)
  Specifies the delay (in milliseconds) before closing the socket after a request is processed. The default value is –1, which disables the delay. Setting it to a non-zero value is useful for debugging client errors that result from unread data in the HTTP request. If unread data arrives just before or during the socket closing, the client browser may get a Connection aborted by peer error.

- `backlog`
  The `backlog` attribute specifies the maximum length of the backlog queue for the Tomcat server socket. The default backlog value is 100. The maximum values that can be passed as the backlog are operating system dependent – some older BSD Unix systems have this as low as 5. Modern operating systems allow for a higher values – Linux for example has a maximum of 128.

- `timeout`
  The `timeout` attribute specifies the socket timeout value in seconds. The default value is `300` seconds.

Thread Pool Properties

The Tomcat thread pool is enabled by the `pools` attribute (below). Tomcat's servlet container uses this thread pool when it needs a new thread. Once it is done with the thread, it is returned to the pool. The other thread pool attributes (`maxThreads`, `maxSpareThreads`, and `minSpareThreads`) are meaningful only if the `pools` attribute is enabled. The default for the `pools` attribute (if it is not specified) is `true`, so thread pools are disabled only if `pools` is explicitly set to `false`.

The thread pool feature was introduced in Tomcat 3.2 – prior to that, each incoming request resulted in a new thread being created. The *Performance Tuning* section at the end of the chapter covers the performance impacts of these thread properties:

- `pools`
  The `pools` attribute enables or disables the use of a thread pool. The default value is `true`. Turning the thread pool off is a bad idea, as it forces Tomcat to allocate a new thread for each incoming connection.

- `maxThreads`
  The `maxThreads` attribute specifies the maximum number of threads in Tomcat's thread pool. The default value is 200.

- `maxSpareThreads`
  This attribute specifies the maximum number of unused threads allowed. Any unused thread in excess of this value is terminated. The default value is 50.

- `minSpareThreads`
  This is the minimum number of spare threads. Additional threads will be created as needed to keep the number of spare threads up to this number. The default value is 4.

SSL Attributes for HTTP/1.0

Tomcat can handle HTTPS requests when the `secure` attribute is enabled. If `secure` is disabled (the default), the rest of the SSL-related attributes are ignored. The sample HTTP connector configuration from `server.xml` shown below gives an example of what the SSL configuration would look like:

```
<Http10Connector port="8443"
                 secure="true"
                 keystore="/path/to/keystore"
                 keypass="keypass"
                 maxThreads="100"
                 maxSpareThreads="50"
                 minSpareThreads="10" />
```

We explain the significance of the `keystore`, `keypass`, and other SSL-related attributes in this section:

- `secure`
  The `secure` attribute enables HTTPS support when set to `true`. The default value is `false`.

- `SSLImplementation` (Tomcat 3.3.1 and later)
  This specifies the Java class that provides the wrapper to the SSL implementation. This class must implement the `org.apache.tomcat.util.net.SSLImplementation` interface.

  Currently, the supported SSL implementations are PureTLS (set `SSLImplementation` to the class name `org.apache.tomcat.util.net.PureTLSImplementation`) and JSSE (set `SSLImplementation` to the class name `org.apache.tomcat.util.net.JSSEImplementation`).

  By default, the `SSLImplementation` attribute is not set. This causes Tomcat to detect the SSL implementation and choose the one that is available. Tomcat does this by using the Java reflection API to see which of these is available in Tomcat's classpath. If both are available, PureTLS is chosen.

- `keystore`
  This attribute specifies the `keystore` containing the server certificates. It defaults to `server.pem` for PureTLS and `.keystore` for JSSE. Both these `keystore` files are assumed to be in the Tomcat user's home directory. The home directory varies with the operating system, and can be overridden by setting the `user.home` Java system property. For example, on Linux the user home would typically be `/home/<username>` where `<username>` is the userid that Tomcat runs as. Similarly, on Windows NT, the default user home directory would be `C:\Winnt\Profiles\<username>`.

- `keypass`
  The `keypass` attribute contains the `keystore` password. The default password is `changeit`. It is recommended for security reasons that we do not to use the default password.

- `clientAuth`
  This is a Boolean attribute that enables or disables the requirement for client authentication. By default, client authentication is disabled. If client authentication is enabled, the client would need to present a certificate too. This is an alternative means of validating the user's credentials as opposed to asking for a username/password combination. It is not commonly used, as it involves installing a certificate on the user's PC.

SSL Implementation-Specific Attributes

The attributes listed below are specific to an SSL implementation (PureTLS or JSSE). The PureTLS attributes are:

- `rootfile`
  The `rootfile` is the file that contains the root certificates. It defaults to `root.pem` in the user's home directory.
- `randomfile`
  The `randomfile` attribute specifies the file used to initialize random number generation. It defaults to `random.pem`.

The attributes specific to JSSE are:

- `algorithm`
  The `algorithm` attribute specifies the algorithm used to encode the certificate. The default value is `SunX509`. SunX509 is Sun's implementation of the X509 protocol. This is the Public Key Infrastructure protocol, and it specifies a format for certificates. More information on X509 is available at http://www.ietf.org/rfc/rfc2459.txt and Chapter 16.
- `keystoreType`
  The `keystoreType` attribute specifies the type of the keystore. It defaults to JKS (Java KeyStore) if not specified.
- `keystorePass`
  The `keystorePass` attribute gives the password for the keystore. If this attribute has not been specified, it is taken to be the same as the `keypass` attribute.
- `protocol`
  This the SSL protocol name. The default value is `TLS`.

Tomcat 4.0: HTTP/1.1 Connector

Tomcat 4.0 introduced a new HTTP/1.1 connector. However, the very next release (4.1) comes with an improved HTTP connector called the Coyote HTTP/1.1 connector that makes the old container obsolete.

HTTP/1.1 Configuration

The configuration attributes for the HTTP/1.1 connector are the same as those of the Coyote HTTP/1.1 connector. Hence, refer to the *Coyote HTTP/1.1 Configuration* section below. The only difference between the two is the value of the `className` attribute.

- `className`
  The `className` attribute specifies the Java class name for the connector implementation. This class must implement the `org.apache.catalina.Connector` interface. For the Tomcat 4.0 HTTP/1.1 connector, this value must be `org.apache.catalina.connector.http.HttpConnector`.

  The default configuration for this connector (from `$CATALINA_HOME/conf/server.xml`) is listed overleaf. As we can see from the configuration, the `port` attribute is set to `8080`. Because of this, Tomcat listens on port 8080 for HTTP requests:

```
<Connector className="org.apache.catalina.connector.http.HttpConnector"
           port="8080"
           minProcessors="5"
           maxProcessors="75"
           enableLookups="true"
           redirectPort="8443"
           acceptCount="10"
           debug="0"
           connectionTimeout="60000"/>
```

The other attributes (`minProcessors`, `maxProcessors`, `enableLookups`, and so on) are discussed in the next section.

Tomcat 4.1: Coyote HTTP/1.1 Connector

Coyote is a new connector architecture introduced in Tomcat 4.1. It has a simplified version of the earlier Tomcat 3.3 connector code and is a higher-performance HTTP/1.1 connector that has been re-written from scratch.

Coyote also comes with adaptors for Tomcat 4.0 and Tomcat 3.x. We will discuss the procedure for using Coyote HTTP in these older Tomcat versions later in the chapter. Older Tomcat versions, such as Tomcat 3.x, can therefore take advantage of the better performance and functionality (such as support for proxy configurations) that Coyote HTTP connector offers.

Coyote HTTP/1.1 Configuration

The default Coyote HTTP/1.1 connector configuration is listed below (from `$CATALINA_HOME/conf/server.xml`):

```
<Connector className="org.apache.coyote.tomcat4.CoyoteConnector"
           port="8080"
           minProcessors="5"
           maxProcessors="75"
           enableLookups="true"
           redirectPort="8443"
           acceptCount="10"
           debug="0"
           connectionTimeout="20000"
           useURIValidationHack="false" />
```

When Tomcat is serving HTML pages, a URL of http://localhost:8080/foo.html refers to the `foo.html` file in the `ROOT` web application (`$CATALINA_HOME/webapps/ROOT`). Similarly, http://localhost:8080/examples/bar.html refers to the `bar.html` HTML file present in the `examples` web application (`$CATALINA_HOME/webapps/examples`).

Let's see what the other configurable attributes for this connector are:

- `className`
  The `classname` attribute is set to Java class implementing the connector. This class must implement the `org.apache.catalina.Connector` interface. For the Coyote HTTP connector, this attribute should be set to the `org.apache.coyote.tomcat4.CoyoteConnector` class.

- `enableLookups`
  When this is set to `true`, all calls to `request.getRemoteHost()` perform a DNS lookup to return the host name for the remote client. When this attribute is `false`, the DNS lookup is skipped and only the IP address is returned. The default value for `enableLookups` is `true`. This attribute can be turned off for performance considerations, so as to avoid the overhead for the DNS lookup. These and other performance considerations are covered later in the *Performance Tuning* section.

- `redirectPort`
  If the connector supports only non-SSL requests, and a user request comes to this connector for an SSL resource, then Catalina will redirect that request to the `redirectPort` port number.

- `scheme`
  The `scheme` attribute is set to the name of the protocol. The value specified in `scheme` is returned by the `request.getScheme()` method call. The default value is `http`. For an SSL connector, we would set this to `https`.

- `secure`
  This attribute is set to `true` for an SSL connector. This value is returned by the `request.getScheme()` method calls. The default value is `true`.

- `acceptCount`
  The maximum queue length for incoming connection requests when all possible request processing threads are in use. Any requests received when the queue is full will be refused. This value is passed as the `backlog` parameter while creating a Tomcat server socket. The default queue length is 10 and the maximum is operating system-dependent.

- `address`
  This attribute specifies the IP address on which the Tomcat server binds. If the `address` attribute is not specified, Tomcat would bind on all addresses (if the host has multiple IP addresses).

- `port`
  The `port` attribute specifies the TCP port number on which this connector will create a server socket and await incoming connections. Only one server application can bind to a particular port number-IP address combination.

- `buffersSize`
  The `bufferSize` attribute specifies the size (in bytes) of the input stream buffer created by this connector. The default value is `2048` bytes.

- `connectionTimeout`
  The number of milliseconds this connector will wait, after accepting a connection, for the request URI line to be presented. The default value is `60000` milliseconds (60 seconds).

- `debug`
  This attribute sets the detail level of the log messages. Higher values will give higher levels of detail – the maximum value for this attribute is not documented, however turning it to 4 or 5 will print most log messages. The default value for this attribute is `zero`, which turns off debugging. All logging and exception information is automatically redirected to the logger component. Logger components can be associated with the related Engine, a virtual host, or even specified for a particular application Context. A sample logger is shown overleaf. This is the default logger that redirects all debug/error messages for this virtual host (in this case `localhost`) into the `$CATALINA_HOME/logs/localhost_log.txt` file.

```
<Host name="localhost" debug="0" appBase="webapps"
      unpackWARs="true" autoDeploy="true">

  <Logger className="org.apache.catalina.logger.FileLogger"
          directory="logs"
          prefix="localhost_log."
          suffix=".txt"
          timestamp="true"/>
```

Logger components are discussed in Chapter 5.

- `maxProcessors`
  Specifies the maximum number of request processing threads to be created by this connector, which determines the maximum number of simultaneous requests that can be handled. If there are more than `maxProcessors` concurrent requests, the remaining incoming requests are queued. See the `acceptCount` attribute on how to specify the queue length. If not specified, this attribute is set to `20`.

- `minProcessors`
  Specifies the number of request processing threads that will be created when this connector is first started. This attribute should be set to a value smaller than that set for `maxProcessors`. The default value is 5.

- `proxyName`
  The `proxyName` attribute, along with the `proxyPort` attribute below, is used when Tomcat is run behind a proxy server. It specifies the server name to be returned for `request.getServerName()` calls. See the section *Running Tomcat Behind a Proxy Server* later for more information on this.

- `proxyPort`
  As mentioned above, the `proxyPort` attribute is used in proxy configurations. It specifies the port number to be returned for `request.getServerPort()` calls. See *Running Tomcat behind a Proxy Server* below for more information on this.

- `tcpNoDelay`
  When this attribute is set to `true`, it enables the `TCP_NO_DELAY` network socket option. This improves the performance as explained later in the *Performance Tuning* section. The default value is `true`.

- `useURIValidationHack`
  The `useURIValidationHack` is an attribute added for a Tomcat 4.0-related fix. This does additional validations and normalization on the URI for security reasons. Some of these normalizations are `/%7E` at the beginning of the URI to `/~` and resolve relative path encoding in the URI (for example, `/. /` and `/./`). This attribute is only required for Tomcat 4.0, and hence can be turned off in Tomcat 4.1. We will later see how the Coyote connector can be used in Tomcat 4.0.

Configure Tomcat 4.x for SSL

The connector for the Catalina instance that supports HTTPS connections must have its `secure` attribute set to `true` and its `scheme` attribute set to `https`. In addition, it must contain a `<Factory>` element with the SSL-related configuration. The `<Factory>` attributes for SSL are listed opposite:

- `algorithm`
  The `algorithm` attribute specifies the certificate encoding algorithm to use. It defaults to `SunX509` if not specified.

- `className`
  The `className` attribute specifies the Java class that implements the SSL server socket factory. This must be set to `org.apache.coyote.tomcat4.CoyoteServerSocketFactory`.

- `clientAuth`
  If the `clientAuth` attribute is set to `true` (the default is `false`), the client needs to have a valid certificate for authenticating itself.

- `keystoreFile`
  This specifies the path name of the keystore file. The default value is a file called `.keystore` in the home directory of the user running Tomcat. The home directory is operating system-specific.

- `keystorePass`
  The `keystorePass` attribute specifies the password for the keystore file. The default password is `changeit`. This password is selected while creating the certificate keystore (see Chapter 16 for more details).

  If we set the password to something other than `changeit` and forget to add a `keystorePass` attribute correctly specifying the keystore password, Tomcat will fail to start with the error:

  ```
  LifecycleException:  Protocol handler initialization failed:
  java.io.IOException: Keystore was tampered with, or password was incorrect.
  ```

- `keystoreType`
  This specifies the type of the keystore file to be used for the server certificate. It defaults to JKS (Java Keystore). Currently, JKS is the only keystore type supported.

- `protocol`
  The `protocol` attribute specifies the version of the SSL protocol to use. It defaults to `TLS` if not specified.

An example connector with SSL configuration is shown below. This configuration is already present in the `$CATALINA_HOME/conf/server.xml` file, but is commented out. All we need to do is uncomment these lines (remove the enclosing `<!--` and `-->` symbols around the connector) and make changes if required. Note that if we change the SSL port (8443) to something else, we need to change the `redirectPort` attribute for all the non-SSL connectors to that port number too. As we mentioned earlier, the non-SSL connectors redirect users to this port if they try to access pages with a security constraint that specifies that SSL is required:

```
<Connector className="org.apache.catalina.connector.http.HttpConnector"
           port="8443"
           minProcessors="5"
           maxProcessors="75"
           enableLookups="true"
           acceptCount="10"
           debug="0"
           scheme="https"
           secure="true">
```

```
  <Factory className="org.apache.catalina.net.SSLServerSocketFactory"
           clientAuth="false"
           protocol="TLS"/>
</Connector>
```

Running Tomcat Behind a Proxy Server

A common deployment scenario involves running Tomcat behind a proxy server. In this kind of environment, the host name and port number that should be returned to the client in the HTTP response should be those specified in the request and not the actual host name and port that Tomcat is running on. These are controlled via the `proxyName` and `proxyPort` attributes that we discussed earlier. These attributes affect the values returned for the `request.getServerName()` and `request.getServerPort()` Servlet API calls.

Apache can be used as the proxy server. If we use Apache, we can use its proxy module (`mod_proxy`) to pass on the servlet requests to the Tomcat server:

```
# Load mod_proxy. The module directory is 'modules'
# on Windows and Tomcat 4.x

LoadModule proxy_module libexec/mod_proxy.so

# Not required for Tomcat 4.x
AddModule mod_proxy.c

# Pass all requests for the context path '/servlets' to Tomcat running at port
8080 on host 'hostname'
ProxyPass /servlets http://hostname:8080/servlets
ProxyPassReverse /servlets http://hostname:8080/servlets
```

And on the Tomcat side, the configuration in `server.xml` for the Coyote HTTP connector:

```
<Connector className="org.apache.coyote.tomcat4.CoyoteConnector"
               port="8080"
               proxyName=www.mydomain.com
               proxyPort="80"
               minProcessors="5"
               maxProcessors="75"
               enableLookups="true"
               redirectPort="8443"
               acceptCount="10"
               debug="0"
               connectionTimeout="20000"
               useURIValidationHack="false" />
```

We could have missed out the `proxyName` and `proxyPort` – in which case the response message would have indicated that it came from `hostname` and 8080 instead of http://www.mydomain.com and port 80.

In the next three chapters we will see how we can use Tomcat connectors to pass requests and responses between Apache and Tomcat.

Using Coyote HTTP with Tomcat 3.3.x

The steps for using the Coyote HTTP connector with Tomcat 3.3.x are listed below. In the instructions that follow, `$TOMCAT_HOME` is the install directory of Tomcat 3.3.x.

- Download the latest stable Coyote release from http://jakarta.apache.org/builds/jakarta-tomcat-connectors/coyote/release/. The release consists of a number of JAR files.
- Copy `tomcat33-resource.jar` to `$TOMCAT_HOME/lib/common`.
- Replace `$TOMCAT_HOME/lib/common/connector_util.jar` with `tomcat-util.jar`.
- Copy `tomcat-http11.jar` to `$TOMCAT_HOME/lib/container`.
- Copy `tomcat-jni.jar` to `$TOMCAT_HOME/bin`.
- Copy `tomcat33-coyote.jar` to `$TOMCAT_HOME/lib/container`.
- Copy `commons-logging.jar` to `$TOMCAT_HOME/lib/container`.
- Add the following XML fragment to `$TOMCAT_HOME/conf/modules.xml`.

```
<module name="CoyoteConnector"
        javaClass="org.apache.coyote.tomcat3.CoyoteInterceptor2"/>
```

- Add the `<CoyoteConnector>` element to `$TOMCAT_HOME/conf/server.xml` as a child of the `<ContextManager>` element. The following is a sample configuration:

```
<ContextManager workDir="work" >
    ...
    <CoyoteConnector   port="8081" secure="false"
                       maxThreads="100" maxSpareThreads="50"
                       minSpareThreads="10" />
    ...
```

The port attribute (`8081` above) is the port number that this connector serves HTTP requests on. The `port` attribute can be modified, but be sure to check with ports used by the other connectors.

Using Coyote HTTP with Tomcat 4.0

The steps for using Coyote HTTP with Tomcat 4.0 are listed below. In the following instructions, `$CATALINA_HOME` is the install directory for Tomcat 4.0:

- Download the latest stable Coyote release from http://jakarta.apache.org/builds/jakarta-tomcat-connectors/coyote/release/. The release consists of a number of JAR files.
- Copy the following JAR files into `$CATALINA_HOME/server/lib`:
  - `commons-logging.jar`
  - `tomcat-coyote.jar`
  - `tomcat-http11.jar`
  - `tomcat-util.jar` (you should overwrite the existing JAR file).

- Copy tomcat-jni.jar to $CATALINA_HOME/bin.
- Add a <Connector> for Coyote to the <Service> element in $CATALINA_HOME/conf/server.xml. An example configuration is shown below. The port attribute for the connector may need to be modified and set to a port number that is available:

```
<Connector className="org.apache.coyote.tomcat4.CoyoteConnector"
           port="8081"
           minProcessors="5"
           maxProcessors="75"
           enableLookups="true" redirectPort="8443"
           acceptCount="10"
           debug="0"
           connectionTimeout="20000"/>
```

Performance Tuning

Earlier in the configuration section we went over some of the attributes that impact performance characteristics of the HTTP connectors. Let's revisit some the attributes that have an impact on performance:

- Turn debug off (Tomcat 4.x)
  The debug attribute in the HTTP/1.1 and Coyote connectors controls the detail level for the log messages. This should be set to zero (the default value) to have minimal logging.
- Set tcpNoDelay to true (Tomcat 3.x and 4.x)
  When this attribute is set to true, it enables the TCP_NO_DELAY network socket option. This improves the performance as it disables the Nagle algorithm. The Nagle algorithm is used to concatenate small buffer messages and thus decrease the number of packets sent over the network. While this may give better response time for a non-interactive network application as it has greater throughput, it results in slower response times in interactive client-server environments (such as a web browser interacting with the web server).
- Set enableLookups to false
  Setting enableLookup to false disables DNS lookups for the request.getRemoteHost() API calls. This improves performance by cutting down the time required for the lookup.
- Use a thread pool
  Tomcat is multi-threaded servlet container, and each incoming request requires a Tomcat thread to handle it. Using a thread pool is hence very important for performance. If the thread pool is disabled, a new thread would be started for every request. If a very large number of requests arrived concurrently, they would cause Tomcat to allocate an equivalent number of threads. This would degrade performance, and could even cause a Tomcat crash.

  To get around this, we should use a thread pool: Tomcat 3.x has a pools attribute that should be set to true while Tomcat 4.x does not have an attribute for switching off thread pool support. In Tomcat 3.x, there are three thread pool-related attributes that can be tuned for performance:

- `maxThreads`
  This is the maximum number of threads. This defines the upper bound to the concurrency, as Tomcat will not create any more threads than this. If there are more than `maxThreads` requests, they will be queued till the number of threads decreases.
- `maxSpareThreads`
  Maximum number of idle threads.
- `minSpareThreads`
  Minimum number of idle threads.

Setting these to appropriate values is a factor of the web site load and the server machine characteristics. A configuration of 50 `maxThreads`, 25 `maxSpareThreads`, and 10 `minSpareThreads` is sufficient for a web site with medium load (say 10-40 concurrent connections). For web sites with greater loads, you would want to increase this limit. Another limiting factor here is the JVM memory settings – for adding a larger number of threads we may need to modify the Tomcat startup scripts (`tomcat.bat/tomcat.sh`) and pass JVM-specific parameters (such as `-Xms` and `-Xmx` to set the initial and maximum heap size) to do this. Please refer to your JVM documentation for additional information.

In Tomcat 4.x, the attributes that control the thread pool behavior are:

- `maxProcessors`
  The maximum number of request processing threads to be created by this connector, which therefore determines the maximum number of simultaneous requests that can be handled. If there are more than `maxProcessors` concurrent requests, the remaining incoming requests are queued. The `acceptCount` attribute then controls the number of requests that get queued.
- `minProcessors`
  The number of request processing threads that will be created when this connector is first started. This attribute should be set to a value smaller than that set for `maxProcessors`.

Summary

In this chapter, we covered the configuration for Tomcat's HTTP connectors. We looked at the connectors for Tomcat 3.x (HTTP/1.0 connectors), Tomcat 4.0 (HTTP/1.1 connector) and the Coyote HTTP/1.1 connector. The Coyote connector supports backward compatibility with Tomcat 3.x and 4.0, and we saw how this is enabled. All three connectors support HTTPS too, but we deferred a discussion of this to Chapter 16.

Finally, we looked at performance tuning measures for the HTTP connectors. However, the HTTP connector is often not used in a production environment where performance is a major concern. The HTTP connectors are useful for test deployments, or where there is not a lot of static content. For production web deployments, it is common to use another web server to serve up static content, and to have Tomcat handle only the dynamic JSP/servlet content. This improves performance, and also allows for integrating existing web applications and scripts, some of which may have been written in other language such as Perl or Python. In the next three chapters, we will cover the web server connectors that allow Tomcat to work with web servers such as Apache and IIS.

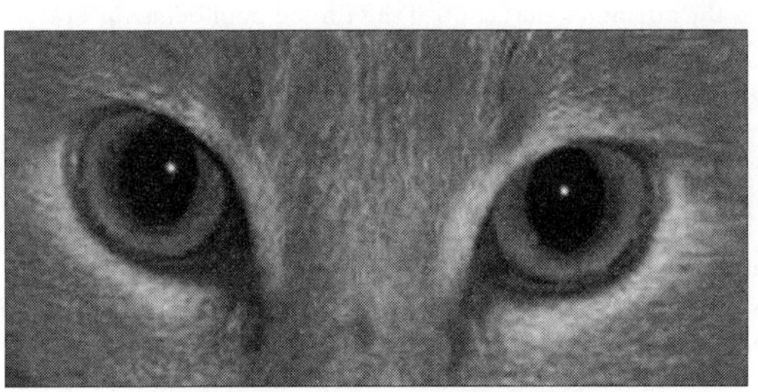

11

Web Server Connectors

In the previous chapter, we examined the HTTP connectors that allow Tomcat to work as a standalone web server. We can also use a web server such as Apache or IIS, along with Tomcat to serve up HTTP content to the user's web browser. In this configuration, the web server and Tomcat communicate with each other using Tomcat's web server connectors.

In this chapter, we will introduce the various Tomcat connectors and the protocols – WARP and AJP. The next two chapters will cover the implementation details of these protocols.

Reasons for Using a Web Server

The obvious question here is – why do we need to use a separate web server when Tomcat already has a HTTP connector? Here are some reasons:

- **Performance**
  Tomcat is inherently slower than a web server, and therefore we want the static content to be served up by the web server, while Tomcat handles the dynamic content (JSP pages and servlets). Passing requests for static HTML pages, images, and stylesheets through a servlet container written in Java is not very performant as compared to a web server.

- **Security**
  A web server like Apache has been around for a lot longer than Tomcat and has far fewer security holes.

- **Stability**
  Apache is much more stable than Tomcat. In an event of a Tomcat crash, the entire web site will not come down – only the dynamic content served by Tomcat would be unavailable.

- **Configurability**
  Apache is also far more configurable than Tomcat. For example, it supports virtual hosts, allowing a single Apache installation to host more than one web site. Using Apache as our front-end allows us to use its rich functionality.

- **Additional functionality**
  Web sites often have legacy code in the form of CGI programs. They might also use scripting languages like Perl or Python to implement specific functionality. Web servers like Apache support CGI programs and have modules for Perl and Python – Tomcat does not. This is yet another reason why we would want to use a web server in addition to Tomcat.

Connector Architecture

All the connectors work on the same principle – they have an Apache module end (`mod_jk`, `mod_jk2`, `mod_webapp`) written in C that gets loaded by Apache (or other supported web servers) the way other Apache modules do.

On the Tomcat end, each servlet container instance has a connector module component written in Java. In Tomcat 4.x, this is a class that implements the `org.apache.catalina.Connector` interface. The connector class for the WARP connector is `org.apache.catalina.connector.warp.WarpConnector` and that for AJP version 13 is `org.apache.ajp.tomcat4.Ajp13Connector`.

The web server handles all requests for static content, as well as all non-servlet/JSP dynamic content (CGI scripts, for example). When it comes across content targeted for the servlet container, it passes the request to the module in question (that is, `mod_jk`, `mod_webapp`, and so on). How does the web server know what content to pass to the connector module? We add directives in the web server's configuration that specify this.

For example, if we are using the `jk` connector, we need to specify this:

```
# Configuration directives in Apache's httpd.conf for mod_jk
# Send all request for JSP (extension *.jsp) or
# servlets (web application path /servlet) to the
# AJP connector
JkMount /*.jsp ajp13
JkMount /servlet/* ajp13
```

Alternatively, if we are using the `webapp` connector, we need to specify this:

```
# Configuration directives in Apache's httpd.conf for mod_webapp
# Send all request in the URL path /servlet to the webapp connector
WebAppDeploy servlet warpConnection /servlet
```

The specifics of these and other directives are covered in the next two chapters.

The connector module then sends the request encoded in a manner specific to a protocol (AJP or WARP) over a network connection to a connector (there can be more than one instance of the servlet container in the back-end). The connector gets the request serviced by the servlet container, and sends the response back to the Apache module. The diagram opposite illustrates this:

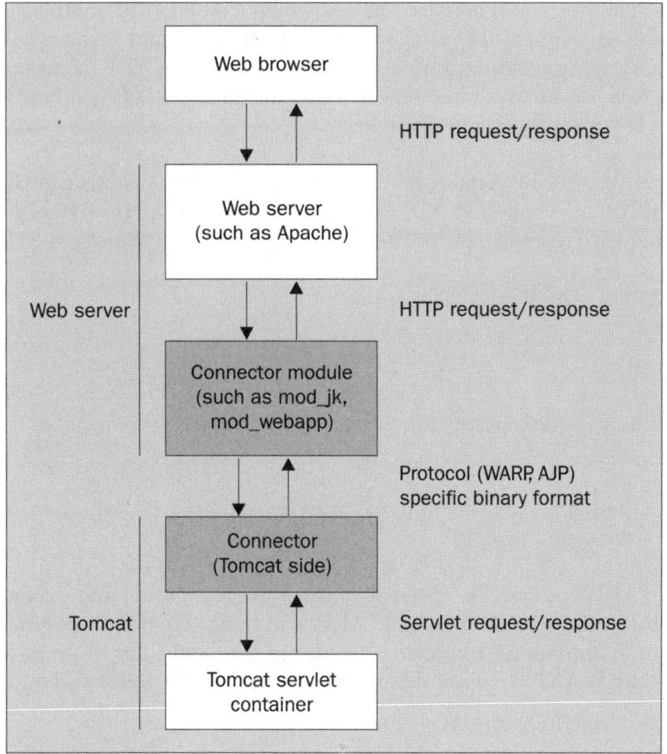

Connector Protocols

Tomcat has two protocols for its web server connectors – AJP and WARP. These protocols essentially define the (binary) format for the data transmitted between the web server and Tomcat, and the control commands.

WARP Protocol

WARP derives its name from the Star Trek television series. WARP is a measure of speed. Traveling at 'WARP speed' means moving faster than the speed of light. Going by the name, the intent of the WARP protocol was to be a very fast mechanism for communication between the web server and the servlet container. WARP also expands as an acronym – the **Web Application Remote access/control Protocol**.

WARP defines a packet structure for transferring data between the web server and the servlet container. This consists of an 8-bit packet-type field, a 16-bit payload length field (to be dropped in new WARP versions), followed by the actual content. All data is transmitted over a network socket (Apache and Tomcat could be on different machines) and encoded in the network byte order (that is, big-endian style).

The packet could contain request data from the user, such as the HTTP method (GET, POST), request URI, query argument, or protocol (HTTP/1.0, HTTP/1). It also could be an admin command that, for example, could deploy an application. On the response side, the WARP packet could contain the response to be sent back to the user's browser or error information. The packet type is used to distinguish between these various types of packets.

The web server parses the HTTP request that it receives. WARP takes this pre-parsed request and transmits it in a format that is encoded such that the connector at the receiving end does not have to parse the data again.

The diagram below shows the WARP packet structure:

Byte #	0	1	2	3 (length+3)
Contents	Packet type	Data length		Actual data payload

As can be seen from the figure, the first byte contains the packet type, which is followed by the payload data length and then the actual payload.

As in the case of the AJP protocol, the specifics of the WARP protocol and packet structure are relevant only to people implementing connectors for WARP, and hence we do not cover them here. Tomcat users have no reason to implement a connector for these protocols. For more information on the protocol, please see the WARP documentation that comes with the webapp connector sourcecode.

AJP Protocol

The **Apache JServ Protocol** (AJP) is a historical name, as AJP10 and AJP11 were the protocols that the now obsolete JServ connector implemented. The current version of AJP is AJP13 and is implemented by the jk and jk2 connectors.

AJP13 uses a binary format for transmitting data between the web server and Tomcat. The earlier versions of AJP (AJP10 and AJP11) used a text-based data format. The communication between the web server and the servlet container is over a network socket, and the same connection is reused for multiple requests and responses. The connection is made persistent for better performance.

The AJP packet format consists of a packet header and then the actual payload. The packet header has the payload size. The type of message is in the first byte of the payload. The message could be an HTTP request/response packet or even a control command (for example, the web server asks the servlet container to shut down). The protocol defines binary encoding for the HTTP commands and headers – for example, the GET command is represented by the byte value 2.

The diagram below shows the AJP packet structure from the web server side to the servlet container:

Byte #	0	1	2	3	4 (length+3)
Contents	0x12	0x34	Data length		Actual data payload

And the diagram below shows the packet structure from the servlet container to the web server:

Byte #	0	1	2	3	4 (length+3)
Contents	A	B	Data length		Actual data payload

As we can see, the binary data packet from the web server side starts with the sequence 0x1234. This is followed by the packet size (two bytes) and then the actual payload data. On the return path, the packets are prefixed by AB (ASCII code for A, ASCII code for B). The protocol then goes on to define the structure for the payload data (type of message is in the first byte of the payload and so on).

Do we, as administrators or web developers need to know the AJP protocol and its packet structure? Luckily for us, we don't. The specifics of the AJP protocol and packet structure are relevant only to people working on (or curious about) Tomcat internals, or interested in implementing a connector for AJP. Users of Tomcat should have no reason to implement a connector.

For further information on the details of AJP, please see the documentation that comes with the `jk` connector source code or at http://jakarta.apache.org/tomcat/tomcat-3.3-doc/AJPv13.html.

Choosing a Connector

Tomcat has a number of connectors available such as `jk`, `webapp`, and `jk2`. In this section we will compare them with the aim of selecting an appropriate connector.

JServ

Apache JServ (http://java.apache.org/jserv/) was a servlet engine that implemented the JavaSoft Servlet API, version 2.0 (the current version of the API is 2.3). JServ is now in maintenance mode, and has been superseded by Tomcat. JServ did not have a HTTP stack, and so came with a connector (`mod_jserv`) that used Apache (versions 1.2, 1.3) for this. This was the origin of `mod_jserv`. This module also works as a connector for Tomcat 3.x and earlier versions, though we should use the `jk` connector for new installations.

Some sample `mod_jserv` directives from Apache's `httpd.conf` are listed below:

```
LoadModule jserv_module libexec/mod_jserv.so
AddModule mod_jserv.c

...
ApJServMount  /examples   ajpv12://tomcat_host_name:8007/examples
```

If we plan to move to the jk connector, we must remove any existing JServ directives from our Apache configuration's `httpd.conf`. This is because the `ApJServMount` directives are not compatible with the `jk` connector. We would have these directives in our `httpd.conf` if our Apache installation had been configured with JServearlier.

`mod_jserv` defined the AJP protocol that specified the packet format for communication between the Apache and Tomcat ends of the connector. `mod_jserv` implemented versions AJP11 and AJP12 of this protocol. This protocol lives on in the `jk` and `jk2` connectors, as we shall see next.

jk

The `jk` connector is a cleaned-up version of the JServ connector, and has a refactored code base. It implements the same protocol (AJP) that JServ did – the versions that it supports include AJP11, AJP12, and AJP13.

`jk` adds support for a lot more web servers than JServ – the supported web servers include Apache 1.3 and 2.x, Netscape, Domino, AOLServer, and IIS. On the servlet side, it supports Tomcat 3.x, 4.x, and JServ. It also supports redirection of incoming requests, and thus we can achieve load-balanced request sessions.

The `jk` connector obsoletes `mod_jserv`. It offers a less complex configuration, and better support for SSL –`mod_jserv` which, for instance, couldn't reliably differentiate between HTTP and HTTPS requests. If you are looking for a stable connector that supports a large(r) number of web servers and Tomcat versions, `mod_jk` is the connector for you. The `jk` connector is covered in greater detail in Chapter 13.

jk2

`jk2` is the next generation for the `jk` connector. It is still under development, and implements the AJP13 protocol. It will support all the web servers that `mod_jk` does (Apache 1.3/2.0, Domino, Netscape, AOLServer, IIS). It also supports the Tomcat 3.x and 4.x servlet containers.

Tomcat 4.1 ships with a `jk2` connector called the Coyote JK2. Coyote is a new architecture/API for the Java code that talks to the connectors. Tomcat 4.1 has a Coyote HTTP/1.1 connector in addition to the Coyote JK2 connector. We covered the Coyote HTTP/1.1 connector in the previous chapter.

`jk2` will eventually obsolete the `jk` connector. It already does so in the Tomcat 4.1 releases.

webapp

The `webapp` connector implements **WARP** for connecting Tomcat and Apache. This protocol has built-in support for auto deployment and web application configuration.

`webapp` uses the **Apache Portable Runtime** (APR) library for operating system portability and therefore can only be used with Apache 1.3 and 2.0. It is limited also by the versions of Tomcat it supports – currently only Tomcat 4.x.

It is also limited in the features it supports – the current version of `webapp` does not support load balancing and fault-tolerance, and has known problems in its Windows support.

`webapp` is an experimental connector, and has a number of known issues. However, it implements the WARP protocol that has been designed with performance as a major consideration.

Summary

In this chapter, we discussed the reasons why we would need to have a web server as the front-end for Tomcat. Next, we looked at the general architecture of a web server connector and examined the two protocols for these connectors – AJP and WARP. Finally, we listed all the available connector implementations and their feature sets.

On comparing all the current implementations, we can see that the `jk` connector is the most stable of the lot and supports more configurations (web servers, servlet containers). Going forward, the `jk2` connector will eventually obsolete `jk`.

In the next chapter we look at the webapp connector in more detail and examine some of the known issues with it.

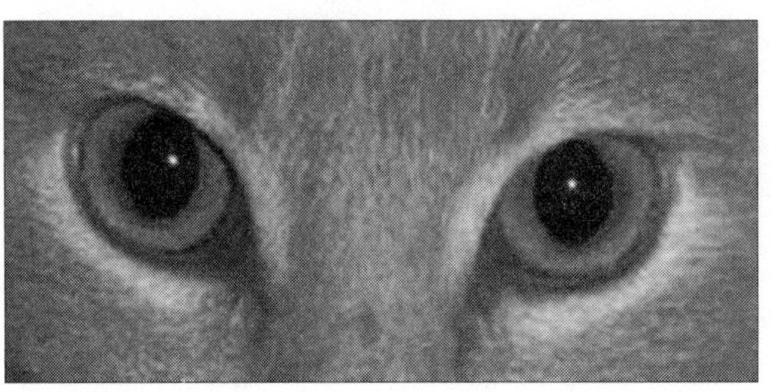

12

The WARP Connector

In the previous chapter, we introduced the Tomcat connectors that provide the communication layer between a web browser and the Tomcat servlet container. There are two defined protocols for connectors – WARP and AJP.

In this chapter, we will cover the webapp connector that implements the WARP protocol. We will explain how to build the connector and configure Apache to direct the JSP and servlet requests to it. Finally, we will explore some known issues with webapp.

Introducing webapp

The webapp connector implements a totally new protocol called **WARP** for connecting Tomcat and Apache. This protocol has built-in support for auto deployment and web application configuration – we will not go into the specifics of the protocol here – this has been covered in the last chapter.

webapp uses the **Apache Portable Runtime** (APR) library for achieving operating system portability and therefore can only be used with Apache 1.3 and 2.0. Also, it supports only the Tomcat 4.x servlet container.

It is also limited in the features it supports – the current version of webapp does not support load balancing and fault-tolerance, and has known problems in its Windows implementation. webapp is an experimental connector, and has a number of known issues with it (we will discuss this at the end of this chapter). However, it implements the WARP protocol that has been designed with performance as a major consideration.

webapp Configuration

Setting up Tomcat and Apache to work with each other is a four-step process:

- Getting the webapp binaries either from an existing binary distribution, or by building it from source
- Configuration changes in Apache
- Configuration changes in Tomcat
- Finally, restarting both Apache and Tomcat for the changes to take effect and testing the installation

This section will cover these steps in more detail. webapp supports only the Tomcat 4.x servlet engine and Apache version 1.3/2.x. All instructions below are specific to these versions.

webapp Binaries

The Tomcat documentation states that the binaries for the Tomcat connector are (or will be) available from the URL http://jakarta.apache.org/builds/jakarta-tomcat-4.0/release/v4.x.y/bin/plaform. Here, x and y are replaced with the Tomcat version number, and platform is one of Linux, Solaris9, Win32, and so on. This download location was empty at the time of writing.

Looking for the connector binaries under the Jakarta project build location (URL: http://jakarta.apache.org/builds/), we found an older version of it in http://jakarta.apache.org/builds/jakarta-tomcat-4.0/archives/v4.0.1/bin/. We are interested in the `mod_webapp.so` binary (and `libapr.dll` for Windows), as well as the `tomcat-warp.jar` file. `mod_webapp.so` is available as a part of the `webapp-module-<version>.tar.gz` (`.zip` on Windows) archive file. `tomcat-warp.jar` should be included in the Tomcat 4.x binary release, so we don't have to do anything here.

After extracting these out, we can copy them to specific locations in the Apache and Tomcat installations:

For Apache 1.3:

```
$ cp mod_webapp.so /path/to/apache1.3/libexec
```

For Apache 2.0:

```
$ cp mod_webapp.so /path/to/apache2.0/modules
```

On Windows, we also need to copy `libapr.dll` into `C:\WINNT\System32` otherwise Apache would not be able to load this module. This DLL (Dynamic Link Library) comes as a part of the binary release.

The Tomcat part of the webapp connector (`tomcat-warp.jar`) is included in the Tomcat 4.x release. In case your installation does not have this, we would need to copy it into the Tomcat installation:

```
$ cp tomcat-warp.jar $CATALINA_HOME/server/lib
```

Building webapp from Source

We would need to build webapp from source if the binaries are outdated (say, a newer version has a bug fix that you want), or if the binary version for our platform is not available.

Building webapp requires a number of GNU/Unix utilities. In case you are doing this on a Windows machine, you would need to install the Cygwin toolkit (http://www.cygwin.com/).

The prerequisites for building the webapp connector from sourcecode are:

- Apache 1.3 or 2.0
- Ant
- CVS
- autoconf 2.52 or above

Remember that mod_webapp only works with Tomcat 4.x.

autoconf

autoconf is an open source program that generates configuration scripts for other programs. We need autoconf version 2.52 or above for building the webapp connector. If your system does not have autoconf at all, or has an older version, you can download it from ftp://ftp.gnu.org/gnu/autoconf/. After installing autoconf, remember to add it to the PATH environment variable. If you install autoconf in a non-standard place, such as your home directory, you need to set the AC_MACRODIR environment variable to point to the autoconf macro file directory:

```
$ PATH=/path/to/autoconf_2-52/bin:$PATH
$ AC_MACRODIR=/path/to/autoconf_2-52_install/share/autoconf
$ export PATH AC_MACRODIR
```

The steps that we follow for building are:

- Download webapp and APR sourcecode, either from a download site or from the Apache CVS repository
- Generate the configure script
- Build the Apache webapp module
- Build tomcat-warp.jar

Download webapp Sourcecode

mod_webapp can be obtained in source form as a part of the Jakarta Tomcat connectors module. This code will eventually be downloadable from http://jakarta.apache.org/builds/jakarta-tomcat-connectors/webapp/. Till then, release snapshots can be obtained from http://nagoya.apache.org/~pier/snapshots/.

We can also download the latest webapp sources from the Apache CVS repository:

```
$ cvs -d :pserver:anoncvs@cvs.apache.org:/home/cvspublic login
```

Enter anoncvs as the CVS password:

```
$  cvs -d :pserver:anoncvs@cvs.apache.org:/home/cvspublic checkout jakarta-tomcat-
connectors/webapp
```

Next, download the APR (Apache Portable Runtime) code:

```
$ cd ./jakarta-tomcat-connectors/webapp
$ cvs -d :pserver:anoncvs@cvs.apache.org:/home/cvspublic checkout apr
```

The APR is a library of C data structures and routines used by webapp and other Apache applications. It provides a portability layer for many operating systems.

Generate Configure Script

Once the code is downloaded, we can create the configure script, configuring both the APR and the webapp modules:

```
$ ./support/buildconf.sh
```

Remember that running the configure script requires autoconf version 2.52 or newer. You will get an error message ("autoconf version 2.52 or newer required to build from CVS") if you use an older version.

Build the Apache webapp Module

The current version of webapp does not come with a script that would allow it to be statically linked with Apache. We therefore will need to have to load it dynamically at runtime as a Dynamic Shared Object (DSO).

There are advantages and disadvantages to using a DSO approach versus a statically linked approach. With DSO, we have a lot of flexibility in adding new third-party modules, or even updating the version of the module. This flexibility is due to the fact that we don't have to rebuild Apache from source each time a new module is to be added. However, a statically compiled Apache (that is, without DSO support) leads to a much faster Apache load time (20% faster) and faster execution time (5% faster).

Since we are building a dynamic module, we need to use the apxs (APache eXtenSion) tool. This tool allows for building and installing Apache extension modules.

We set the system path to include the axps program directory:

```
$ PATH=/path/to/apache/bin
$ export PATH
```

If your Apache installation doesn't have the apxs program, it might mean that Apache was built without support for dynamic module loading. We can check this using the following command:

```
$ /path/to/apache/bin/httpd -l | grep mod_so.c
```

If this comes back with a matched output, it means that Apache has DSO support configured. Otherwise, if nothing is printed out, it means that your Apache installation does not support DSO. In this case we need to rebuild Apache from source to allow dynamically loaded modules.

For this, we download the Apache code from http://www.apache.org/dist/httpd/ and then configure it appropriately:

```
$ cd /path/to/apache_src
$ ./configure --enable-module=so
$ make
```

Apache 2.0 enables `mod_so` (the module that allows dynamic loading of other modules) by default, unlike Apache 1.3. You could refer to *Professional Apache 2.0* from *Wrox Press (ISBN 1-86100-722-1)* or http://httpd.apache.org/ for more information on Apache.

Once we have an Apache configuration with DSO support built in, we can build the `mod_webapp` connector. We change directory to `jakarta-tomcat-connectors/webapp` and run the `configure` script for the `webapp` connector:

```
$ ./configure --with-apxs
```

The `--with-axps` option specifies that the Apache module should be built. If this is not specified, only the `webapp` libraries and APR will be built. We can also pass the path to the `apxs` executable to this command (instead of setting the `PATH` as we did earlier):

```
$ ./configure --with-apxs=/path/to/apxs
```

If the path to `apxs` is not set correctly, the `configure` script will come back with a "configure: error: cannot find apxs "apxs"" error message. Correct this by supplying the appropriate path.

If you get a "configure: error: apxs is unworkable" error from the `configure` script, it means that Apache was built without DSO support. We explained earlier how to check for this, and how to rebuild Apache for DSO support.

Some other useful options of the connector `configure` script are listed below:

- `--with-apr=DIR`
  This allows us to use an existing APR source directory (the default is `jakarta-tomcat-connectors/webapp/apr`). APR is a common constituent of other Apache programs too, and it is likely that this may be already installed elsewhere:

- `--enable-debug`
  If this option is used, the Apache `webapp` module and the Java component used by Tomcat are both built with debugging output enabled. This will create a lot of output to the log files, and will be bad for performance (though useful for test/debug installations).

The `configure` script generates the `Makefile`, and writes out the `build.properties` in the `jakarta-tomcat-connectors/webapps` directory using the template (`build.properties.in`). Now edit the `build.properties` file and set the `basedir`, `targdir`, `version`, and `catalina.home` properties. The only mandatory attribute is `catalina.home` – this needs to be set to the Tomcat 4.x installation directory:

```
# The full path of the sources directory
# (defaults to the directory where build.xml resides)
basedir=/path/jakarta-tomcat-connectors/webapp

# The full path of the targets directory
# (defaults to the current directory)
targdir=/path/jakarta-tomcat-connectors/webapp

# The version of the WebApp module
# (defaults to "unknown")
version=mod_webapp/1.2.0-dev

# The full path of a Tomcat 4.x distribution
# (no default - compilation will fail)
catalina.home=/path/to/jakarta-tomcat-4.1.3-LE-jdk14
```

Once the `build.properties` file has been edited, we can build the `webapp` module using the `make` command:

```
$ make
```

The `mod_webapp` DSO module would get built in the `jakarta-tomcat-connectors/webapp/apache-1.3` or `jakarta-tomcat-connectors/webapp/apache-2.0` directory depending on the `apxs` version. We then copy this to the Apache module directory.

For Apache 1.3:

```
$ cd jakarta-tomcat-connectors/webapp/apache-1.3
$ cp mod_webapp.so /path/to/apache1.3/libexec
```

For Apache 2.0:

```
$ cd jakarta-tomcat-connectors/webapp/apache-2.0
$ cp mod_webapp.so /path/to/apache2.0/modules
```

On Windows (even for Apache 1.3), the `mod_webapp.so` should be copied to the `modules` directory. In addition, we must also copy `libapr.dll` into `C:\WINNT\System32`, otherwise Apache would not be able to load this module.

Build tomcat-warp.jar

The Tomcat 4.1.x binary distribution already comes with the `tomcat-warp.jar` file, and so this step can be skipped. Look in your Tomcat installation under `$CATALINA_HOME/server/lib` to confirm if you have this JAR file.

We are now ready to build the `tomcat-warp.jar` file. This JAR file contains the Tomcat side of the `webapp` connector.

The build.properties configuration file is used during this build process. Please make sure that it has been edited and the catalina.home property set appropriately. This file was used during the mod_webapp build process too, so if that went through fine, it means that build.properties is correct. We use Ant to build the JAR file (make sure you are back in jakarta-tomcat-connectors/webapp to run this command):

```
$ ant
```

Once the JAR file is created, we need to copy it to the $CATALINA_HOME/server/lib directory:

```
$ cp build/tomcat-warp.jar $CATALINA_HOME/server/lib
```

Configuration Changes in Apache

After building the mod_webapp DSO, we would need to configure Apache to load the module. This means adding the following lines to be added to Apache's httpd.conf configuration file.

For Apache 2.0:

```
LoadModule webapp_module modules/mod_webapp.so
```

For Apache 1.3 on Unix:

```
LoadModule webapp_module libexec/mod_webapp.so
AddModule mod_webapp.c
```

For Apache 1.3 on Windows:

```
LoadModule webapp_module modules/mod_webapp.so
AddModule mod_webapp.c
```

The LoadModule directive dynamically links in the object file corresponding to the module, and adds it to the list of active modules. The AddModule directive was required in Apache 1.3 to ensure that modules get loaded in the correct order – it is not required in Apache 2.0.

We can use the apachectl command (in $APACHE_HOME/bin directory) to ensure that the Apache configuration is correct:

```
$ apachectl configtest
```

The output of this command should be a "Syntax OK" message string.

Finally, we add our web application connections and context into the Apache configuration (httpd.conf). The directives for these are WebAppConnection, WebAppDeploy, and WebAppInfo.

WebAppConnection

This directive is recognized by mod_webapp as the definition of a connector it must create for forward requests. The format of the WebAppConnection directive is:

```
WebAppConnection [connection name] [provider] [host:port]
```

The following is a brief description of its parameters:

- **connection name**
  This is a unique name for the connection to be created between Apache and Tomcat.
- **provider**
  The name of the provider used to connect to the servlet container. Currently only the `warp` provider is available.
- **host:port**
  The host name and port number to which the WARP connection must attempt to connect. The port is specified in our `server.xml` file for the `WarpConnector` (described below). The default value for this is `localhost:8008`.

WebAppDeploy

This directive tells `mod_webapp` to forward all requests for a particular directory to the application server. The following is its format and a brief description of its parameters:

```
WebAppDeploy [application name] [connection name] [url path]
```

- **application name**
  This is the application name as specified in our `webapps` directory in Tomcat. For example, if we want to deploy a WAR-based web application called `myApplication.war`, our application name would be `myApplication`.
- **connection name**
  This specifies the name of a previously declared `WebAppConnection` directive.
- **url path**
  The URL path where this application will be deployed. All URLs that are prefixed by this URL path are passed through the `webapp` connector. Does this URL path have any relation to the web application context path? No, it does not – it can be anything.

WebAppInfo

This directive points to information on all configured connections and deployed applications. These are made available at the URL http://server.name:port/path/. This is not a mandatory directive, and can be skipped:

```
WebAppInfo /path
```

The following is an example of configuration statements added to Apache's `httpd.conf`:

```
LoadModule webapp_module libexec/mod_webapp.so
ServerName myhost.mydomain.com:80
WebAppConnection conn warp localhost:8008
WebAppDeploy examples conn /examples
WebAppInfo /webapp-info
```

Here, we are instructing the `webapp` connector to connect to the servlet container waiting for requests on this machine itself (`localhost`) and bound to port 8008. The `8008` port is the port specified in Tomcat's `server.xml` file for the `org.apache.catalina.connector.warp.WarpConnector` connector (see opposite).

> **Note the `ServerName` directive before the `webapp` connector directives. This is due to a known problem with `webapp` – it is unable to determine the default value of the host and port. This problem is being fixed at the time of writing.**

```
ServerName host:port
```

Here `host:port` is the host and port number that Apache runs on. If you are running Apache as a non-privileged user (that is a user other than `root` on Unix systems), you need to use a port number greater that 1024. Also, ensure that the port being used by Apache does not conflict with a port in use in Tomcat's configuration. For example, the default standalone connector in Tomcat runs on port 8080. If you run Apache on this port too, remember to change the port number in Tomcat's configuration (`$CATALINA_HOME/conf/server.xml`) or comment out the standalone HTTP connector in `server.xml` altogether.

Configuration Changes in Tomcat

The configuration on the Tomcat end involves configuring a connector for `webapp` in the `$CATALINA_HOME/conf/server.xml` file.

A connector represents the interface between external clients sending requests to (and receiving responses from) a particular service in the server. Each connector passes the request to the engine associated with the service containing the connector. As a reminder, all of the types of connectors have the following attributes in common:

- `className`
  This specifies the Java class name of the implementation to use. This class must implement the `org.apache.catalina.Connector` interface.
- `enableLookups`
  The value is `true` if the server is to be configured so that calls to `request.getRemoteHost()` perform DNS lookups to return the actual host name of the remote client. The default value is `true`.
- `redirectPort`
  If this connector supports non-SSL requests, and a request is received for which a matching `<security-constraint>` requires SSL transport, Catalina will automatically redirect the request to the port number specified here.
- `scheme`
  This attribute is set to the name of the protocol we wish to have returned by calls to `request.getScheme()`. For example, this attribute will be set to `https` for an SSL connector. The default value is `http`.
- `secure`
  Set this attribute to `true` if you wish to have calls to `request.isSecure()` to return `true` for requests received by this connector (for an SSL connector). The default value is `false`.

In addition to these attributes, there are additional connector attributes specific to the webapp connector:

- acceptCount
  The acceptCount attribute specifies the maximum queue length for incoming connection requests when all possible request processing threads are in use. Any requests received when the queue is full will be refused. The default value is 10.

- debug
  The debugging detail level of log messages generated by this component, with higher numbers creating more detailed output. The default value is 0.

- maxProcessors
  The maximum number of request processing threads to be created by this connector, which therefore determines the maximum number of simultaneous requests that can be handled. If not specified, this attribute is set to 20.

- minProcessors
  The number of request processing threads that will be created when this connector is first started. This attribute should be set to a value smaller than that set for maxProcessors. The default value is 5.

- port
  The TCP port number on which this connector will create a server socket and await incoming connections. Your operating system will allow only one server application to listen to a particular port number on a particular IP address.

- appBase
  Set the application base directory for hosts created via WARP. The default value is webapps.

A sample connector directive for the WARP connector in $CATLINA_HOME/conf/server.xml file is shown below:

```
<Connector className="org.apache.catalina.connector.warp.WarpConnector"
           port="8008" minProcessors="5"
           maxProcessors="75"
           enableLookups="true"
           appBase="webapps"
           acceptCount="10" debug="0"/>
```

The port number (8008) must be the same as the one we specified earlier while configuring Apache.

webapp has an engine implementation (org.apache.catalina.connector.warp.WarpEngine) that can be used along with the webapp connector service. It supports all the standard <Engine> element attributes. The sample configuration from the Tomcat 4.1 server.xml file for the webapp connector and WarpEngine is listed below. The <Engine>, <Service>, <Logger>, and <Realm> elements shown below are discussed in detail in Chapter 5:

```
<Service name="Tomcat-Apache">
  <Connector className="org.apache.catalina.connector.warp.WarpConnector"
             port="8008" minProcessors="5" maxProcessors="75"
             enableLookups="true" appBase="webapps"
             acceptCount="10" debug="0"/>

  <Engine className="org.apache.catalina.connector.warp.WarpEngine"
          name="Apache" debug="0">
```

```
    <Logger className="org.apache.catalina.logger.FileLogger"
            prefix="apache_log." suffix=".txt"
            timestamp="true"/>
    <Realm className="org.apache.catalina.realm.MemoryRealm" />
  </Engine>
</Service>
```

Testing the Installation

Once these configuration steps are complete, we need to restart Tomcat and Apache:

```
$ cd $CATALINA_HOME/bin
$ ./shutdown.sh
$ ./startup.sh
$ cd /path/to/apache/bin
$ ./apachectl restart
```

Now that this has been done, we can browse to the URL http://host:port/examples/ and run the example servlets (and JSP pages) that came with Tomcat. Here, host and port are the hostname and port number that Apache runs on, and examples is the web application that we had configured in `httpd.conf` (see below):

```
WebAppDeploy examples conn /examples
```

We can now remove (or comment out) the HTTP connector for Tomcat that runs on port 8080 from `server.xml` since we do not need it anymore, and restart Tomcat.

Is there an order in which the two need to be started? Users have reported problems with `webapp` if Apache is started before Tomcat. They even recommend that there be a few seconds delay between the time Tomcat completes initialization and Apache starts, and maintaining this order even for restarts (that is when Tomcat is to be restarted). However, on testing this out, we did not face this problem, though Tomcat did take a little extra time to initialize if Apache was already started.

webapp Bugs and Issues

Some of the commonly faced issues with the `webapp` connector at the time of writing are listed below:

- The `webapp` connector handles all requests for static resources (such as an HTML file or an image) to Tomcat, instead of passing it through Apache.

  This is a serious performance issue, because if the request for every image, CSS file, and so on is passed through the servlet container, performance would be seriously affected.

  One workaround for this is to move the static resource URLs outside the web application path. For example, if the web application's JSP pages and servlets are deployed under the URL path `/foobar`, move all static content out of this path. However, the servlets or JSP pages themselves may contain embedded image or stylesheet tags (shown below). The request for this image is passed through Tomcat too:

```
<img src="/images/logo.gif" ...>
```

Another workaround for this is proposed by one of the authors of the webapp module (*Pier Fumagalli*). He proposes using custom JSP tags. For example, instead of the <img> tag, the JSP could contain a custom image tag as shown:

```
<myTag:img src="/logo.gif" ...>
```

This custom image tag could expand to something like that given below:

```
<img src="http://apache-image-server.domain.com/images/logo.gif" ...>
```

Here http://apache-image-server.domain.com is the fully qualified URL of a web server (say, Apache) that serves up the images (and other bandwidth-hungry content). This approach has the additional advantage of improving the scalability of the web site as the load is distributed. Also, changing the location of the image server requires nothing more than changes in one tag library.

- `ServerName` needs to be added before any `webapp` directives (see the reason for this earlier in the chapter).

- Apache 2.0.35 fails to start with the `webapp` connector configured – the `apachectl start` command (and `configtest`) fail with an "Invalid virtual host name" error. By adding the `ServerName` directive, the `apachectl configtest` no longer reports the error, however Apache still fails to start. In case you face this issue, please upgrade to the latest version of `mod_webapp`. We tried with Apache 2.0.39, and this worked fine after the `ServerName` directive was added.

- If the Apache 1.3 start fails with a "libexec/mod_webapp.so: undefined symbol: apr_atomic_set" error, you should rebuild the `webapp` module with another (older/newer) version of APR. This bug is specific to Linux and is caused by the `configure` script disabling thread support where `mod_webapp` is built on Linux for Apache 1.3. The workaround is to either move to another APR version (we detected the problem with APR version 0.9), or edit the `configure` script in `jakarta-tomcat-connectors/webapp` and remove the `--disable-threads` option that gets tacked on by default. We then have to do a `make clean`, followed by redoing the steps mentioned in the *Build the Apache webapp Module* section.

  In case we need to move to another version of APR, we could use configure `--with-apxs --with-apr=DIR` for configuring the connector code to point at another version of APR, and then rebuild the connector code.

- Apache has a very fast startup – not so with Tomcat. Tomcat and `webapp` connector startup takes some time. Trying to access a web application resource in the duration gives a HTTP 500 error ("`Cannot open connection <connection name>`") back to the browser.

- Apache does not know if an error (for example 404 or web page not found) occurred if Tomcat is configured to handle errors. It is common practice in Tomcat to specify a page to be displayed for error handling in the deployment descriptor file. The sample `web.xml` extract below shows this being done:

```
<error-page>
  <error-code>404</error-code>
  <location>/error.html</location>
</error-page>
```

Because of this, a valid page response is returned to Apache and it does not know of the error. In case we want Apache to handle this error (say we have a common error-handling page for all errors – whether in static or dynamic content), we should remove these directives in `web.xml`.

- The `webapp` module support on Windows is a work in progress, and common reported problems include web server hangs and/or images not getting displayed.

Summary

In this chapter, we examined the installation and configuration steps for the `webapp` connector that implements the WARP protocol. We then saw a sample deployment scenario that simulated a real-life web site with Apache and Tomcat connected using the `webapp` connector.

`webapp`, as we mentioned earlier, has a lot of 'work-in-progress' code, a number of known issues, and limited support for web servers. In the next chapter we will look at the more widely used AJP protocol and the connectors (`jk`, `jk2`) that implement that protocol.

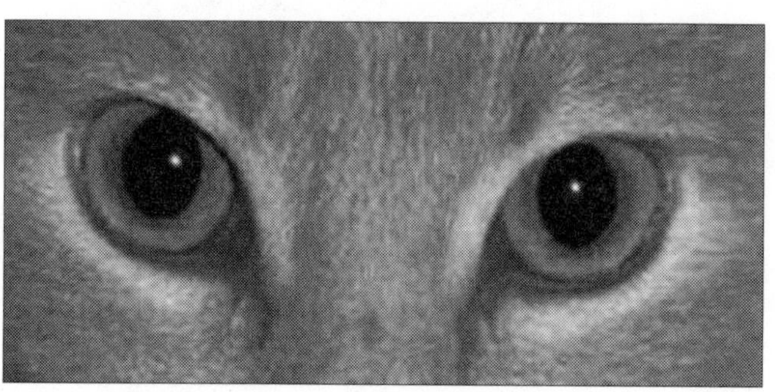

13

The AJP Connector

In the last chapter, we saw how to implement the WARP protocol using the `webapp` connector. In this chapter, we will discuss how to implement `mod_jk` to deploy our web applications with the combination of Tomcat with Apache. Here's what we'll discuss in this chapter:

- We will introduce `mod_jk`
- We will see how to integrate Tomcat with Apache
- We will see how to perform load balancing of multiple Tomcat instances with Apache

In this chapter, we'll use Tomcat 4.0.4 and Apache 2.0.39. The discussions here are also applicable to other versions of Tomcat (such as 3.x) and Apache (such as1.3.x), with a few appropriate changes; these will be mentioned wherever applicable. We'll assume a basic knowledge of Apache; the following URL may be of use as a quick reference: http://httpd.apache.org/docs/install.html.

mod_jk

As we saw in Chapter 11, to integrate Tomcat with a web server we need a redirector module that will forward client requests for JSP pages and servlets from the web server to Tomcat. This is done by matching the URL pattern of the request to a mapping in a configuration file. The JSP pages/servlets then handle the forwarded request, generate an appropriate dynamic response and send it back to the client via the module. To address this requirement, Apache's Jakarta project provides a module called **mod_jk**.

The following schematic diagram indicates the role of mod_jk in the combination of Tomcat and Apache. Here we see that Apache, with the help of mod_jk, redirects all requests for any JSP/servlet components. There may be one or more running instances of Tomcat that will serve these client requests. The redirector usually comes as a DLL or shared object module (.dll for Windows and .so file for Unix/Linux) that plugs into the web server, so Tomcat is said to be a **plug-in** for Apache:

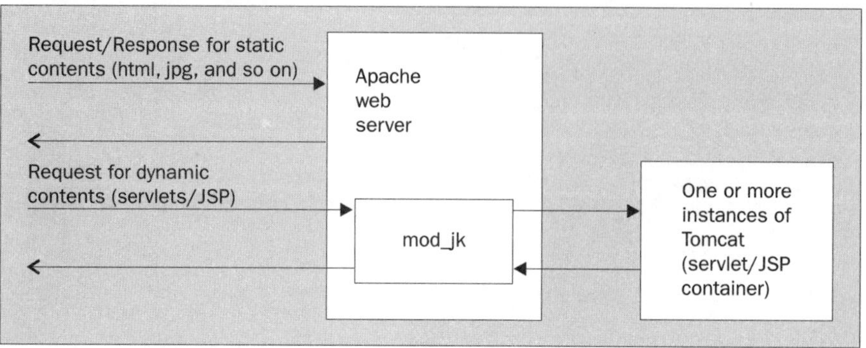

> *If you've previously configured Apache to use `mod_jserv`, remove any `ApJServMount` directives from your `httpd.conf` file. If you're including `tomcat-apache.conf` or `tomcat.conf`, you'll want to remove them as well as they are specific to `mod_jserv`. These steps are necessary because the `mod_jserv` configuration directives are not compatible with `mod_jk`.*

The Apache JServ Protocol

The Apache JServ Protocol (AJP) is a packet-oriented, TCP/IP-based protocol. It provides a communication channel between the Apache web server process and the running instances of Tomcat. Various versions of this protocol are available, including versions 1.2, 1.3, and 1.4. As AJP 1.3 is the most commonly used and well-tested version, we'll use it for our discussion here. Some of the noticeable features of AJP 1.3) are:

- Good performance
- Support for SSL
- The facility to get information about encryption and client certificates

AJP increases performance by making the web server reuse already open TCP-level connections with the Tomcat container, and as such, saves the overhead of opening new socket connections for each request. This is a concept similar to that of a connection pool. In the request-response cycle (completion of a request by getting a response corresponding to it), when a connection gets assigned to a particular request, it will not be reused until that request-response cycle is completed. This makes things simple by avoiding the cost of some more opened connections.

The AJP Connector

Tomcat provides a connector that implements the AJP protocol. Most versions of Tomcat support multiple versions of AJP (for example, Tomcat 3.x supports 1.2 and 1.3 whereas Tomcat 4.1.x supports 1.3 and 1.4) and for each AJP version, a connector Java class is provided in the Tomcat installation. Such a class is called an **AJP connector.**

It is easy to find out which class is providing support for which version of AJP because the class name itself contains the AJP version. For example, in Tomcat 4.0, we'll find a class called `org.apache.ajp.tomcat4.Ajp13Connector`, which will support AJP version 1.3. Similarly, for AJP version 1.4, Tomcat provides a class named `org.apache.ajp.tomcat4.Ajp14Connector`. This AJP connector can be configured in the `server.xml` file of Tomcat. We'll soon cover how to define the AJP connectors.

The New mod_jk2

We have already seen how Tomcat 4.0 provides an AJP connector for coupling Tomcat with a web server like Apache. In Tomcat 4.1.x, a new type of connector called JK2 has been introduced. The functional objective of this connector is the same as that of the original AJP connector, that is, to support the coupling of Tomcat with a web server like Apache. However, it is modified and improved to support the new architecture of Tomcat 4.1.x. This new type of connector supports AJP versions 1.3 and 1.4. Tomcat 4.1.x provides an implementation of this connector as the Coyote connector.

As we know, `mod_jk` is the module that provides the bridge between Tomcat and Apache. JK2 is the next generation and the corresponding module for Apache is available as `mod_jk2`.

Worker Implementations with mod_jk

A **worker** is a Tomcat instance that is running to serve JSP/servlet requests coming from another web server. In most cases, there is only a single Tomcat process, but sometimes we will need to run multiple workers to implement load balancing or site partitioning (mainly required for sites with heavy traffic). We'll see how to achieve this in the *Tomcat Load Balancing with Apache* section.

Each worker is identified by a host name/IP and port number combination. Here host means the machine name on which the given Tomcat instance is running and port refers to the port on which that instance is listening for any requests.

Plug-In vs. In-Process

Worker implementation in Tomcat with a web server can be done in two ways:

- **Using Tomcat as a plug-in**
  The most common implementation of Tomcat with Apache is using the Tomcat process as a plug-in to the running web server process. In this case, `mod_jk` is required as a redirector component. We'll need to configure the web server plug-in so that it can look up the different Tomcat workers and forward requests to them.

- **Using Tomcat as an in-process worker**
  This is a special type of worker implementation. In this case, the web server opens a JVM in its own process and executes Tomcat. Here Tomcat shares the same address space as that of the server process. This is a special type of deployment that provides an advantage in terms of request processing speed and better use of resources. We are not going to cover in-process workers in this chapter because, although Tomcat 3.x supports them, Tomcat 4.x doesn't and there are no plans to implement them in the future.

Multiple Tomcat Workers

There are a number of situations where we may use a multiple worker setup:

- We may want different contexts to be served by different Tomcat workers. This setup will provide a development environment where all the developers share the same web server but own a Tomcat worker of their own.
- We may want different virtual hosts served by different Tomcat processes to provide a clear separation between sites belonging to different entities.
- We may want to provide load balancing, where we run multiple Tomcat workers each on a machine of its own (or maybe on the same machine) and distribute the requests between them.

Getting mod_jk

For Windows, we need the `mod_jk.dll` for Apache. The Apache 1.3 version is available from the download directory on the Jakarta Project web site: http://jakarta.apache.org/builds/jakarta-tomcat/release/v3.2.3/bin/win32/i386/. After downloading it, just copy the `mod_jk.dll` to the `modules` subdirectory of Apache. The Apache 2.0 version is available here: http://www.acg-gmbh.de/mod_jk/.

> **The version of `mod_jk` is not dependent on the version of Tomcat. The Tomcat 3.3 distribution of `mod_jk` will function correctly with Tomcat 4.x and other 3.x versions of Tomcat, such as Tomcat 3.2.1. This is quite logical when we think about it; it's a redirector module residing in the web server process and providing a standard interface for the Tomcat container.**

For other platforms, we can get `mod_jk.so` for Apache 1.3.x from its appropriate download directory: http://jakarta.apache.org/builds/jakarta-tomcat/release/v3.2.3/bin/linux/i386/. After downloading it, just copy it to the `libexec` subdirectory of Apache.

The Tomcat connectors are handled by a separate subproject of Jakarta, and as such, so are `mod_jk` and `mod_jk2`. To make the availability of the Tomcat connectors streamlined, the Jakarta Project has put up a separate URL that is expected to have both the versions of the module (binary and source). The URL is: http://jakarta.apache.org/builds/jakarta-tomcat-connectors/. However, at the time of writing, this download area is largely empty, with only a few connectors and platforms represented.

For the new version of Apache (2.0) the complete range of binaries/sources is not yet populated at the above location, although there are a couple of resources for `mod_jk` apart from Apache's site. You can get the `mod_jk` module by either downloading a binary or you could build one of your own.

Building mod_jk On Windows

Here are some basic steps for building `mod_jk.dll` on Windows:

- Download the source of the latest Apache web server from the Apache site (http://www.apache.org/dist/httpd/) and unpack the distribution into any convenient directory such as `C:\Apache`

- Download the latest connectors source from the Jakarta site (http://jakarta.apache.org/builds/jakarta-tomcat-4.0/release/v4.0.4/src/jakarta-tomcat-connectors-4.0.4-src.zip) and unpack it to a convenient directory such as `C:\ jakarta-tomcat-connectors-4.0.4-src`
- Set the environment variables:
  - `%APACHE2_HOME%` – for the Apache source distribution
  - `%JAVA_HOME%` – for the J2SE installation
- Now with Microsoft Visual C++, open the DSP file in `C:\jakarta-tomcat-connectors-4.0.4-src\jk\native\apache-2.0\mod_jk.dsp` or `C:\jakarta-tomcat-connectors-4.0.4-src\jk\native\apache-1.3\mod_jk.dsp` depending on your server
- Using the build option, build the `mod_jk.dll`
- Copy `mod_jk.dll` to the `modules` directory of the binary Apache installation

The `mod_jk2` source is also in this distribution; use the `C:\jakarta-tomcat-connectors-4.0.4-src\jk\native2\server\apache2\mod_jk2.dsp` file.

Building mod_jk on Unix/Linux

Here are some basic steps for building `mod_jk.so` on Linux:

- We can get the needed source for the connectors from the Jakarta site: http://jakarta.apache.org/builds/jakarta-tomcat-4.0/release/v4.0.4/src/jakarta-tomcat-connectors-4.0.4-src.tar.gz.
- Create a convenient directory for building the connector like `/usr/local/src/jakarta-tomcat-connectors`. We'll refer to this as `$CONNECTOR_HOME`.
- Change to the directory `$CONNECTOR_HOME/jk/native`.
- Run `./buildconf.sh` to create a `configure` script.
- Run `./configure --with-apxs=<APACHE_HOME>/bin/apxs`. This command will configure `mod_jk.so` for the version of Apache that `apxs` belongs to.
- Now run `make`.
- We'll see `mod_jk.so` in `$CONNECTOR_HOME/jk/native/apache-<verison>`, where `<version>` is the version of Apache we configured for.
- `make install` isn't implemented yet, so copy `mod_jk.so` to the `libexec` (Apache 1.3) or `modules` (Apache 2.0) directory.

`mod_jk2` has a similar procedure:

- Change to the directory `$CONNECTOR_HOME/jk/native2`
- Run `./buildconf.sh` to create a `configure` script
- For Apache 1.3 run `./configure --with-apxs=<APACHE_HOME>/bin/apxs` and for Apache 2.0 run `./configure --with-apxs2=<APACHE_HOME>/bin/apxs`

- Now run make
- We'll see mod_jk2.so in $CONNECTOR_HOME/jk/build/jk2/apache2
- Copy mod_jk2.so into libexec or modules as appropriate for your version of Apache

Both modules also come with Ant build scripts. Go into the jk directory, edit build.properties, and run:

```
$ ant
$ ant native
```

Providing you have libtool, the native code for the connectors should be compiled.

Integrating Tomcat with Apache

When integrating Tomcat with Apache, we will need to modify the following files:

- server.xml
  Tomcat's main configuration file. Found in $CATLINA_HOME/conf.
- worker.properties
  Tomcat's configuration file for setting instances/workers. This can be placed anywhere that mod_jk has read access.
- mod_jk.conf
  Tomcat's configuration file for integration with Apache. Found in $CATALINA_HOME/conf/auto.
- httpd.conf
  Apache's main configuration. Found in $APACHE_HOME/conf.

Configuring the AJP Connector in server.xml

We start with setting the AJP connector in server.xml, where we'll see a typical entry for an AJP connector. Usually we'll find that these lines are already present in the file, but will be commented out. This makes configuration very easy, as all we need to do is find them and uncomment them.

For Tomcat 4.x

Here we define an AJP connector that will use AJP version 1.3 and listen on AJP's default port (8009). We can set some other attributes for it, which we'll cover in the upcoming section:

```
<Connector className="org.apache.ajp.tomcat4.Ajp13Connector"
           port="8009"
           minProcessors="5"
           maxProcessors="75"
           acceptCount="10"
           debug="0"/>
```

Every Tomcat connector supports the following attributes, so we won't look at them here. If you need more information on these, see Chapter 10:

- `className`
- `enableLookups`
- `redirectPort`
- `scheme`
- `secure`

The class `org.apache.ajp.tomcat4.Ajp13Connector` is the standard implementation of the AJP connector. This implementation supports the following attributes, in addition to the attributes mentioned above:

- `acceptCount`
  The maximum queue length for incoming connection requests when all possible request processing threads are in use. Any requests received when the queue is full will be refused. The default value is 10.
- `address`
  For servers with more than one IP address, this attribute specifies the address that will be used for listening to a specified port. By default, this port will be used on all IP addresses associated with the server.
- `debug`
  The debugging detail level of log messages generated by this component, with higher numbers creating more detailed output in the log files. The values range from 0 to 4 (the default value is 0). 0 corresponds to 'off', while 1-4 are emergency, error, information, and debug respectively. Higher levels will provide more details with more depth in code execution hierarchy. The location of these logs can be set in the Apache configuration files, as we shall see later.
- `maxProcessors`
  The maximum number of request processing threads to be created, which therefore determines the maximum number of simultaneous requests that can be handled. The default value is 20. A good rule of thumb for this attribute is to set it to the average number (plus a bit) of expected simultaneous requests, and then set the `acceptCount` to make up the difference between this and the maximum number expected.
- `minProcessors`
  The number of request processing threads that will be created when this connector is first started. This attribute should be set to a value smaller than that set for `maxProcessors`. The default value is 5.

The values for `maxProcessors` and `minProcessors` can be fine-tuned to suit the requirement of a specific application. They will be directly affected by factors like maximum expected client request load, system resources available, and response time expected by the client.

- port
  The TCP port number on which the connector will create a server socket and await incoming connections. The operating system will allow only one server application to listen to a particular port number on a particular IP address.
- tomcatAuthentication
  This attribute indicates whether or not Tomcat should handle authentication. If the attribute value is true (the default), any authentication carried out by the forwarding web server will be ignored and Tomcat will take care of the authentication. If the attribute value is false, Tomcat will not attempt authentication if the forwarding web server has already carried it out.

For Tomcat 3.x

We can set an AJP connector for Tomcat 3.x easily, by including the following lines in server.xml; this entry for AJP 1.2 comes after the <ContextInterceptor> entry. Usually an entry for AJP 1.2 is provided and we can create a similar one for AJP 1.3:

```
<Connector className="org.apache.tomcat.service.PoolTcpConnector">
  <Parameter name="handler"
       value="org.apache.tomcat.service.connector.Ajp13ConnectionHandler"/>
  <Parameter name="port" value="8009"/>
</Connector>
```

For mod_jk2

mod_jk2 supports AJP versions 1.3 and 1.4. In Tomcat 4.1.x, the implementation of this connector is called Coyote. It is made available as a Java class called org.apache.coyote.tomcat4.CoyoteConnector. Let's see how we can actually use mod_jk2.

We start by setting the value of the protocolHandlerClassName attribute of the <Connector> entry in server.xml. Its value should be set to org.apache.jk.server.JkCoyoteHandler. By doing this we are informing <Connector> of the correct protocol to use. Here is the complete entry:

```
<!-- Please note that for AJP 1.3 8009 is its default port -->
<Connector className="org.apache.ajp.tomcat4.Ajp13Connector"
           port="8009"
           protocolHandlerClassName="org.apache.jk.server.JkCoyoteHandler"
           ...
           ...
/>
```

The rest of the configuration steps for the JK2 connector are the same as for mod_jk. We cover the complete configuration of mod_jk in detail in the upcoming section.

Setting the workers.properties File

Each running Tomcat instance is represented as a single worker. Tomcat workers can be set up for the web server plug-in by using a simple properties file. This file, called workers.properties, is usually kept in the $CATALINA_HOME/conf/jk directory. This file consists of entries that will convey information to the web server plug-in about any available Tomcat workers.

Format of workers.properties File

The format used by `workers.properties` for defining a list of available workers is:

```
worker.list = <a comma separated list of worker names>
```

For example, here we define two workers named `testWorker1` and `testWorker2`:

```
worker.list = testWorker1, testWorker2
```

We can also define a property for a given worker:

```
worker.<worker name>.<property> = <property value>
```

For example, we can assign the value `myMachine` to the `host` attribute of `testWorker1`:

```
worker.testWorker1.host = myMachine
```

Types of Workers

Any defined Tomcat worker needs to be assigned a type. The following types can be assigned to various Tomcat workers:

- **ajp12**
  This type of worker uses the AJP 1.2 protocol to forward requests to out-of-process Tomcat workers.
- **ajp13**
  This type of worker uses the AJP 1.3 protocol to forward requests to out-of-process Tomcat workers.
- **jni**
  This worker knows how to forward requests to in-process Tomcat workers using JNI. As of now, this type is supported by Tomcat 3.x only.
- **lb**
  This type of worker is used for **load balancing**. In a load-balancing scenario, this type of worker doesn't handle any actual processing, rather it just handles the communication between a web server and other defined Tomcat workers of type `ajp12` or `ajp13`. This kind of worker supports round-robin load balancing with a certain level of fault tolerance. We'll see this in more detail when we come back to load balancing.

For example, the following line sets the `type` of `testWorker1` to `ajp13`, meaning it will use the AJP 1.3 protocol:

```
worker.testWorker1.type=ajp13
```

Worker Properties

After we have set a worker's type, we can set a number of other properties.

The port on which the worker listens can be set as shown below. For example, if our worker is of type `ajp13`, it will listen for AJP requests, by default, on port 8009:

```
worker.testWorker1.port=8009
```

Next we configure the host where the Tomcat worker is listening for requests. For example, if `testWorker1` is running on `localhost` then set the entry as:

```
worker.testWorker1.host=localhost
```

When working with a load balancer worker, we need to set the load-balancing factor for this worker. For example, if `testWorker1` is running with a load balancer, then, depending on the hardware condition of the machine, the corresponding load factor can be set (we'll see more of this when we cover load balancing):

```
worker.testWorker1.lbfactor=5
```

Some web servers, for example Apache 2.0 and IIS, are multi-threaded and Tomcat can take advantage of this by keeping a number of connections open as a cache. An appropriately high value based on the average number of concurrent users for Tomcat can prove very beneficial from a performance point of view (the default is 1):

```
worker.testWorker1.cachesize=20
```

An Example Tomcat Worker

For any defined worker, if we want to use a certain protocol version, for example, AJP 1.3, the corresponding AJP connector needs to be configured in the `server.xml` of the worker. Now let's have a look at a sample `workers.properties` file.

For Windows:

```
# Setting Tomcat & Java Home
workers.tomcat_home="c:\jakarta-tomcat4"
workers.java_home="c:\j2sdk1.4.0"
ps=\
worker.list=testWorker1
# Settings for testWorker1 worker
worker.testWorker1.port=8009
worker.testWorker1.host=localhost
worker.testWorker1.type=ajp13
```

The `ps=\` line sets the **path separator** for the OS that Tomcat is running on.

For Linux/Unix systems:

```
# Setting Tomcat & Java Home
workers.tomcat_home=/usr/java/jakarta-tomcat4
workers.java_home=/usr/java/j2sdk1.4.0
```

```
ps=/
worker.list=testWorker1
# Settings for testWorker1 worker
worker.testWorker1.port=8009
worker.testWorker1.host=localhost
worker.testWorker1.type=ajp13
```

Configuration Settings for Apache

Tomcat and Apache can communicate once the information about the available Tomcat workers is included in the `httpd.conf` Apache web server configuration file. There are two ways in which we can do this, both of which are discussed below. We will use Tomcat's `example` web application throughout this section to show how the configuration is done.

Auto-Generating Configuration Settings

Tomcat can be configured to automatically generate the Apache configuration file, called `mod_jk.conf`.

> **The `mod_jk.conf` file is created every time Tomcat starts, so make sure that you really can afford this overhead. Also, this will reset all of our deployment settings, as Tomcat overwrites the file every time.**

For Tomcat 4.x

To make Tomcat 4.x generate the configuration file every time it starts, we will need to add a special listener at the server and host level. This will then update the auto-generated `mod_jk.conf` file with all the needed attributes. Just add the following lines immediately after the `<Server port="8005" ...>` declaration.

```
<Listener className="org.apache.ajp.tomcat4.config.ApacheConfig"
    modJk="/usr/apache2/modules/mod_jk.so"
    workersConfig="/usr/java/jakarata-tomcat4/conf/jk/workers.properties"
    jkLog="/usr/java/jakarta-tomcat4/logs/mod_jk.log"
    jkDebug="info"
/>
```

In this declaration we have provided the necessary information in terms of attribute values to the listener class called `ApacheConfig`. It will create appropriate entries, such as the `LoadModule modules/mod_jk` declaration, in the auto-generated `mod_jk.conf` file using this information. Here we have provided the location of the `workers.properties` file, the location of the `mod_jk` module, the location of the log file, and the level of logging information we require.

> **Windows users may have to edit `mod_jk.conf` to include the module path in double quotes, especially when the installation path of Apache contains spaces in the directory names, otherwise this module will not get loaded and the server will throw a module not found error.**

The attributes that are supported by the `ApacheConfig` listener are:

- `configHome`
  This is the default parent directory for all the paths provided as attribute values. If not set, this defaults to `$CATALINA_HOME`. It gets overridden when absolute paths are provided for any attribute value.

- `jkConfig`
  The location to where we will write the Apache `mod_jk.conf` file. If not set, this defaults to `$CATALINA_HOME/conf/auto/mod_jk.conf`.

- `workersConfig`
  The path to the `workers.properties` file used by `mod_jk`. If not set, this defaults to `$CATALINA_HOME/conf/jk/workers.properties`.

- `modJk`
  The path to the Apache `mod_jk` module. If not set, this defaults to `modules/mod_jk.dll` on Windows, and `modules/mod_jk.so` on Linux/Unix systems.

- `jkLog`
  The path to the log file that `mod_jk` uses.

- `jkDebug`
  The level of logging to be done by `mod_jk`. May be `debug`, `info`, `error`, or `emerg`. If not set, this defaults to no log.

- `jkWorker`
  The desired worker. This must be set to one of the workers defined in the `workers.properties` file and defaults to `ajp13`.

- `forwardAll`
  If this is set to `true` (the default), `mod_jk` will forward all requests to Tomcat. This ensures that all the behavior configured in `web.xml` functions correctly. If `false`, Apache will serve static resources. Note that when set to `false`, some of Tomcat's configuration may not be duplicated in Apache, so check the generated `mod_jk.conf` file to see what configuration is actually being set in Apache.

- `noRoot`
  If this attribute is set to `true`, the `ROOT` context is not mapped to Tomcat. If set to `false`, and `forwardAll` is set to `true`, all requests to the `ROOT` context are mapped to Tomcat. If `false` and `forwardAll` is `false`, only JSP page and servlet requests to the `ROOT` context are mapped to Tomcat. When `false`, to correctly serve Tomcat's `ROOT` context you must also modify the `DocumentRoot` setting in Apache's `httpd.conf` file to point to Tomcat's `ROOT` context directory. Otherwise, Apache will serve some content, such as `index.html`, before `mod_jk` can get the request and pass it on to Tomcat. The default is `true`. We shall see all the variations of this in Chapter 19 when we discuss shared hosting.

- `append`
  Append the generated configuration file to the current configuration file. The default is `false`. Therefore it is a good idea to back up the values in another file and reference it from Apache.

For creating the appropriate mappings for Apache `<VirtualHost>` entries in the resultant `mod_jk.conf` file, add a listener below each `<Host>` entry. A sample is provided opposite:

```
<Host name="localhost" debug="0" appBase="webapps" unpackWARs="true">
<Listener
className="org.apache.ajp.tomcat4.config.ApacheConfig" append="true" />
```

This corresponds to the entire Tomcat installation, but we can choose single Tomcat contexts by adding the listener after the `<Context>` entry we are interested in. Once we do this, the `mod_jk.conf` file will automatically reflect the corresponding mapping as shown below.

For Windows:

```
# Load mod_jk
LoadModule jk_module "c:\Program Files\Apache Group\apache\modules\mod_jk.dll"

# Configure mod_jk
JkWorkersFile "c:\jakarta-tomcat4\conf\jk\workers.properties"
JkLogFile "c:\jakarta-tomcat4\logs\mod_jk.log"
JkLogLevel info

# Virtual Host.
<VirtualHost localhost>
  ServerName localhost
  JkMount /examples/*.jsp testWorker1
  JkMount /examples/servlet/* testWorker1

  ... other contexts ...
</VirtualHost>
```

For Linux:

```
# Load mod_jk
LoadModule jk_module modules/mod_jk.so

# Configure mod_jk
JkWorkersFile /usr/java/jakarta-tomcat4/conf/jk/workers.properties
JkLogFile /usr/apache2/logs/mod_jk.log
JkLogLevel info

# Virtual Host.
<VirtualHost localhost>
  ServerName localhost
  JkMount /examples/*.jsp testWorker1
  JkMount /examples/servlet/* testWorker1

  ... other contexts ...
</VirtualHost>
```

Note that you may have to edit this file to add the `testWorker1` values.

The `JkMount` directive 'mounts' a Tomcat directory onto the Apache root web context. In the files above, the line:

```
JkMount /examples/*.jsp
```

mounts every file in `$CATALINA_HOME/webapps/examples` that matches the `*.jsp` wildcard. This means that any URL that matches http://localhost/examples/*.jsp will go to Tomcat and everything else will be served by Apache. In combination with the `/examples/servlet/*` pattern, this will ensure all dynamic content comes from Tomcat and all static content comes from Apache.

The other three JK directives are pretty self-explanatory:

```
JkWorkersFile /usr/java/jakarta-tomcat4/conf/jk/workers.properties
JkLogFile /usr/apache2/logs/mod_jk.log
JkLogLevel info
```

The log file is where any AJP protocol-specific information is placed. Access logs for resources on Tomcat and Apache function as normal.

Each time Tomcat is started, it will write the configuration file to `$CATALINA_HOME/conf/auto/mod_jk.conf`. As a result, our settings will be overwritten. Therefore, we should either disable the auto-generation option by commenting out the directive in the `server.xml`, or make a custom setting file and include it in `httpd.conf`.

For Tomcat 3.x

In Tomcat 3.3 the `server.xml` `<ApacheConfig>` element controls the form of the `mod_jk.conf` file, which we generate on demand. It accepts all the same attributes as the listener we described for Tomcat 4.x except for `append`. This feature is new in Tomcat 3.3 and older versions automatically generate the configuration file every time they start. If you are using an older version, be sure and back up your settings in another file so that they are not lost every time Tomcat starts up.

To generate the configuration file with Tomcat 3.3, on Linux run:

```
$ $TOMCAT_HOME/bin/startup.sh jkconf
```

or on Windows run:

```
> %TOMCAT_HOME%/bin/startup jkconf
```

Note that the Windows version will cause the Tomcat window to appear and then rapidly disappear as if Tomcat had crashed. This is perfectly normal, but if you are worried, run `tomcat jkconf` to see the results in the current window.

This will create the file in `$TOMCAT_HOME/conf/auto`.

Manually Adding Configuration Settings

If we don't use `ApacheConfig`, we need to append the following lines at the end of our `httpd.conf` or save them as `mod_jk.conf` in `$CATALINA_HOME/conf/auto`. As we are only really interested in the `examples` web application, we won't add a virtual host this time.

For Windows:

```
# Load mod_jk
LoadModule jk_module "c:\Program Files\Apache Group\apache\modules\mod_jk.dll"

# Configure mod_jk
JkWorkersFile "c:\jakarta-tomcat4\conf\jk\workers.properties"
JkLogFile "c:\jakarta-tomcat4\logs\mod_jk.log"
JkLogLevel info

JkMount /examples/*.jsp testWorker1
JkMount /examples/servlet/* testWorker1
```

For Linux/Unix Systems:

```
# Load mod_jk
LoadModule jk_module modules/mod_jk.so

# Configure mod_jk
JkWorkersFile /usr/java/jakarta-tomcat4/conf/jk/workers.properties
JkLogFile /usr/apache2/logs/mod_jk.log
JkLogLevel info

JkMount /examples/*.jsp testWorker1
JkMount /examples/servlet/* testWorker1
```

Creating an Alias for the Tomcat Context

Finally, we'll need to create an alias for the Tomcat `examples` web application context so that Apache serves any static resources it contains. Using this alias Apache will forward all requests that map to a JSP page/servlet under `examples` to the appropriate Tomcat instance:

```
# Create an Alias for examples
Alias /examples/ "/usr/java/jakarta-tomcat4/webapps/examples/"

# Now allow access to this directory by setting
# the required Apache directives.
<Directory "/usr/java/jakarta-tomcat4/webapps/examples/">
  Options Indexes FollowSymLinks
  AllowOverride None
  Order allow,deny
  Allow from all
</Directory>

# Now prevent any unauthorized access to the contents of WEB-INF
<Location /*/WEB-INF/*>
  AllowOverride None
  Deny From All
</Location>
```

If we use the `ApacheConfig` directive, then we'll just need to append the following line to our `httpd.conf` file. It will include the auto-generated `mod_jk.conf` file in our `httpd.conf` file:

```
# Here please replace $CATALINA_HOME with the actual value of the
# Tomcat installation directory
Include $CATALINA_HOME/conf/auto/mod_jk.conf
```

Testing the Final Setup

In this section, we'll see how Apache accepts every request. All the requests for any dynamic processing, like JSP pages or servlets, will be handed over to Tomcat. Similarly, any response from them will be sent back to the client through Apache.

The first step for testing will be to check we can see the `examples` web application by pointing a browser at http://localhost/examples/. If everything is set up correctly, you should see something like the following:

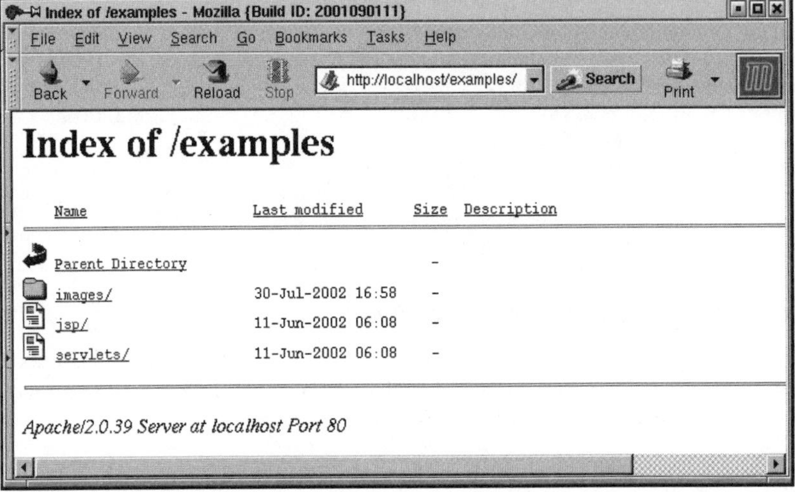

This shows that the integrated combination of Tomcat and Apache is working fine for serving static content. Let's cross-check whether `mod_jk` is doing its job equally well for serving dynamic content. We do this by pointing our browser to one of the examples that are installed with Tomcat. For example, http://localhost/examples/jsp/dates/date.jsp:

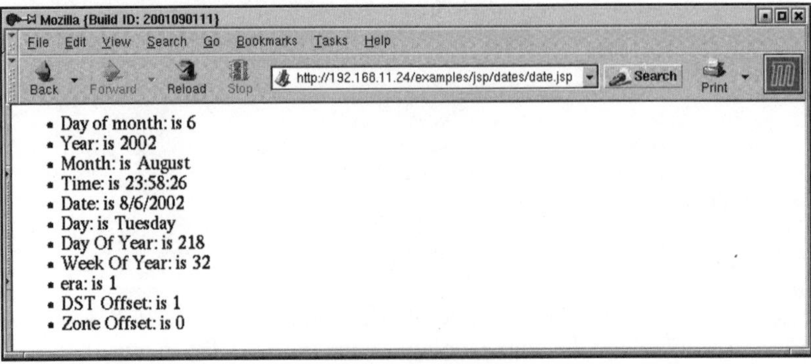

After testing the deployment from a local machine, test the installation from any other machine across the network. This will make sure that the settings we made are working as expected.

Tomcat Load Balancing with Apache

Every enterprise web application needs to have fast, scalable, reliable, and fail-safe behavior once it has been deployed. On busy sites, whenever a request call is delegated from the Apache server to Tomcat, it's a good idea to route these requests to multiple Tomcat servers rather than to a single one. Using the same Apache module (`mod_jk`), we can do this. `mod_jk` manages the task of load balancing with support for **seamless sessions** and round-robin scheduling.

Let's first look at the concept of a seamless session (also known as **session affinity** or **sticky session**). When a client requests any dynamic resource, like a JSP page, for the first time, the load balancer will route this request to any of the available Tomcat instances. Now, any further request from the same browser session should get routed to the same Tomcat container instance to keep the user session alive. If the maximum number of connections to that worker has been reached before this call, then `mod_jk` waits for the appropriate worker to become free. This is known as a seamless session because the client sees no break in the application's function.

Now we'll see how to configure `mod_jk` to handle client requests with this kind of functionality. Here, the Tomcat instances are listening to different ports (if they are running on the same machine) or are running on different machines. We are going to test both these conditions simultaneously.

Preparing for Load Balancing

The first step in setting up load balancing is to designate a load-balancing (lb) worker. The load-balancing worker is responsible for the management of several actual request-processing workers. The lb worker handles:

- Instantiating the workers in the web server
- Using the workers' load-balancing factor to perform weighted round-robin load balancing where a high lb factor means a more powerful machine that can handle more requests than others in the group
- Keeping requests belonging to the same session executing on the same Tomcat worker, that is, keeping session affinity
- Identifying failed Tomcat workers, suspending requests to them, and falling back to other workers managed by the lb worker

The overall result is that workers managed by the same lb worker are load-balanced (based on their lb factor and current user session) and also covered by a fall-back mechanism so that a single Tomcat process death will not bring down the entire deployment. Note that these workers should not appear in the `worker.list` property. A comma-separated list of workers that the load balancer needs to manage is set as shown below:

```
worker.loadbalancer.balanced_workers=testWorker1,testWorker2
```

The Workers

In this example, we'll install and run different Tomcat instances on our test machine (`localhost`), as well as one more on a remote machine (which is accessible over the network). Let's install two different Tomcat instances, say `tomcat1` and `tomcat2`, on the test machine at `$CATALINA_HOME1` and `$CATALINA_HOME2`. Apache is also running on this machine.

Also, install Tomcat (`tomcat3`) on a different machine, available over the network. Let's say `tomcat3` is running at `$CATALINA_HOME3` on its machine.

We'll configure all these Tomcat instances as needed by the load balancing mechanism and then return to the `workers.properties` file as the final step. However, we should keep the following things in mind:

- Each Tomcat instance running on the same machine should listen to a unique port. However, two Tomcat instances running on two different machines (which are participating in the same load balancing mechanism as two workers) can listen on the same port number.
- The AJP connector of each Tomcat instance running on the same machine should listen to a unique port. However, the AJP connectors of two Tomcat instances running on two different machines (which are participating in the same load balancing mechanism as two workers) can run on the same port.

Configuring the AJP Connector Ports

As stated above, we know that the two workers, `tomcat1` and `tomcat2`, are running on the local machine. We'll set the AJP connector of `tomcat1` to run on port 8009 and for `tomcat2` it will be 8010. Let's configure the AJP connector for `tomcat3` running on port 8010. This way we can also test that the AJP connectors of two different Tomcat instances can run on the same port when they are on different machines.

Now edit the `$CATLINA_HOME/conf/server.xml` file of each Tomcat worker and set the AJP port for each of them as we decided above. So search for the entry below and replace the `port` attribute's value with the appropriate value for the Tomcat instance you are dealing with:

```
<Connector className="org.apache.ajp.tomcat4.Ajp13Connector"
              port="8009" minProcessors="5" maxProcessors="75"
              acceptCount="10" debug="0"/>
```

Modify the AJP connector port for each Tomcat worker/instance as below:

- For `tomcat1`: 8009
- For `tomcat2`: 8010
- For `tomcat3`: 8010

Tomcat 3.x

Note that for Tomcat 3.x the setting of the AJP connector is a little different and can easily be done by including the following lines in `server.xml`. An entry for AJP 1.2 comes after the `<ContextInterceptor>` entry. Usually an entry for AJP 1.2 is provided and we can create a similar one for AJP 1.3 as mentioned opposite:

```
<Connector className="org.apache.tomcat.service.PoolTcpConnector">
  <Parameter name="handler"
        value="org.apache.tomcat.service.connector.Ajp13ConnectionHandler"/>
  <Parameter name="port" value="8009"/>
</Connector>
```

Configuring the Server Port

We now make sure that each Tomcat worker is running on a non-clashing port. So, in `server.xml`, set each Tomcat worker's server port as detailed below. To do this, search for the following entry:

```
<Server port="8005" shutdown="SHUTDOWN" debug="0">
```

and set the server port for each Tomcat worker as below:

- For `tomcat1`: 8005
- For `tomcat2`: 8006
- For `tomcat3`: 8005

> **Note that multiple WARP connectors could cause problems if they are all listening on the same port. As we have no need for a WARP connector in this example, it is best if all WARP connector configurations are removed.**

Tomcat 3.x

For Tomcat 3.x, instead of the `<Server>` tag, we need to refer to the following entry and change the port for load balancing:

```
<Connector className="org.apache.tomcat.service.PoolTcpConnector">
  <Parameter name="handler"
             value="org.apache.tomcat.service.http.HttpConnectionHandler"/>
  <Parameter name="port"
             value="8080"/>
</Connector>
```

> **As we'll be running the Tomcat workers in conjunction with the load balancer worker, it's possible that someone could directly access any of the available workers by bypassing the load balancer path. We can easily solve this problem by removing the HTTPConnector configuration of all the Tomcat workers.**

Setting the jvmRoute Option

For load balancing, we'll also need to specify the `jvmRoute` attribute to the `<Engine>` directive in `server.xml` for each Tomcat worker. This unique ID ensures the seamless session feature is activated and it must be unique across all the available Tomcat workers participating in the load-balancing cluster.

This unique identifier will be appended to the session ID generated for that Tomcat worker. Using this, the front-end server can, and will, forward any particular session request to the appropriate Tomcat worker.

So let's add a unique `jvmRoute` attribute to each Tomcat worker's `server.xml` file as detailed below. For `tomact1` and `tomcat2` on the local machine the entries will be:

```
<Engine jvmRoute="tomcat1"
name="Standalone"
defaultHost="localhost"
debug="0">

<Engine jvmRoute="tomcat2"
name="Standalone"
defaultHost="localhost"
debug="0">
```

For `tomact3` running on the remote machine the entry will be:

```
<Engine jvmRoute="tomcat3"
name="Standalone"
defaultHost="localhost"
debug="0">
```

The workers.properties File

We'll now define a simple `workers.properties` file for the load balancing. Here, we'll define a single worker in the `worker.list` option as the load-balancing worker. This worker will be the single access point for any requests delegated by Apache and will handle the other workers. We'll call it `loadbalancer`, although we can name it whatever we want.

For each Tomcat worker, let's define the standard parameters: the host and port on which it will be running, the version of the AJP protocol (AJP 1.3 or AJP 1.4) it will be using, the load balancing factor which should be applied, and the number of open connections accepted in the form of cache:

```
# Define the path separator appropriate to the platform we are using
# For Windows Systems
#ps=\

# For Linux /Unix Systems
ps=/

# Define the load balancing worker only, and not other workers.
worker.list= loadbalancer

# -------------------------------------------------------------------------
# First Tomcat instance running on local machine (localhost)
# -------------------------------------------------------------------------
# Set the port on which it will listen
worker.tomcat1.port=8009
# Set the host on which the Tomcat worker is running
```

```
worker.tomcat1.host=localhost
# Set the type of worker, here we are using ajp13
worker.tomcat1.type=ajp13
# Specify the load-balancing factor, any value greater than 0
worker.tomcat1.lbfactor=10
# Specify the size of the open connection cache.
worker.tomcat1.cachesize=5

# -------------------------------------------------------------------------
# Second Tomcat instance running on local machine (localhost)
# -------------------------------------------------------------------------
# Set the port on which it will listen
worker.tomcat2.port=8010
# Set the host on which the Tomcat worker is running
worker.tomcat2.host=localhost
# Set the type of worker, here we are using ajp13
worker.tomcat2.type=ajp13
# Specify the load-balancing factor , any value greater than 0
worker.tomcat2.lbfactor=10
# Specify the size of the open connection cache.
worker.tomcat2.cachesize=5

# -------------------------------------------------------------------------
# Remote Tomcat instance running on some other machine, say "remote"
# -------------------------------------------------------------------------
# Set the port on which it will listen
worker.tomcat3.port=8010
# Set the host on which the Tomcat worker is running
worker.tomcat3.host=remote
# Set the type of worker, here we are using ajp13
worker.tomcat3.type=ajp13
# Specify the load-balancing factor, any value greater than 0
worker.tomcat3.lbfactor=10
# Specify the size of the open connection cache.
worker.tomcat3.cachesize=5
```

The `loadbalancer` worker is of type `lb` and uses a weighted round-robin algorithm for load balancing with support for seamless sessions as discussed earlier. If a worker dies, the `loadbalancer` worker will check its state over small time intervals. Until it is back online, all work is redirected to the other available workers:

```
# ------------------------
# Load Balancer worker
# ------------------------

worker.loadbalancer.type=lb
# State the comma-separated name of workers that will form part of this
# load balancing mechanism
worker.loadbalancer.balanced_workers=tomcat1, tomcat2, tomcat3
```

DocumentRoot

For the load balance testing, we are assuming that Apache is serving from its default directory. So cross-check that the appropriate DocumentRoot and <Directory> settings are present in the httpd.conf file. If they are not present, put them back to their default settings until the load balancing is tested. The defaults will be something like this:

```
# The default entry for the DocumentRoot
DocumentRoot "usr/apache2/htdocs"

# This should be changed to whatever you set DocumentRoot to.
<Directory "usr/apache2/htdocs">
```

Setting the JkMount Directive

We have gone through the basic steps for integrating Tomcat and Apache, but perhaps the most important step is to tell Apache about the URL patterns that it should hand over to Tomcat:

```
# Mappings for the requests to JSP and servlets
JkMount /servlet/*  loadbalancer
JkMount /*.jsp loadbalancer
```

So mod_jk will forward any requests that match these patterns to the loadbalancer worker. A couple of examples are:

- http://localhost/examples/jsp/test.jsp
- http://localhost/examples/servlet/myServlet

Once the request processing is done, the response is sent back to the corresponding client.

Including the mod_jk Settings

Here, we'll need to include the settings for mod_jk, the defined Tomcat loadbalancer worker, and a few other settings like the location of the log file, the log level, and mappings for the various resources that mod_jk will ask Tomcat to provide.

Insert the lines below at the bottom of the httpd.conf configuration file:

```
# Configure mod_jk
LoadModule jk_module modules/mod_jk.so
# Include the workers.properties file
JkWorkersFile /usr/apache2/conf/workers.properties
# Location for the Log File
JkLogFile /usr/apache2/logs/mod_jk.log
# Logging level like emerg, info, debug
JkLogLevel emerg

# Mappings for the requests to JSP and servlets
JkMount /servlet/*  loadbalancer
JkMount /*.jsp loadbalancer
```

Before we run the Tomcat workers for testing, we'll need to handle the `$CATALINA_HOME` environment variable. In most cases, when we run a single Tomcat instance, we set the `$CATALINA_HOME` as an environment variable so that it will be available once our system boots up. This can create a problem when we want to run two instances of Tomcat on the same machine (in our case `tomcat1` and `tomcat2`). This is because each of the Tomcat instances will need its own unique `$CATALINA_HOME` variable.

This can be handled by resetting `$CATALINA_HOME`. If we had set it when we were using a single instance, then for each of the Tomcat instances, edit the `catalina.sh` (or `catlina.bat` for Windows) file located in `$CATALINA_HOME/bin` and add the following two lines at the start of it.

For Linux/ Unix Systems:

- `$JAVA_HOME=/usr/java/j2sdk1.4.0`
- `$CATALINA_HOME=/usr/java/jakarta-tomcat4X`

For Windows:

- `%JAVA_HOME%=c:\j2sdk1.4.0`
- `%CATALINA_HOME%=c:\Jakarta-tomcat4X`

Sample Files for Load Balance Testing

Now that we've finished configuring our load-balancing setup, we need to make sure that all the Tomcat instances are up and running properly. To do this, we'll create a file named `index.jsp` with the following contents and put it in the `ROOT` context of `tomcat1` (at `$CATALINA_HOME1/webapps/ROOT/index.jsp`):

```
<%@ page language="java" %>
<html>
  <body>
    <h1><font color="red">Session Served By Tomcat 1</font></h1>
    <table align="centre" border="1">
      <tr>
        <td>Session ID</td>
        <td><%= session.getId() %></td>
      </tr>
      <tr>
        <td>Created on</td>
          <td><%= session.getCreationTime() %></td>
      </tr>
    </table>
  </body>
</html>
```

Copy this file into the `ROOT` context of the other two Tomcat installations. To help us see which Tomcat instance has processed our request, edit `index.jsp` by changing the line:

```
<h1><font color="red">Session Served By Tomcat 1</font></h1>
```

to:

```
<h1><font color="blue>"Session Served By Tomcat 2</font></h1>
```

for tomcat2 ($CATALINA_HOME2/webapps/ROOT/index.jsp), and:

```
<h1><font color="green">Session Served By Tomcat 3</font></h1>
```

for tomcat3 ($CATALINA_HOME3/webapps/ROOT/index.jsp).

Testing the Load Balancing Behavior

Let's test our setup for load balancing. To do this, first verify that Apache is serving the static content properly by browsing to the URL http://localhost/. You should see the default Apache index.html page. Now, test that Tomcat is serving the index.jsp page by browsing to the URL http://localhost/index.jsp. We will be served by any of the three Tomcat instances. If tomcat1 served that page, we'll get the page as shown below:

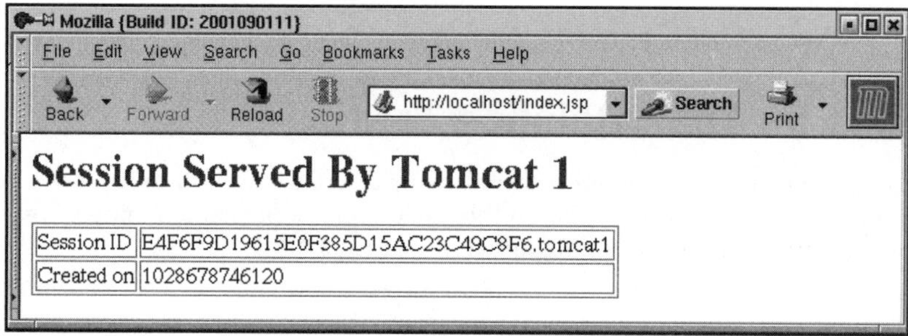

Similarly, if the tomcat2 worker serves our request, we'll get the page with the blue heading and the Session Served By Tomcat 2 message followed by its session data. Finally, if our request gets routed to the remote Tomcat instances we'll get the page with the green heading and the message Session Served By Tomcat 3 followed by its session data.

Let's see how seamless session is supported by the Tomcat load balancer implementation. Notice the page we get in the browser window. We will find the session ID mentioned in the first row of the table. Make a note of it. Refresh your browser, and you'll notice that for any number of hits, the session ID remains the same. This indicates that the load balancer is keeping the current session contents intact.

Let's try something more to test the load balancing behavior of our implementation. This time, open another window with the same URL (http://localhost/index.jsp). We'll see that this time our request will be handled by some other Tomcat worker, maybe tomcat2 or tomcat3, but certainly not by the worker which served the earlier request (tomcat1). This is because our implementation uses mod_jk's round-robin algorithm.

Now let's take our testing to the next level. This time, if we keep our browser windows open, we'll notice that all three Tomcat workers will serve the incoming requests in a round-robin fashion. This means that the first request will be served by say tomcat1, the second will be served by tomcat2, and the third will be served by tomcat3. The fourth request will be again served by tomcat1. This is shown in the table opposite:

tomcat1	tomcat2	tomcat3
1	2	3
4	5	6
7	8	9
-	-	-

Now, stop the `tomcat2` worker and try the same thing. This time Apache uses the round-robin rule for the remaining two Tomcat workers. The following table represents the request processing:

tomcat1	tomcat2	tomcat3
1	X	2
3	X	4
5	X	6
-	X	-

What happens if we start `tomcat2` again? Does the load balancer realize that `tomcat2` is again available? Also, when will the load balancer start using it? The answer is that the load balancer will start using `tomcat2` as soon as it finds that the server is up. It periodically checks the status of the worker, and will start using it as soon as it is made available. We can cross-check this by starting `tomcat2` again and continue our testing cycle. We would get a response something like this:

tomcat1	tomcat2	tomcat3
1	X	2
3	X	4
5	6	7
8	9	10

Testing Further with Load Factor

We looked at load balance testing with the same load factors for all the workers. Let's look at a more realistic situation and how the `lbfactor` attribute of the worker will play a role. To carry out this test we'll need to change the corresponding `lbfactor` settings in `workers.properties`. Here we'll turn `tomcat3` (located on a remote machine) off. For this test, modify the following entries shown in the `workers.properties` file:

```
# modify the load-balancing factor for Tomcat 1
worker.tomcat1.lbfactor=2
# modify the load-balancing factor for Tomcat 2
worker.tomcat2.lbfactor=4
```

Now, restart Tomcat workers 1 and 2. Keep tomcat3 off and finally restart Apache. Then do the same steps of testing as we did for the earlier setup. Visit http://localhost/index.jsp a number of times and note the behavior.

In this case you should notice the behavior has changed. This is because the lbfactor is causing mod_jk to distribute the request load proportionally. So tomcat1 and tomcat2 will not get the hits as before and the pattern will be like this:

tomcat1	tomcat2
1	2
3	X
4	5
6	X
7	8
9	X

Why Set a Different lbfactor for Each Worker?

Typically, in a real-world deployment scenario, we'd find that the hardware configurations of our machines are not the same. In addition, there is a good chance that even though the hardware configurations are the same, the machines may be serving other online content. So every machine may not be in a position to contribute exactly the same resources as the others in the final load balancing setup. This can be handled by setting an appropriate lbfactor for each of them. Accordingly, the runtime load balancer will distribute the request load appropriately.

Summary

In this chapter we have enhanced our skills for handling web application deployment. We started with a quick discussion of the AJP connector before going on to obtain mod_jk, the Apache redirector module. We discussed the binary distribution as well as going through how to build from source on both Windows and Unix systems. We also discussed the next generation redirector module, mod_jk2, and saw how its configuration is very similar to that of mod_jk.

We saw how mod_jk acts as a redirector component to route requests for dynamic content to Tomcat workers. Also, we have acquired skills to exploit the strengths of integrating Tomcat with Apache. We have implemented and tested load balancing using mod_jk for properly routing traffic between multiple instances of Tomcat and Apache. We can now fine-tune our application deployment with the various available options.

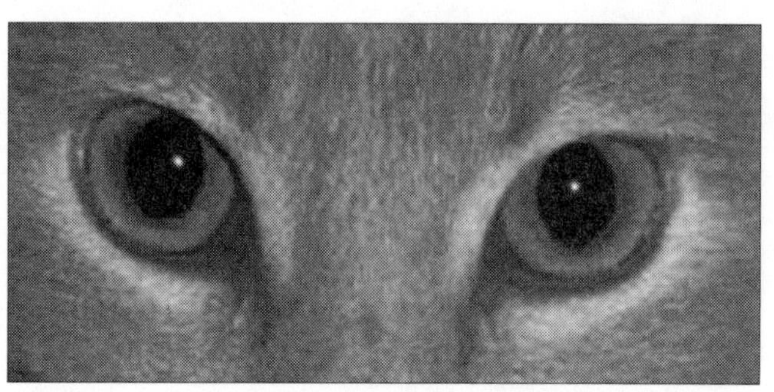

14

Tomcat and IIS

Internet Information Services (IIS) is Microsoft's implementation of a web server and is optimized for the Windows operating system. Why would we want to run IIS with Tomcat? We may want to do this in an environment that needs to be capable of supporting multiple development platforms such as Microsoft's Active Server Pages and the alternative JavaServer Pages. Also, we get better performance on Windows by using the web serving capability of IIS and Tomcat as the servlet/JSP container instead of using Tomcat as both a web server and a servlet container.

IIS is a web server but can also process Active Server Pages, which is Microsoft's answer to server-side scripting. It does not have a servlet container and cannot by default process JSP and servlets. However, IIS can be extended by adding **ISAPI** filters, using which we can use third-party components such as servlets and JSPs. ISAPI filters are plug-ins to IIS that can filter incoming requests, perform custom processing, call other applications, and perform filtering functions on output that is to be sent back to the HTTP client. The Apache Group has created an ISAPI filter that can be added to IIS and configured so that IIS handles all requests except for JSP and servlets, which it redirects to Tomcat.

In this chapter, we will look at how we can configure IIS and Tomcat to work together. We'll also discuss in detail the installation of the ISAPI filter for IIS and configuration changes that are necessary for Tomcat. We'll further discuss the necessary troubleshooting tips wherever applicable.

This chapter focuses on the integration points between IIS and Tomcat. As such, it is not a primer for either IIS or Tomcat. Instead, it focuses on the intermediate components that make this integration magic happen.

Concepts

Before starting on the installation procedures, it is worth reviewing the fundamentals of this technology:

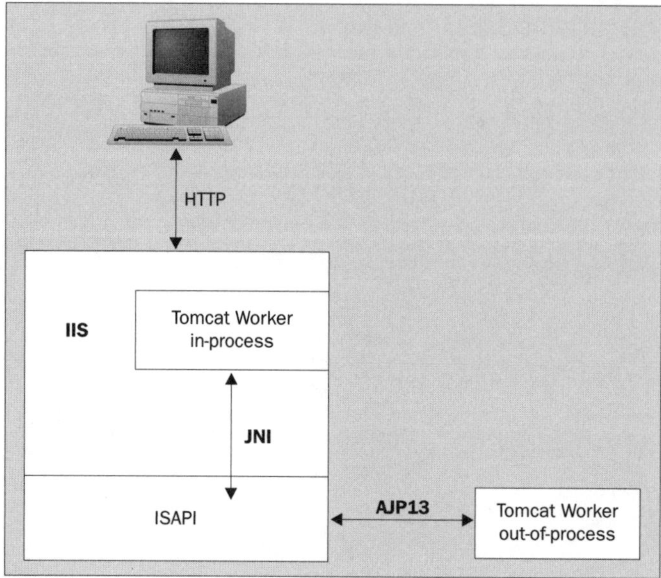

As illustrated in the diagram above, the core component that enables integration between IIS and Tomcat is the ISAPI redirector and it is available for download as a DLL called `isapi_redirect.dll`. ISAPI is Microsoft's answer to CGI. It is a way for Microsoft to customize and extend the functionality of IIS. The component `isapi_redirect.dll` is referred to as a redirector because it filters incoming URL requests and redirects some of these requests to Tomcat using a protocol such as AJP 1.3 or Java's JNI. Note that the AJP protocol is also used to connect Tomcat to Apache. For more information on AJP connectors, refer to Chapter 13.

The filters processed by `isapi_redirect.dll` are configurable. These are specified in a file called `uriworkermap.properties`. We can specify which incoming requests should be forwarded to Tomcat by IIS by editing the contents of this file. The Tomcat process that receives and processes requests from the ISAPI redirector is called the worker. The Tomcat worker either exists as out-of-process, that is, as a distinct process within the operating system, or in-process – within IIS where it (IIS) opens an instance of the JVM in its address space. We can configure Tomcat workers to be in-process or out-of-process and we will see how we can do this soon. In-process and out-of-process Tomcat workers differ from each other in the way that they perform Inter Process Communication (IPC) with the ISAPI redirector.

The ISAPI redirector communicates with an out-of-process Tomcat worker over TCP/IP using a proprietary protocol called AJP and it communicates with an in-process Tomcat worker using Java's JNI. For both – out-of-process and in-process workers – the ISAPI redirector must know the specifics of the Tomcat worker. The specific configuration information could be an IP port number and machine name for an out-of-process worker or it could be the location of the JDK and Tomcat binaries for an in-process worker. The administrator configures this specific information in the file, `workers.properties`. This file also has as a list of the defined workers. Note that since the AJP 1.3 protocol runs over TCP/IP, it lends itself to distributed client-server configurations.

In general, even though each instance of an out-of-process Tomcat worker may be marginally slower that its in-process counterpart, out-of-process Tomcat workers provide for a more robust implementation and are more scalable because architectures based on out-of-process Tomcat workers can be arranged in a heterogeneous environment where you can have Tomcat on Unix and IIS on Windows. We will see how to do that later in the chapter. Note that the in-process working of Tomcat is not supported in version 4. We have included a section in this chapter on the in-process configuration, but we have only done this to be thorough in our coverage and to illustrate some interesting concepts. We recommend that you use the out-of-process configuration.

Configuring IIS for Tomcat Out-of-Process

In this section, we will go over the software that needs to be installed and the configuration changes that need to be made to IIS for it to hand off servlet/JSP requests to Tomcat. The instructions are for a configuration where we have IIS and Tomcat running on the same machine. We will take a look at a distributed configuration in a later section. For the purposes of this install, we used the following configuration:

- Operating system: Windows 2000 SP2
- Web Server: IIS 5.0
- Tomcat: 4.0.4
- JAVA: JDK1.3
- Connectivity: AJP 1.3

A quick word about versions before moving on – IIS 4 and 5 will work with Tomcat 3 and 4 and JDK 1.2 onwards. If possible, it is best to use the most recently release versions. Hence we would recommend that you use Tomcat 4 with IIS 5. In regard to the operating system, Windows 2000 and Windows NT provide more robust alternatives to Windows 98.

The installation of the ISAPI redirector can be quite tricky. You may want to follow instructions, step by step, as they're outlined here to start with. We would encourage you to use the same platform as used above during your first install. Once you've had a successful install, you can then attempt your own variations. As we proceed through out this chapter, we will discuss concepts as they come up and you should be able to use this as a foundation to create your own customized configurations.

Install Tomcat and IIS

Follow the instructions given in Chapter 3 to install Tomcat. Verify that Tomcat is working properly; by browsing to the URL: http://localhost:8080/, you should get the default Tomcat home page. Check to verify that IIS is installed on the server. If not, we will need to install IIS by going to Start | Setting | Control Panel and selecting the Add/Remove programs applet. Look under the Add/Remove Windows Components section to install IIS.

> **Also make sure that the directory to the `bin` directory of the JDK was appended to the `PATH` environment variable.**

Download isapi_redirect.dll

Once Tomcat and IIS are installed, the next thing to do is to download the ISAPI redirector (`isapi_redirect.dll`). The binary can be downloaded from http://jakarta.apache.org/builds/jakarta-tomcat/release/v3.3/bin/win32/i386/. This file (`isapi_redirect.dll`) needs to be placed in the `%CATLINA_HOME%\bin` directory.

> **You may have noticed that we obtained the `isapi_redirect.dll` from the Tomcat 3.3 release directory, even though we are using Tomcat 4.0.4. This is because the latest version of `isapi_redirect.dll` was released with Tomcat 3.3. Nevertheless, this version of the `isapi_redirect.dll` is the correct version to use with Tomcat 4 and IIS 5.**

Note that we can also build a copy of this `.dll` from sourcecode, but the easiest thing to do is to download the binary version from a trusted source.

Verify That Tomcat Is Configured To Use the AJP13 Connector

This step does not require you to make any changes. Here, we will take a look at a configuration setting in the `%CATLINA_HOME%\conf\server.xml` file, so that we can see what is happening behind the scenes. Tomcat 4.0.4 will communicate with IIS via the AJP 1.3 protocol. The Stand-Alone Tomcat server must be configured to use the AJP 1.3 connector, which is a Java interface that enables communication using the AJP 1.3 protocol. Note that Tomcat 4 will not work with previous versions of the AJP protocol such as AJP 1.2. To verify that Tomcat is using the AJP 1.3 connector, check that the AJP 1.3 connector is declared in `server.xml` under the section for the Tomcat Stand-Alone service.

```
<!-- Define the Tomcat Stand-Alone Service -->
<Service name="Tomcat-Standalone">

  <Connector className="org.apache.ajp.tomcat4.Ajp13Connector"
             port="8009"
             minProcessors="5"
             maxProcessors="75"
             acceptCount="10"
             debug="0" />
```

With the above configuration, the connector will listen to incoming requests on port 8009. A minimum of 5 threads will be created to process incoming requests. A maximum of 75 requests can be processed concurrently and in such a situation up to 10 requests can be queued.

Create the Registry Entries for ISAPI Redirector

The ISAPI redirector (`isapi_redirect.dll`) uses certain registry entries to initialize its configuration. These entries need to be created so that Tomcat can locate the configuration files that tell the redirector where to send incoming requests for servlets and how to log messages.

As of Tomcat 3.3, we can have Tomcat generate a `.reg` file that can be executed to create these registry keys. To do this, find this line, in the `server.xml` file:

```
<Server port="8005" shutdown="SHUTDOWN" debug="0">
```

Add this line, under the line above:

```
<Listener className="org.apache.ajp.tomcat4.config.IISConfig" />
```

Shut down and restart Tomcat. Two directories `auto\` and `jk\` are created under the `%TOMCAT_HOME\conf\` directory as shown in the screenshot below:

```
Tomcat
Generating IIS registry file = ..\conf\auto\iis_redirect.reg
Generating IIS URI worker map file = ..\conf\auto\uriworkermap.properties
Starting service Tomcat-Standalone
Apache Tomcat/4.0.4
Starting service Tomcat-Apache
Apache Tomcat/4.0.4
```

Open the `iis_redirect.reg` file in a text editor and view the contents. Modify the `iis_redirect.reg` file so that it reflects the specifics of your configuration. Use absolute path names such as `C:\Tomcat4.0.4`. Do not use relative path names. Most problems with registering the `isapi_redirect.dll` filter in IIS are associated with incorrect path names in the registry.

Here is a sample of the file:

```
REGEDIT4

[HKEY_LOCAL_MACHINE\SOFTWARE\Apache Software Foundation\Jakarta Isapi
Redirector\1.0]
"extension_uri"="/jakarta/isapi_redirect.dll"
"log_file"="C:\\Tomcat4.0.4\\logs\\iis_redirect.log"
"log_level"="emerg"
"worker_file"="C:\\Tomcat4.0.4\\conf\\jk\\workers.properties"
"worker_mount_file"="C:\\Tomcat4.0.4\\conf\\auto\\uriworkermap.properties"
```

Let's take a look at each of the registry entries:

- `extension_uri`
  This is the URL to the `isapi-redirector` extension. Note that `jakarta` is a virtual directory within IIS that we will create later in the installation procedure.
- `log file`
  This is the path to the log generated by the ISAPI redirector.
- `log_level`
  This tells IIS as to what level of detail the ISAPI redirector will log to the log file? Valid values are: `debug`, `info`, `error`, and `emerg`. The default value with Tomcat 4 is `emerg`. You will get the most detailed information in the log file with the `debug` option and the least information with the `emerg` option.
- `worker_file`
  This is the path to the `workers.properties` file. We'll look at this in a later section.

- `worker_mount_file`
  This is the path to the `uriworkermap.properties` file which we will talk about in the next section.

To create the registry entries, double-click the on the `iis_redirect.reg` file and you'll get a message box as below:

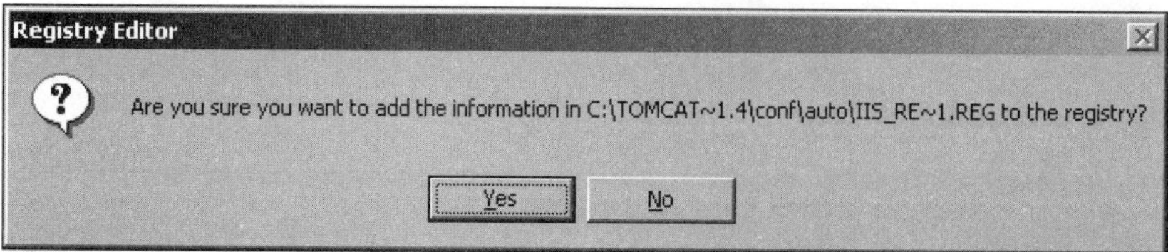

Select Yes to create the registry entries and the script will create the values in the registry. At this point, you should open up the registry using the `regedt32` utility and verify the registry entry keys that were created for you under `HKEY_LOCAL_MACHINE\SOFTWARE\Apache Software Foundation\Jakarta Isapi Redirector\1.0`:

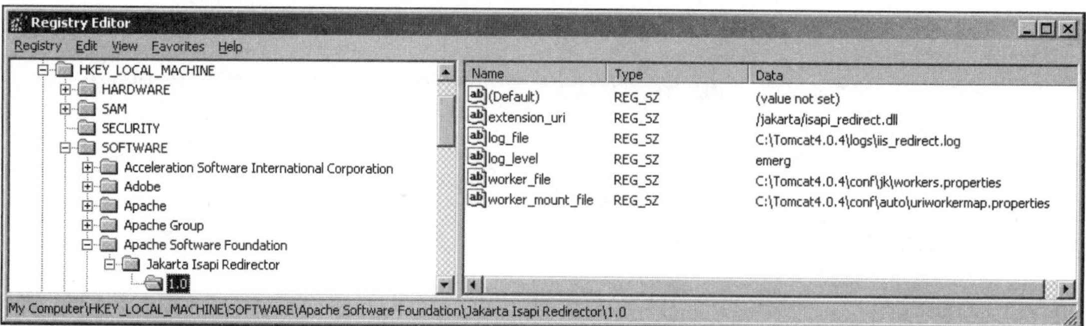

Note that we could also have created these entries manually, but the above procedure creates an easy starting point. If you need to uninstall Tomcat at some point, you can remove these registry entries manually by deleting them using the `regedt32` utility.

> **Note that you should be cautious while modifying the registry, as mistakes can prevent a Windows application from working correctly.**

Earlier in this section, we created the following entry in `server.xml`:

```
<Listener className=" org.apache.ajp.tomcat4.config.IISConfig" />
```

We did this so that Tomcat would generate the `iis_redirect.reg` file and the `uriworkermap.properties` files. Remove this entry from the `server.xml` file so that Tomcat does not repeatedly regenerate these files at startup and replace the changes that we have made to these files. After making these changes to `server.xml`, restart Tomcat.

Create the uriworkermap.properties File

This is a configuration file required by the connector. It maps incoming request URIs to Tomcat workers, which will process this request. A worker is an instance of Tomcat that will service requests initiated by a web server. The worker can reside on a separate computer or on the same computer as the web server. As of Tomcat 4, Tomcat itself can generate this configuration file. In fact, the procedure that we followed earlier to create the registry entries will also generate a file called `uriworkermap.properties` under the `conf\auto` directory. This is just a sample file. We can open and take a look at it. However, we will need to create our own version of this file to configure the specifics of our environment.

To test our install of the ISAPI redirector, we will configure Tomcat to serve up content from the `examples` web application that is shipped with Tomcat. To do this, rewrite the `uriworkermap.properties` file so that it contains a single line as shown below:

```
/examples/*=myworker
```

This line tells the ISAPI redirector to forward all requests for the `examples` web application to Tomcat for processing. Note that at this point in the install, we should have already set up the registry key corresponding to the worker mount file to point to `uriworkermap.properties`.

Create the workers.properties Configuration File

This configuration file tells `isapi_redirect.dll` where to look for the Tomcat worker that will service the web server request. In the previous step, we had configured web server requests for the `examples` application to be processed by a Tomcat worker called `myworker`. In this section we identify the specifics about the worker (`myworker` in this case) that will process requests for the `examples` web application.

This file needs to be placed in the directory specified by the registry entry created for it in the *Create the Registry Entries for ISAPI redirector* section. The path in the registry to this key is: `HKEY_LOCAL_MACHINE\SOFTWARE\Apache Software Foundation\Jakarta Isapi Redirector\1.0\worker_file`. In this case, with the default Tomcat 4 install, the directory is the `%CATLINA_HOME%\conf\jk` directory.

A sample of the `worker.properties` file can be found in the Apache web site, under the AJP connector section (http://jakarta.apache.org/tomcat/tomcat-4.0-doc/config/ajp.html). Here we've included a modified version for our specific configuration. It is a small version of the file, however it is an excellent starting point. As we proceed with the chapter, we will define concepts that will show you how to add to this configuration. For example, in the section *Scalable Architectures with Tomcat*, we will show you how to add additional workers to build a more scalable architecture. To get started however, it is best to define just a single worker as shown below. In the `workers.properties` file, as a minimum, we will need to specify:

- The definition of the worker, example name, and the connector type (ajp13)
- The port where the AJP connector is running.

Note that this `workers.properties` file is quite different from the sample `workers.properties` file that is supplied by the Apache group (see the previous chapter for details). For simplicity, we have defined a single worker called `myworker`:

```
# ************ Begin worker.properties **************

# define a worker named myworker of type ajp13
worker.myworker.type=ajp13

# We should configure our environment slash... ps=\ on NT and / on UNIX
# and maybe something different elsewhere.
ps=\
#------ worker list ------------------------------------------
#-----------------------------------------------------------------------
# The worker that our plugins should create and work with
worker.list=myworker

#------ WORKER DEFINITION ------------------------------
#-----------------------------------------------------------------------
# Defining a worker named myworker and of type ajp13
# Note that the name and the type do not have to match.
worker.myworker.port=8009
worker.myworker.host=localhost

# ************ End worker.properties **************
```

In this example, we have created a `workers.properties` file that defines a Tomcat worker named `myworker` that uses the AJP1.3 protocol. This worker runs on the local server and is bound to port 8009. Note that we have not configured load balancing between multiple workers. This was covered in Chapter 13, and this is similar regardless of the web server that we are using (Apache or IIS).

Create a Virtual Directory within IIS

We need to create a virtual directory within IIS for the ISAPI redirector. We need to do this because the IIS redirector is an IIS plug-in, that is, it is a filter and an extension. IIS calls the filter function for incoming requests. If the incoming URL matches the list of filters maintained in `uriworkermap.properties`, control is transferred to the extension in the form `/jakarta/isapi_redirect.dll` – you may remember this entry from the registry setting for the `extension_uri` that we set up. To create the virtual directory, we should do the following:

- Open up IIS Manager (Internet Services Manager).
- Right-click on the **Default Web Site** and select **New** and **Virtual Directory**.
- The Virtual Directory Creation Wizard will pop open. Use `jakarta` as the name of the virtual directory alias. Note that the name of the virtual directory has to be `jakarta` because we had mentioned this in the registry entry before.
- The wizard will prompt us for a directory. Specify the directory of the installed `isapi_redirect.dll`. This is the `bin\` directory under the root Tomcat install.
- The wizard will prompt us for access permissions. The access permissions should be just read and execute.

Once you have created the `jakarta` virtual directory, it is a good idea to open it to review the properties you have set for the virtual directory. You can do this by right-clicking on the virtual directory and selecting properties. This is what you should see in the properties window:

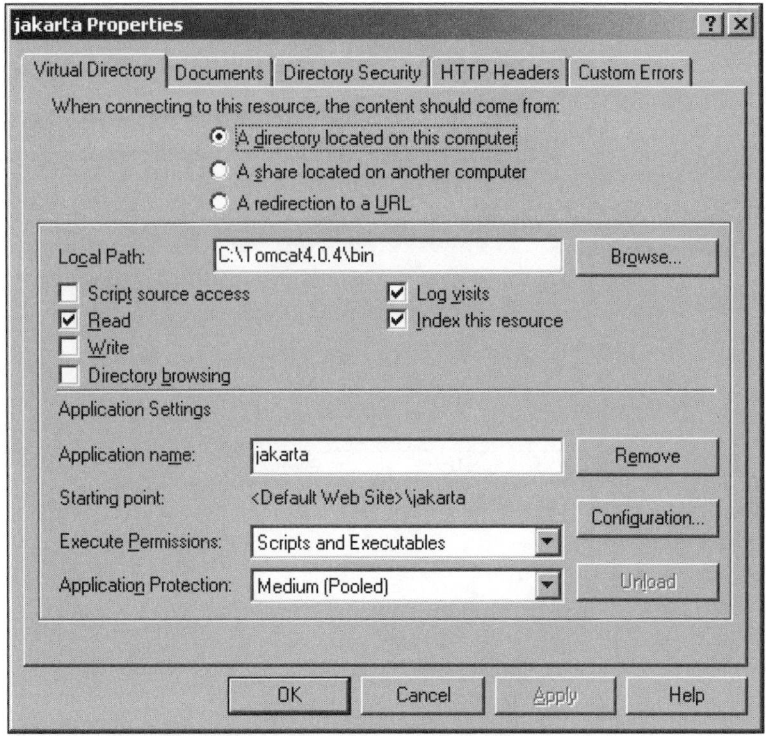

Install the ISAPI Redirector

We now install the ISAPI redirector in IIS. To do this:

- In IIS Manager, right-click on the Default Web Site, select Properties from the drop-down menu and click on it to open up the properties window
- In the properties window, click on the ISAPI Filters tab
- Click on the Add button

You will be prompted for the name of the filter and the location of `isapi_redirect.dll`. For the name of the filter use `jakarta`. Use the browse button to select `isapi_redirect.dll`, which is in `%TOMCAT_HOME%\bin` directory.

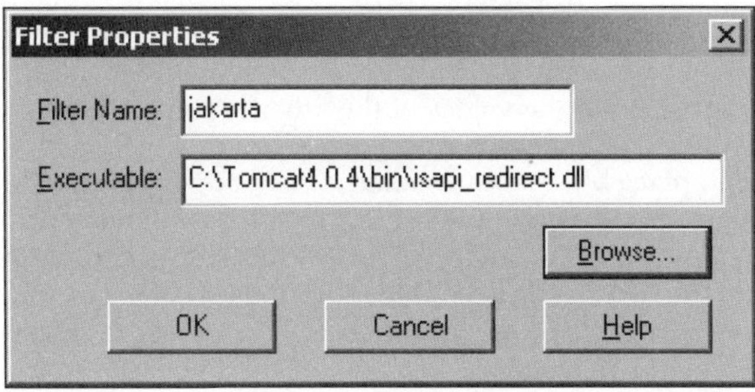

- Close IIS Manager if you have it open. Shut down and restart IIS. Make sure you do this using the services applet in the control panel. Do not do this using IIS Manager. You will need to shut down and start two services – these are the IIS Admin service and World Wide Web publishing service.

After you have restarted IIS, open up IIS Manager, check to see that there is a green arrow pointing upwards next to the ISAPI redirector that we have just installed.

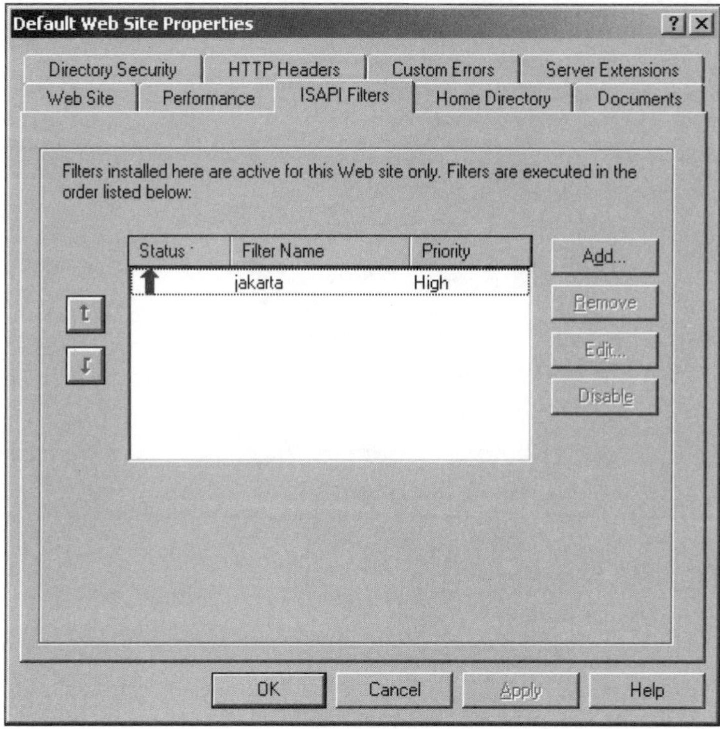

If you do not see the green arrow, then there is a problem with the install of the ISAPI redirector. This is a common error encountered during a first install.

Here is a list of things to check:

- Check your registry entries and the configuration files. Nine times out of ten, problems with this part of the install occur because the paths set in the registry settings for `worker_file` (`workers.properties`) or `worker_mount_file` (`uriworkersmap.properties`) are wrong. If these files are in the correct locations and the registry keys are defined properly, that is, names are spelled correctly, the ISAPI redirector should load regardless of the content in these files and regardless of the values of the other registry settings.

  As an experiment, place blank files for `workers.properties` and `uriworkermap.properties` in the correct locations and restart IIS. The ISAPI redirector loaded correctly if you get a green arrow, so for this step, the contents of these files do not matter, however, the files need to be in the locations specified in the registry. Note that if the contents of the `workers.properties` and `uriworkermap.properties` files are incorrect, you will have problems later on.

- Restart IIS by restarting the IIS Admin service and the World Wide Web publishing service.
- Verify that the path you have specified to the `isapi_redirect.dll` when adding the filter is valid.

Testing and Troubleshooting

We can test if our installation is correct by browsing to the URL: http://localhost/examples/servlets/index.html. If every thing went fine, you should be able to execute the examples on that page.

If the page is not displayed, then go through the following troubleshooting procedure:

- Verify that IIS is running. You can do this in the services applet. At a minimum, you need to have the IIS Admin service and the World Wide Web Publishing service running.
- Within IIS check that the ISAPI redirector is properly installed. If it is properly installed, it should have a green arrow next to it.
- Verify that the `jakarta` virtual directory is defined properly in IIS. If there is something wrong with it, IIS will indicate this by flagging it with a red symbol. Note also that the name of this virtual directory has to be `jakarta`.
- Verify that a log file has been created by `isapi_redirect.dll`. This was set in the *Create the Registry Entries for ISAPI Redirector* section as the `log_file` entry in the registry. If the log file does not exist, then you need to check that the ISAPI redirector was properly configured as specified in the previous step. Check to see if there are any error messages in this file. You could also try setting the `log_level` registry setting to the value `debug`. Be sure to restart IIS after you do this. This generates a large number of messages but it may help you troubleshoot this problem.
- Look within the IIS log. The IIS Log is by default located in `C:\WINNT\system32\LogFiles\W3SVC1\`; you can also click on the Properties button in the web site properties window to see where it is. By default a different log file is generated every day. In the log file you should see the following entry:

```
01:10:33 127.0.0.1 GET /jakarta/isapi_redirect.dll 200
```

  If this entry does not exist in the IIS Log, then the ISAPI redirector is not being called by IIS. The value 200 is the HTTP status code. If the call to `isapi_redirect.dll` exists but you are getting a status code such as 400, 404, and 500, then you have an error. Please refer to the section *IIS Log* for a detailed description of how you can interpret the messages in the IIS log as it relates to this installation procedure.

- Make sure Tomcat is running and that the AJP13 connector is listening on the correct port. This is port 8009 by default and is defined in the `server.xml` file. We had reviewed this configuration in the section *Verify That Tomcat Is Configured To Use AJP 13 Connector*. You can also review this by opening up a DOS prompt and running the command `netstat -a` from the command line. You should see a line similar to the line below as one of the entries:

```
TCP  localaddress:8009 foreignaddress:0  LISTENING
```

- Verify that the registry settings are correct.
- You may want to check that you do not have any additional filters defined besides the ISAPI redirector, which may be creating a conflict. If you do have additional filters defined in IIS, you may want to try removing them.
- Verify the content of the `workers.properties` file. It should be defined exactly as in the *Create the workers.properties Configuration File* section. Check that you have defined the worker correctly. Make sure the worker that you have defined in the `workers.properties` file is also the worker that is mapped to receive requests in the `uriworkermap.properties` file.

Adding Your Own Web Applications

In the last section, we looked at installing the ISAPI redirector and then we added the `examples` web application to test our install. Now that the ISAPI redirector is installed, let's look at how we can add other web applications to the configuration. Tomcat refers to this as adding an additional Context. Chapter 5 covers this topic in detail, and since this task remains the same regardless of which web server we are using, we will not go over this topic again in this chapter.

Configure the ISAPI Redirector

Make a change to the `uriworkermap.properties` file. In this file, add the following line:

```
/webapp/*=worker_name
```

Here, `webapp` is the name of the new web application and `worker_name` is the name of the Tomcat worker that will do the processing. We will need to restart IIS for this to take effect. Note that `worker_name` must be defined in the `workers.properties` file.

To further illustrate this concept, let's look at a scenario specific to the install that we have just completed. In the out-of-process installation section, we have defined a worker named `myworker`. We want `myworker` to process both the `examples` and the `webapp` web applications. The `workers.properties` file remains the same. This is what the `uriworkermap.properties` file looks like:

```
/examples/*=myworker
/webapp/*=myworker
```

Configure IIS To Serve Pages from the Tomcat Web Application

This step is optional. So far we have talked about configuring IIS to serve up static content from all directories but the Tomcat web applications. In this configuration, Tomcat is still responsible for serving content that resides in the web application directories. If we want to improve on this configuration, we can also configure IIS to serve up the static content from the web application directory itself while Tomcat continues to serve up the servlets and JSP. This may result in better performance because Tomcat will be relieved of the heavy lifting associated with serving up images and HTML files, and Tomcat can be used for what it does best, that is, process servlets and JSP. In this configuration, IIS will be used for serving up static content and Tomcat will be used for serving up the dynamic content.

To configure IIS in this manner, we create a virtual directory in IIS corresponding to the Tomcat web application directory. For example, if we were to do this for the webapp application:

- Set up a virtual directory in IIS called webapp. As a reference, see the section *Create a Virtual Directory within IIS* in the *Configuring IIS for Tomcat Out of Process* installation section
- Start the Virtual Directory Creation Wizard
- Select the path to the webapp directory
- Select the options for read and execute scripts for the access permissions to this directory

Edit the `uriworkermap.properties` file so that Tomcat serves up the JSP and servlets and IIS serves up all the other content:

```
/webapp/servlet/*=worker_name
/webapp/*.jsp=worker_name
```

These should be the only lines in the `uriworkermap.properties` file for the webapp web application. Note that `worker_name` is a worker that we defined elsewhere in the `workers.properties` file. After doing these changes, restart IIS.

Scalable Architectures with IIS and Tomcat

So far, we have talked about setting up a configuration where we have both IIS and Tomcat running on the same physical server. This is useful for smaller implementations. However, in a production environment, we may be interested in a more scalable solution where we would like to partition our architecture into multiple tiers so that the presentation layer or static HTML pages are served up by IIS and the web applications are hosted by Tomcat workers each residing on a separate server. This makes the system more scalable because you will have dedicated machines performing dedicated tasks, that is, serving static content and processing web applications.

In addition to scalability, we may also be interested in a distributed configuration to support multiple development and test environments, virtual hosting, and load-balanced Tomcat workers. In this section, we build on the concepts that we have already talked about and we take a look at the configuration changes required to build scalable distributed configurations of IIS and Tomcat:

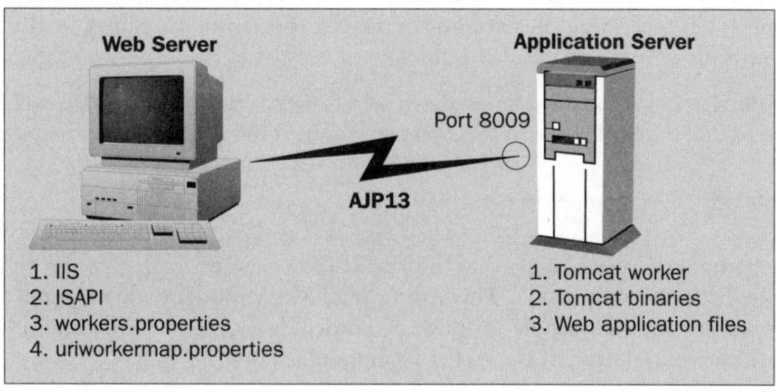

Let's start with a simple example and build on it. Consider the previous figure, where we have IIS on one server and a Tomcat worker running on a different server. How would we configure IIS and Tomcat to work with this configuration? The client server design of the AJP13 protocol makes this quite simple to configure.

First, let's look at the software stack on each sever. The Web Server, which has IIS running on it, will also have the isap_redirect.dll and the configuration files (uriworkermap.properties and workers.properties). Note that the JDK and the Tomcat binaries are not required on the web server. The Application Server will have the full Tomcat install. The AJP13 connector must be configured on the application server and a Tomcat worker must be running on a known port on the application server. Note that if you had multiple application servers with Tomcat workers distributed across these application servers servicing the same web application, you would want to duplicate the web application files across all these servers.

Next, let's look at the configuration changes required. From a conceptual perspective, it is probably instructive to look at a non-distributed configuration where we have everything on one box and then to examine what needs to be done to split it up into a distributed configuration. Let's look at a specific example, where we have a single worker called myworker servicing the examples application. This is a good example, because we have already gone through the steps required to install this specific configuration on a single box in an earlier section. Now let's look at the changes that would be required if we were to install this configuration on a web server and an application server:

- Install the software on the appropriate servers.
- Install the software as shown in the previous figure.
- Modify the uriworkermap.properties file. This file should look like this:

```
/examples/*=myworker
```

  Note that with the above, all resources in the examples directory are being sent to myworker, which runs on the application server. Alternatively, if we wanted IIS to service static HTML files, we could have had the following:

```
/examples/servlet/* = myworker
/examples/*.jsp=myworker
```

  Note that this configuration makes the application a little bit more complicated for the developers, because some files are on the examples virtual directory in IIS and others are in the examples web application in Tomcat.

- Modify the workers.properties file. The workers.properties file will have to be changed so that the host name of the Tomcat worker is the application server, as shown below:

```
worker.myworker.host=myappserver
```

All other entries remain the same. Note that the application server myappserver in this example must be IP addressable, from the web server. This example of a distributed configuration of a server running IIS and another server running a single instance of Tomcat is a good demonstration of the client server concepts that form the foundation of the AJP 1.3 protocol.

You could have multiple web servers that make up a web server farm, that is load balanced using a load-balancing switch. You could have multiple application servers each running a Tomcat worker. You could have multiple Tomcat workers running on each application server. You could have a web application serviced by multiple Tomcat workers – in this scenario the Tomcat workers would have to be load balanced. All these configurations are possible with the AJP protocol and the concepts remain the same whether you are using Apache or IIS as the web server. Chapter 13 has covered the concepts required to implement these configurations.

Finally, notice that once you begin partitioning your architecture into web server and application server configurations, you have paved the way for a heterogeneous system, so even though you use IIS for the web server, your application server can be Unix/Linux based.

Running Tomcat In-Process

With IIS, we have the option of installing Tomcat in-process or out-of-process. With the out-of-process option, Tomcat and IIS will run as separate processes in Win2K. The Inter Process Communication mechanism (IPC) between IIS and Tomcat occurs via TCP/IP. It is for this reason that we have to configure the port and host of the AJP13 worker in the `worker.properties` file. In an in-process configuration, IIS opens up a JVM in-process within the IIS address space and executes Tomcat within this JVM. Requests from IIS are forwarded to Tomcat using JNI. This approach results in faster response times, but may cause instability because both IIS and Tomcat are running within the same address space.

The in-process configuration is fully supported in Tomcat 3.3.1. Tomcat 4 does not support the configuration of an in-process worker at this time of writing. For the purposes of this configuration, we have used the following:

- Operating system: Windows 2000 SP2
- Web server: IIS 5.0
- Tomcat: 3.3.1
- JAVA: JDK1.3

Configure the ISAPI Redirector for IIS

Configure `isapi_redirect.dll`. This includes:

- Setting up the registry entries
- Defining a `workers.properties` file
- Defining the `uriworkermap.properties` file

The steps above are similar to the ones we followed while configuring Tomcat out-of-process. It is advisable (but not required) to set up and test an out-of-process worker first using the `ajp13` connector before configuring Tomcat for in-process execution.

Download the In-Process Adapter

We can download jni_connect.dll from the binary distribution list in http://jakarta.apache.org/builds/jakarta-tomcat/release/v3.3/bin/win32/i386/. Copy jni_connect.dll to the %TOMCAT_HOME%\bin\native directory.

Update the workers.properties File

Tomcat 3.3.1 has a sample workers.properties file that has the commands configured for the in-process worker. Open up the workers.properties file and make the following modifications:

Verify that the Tomcat home directory is correct. This should already be done as part of the configuration of the isapi_redirector.dll:

```
# workers.tomcat_home should point to the location where Tomcat is
# installed. This is where we have the conf, webapps, and lib directories.
workers.tomcat_home=c:\jakarta\jakarta-tomcat-3.3.1
```

Verify that the Java JDK directory is correct. This should already be done as part of the configuration of the isapi_redirector.dll:

```
# workers.java_home should point to the Java installation. Normally
# we should have the bin and lib directories beneath it.
workers.java_home=c:\jdk1.3
```

Add the in-process worker to the worker list:

```
# Add 'inprocess' if we want JNI connector
worker.list= inprocess
```

Declare the in-process worker and declare it to be of type jni:

```
#------ DEFAULT JNI WORKER DEFINITION---------------------------------
#---------------------------------------------------------------------
# Defining a worker named inprocess and of type jni.This
# declares that the worker is of type "in process".
# Note that the name and the type do not have to match.
worker.inprocess.type=jni
```

Declare the path to tomcat.jar located in the lib/ directory under the root Tomcat install directory. This varies for the different versions of Tomcat. The path that we see below is specific to Tomcat 3.3.1:

```
#------ CLASSPATH DEFINITION -----------------------------------------
#---------------------------------------------------------------------
#
# Additional classpath components. Note that the $variable values will be
# the actual values specific to the configuration.
worker.inprocess.class_path=$(workers.tomcat_home)$(ps)lib$(ps)tomcat.jar
```

Set the command line for Tomcat when it starts up in-process. We will see these lines in the sample file, but they are commented out. All we have to do is remove the comments:

```
# Setting the command line for Tomcat.
# Note: The cmd_line string may not contain spaces.
worker.inprocess.cmd_line=start

# Not needed, but can be customized.
worker.inprocess.cmd_line=-config
worker.inprocess.cmd_line=$(workers.tomcat_home)$(ps)conf$(ps)server.xml
worker.inprocess.cmd_line=-home
worker.inprocess.cmd_line=$(workers.tomcat_home)
```

Set the path to the JVM. The path to the JVM varies between the different JDKs:

```
worker.inprocess.jvm_lib=c:\jdk1.3\bin\hotspot\jvm.dll
```

Set the path to the log files used by the `jni` adapter. These lines were already set in the configuration file – we used the defaults:

```
# Setting the place for the stdout and stderr of Tomcat
worker.inprocess.stdout=$(workers.tomcat_home)$(ps)logs$(ps)inprocess.stdout
worker.inprocess.stderr=$(workers.tomcat_home)$(ps)logs$(ps)inprocess.stderr
```

Update the uriworkermap.properties File

This file tells the `isapi_redirector.dll` about which incoming requests to forward to which Tomcat worker. We may have already configured this file if the `isapi_redirector.dll` was set up. Add a line to the `uriworkermap.properties` file indicating which web application will be processed by the in-process worker. In our case, we wanted the `examples` web application to be processed by the in-process worker:

```
/examples/*=inprocess
```

Final Steps

Finally, make sure we have done the following:

- Verify that the registry entries for the ISAPI redirector point to the correct `uriworkermap.properties` and `workers.properties` files.
- Restart IIS.
- Verify that the ISAPI redirector filter in IIS has a green arrow next to it.
- Note that Tomcat does not have to be running, since IIS will open up a JVM and execute Tomcat within that JVM.

Testing and Troubleshooting

Once we've gone through the above steps, we can test it by typing the URL: http://localhost/examples/jsp/index.html. We may also want to look at the log files for errors. We had defined the log file for the JNI adapter in the workers.properties file. By default, these are present in the %TOMCAT_HOME%\logs directory, and they are called inprocess.stdout and inprocess.stderr. We may also want to look at messages created by the isapi_redirector.dll. Again, this log is in the logs directory by default.

Here are some typical things to look for in case things go wrong:

- Make sure IIS has loaded the ISAPI redirector correctly.
- Make sure the jni_connect.dll has been copied to the bin\native directory.
- Ensure that the path to the JVM is correct in the workers.properties file. This is the path to jvm.dll and it is set in workers.properties with the following statement:

```
worker.inprocess.jvm_lib=c:\jdk1.3\bin\hotspot\jvm.dll
```

With this type of error, you will see the following entry in isapi_redirect.log, when the log level is set to debug:

```
[Sun Aug 04 00:07:59 2002] [jk_jni_worker.c (384)]: Fail-> no jvm_dll_path
```

- Ensure the uriworkermap.properties is set to use the correct worker. With this type of error, you will see the following entry in isapi_redirect.log:

```
[Sun Aug 04 00:59:21 2002] [jk_worker.c (127)]: wc_get_worker_for_name, done did
not found a worker
```

Log Files

There are a number of log files that we can look at to monitor the system. These log files give us information about the system and also provide us with useful information on whether specific components are starting up or failing to load. Let's follow the data flow of an incoming HTTP request and view the different footprints made by this request.

IIS Log

IIS will be the first entity to receive the HTTP request. If the filter matches the incoming request with an entry in the uriworkermap.properties file, then it will call the extension. It will log this request in the IIS Log, which is by default located in the C:\WINNT\sytem32\LogFiles\W3SVC1\ directory. The configured logs directory can be viewed or changed in the IIS Manager by selecting **Properties** on the web site, usually **Default Web Site**, unless we have explicitly created a new one. In the **Web Site Properties** window, look under the **Web Site** tab and we'll see the **Properties** button under the **Logging** section. Click on the button to view or change the location of the IIS Log Files.

By default a different IIS log file is generated every day. The following entry in the log file indicates that the ISAPI redirector is functioning normally:

```
01:10:33 127.0.0.1 GET /jakarta/isapi_redirect.dll 200
```

This line in the IIS Log File shows time, client IP address, HTTP Method, URL requested, and HTTP status code. This footprint in the IIS log is the call to the ISAPI extension. Remember that `isapi_redirect.dll` is both a filter and an extension, and it indicates the ISAPI redirector is handling the call. Note the HTTP return code. In this case an HTTP return code of 200 indicates that everything is okay. If you do not see any such entry in the IIS Log, then perhaps your ISAPI redirector has failed to load, in which case; you need to check that you have set up the filters correctly in the `uriworkermap.properties` file. If the ISAPI redirector decides not to intercept the request, then IIS will attempt to service it, and when it does not find the resource it will terminate with an HTTP return code of 404. For example:

```
01:10:33 127.0.0.1 GET /examples/servlets/index.html_400
```

Since we are discussing possible errors in the IIS Log, let's look at some others.
If you get an return code of 500, check the `extension_uri` setting in the registry, the state of the `jakarta` directory, and the `workers.properties` file to see if the Tomcat worker is running on the expected ports. If Tomcat is not running at all, you will also get an return code of 500.

isapi_redirect.log

IIS passes control to the ISAPI filter, which then looks at the URL, filters it, and passes control back to IIS or Tomcat. If errors occur, it logs these in the `isapi_redirect.log`, which we configured in the registry. If this log file is empty, we do not have any errors with the configuration. If this log file does not show up at all, then the ISAPI redirector has probably not loaded correctly. Let's look at some of the messages that show up in this file, when things are working fine. Note that this trace was taken with the log level set to `debug`. The other log levels do not generate so many messages. In general, you will not want to run a production instance with the log level set to `debug`, but it is quite handy for troubleshooting purposes.

Here is a part of a successful startup sequence:

```
[Sun Aug 04 02:19:05 2002] [jk_isapi_plugin.c (814)]: Using registry.
[Sun Aug 04 02:19:05 2002] [jk_isapi_plugin.c (816)]: Using log file
c:\tomcat\logs\iis_redirect.log.
[Sun Aug 04 02:19:05 2002] [jk_isapi_plugin.c (817)]: Using log level 0.
[Sun Aug 04 02:19:05 2002] [jk_isapi_plugin.c (818)]: Using extension uri
/jakarta/isapi_redirect.dll.
..........          ..........          .................
..........          ..........          .................
..........          ..........          .................
```

Here is an error message when the JVM required by the in-process worker could not be found:

```
[Sun Aug 04 00:07:59 2002] [jk_jni_worker.c (384)]: Fail-> no jvm_dll_path
[Sun Aug 04 00:07:59 2002] [jk_jni_worker.c (568)]: Into destroy
[Sun Aug 04 00:07:59 2002] [jk_jni_worker.c (579)]: In destroy, JVM not
intantiated
[Sun Aug 04 00:07:59 2002] [jk_worker.c (164)]: wc_create_worker validate failed
for inprocess
[Sun Aug 04 00:07:59 2002] [jk_worker.c (229)]: build_worker_map failed to create
workerinprocess
```

Here is an error message when the Tomcat worker was not running and `isapi_redirect.dll` could not contact the worker using AJP 1.3:

```
[Sun Aug 04 02:25:50 2002] [jk_ajp13_worker.c (635)]: Error connecting to the
Tomcat process.
```

The JNI Adapter Logs

If we are running Tomcat in-process, the system will create the JNI adapter logs. These are called `inprocess.stderr` and `inprocess.stdout` by default in Tomcat 3.3.1 and these are configured in the `workers.properties` file (see the section *Update the workers.properties File* subsection of the section *Running Tomcat In Process*). Typically, `stderr` and `stdout` refer to the default error stream and default output stream configured for that particular program. However, the JNI adapter seems to log normal operations processing in the `stderr` log also. During the install process, the generation of these files is a good indication that Tomcat is running in-process. These files can be found in the `%TOMAT_HOME%\logs` directory.

Performance Tuning

We have some options for tuning the IIS and ISAPI redirector configuration to improve performance. In this section, we take a look at the different options that are available.

Web Site Hits Per Day

We can configure IIS for the expected number of hits on the web site. We can do this by selecting Properties and selecting the Performance tab on the IIS web site (usually Default Web Site unless you have customized your IIS configuration to include additional web sites). The screenshot opposite shows the tab where you would adjust this setting. You should adjust the expected number of hits per day to be slightly higher than what you expect. If you adjust it correctly, performance will improve because web connections will be made faster. If you set it too high, then you will waste server memory and performance will degrade.

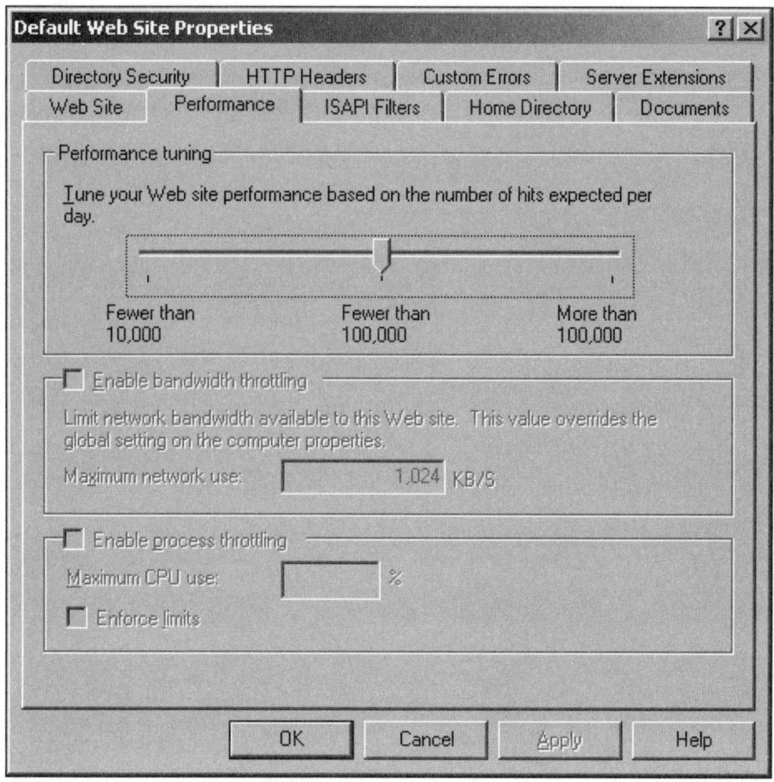

Keep Alive and TCP Connection Timeout

You can configure IIS to enable Keep Alive. This is set by default. HTTP is a stateless protocol and as such, the HTTP request between client and web server is established, serviced, and closed per request. If the web server were to set up and break down TCP connections for each HTTP request, then this would be a serious performance degradation. When you enable Keep Alive, the web server keeps the TCP connection open for a period of time to optimize performance for back-to-back HTTP requests between client and web server.

In the screenshot overleaf, you will also see a TCP connection timeout parameter. This is the amount of time that idle TCP connections will be left open. The default value is 900 seconds. You may consider reducing this value to 60 seconds and viewing the impact on your web site:

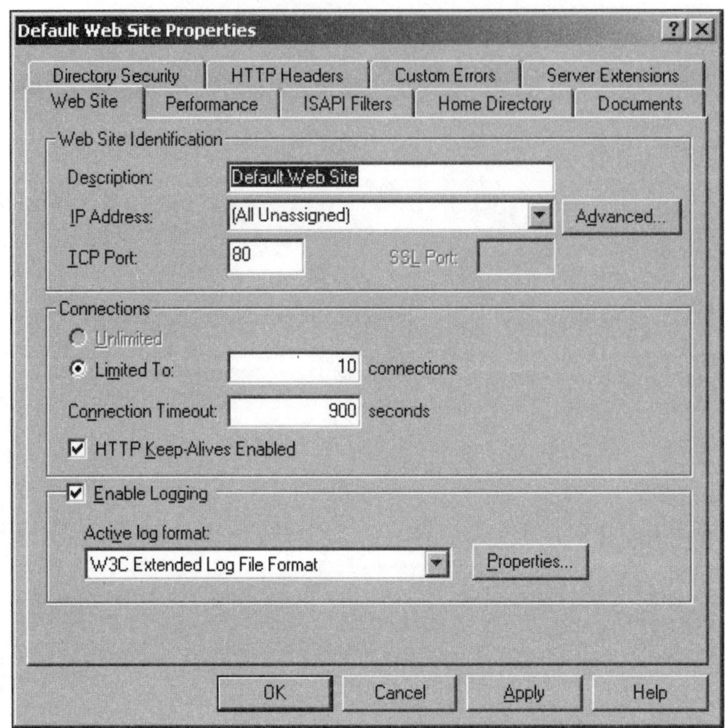

Caching in IIS

You can control caching in IIS by using three settings. The settings listed in the table below are to be created under `HKEY_LOCAL_MACHINE \SYSTEM\CurrentControlSet\Services\Inetinfo\Parameters`:

Setting	Data Type	Description	Default
`ObjectCacheTTL`	`REG_DWORD`	Time to Live Per object, that is, how long is each object cached in memory	30 seconds
`MemCacheSize`	`REG_DWORD`	Maximum size of IIS cache	50% of system memory
`MaxCachedFileSize`	`REG_DWORD`	Maximum size of files that will be cached.	256 KB

You can adjust each of these parameters to optimize the performance of your web server. When used with Tomcat, IIS will primarily serve up static content. Assuming that we are using a distributed configuration, you should set `ObjectCacheTTL` and `MemCacheSize` aggressively to tune for static content. The exact configuration will depend on the specifics of your web site. The best approach is to try out a number of different values for these settings and see for yourself how things are working. If you are going to set these values aggressively, you need to have IIS running on its own W2K box, because this might affect other applications.

Network

Set the receive buffers on the Network Interface Card on the Web server to a maximum. This reduces the number of dropped packets and reduces TCP retransmissions. You can set this parameter by going to Start | Settings | Control Panel | Network and Dial Up Connections. Select the active LAN Connection typically called Local Area Connection. Right click to select Properties. Click on the Configure button next to the Network Interface Card. Set the receive buffers to the maximum value 1024.

To ensure that we do not run out of user ports required to set-up TCP connections, set the `MaxUserPorts` parameter. This can be done by setting this value in the registry – `Hkey-Local-Machine\System\CurrentControlSet\Services\TCPIP\MaxUserPort` to `0xfffe`.

On high-speed networks, set the TCP window size to a maximum. You can do this by setting the value of the registry key `Hkey-Local-Machine\System\CurrentControlSet\Services\TCPIP\TcpWindowSize` to `0x4470`.

You may be wondering about the trade-offs in doing the above. The trade-off is that the operating system will need to allocate more memory for NIC receive buffers and user ports.

AJP Socket Pooling

AJP13 worker can be configured to keep a pool of sockets open. We can experiment with this value, but a rule of thumb is to set it to the number of concurrent users. This configuration setting is defined in the `workers.properties` as shown below:

```
worker.ajp13.cachesize = 30
```

If you set this value too low, you will have an impact on performance. If you set it too high, the operating system will need to allocate more memory to track this information.

Load-Balanced AJP Workers

We can define a load-balanced worker consisting of a number of `ajp13` workers. Chapter 13 describes load balancing with AJP in detail and the concepts are similar regardless of the web server that we're using. To give a quick overview, we will define a number of AJP connectors running on different ports and on different machines. On the IIS web server, in the `workers.properties` file we will declare a worker of type `lb` (or load balancer). Load balancing across the different Tomcat workers increases the throughput of the system.

Tuning the AJP Connector

On the application server where the Tomcat workers are running, we can tune the number of operating system threads used by the AJP13 connector to process incoming requests. The AJP13 connector is defined in the `server.xml` file. Here is the default definition:

```
<Connector className=" org.apache.ajp.tomcat4.Ajp13Connector"
           port=" 8009"
           minProcessors=" 5"
           maxProcessors=" 75"
           acceptCount=" 10"
           debug=" 0" />
```

We can adjust the values for `minProcessors`, `maxProcessors`, and `acceptCount` to tune the number of threads initialized at startup, at peak usage, and the number of requests queued. A general rule of thumb is to set the number of `maxProcessors` to the maximum number of concurrent users expected per Tomcat worker. Set `minProcessors` to the average number of concurrent users expected per Tomcat worker. Note that if you set these values too high, you burden the operating system with the overhead required allocating memory and CPU for these threads. If you set these values too low, user requests will be queued or not serviced at all.

Summary

In this chapter, we've seen how IIS can be configured to work with Tomcat. We first saw how ISAPI works as a redirector to forward requests to Tomcat as an out-of-process worker. Tomcat can also be used as an in-process worker. The difference between these approaches is that, if Tomcat is used as an out-of-process worker, ISAPI communicates with Tomcat over TCP/IP using the proprietary protocol called AJP. On the other hand, if Tomcat is used as an in-process worker, it communicates using Java's JNI. We recommend that you use Tomcat out-of-process because this lends itself to more scalable architectures.

We examined a number of different ways of setting up our architecture using application servers, web server farms, and multiple dedicated Tomcat workers to provide a more scalable architecture. We examined tuning parameters for IIS and the ISAPI redirector.

In the next chapter, we'll look at how Tomcat communicates with different databases using JDBC.

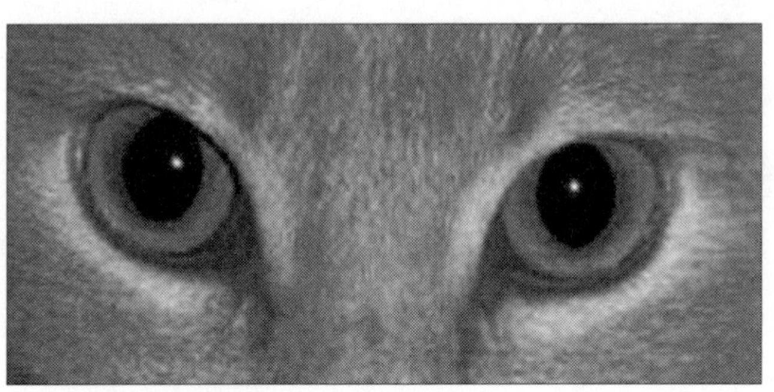

15

JDBC Connectivity

Most applications, including web applications, work on processing data. Most of the data that is processed today originates from a database. The most popular database management systems are based on relational concepts – and are appropriately called Relational DataBase Management Systems (or RDBMS).

All popular databases, including Oracle, MySQL, SQL Server, Sybase, Interbase, PostgreSQL, and DB2 are relational databases. As Tomcat administrators, we must be well-versed in RDBMSs. In addition, we need to understand the nature of interactions between an RDBMS and Tomcat to better understand the requirements that may arise.

This chapter aims to provide the following information:

- JDBC, Java's database connectivity API
- Connection pooling
- Interactions between RDBMS and Tomcat
- Why JNDI-based JDBC configurations are preferred
- How to configure a JDBC data source the preferred way
- Why alternative JDBC configurations may be required
- How to configure alternative JDBC access

We will see the variety of situations that may arise when configuring Tomcat to work with relational databases. More importantly, we will gain some hands-on experience configuring several of the examples in the discussion. Special emphasis will be placed on the recommended or preferred way of interacting.

By the end of this chapter, you will be comfortable with the integration of RDBMSs with Tomcat and will be able to handle the most common requests for configuring RDBMSs to work with the Tomcat server.

JDBC Basics

JDBC is a programming interface for accessing RDBMSs. Its operation is based on the transmission and execution of Structured Query Language (SQL) on the database server. SQL is a text-based query language for performing operations with data stored in a relational database. In fact, JDBC is based on a Call-Level Interface (CLI) to an engine that processes SQL statements. More specifically, JDBC uses the X/Open SQL CLI (X/Open is an international standards organization) conforming to the SQL92 language syntax standard. The figure below illustrates how SQL CLI, and therefore JDBC, operates underneath the hood:

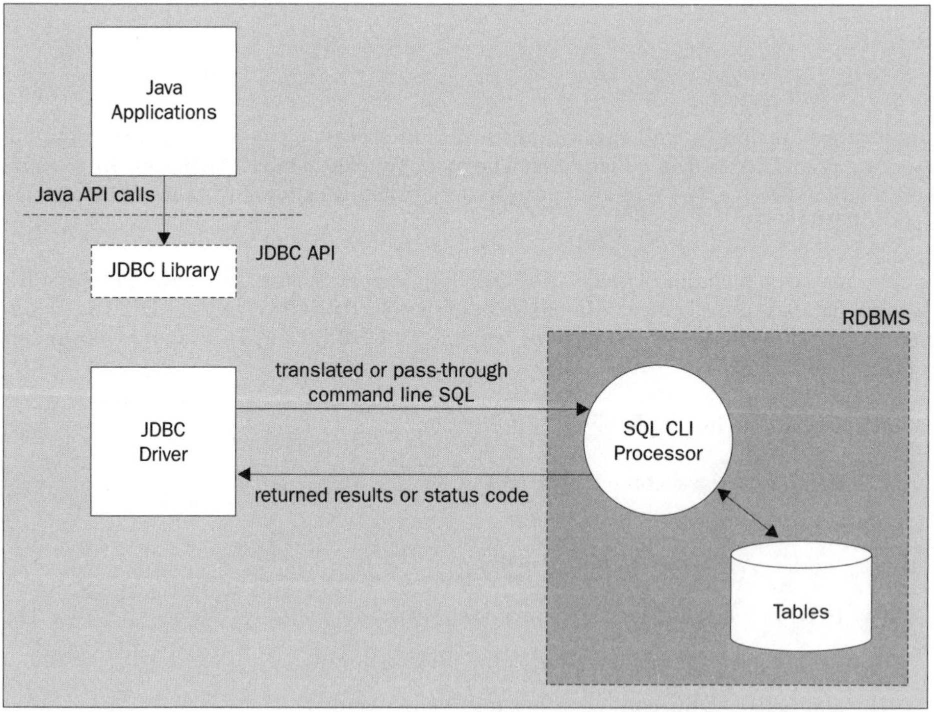

We can see in the figure that the JDBC engine submits SQL query statements to the remote SQL processing engine (part of the RDBMS and typically handles multiple simultaneous connections via a connection manager), and the SQL processing engine returns the result of the query in a set of data called a **result set**. A result set is typically zero or more rows of data; one can think of result sets as temporarily created tables.

Therefore, JDBC operations are designed to:

- Take the JDBC API calls and transform them into a SQL query
- Submit that query to the SQL processing engine on the RDBMS
- Retrieve the result set that is returned from the query and transform it into a Java accessible data structure

Not all statements return a result set. Even if we conduct a search that is not successful, the returned result set will be empty (called a `NULL` result set). In addition, the SQL language includes statements that are used to create tables, update data, delete rows, and so on; these statements also do not return any result sets.

Basic JDBC Operations

In JDBC programming, the typical steps that the developers must follow are:

- Obtain a connection to the remote database server (in JDBC 1.x, it is necessary to instantiate a database driver prior to obtaining a connection)
- Create and prepare a SQL statement for execution (or call a stored procedure in the RDBMS)
- Execute the SQL statement
- Obtain the returned result set (if any) and work on it
- Disconnect from the remote database

As administrators, we are most interested in facilitating the first step – obtaining a connection to the desired database. Let's examine this step in more details.

Establishing and Terminating Connections To RDBMSs

Other than providing a unified way of accessing, modifying, and manipulating data in RDBMSs, JDBC also provides a unified way of connecting to RDBMSs from different vendors. While normal native connections to Oracle will be very different from connections to MySQL, which will yet be different from when working with Microsoft's SQL Server, connecting to any of these RDBMSs can be accomplished using the same JDBC API calls.

Evolving JDBC Versions

In the early days of JDBC, most RDBMS vendors and JDBC developers were coding to the JDBC 1.0 standard. Under this standard, the code to establish a connection to an RDBMS, as well as the code to disconnect from the RDBMS, was all written by the developers. In fact, even the code to select and activate a JDBC driver was coded by the developers.

While simple and straightforward to code, this approach created a problem; in some cases where the driver used was hard-coded by the developers, the database access code only worked with specific RDBMSs from the vendor.

With the arrival of JDBC 2.0, this restriction was relaxed. JDBC 2.0 introduced the concept of a **data source**. This is an indirect way of specifying the JDBC driver to be used for making the connection. Developers can now obtain a connection on the data source in their code, allowing the same JDBC code to work with drivers from any vendor. Meanwhile, an administrator can switch database vendor support by simply configuring a different data source and no code changes are needed.

While JDBC 2.0's introduction of data source and connection pooling support (covered a little later) opens up new possibilities for RDBMS developers, it falls short of specifying standard ways that these features should or must be used. As a result, many of the architectural issues are left for the JDBC driver writers to solve – and code can quickly become vendor-specific again (this time depending on the JDBC driver vendor).

JDBC 3.0 is the first specification that clearly spells out the different architectures that JDBC can operate in – including two-tier and three-tier models. The three-tier model corresponds to the application server model and the model of operation favored by J2EE applications.

The specification also attempts to accommodate JDBC 1.x and 2.x drivers and model of operations, while formalizing JNDI as the preferred way for applications to obtain a data source. It also formalizes connection pooling as a value-added service of the application server or servlet container. At the time of writing, JDBC 3.0 is a recently finalized standard and there are not yet many vendors with products that support it.

Regardless of the JDBC version, the JDBC driver still has to translate the unified JDBC commands into native commands to connect to the different servers. JDBC drivers have evolved significantly over the past few years and most of them today are high-performance Type IV drivers (explained in the next section). However, some legacy systems still exist that support only the older Type I to Type III drivers. It is a good idea to gain some familiarity with different types of JDBC drivers that may be around.

JDBC Driver Type

There are four different types of JDBC drivers: Type I to Type IV. In general, the higher driver types represent an improvement on performance:

- **Type I**
  These drivers are the most primitive JDBC drivers as they are essentially data access adapters. They adapt another data access mechanism (such as ODBC) to JDBC. These drivers completely rely on the other data access mechanism to work and as such have double the administrative and maintenance headaches. These drivers are also typically hardware/OS-specific (due to the data access mechanism that they depend on), making them completely non-portable.

- **Type II**
  These drivers are partially written in Java and partially written in native data access languages (typically C or C++). The non-Java portion of these drivers limits the portability of the final code and platform migration possibilities. The administrative and maintenance burden of Type I still exists.

- **Type III**
  These drivers are pure Java drivers on the client side, which gives them the portability benefit of Java. However, they rely on a middleware engine running externally to operate. The client code communicates with the middleware engine, and the engine talks to the different types of databases. The administration and maintenance burden is somewhat reduced, but far from eliminated.

- **Type IV**
  These drivers are 100% Java client drivers that talk directly to the network protocols supported by the RDBMSs. This results in the highest performance connection and the most portable application code. Administration and maintenance is greatly simplified (only the driver needs to be updated).

Fortunately, most modern day JDBC drivers are of the Type IV variety. All of the major RDBMSs available today (MySQL, Oracle, DB2, and MS SQL Server) have Type IV JDBC drivers available, either through the database vendors themselves or via a third-party driver vendor.

Database Connection Pooling

When a web application accesses a remote RDBMS, it may do so through a **JDBC connection**. Typically, a physical JDBC connection is established between the client application and the RDBMS server via a TCP/IP connection. The action of establishing such a connection is both CPU-and time-intensive. It involves multiple layers of software, and the transmission and receipt of network data. A typical physical database connection may take seconds to establish.

Modern web applications consist of JSP pages and servlets that may need data from a database on every HTTP request; for example, a servlet that prints the current employees from a specific department or an electronic auction system where you can see all your current open auctions. On a well-loaded server, the time it takes to establish, disconnect, and re-establish actual connections (physical connections) can substantially slow down web application performance.

To create high-performance and scalable web applications, JDBC driver vendors and application servers are incorporating database connection pooling into their products.

Connection pooling reduces expensive session establishment time by creating a pool of physical connections when the system starts up. When an application requires a connection, one of these physical connections is provided. When the application finishes using the connection, normally it would be disconnected. However, in the case of a logical connection, it is merely returned to the pool and awaits the next application request. The figure overleaf illustrates database connection pooling:

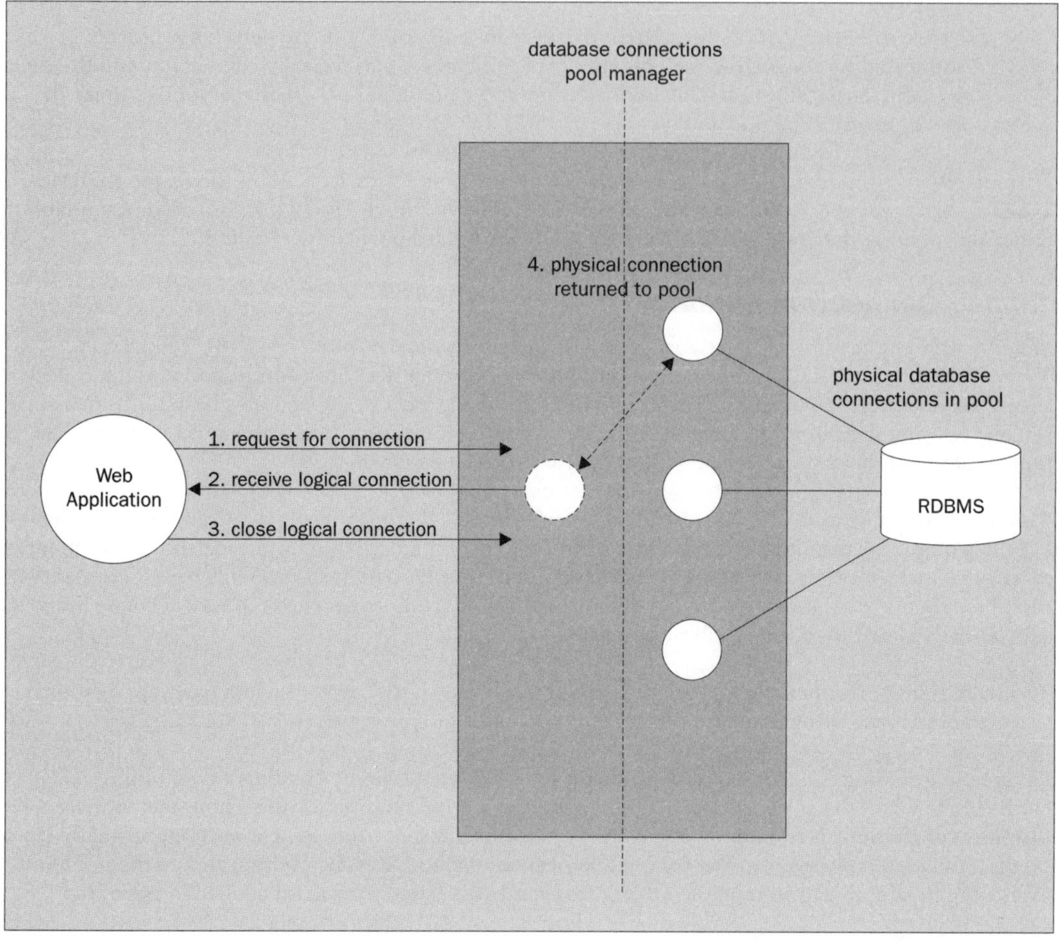

We can see that a **pool manager** creates the initial physical connections, manages the distribution of the physical connections to the web applications in the form of a logical connection, returns any closed logical connection to the pool, and handles any exception or error that may arise – potentially disconnecting the physical connection or recovering from error conditions. Note that closing a logical connection does not actually close any physical connection, but merely returns the connection back to the pool. This pool manager functionality may be provided by one of the three sources:

- The JDBC driver vendor
- A third-party pool manager software vendor
- An application server such as Tomcat

When configuring web applications to run on Tomcat, the preferred and the recommended pool manager to use is one that is supplied with the Tomcat server. We will discuss the how and why in a later section.

Tomcat and the JDBC Evolution

Application developers and system designers using Tomcat 3.x and 4.x have a wide choice of JDBC support mechanisms to choose from. Tomcat 3.3+ and 4.x servers are compliant with the J2EE specifications and offer JDBC 2.1, while the remaining are compatible with JDBC 1.0. We will be examining the recommended mechanism to access JDBC resources while working with Tomcat, as well as exploring one alternative access mechanism, within this chapter.

Meanwhile, the specifications for JDBC 3.0 have already been finalized and the new features will give even more flexibility. Future releases of Tomcat may be synchronized with JDBC 3.x standards, as many of the features of JDBC 3.0 are already adopted by Tomcat 4.1.x (the latest beta available at the time of writing).

Some of the JDBC 3.x features that are already part of Tomcat 4.1.x include:

- **Application server-managed database connection pools**
  Tomcat 4.1.x uses Jakarta Commons DBCP pooling to provide container-managed connection pooling. DBCP is short for DataBase Connection Pooling. This also enables simplified configuration for the pooling mechanism: only four parameters for configuration of the DBCP pool behavior (see the *Resource and ResourceParams* section later). JDBC 3.0 is the first specification that specifies more standard configuration parameters for pooling (like `maxStatements`, `initialPoolSize`, `minPoolSize`, `maxPoolSize`, `maxIdleTime`, and `propertyCyle`), making the mechanism more configurable in a standards-compliant manner.

- **Using the JNDI-API to look up data sources within an application server**
  Tomcat 4.x emulates JNDI to provide web applications running under it, which is a portable and configurable way of obtaining data sources for JDBC operations without hard-coding the driver and associated properties. This makes the selection of the JDBC driver and RDBMS instance a deferred deployment-time decision. JDBC 3.0 specifies JNDI as the preferred method for applications to locate a data source.

- **Ease of migration to the connector architecture**
  The Tomcat 4 architecture makes extensive use of connectors to decouple the external connection requirements from the design of the engine. JDBC 3.0 recommends the gradual migration of JDBC drivers to the connectors architecture, which is on the road to standardizing J2EE connectivity and easing manageability and maintainability of J2EE systems. See the J2EE Connector Architecture (JCA) document for more details (URL http://java.sun.com/j2ee/connector/).

These are a few administrator-visible improvements that JDBC 3.0 supplies, and which Tomcat already implements. As more and more RDBMS vendors and third-party driver vendors move to embrace JDBC 3.0, we will see a gradual shift from today's JDBC 2.1 dominated landscape to JDBC 3.0. In general, this will give Tomcat administrators and developers alike a more flexible and robust connection to RDBMS data sources.

Tomcat and JDBC

Tomcat provides valuable services for hosted web applications that use JDBC connections. More specifically, Tomcat will enable running web applications to:

- Access JDBC data sources using standard JNDI lookup
- Use connection pooling value-added service

Web Containers and RDBMSs

The role of a web container as an intermediary between client web applications and an RDBMS is defined by the set of J2EE specifications – most recently in the Servlet 2.3 specification and JDBC 3.0 specification (both are now final and can be located at http://jcp.org/aboutJava/communityprocess/first/jsr053/index.html and http://java.sun.com/products/jdbc/download.html#corespec30 respectively). The value added service that Tomcat provides is compliant with these specifications, and is documented as three-tier architecture. The figure below illustrates this:

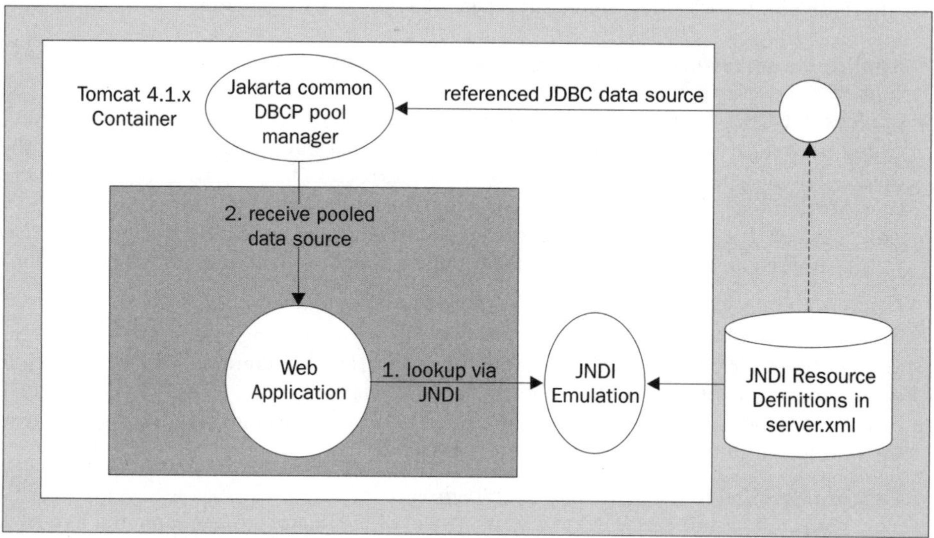

Here we can see that JDBC drivers are configured with Tomcat as JNDI resources. These resources are made available during web application runtime via standard JNDI lookups. The steps are depicted in the diagram:

- First, a web application obtains a JNDI `InitialContext` from Tomcat; it then performs a lookup on the resource (JDBC data source) by name.
- Next, Tomcat handles the JNDI lookup by consulting the configuration files (`server.xml` and `web.xml`) to determine the JDBC driver to use for obtaining a data source. Tomcat will also use DBPC to pool the connections made; the connections obtained from Tomcat are logical connections.

Even though no true JNDI-compatible directory services are involved, the Tomcat container emulates the action of a JNDI provider. This enables code that is written with JNDI as the JDBC data source lookup mechanism to work within the Tomcat container (and other Servlet 2.3-compliant application servers).

Also from the previous figure, we can see that Tomcat 4 does more than merely provide JNDI emulation: it also provides database connection pooling. Tomcat 4.1.x uses another Apache Jakarta project, called the Commons DBCP (Database Connection Pooling), for its built-in pool manager functionality.

Preferred Configuration: JNDI Resources

Using JNDI resources in Tomcat to configure JDBC data sources is the recommended way to provide web applications with access to JDBC connections. While other methods are possible – and we will cover at least one alternative later – this approach will lead to code that is portable to other web containers.

Here are the steps that we must follow to configure JNDI resource for a JDBC data source:

- Add `<Resource>` and `<ResourceParams>` tags in the `<Context>` element of the web application, or in a `<DefaultContext>` subelement of the `<Host>` element to configure the JNDI resource
- Ensure that a `<resource-ref>` element is defined, corresponding to the `<Resource>` from above, in the `web.xml` file of the web application using the JDBC resource (note that the `web.xml` file is typically maintained by the application developer)
- Use JNDI calls in the application code to look up the JDBC data source

Resource and ResourceParams

The `<Resource>` tag is used to specify the JNDI resource that represents a JDBC data source, and the `<ResourceParams>` tag is used to configure the associated data source factory. Here is a typical `<Resource>` element found in the `server.xml` configuration file:

```
<Resource name="jdbc/WroxTC41" auth="Container"
          type="javax.sql.DataSource"/>
```

What this resource statement says is:

- Create a JNDI resource that is accessible from the context `java:comp/env/jdbc/WroxTC41` by the web application. The web application can use this context (logical name) to look up the data source. The type of resource that will be returned during this lookup is a `javax.sql.DataSource`. It also specifies that the container should authenticate against the RDBMS on behalf of the web application.

You may want to check Chapter 8 for detailed examination of the attributes allowed in the `<Resource>` element. A `<ResourceParams>` element is associated with the `<Resource>` element. The `<ResourceParams>` element, also covered in Chapter 8, is used to parameterize the associated resource. For example, we may have the following `<ResourceParams>` for the previously defined `<Resource>` element (note that this is where we become database-specific):

```
<ResourceParams name="jdbc/WroxTC41">
  <parameter>
    <name>driverClassName</name>
```

```
      <value>org.gjt.mm.mysql.Driver</value>
    </parameter>
    <parameter>
      <name>url</name>
      <value>jdbc:mysql://localhost/wroxtomcat</value>
    </parameter>
    <parameter>
      <name>username</name>
      <value>empro</value>
    </parameter>
    <parameter>
      <name>password</name>
      <value>empass</value>
    </parameter>
    <parameter>
      <name>maxActive</name>
      <value>20</value>
    </parameter>
    <parameter>
      <name>maxIdle</name>
      <value>30000</value>
    </parameter>
    <parameter>
      <name>maxWait</name>
      <value>100</value>
    </parameter>
  </ResourceParams>
```

Note that the name attribute of the <ResourceParams> element must match the <Resource> element that it is configuring. The actual name and value of the parameters depends on the data source connection factory that is used. The settings above assume that we are configuring a DBCP factory. We will see how we make this resource available to web application code (JSP pages and servlets) later. First, let us find out what a DBCP factory is.

The DBCP factory will work with JDBC drivers for any RDBMSs, for example, here is the setting for accessing an Oracle database:

```
  <ResourceParams name="jdbc/WroxTC41">
    <parameter>
      <name>driverClassName</name>
      <value>oracle.jdbc.driver.OracleDriver</value>
    </parameter>
    <parameter>
      <name>url</name>
      <value>jdbc:oracle:thin:@xpserver:1521:ORCL</value>
    </parameter>
    <parameter>
      <name>username</name>
      <value>empro</value>
    </parameter>
    <parameter>
      <name>password</name>
```

```
      <value>empass</value>
    </parameter>
    <parameter>
      <name>maxActive</name>
      <value>20</value>
    </parameter>
    <parameter>
      <name>maxIdle</name>
      <value>30000</value>
    </parameter>
    <parameter>
      <name>maxWait</name>
      <value>100</value>
    </parameter>
  </ResourceParams>
```

Data Source Factory

A data source factory is a Java class that will hand out data sources. In some sense, this class manufactures data sources; hence the factory name. In actual operations, however, it may simply supply a customized data source class that will work with, as well as hand out, pooled data sources.

DBCP – Jakarta Commons Pooling Support

To return a JDBC data source to the application, Tomcat 4 uses a data source factory to create the data source. While it is not well-documented, Tomcat 4.1.x uses the Jakarta Commons DBCP (by default) to supply a data source factory and implement connection pooling.

Tomcat 4.0.4, on the other hand, uses the third-party licensed Tyrex data source factory. Although it is relatively easy to override the default data source factory, the procedure is not well-documented. For example, to make Tomcat 4.0.4 use the DBCP mechanism, we must add the following `<parameter>` element in the `<ResourceParams>`:

```
<parameter>
  <name>factory</name>
  <value>org.apache.commons.dbcp.BasicDataSourceFactory</value>
</parameter>
```

You may consider using DBCP pooling even if you use Tomcat 4.0.4 since it will be the default (and pool manager of choice for the Tomcat distribution) for all future 4.x-level releases. We will use this technique to configure our own data source factory in a later example.

Transactions and Distributed Transactions Support

RDBMSs offer varying levels of support for transactions. A transaction can be viewed as a unit of work that can be composed of multiple operations, but can only be committed (all operations complete successfully) or rolled back (no operation completed).

When a transaction involves work that crosses multiple physical RDBMSs, it is called a distributed transaction. One standard that enables RDBMSs (and other products supporting transactions, such as Message Queue Servers) from different vendors to participate in the same distributed transaction is called XA.

In the XA operation model, an external **transaction manager** coordinates a two-phase-commit protocol between multiple **resource managers** (RDBMSs in our case). The two-phase-commit protocol ensures that the pieces of work, scattered across multiple physical RDBMSs, are either all completed or all rolled back.

JDBC 2.1 and 3.0 accommodates data sources that support XA operations. Administrators who work with XA data sources and data source factories should consult the vendor's documentation for proper parameterization and ensure they work with Tomcat.

Hands-On JNDI Resource Configuration

Now it's time to put theory into practice. We will work through an actual example that configures a DBCP data source, through Tomcat 4.1.3's JNDI resources support, with a Type IV JDBC driver. We will base our example on a popular, widely available, RDBMS – MySQL.

Installation and configuration of the MySQL database is beyond the scope of this chapter, but see *Beginning Databases with MySQL* from *Wrox Press (ISBN 1-86100-692-6)*. This chapter will assume that you have MySQL already configured and tested, and that you have an account with privileges to create tables and add records to create the test database. The latest version of MySQL is available for download from: http://www.mysql.com/.

The Type IV JDBC driver that we will use is the `mm.mySQL` server, created and maintained by Mark Matthews. This driver is open source, and is widely used by the MySQL community. You can download the latest version of the driver via this URL: http://mmmysql.sourceforge.net/.

The latest version available at the time of writing is 2.0.14, and is the version that this example is based on.

> **Note, you must unzip the driver JAR file from the download and use the `mm.mysql-2.0.14-bin.jar` file within it. In our example, place this file under `$CATALINA_HOME/common/lib`, `$CATALINA_HOME/shared/lib`, or the web application's `lib` directory so as to make the file visible to one of the class loaders.**

Creating the MySQL Test Database

First, we will need to create the database that we will work with on the MySQL database. The employee database contains the number of employees from different branches of a company and their details. Assuming you have a MySQL user who has create table privilege on a database called `wroxtomcat`, we will create the three tables.

If you have database system administrator privilege on MySQL, this can be done via the command line:

```
mysql> GRANT ALL ON wroxtomcat.* TO
    -> 'mike'@'localhost' IDENTIFIED BY 'abc123';
```

This will enable the user `mike` to connect from `localhost` and create tables in the `wroxtomcat` database. The user `mike` must log on using the password `abc123`.

To make things easy, here is a makedb.sql script to create all the tables required:

```
CREATE DATABASE IF NOT EXISTS wroxtomcat;

USE wroxtomcat;

CREATE TABLE employee (
   employeeid VARCHAR(10) NOT NULL,
   name VARCHAR(50) NOT NULL,
   phone VARCHAR(15) NOT NULL,
   department VARCHAR(15) NOT NULL,
   password VARCHAR(15) NOT NULL,
   PRIMARY KEY (employeeid)
);

CREATE TABLE vacation (
   employeeid VARCHAR(10) NOT NULL,
   fiscal INT(3) NOT NULL,
   approved CHAR(1) NOT NULL,
   PRIMARY KEY (employeeid, fiscal)
);

CREATE TABLE dept (
   department VARCHAR(15) NOT NULL,
   address VARCHAR(30) NOT NULL,
   zipcode VARCHAR(6) NOT NULL,
   PRIMARY KEY (department)
);
```

Use makedb.sql to create the database as follows:

```
$ mysql < makedb.sql
```

Next, we can load the tables with the data that we will use. This is performed via the SQL script loaddb.sql, which contains:

```
USE wroxtomcat;

INSERT INTO dept (department, address, zipcode) VALUES ( 'Engineering', '33
Mexicali Road', '25763');
INSERT INTO dept (department, address, zipcode) VALUES ( 'Sales', '15 Navel
Circle', '98322');
INSERT INTO dept (department, address, zipcode) VALUES ( 'Administration', '1
Lawless Court', '66699');
INSERT INTO employee (employeeid, name, phone, department, password) VALUES (
'2901', 'Joe', '333-3331', 'Engineering', 'junior');
INSERT INTO employee (employeeid, name, phone, department, password) VALUES (
'2202', 'Matt', '434-3333', 'Engineering', 'perlguru');
INSERT INTO employee (employeeid, name, phone, department, password) VALUES (
'3021', 'Jane', '231-0001', 'Sales', 'milseller');
INSERT INTO employee (employeeid, name, phone, department, password) VALUES (
'0001', 'Bill', '343-0012', 'Administration', 'gatorshaq');
```

```
INSERT INTO employee (employeeid, name, phone, department, password) VALUES (
'0015', 'Steve', '342-2212', 'Administration', 'billion');
INSERT INTO vacation (employeeid, fiscal, approved) VALUES ( '0001', '1', 'Y');
INSERT INTO vacation (employeeid, fiscal, approved) VALUES ( '0001', '2', 'Y');
INSERT INTO vacation (employeeid, fiscal, approved) VALUES ( '0001', '3', 'Y');
INSERT INTO vacation (employeeid, fiscal, approved) VALUES ( '0001', '4', 'Y');
INSERT INTO vacation (employeeid, fiscal, approved) VALUES ( '2901', '12', 'N');
INSERT INTO vacation (employeeid, fiscal, approved) VALUES ( '2202', '51', 'N');
```

This script simply fills the table with the data. Run the script from the console using the command:

```
$ mysql < loaddb.sql
```

Now that we have created the tables and populated them with data, we need to create a user that the developers will use to access the data in the database. Since our web application functionality requires only read access to the data, we will create a read-only user for developer access. This will ensure that data cannot be accidentally or maliciously modified or altered.

Setting up the Read-Only User

If you do not have privilege as the database system administrator, you will need to seek help. You need the following user setup:

User Property	Value
Username	empro
Password	empass
Access	SELECT privilege only on the wroxtomcat database (that is use: GRANT SELECT ON wroxtomcat.* TO 'empro'@'localhost' IDENTIFIED BY 'empass';)

This will create a user that has read-only access to the wroxtomcat tables, which the developer will be using to access the data in the table, since they do not perform any modifications to the underlying RDBMS in this case.

Adding the JDBC JNDI Resource To the Default Context

Finally, we configure the JNDI resource for the data source. We will follow the three steps approach detailed earlier.

Step 1 – <Resource> and <ResourceParam>

We will make this JNDI data source accessible to all the web applications running on this host. By adding the resource definition in the <DefaultContext> section, all of the web application can have access to this resource.

In the $CATALINA_HOME/conf/server.xml configuration file, within the scope of the localhost <Host> container, add the following <DefaultContext> element:

```
<DefaultContext>
  <Resource name="jdbc/WroxTC41" auth="Container"
            type="javax.sql.DataSource"/>
  <ResourceParams name="jdbc/WroxTC41">
    <parameter>
      <name>driverClassName</name>
      <value>org.gjt.mm.mysql.Driver</value>
    </parameter>
    <parameter>
      <name>url</name>
      <value>jdbc:mysql://localhost/wroxtomcat</value>
    </parameter>
    <parameter>
      <name>username</name>
      <value>empro</value>
    </parameter>
    <parameter>
      <name>password</name>
      <value>empass</value></parameter>
    <parameter>
      <name>maxActive</name>
      <value>20</value></parameter>
    <parameter>
      <name>maxIdle</name>
      <value>30000</value></parameter>
    <parameter>
      <name>maxWait</name>
      <value>100</value>
    </parameter>
  </ResourceParams>
</DefaultContext>
```

> **The `url` parameter is often named `driverName` in old documentations for legacy reasons (older version name), and can still be specified using the old name. For all new work, use `url`.**

The above configuration will work fine with Tomcat 4.1.3 or later releases, as they use DBCP connection pooling. However, if you are using a Tomcat release that uses the Tyrex (licensed) data source factory by default (Tomcat 4.0.4 or later up to 4.1.3), you will need to add the following parameter to the `<ResourceParams>` element:

```
<ResourceParams name="jdbc/WroxTC41">
  <parameter>
    <name>factory</name>
    <value>org.apache.commons.dbcp.BasicDataSourceFactory</value>
  </parameter>
  ...
```

In addition, since Tomcat 4.0.4 does not include the Jakarta Commons libraries by default, you will need the DBCP and dependent libraries in the `$CATALINA_HOME/common/lib` directory. Make sure you have the following binaries downloaded from Jakarta Commons area (http://jakarta.apache.org/commons/):

- `commons-dbcp.jar`

- ❑ commons-collection.jar
- ❑ commons-pool.jar

Tomcat 4.1.3 or later already uses the DBCP library code as the default data source factory (eliminating a licensed software dependency), and the required Commons libraries are already included.

Step 2 – Add the <resource-ref/> Entries To web.xml

Instead of creating our own web application, we'll take an easy way out and borrow the existing example application from Tomcat. To do this, change directory to $CATALINA_HOME/webapps/examples/WEB-INF and edit the web.xml file (this is the deployment descriptor of the examples web application). Add the following highlighted code to web.xml; note that it should be added immediately to the end of the existing <resource-ref> already in the file:

```
...
<resource-ref>
  <res-ref-name>mail/Session</res-ref-name>
  <res-type>javax.mail.Session</res-type>
  <res-auth>Container</res-auth>
</resource-ref>
<resource-ref>
  <res-ref-name>jdbc/WroxTC41</res-ref-name>
  <res-type>javax.sql.DataSource</res-type>
  <res-auth>Container</res-auth>
</resource-ref>
```

This <resource-ref> makes the jdbc/WroxTC41 context, via JNDI APIs, available to the examples web application.

Step 3 – Use JNDI To Look Up a Data Source

Finally, yet importantly, we need some code that will look up the data source and start querying the database. The JSP below, JDBCTest.jsp, will do exactly that. Put it into the $CATALINA_HOME/webapps/examples/jsp directory. Pay special attention to the way JNDI is used to obtain the data source (code highlighted):

```
<html>
  <head>
    <%@ page errorPage="errorpg.jsp"
             import="java.sql.*,
                     javax.sql.*,
                     java.io.*,
                     javax.naming.InitialContext,
                     javax.naming.Context" %>
  </head>
  <body>
    <h1>JDBC JNDI Resource Test</h1>

    <%
    InitialContext initCtx = new InitialContext();
    DataSource ds = (DataSource)
                    initCtx.lookup("java:comp/env/jdbc/WroxTC41");
```

```
    Connection    conn = ds.getConnection();

    Statement stmt = conn.createStatement();
    ResultSet rset = stmt.executeQuery("select * from employee;");
    %>
    <table width='600' border='1'>
      <tr>
        <th align='left'>Employee ID</th>
        <th align='left'>Name</th>
        <th align='left'>Department</th>
      </tr>
      <%
      while (rset.next()) {
      %>
        <tr><td> <%= rset.getString(1)  %></td>
          <td> <%= rset.getString(2)  %></td>
          <td> <%= rset.getString(4)  %></td>
        </tr>
      <%  }
      conn.close();
      initCtx.close();
      %>
    </table>
  </body>
</html>
```

The JNDI code highlighted above first obtains the `InitialContext` from Tomcat. It then uses this context to look up the JNDI resource that we have configured. Note that all Tomcat JNDI resources are found relative to `java:comp/env/`. Once the data source is obtained through JNDI, it is used to create a connection (actually pooled through DBCP). The JSP page then performs a `SELECT *` on the `employee` table, and then prints out all the rows that are retrieved. Finally, it creates an HTML table containing all the table rows.

Any exception caught during execution of this JSP page is redirected to a very simple error-handling page called `errorpg.jsp` file. This file is specified via the `errorPage` attribute of the `@page` directive. Here is the content of `errorpg.jsp`:

```
<html>
  <body>
    <%@ page isErrorPage="true" %>
    <h1> An error has occurred </h1>
    <%= exception.getMessage() %>
  </body>
</html>
```

This page will simply display a message indicating the exception caught.

Testing the JNDI Resource Configuration

Now that we have set up the JNDI resources, populated the database tables, added the `<resource-ref>` to the deployment descriptor, and created a servlet that will use JNDI to obtain a JDBC data source, we are ready to give the new JSP code a test.

Start Tomcat and then, from a browser, attempt to reach the following URL: http://localhost:8080/examples/jsp/JDBCTest.jsp.

This will compile and execute the JSP code. If everything is configured correctly and working, you should see the page below:

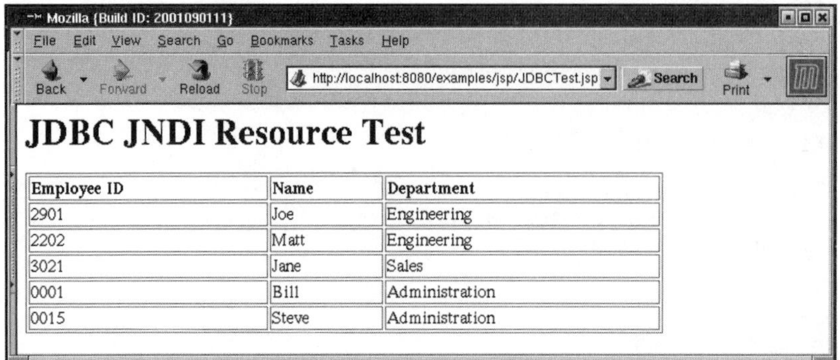

The web page generated above is the result of a JDBC query to the MySQL database data, via a connection obtained from the JNDI lookup.

> **You may face exceptions like, Server denies access to data source or some server connection failures, which are due to the MySQL user not having enough privileges.**

Alternative JDBC Configuration

We have been mentioning that the JNDI API is the preferred and recommended way to pass a JDBC data source to our web applications. It is likely to become the best-supported mechanism to access JDBC data sources.

However, in production, there can often be situations when we must consider alternative means of JDBC data source/connection configuration.

The Need for Alternative Configuration

There is no justifiable reason why newly developed database access code slated for web application deployment should not use the preferred JNDI mechanism for data access.

However, since JDBC 1.0 was a widely used and highly functional API long before the arrival of JDBC 2.x and beyond, there exists a large legacy base of working JDBC code that does not know about features such as connection pooling.

There may be circumstances where you must integrate legacy code, and the sourcecode is either not available or cannot be changed. Legacy JDBC 1.0 code typically has both, the JDBC driver and the URL of the database used hard-coded. Thankfully, JDBC 2.x and JDBC 3.x continue to maintain backward compatibility with JDBC 1.0 – this means that legacy code can continue to run, even in Tomcat 4.1.x servers.

Another major reason for deviating from the recommended configuration is the deployment of an alternative connection-pooling manager. There is a major debate between developers preferring one pool manager to another.

Alternative Connection Pool Managers

Up until Tomcat 4.1.x (still in beta at the time of writing), connection-pooling implementation on Tomcat servers has evolved in a roll-your-own manner. Since Tomcat did not provide default support, anyone who needed the functionality (that will include anyone who deployed any large or medium scale web application) had to write their own code, or find a third-party solution to the problem.

As a result, it is highly likely that any existing project on Tomcat is already using some alternative connection-pooling manager with its own requirement on data source configuration.

Let us examine one such pool manager, and see how its configuration and access differs from the preferred method. The pool manager we will work with is `DBConnectionBroker` from Java Exchange (http://www.javaexchange.com/).

About DBConnectionBroker

The `DBConnectionBroker` provides pooling of JDBC connections by managing pools for individual servlets. This means that all concurrent instances of the same servlet will be sharing the same connection pool. It also means that different servlets running on the same machine will not share a JDBC connection at all. There is no global view or control of the JDBC connection pools created. Most web applications running on a web server have a fixed set of servlets; the ones subjected to the most concurrent access will benefit the most from the `DBConnectionBroker` design.

This differs markedly from the DBCP approach of Apache Commons or Tomcat 4.1.x, where the total number of connections in the pool can be controlled globally – regardless of the number of different servlets that may be running.

> **The advantage of one design or approach over another is highly dependent on the application, the system configuration, and the access pattern.**

Deploying DBConnectionBroker

The `DBConnectionBroker` requires no `server.xml` configuration. As such, it can actually be used simultaneously with JNDI/DBCP-based connection pooling on the same Tomcat instance.

To install `DBConnectionBroker`, we only need to make sure the `DBConnectionBroker.class` is located in the `$CATALINA_HOME/webapps/examples/WEB-INF/classes/com/javaexchange/dbConnectionBroker` directory. This will allow the web application to locate the class.

Let us look at `JDBCBrokerTest.jsp`. This is a rewrite of the `JDBCTest.jsp` – but using the `DBConnectionBroker` pool manager instead.

Obtaining Connections Via the DBConnectionBroker

We can see that the JDBC manipulation code remains the same. However, the method used in obtaining a data source varies greatly. In this case, we actually need to hard-code the configuration into the JSP page. The highlighted code is `DBConnectionBroker`-specific:

```
<html>
  <head>

    <%@ page errorPage="errorpg.jsp"
             import="java.sql.*,
                     javax.sql.*,
                     java.io.*,
                  com.javaexchange.dbConnectionBroker.DbConnectionBroker" %>
  </head>
  <body>
    <h1>JDBC JNDI Resource Test</h1>
    <%!
    DbConnectionBroker myBroker;
    public void jspInit() {
      try {
        String filesep = System.getProperty("file.separator");
        myBroker =
   new DbConnectionBroker("org.gjt.mm.mysql.Driver",
                       "jdbc:mysql://localhost/wroxtomcat",
                       "empro","empass",2,8,
                       filesep + "tmp" + filesep + "JDBCBrokerTest.log",
                       1.0);
      } catch (IOException ex) {
        // JSP init() cannot throw any exception
        // check JDBCBrokerTest.log for information
      }
    }

    public void jspDestroy() {
      myBroker.destroy();
    }
    %>
```

The `DbConnectBroker` needs to monitor a servlet's lifecycle (by overriding the `jspInit()` and `jspDestroy()` methods) since it creates one connection pool per JSP page or servlet. Note how the broker is initialized in the code with the JDBC driver, URL, username, and password information. In addition, the initialization also specifies a minimum of 2 connections in the pool, a maximum of 8, a log file in the `tmp` directory, and that the connections should all be refreshed every day (the final `1.0`):

```
    <%
    Connection    conn = myBroker.getConnection();

    Statement stmt = conn.createStatement();
    ResultSet rset = stmt.executeQuery("select * from employee;");
    %>
    <table width='600' border='1'>
      <tr>
```

```
        <th align='left'>Employee ID</th>
        <th align='left'>Name</th>
        <th align='left'>Department</th>
      </tr>

      <%
      while (rset.next()) {
      %>
        <tr><td> <%= rset.getString(1)    %></td>
          <td> <%= rset.getString(2)  %></td>
          <td> <%= rset.getString(4)  %></td>
        </tr>
      <%  }
      if (stmt != null)
        stmt.close();
      myBroker.freeConnection(conn);
      %>
    </table>
  </body>
</html>
```

Note that once the connection to the database is obtained, the code is almost identical to that of `JDBCTest.jsp`.

Testing the DBConnectionBroker

Make sure you have the `DBConnectionBroker.class` file in the `$CATALINA_HOME/webapps/examples/WEB-INF/classes/com/javaexchange/dbConnectionBroker` directory, then you can start Tomcat 4 and try to access the JSP page via the URL: http://localhost:8080/examples/jsp/JDBCBrokerTest.jsp.

The first time this URL is accessed, Tomcat will compile the JSP page and call `jspInit()`, creating the JDBC connection pool for this JSP page. You should see the `employee` table as below:

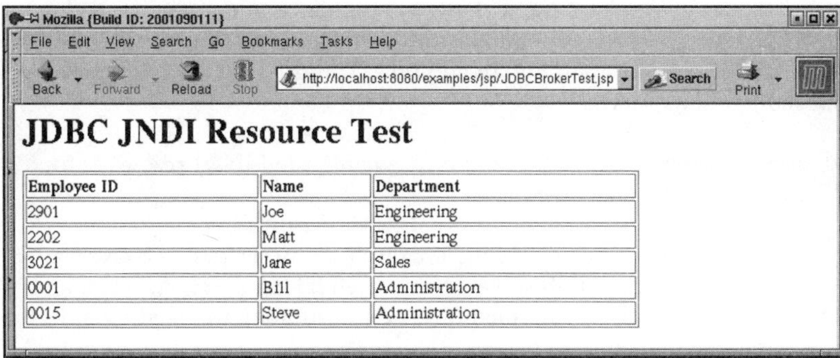

This behavior is identical to our earlier JNDI example. We have successfully deployed an alternative pool manager and utilized an alternative means of obtaining pooled JDBC data sources.

Deploying Third-Party Pools

Having seen how seemingly easy it is to integrate third-party pool managers, we must give careful thought to the consequences of doing so before proceeding.

Here are some hard questions that we must ask ourselves:

- **Support**
  How well is the third-party pool manager supported? If there is any future incompatibility with Tomcat, who will resolve it and how soon?
- **Code portability**
  Does using the pool manager force us to sacrifice configuration flexibility? Do we need to hard-code driver and data source information?

Since DBCP is an Apache Commons project, it is used by many Apache Jakarta projects. As such, it is likely to evolve and stabilize rapidly with contributions from the Jakarta community. Third-party connection pool managers are unlikely to enjoy the same level of contribution and support.

As it is a part of Tomcat 4.1.x, DBCP technology is likely to track Tomcat evolution and will always be tested for compatibility with every new Tomcat release.

Summary

In this chapter, we have examined JDBC connectivity in the context of Tomcat. The most obvious interaction is the need of web applications to connect to relational database sources.

We started our examination with a discussion of Java's support for accessing RDBMSs, in the form of JDBC. We tracked the JDBC version evolution and talked briefly about the different types of JDBC drivers that are available.

Next, we drew on the latest Servlet 2.3 and JDBC 3.0 standards and ended up with a recommended way of providing a JDBC data source to web applications, which involved the configuration of JNDI resources in the Tomcat configuration file. In addition, Tomcat 4.1.x also provides a value-added database connection pooling service.

Using MySQL and the popular `mm.mySQL` driver, we configured JNDI resources for a custom servlet that accessed RDBMS tables we created.

Database connection pooling is a required functionality for any serious web application, but standard connection pooling with respect to web servers has started taking place. As a result, many third-party solutions exist that are not standards-compliant. As administrators, we need to know that such alternatives exist, and understand their nature.

As an exercise, we deployed a third-party pool manager from http://www.javaexchange.com/. We observed that the pool manager uses a non-standards-compliant mechanism for providing configuration and data source access to a web application. As a result, the web application becomes specific to the pool manager, despite the fact that most of the application code can be reused. This raises serious questions about the actual value of a third-party pool manager. However, since the DBCP Jakarta Commons technology is still in its infancy, it is good to know that there are viable and mature alternatives should the situation demand them.

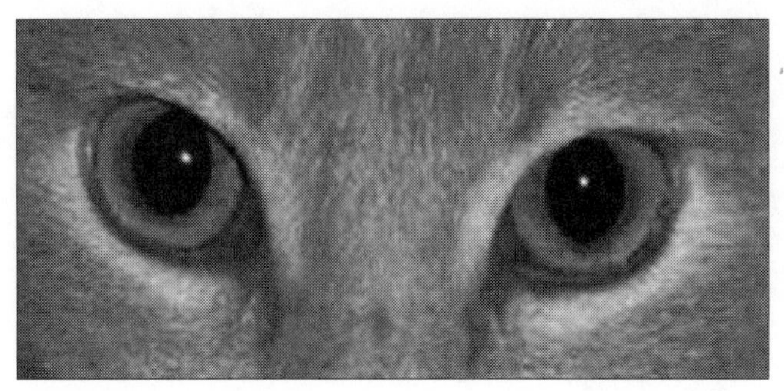

16

Tomcat Security

There is perhaps no topic in the computing industry that receives more emphasis than security. In the context of this Tomcat book, security has a definite place. Should rogue developers or malicious hackers gain access to your Tomcat installation, they could equally gain full access to your machine if you haven't taken proper security precautions.

So, what are those proper security precautions?

This chapter will divide the topic of securing Tomcat into four subtopics:

- Securing your computer's filesystem against Tomcat
- Restricting the operations that Tomcat is allowed to perform.
- Securing access to web applications using authentication realms
- Securing the data channel between Tomcat and the client using SSL

The first of these subtopics is really not specific to Tomcat at all; it involves precautions that any system administrator should take when securing any daemon/server application. Before we discuss these topics, we will look at some basic security considerations.

Some Basic Security Considerations

In this section, we will detail tightening up the default installation by editing the configuration files and managing the applications that are present by default in the `webapps` folder. This will remove some of the most vulnerable entry points for attacks against the server.

As discussed in Chapter 7, by default, the manager application is not enabled because there are no users with manager privileges set up to begin with. Therefore, since this application is disabled, it is relatively safe to keep it unless we specifically assign a user with the appropriate rights.

To be completely safe we can place the manager folder and its contents elsewhere; as long as it is not within the webapps directory for Tomcat then it can never be enabled by just adding an entry into tomcat-users.xml. However, it is still possible to enable the application by modifying the server.xml file and modifying the manager context's docBase attribute. As long as the manager folder is on the same machine as the server installation it is possible to set the manager up again.

In fact, since the most insecure aspect of any installation is the internal access controls for the installation machine, it is best to begin by locking the application down entirely by revoking read/write rights for the folder and its contents from any user except ours or perhaps for all of them. We shall cover this in the next section.

Now in addition to the unpacked manager web application, it may be worth checking for the packaged version of the application in the webapps (manager.war). If it is there, Tomcat will expand it and install the web application it contains on every startup. For security, it is worth checking that there are no other unwanted or unexpected .war files in the webapps directory. This is mainly a problem in Tomcat 3.x, as in Tomcat 4 the default web applications are only supplied in their expanded form (though of course this may change).

The next application to consider is the examples folder that includes fairly innocuous example servlets and JSP files. There is no real threat provided in any of these examples, but, as they are not tested for a deployment environment, and as they are not really necessary, it would be better to also remove this folder. Denial of Service attacks that flood these rather simple examples with many requests or with very large form data submissions are possible.

The Tomcat documentation is now provided as a web application named tomcat-docs, which is an entirely static web application with no JSP pages or servlets. Whether you leave this in place or not is up to you, as it may be useful for developers to have a local copy of the documentation, whether to save network traffic or in case there are problems connecting to the outside world.

A WebDAV application (webdav) that allows clients to remotely author web sites is also provided by default. WebDAV is supported by a handful of browsers including Microsoft Office and IE5.x on Windows 2000, Photoshop, GoLive, and a number of specialised DAV explorers. This application is enabled by default and so will handle requests made with the WebDAV protocol, but the files are read only. WebDAV must be set up for each folder, so no real damage should be possible. If you want to play safe, then remove this web application, any WAR file also present, and lock down the read/write privileges according to the abilities of your operating system.

Depending on your choice of installation, you may also have a test application that is used to unit test Tomcat. Follow the general advice given for the previous default applications.

It may also be worth disabling the default ROOT web application if you don't have one of your own. If your applications will be accessed by a web application URL (such as examples) then it may be worth replacing the contents of the ROOT folder with an empty index.html file. As we saw in Chapter 5, it is also possible to disable directory browsing on certain directories. We can then supply an empty web application that would show access restriction error messages to clients who attempt to access the directory.

Alternatively, we can also disable unauthorized access to the web application. Thus it is possible to restrict access to the `ROOT` application to internal clients, such as the developer group. We'll see more on access permissions in the next section.

Note that for security reasons, requesting the `ROOT` application using a URL such as the following, http://localhost:8080/ROOT/, will not resolve to the `ROOT` directory contents. This is an exception to the rule that all folders within the `webapps` directory are named after their parent folder.

A honey pot (a dummy, apparently insecure web application with no meaningful functionality used to lure hackers away from the real application) may also be set up at this directory if there is no default web application for the server. However, it is usually better to isolate honey pots on a separate machine.

Securing the Filesystem

As a security-conscious system administrator, one of the most important things you can do is restrict an application's access to your server's filesystem. If a program obtained free rein over the filesystem, it could relay sensitive information to outsiders, propagate a virus or worm, or simply delete critical system files.

Fortunately, both Windows NT/2000 and Unix-derived operating systems (including Linux and Mac OS X) have powerful security mechanisms built into them that allow administrators to apply just such a restriction in a fine-grained manner. Note that if you're using Windows 95/98/ME, you can skip this section; there's nothing you can do to restrict an application's access to the filesystem. These older, consumer-oriented Windows versions should not be used for any type of production-grade Tomcat deployment.

For simplicity, throughout the rest of this chapter we will use the term "Windows" to refer to any of the Windows NT-based operating systems (NT, 2000), and "Unix" to refer to any of the Unix-derived operating systems (Linux, Solaris, FreeBSD, Mac OS X).

Users, Groups, and Permissions

Both Windows and Unix make use of three basic concepts when it comes to securing the filesystem:

- **Users** are the individuals making use of an operating system. In Unix, every file is owned by a user.
- **Groups** are collections of zero or more users. Users can belong to multiple groups. In Unix, every file is associated with a group. In Windows, files can be owned by either a user or a group, but there is no requirement for an owner **and** a group to be associated with a file.
- **Permissions** determine what users and groups are able to do to a file. While various flavors of Unix and Windows differ in the specific permissions available, three basic permissions shared by all of these operating systems are:
    - The ability to read a file
    - The ability to write to a file
    - The ability to execute a file

A Permissions Example

To better understand how these three concepts interrelate, let's see an example. Imagine a computer with three different users: mom, dad, and kid. Let us further suppose that there are three different groups: parents, children, and family. The users mom and dad are members of the parents group, kid is a member of the children group, and all three users are members of the family group.

mom and dad have two different files on their computer: birthday_gifts.txt and emergency_plan.txt. The file birthday_gifts.txt contains a list of all the presents that mom and dad are planning on giving kid, and they would therefore like to block kid from reading (or manipulating) that file. To accomplish this, they modify the permissions of birthday_gifts.txt so that only members of the parents group may read and modify the file.

On the other hand, mom and dad want everyone in the family to be able to view and modify the emergency_plan.txt file. To accomplish this, they give the family group permissions to read and write the file.

Configuring Users, Groups, and Permissions

Now that we've covered the high-level concepts involved in securing filesystems (that is: users, groups, and permissions), let's review how to interact with this security model in Windows and Unix systems. Unfortunately, all variations of Windows and Unix are slightly different in how they are configured. Reviewing each and every operating system flavor would be nice, but is sadly impractical. We will take a look at Windows 2000 Professional and Red Hat Linux; other operating systems may vary slightly from these instructions.

Red Hat Linux 7.3

Linux and other Unix operating systems have three basic permissions that can be assigned to a file: read, write, and execute. Furthermore, each of these permissions can be set for a single user who owns the file, a specific group, and everyone else. Thus, given a file file.txt, we can set that the owner can read and write to the file, members of a certain group can only read the file, and everyone else can't read, write, or execute the file.

Viewing Permissions

The permissions of a file in Linux can be viewed with the ls command, using the -l parameter. The output of this command looks like the following:

```
$ ls -l
drwxr-xr-x    2 tomcat    tomcat        4096 Aug 13 01:28 bin
drwxr-xr-x    2 tomcat    tomcat        4096 Jun 10 23:09 classes
drwxr-xr-x    4 tomcat    tomcat        4096 Jun 10 23:09 common
drwxr-xr-x    2 tomcat    tomcat        4096 Aug 13 01:28 conf
drwxr-xr-x    2 tomcat    tomcat        4096 Aug 13 01:28 lib
-rw-r--r--    1 tomcat    tomcat        4568 Jun 10 23:09 LICENSE
...
```

In this output, we see a series of columns that correspond to each file or sub-directory in the current directory. We're only concerned with the first, third, fourth, and last columns. Let's define each of these, and drop out the other columns which are irrelevant to our discussion:

```
Permissions  Owner   Group   Filename
========================================
drwxr-xr-x   tomcat  tomcat  bin
drwxr-xr-x   tomcat  tomcat  classes
drwxr-xr-x   tomcat  tomcat  common
drwxr-xr-x   tomcat  tomcat  conf
drwxr-xr-x   tomcat  tomcat  lib
-rw-r--r--   tomcat  tomcat  LICENSE
```

Now, let's break down the values of each entry in the permission column. At first glance, they may seem somewhat cryptic, but they're actually quite simple. The permissions column can itself be viewed as four separate columns: file type, owner permissions, group permissions, and public permissions. Let's take the first and last files from our list above and break down the permissions column for each:

```
File Type   Owner P.  Group P.   Public P.   Filename
=====================================================
d           rwx       r-x        r-x         bin
-           rw-       r--        r--         LICENSE
```

The first sub-column of the permissions column dictates the file type, which can be `d` for directory, `l` for link, and `-` for a normal file. All of the remaining columns display whether or not the user, group, or public have read (`r`), write (`w`), or executable (`x`) access to that file (for directories, the executable property indicates whether the user has access to the directory). In the case of `bin`, the first file, all three of these groups have read and execute rights, but only the owner of the `bin` directory can write to the directory. For the second file, `LICENSE`, the owner, group, and public can read the file, but only the owner can modify the file.

Changing Permissions

To change the permissions of a file, the `chmod` utility is used. For example, we can change the permissions of the `LICENSE` file so that every user can read and write to the file by executing `chmod` with the following parameters:

```
$ chmod u=rw,g=rw,o=rw LICENSE
```

The `u` parameter is used to set the permissions for the owner of the file, the `g` parameter is used to set the permissions for the group associated with the file, and `o` is used to set the permissions for everyone else. This is a somewhat confusing choice of parameter names, so just remember that `u` stands for "user" and `o` stands for "others". You can use one, two, or all three of these parameters. Let's see the results of our operation:

```
$ ls -l | grep LICENSE
-rw-rw-rw- ... LICENSE
```

A handy recursive parameter lets us change the ownership of an entire directory hierarchy in one command. It's used like this:

```
$ chmod -R [permissions] [file/directory]
```

Changing File Ownership

To change the owner of a file, and the group that the file is associated with, the chown command is used. The syntax of chown is:

```
chown user[:group] filename
```

So, if we want to change the owner of the LICENSE file from tomcat to bobcat, we would issue this command:

```
$ chown bobcat LICENSE
```

chown can also use the -R recursive parameter.

Creating New Users and Groups

There are several utilities used for the creation, modification, and deletion of users and groups. These utilities are summarized below:

Utility	Purpose
useradd	Add new users
userdel	Delete existing users
usermod	Modify existing users
groupadd	Add new groups
groupdel	Delete existing groups
groupmod	Modify existing groups

Creating new users with the useradd command is as simple as:

```
useradd [username]
```

Each user must belong to at least one group. The group can be specified when the user is created with the -g parameter, like this:

```
useradd -g [groupname] [username]
```

If the -g parameter is not used, a new group is created with the same name as the username.

superuser Account

The Linux superuser user account, also known as root, has complete and unrestricted access to all files, regardless of any permissions that may have been set.

Additional Information

We've summarized the basics on how Red Hat Linux handles security. All of the commands we've reviewed in this section have various parameters that affect their operation, but going into more detail is beyond the scope of this book. To learn more about these commands, see the online documentation, accessed with the `man` command. For example, to learn more about `useradd`, type in:

```
$ man useradd
```

The information we've covered here will be used shortly in this chapter to teach you how to secure your files.

Windows 2000 Professional

Like Unix, Windows 2000 Professional (hereafter Win2k) allows users to configure the permissions of files. However, Win2k's permission model is a bit more complicated than that of Unix.

Viewing and Changing Permissions

To illustrate, let's first take a look at the permissions of a directory. This is done by right-clicking on a directory and selecting Properties from the popup menu. This will bring up a Properties window. By clicking on the Security tab, we can view the permissions of a file:

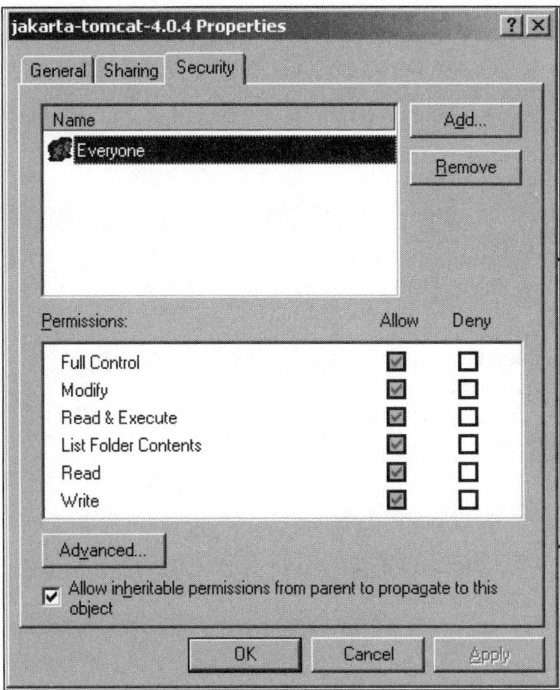

What we see in the screenshot above is that Windows allows administrators to specify permissions for a file or directory based on groups or individual users. The top-most box lists the users or groups for which the permissions apply; we can add additional users or groups and give them specific permissions. The bottom-most box contains the permission settings for the selected user/group in the top-most box.

Pay special attention to the checkbox at the bottom of the Properties window: Allow inheritable permissions from parent to propagate to this object. By default, files in Windows simply inherit the permissions given to their parent object. If this checkbox is unchecked, notice the difference in the window:

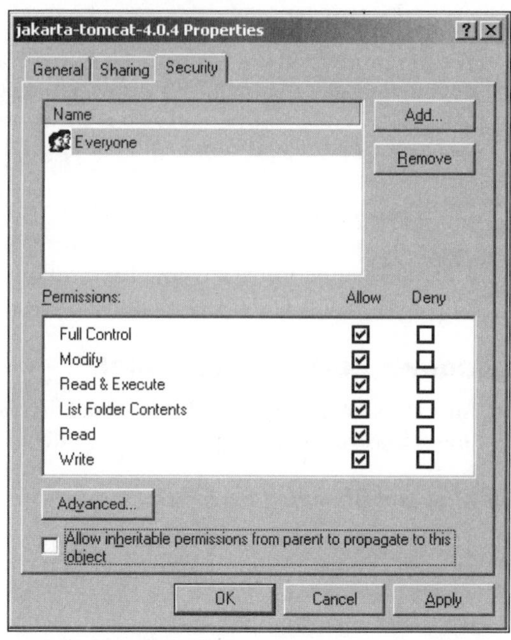

Note that the Allow permissions column is no longer grayed out. This indicates that the permissions of this directory are now independent of those of its parent.

Administrators can add or remove users from the top-most box and set permissions accordingly.

Changing File Ownership

Ownership of files is controlled with the Advanced... button on the Security tab of the Properties window. The button is shown in the preceding screenshot. Clicking on the button will display an Access Control Settings window with an Owner tab. Clicking on the Owner tab will show a screen similar to the following:

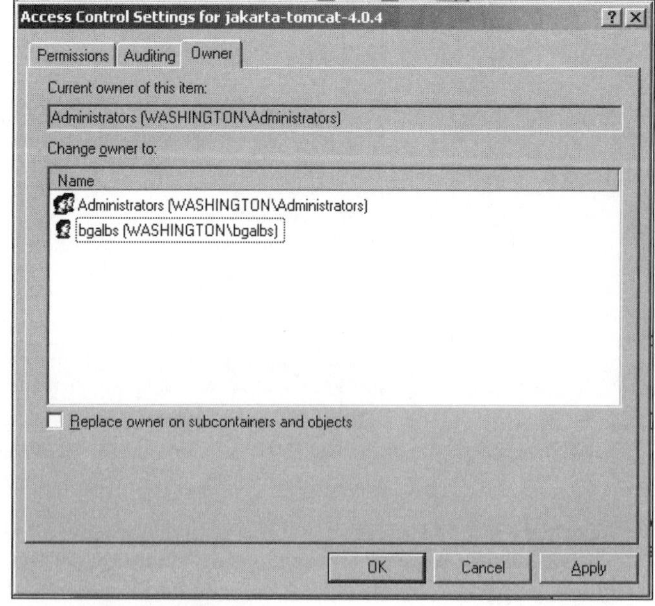

Creating New Users and Groups

New users can be created with the Users and Passwords control panel. For more options on manipulating users, and creating and manipulating groups, the Advanced tab of the Users and Passwords control panel can be used to launch an Advanced user/group management interface, as shown in the screenshot below:

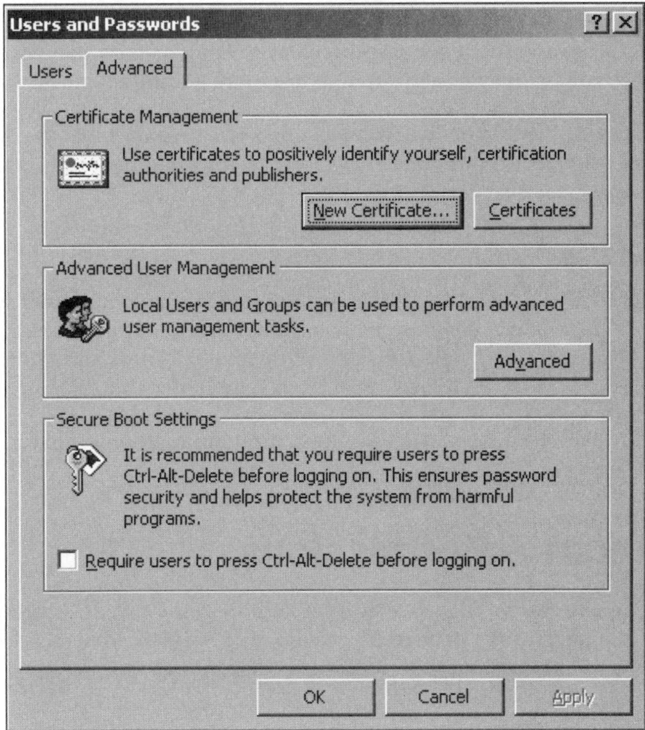

Superuser Account

Windows 2000 ships with a standard superuser account named `Administrator` that has complete access to all files, regardless of any permission settings. Additionally, any members of the `Administrators` group have the same unfettered access.

Additional Information

For more information on the Windows 2000 file security model, see the following link: http://www.microsoft.com/windows2000/en/server/iis/default.asp?url=/WINDOWS2000/en/server/iis/htm/core/iidfpsc.htm.

Recommended File Security Practices

Now that we've covered the basics of how the file security model works in Windows and Unix and how to configure it, let's talk about some recommended practices for using Tomcat with this model.

Do Not Run Tomcat with a Superuser Account

Because the superuser account (`root` on Unix, `Administrator` or member of `Administrators` on Windows) has complete, unrestricted access to all files, it is never a good idea to run Tomcat when logged in as this account. Should Tomcat be compromised, it would have unlimited access to compromise your entire machine.

A far better idea is to create a separate user account with the express purpose of running Tomcat and changing all Tomcat files and the root Tomcat directory to be owned by that account. Ensure that the Tomcat user account is not assigned to a group that has more additional permissions than you intend.

If you're using Windows and you launch Tomcat as a service, be aware that you can modify each service to be launched using an account that you specify. This is configured using the Log On tab of the Properties window for any service.

Protect Sensitive Files

By default, most files are read-accessible by any account on Unix and Windows systems. If your server has sensitive information, such as a database with customer information or e-mail files, seriously consider eliminating read access from all users except the explicit users and groups associated with the files in question.

Consider marking all of the files in `$CATALINA_HOME/conf` as read-only; that is, remove the write privilege from the files' owner.

Securing Tomcat's Permissions

Configuring your filesystem for maximum security is an important part of securing your Tomcat deployment, but it is only half of the picture. By using Java's Security Manager architecture, you can restrict those features of the Java language that Tomcat is able to access.

The Java Security Manager

As mentioned in the beginning of this chapter, the Java Security Manager architecture allows system administrators to impose fine-grained security restrictions to all Java applications. This security architecture is turned off by default, but it can be turned on at any time. In this section we will talk briefly about the Security Manager architecture in general terms, and then look at how this architecture specifically applies to Tomcat.

Overview of the Security Manager

The Security Manager architecture works on the notion of permissions. Once the Security Manager is turned on (using a command-line switch that we'll discuss a little later), applications must have **explicit permission** to perform certain security-sensitive tasks, such as creating a custom class loader or opening a socket to servers.

To make effective use of the Security Manager architecture, it is therefore necessary to know how applications can be given permissions and what the possible permissions are.

Granting Permissions To Applications

Policy files are the mechanism that the Security Manager uses to grant permissions to applications. Policy files are nothing more than simple text files composed of individual actions that applications are allowed to perform.

A policy file is composed of `grant` entries, which look like this:

```
// first grant entry
grant {
  permission java.lang.RuntimePermission "stopThread";
}

// second grant entry
grant codeBase "file:${java.home}/lib/ext/*" {
  permission java.security.AllPermission;
};
```

The first `grant` entry demonstrates the simplicity of the syntax. It grants all applications the ability to access the deprecated `Thread.stop()` method.

The second `grant` entry illustrates that code in specific locations can also be granted permissions. This is of course useful when we want to extend permissions to certain trusted code whilst denying permissions to all other code. In this case, all code in the `$JAVA_HOME/lib/ext` directory is granted all permissions, which effectively disables the Security Manager architecture for that code.

Grant Entry Syntax

Each `grant` entry must be composed of the following syntax:

```
grant codeBase "URL" {
  // this is a comment
  permission permission_class_name "target_name", "action";
  ...
};
```

Note that comments in policy files must begin with "//" on each line. As we saw in the first `grant` entry above, the `codeBase` attribute is optional. `codeBase` specifies a URL to which all the permissions should apply. The syntax is as follows:

codeBase Example	Description
`file:/C:/myapp/`	Indicates that code in the directory `c:\myapp` will be assigned the permissions in the `grant` block. Note that the slash "/" indicates that only class files in the directory will receive the permissions, not any JAR files or subdirectories.
`http://java.sun.com/*`	All code from the specified URL will be granted the permissions. In this case, the "/*" at the end of the URL indicates that all class files and JAR files will be assigned the permissions, but not any subdirectories.

Table continued on following page

codeBase Example	Description
`file:/funstuff/-`	All code in the `/funstuff` directory will be granted the permissions. The `"/-"` indicates that all class files and JAR files in the directory and its subdirectories will be assigned the permissions.

Within the `grant` block, one or more permissions can be assigned. Each permission consists of a permission class name and, in some cases, an additional **target** that identifies a specific permission within the permission class. Some permission targets can additionally take parameters, called **actions**. Here are examples of permissions:

```
grant {
  // allows applications to listen on all ports
  permission java.net.SocketPermission "localhost", "listen";

  // allows applications to read the "java.version" property
  permission java.util.PropertyPermission "java.version", "read";
}
```

Available Permissions

Permissions are defined by special classes that ultimately inherit from the abstract class `java.security.Permission`. Most permission classes define special targets that represent a security permission that can be turned on and off.

For example, the `java.lang.RuntimePermission` class defines the following targets (this is not a complete list):

Target Name	Description
`createClassLoader`	Allows an application to create a custom class loader
`exitVM`	Allows an application to exit the JVM via the `System.exit()` method

As of Java 1.4, there are 19 different permission classes offering control over various permissions. We will provide a list of these classes to demonstrate what is possible with permissions, but will not provide an extensive listing of the permission targets. The complete list of permission classes and their targets can be viewed at http://java.sun.com/j2se/1.4/docs/guide/security/permissions.html:

Permission Class	Description
`java.security.AllPermission`	By granting this permission, all other permissions are also granted. Granting this permission is the same as disabling the Security Manager for the affected code.

Permission Class	Description
`java.security.SecurityPermission`	Allows programmatic access to various security features of the Java language.
`java.security.UnresolvedPermission`	This permission class is not defined in policy files; rather, it is used as a place holder for when a policy file makes reference to a user-defined permission class that had not been loaded at the time of processing the policy file. This permission is only relevant to those interacting with the Security Manager system programmatically at run time.
`java.awt.AWTPermission`	Controls various AWT permissions.
`java.io.FilePermission`	Restricts read, write, execute, and delete access to files in specified paths.
`java.io.SerializablePermission`	Allows serialization permissions.
`java.lang.reflect.ReflectPermission`	Allows applications to circumvent the `public` and `private` mechanism's access checks and reflectively access any method.
`java.lang.RuntimePermission`	Allows access to key runtime features, such as creating class loaders, exiting the VM, and reassigning `STDIN`, `STDOUT`, and `STDERR`.
`java.net.NetPermission`	Allows various network permissions.
`java.net.SocketPermission`	Allows incoming socket connections, outgoing connections, listening on ports, and resolving hostnames. These permissions can be defined on specific hostnames and port combinations.
`java.sql.SQLPermission`	While this sounds intriguing, don't get too excited; it only controls a single permission: setting the JDBC log output writer. This file is considered sensitive because it may contain usernames and passwords.
`java.util.PropertyPermission`	Controls whether properties can be read from or written to.
`java.util.logging.LoggingPermission`	Allows the ability to configure the logging system.
`javax.net.ssl.SSLPermission`	Allows the ability to access SSL-related network functionality.
`javax.security.auth.AuthPermission`	Controls authentication permissions.

Table continued on following page

Permission Class	Description
`javax.security.auth.PrivateCredentialPermission`	Controls various security permissions.
`javax.security.auth.kerberos.DelegationPermission`	Controls various security permissions related to the Kerberos protocol.
`javax.security.auth.kerberos.ServicePermission`	Controls various security permissions related to the Kerberos protocol.
`javax.sound.sampled.AudioPermission`	Controls access to the sound system.

Enabling the Security Manager System

The Security Manager system is enabled by passing the `-Djava.security.manager` parameter to the Java Virtual Machine at startup, in this manner:

```
$ java -Djava.security.manager MyClass
```

By default, Java looks for the file `$JAVA_HOME/lib/security/java.policy` to determine what permissions to grant when the Security Manager is turned on.

For more information on enabling the Security Manager and using your own policy files, see http://java.sun.com/j2se/1.4/docs/guide/security/PolicyFiles.html.

Advanced Security Manager Topics

There are additional Security Manager topics that are simply beyond the scope of this chapter. For example, it is possible to subclass the default Java Security Manager implementation to provide for your own permission classes. It is further possible to define `grant` blocks in policy files based on code signatures. For information on these and other advanced topics, check out http://java.sun.com/j2se/1.4/docs/guide/security/.

Using the Security Manager with Tomcat

Now that we've covered the basics of the Security Manager system, let's talk about how to use it with Tomcat.

Enabling Tomcat's Security Manager

The preferred way to start Tomcat with the Security Manager enabled on Unix systems is the following:

```
$ $CATALINA_HOME/bin/catalina.sh start -security
```

On Windows systems, you'd issue this command:

```
> %CATALINA_HOME%\bin\catalina start -security
```

Tomcat's Policy File

Tomcat uses the `$CATALINA_HOME/conf/catalina.policy` file to determine its own permissions and those of its web applications.

What follows is the file as of Tomcat 4.0.4. Note that it is divided into three sections: system code permissions, Catalina code permissions, and web application code permissions. We'll explain each section under its own heading and then move on to the next one:

```
============================================================================
// catalina.corepolicy - Security Policy Permissions for Tomcat 4.0
//
// This file contains a default set of security policies to be enforced
// (by the JVM) when Catalina is executed with the "-security" option.
// In addition to the permissions granted here, the following additional
// permissions are granted to the codebase specific to each web
// application:
//
// * Read access to the document root directory
//
// $Id: catalina.policy,v 1.14.2.1 2001/10/06 18:51:03 remm Exp $
// ============================================================================
```

System Code Permissions

Tomcat's policy file grants all permissions to the `javac` tool, which is used to compile JSP pages into servlets, and also grants all permissions to any Java standard extensions. Four `grant` lines are used instead of two to deal with multiple path possibilities. Note that you may need to add additional `grants` to this section if your JVM uses different paths for its standard extensions (Mac OS X needs additional grants for example) and you're actually putting JARs or classes in those paths:

```
// ========== SYSTEM CODE PERMISSIONS =====================================

// These permissions apply to javac
grant codeBase "file:${java.home}/lib/-" {
  permission java.security.AllPermission;
};

// These permissions apply to all shared system extensions
grant codeBase "file:${java.home}/jre/lib/ext/-" {
  permission java.security.AllPermission;
};

// These permissions apply to javac when ${java.home} points
// at $JAVA_HOME/jre
grant codeBase "file:${java.home}/../lib/-" {
  permission java.security.AllPermission;
};

// These permissions apply to all shared system extensions when
// ${java.home} points at $JAVA_HOME/jre
grant codeBase "file:${java.home}/lib/ext/-" {
  permission java.security.AllPermission;
};
```

Catalina Code Permissions

Note that Catalina grants all permissions to:

- Tomcat's startup classes (`$CATALINA_HOME/bin/bootstrap.jar`)
- The shared class loader files (`$CATALINA_HOME/lib` and `$CATALINA_HOME/classes`)
- The common class loader files (`$CATALINA_HOME/common/lib` and `$CATALINA_HOME/common/classes`)
- The server class loader files (`$CATALINA_HOME/server/lib` and `$CATALINA_HOME/server/classes`)

```
// ========== CATALINA CODE PERMISSIONS ===================================

// These permissions apply to the server startup code
grant codeBase "file:${catalina.home}/bin/bootstrap.jar" {
  permission java.security.AllPermission;
};

// These permissions apply to the servlet API classes
// and those that are shared across all class loaders
// located in the "common" directory
grant codeBase "file:${catalina.home}/common/-" {
  permission java.security.AllPermission;
};

// These permissions apply to the container's core code, plus
// any additional libraries installed in the "server" directory
grant codeBase "file:${catalina.home}/server/-" {
  permission java.security.AllPermission;
};

// These permissions apply to shared web application libraries
// including the Jasper page compiler in the "lib" directory
grant codeBase "file:${catalina.home}/lib/-" {
  permission java.security.AllPermission;
};

// These permissions apply to shared web application classes
// located in the "classes" directory
grant codeBase "file:${catalina.home}/classes/-" {
  permission java.security.AllPermission;
};
```

Web Application Permissions

Tomcat allows read access to various system properties. Note also the following `grant`:

```
permission java.lang.RuntimePermission
    "accessClassInPackage.sun.beans.*";
```

The `accessClassInPackage.*` target of `RuntimePermission` allows classes to see other classes that it normally would not have access to. In this case, Tomcat is giving all web applications access to the `sun.beans.*` package.

```
// ========== WEB APPLICATION PERMISSIONS =================================

// These permissions are granted by default to all web applications
// In addition, a web application will be given a read FilePermission
// and JndiPermission for all files and directories in its document root.
grant {
  // Required for JNDI lookup of named JDBC DataSource's and
  // Javamail named MimePart DataSource used to send mail
  permission java.util.PropertyPermission "java.home", "read";
  permission java.util.PropertyPermission "java.naming.*", "read";
  permission java.util.PropertyPermission "javax.sql.*", "read";

  // OS Specific properties to allow read access
  permission java.util.PropertyPermission "os.name", "read";
  permission java.util.PropertyPermission "os.version", "read";
  permission java.util.PropertyPermission "os.arch", "read";
  permission java.util.PropertyPermission "file.separator", "read";
  permission java.util.PropertyPermission "path.separator", "read";
  permission java.util.PropertyPermission "line.separator", "read";

  // JVM properties to allow read access
  permission java.util.PropertyPermission "java.version", "read";
  permission java.util.PropertyPermission "java.vendor", "read";
  permission java.util.PropertyPermission "java.vendor.url", "read";
  permission java.util.PropertyPermission "java.class.version", "read";
  permission java.util.PropertyPermission "java.specification.version", "read";
  permission java.util.PropertyPermission "java.specification.vendor", "read";
  permission java.util.PropertyPermission "java.specification.name", "read";

  permission java.util.PropertyPermission "java.vm.specification.version", "read";
  permission java.util.PropertyPermission "java.vm.specification.vendor", "read";
  permission java.util.PropertyPermission "java.vm.specification.name", "read";
  permission java.util.PropertyPermission "java.vm.version", "read";
  permission java.util.PropertyPermission "java.vm.vendor", "read";
  permission java.util.PropertyPermission "java.vm.name", "read";

  // Required for getting BeanInfo
  permission java.lang.RuntimePermission "accessClassInPackage.sun.beans.*";

  // Allow read of JAXP compliant XML parser debug
  permission java.util.PropertyPermission "jaxp.debug", "read";
};

...
```

Note that system administrators are not only free to modify Tomcat's policy file; they are encouraged to. Once the Security Manager has been enabled, you'll likely need to make changes to Catalina's policy file for certain aspects of your web applications to function.

Recommended Security Manager Practices

Now that you know how to turn on the Security Manager with Tomcat, and also where Tomcat stores its policy file, we can discuss recommended practices for granting permissions to your applications.

Use the Security Manager

If you don't turn on Tomcat's Security Manager, any JSP or class file is free to perform any action it likes. This includes opening unauthorized connections to other network hosts, destroying your filesystem, or even abnormally terminating Tomcat itself by issuing the `System.exit()` command.

To maintain a secure Tomcat installation, you should don your paranoid hat and assume that at some point, a hacker will be able to deploy malicious code into one of your Tomcat web applications.

By turning the Security Manager on, you gain explicit control over what your web applications are allowed to do.

Be Mindful of Shared Code

Placing code into Tomcat's shared class loader directories (`$CATALINA_HOME/classes` and `$CATALINA_HOME/lib`) is a good way to share common libraries amongst web applications. However, because of Tomcat's liberal permission grants for this class loader (all permissions are granted), you may want to think twice before you make a habit out of placing code in this class loader.

You must either:

- Ensure that all code placed in this class loader is trusted.
- Change Tomcat's policy file to be much more restrictive with its permission grants to the shared class loader. Be careful, however, not to muck around with the permissions assigned to the other class loaders as Tomcat may cease to function.

Know Your Application's Requirements

As mentioned above, turning the Security Manager on gives you complete control over what your web applications are allowed to do. The flipside of this security coin is that your web applications will find themselves unable to do some things that they may have taken for granted before. Consider the following tasks that are unauthorized with Tomcat's default policy configuration:

- Creating a class loader
- Accessing a database via a socket (for example, the MySQL JDBC driver trying to establish a connection with a MySQL database)
- Sending an e-mail via the JavaMail API
- Reading or writing to files outside of the web application's directory

In truth, there are a myriad of permissions that your applications may require. The trick is to communicate with the developers and know what permissions the web applications will require.

We will look at some examples for enabling some of the common permissions listed above; for others, check out the Java Security documentation links from earlier in the chapter.

Enabling Creation of a Class Loader

The following example shows how to give a specific web application, `yourWebApp`, the ability to create a class loader:

```
grant codeBase "file:${catalina.home}/webapps/yourWebApp/WEB-INF/-" {
  permission java.lang.RuntimePermission "createClassLoader";
};
```

> **Note that this is an extremely dangerous permission to grant. An application that can instantiate its own class loaders can, by definition, load its own classes into the system. As mentioned earlier, malicious classes could then be used to compromise your system in a number of ways.**

Enabling JDBC Drivers To Open Socket Connections To Databases

The following example shows how to allow all web applications access to a specific database running on the host `db.server.com` on port 54321:

```
grant codeBase "file:${catalina.home}/webapps/-" {
  permission java.net.SocketPermission "db.server.com:54321", "connect";
};
```

Note that this example allows all code in all of your web applications to connect to `db.server.com:54321`. If this is too much of a security risk for you, you have a few alternative options:

- Explicitly assign permission to each web application's JDBC driver individually:

```
grant codeBase "file:${catalina.home}/webapps/webAppName/WEB-INF/lib/JDBC.jar" {
  permission java.net.SocketPermission "db.server.com:54321", "connect";
};
```

- Place the JDBC driver into the shared class loader, which has all permissions granted to it

Sending an E-Mail with JavaMail

Sending e-mail requires that your web application have access to port 25 on an SMTP server. The following example shows how to grant this permission to all classes in a web application:

```
grant codeBase "file:${catalina.home}/webapps/myWebApp/WEB-INF/classes/-" {
  permission java.net.SocketPermission "mail.server.com:25", "connect";
};
```

Reading or Writing To Files Outside of the Web Application's Directory

We spent a considerable amount of time earlier discussing how to use the standard facilities of the Windows and Unix operating systems to restrict the files that your web applications have access to. If you wish to use your operating system to control file access, rather than Java's permissions, you can give your web applications free rein once again with the following example:

```
grant {
  java.io.FilePermission "<<ALL FILES>>", "read,write,execute,delete";
};
```

Note that if you do not grant at least some file permissions to your web application, your web applications will be shut out from accessing your filesystem. So, should you still bother securing it using your operating system's file permissions? Yes. Why? Remember that even though your web applications may be shut out, Tomcat itself has full permissions and should a malicious hacker modify Tomcat somehow, they could still access your filesystem.

> **If you haven't tightened the security around the shared class loader, rogue classes in its scope would also have full filesystem access.**

Finally, Tomcat is probably not the only exploitable application on your machine, and thus you should use the filesystem permissions to restrict other potential offenders.

Also note that by default, all Java applications do have read access to the directory in which they are located and its subdirectories.

Security Realms

Recall that a realm is a programming interface that is used to authenticate users and implement container-managed security based on roles. The actual mapping of users to roles can be specified at deployment time – and can be changed dynamically without having to change the application code. We saw in Chapter 8 that memory realms can be utilized readily in Tomcat 4.0, while Tomcat 4.1 has an updatable, robust implementation called the `UserDatabase`. However, we purposely deferred a detailed discussion of this form of security to this chapter. We will now look at a couple of secure authentication schemes:

- File-based realms with digested passwords
- JDBC realms with secure database users and digested passwords

Both of these are more secure than their default counterparts, but the database version is a better option for production systems.

Message Digests

Before we start, we need to discuss **message digests** as they will play a role in the upcoming section. A message digest, also called a **hash**, is used to provide proof that the data we are dealing with hasn't been altered or tampered with.

A hashing algorithm takes some data as input and creates a unique fingerprint of it (which is usually 16 or 20 bytes long). This is a one-way process, meaning that the digest cannot be undigested to discover the original data. As each fingerprint is unique, we can compare the digest of our original data with a digest of the data we are testing. If they match, then the data we are testing is the same as the digest data and therefore hasn't been changed.

We can apply this to passwords by digesting the cleartext password and storing it on file. This means that even if the password file is compromised, an attacker cannot read or undigest the passwords it contains and they will be unusable. To check a user's password against the stored digest, we simply digest the value entered and compare it with the value on file. If they match, it is the same password.

There are two message digest algorithms supported by Java:

- **MD5**
  This algorithm is used in a number of password storage mechanisms, including many Unix systems. MD5 produces a 16 byte message digest.

- **SHA**
  This algorithm is more secure than MD5 as it uses a 20 byte message digest.

Now that we know about message digests, we can get on with authenticating users.

Users and Roles

We must find out which users and roles are to have access to the web application before we can set them. This information is stored in the web application's `web.xml` file under the `<security-constraint>` element. The application's developer should provide you with this information, but it's a good idea to be familiar with the options that can be used in a web application. The examples we talk about here will be carried into our configuration examples later on.

We have touched on most of these settings in Chapter 6, so we won't go into too much detail. Besides, this is the developer's job to get right; we just have to set up the server appropriately. The first element, `<web-resource-collection>`, is a convenient way to group web resources together so that security can be applied uniformly. Inside this element, we must specify the name of the resource and the URL pattern(s) to cover.

The `<role-name>` element of `<auth-constraint>` specifies a role that is allowed to access this section of the web application; any user belonging to this role may log in, providing they give a valid password. This is the domain of the administrator, as users and roles are defined in realms in `server.xml` The web application doesn't care what realm is used, as long as the user is configured in one of them. There are a couple of other sub-elements of `<web-resource-collection>`, `<description>` and `<http-method>`, which we don't have to consider just now as we are going to restrict access to the whole application for all HTTP methods:

```
<?xml version="1.0" encoding="ISO-8859-1"?>

<!DOCTYPE web-app
    PUBLIC "-//Sun Microsystems, Inc.//DTD Web Application 2.3//EN"
    "http://java.sun.com/dtd/web-app_2_3.dtd">

<web-app>
  <security-constraint>
    <web-resource-collection>
      <web-resource-name>Entire Application</web-resource-name>
      <url-pattern>/*</url-pattern>
    </web-resource-collection>
    <auth-constraint>
       <role-name>admin</role-name>
    </auth-constraint>
```

So, in the example above, the entire web application is protected by the security constraint: `/*` is the regular expression that matches all requests. However, the only role that is allowed access is `admin`. We shall therefore have to create an `admin` role in `server.xml` to allow this web application to run.

The two elements mentioned are the only two sub-elements of `<security-constraint>` that apply to realm configuration, but there is another element in `web.xml` that has a small association with realms:

```
    <login-config>
      <auth-method>FORM</auth-method>
      <realm-name>Tomcat Manager Application</realm-name>
      <form-login-config>
        <form-login-page>/login.jsp</form-login-page>
        <form-error-page>/notAuthenticated.jsp</form-error-page>
      </form-login-config>
    </login-config>
  </web-app>
```

`<login-config>` sets the type of login and authentication that the application needs. In this case, the application has `FORM`-based authentication, which means that the developers will have supplied a custom login page for this application. Note that this may also be `BASIC`, `DIGEST`, or `CLIENT-CERT`. As it stands, `FORM`-based authentication is a good option for a few reasons:

- The server handles the user information. In the other forms of authentication, the browser caches the authentication information. While this is convenient for the user, it is not as secure as if the server held on to this information.
- `BASIC` authentication is easy to decode as it is sent as a cleartext, base64-encoded string.
- Not all browsers supported `DIGEST` authentication, so you can't guarantee that all clients will be able to authenticate. However, if the application is in a closed environment, such as a corporate intranet, it is easier to control the choice of browser. Internet Explorer and Konqueror are two browsers that do support `DIGEST` authentication. Mozilla 1.0 claims to recognize the `DIGEST` request (0.9 doesn't even recognize this), but can't authenticate.
- `DIGEST` authentication doesn't work if the passwords are digested on the Tomcat side (so that they can't be read as cleartext) because of the way that the `DIGEST` mechanism calculates its digest. First of all the browser calculates a digest of the username, the password, the URL, the HTTP method, and a random string sent to it by the server. Likewise, the server creates a digest to verify that the details entered by the user are correct. However, as the password is already digested on the server, and thus completely different from the cleartext version entered into the browser, the two digests will be different, and authentication will fail. As digesting the passwords on the server side is a sensible precaution, we will avoid `DIGEST` authentication for the moment. We'll see more about digested passwords in the upcoming sections.
- `CLIENT-AUTH` is really only necessary in business-to-business transactions, and so does not appear in most web applications that you will come across.

If you wish to add `FORM`-based authentication to a web application in place of some other type supplied by the developers, here is an example login page:

```
  <html>
    <head><title>Please Log In</title>
    <body>
      <form method="POST"
            action='<%= response.encodeURL("j_security_check") %>' >
        <table border="0" cellspacing="5">
          <tr>
```

```
            <th align="right">Username:</th>
            <td align="left"><input type="text" name="j_username"></td>
          </tr>
          <tr>
            <th align="right">Password:</th>
            <td align="left"><input type="password" name="j_password"></td>
          </tr>
          <tr>
            <td align="right"><input type="submit" value="Log In"></td>
            <td align="left"><input type="reset"></td>
          </tr>
        </table>
      </form>
    </body>
  </html>
```

And an example error page:

```
<html>
  <head><title>Error: Login Failure</title></head>
  <body>
    Log in failed, please try
    <a href='<%= response.encodeURL("login.jsp") %>'>again</a>.
  </body>
</html>
```

Add these to the web application you wish to use FORM-based authentication in and update web.xml to reflect their positions.

We'll use these pages as an example once we have configured some users and roles, so place them in a directory under webapps called secure. Also make sure that the web.xml file we saw above is in the secure/WEB-INF directory.

To test our configuration later on, we'll need a resource to protect, so here's a simple web page (secure/index.html):

```
<html>
  <head><title>Wrox Administration Application</title></head>
  <body>
    <h1>Wrox Administration Application</h1>
  </body>
</html>
```

Now let's set up the users and roles using realms.

File-Based Realms

We saw file-based realms in Chapter 8, where we looked at Tomcat 4.0's memory realm and Tomcat 4.1's UserDatabase realm. What we didn't look at, however, was how to make them more secure. The ideal solution for authentication is to use a database (covered next), but if you wish to use a memory or UserDatabase realm you should secure it as much as possible.

The default file-based realms store passwords in cleartext in the `tomcat-users.xml` file. This is obviously not ideal. Therefore, we must find a way to store these passwords in a less readable format. There are four steps to configuring a secure file-based realm in Tomcat:

- Select the password digest algorithm
- Create a digested password
- Add the digested password to the realm
- Test the digested password

These steps will ensure that users' passwords are not stored in cleartext anywhere on the system. The steps are the same for both Tomcat 4.0 and Tomcat 4.1; only the details of those steps differ between the two versions.

Tomcat 4.0

First we'll configure Tomcat 4.0's memory realm to use a more secure version of authentication.

Select the Digest Algorithm

The choice of digest algorithm is limited to those supported by the `java.security.MessageDigest` class (SHA or MD5). All we have to do is set the `digest` attribute in the `<Realm>` element. In our example, we will use MD5:

```
<!-- Tomcat 4.0 -->
<Realm className="org.apache.catalina.realm.MemoryRealm" digest="md5"/>
```

Whenever a user enters their password at the authentication stage, Tomcat will digest it with the algorithm specified here and then compare it with the value stored in the authentication file.

Create a Digested Password

We now need to create a digested version of our password. Tomcat 4.0 comes with a class that will do all the hard work for us, `org.apache.catalina.realm.RealmBase`. We have to specify the algorithm (MD5 in this case) and the string we want to digest (`tomcat`, which will be our password):

```
$ java -classpath $CATALINA_HOME/server/lib/catalina.jar
org.apache.catalina.realm.RealmBase -a md5 tomcat
catalina:1b359d8753858b55befa0441067aaed3
```

The output (highlighted in bold) is the string we entered, followed by a colon and the MD5 hash we need.

Add the Digested Password To the Memory Realm

The final step is to add the digested password to the memory realm for our Tomcat installation. Copy the digested output of the previous step and add it as the `password` attribute of a user in `tomcat-users.xml`:

```
<!-- Tomcat 4.0 -->
<tomcat-users>
  <user name="admin"
        password="1b359d8753858b55befa0441067aaed3"
        roles="manager"/>
</tomcat-users>
```

Here, we've added a user called admin with the admin role so that we can test our secure password with our test application we set up above.

Test the Digested Password

Now we need to make sure that the new password works. Restart Tomcat and browse to http://localhost:8080/secure/. You will be shown the form we configured earlier. Enter **admin** as the **Username** and **tomcat** as the **Password**:

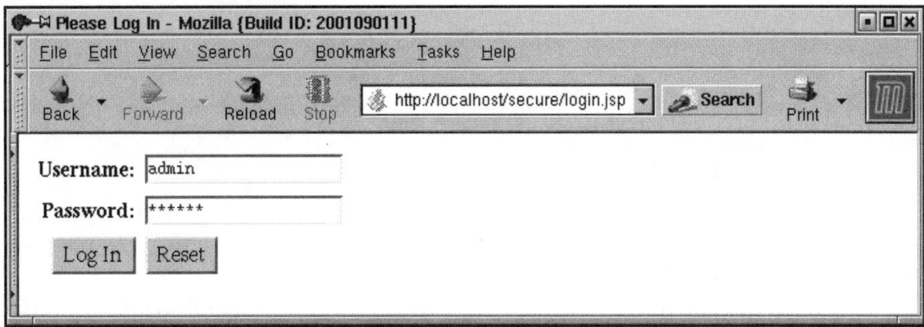

Tomcat will then digest this password and compare it with the value in tomcat-users.xml. If all is well, you will then be shown our index page. If you enter the wrong details, then you will be shown the error page that we configured above.

Tomcat 4.1

The steps for Tomcat 4.1 are exactly the same as for Tomcat 4.0, but the commands and configuration directives are slightly different.

Select the Digest Algorithm

The choice of digest algorithm is limited to those supported by the java.security.MessageDigest class (SHA or MD5). All we have to do is set the digest attribute in the <Realm> element. In our example, we will use SHA:

```
<!-- Tomcat 4.1 -->
<Realm className="org.apache.catalina.realm.UserDatabaseRealm"
       debug="0" resourceName="UserDatabase" digest="sha"/>
```

Whenever a user enters their password at the authentication stage, Tomcat will digest it with the algorithm specified here and then compare it with the value stored in the authentication file.

Create a Digested Password

We now need to create a digested version of our password. Tomcat 4.1 comes with a script called `digest.sh` (`digest.bat` on Windows) located in `$CATALINA_HOME/bin` that calculates the digested value for us. We need to specify the algorithm (SHA in this case) and the string we wish to digest (`tomcat`, which is our password):

```
$ $CATALINA_HOME/bin/digest -a sha tomcat
catalina:536c0b339345616c1b33caf454454d8b8a190d6c
```

The output (highlighted in bold) is the string we entered, followed by a colon and the SHA hash we need.

Add the Digested Password To the UserDatabase realm

The final step is to add the digested password to the UserDatabase realm for our Tomcat installation. Copy the digested output of the previous step and add it as the `password` attribute of a user in `tomcat-users.xml`:

```
<!-- Tomcat 4.1 -->
<?xml version='1.0'?>
<tomcat-users>
  <role rolename="admin"/>
  <user username="admin"
        password="536c0b339345616c1b33caf454454d8b8a190d6c"
        roles="admin"/>
</tomcat-users>
```

Here we've added a user called `admin` with the role of `admin`. This role allows the user to access our example application (as well as the `admin` application that ships with Tomcat 4.1).

Test the Digested Password

We'll test the digested password by trying to access our example web application. Browse to http://localhost:8080/secure/ and you should be presented with the login page. Enter **admin** as the **Username** and **tomcat** as the **Password** and hit the **Log In** button. If all goes well, you should be granted entry to the application. If not, you will be shown the error page we defined above.

JDBC Realms

In this section we will set up a secure JDBC realm using a MySQL database. By the end of it, we will be able to:

- Set up a password-protected user in MySQL
- Set up MySQL to provide secure authentication information for Tomcat
- Give a MySQL user limited access to the authentication information

Requirements

For JDBC authentication Tomcat requires a database with at least two tables, each of which must have at least two columns. It is the contents of these tables that are important, not their names as these can be changed in `server.xml`:

Table Name	Description
users	Contains username and password information
user_roles	Contains user to roles mapping information

The users table is expected to contain the following two columns at a minimum:

Column	Type	Length
user_name	VARCHAR(15) NOT NULL PRIMARY KEY	15
user_pass	VARCHAR(32) NOT NULL	32

The user password will be an MD5 digest password, and as such will be 16 bytes long.

The user_roles table is expected to contain the following two columns at a minimum:

Column	Type	Length
user_name	VARCHAR(15) NOT NULL PRIMARY KEY	15
role_name	VARCHAR(15) NOT NULL	15

The exact length of the VARCHAR is not important, but we must create columns in our tables that match the required view.

In our example, we will call this database authority, as this is the default name in server.xml. Here's the SQL to create the database:

```
CREATE DATABASE IF NOT EXISTS authority;

USE authority;

CREATE TABLE users (
   user_name VARCHAR(15) NOT NULL PRIMARY KEY,
   user_pass VARCHAR(32) NOT NULL
);

CREATE TABLE user_roles (
   user_name VARCHAR(15) PRIMARY KEY NOT NULL REFERENCES users(user_name),
   role_name VARCHAR(10) NOT NULL
);
```

Either type this into the MySQL prompt, or run it as a script:

```
$ mysql < authority.sql
```

Now we need to add some users and roles. To make the installation even more secure, we will encrypt all the passwords of the users stored in the authority table. Most databases provide functions for encrypting information, and MySQL is no exception. We will use the MD5() function in this case. Here's the SQL to add an admin user:

```
INSERT INTO users (user_name, user_pass) VALUES ('admin', MD5('tomcat'));
```

The JDBC realm has an attribute called digest that is used to specify the encryption algorithm to use on the password entered at the authentication stage. The encrypted version is then compared with the password in the table.

Finally, we must populate the role table. We'll use the admin role, as it will grant access to our example application:

```
INSERT INTO user_roles (user_name, role_name) VALUES ('admin', 'admin');
```

Adding a Tomcat User To MySQL

Tomcat uses the username and password specified in $CATALINA_HOME/conf/server.xml to connect to the database in a JDBC realm:

```
<Realm className="org.apache.catalina.realm.JDBCRealm" debug="99"
       driverName="org.gjt.mm.mysql.Driver"
       connectionURL="jdbc:mysql://localhost/authority"
       connectionName="test" connectionPassword="test"
       userTable="users" userNameCol="user_name" userCredCol="user_pass"
       userRoleTable="user_roles" roleNameCol="role_name" />
```

Therefore we need to have this user in the mysql.user table. The best way to create a new user is to use the GRANT command:

```
GRANT priv_type [(column_list)] [, priv_type [(column_list)] ...]
    ON {tbl_name | * | *.* | db_name.*}
    TO user_name [IDENTIFIED BY 'password']
        [, user_name [IDENTIFIED BY 'password'] ...]
```

There are a large number of other options for this command, but we shall only use a few of them in this example, as detailed MySQL explanations are not the point of this chapter.

This command creates a user in the mysql.user table. MySQL uses this table to determine access rights to its databases. It is important to restrict access to this table, as unlimited access would allow anyone to change the access rights to every database on the server. It is a good idea to limit the access to root and root alone.

We don't want our users' passwords stored in cleartext, but luckily MySQL encrypts them automatically when you specify them with GRANT. For this example, we will be creating a user called tomcat who will be accessing the database from the local machine with the password tomcat:

```
mysql> GRANT SELECT ON authority.*
    -> TO 'tomcat'@'localhost' IDENTIFIED BY 'tomcat';
mysql> FLUSH PRIVILEGES;
```

Here we give tomcat SELECT privileges on all tables in the authority database because the JDBC realm only needs read access. Other applications may well need more access if they need to add more users. The IDENTIFIED BY clause specifies the user's password. MySQL automatically obfuscates this value and inserts it into the user table like so:

```
mysql> SELECT * FROM mysql.user;
+---------------+----------+------------------+------------+-------------+
| Host          | User     | Password         | Select_priv | Insert_priv |
+---------------+----------+------------------+------------+-------------+
| localhost     | tomcat   | 22e3be3e311d37ea | N          | N           |
+---------------+----------+------------------+------------+-------------+
```

Note that there will be a lot more information than this, but most of it relates to access privileges on the mysql database and as such doesn't concern us here.

Older versions of MySQL might not do this automatically, so the following command is needed:

```
mysql> GRANT SELECT ON authority.*
    -> TO 'tomcat'@'localhost' IDENTIFIED BY PASSWORD('tomcat');
mysql> FLUSH PRIVILEGES;
```

Remember the FLUSH PRIVILEGES line, as MySQL won't update its privileges tables without being explicitly told to. Another way to update the privileges is to use the MySQL administration tool:

```
$ mysqladmin reload
```

The SET command can be used to change the password of a user without having to create it afresh:

```
SET PASSWORD FOR 'tomcat'@'localhost' = PASSWORD('new_password');
```

To see that the tomcat user has indeed been given the appropriate privileges on authority, run the following query and look for the authority database in the Db column:

```
mysql> SELECT * FROM mysql.db;
+---------------+-----------+--------+-------------+-------------+
| Host          | Db        | User   | Select_priv | Insert_priv |
+---------------+-----------+--------+-------------+-------------+
| localhost     | authority | tomcat | Y           | N           |
+---------------+-----------+--------+-------------+-------------+
```

Here, the Y in the Select_priv column indicates that the user in the User column (tomcat) has SELECT privileges on the table in the Db column (authority).

If you wish to cancel a user's privileges, use the REVOKE command as follows:

```
mysql> REVOKE SELECT ON authority.* FROM 'tomcat'@'localhost';
mysql> FLUSH PRIVILEGES;
```

Now that we have set up a user for Tomcat, we should configure a realm that uses it.

Defining the MySQL-Based JDBC Realm

To define the JDBC realm, we must first remove the default `MemoryRealm` (`UserDatabase` in Tomcat 4.1) realm. Look in the `server.xml` file and comment out the reference to the global `MemoryRealm` (`UserDatabase`) realm as follows:

```
<!-- Tomcat 4.0 -->
<!--
<Realm className="org.apache.catalina.realm.MemoryRealm" />
-->
```

```
<!-- Tomcat 4.1 -->
<!--
<Realm className="org.apache.catalina.realm.UserDatabaseRealm"
       debug="0" resourceName="UserDatabase"/>
-->
```

Next, define a JDBC realm, mapping our tables and columns from the `authority` database:

```
<Realm className="org.apache.catalina.realm.JDBCRealm" debug="99"
       driverName="org.gjt.mm.mysql.Driver"
       connectionURL="jdbc:mysql://localhost/authority"
       connectionName="tomcat" connectionPassword="tomcat"
       userTable="users" userNameCol="user_name" userCredCol="user_pass"
       userRoleTable="user_roles" roleNameCol="role_name"
       digest="md5"/>
```

Note that we have configured the `mm.mysql` driver for the JDBC driver from http://mmmysql.sourceforge.net/ as detailed in the previous chapter. The `connectionURL` points to the database that contains the authentication details, which is accessed using the credentials supplied in the `connectionName` and `connectionPassword` attributes.

The lines beginning with `userTable` and `userRoleTable` specify which tables in the database we should be using to look up the user and role for authentication purposes. The `digest` attribute is the algorithm that Tomcat uses to digest the password entered by the user, in this case MD5. As mentioned earlier, this attribute can be one of the two digest algorithms supported by `java.security.MessageDigest` (SHA or MD5).

Testing the JDBC Realm

To see the realm in action, start Tomcat and connect to our example web application: http://localhost:8080/secure/. You should be challenged with the login screen. Enter **admin** as the **Username** and **tomcat** as the password:

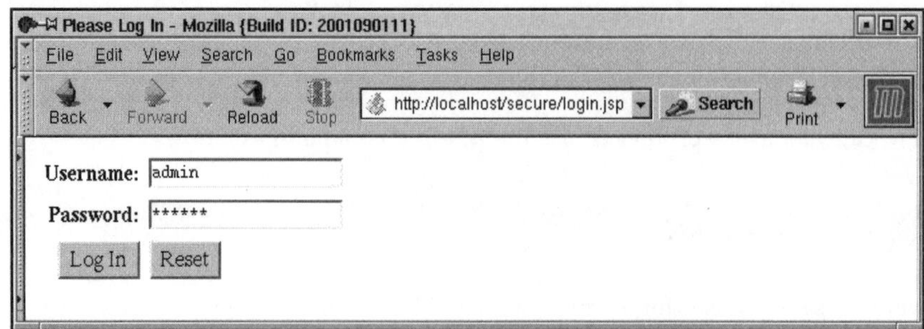

Using the JDBC realm, authentication is now performed against MySQL instead of against the `tomcat-users.xml` file. By replacing the JDBC driver, and changing the table/column mappings, we can use data from other databases (for example, Oracle) with a completely different schema. As long as the username and password are stored somewhere in one table, and the username and role are stored somewhere in another, Tomcat can use the database for authentication.

As we have demonstrated so far, changing the authentication method is easy without having to alter any code in the web application. In fact, we have even added a custom login form to a web application, as we wanted the advantages of `FORM`-based authentication. We've also seen some methods for making the authentication process a lot more secure, most of which involve scrambling passwords so that they can't be read or cracked easily. Next we will examine SSL, which will make our application even more secure by preventing prying eyes looking at our data in transit.

SSL

Secure Sockets Layer (SSL) is a protocol that allows for secure communication between clients and servers in a network environment. Originally developed by Netscape, it has since been adopted as an Internet standard. In addition to encryption of data (and hence secure communication), SSL also provides for authentication.

The security protocols on which SSL is based are **public key encryption** and **symmetric key encryption**. In public key encryption, there is a pair of encryption keys used for encoding a message – one publicly available key, and the other a private key that is not disclosed to anyone else. Anyone wanting to send a message to an application that has a known public key would need to encrypt it with that key. Only the corresponding private key can then decrypt the message, and thus the transmission is secure. Symmetric key encryption on the other hand uses the same (secret) key for both encryption and decryption. This algorithm, however, needs a reliable way to exchange the secret key between the two end points in the transmission.

When a client opens an SSL connection with a server, a **SSL Handshake** is performed. The procedure for a SSL Handshake is as follows:

- The server sends over its digital certificate. This contains the public key of the server, the information about the server, the authority that issued the certificate to the server, and the (time) validity of the certificate.
- The client then authenticates the server based on the validity of the certificate and trustworthiness of the authority that issued the certificate. Certificates issued by well-known (and trusted) **Certificate Authorities** (CA), such as VeriSign and Thawte, are recognized by most web browsers. If the certificate cannot be validated, the user is warned, and they can choose to either accept the certificate, or deny it.
- A session key is then generated and exchanged over the connection. The connection is at this point secured by the public key encryption mechanism, and so the exchange is secure. The session key is a symmetric key and is used for the duration of the session to encrypt all subsequent data transmissions.

The server configuration may also require the client to present its own authentication. We shall see later how the `clientAuth` Tomcat attribute is used to specify this. In this situation, another step is introduced in the SSL Handshake. Such a requirement is not common, and is used only in some business-to-business application environments.

The HTTPS (HTTP over SSL) protocol, as the name suggests, uses SSL as a layer under HTTP. Transport Layer Security (TLS) is the IETF (Internet Engineering Task Force) version of SSL protocol. It is defined by RFC 2246 (http://www.ietf.org/rfc/rfc2246.txt), and is intended to eventually supersede SSL.

Adding support for SSL or TLS in Tomcat is a four-step process:

- First, we download and install an SSL/TLS implementation (for example, PureTLS, JSSE)
- We then create the certificate **keystore** containing a self-signed certificate. This certificate is called a self-signed certificate because we generate it for ourselves, and it is not guaranteed by anyone else, such as a CA.

  We can then obtain a certificate from a CA like VeriSign (http://www.verisign.com/), Thawte (http://www.thawte.com/), or Trustcenter.de (http://www.trustcenter.de/). We use the self-signed certificate created above to generate a certificate-signing request and submit it to the CA to get a certificate digitally signed by them. This certificate, when presented to a user, guarantees them (the CA) that we are whom we claim to be.

  If we are using Tomcat in a test/development environment, we can skip this step. We would need a certificate for a production deployment though, as users might not be willing to accept our self-signed certificate.
- Finally, we make the Tomcat configuration changes for SSL. These are Tomcat version-specific and covered later in the chapter.

JSSE

Java Secure Socket Implementation (JSSE) is Sun's implementation of the SSL and TLS protocols. JSSE is available for free, but is not open source. For more information on JSSE, please see http://java.sun.com/products/jsse/.

Installing JSSE

We have to install JSSE if we are using JDK 1.2 or 1.3. JDK 1.4 has JSSE bundled along with it, so you should skip the step below if you have JDK 1.4 installed.

Download JSSE from http://java.sun.com/products/jsse/. The three JSSE JAR files (`jsse.jar`, `jnet.jar`, and `jcert.jar`) need to be in Tomcat's classpath. This can be done by copying them to the `$JAVA_HOME/jre/lib/ext` directory as shown below:

```
$ cd $JSSE_HOME/lib
$ cp *.jar $JAVA_HOME/jre/lib/ext
```

We could alternatively add them to the classpath in Tomcat's startup script. In Tomcat 3.x, we need to edit the `tomcat.bat` (`tomcat.sh` on Unix) file. The corresponding file for Tomcat 4.x is `catalina.bat` (`catalina.sh` on Unix).

On Unix/Linux:

```
$CLASSPATH=$CLASSPATH:$JSSE_HOME/lib/jsse.jar:$JSSE_HOME/lib/jnet.jar:$JSSE_HOME/l
ib/jcert.jar
```

On Windows:

```
$CLASSPATH=%CLASSPATH%;%JSSE_HOME%/lib/jsse.jar;%JSSE_HOME%/lib/jnet.jar;%JSSE_HOM
E%/lib/jcert.jar
```

Prepare the Certificate Keystore

The steps for preparing a certificate keystore are listed below.

On UNIX/Linux:

```
$ $JAVA_HOME/bin/keytool -genkey -alias tomcat -keyalg RSA
```

And on Windows:

```
> %JAVA_HOME%\bin\keytool -genkey -alias tomcat -keyalg RSA
```

The `-genkey` option specifies that a key pair (private key, public key) needs to be created. This key pair is enclosed in a self-signed certificate. The `-keyalg` option specifies the algorithm (which in this case is RSA) to be used for the key pair. All keystore entries are accessed via unique aliases using the `-alias` option – here the alias is specified as `tomcat`.

The `keytool` command will ask for a password. We can either enter the default password (`changeit`) or specify any other password. If the password is something other than the default, we will have to configure the `keystorePass` attribute in Tomcat's configuration – we shall see this a bit later.

The default name for the keystore file is `.keystore` and it is stored in the Tomcat user's home directory. This directory will vary depending on the operating system. For example, if you install Tomcat as userid `web` on Linux, the `keystore file` would need to be in `/home/web` (the home directory of the user web). Similarly, if you install it as userid `web` on Windows NT, the `keystore` file would be in `C:\WINNT\Profiles\web`. We could have also specified an alternative keystore filename and password using the `-keystore` and `-keypass` options:

```
$ $JAVA_HOME/bin/keytool -genkey -alias tomcat -keyalg RSA -keypass somepass -
keystore /path/to/keystorefile
```

The screenshot below shows the keytool command being run:

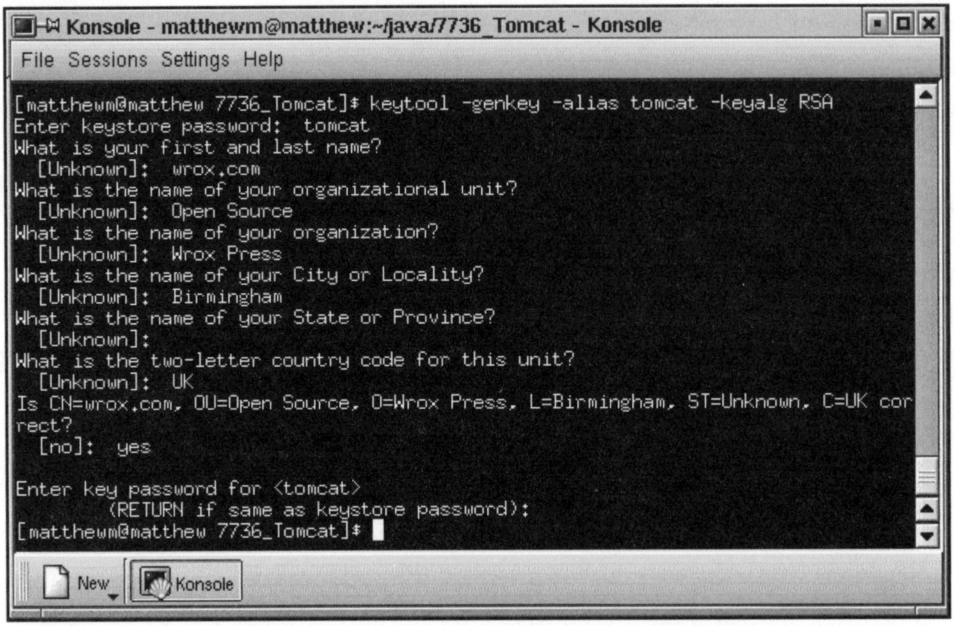

```
Konsole - matthewm@matthew:~/java/7736_Tomcat - Konsole
File Sessions Settings Help
[matthewm@matthew 7736_Tomcat]$ keytool -genkey -alias tomcat -keyalg RSA
Enter keystore password:  tomcat
What is your first and last name?
  [Unknown]:  wrox.com
What is the name of your organizational unit?
  [Unknown]:  Open Source
What is the name of your organization?
  [Unknown]:  Wrox Press
What is the name of your City or Locality?
  [Unknown]:  Birmingham
What is the name of your State or Province?
  [Unknown]:
What is the two-letter country code for this unit?
  [Unknown]:  UK
Is CN=wrox.com, OU=Open Source, O=Wrox Press, L=Birmingham, ST=Unknown, C=UK cor
rect?
  [no]:  yes

Enter key password for <tomcat>
        (RETURN if same as keystore password):
[matthewm@matthew 7736_Tomcat]$
New Konsole
```

Notice the Common Name (CN) field that we have entered as wrox.com. This needs to be of the format www.domainname.com, hostname.domainname.com or just domainname.com. This name is embedded in the certificate. The CN should be the fully qualified hostname for the machine where Tomcat is deployed. If this is not so, then users will get a warning message in their web browser when they try to access a secure page from our web site.

If this is a test/development environment, or we do not want a certificate from a CA, we can stop here as far as the SSL setup is concerned. We are now ready to make Tomcat-related setup changes.

If we were deploying in a production environment, we would need to get a certificate that is validated by a CA. The steps for these are covered in the next section.

Installing a Certificate from a Certificate Authority

The steps involved in obtaining a certificate from a CA are as below.

Create a Certificate Signing Request (CSR)

We first create a local certificate as before using the keytool command:

```
$ keytool -genkey -alias tomcat -keyalg RSA -keystore <your_keystore_filename>
```

Next, we use this certificate to create a CSR:

```
$ keytool -certreq -keyalg RSA -alias tomcat -file certreq.csr -keystore
<your_keystore_filename>
```

The keytool option (-certreq) creates a CSR file called certreq.csr that can be submitted to the CA to get a certificate. Getting a certificate would require payment to the CA for the authentication services. Some CAs have test certificates available for download at no cost. These usually have limited time validity.

If the keystore file is the default (that is, a file named .keystore in the home directory), then the -keystore <your_keystore_filename> option can be skipped, as is shown in the screenshot below:

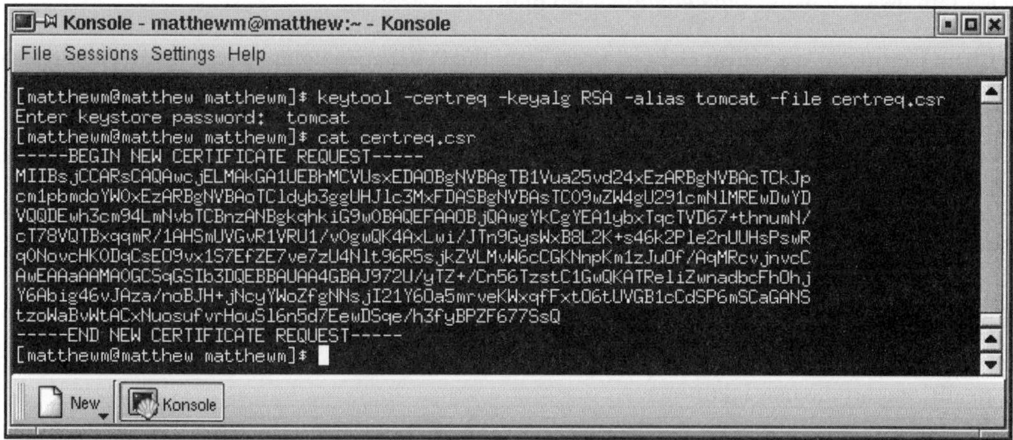

The screenshot below shows the process for getting a certificate from a CA (in this VeriSign):

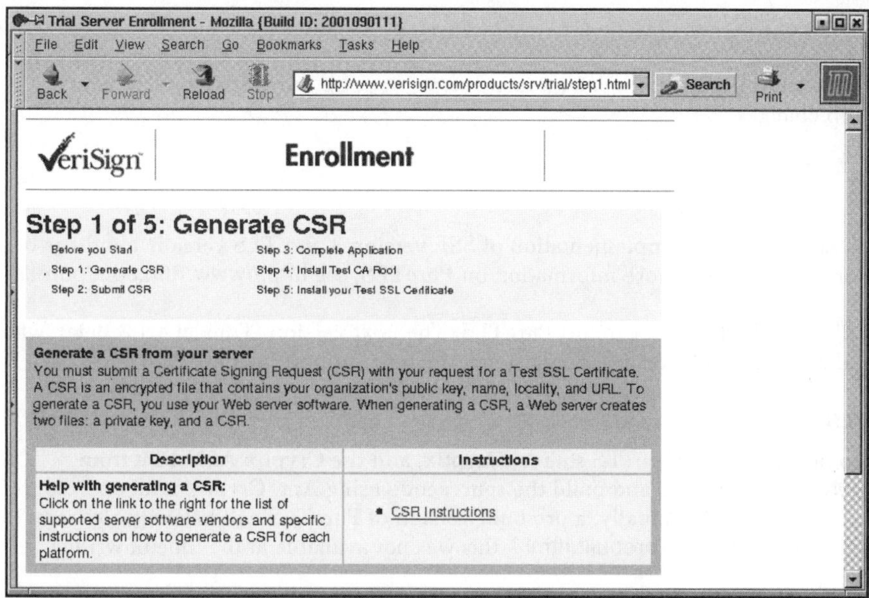

The contents of the CSR that we generated above (certreq.csr) should be copied into the web form in step two of the above page. Clicking on the Continue button does this.

Import the Certificate

After we have the certificate from the CA, we need to get the Chain Certificate (also called the Root Certificate) from them. This can be downloaded from the following sites (depending on the CA):

- http://www.verisign.com/support/install/intermediate.html
- http://www.trustcenter.de/set_en.htm
- http://www.thawte.com/certs/trustmap.html

The Chain Certificate is a self-signed certificate from the CA that contains its well-known public key. We can view the contents of a certificate using the `-printcert` option:

```
$ keytool -printcert -file /path/to/certificate
```

This is good practice before importing a third-party certificate into the keystore. We then import the Chain Certificate into the keystore:

```
$ keytool -import -alias root -keystore <your_keystore_filename> -trustcacerts -
file <filename_of_the_chain_certificate>
```

And finally, import the new certificate:

```
$ keytool -import -alias tomcat -keystore <your_keystore_filename> -trustcacerts -
file <your_certificate_filename>
```

Here, the `<filename_of_the_chain_certificate>` contains the Chain Certificate that we got from the CA. As we mentioned earlier, the `-keystore <your_keystore_filename>` option is not required if the keystore file has a default name (`.keystore`). We are now ready to make Tomcat-related setup changes.

PureTLS

PureTLS is an open source implementation of SSL version 3 and TLS version 1 and has been developed by Claymore Systems. For more information on PureTLS, see http://www.rtfm.com/puretls/.

Tomcat 4.x currently does not support PureTLS. The next version (Tomcat 4.1.8 Beta), which was not yet released at the time of writing, is expected to include support for PureTLS.

Install PureTLS

We need to download the PureTLS source, Cryptix, and the Cryptix ASN.1 kit from http://www.rtfm.com/puretls/ and build the sourcecode using Ant. Cryptix is an open source library for cryptographic routines. Eventually, a pre-built version of PureTLS will be available from http://www.rtfm.com/puretls/prebuilt.html – this was not available at the time of writing.

The PureTLS and Cryptix JAR files need to be in Tomcat's classpath. We could do this by making them available at an installed extension by copying them to the `$JAVA_HOME/jre/ext/lib` directory:

```
$ cp cryptix32.jar puretls.jar cryptix-asn1.jar $JAVA_HOME/jre/lib/ext
```

Alternatively, we could edit `tomcat.sh` and add the TLS JAR files to the classpath. A similar change needs to be made for the `tomcat.bat` script in Windows:

```
CLASSPATH=${TOMCAT_INSTALL}/lib/tomcat.jar:/path/to/cryptix32.jar:
/path/to/puretls.jar:/path/to/cryptix-asn1.jar
```

Prepare the Certificate Keystore

PureTLS uses OpenSSL-style keyfiles. To generate these key files, we would need to download and install the OpenSSL tool (http://www.openssl.org/). This tool is installed by default on Linux systems. On other platforms, we would need to build it from source. Installing OpenSSL on Windows requires Perl.

Using this tool, we can generate a new certificate request and key:

```
$ openssl req -new -out REQ.pem -keyout KEY.pem
```

We can then generate a self-signed X509 certificate from a certificate request using a supplied key:

```
$ openssl req -x509 -in REQ.pem -key KEY.pem -out CERT.pem
```

X509 is the Public Key Infrastructure protocol, and it specifies a format for certificates.

Finally, we import the certificate into the keystore using the Java `keytool` command:

```
$ keytool -import -alias tomcat -keystore server.pem -trustcacerts -file CERT.pem
```

The keystore file (default name `server.pem`) needs to be available in the Tomcat user's home directory.

Obtain and Install a Certificate from a Certificate Authority

We may want to have the server certificate signed by a CA. This is an optional step and may be required only for web applications in production environments. To do this, we need to submit the Certificate Signing Request to a CA, such as VeriSign, Thawte, or Trustcenter.de as explained above.

The OpenSSL command listed below prints the contents of the certificate request. We can then go to the web site of one of the CA companies, and fill in a web form:

```
$ openssl req -text -in REQ.pem
```

After purchasing the certificate, we get back a valid certificate that we can import into our keystore as before using the `keytool -import` command. As we mentioned earlier, we can also get a test certificate from some CAs at no cost.

We also have to get the Root Certificate (also called the Chain Certificate) from the CA. This can be downloaded from the sites listed earlier.

Protecting Resources with SSL

We can protect resources with SSL just as we can protect resources with authentication constraints. The `<user-data-constraint>` sub-element of `<security-constraint>` in `web.xml` is used to specify the guaranteed integrity of the data flowing between the client and the server for this resource. There are three levels of integrity: `NONE`, `INTEGRAL`, and `CONFIDENTIAL`.

`NONE` means there is no guarantee that the data has not been intercepted and tampered with, while `INTEGRAL` guarantees the integrity of the data, meaning that the data has not been interfered with. The strongest guarantee is `CONFIDENTIAL`, which guarantees that a thirdparty has not intercepted the data. If we specify `INTEGRAL` or `CONFIDENTIAL`, the server will use SSL for all requests to this resource by redirecting the client to the SSL port of the server. The redirection port is configured in the `redirectPort` attribute of the HTTP connector.

For our secure resource, we want to be sure that all the data we transfer is safe, so we will use the `CONFIDENTIAL` level. Simply add the following element to the `<security-constraint>` in our example `web.xml` file:

```
<security-constraint>
  ...
  <user-data-constraint>
    <description>
     Constrain the user data transport for the whole application
    </description>
    <transport-guarantee>CONFIDENTIAL</transport-guarantee>
  </user-data-constraint>
</security-constraint>
```

This will force all requests for our `secure` web application to use HTTPS, even if the original came in over HTTP. This is the only setup required in `web.xml`, so now we'll look at `server.xml`.

Tomcat 4.x Setup

The setup procedure for Tomcat 4.x is very straightforward. The default `server.xml` file comes with a handy HTTP connector set up for SSL already, so we will simply modify it (note that this is the setting for Tomcat 4.1, but the only difference in Tomcat 4.0 will be the `className` attribute):

```
<!--
<Connector className="org.apache.coyote.tomcat4.CoyoteConnector"
           port="8443" minProcessors="5" maxProcessors="75"
           enableLookups="true"
           acceptCount="10" debug="0" scheme="https" secure="true"
           useURIValidationHack="false">
  <Factory className="org.apache.coyote.tomcat4.CoyoteServerSocketFactory"
           clientAuth="false" protocol="TLS" />
</Connector>
-->
```

The SSL-related settings are within the `<Factory>` element. We'll add the password we specified above, as well as the location of the keystore file:

```
<Factory className="org.apache.coyote.tomcat4.CoyoteServerSocketFactory"
         clientAuth="false" protocol="TLS"
         keystoreFile="/home/tomcat/.keystore"
         keystorePass="tomcat" />
```

Now start Tomcat and point a browser to https://localhost:8443/secure/ and you will be presented with a warning about our suspicious certificate (note that this warning may vary depending on your browser):

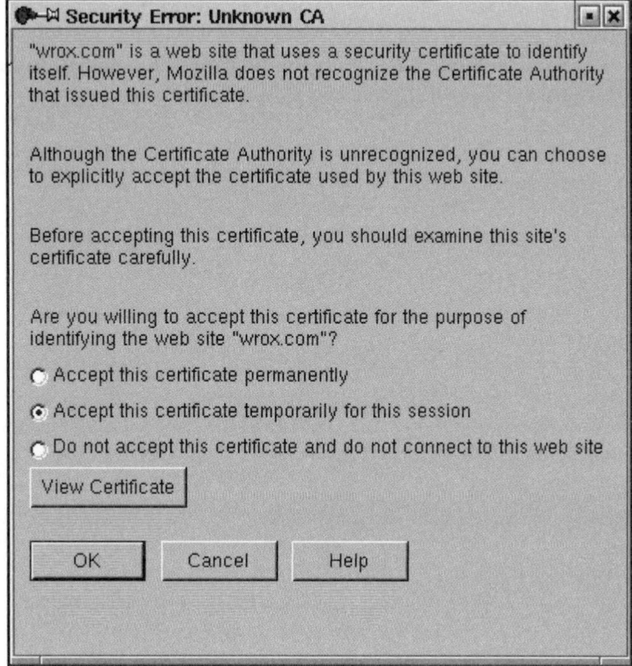

You can choose to view the certificate to see the details of the issuer. These details will match those we specified earlier. Before you proceed your browser will give you the option to install this certificate forever (you will have to view the certificate with Internet Explorer to do this), which means that you trust this site and won't be shown the security warning again.

Once you have confirmed you are happy with accepting this certificate, the default Tomcat page will be shown as normal, only this time our session will be conducted over SSL.

SSL with Apache

We've seen how the standalone HTTP connector handles SSL. Another approach that is more widely used is to have the web server handle the SSL-related functionality. This is a more stable configuration, and advised for performance reasons. In this configuration, the communication between the user's browser and web server is encrypted over SSL, but the communication between the web server and Tomcat is not. The next section illustrates using Apache with SSL support and Tomcat.

Deploying a Web Application

Let us now examine how to deploy a web application by integrating Apache and Tomcat. Our web site consists of one instance of Tomcat that serves up content for general Internet users (the company brochures, other general web content, and so on) as well as privileged content (for example, timesheet forms) meant for employees of the company. The latter is protected by SSL to ensure that the data communicated is secure.

Configuring Apache

We begin by configuring Apache. Since we are responding to user requests on port 80 (the default port) as well as the SSL port (default value 443), we need to listen on both these ports:

```
# Listen on port 80 and 443 (the SSL port)
Listen 80
Listen 443
```

Next, we add a `LoadModule` directive in the `LoadModule` section of the `httpd.conf` configuration file:

```
# Load the webapp module
LoadModule webapp_module modules/mod_webapp.so
```

If we are using Apache 1.3, the `modules` directory would be called `libexec` instead, and we would have to add an `AddModule` directive too:

```
# Load the webapp module. Apache 1.3 only
LoadModule webapp_module libexec/mod_webapp.so
AddModule mod_webapp.c
```

We then add a `ServerName` directive before any other `webapp` directives. This is required for a known `webapp` bug as discussed in Chapter 12. You could try skipping this and see if the problem has been fixed in the latest `webapp` version:

```
# Set the server name before all webapp directives -
# this is required for webapp bug workaround
ServerName myhost.mydomain.com:80
```

Next, we specify the connections for the WARP connector:

```
WebAppConnection ssl_conn     warp localhost:8009
WebAppConnection non_ssl_conn warp localhost:8008
```

The port numbers specified here (8008, 8009) will be set as the port number for the `webapp` connector in the Tomcat configuration. We need not have Tomcat run on the same machine as Apache (although it does in this example).

We also could have multiple instances of Tomcat running – one for the SSL content and one for the non-SSL content. We also could have these instances distributed on different hosts for load balancing. The directives opposite show how this could be done:

```
WebAppConnection ssl_conn     warp host1.domain.com:8008
WebAppConnection non_ssl_conn warp host2.domain.com:8008
```

We now have to make the SSL-related settings in Apache. The details of SSL configuration in Apache are not covered here; you will find them in Appendix B:

```
# SSL-related setting - the certificate and private key
# We are using the same certificate for all virtual hosts
SSLCertificateFile /path/to/file.crt
SSLCertificateKeyFile /path/to/file.key
```

Next, we have the two virtual host definitions – one with SSL, and the other without. The (fictitious) IP address of our site is 192.168.1.1:

```
# Virtual host using SSL
<VirtualHost 192.168.1.1:443>
    # Switch on the SSL Engine
    # The Apache 1.3 version of this directive is SSLEnable
     SSLEngine on
     ServerName myhost.mydomain.com
     DocumentRoot /some/path/here

     WebAppDeploy sslservlets ssl_conn /sslservlets
     [...]
</VirtualHost>

# Virtual host not using SSL
<VirtualHost 192.168.1.1:80>
     ServerName myhost.mydomain.com
     DocumentRoot /someother/path/here

     WebAppDeploy servlets non_ssl_conn /servlets
     [...]
</VirtualHost>
```

Configuring Tomcat

After completing the Apache configuration, we need to make changes to Tomcat's `server.xml` file where we define two connectors. The first is the SSL connector with `port` set to 8009 (the same as that specified in the `WebAppConnection` directive in Apache's `httpd.conf`), `scheme` set to `https`, and `secure` set to `true`. There is an `<Engine>` element defined for the connector, with settings for the logger and (virtual) host:

```
<!-- WARP Connector Service for SSL connection-->
<Service name="HTTPS-Connector">
  <!-- the connector for https traffic -->
  <Connector className = "org.apache.catalina.connector.warp.WarpConnector"
             port="8009"
             minProcessors="5"
             maxProcessors="20"
             scheme="https"
             secure="true"
             enableLookups="true"
             appBase="webapps"
             acceptCount="10"
```

```
            debug="0"/>

    <!-- WarpEngine definition required for virtual hosts -->
    <Engine className = "org.apache.catalina.connector.warp.WarpEngine"
            name="HTTPS-Connector"
            debug="0">

      <Logger className = "org.apache.catalina.logger.FileLogger"
              prefix="my_https_log."
              suffix=".txt"
              timestamp="true"/>

      <Realm className = "org.apache.catalina.realm.MemoryRealm" />

      <!-- Define all virtual hosts for this connection -->
      <Host className = "org.apache.catalina.connector.warp.WarpHost"
            name="myhost1.mydomain.com"
            debug="0"
            appBase="webapps/sslservlets"
            unpackWARs="true" >

        <Context path="" docBase="https" debug="0"/>

      </Host>
    </Engine>
  </Service>
```

On similar lines, we have the non-SSL connector with `port` set to 8008 (same as that specified in the `WebAppConnection` directive in Apache's `httpd.conf`), `scheme` set to `http`, and `secure` set to `false`. There is an `<Engine>` element defined for the connector, with settings for the logger and (virtual) host:

```
  <!-- WARP Connector Service for non-SSL connection-->
  <Service name="HTTP-Connector">
    <!-- the connector for non-https traffic -->
    <Connector className = "org.apache.catalina.connector.warp.WarpConnector"
               port="8008"
               minProcessors="2"
               maxProcessors="10"
               scheme="http"
               secure="false"
               enableLookups="true"
               appBase="webapps"
               acceptCount="10"
               debug="0"/>

    <!-- WarpEngine definition required for virtual hosts -->
    <Engine className = "org.apache.catalina.connector.warp.WarpEngine"
            name="HTTP-Connector"
            debug="0">

      <Logger className = "org.apache.catalina.logger.FileLogger"
              prefix="my_http_log."
              suffix=".txt"
              timestamp="true"/>

      <Realm className = "org.apache.catalina.realm.MemoryRealm" />
```

```
    <Host className = "org.apache.catalina.connector.warp.WarpHost"
          name="myhost2.mydomain.com"
          debug="0"
          appBase="webapps/servlets"
          unpackWARs="true" >

      <Context path="" docBase="http" debug="0"/>

    </Host>
  </Engine>
</Service>
```

Testing the Installation

After making these changes, restart Tomcat and Apache. If the configuration was done properly, we should be able to access the secure part of the dynamic web site at https://myhost.mydomain.com/sslservlets/<servletname> and the non-secure part at http://myhost.mydomain.com/servlets/<servletname>.

A common problem in the setup is related to SSL configuration on Apache – Apache might fail to start or not serve up SSL content. If you face this problem, first check the new directives added to httpd.conf:

```
$ cd /path/to/apache/bin
$ ./apachectl configtest
```

Any errors related to directive syntax should be uncovered here. Next, look for Apache error messages logged in $APACHE_HOME/logs/error_logs. We can control logging by the mod_ssl module via the SSLLog and SSLLogLevel Apache directives:

```
SSLLog logs/ssl_errors.log
SSLLogLevel warn
```

The log levels defined for SSL logging are debug, trace, info, warn, error, and none. A debug level of none turns off all logging. The log levels are in order of priority and setting logging to a certain level shows messages of that and above levels. For example, the warn level shows warnings and error messages.

What about errors at the Tomcat end? We had added a <Logger> element for the webapp connector in our server.xml configuration (repeated again below):

```
<Logger className = "org.apache.catalina.logger.FileLogger"
        prefix="my_https_log."
        suffix=".txt"
        timestamp="true"/>
```

The setting above sends all webapp log messages to the $CATALINA_HOME\logs\my_https_log.yyyy-mm-dd.txt file.

Summary

This chapter we have had a look at various security topics with respect to Tomcat. First of all we looked at general Tomcat security: removing or disabling the default web applications and locking up the filesystem. Both of these are procedures are common practice in all server installations and so should fit into your general security policy without too much trouble.

We then moved on to the Tomcat-specific security. First of all we talked about Java's Security Manager and its role in controlling access to system resources. Tomcat can take advantage of this feature to prevent web applications from carrying out potentially dangerous actions. A rogue servlet could easily take down the filesystem if measures are not taken to restrict access.

Next we looked at realms and their role in authentication. Realms use various means to store user passwords, but the default method stores passwords in cleartext in a file on the filesystem. A better option would be to digest the password so that casual readers can't use it and attackers can't decode it. The other option we looked at was storing digested passwords in a database protected by another digested password. This is a more robust secure solution.

Our final topic was securing the data channel between Tomcat and the client using SSL. SSL prevents third parties from listening in on our data transfers between the server and the client. When dealing with sensitive data it is always wise to use SSL. We saw Tomcat's implementation of SSL as well as looking at using Apache as the SSL front-end for Tomcat.

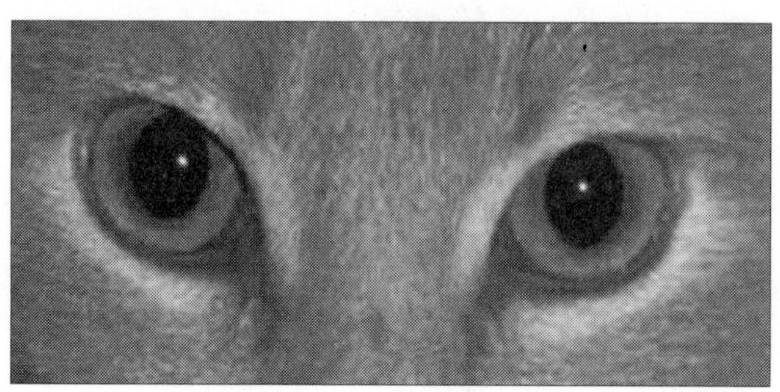

17

Additional Uses for Ant

In Chapter 7, we covered the Tomcat `manager` web application and saw how we could use it to deploy and undeploy web applications without the need to restart Tomcat. We also briefly glanced at the Tomcat Ant tasks, which allowed us to perform the same operations via the Ant script.

Ant is quickly becoming the de facto standard for creating cross-platform build files for Java applications. One important factor that has led to its popularity is the ability for developers to extend Ant via custom tasks. Tomcat too has introduced several Ant tasks from version 4.1.x onwards. These Tomcat-specific Ant tasks provide access to the `manager` application functions via Ant. This means that we can not only build the web application using the Ant build script, but also go a step further by installing, removing, or reloading the application while running Tomcat.

In this chapter, we shall cover the following:

- A quick introduction to Ant
- A sample web application and its associated Ant build script (`build.xml`) that is primarily used to compile the application and get it ready for deployment to a Tomcat instance.
- Discuss how we can e-mail the results of the build process back to the developers.
- Discuss the Tomcat Ant tasks
- Enhance the `build.xml` file to include the Tomcat Ant tasks so that we can install, remove, or reload the application without stopping Tomcat.
- Demonstrate additional Tomcat Ant tasks that a system administrator could use to get information from Tomcat, such as listing all the applications, starting/stopping applications, retrieving information about sessions, security roles, and so on.

Prerequisites

Before we discuss the Ant build scripts and Tomcat Ant tasks, we need to be aware of a few prerequisites for using Ant:

- Make sure you have both Tomcat version 4.x and Ant version 1.5 installed on your machine. For the remainder of the chapter, we will refer to `$ANT_HOME` as the environment variable that points to the root installation directory of Ant. Ant version 1.5 is needed for the *E-Mail Notifications* section of this chapter. This is because version 1.5 uses the new `MailLogger` class. However, you could use Ant version 1.4 for the other features covered in this chapter.
- Add `$ANT_HOME/bin` to the system `PATH` environment variable.
- The Tomcat Ant tasks are packaged in `catalina-ant.jar`, which is present in `$CATALINA_HOME/server/lib` directory. Copy the `catalina-ant.jar` file to the `$ANT_HOME/lib` directory.
- Add a user with the `manager` role in Tomcat's user database if such a user does not exist (refer to Chapter 7 for information on this).

Introduction To Ant

Ant is a platform-independent build tool written in Java. It uses an XML configuration file to perform **tasks**. This file contains the list of tasks that we want to perform. The general structure of an Ant build file is shown below:

```
Project
 |
 |_ Property (1..n)
 |
 |_ Target(1..n)
          |
          |_ Property (1..n)
          |
          |_ Path (1..n)
          |
          |_ Task (1..n)
 |
 |_ Path (1..n)
 |
 |_ Task Definition (1..n)
```

A Project consists of a number of properties, targets, paths, and task definitions. Properties at the project level are name-value pairs that are available throughout the project and to each target.

A Target consists of a series of tasks. A Target can define its own set of Properties, which could override the global project properties. A Target can depend on other targets, which means that all targets that it depends upon will execute first before running the tasks associated with it. Ant comes with several built-in tasks that we can call. Some of the built-in tasks include creating directories, copying files, compile Java source files, and so on.

The built-in tasks would have severely limited the applicability of Ant to diverse project requirements. As a result, Ant also allows us to create our own user-defined tasks. These are known as **optional tasks** and we can reference them via the task definition element for the root project element as shown above. Once we have referenced a task definition element, we can use it like any other ordinary task in our target. The Tomcat Ant tasks, which we will see later on in the chapter, are optional tasks.

We can also define path elements at both the Project level and Target level. A path is used to include/exclude certain files/directories. For example, we can construct a path element to contain the directories / JAR files that comprise the classpath.

Let us take a look at a simple Ant file (`mybuild.xml`). This build file creates a directory and then copies a file to that directory.

We begin by specifying a `<project>` element:

```
<project name="MyAntProject" basedir="." default="copyfile">
```

The `<project>` element has an attribute `name` having a value of `MyAntProject`. The `basedir` attribute indicates the root directory, which will be used as a reference for all the tasks present in this project. The `default` attribute indicates the target that will be executed by default if none is specified while running Ant.

Next, we define the properties for the project:

```
<property name="dir.name" value="${basedir}\mydir"/>
<property name="file.name" value="file1.txt"/>
```

Here, we have defined two global properties: `dir.name` and `file.name`. The `dir.name` property specifies the name of the directory that we wish to create, and `file.name` is the file that we wish to copy.

We now specify the tasks that we wish to perform. This includes creating a directory (`mydir`) and copying the file (`file1.txt`) into the newly created directory:

```
  <target name="makedirectory" description="Create directory mydir">
    <mkdir dir="${dir.name}"/>
  </target>

  <target name="copyfile" depends="makedirectory" description="Copy files">
    <copy file="${file.name}" todir="${dir.name}"/>
  </target>

</project>
```

In the two targets above, `makedirectory` and `copyfile`, note that the task `copyfile` is made dependent on the task `makedirectory`. So even if we specify the `copyfile` target, Ant will make sure that all the dependencies are run first, and `makedirectory` will be executed irrespective of the situation.

The target `makediretory` creates the directory. Note how we are referencing the directory name via the `${dir.name}` property. We used the built-in tasks `<mkdir>` and `<copy>` to perform the functions of making a directory and copying the file. The syntax of the `ant` command is as overleaf:

```
ant -buildfile <filename> <target-name>
```

If the -buildfile option is not used, Ant will look for the build.xml file in the directory from which we issued the ant command. If we do not specify the target name, Ant will look for the default target to execute as specified by the default attribute of the root project element.

To run our example, all we have to do is the following:

```
$ant -buildfile mybuild.xml

Buildfile: mybuild.xml

makedirectory:
    [mkdir] Created dir: /usr/chapter17/mydir

copyfile:
     [copy] Copying 1 file to /usr/chapter17/mydir

BUILD SUCCESSFUL
Total time: 1 second
```

After completing successfully, file1.txt has been copied to the mydir directory. Now that we are familiar with Ant, let us move on understanding the Ant build file that we will use to compile and prepare our web application for deployment.

Ant Build Process

In this section, we'll discuss a sample web application along with the Ant build file to build the application. We build the application by compiling the files and creating the appropriate directory structure (WAR) to get the application ready for deployment.

We will not go in the details of the structure of a web application, since it is primarily the developer's concern. We are more interested in how we can use Ant to deploy our applications. So, we would expect to receive the web application to be deployed in one of these forms:

- **Custom directory structure**
  In this scenario, the development team has its own directory structure and an associated Ant build file that compiles the application and creates an expanded directory structure that confirms to a WAR and/or a .war file (as mentioned below), which can be deployed.
- **WAR file**
  In this scenario, we receive the web application as a pre-compiled and packaged WAR file (.war).
- **Expanded directory structure**
  In this scenario, we receive the web application in a fully expanded directory structure that confirms to a WAR as shown here:

```
<webapplication>
                 /WEB-INF
                          /web.xml
                          /classes/*
                          /lib/*
```

We will now list the Ant build script (`build.xml`) that covers the custom directory structure. This build script has Ant targets that can produce both the expanded directory structure and the WAR file.

The directory structure of a web application that we may receive from the developers is as shown below:

```
usr/
    Chapter17/
        build.xml
        build/
        dist/
        src/
            com/
                wrox/
                    apachetomcat/
                                LoginServlet.java
        web/
            login.jsp
            main.jsp
            error.jsp
            images/
                    wroxlogo.gif
            WEB-INF/
                    web.xml
```

The main build file (`build.xml`) is present in the `<root-directory>/usr/chapter17` directory. Let us describe the directories under the `Chapter 19` directory and their purpose in brief:

Directory Name	Description
`src`	This directory contains the package structure of all the Java source files/classes of the web application.
`web`	This directory contains the HTML and JSP files. Also, it contains any other resource directories, for example, `images`. It also contains the `WEB-INF` directory.
`build`	This directory contains the expanded WAR structure. The `compile` target in the Ant build script (`build.xml`) shown below generates it.
`dist`	This directory contains the WAR file that is generated from the `build` directory shown above. The `dist` target in the Ant build script shown below generates this file.

The `build.xml` file is shown below. Note that we might have to change some of these properties to suit our environment. The `catalina.home` property should point to the root directory of our Tomcat installation. A preferred practice is not to put the global project properties at the top of our Ant build file. Instead, move them to a separate properties file that will contain the name/value property pairs. We can then invoke the Ant build process. The general format of an `ant` command is shown below:

```
ant -buildfile <filename> <target-name> -propertyfile <properfilename>
```

This will execute the default target in the build.xml file and will initialize the properties from the build.properties file. These properties will then be available to all the elements in the build file. Let us quickly go through the Ant build script:

```
<!-- Ant build file for Wrox Intranet Application -->
<project name="WroxIntranet" default="compile" basedir=".">
```

The default target in the build file is the compile target. The section below initializes the global properties that we shall use through all the targets:

```
      <property name="catalina.home"
                               value="/usr/chapter17/jakarta-tomcat4.1.7"/>
      <property name="app.name"     value="wrox"/>
      <property name="app.path"     value="/${app.name}"/>
      <property name="src.home"     value="${basedir}/src"/>
      <property name="web.home"     value="${basedir}/web"/>
      <property name="docs.home"    value="${basedir}/docs"/>
      <property name="build.home"   value="${basedir}/build"/>
      <property name="dist.home"    value="${basedir}/dist"/>
      <property name="war.file"     value="${dist.home}/${app.name}.war"/>
```

The clean target deletes the build and dist directories and all subdirectories within them. This target is useful if we want to build the entire application instead of doing an incremental build.

```
<!-- ====== Clean Target ====== -->
  <target name="clean"
          description="Deletes the build and dist directories">
    <delete dir="${build.home}"/>
    <delete dir="${dist.home}"/>
  </target>
```

The prepare target creates the expanded WAR directory structure and copies the static web files from web and its subdirectories:

```
<!-- ====== Prepare Target ====== -->

  <target name="prepare">
    <mkdir  dir="${build.home}"/>
    <mkdir  dir="${build.home}/images"/>
    <mkdir  dir="${build.home}/WEB-INF"/>
    <mkdir  dir="${build.home}/WEB-INF/classes"/>

    <!-- Copy static content of this web application -->
    <copy todir="${build.home}">
      <fileset dir="${web.home}"/>
    </copy>

  </target>
```

The compile target compiles all the Java source files present in the src directory. The destination directory for the class files is ./build/WEB-INF/classes:

```
<!-- ====== Compilation  ====== -->
    <target name="compile" depends="prepare">

        <javac srcdir="${src.home}" destdir="${build.home}/WEB-INF/classes"
               debug="true" deprecation="true">
        <classpath>
            <fileset dir="${web.home}/WEB-INF/lib">
               <include name="*.jar"/>
            </fileset>

          <pathelement location="${catalina.home}/common/classes"/>
            <fileset dir="${catalina.home}/common/endorsed">
                 <include name="*.jar"/>
            </fileset>

            <fileset dir="${catalina.home}/common/lib">
                 <include name="*.jar"/>
            </fileset>

            <pathelement location="${catalina.home}/shared/classes"/>

            <fileset dir="${catalina.home}/shared/lib">
                 <include name="*.jar"/>
            </fileset>

        </classpath>
        </javac>

        <!-- Copy application resources -->
        <copy  todir="${build.home}/WEB-INF/classes">
             <fileset dir="${src.home}" excludes="**/*.java"/>
        </copy>
    </target>
```

The `dist` target creates a WAR file out of the expanded WAR directory structure present in the `build` directory:

```
<!-- ====== Dist Target ====== -->

    <target name="dist" depends="compile"
          description="Create WroxIntranet WAR file">

       <!-- Create WroxIntranet Application WAR -->
       <mkdir dir="${dist.home}"/>
       <jar jarfile="${war.file}"  basedir="${build.home}"/>
    </target>
```

The `all` target runs all the targets. Ant will run each target once in the order specified in the `depends` attribute as `all` depends on them completing successfully:

```
<!-- ====== All Target ====== -->

    <target name="all" depends="clean, prepare, compile, dist"
          description="Builds the entire application by cleaning the build
                       and dist directories"/>

</project>
```

Let us run the different targets now to make sure that our environment is set up to run Ant correctly. We shall execute the clean and dist targets as shown below:

- clean
  Open the console window and go to usr/chapter17 folder and run the clean target as shown below. Note that if we run the clean target after running the compile or dist targets, we will find the build and dist directories getting cleared in the clean target:

```
$ant clean
Buildfile: build.xml

clean:

BUILD SUCCESSFUL
Total time: 2 seconds
Buildfile: build.xml

clean:
   [delete] Deleting directory /usr/chapter17/wrox/build
   [delete] Deleting directory /usr/chapter17/wrox/dist

BUILD SUCCESSFUL
Total time: 2 seconds
```

- dist
  The dist target is responsible for generating the WAR file. Since the dist target depends on the compile target too, by running it, we can ensure that not only will the files get compiled and copied into an expanded WAR directory structure in build/, but the WAR file also gets generated. We can execute this target as shown below:

```
$ ant dist
Buildfile: build.xml

prepare:
    [mkdir] Created dir: /usr/chapter17/wrox/build
    [mkdir] Created dir: /usr/chapter17/wrox/build/images
    [mkdir] Created dir: /usr/chapter17/wrox/build/WEB-INF
    [mkdir] Created dir: /usr/chapter17/wrox/build/WEB-INF/classes
     [copy] Copying 5 files to /usr/chapter17/wrox/build
     [copy] Copied 1 empty directory to /usr/chapter17/wrox/build

compile:
    [javac] Compiling 1 source file to /usr/chapter17/wrox/build/WEB-
INF/classes
     [copy] Copying 1 file to /usr/chapter17/wrox/build/WEB-INF/classes

dist:
    [mkdir] Created dir: /usr/chapter17/wrox/dist
      [jar] Building jar: /usr/chapter17/wrox/dist/wrox.war

BUILD SUCCESSFUL
Total time: 4 seconds
```

So now we not only have the expanded WAR directory structure in `build` but also the WAR file for the web application in the `dist` directory. At this stage we can deploy this application in two ways:

- Copy the WAR file to `$CATALINA_HOME/webapps` directory.
- Create a context for our web application by making a directory within `$CATALINA_HOME/webapps`, for example, `$CATALINA_HOME/webapps/wrox`, and copy the expanded WAR directory structure of `build` to the `$CATALINA_HOME/webapps/wrox`. This is suitable provided we don't need to configure a data source or anything similar for this application. In that case, we would need an entry in `server.xml` or an application configuration XML file in `%CATALINA_HOME%/webapps`.

However, there is a third way as well: the Tomcat Ant tasks which we shall cover in the later sections. These tasks provide some advantages as we can extend the build file that we wrote for deployment as well. This makes deployment easier as we can automate it via scheduled tasks, providing a central resource to build and deploy our application and making the process less error-prone.

Before covering the Tomcat Ant tasks, let's see how we could use an e-mail to notify build results. Depending on the process in our organization, it might be mandatory to have an e-mail notification irrespective of a build success or failure.

Ant Build Status – E-Mail Notifications

Ant 1.5 provides a built-in class named `MailLogger` that can be used to e-mail results of the build process. The fully qualified name of the `MailLogger` is `org.apache.tools.ant.listener.MailLogger`. We can associate a logger with our build process by invoking Ant as shown below:

```
$ant -logger <loggername>
```

Here `<loggername>` is the fully qualified class name of the logger that we wish to use.

When the build file finishes executing, the `org.apache.tools.ant.listener.MailLogger` sends an e-mail of the build status. We can control the e-mail task via several properties that the `MailLogger` looks for. These properties are given below:

Property Name	Description
`MailLogger.mailhost`	The outgoing SMTP mail server that is used to send the e-mail. For example, `smtp.myisp.com`. This property is mandatory.
`MailLogger.from`	The e-mail address of the account from which the e-mail is sent. This property is mandatory.
`MailLogger.failure.notify`	This Boolean property indicates whether an e-mail notification needs to be sent in case the build fails. This property is optional and it is enabled by default.

Table continued on following page

Property Name	Description
`MailLogger.success.notify`	This Boolean property indicates whether an e-mail notification needs to be sent in case the build succeeds. In case we are interested in sending an e-mail only when there is a failure, we can set this property value to `false`. This property is optional and has a default value of `true`.
`MailLogger.failure.subject`	The subject of the e-mail in case the build fails. This property is optional and its default value is `Build Failure`.
`MailLogger.failure.to`	The e-mail address to which the build results need to be sent in case of a failure. We can send the results to multiple e-mail addresses by separating them by commas. This property is only needed if we need to send an e-mail in case of a failure.
`MailLogger.success.subject`	The subject of the e-mail in case the build succeeds. This property is optional and its default value is `Build Success`.
`MailLogger.success.to`	The e-mail address to which the build results need to be sent in case of success. We can send the results to multiple e-mail addresses by separating them by commas. This property is mandatory only if we need to send an e-mail if the build is successful.

The source for this chapter comes along with a `MailLogger.properties` file that we will use to pass to the Ant build process so that the `MailLogger` is able to get these properties. The `MailLogger.properties` file is shown below:

```
MailLogger.mailhost=<your-smtp-servername>
MailLogger.from=<youraccount@someserver.com>

MailLogger.failure.subject=BUILD FAILURE : Wrox Intranet Application
MailLogger.failure.to=<youraccount@someserver.com>

MailLogger.success.subject=BUILD SUCCESSFUL : Wrox Intranet Application
MailLogger.success.to=<youraccount@someserver.com>
```

Set the `MailLogger.mailhost` property to the appropriate SMTP server and the `from` and `to` e-mail addresses to the appropriate e-mail addresses.

Note that you might not have a local SMTP server running, in which case you will have to use the outgoing SMTP server of your service provider.

Let us now see all this working. What we will do is edit one of the Java source files present in the src directory so that we are certain that it will not compile. We will then run the Ant build.xml file again, this time by specifying the MailLogger as the logger and also provide it the MailLogger.properties file. The build process will obviously fail and the result of this will be e-mailed to the account that we specify in the MailLogger.failure.to property.

The steps to verify this are given below:

- Go to /src/com/wrox/apachetomcat. Open the LoginServlet.java file; you will find the following line:

```
public void destroy() {}
```

  Change this line to:

```
public void des troy() {}
```

  Save the file and close the editor.

- Go to the console window and navigate to usr/local/lib/Ant. You will find the MailLogger.properties file that we discussed. Edit the properties as discussed to match your SMTP server and e-mail address.
- Execute the clean target to clean up all the build and dist directories as discussed earlier:

Now run the Ant build file as shown below:

```
$ ant dist -logger org.apache.tools.ant.listener.MailLogger -propertyfile
MailLogger.properties
Buildfile: build.xml

prepare:

compile:
    [javac] Compiling 1 source file to /usr/chapter17/wrox/build/WEB-INF/classes
    [javac] /usr/chapter17/wrox/src/com/wrox/apachetomcat/LoginServlet.java:12:
'(' expected
    [javac]     public void dest roy() {}
    [javac]                      ^
    [javac] 1 error

BUILD FAILED
file:/usr/chapter17/wrox/build.xml:45: Compile failed; see the compiler error
output for details.
Total time: 4 seconds
```

You can see that there was a problem in the compile operation. At the same time, Ant has also sent us an e-mail. The e-mail that we receive in the account that we specified in the MailLogger.failure.to property is shown overleaf:

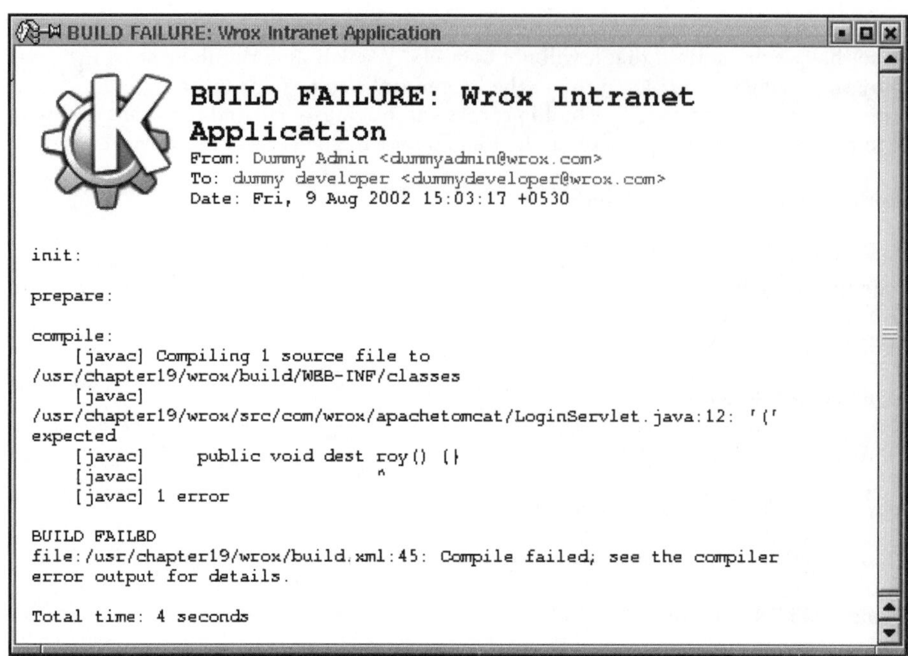

Don't forget to revert the changes you have made in the `LoginServlet.java` file present in `/src/com/wrox/apachetomcat`.

Tomcat Ant Tasks

From Tomcat 4.1 onwards, we have Ant tasks that allow us to invoke the functionality provided by the `manager` web application via an Ant script. As we saw in Chapter 7, the different tasks that we can perform with the `manager` application are:

- `install` and `remove` a web application
- `start`, `stop`, and `reload` a web application
- `deploy` and `undeploy` a web application
- `list` all JNDI resources and security `roles`

Each of these tasks present is available in the `$CATALINA_HOME/server/lib/catalina-ant.jar` file. Note that there are no Ant tasks equivalent to the manager `/sessions` command.

Let us now go into the details for each of the tasks. We will use these tasks in conjunction with the web application that we have already built and got ready for deployment, as discussed in the previous sections.

Tomcat Ant Tasks – Build File Definitions

Since we are going to be dealing with the Tomcat `manager` web application, it is necessary to define 3 additional properties in the `build.xml` file as given below:

```
<!-- ====== Init Target (Property Definitions) ====== -->
  <target name="init">
    <property name="catalina.home"
              value="/usr/chapter17/jakarta-tomcat-4.1.7"/>
    <property name="app.name"      value="wrox"/>
    <property name="app.path"      value="/${app.name}"/>
    <property name="src.home"      value="${basedir}/src"/>
    <property name="web.home"      value="${basedir}/web"/>
    <property name="docs.home"     value="${basedir}/docs"/>
    <property name="build.home"    value="${basedir}/build"/>
    <property name="dist.home"     value="${basedir}/dist"/>
    <property name="war.file"      value="${dist.home}/${app.name}.war"/>
    <property name="managerapp.url" value="http://localhost:8080/manager"/>
    <property name="managerapp.userid"     value="admin"/>
    <property name="managerapp.password"   value="admin"/>
  </target>
```

The `managerapp.url` property specifies the URL at which the `manager` web application is available; make sure to change this value to match your local configuration. The `managerapp.userid` and `managerapp.password` properties represent the userid and password of a user having a `manager` role in the Tomcat `Users` database. You need to change these values to the appropriate userid and password for security and make sure that the role is `manager`.

Next we need to add the custom Ant task definitions via the `<taskdef>` element in Ant as shown below in the `build.xml` file. These tasks reference the appropriate Java classes present in the `catalina-ant.jar` file:

```
<project ... >
<!-- ================= Custom Ant Task Definitions =================== -->
<taskdef name="deploy"   classname="org.apache.catalina.ant.DeployTask"/>
<taskdef name="install"  classname="org.apache.catalina.ant.InstallTask"/>
<taskdef name="list"     classname="org.apache.catalina.ant.ListTask"/>
<taskdef name="reload"   classname="org.apache.catalina.ant.ReloadTask"/>
<taskdef name="remove"   classname="org.apache.catalina.ant.RemoveTask"/>
<taskdef name="undeploy" classname="org.apache.catalina.ant.UndeployTask"/>
<taskdef name="start"    classname="org.apache.catalina.ant.StartTask"/>
<taskdef name="stop"     classname="org.apache.catalina.ant.StopTask"/>
<taskdef name="resources"
                         classname="org.apache.catalina.ant.ResourcesTask"/>
<taskdef name="roles"    classname="org.apache.catalina.ant.RolesTask"/>
....        ....     ....          ....          ....          ....
</project>
```

Note that the `build.xml` *file that you'll find on our site will have all these entries present, so you need not add them.*

We shall now go through each of the Tomcat Ant tasks. Note that we will be covering the tasks from the viewpoint of an Ant project. For further details about what these tasks do and what their limitations are, refer to Chapter 7.

Each of the tasks shown previously has attributes that correspond to the request parameters that are included with the HTTP requests that are sent to the Tomcat manager web application. The commonly used attributes for the Tomcat Ant tasks are shown below:

Task Attribute	Description
url	This is the URL of the manager web application. If not specified, defaults to http://localhost:8080/manager.
username	This is the username in the Tomcat user database, having the manager role.
password	This is the password for the username in the Tomcat user database, having the manager role.
config	This is a URL pointing at the context configuration file (that is a file containing only the <Context> element, and its nested elements, from server.xml for a particular web application). This attribute is supported only on the install target, and is required only if we wish to install an application with non-default configuration characteristics. For example if our application has a data source.
path	This is the context path (prefixed with a leading slash) of a web application that the manager application has to execute commands to. In our build file, the path is wrox and it is represented by the app.path property.
war	A jar:URL that points to a WAR file or a file:URL that points to an unpacked directory containing the web application. For example, if we want to specify the WAR file for our project, this attribute will have the following value: jar:file:/${dist.home}/${app.name}.war!/ and if we want to provide an unpacked directory containing our web application, its value will be: file:/${build.home}.

Install

The install task is used to install and start a web application. We can install the web application from an expanded WAR directory structure (present in build directory in our case) or from a WAR file wrox.war present in dist directory in our case.

The install task does not edit the $CATALINA_HOME/conf/server.xml file. As a result of this, if we restart the Tomcat server, the web application will not be available. If we want to permanently deploy the web application, then we will need to use the deploy task that is covered later on. It makes changes to the $CATALINA_HOME/conf/server.xml, that is, it adds a context entry to it, so that even in the case of a Tomcat server restart, the application is available.

Each application has its own benefits. If we just want to test the application without making any changes to the Tomcat configuration files, then we can use the install task. On the other hand if we have tested our application and everything works fine and we plan to go ahead and permanently deploy the application, then use the deploy task instead.

Expanded WAR Directory Structure

The install target shown below is used to install a web application from an expanded WAR directory structure. As you can see, we have made this target depend on the compile target, so that we compile the application in case any changes were made:

```
<!-- ======== Install Target (Tomcat Ant Task) =========== -->

  <target name="install" depends="compile"
          description="Install application to servlet container">
      <install url="${managerapp.url}"
               username="${managerapp.userid}"
               password="${managerapp.password}"
               path="${app.path}"
               war="file://${build.home}"/>
  </target>
```

> **Before executing any of the Tomcat Ant tasks, make sure that you have an instance of the Tomcat server running.**

To run this target, execute the `ant install` command as shown below:

```
$ant install
Buildfile: build.xml

prepare:

compile:

install:
  [install] OK - Installed application at context path /wrox

BUILD SUCCESSFUL
Total time: 3 seconds
```

This has installed the web application at the context path `wrox`. We can now verify if the application is indeed installed by using a browser and visiting the URL as shown below. The screenshot below shows the simple Wrox Intranet application, where you may log in using the username/password of `wrox/wrox`. Any other username/password combination will result in an error page:

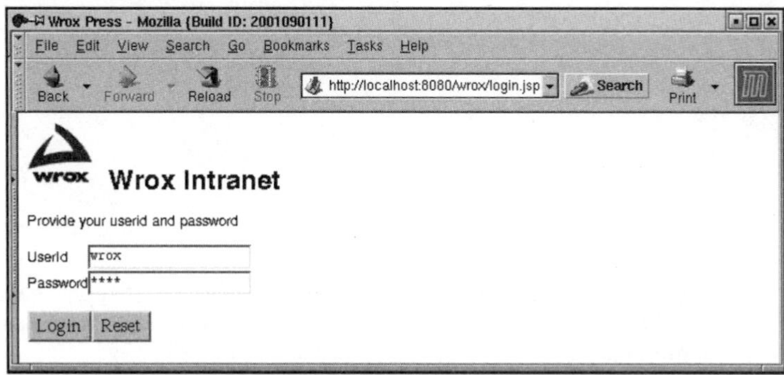

On successful login you will see the `main.jsp` page that provides further links. The application has been kept simple to focus on the Tomcat Ant tasks.

Installing a Web Application from a WAR File

We could have done the same task by installing the web application from a WAR file. As we saw, the `dist` target in the `build.xml` file generates the `wrox.war` file for us in `dist` directory. We could use the `jar:URL` format to point to our WAR file. Please note that the WAR file names end in `!/`. The `jar URL!/` indicates to Ant that the data that it needs to find is to be found at the root of a JAR file:

```
<!-- ======= Install WAR file Target (Tomcat Ant Task) ============= -->

  <target name="installwar" depends="dist"  description="Install WAR to servlet
container">
        <install url="${managerapp.url}"
                 username="${managerapp.userid}"
                 password="${managerapp.password}"
                 path="${app.path}"
                 war="jar:file:/${war.file}!/"/>
  </target>
```

List

The `list` task will list all the currently running web applications. These applications could be loaded at startup time or installed dynamically (we did this via the `install` task in the previous section).

The `list` target is shown below. It does not take any additional attributes apart from the `manager` application details:

```
<!-- ========== List Target (Tomcat Ant Task) =============== -->

  <target name="list"
          depends="init"
         description="List installed applications on servlet container">

<list    url="${managerapp.url}"
             username="${managerapp.userid}"
             password="${managerapp.password}"/>
  </target>
```

The list task is run as shown below:

```
$ant list
Buildfile: build.xml

list:
     [list] OK - Listed applications for virtual host localhost
     [list] /examples:running:0:examples
     [list] /webdav:running:0:/usr/jakarta-tomcat-4.1.7/webapps/webdav
     [list] /tomcat-docs:running:0:/usr/jakarta-tomcat-4.1.7/webapps/tomcat-docs
     [list] /manager:running:0:../server/webapps/manager
```

```
    [list] /admin:running:0:../server/webapps/admin
    [list] /wrox:running:1:/usr/chapter17/wrox/build
    [list] /:running:0:/usr/jakarta-tomcat-4.1.7/webapps/ROOT

BUILD SUCCESSFUL
Total time: 2 seconds
```

As you can see, our new application wrox is also listed in the web applications. Note that the other applications were defined in the server.xml file in $CATALINA_HOME/conf, while our application was installed dynamically.

The list task also provides the following details about each application in the following format:

- **Application context**
  This is the context name of the web application. In our case, it is wrox and you can see other applications like manager and tomcat-docs.
- **Application status**
  This indicates whether the application is running or stopped. If the application is running, users can access the application. If the application is stopped, users cannot access the application. We shall see later how we can use the start and stop commands to start and stop applications dynamically.
- **Active sessions**
  It represents the number of active sessions for an application. As we accessed our application, there is one active session. Note that we invalidate a session in the error.jsp page if a wrong username/password is entered; here the active sessions will be 0, unless you are accessing the application via other browser instances.
- **Application root directory**
  This is the root directory of an application. In our case, /usr/chapter17/build, we had installed it from the expanded WAR directory structure.

Stop

The stop task is used to stop a running application. This application will no longer be accessible by the clients.

The stop target is shown below. In addition to the manager application attributes, we need to provide the path attribute, which basically indicates the context name of the web application that we wish to stop:

```
<!-- ========== Stop Target (TOMCAT Ant Task) ================= -->
  <target name="stop"  depends="init"
                       description="Stop application on servlet container">
    <stop url="${managerapp.url}"
          username="${managerapp.userid}"
          password="${managerapp.password}"
          path="${app.path}"/>
  </target>
```

${app.path} in our build file corresponds to the value of wrox, so what we will do now is stop our running /wrox application.

To run the stop target, give the command as shown below:

```
$ ant stop
Buildfile: build.xml

stop:
     [stop] OK - Stopped application at context path /wrox

BUILD SUCCESSFUL
Total time: 2 seconds
```

Now, we can verify if the application has indeed stopped in one of the following two ways:

By using the browser to access the application you will find that we get an HTTP 404 – Application Not Found error. Another way of making sure, which continues the topic of the chapter, is to use the list target that we already know about.

Let us run the list target as shown below:

```
$ant list
Buildfile: build.xml

list:
     [list] OK - Listed applications for virtual host localhost
     [list] /examples:running:0:examples
     [list] /webdav:running:0:/usr/jakarta-tomcat-4.1.7/webapps/webdav
     [list] /tomcat-docs:running:0:/usr/jakarta-tomcat-4.1.7/webapps/tomcat-docs
     [list] /manager:running:0:../server/webapps/manager
     [list] /admin:running:0:../server/webapps/admin
     [list] /wrox:stopped:0:/usr/chapter17/wrox/build
     [list] /:running:0:/usr/jakarta-tomcat-4.1.7/webapps/ROOT

BUILD SUCCESSFUL
Total time: 2 seconds
```

You will find that the wrox application is shown as stopped.

Start

The start task as the name suggests is used to start a stopped web application. The start target is shown below. The attributes are identical to the ones for the stop target:

```
<!--  ======== Start Target (TOMCAT Ant Task) ========================== -->
  <target name="start"  depends="init"
          description="Start application on servlet container">
    <start url="${managerapp.url}"
           username="${managerapp.userid}"
           password="${managerapp.password}"
           path="${app.path}"/>
  </target>
```

We can start our stopped wrox application by executing the start target as shown below:

```
$ant
Buildfile: build.xml

start:
    [start] OK - Started application at context path /wrox

BUILD SUCCESSFUL
Total time: 3 seconds
```

You can now use the list target or your favorite browser to verify if the application has indeed started.

Reload

The reload task shuts down an application and restarts it. It is especially useful if we make changes to our application and would like Tomcat to reload the application. Changes include any modification to the web files, source files (.java), or even web.xml.

The reload target is shown below. We need to provide the path that is the context that we wish to reload:

```
<!-- ======== Reload Target (Tomcat Ant Task) ================= -->
  <target name="reload" depends="compile"  description="Reload application on
servlet container">
    <reload url="${managerapp.url}"
            username="${managerapp.userid}"
            password="${managerapp.password}"
            path="${app.path}"/>
  </target>
```

We can try out the reload task by changing one of the JSP files and running ant reload.

Remove

The remove task is used to remove or to uninstall an application. The remove task just removes the application context from the Tomcat server's memory. No changes are made to the configuration file $CATALINA_HOME/conf/server.xml. The remove task is therefore used in conjunction with the install task. On the other hand if we used the deploy task, we would need to use the undeploy task (covered later), which makes permanent changes to the $CATALINA_HOME/conf/server.xml by removing the context entries for our web application.

The remove target is shown below. In addition to the manager application attributes, we need to provide the path attribute, which indicates the application that we wish to remove:

```
<!-- ========= Remove Target (TOMCAT Ant Task) ================ -->

  <target name="remove"
          depends="init"
          description="Remove application on servlet container">
```

```
        <remove url="${managerapp.url}"
                username="${managerapp.userid}"
                password="${managerapp.password}"
                path="${app.path}"/>
    </target>
```

To remove the wrox application, run the remove target as shown below:

```
$ant remove
Buildfile: build.xml

remove:
   [remove] OK - Removed application at context path /wrox

BUILD SUCCESSFUL
Total time: 2 seconds
```

We can now use the list target or a browser to verify if the application has indeed been removed.

Deploy

The deploy task works in almost the same way as the install task, but with a few important differences.

As discussed in Chapter 7, the install command to the Tomcat manager web application does a dynamic installation of our web application to a running instance of Tomcat. If you restart Tomcat, the web application that we just installed will not be available, which makes this task less useful for administration.

In terms of Tomcat, no <Context> element was added to the $CATALINA_HOME/conf/server.xml for the application. As a result of this, Tomcat does not load our application at startup and it starts afresh. This behavior of the install task has its benefits too since it allows us to compile, deploy, and test the application without making any permanent changes to the Tomcat configuration files. It also allows us to do all this without stopping or restarting the Tomcat server.

However, if we wish to permanently deploy our web application so that Tomcat knows about it even after a restart, we might want to use the deploy task instead. The deploy task uploads the WAR file to the webapps directory, creates the <Context> entry in $CATALINA_HOME/conf/server.xml, and starts the application making it available for clients. By making the <Context> entry in the server.xml file, it ensures that Tomcat will initialize the application even in the case of a restart. Our WAR file can even contain a META-INF/context.xml file that contains a context configuration file to configure the application.

The deploy target in the build.xml file is shown below. It has the same parameters as the install task except that the war attribute needs to point to the file URL exactly as shown. Do not add !/ at the end of the war file name because we are just providing the JAR filename for the deploy task:

```
<!-- ========== Deploy Target (TOMCAT Ant Task) ================ -->
  <target name="deploy"
          depends="dist"
          description="Deploys application to servlet container">
```

```
        <deploy url="${managerapp.url}"
                username="${managerapp.userid}"
                password="${managerapp.password}"
                path="${app.path}"
                war="file:/${war.file}"/>
    </target>
```

To deploy the same wrox application to the Tomcat instance, make sure that you have removed the application first by using ant remove. Then we can deploy the application by executing the target as shown below:

```
$ant deploy
Buildfile: build.xml

prepare:

compile:

dist:

deploy:
   [deploy] OK - Installed application at context path /wrox


BUILD SUCCESSFUL
```

Once the application is installed, you will find that you can access the application via the browser.

> **Note that the WAR file did not get moved to the webapps directory. The WAR file in fact got copied to the $CATALINA_HOME/work/Standalone/localhost/manager directory and then it was automatically expanded into the $CATALINA_HOME/work/Standalone/localhost/wrox directory.**

We could also use ant list to verify that the application is running. We can test if the application is available even after restarting Tomcat by shutting down Tomcat, restarting it, and executing the ant list task to check if the wrox application is available.

Undeploy

The undeploy task is to the deploy task, what the remove task is to the install task.

Its parameters are the same as the remove task. The difference is in the functionality as the remove task simply made the context (/wrox) available. The undeploy task on the other hand, not only makes the context (/wrox) available for reuse but it also removes any entries from the $CATALINA_HOME/conf/server.xml and the WAR file and its unpacked contents if any under the webapps directory.

The `undeploy` target is shown below:

```
<!-- ======== Undeploy Target (TOMCAT Ant Task) =================== -->
  <target name="undeploy"
          depends="compile"
         description="Undeploy the application from the servlet container">

      <undeploy url="${managerapp.url}"
                username="${managerapp.userid}"
                password="${managerapp.password}"
                path="${app.path}"/>
  </target>
```

We can run the target as shown below:

```
$ant undeploy
Buildfile: build.xml

undeploy:
 [undeploy] OK - Undeployed application at context path /wrox


BUILD SUCCESSFUL
```

Resources

The `resources` task will list all the available JNDI resources. The resources target is shown below:

```
<!-- ======== Resources Target (TOMCAT Ant Task) =============== -->
  <target name="resources"
         depends="init" description="List all the JNDI Resources">
    <resources url="${managerapp.url}"
               username="${managerapp.userid}"
               password="${managerapp.password}"/>
  </target>
```

To run the target, give the command as shown below:

```
$ant resources
Buildfile: build.xml

resources:
[resources] OK - Listed global resources of all types
[resources] UserDatabase:org.apache.catalina.users.MemoryUserDatabase
[resources] simpleValue:java.lang.Integer

BUILD SUCCESSFUL
Total time: 2 seconds
```

We could also list JNDI resources by a specific type. For instance, if we want to list all JDBC data sources, the type will be `javax.sql.DataSource`.

The `resourcesbytype` target is shown below. We can accordingly provide different types if we want to:

```
<target name="resourcesbytype"  depends="init" description="List all the JNDI
Resources by Type">
    <resources url="${managerapp.url}"
               username="${managerapp.userid}"
               password="${managerapp.password}"
               type="javax.sql.DataSource"/>
  </target>
```

Roles

The `roles` target lists all the security roles that we have current configured for Tomcat. These roles are present in the `$CATALINA_HOME/conf/tomcat-users.xml` file.

```
<!-- ======== Roles Target (TOMCAT Ant Task) ============== -->
  <target name="roles"  depends="init" description="List all the User Roles">
    <roles url="${managerapp.url}"
           username="${managerapp.userid}"
           password="${managerapp.password}"/>
  </target>
```

To run the target, give the command as shown below:

```
$ant roles
Buildfile: build.xml

roles:
    [roles] OK - Listed security roles
    [roles] manager:
    [roles] role1:
    [roles] tomcat:

BUILD SUCCESSFUL
Total time: 2 seconds
```

Summary

In this chapter, we introduced Ant and discussed the structure of the Ant build script. We then saw how a system administrator could use the `MailLogger` class in Ant 1.5 to notify groups of users by e-mail, in case of build failures.

We also covered the Ant tasks which we can use to give commands to the Tomcat `manager` web application via an Ant script. These tasks help us not only to build our web application via the Ant script, but also to deploy it at the same time to a running Tomcat instance. This gives us an ability to test out our application before making any permanent changes to the Tomcat setup with respect to our application deployment. The Ant tasks for Tomcat thus help us to automate the deployment tasks thereby resulting in a less error-prone process.

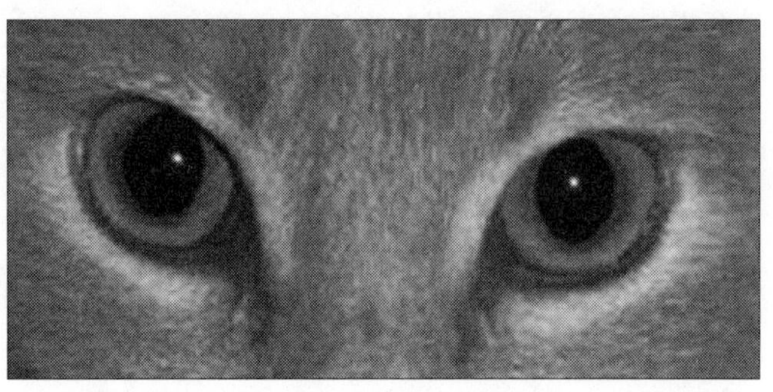

18

Log4J

Logging is an essential part of administrating any web application. It allows us to see what is happening and when it is happening. In this chapter we will look at an open source Java framework for logging: Log4J from the Jakarta Project.

We shall cover the following subjects in this chapter:

- The basics of Log4J
- Logging to a file
- Logging to the console
- Logging to system tools such as `syslog` and the WinNT Event Logger
- Logging to multiple destinations from a single application

Log4J

Log4J (http://jakarta.apache.org/log4j/) is a logging API developed as an alternative to `System.out.println()`. It has grown into a sophisticated suite of tools that allow us to log to anything from a simple text file to the Unix `syslog` or WinNT's Event Logger.

There are three main components in Log4J:

- Loggers
- Appenders
- Layouts

We shall be covering each of these in turn. Note that Loggers replace the deprecated Categories from Log4J 1.2 onwards. Categories will still function until mid-2003, but the Log4J developers strongly advise against their use in new code. As we cover Log4J 1.2.6 in this chapter, we will deal with Loggers.

As a Java framework, Log4J implements each of these components as a Java class and uses inheritance to implement more specific functionality. In fact, Log4J uses a hierarchical model for its internal structures as well. We shall discuss this further at the end of this section.

Loggers

Loggers are the main components in Log4J; they do the hard work of logging. Each Logger is assigned a name by which it is referenced. The form of the name is analogous to the Java package naming conventions and is an important part of the hierarchical model that Log4J follows. For example, here is how we would specify a Logger in a Log4J configuration file (we'll see more on configuration files later):

```
log4j.logger.wrox.simple=DEBUG, simple
```

The `log4j.logger` portion is required to let Log4J know we are configuring a Logger. The next section, `wrox.simple`, is the name of the Logger. The section after the equals sign states the Level of messages that this Logger will log and the name of the Appender to use when logging a message. Both of these concepts will be covered later in this section.

Levels

Log4J uses the notion of Levels to decide whether or not a particular Logger should log an event or not. A Logger is given a logging level and only logs messages with a level less than or equal to this value. The following table describes the levels in ascending order:

Level	Description
`ALL`	The `ALL` level is designed to switch all logging on.
`DEBUG`	`DEBUG` is designed for application development and as such should not be used once an application is deployed. As the name suggests, this level is designed for debugging and should log relatively fine-grained events.
`INFO`	`INFO` is used to track the progress of a running application. Therefore, `INFO` events should be coarse-grained enough to mark major points in an application, such as startup and shutdown.
`WARN`	`WARN`-level events are potentially harmful situations in an application. The application can continue running.
`ERROR`	`ERROR`-level events are serious problems in an application but they may still allow it to continue functioning in some limited capacity.
`FATAL`	`FATAL`-level events will undoubtedly lead to an application crash and should be reserved for the most serious of circumstances.
`OFF`	The `OFF` level is designed to switch all logging off.

Appenders

Appenders are used to write log messages to various output destinations. These range from simple text files to system-level applications such as `syslog` and WinNT's Event Logger. An Appender is assigned to a Logger to allow the Logger to log messages.

It is the Appender that formats the logging messages and routes them to the appropriate destination. Appenders are generally given a target and have a Layout assigned to them to allow them to function. We shall describe Layouts next.

Here is an example of an Appender that writes logging messages from our `wrox.simple` Logger to a file called `log4jsimple.log`. This file can be specified with an absolute or relative path. This example will log to a file in the directory from which the code is called:

```
log4j.appender.simple=org.apache.log4j.FileAppender
log4j.appender.simple.File=log4jsimple.log
```

Layouts

Layouts specify the format that the log message will have once it reaches its destination. There are a number of different formats that range from a default simple format, to custom formats, to nicely formatted HTML tables. Layouts are added to Appenders during configuration.

Here is our simple Logger again. This time we'll specify that the format of the log messages is the `SimpleFormat`:

```
log4j.appender.simple.layout=org.apache.log4j.SimpleLayout
```

This is the final step in configuring a Logger. When an event of `WARN` level is triggered (a `NullPointerException` for example), the message will be logged to `log4jsimple.log` in the following format:

```
WARN - Warning: NullPointerException
```

Custom Layouts

Custom Layouts can be configured to display just about anything you like. They accept format modifiers and conversion characters that are similar to those used in C. For example, the following will display the date in ISO8601 format, a logging message, the method that called the logging method, and the platform's newline character:

```
%d %m : %M %n
```

We'll see more examples of this later when we come to the `PatternLayout` later in this chapter.

Configurators

Before a Logger can be used to log messages, it must be configured. There are three ways to do this:

- Programmatically
- With an XML file
- With a Java properties file

We'll see how each of these methods can configure the example Logger we saw above.

Programmatically

A Java program can create a new `Logger` object and set each of its configuration options in much the same way as any other Java object. Here is a simple Java class that shows a Logger being created and configured to log messages:

```
package wrox;

import org.apache.log4j.Logger;
import org.apache.log4j.Level;
import org.apache.log4j.SimpleLayout;
import org.apache.log4j.FileAppender;

import java.io.IOException;

public class Log4JTest {

  public static void main(String[] args) {
```

As we are creating a Logger from scratch, we have to assign its name in the code:

```
    Logger logger = Logger.getLogger("wrox.simple");
```

Once we have created a Logger, we need to set its logging level. In this case we use the `Level.DEBUG` constant to set the level to `DEBUG`:

```
    logger.setLevel(Level.DEBUG);
```

Next we create a `SimpleLayout` as we will be using it when creating the `FileAppender` later:

```
    try {
      SimpleLayout simpleLayout = new SimpleLayout();
```

Now that we have a `SimpleLayout`, we can create a `FileAppender` to assist our Logger. Here we also set the file that the log messages will be sent to. In this case, a file called `log4j.log`:

```
      FileAppender fileAppender =
                             new FileAppender(simpleLayout, "log4j.log");
```

The final configuration step is to attach the `FileAppender` to our Logger:

```
      logger.addAppender(fileAppender);
```

Now we can send some logging messages to the file used by our `FileAppender`. Each of the methods below sends a message of the appropriate level:

```
        logger.debug("A debug message");
        logger.info("An info message");
        logger.warn("A warn message");
        logger.error("An error message");
        logger.fatal("A fatal message");
```

The following `catch` block shows a nice piece of Log4J's functionality. Each of the logging methods also has an overloaded version that accepts a `Throwable` object whose stack trace will appear in the log file along with the message:

```
      } catch (IOException ex) {
        logger.warn("An IOException was thrown", ex);
      }
    }
  }
```

An XML File

Log4J can use an XML file for Logger configuration. Here is the XML file that is equivalent to our programmatic configuration above.

First we have the XML declaration and the DTD declaration. This ensures that the XML configuration file conforms to the syntax understood by Log4J:

```
<?xml version="1.0" encoding="UTF-8" ?>
<!DOCTYPE log4j:configuration SYSTEM "log4j.dtd">
```

The opening element is `<log4j:configuration>`, which is then followed by our Appender declaration. Inside this, we set the `File` parameter and add a Layout:

```
<log4j:configuration>
  <appender name="simple" class="org.apache.log4j.FileAppender">
    <param name="File" value="log4j.log"/>
    <layout class="org.apache.log4j.SimpleLayout"/>
  </appender>
```

Finally we declare our Logger. We set its level with the `<level>` element's `value` attribute and attach the Appender with the `<appender-ref>` element. Note that the `ref` attribute corresponds with the `name` attribute of the `<appender>` element above:

```
  <logger name="wrox.simple" >
    <level value="debug"/>
    <appender-ref ref="simple" />
  </logger>
</log4j:configuration>
```

The only steps left are to load the configuration into the application. Our vastly simplified `main()` method is as follows:

```
public static void main(String[] args) {
  DOMConfigurator.configure("log4j.xml");

  Logger logger = Logger.getLogger("wrox.simple");

  logger.debug("A debug message");
  logger.info("An info message");
  logger.warn("A warn message");
  logger.error("An error message");
  logger.fatal("A fatal message");
}
```

As you can see, this method of configuration is a lot cleaner and keeps the details out of the code. The `configure()` method takes a filename, URL, or XML configuration element.

A Java Properties File

The third and final way to configure a Logger is with a Java properties file. The mechanics of this method are very similar to those of the XML method. Our early examples in this chapter were from a properties file, and the main examples later in the chapter will also follow this format. However, we'll quickly go over the full properties file for our simple example:

```
# A simple logger
log4j.logger.wrox.simple=DEBUG, simple

# This simple example will log to a file
log4j.appender.simple=org.apache.log4j.FileAppender
log4j.appender.simple.File=log4jsimple.log

# We will use a simple layout for this example
log4j.appender.simple.layout=org.apache.log4j.SimpleLayout
```

The lines marked with # are comments and will be ignored by Log4J.

To configure a Logger with this properties file, we would use the following line of code:

```
PropertyConfigurator.configure("log4j.properties");
```

The rest of the operation would continue as in our two other examples.

Hierarchies

As mentioned earlier, Log4J follows a hierarchical model. Log4J hierarchies are similar in concept to Java packages. For example, our `wrox.simple` Logger would be the parent of a Logger called `wrox.simple.child`. As such, any properties set on `wrox.simple` will be inherited by `wrox.simple.child`. This means that if a Logger has not had its Level or Appender set explicitly, it will take these values from its parent.

Let's extend our simple example:

```
# A simple logger
log4j.logger.wrox.simple=DEBUG, simple

# A child for wrox.simple
log4j.logger.wrox.simple.child

# This simple example will log to a file
log4j.appender.simple=org.apache.log4j.FileAppender
log4j.appender.simple.File=log4jsimple.log

# We will use a simple layout for this example
log4j.appender.simple.layout=org.apache.log4j.SimpleLayout
```

Here `wrox.simple.child` will have a Level of `DEBUG` and use the same FileAppender as its parent.

Log4J in a Web Application

Now that we have the basics of Log4J we shall move on to using it in a Java web application. The developer of the application would usually add the logging statements before it is handed to the administrator. However, it is useful to know the syntax and usage of the different options available. We'll start off by using the simple example again, but this time we'll use it from a JSP page in a web application called `logging`. First though, we need to configure the Logger.

Configuring a Logger in a Web Application

As we saw earlier, the easiest way to configure a Logger was to use a configuration file. When using Log4J in a web application it is a good idea to set up a Logger for the entire web application at startup. This can be achieved by using an initialization servlet that loads the configuration file into the web application.

The Initialization Servlet

Here is the initialization servlet:

```
package wrox;

import javax.servlet.ServletException;

import javax.servlet.http.HttpServlet;
import javax.servlet.http.HttpServletRequest;
import javax.servlet.http.HttpServletResponse;

import java.io.PrintWriter;
import java.io.IOException;

import org.apache.log4j.PropertyConfigurator;

public class Log4JInitServlet extends HttpServlet {
```

The application-wide configuration happens in the `init()` method. This method is called as the servlet is first loaded by Tomcat, making the Logger available from startup:

```
    // Initialize the servlet by loading the Log4J properties file
    public void init() throws ServletException {
```

The properties file will be stored in the `$CATALINA_HOME/webapps/logging/WEB-INF/classes` directory of our web application. We need to get the path to the properties file before we can load it, so we get the full path to the web application on the filesystem and then append the name of the file. In this case, the name of the file comes from the `properties` initialization parameter specified in `web.xml`. This allows us to specify the location of the properties file outside of the application's code:

```
      // First we get the fully qualified path to the web application
      String path = getServletContext().getRealPath("/");
      String properties = path + getInitParameter("properties");
```

The final step is to call the `configure()` method to make the Logger available for all the other files in the application:

```
      // Next we set the properties for all the servlets and JSP
      // pages in this web application
      PropertyConfigurator.configure(properties);
      }
```

The final methods are required to be in any servlet:

```
    // The doPost() method forwards all requests to the doGet() method
    public void doPost(HttpServletRequest req, HttpServletResponse resp) throws
  ServletException, IOException {
      doGet(req, resp);
    }

    // The doGet() method informs users of the purpose of this servlet
    public void doGet(HttpServletRequest req, HttpServletResponse resp) throws
  ServletException, IOException {
      PrintWriter out = resp.getWriter();

      out.println("Initialization servlet for Log4J");
    }

    public void destroy() {}
  }
```

Compile this class and place it in `$CATALINA_HOME/webapps/logging/WEB-INF/classes/wrox`.

web.xml

Next we need a `web.xml` file for our web application so that we can specify the location of our properties file:

```
<?xml version="1.0" encoding="ISO-8859-1"?>

<!DOCTYPE web-app
    PUBLIC "-//Sun Microsystems, Inc.//DTD Web Application 2.3//EN"
    "http://java.sun.com/dtd/web-app_2_3.dtd">

<web-app>
  <servlet>
    <servlet-name>log4Jinit</servlet-name>
    <servlet-class>wrox.Log4JInitServlet</servlet-class>
    <init-param>
      <param-name>properties</param-name>
      <param-value>WEB-INF/classes/log4j.properties</param-value>
    </init-param>
    <load-on-startup>1</load-on-startup>
  </servlet>
</web-app>
```

The `<load-on-startup>` element loads the servlet when Tomcat is started. This is exactly what we want as we need the Logger to be available to the web application as soon as Tomcat starts.

Logging To Files

In this section we will start with a simple file example, then show the following formats that are made available to Log4J:

- `HTMLFormat`
- `PatternFormat`

Simple File

The configuration file for this first example is very similar to the one we saw before. However, this time we'll log to the `$CATALINA_HOME/logs` directory:

```
# A simple logger
log4j.logger.wrox.simple=DEBUG, simple

# This simple example will log to a file
log4j.appender.simple=org.apache.log4j.FileAppender
log4j.appender.simple.File=<CATALINA_HOME>/logs/log4jsimple.log

# We will use a simple layout for this example
log4j.appender.simple.layout=org.apache.log4j.SimpleLayout
```

Note that Log4J does not consider `<CATALINA_HOME>` to be a shortcut; it is merely a neat piece of notation for us. Be sure and provide the full path in your files.

Save this file as `log4j.properties` in `logging/WEB-INF/classes`.

Finally, we need a JSP page to use the Logger (`logsimple.jsp`):

```
<%@ page import="org.apache.log4j.Logger" %>
<html>
  <head><title>Logging with Log4J</title></head>

  <%
  Logger logger = Logger.getLogger("wrox.simple");

  logger.debug("A debug message");
  logger.info("An info message");
  logger.warn("A warn message");
  logger.error("An error message");
  logger.fatal("A fatal message");
  %>

  <body>
    <h1>Logging completed</h1>
  </body>
<html>
```

Place this in `$CATALINA_HOME/webapps/logging`. Now, point your browser at http://localhost:8080/logging/logsimple.jsp. You should see the confirmation message. This should have set off the Logger and written the logging messages to `$CATALINA_HOME/logs/log4jsimple.log`.

HTML

Now we will look at a different kind of Layout, the HTMLLayout. This Layout formats the logging information into HTML tables that can be customized to fit most needs. We shall send the logging information to an HTML file in the `logging` web application so that we can view it online. However, it would be possible to put this file under a password-protected context, such as `admin` in Tomcat 4.1.3 onwards.

Here is the configuration file:

```
# An HTML logger
log4j.logger.wrox.html=DEBUG, html

# This simple example will log to an HTML file
log4j.appender.html=org.apache.log4j.FileAppender
log4j.appender.html.File=<CATALINA_HOME>/webapps/logging/log.html

# This line stops additional log sessions being appended to the end
# of the file
log4j.appender.html.Append=false

# We will use an HTML Layout for this example
log4j.appender.html.layout=org.apache.log4j.HTMLLayout

# This line shows where in the servlet/JSP page the logging
# statement is placed
log4j.appender.html.layout.LocationInfo=true

# The Title parameter sets the HTML <title> tag for the HTML page
log4j.appender.html.layout.Title=Wrox Log
```

The JSP page for this example, `loghtml.jsp`, has only one change:

```
<%@ page import="org.apache.log4j.Logger" %>
<html>
  <head><title>Logging with Log4J</title></head>

  <%
  Logger logger = Logger.getLogger("wrox.html");

  logger.debug("A debug message");
  logger.info("An info message");
  logger.warn("A warn message");
  logger.error("An error message");
  logger.fatal("A fatal message");
  %>

  <body>
    <h1>Logging completed</h1>
  </body>
<html>
```

Access this page at http://localhost:8080/logging/loghtml.jsp and then view http://localhost:8080/logging/log.html. You should see something similar to the following:

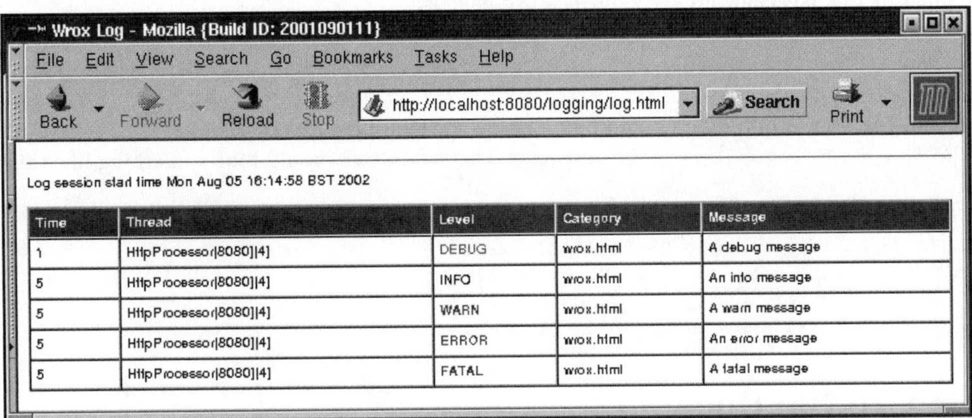

Pattern

The final Layout that we will look at is the `PatternLayout`. This Layout allows us to specify a custom format for the logging messages. The format can be configured in a number of ways with various format modifiers and conversion characters playing their part. We saw one example earlier, but here is the example we will be using in this section:

```
%-5p : %m %d{dd-MM-yy HH:mm:ss}%n
```

We have already seen the `%m` and `%n` conversion characters, as well as a different version of the `%d` character. This time we have specified a custom format for the date between the `{}` markers. The initial `%-5p` section can be further broken down into the `-5` and `%p` blocks. `%p` displays a string representation of the priority (a throwback to earlier versions of Log4J when a Priority did the same job as a Level), that is, '`DEBUG`', '`WARN`', and so on. `-5` is a format modifier that says 'right pad with spaces if the priority is less than 5 characters long'.

A full list of the format modifiers and conversion characters is available in the Log4J documentation: http://jakarta.apache.org/log4j/docs/api/org/apache/log4j/PatternLayout.html.

We specify this pattern for our file as follows:

```
# A pattern logger
log4j.logger.wrox.pattern=DEBUG, pattern

# This simple example will log to a custom format file
log4j.appender.pattern=org.apache.log4j.FileAppender
log4j.appender.pattern.File=<CATALINA_HOME>/logs/log4jpattern.log

# We will use a custom layout for this example
log4j.appender.pattern.layout=org.apache.log4j.PatternLayout
# Here we set our custom pattern
log4j.appender.pattern.layout.ConversionPattern=%-5p : %m %d{dd-MM-yy HH:mm:ss}%n
```

The only line that has changed since our last JSP page is:

```
  Logger logger = Logger.getLogger("wrox.pattern");
```

Point your browser to http://localhost:8080/logger/logpattern.jsp and then view `$CATALINA_HOME/logs/log4jpattern.log`. The log entries should look something like this:

```
DEBUG : A debug message 06-08-02 01:54:21
INFO  : An info message 06-08-02 01:54:21
WARN  : A warn message 06-08-02 01:54:21
ERROR : An error message 06-08-02 01:54:21
FATAL : A fatal message 06-08-02 01:54:21
```

Logging To the Console

Log4J allows us to log to other destinations other than files. In this section we shall send logging messages to the console. This allows an application to instantly notify the administrator of any problems that occur. To log to the console we need to attach a ConsoleAppender to our Logger:

```
# A console Logger
log4j.logger.wrox.console=DEBUG, console

# This simple example will log to the console
log4j.appender.console=org.apache.log4j.ConsoleAppender
# Set the target to Sysytem.out
```

```
log4j.appender.console.Target=System.out

# We will use the simple format for the console example
log4j.appender.console.layout=org.apache.log4j.SimpleLayout
```

The `Target` parameter must be one of `System.out` (the default) or `System.err`. ConsoleAppenders accept the same Layouts as FileAppenders: in this case we are using a `SimpleLayout`.

Again, our JSP page (`logconsole.jsp`) only needs one change:

```
Logger logger = Logger.getLogger("wrox.console");
```

Accessing http://localhost:8080/logging/logconsole.jsp will cause the log messages to be logged to Tomcat's console:

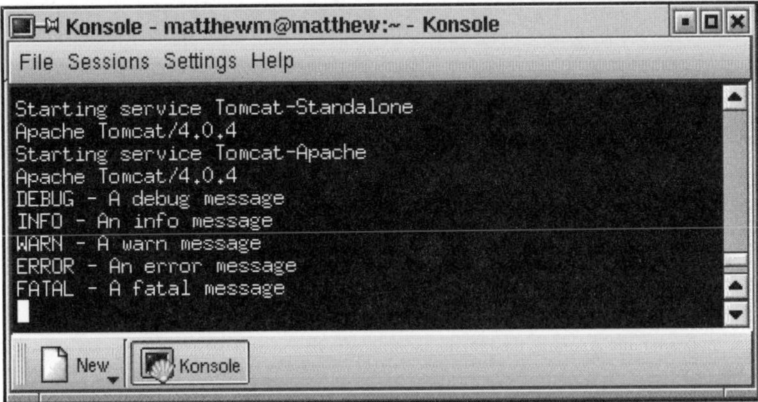

Logging To Multiple Destinations

One of the more useful features of Log4J is the ability to log to several destinations at once. This can allow us to send serious error messages to a location where they will be instantly noticed, for example the console, while other more routine messages can be sent to a regular logging file.

We shall look at the following examples in this section:

- Logging `FATAL` events to the console and all events to a file
- Logging `FATAL` events to the console and all events to Unix's `syslog` system Logger
- Logging `FATAL` events to the console and `FATAL` and `ERROR` level events to WinNT's Event Logger

Console and a File

Our first example will log all `FATAL` level events to the console so that an administrator will be instantly alerted to any serious problems with an application. Also, we still need a record of other events (and a permanent record of `FATAL` events) so we will log all events to a file.

First we assign two Appenders to the `wrox.multifile` Logger: `fatalconsole` and `errorfile`. We also set the default logging level:

```
# A multi-destination logger
# FATAL errors will go to the console
# All errors will go to a file
log4j.logger.wrox.multifile=DEBUG, fatalconsole, errorfile
```

Now we set the `fatalconsole` Appender's type to ConsoleAppender, set the target to `System.out`, and set the logging level to `FATAL`, using the `Threshold` parameter of the Appender:

```
# All fatal messages for this example go to the console
log4j.appender.fatalconsole=org.apache.log4j.ConsoleAppender
log4j.appender.fatalconsole.Target=System.out
log4j.appender.fatalconsole.Threshold=FATAL
```

Next we set up the file where all log messages will be sent. We also set the logging level to `DEBUG`:

```
# All messages go to a file
log4j.appender.errorfile=org.apache.log4j.FileAppender
log4j.appender.errorfile.File=<CATALINA_HOME>/logs/log4jerrors.log
log4j.appender.errorfile.Threshold=DEBUG

# We will use simple layouts for both the console and the file
log4j.appender.fatalconsole.layout=org.apache.log4j.SimpleLayout
log4j.appender.errorfile.layout=org.apache.log4j.SimpleLayout
```

Now all we need to do to set up this example is change the same line of code in our JSP page (`fatalconsole.jsp`):

```
  Logger logger = Logger.getLogger("wrox.multifile");
```

The logging method calls remain the same. Now each time a logging message is logged by the `wrox.multifile` Logger it is compared to the level of each Appender and only sent to its destination if it is less than or equal to this level.

Now if you point a browser at http://localhost:8080/logging/fatalconsole.jsp you should see the following in the Tomcat console:

Now look at `$CATALINA_HOME/logs/log4jerrors.jsp`:

```
DEBUG - A debug message
INFO - An info message
WARN - A warn message
ERROR - An error message
FATAL - A fatal message
```

As you can see, Log4J has only sent `FATAL` level messages to the console, but has sent all messages to the regular logging file.

Console and Syslog

The Unix `syslog` program is an integral part of all Unix systems. It was designed with two important functions in mind: liberating programmers from having to write log files and putting logging in the hands of the administrator.

Log4J provides the SyslogAppender for working with `syslog`. It needs a bit more configuring than the other Appenders we have seen before, but it is still relatively straightforward. In this example, we will again send `FATAL` level events to the console, but this time we will send all events to `syslog` as user-level events:

```
# A multi-destination logger
# FATAL errors will go to the console
# All errors will go to syslog
log4j.logger.wrox.multisyslog=DEBUG, fatalconsolesys, syslog

# All fatal messages for this example go to the console
log4j.appender.fatalconsolesys=org.apache.log4j.ConsoleAppender
log4j.appender.fatalconsolesys.Target=System.out
log4j.appender.fatalconsolesys.Threshold=FATAL
```

Here is the SyslogAppender configuration. After setting the `syslog` Appender type, we set its logging level. We then need to set the `syslog` facility using the SyslogAppender's `Facility` parameter. `syslog` uses facilities alongside a severity index to decide where the logging message should be sent, much like Log4J does with the logging level and Appender name. Many system functions have their own facility, for example `sendmail` has the `mail` facility and the kernel has the `kern` facility. In our example we will use the `user` facility that is designed for user-level processes.

The final piece of configuration for a SyslogAppender is the `SyslogHost` parameter. This should specify the central logging host of your network, or `localhost` if you are logging to the local machine:

```
# All messages go to syslog
log4j.appender.syslog=org.apache.log4j.net.SyslogAppender
log4j.appender.syslog.Threshold=DEBUG
log4j.appender.syslog.Facility=USER
log4j.appender.syslog.SyslogHost=localhost

# We will use simple layouts for both the console and syslog
log4j.appender.fatalconsolesys.layout=org.apache.log4j.SimpleLayout
log4j.appender.syslog.layout=org.apache.log4j.SimpleLayout
```

> **Note that if `syslog` is running on a Linux box over a network, you will have to start it with the `-r` switch to enable network logging. This can be set in the `/etc/init.d/syslog` file. Run `/etc/init.d/syslog restart` to restart `syslog`.**

Again, there is only one change to the JSP file:

```
Logger logger = Logger.getLogger("wrox.multisyslog");
```

Point a browser at http://localhost:8080/logging/fatalsyslog.jsp and then examine the log file where `syslog` sends all user-level log messages. You should see the messages listed in `syslog`'s format, which should look like the following:

```
Aug 5 16:48:40 matthew user: DEBUG - A debug message
```

Console and WinNT Event Logger

Our final example will be logging messages to the console and WinNT's Event Logger. The Event Logger can be found under Start | Settings | Control Panel | Administrative Tools | Event Viewer. This is where WinNT logs its system messages. These messages include serious errors in applications like Internet Explorer, as well as less important messages such as print job completion messages. WinNT messages have error types that are similar in concept to Log4J Levels. For example, WinNT Errors correspond to Log4J's `FATAL` and `ERROR` levels.

In this example, we will again send only `FATAL` errors to the console, but this time only `FATAL` and `ERROR` messages will be sent to the Event Logger:

```
# A multi-destination logger
# FATAL errors will go to the console
# FATAL and ERROR will go to the NT Event Logger
log4j.logger.wrox.multiwinnt=DEBUG, winntconsole, winntlogger

# All fatal messages for this example go to the console
log4j.appender.winntconsole=org.apache.log4j.ConsoleAppender
log4j.appender.winntconsole.Target=System.out
log4j.appender.winntconsole.Threshold=FATAL
```

Here is where we configure the `NTEventLogAppender` that allows us to write to the Event Logger:

```
# All fatal and error messages go to the WinNT logger
log4j.appender.winntlogger=org.apache.log4j.nt.NTEventLogAppender
log4j.appender.winntlogger.Threshold=ERROR
```

The Event Logger displays the source of the message in its window. By default, Log4J messages are given the name `'log4j'`. This isn't very useful if we have a number of applications using Log4J, so we will add our own source name:

```
# We will set the Source parameter so we know which application
# this message came from
log4j.appender.winntlogger.Source=Wrox Logging
```

The Event Logger can take the same Layouts as other Layouts, but only `SimpleLayout` and `PatternLayout` make sense in this situation (as we shall see when we examine the log message):

```
# We will use a simple layout for both the console and the Event Logger
log4j.appender.winntconsole.layout=org.apache.log4j.SimpleLayout
log4j.appender.winntlogger.layout=org.apache.log4j.SimpleLayout
```

Here's that line of code again:

```
Logger logger = Logger.getLogger("wrox.multiwinnt");
```

Viewing the page http://localhost:8080/logging/fatalwinnt.jsp will send the usual `FATAL` message to the console as well as an `ERROR` message and a `FATAL` message to the Event Logger:

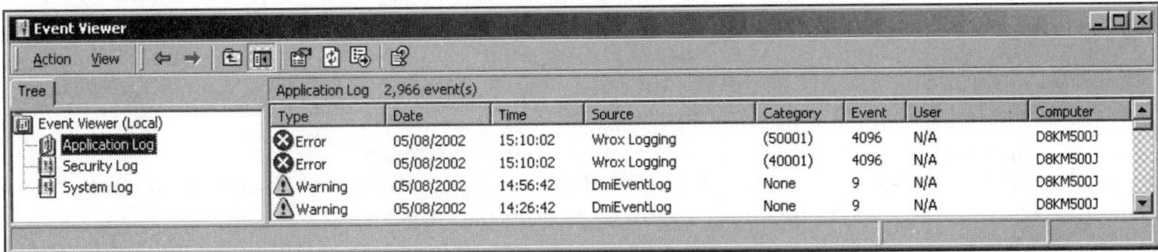

Both messages are logged as WinNT errors, but are given different categories. Double-clicking on a log message will show its properties:

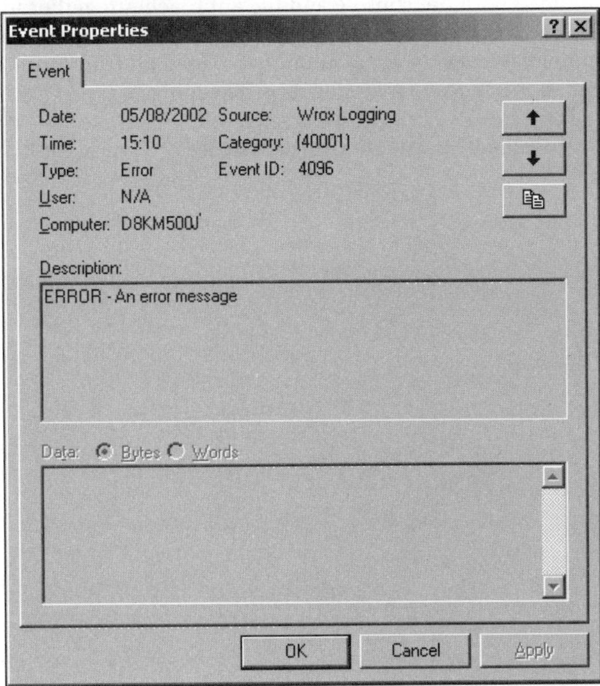

The Description box explains why the `SimpleLayout` and `PatternLayout` are the only sensible options for this kind of Appender: putting HTML tables into this box would make it almost unreadable.

Summary

In this chapter we had a look at the basics of Log4J, an open source Java logging framework from the Jakarta Project. We saw how it is structured and how the various components rely on one another to create a flexible logging system.

The main component of Log4J is the Logger. Once we have a Logger, we must add an Appender that specifies the type of destination for the logged messages. The final central component is a Layout that formats the message before it is finally written to its destination. These three components belong to a hierarchical model: Loggers without specific Appenders and Layouts inherit them from their parent Logger.

We also saw Log4J in action. First we showed how to set up a Logger for an entire web application using an initialization servlet. This ensures that the same Logger logs all the JSP pages and servlets in the same web application, making administration easier.

The final section of the chapter looked at various kinds of destinations and formats that could be used. We started with simple files, before moving on to custom patterns and HTML. These formats are fine for regular logging, but not so good for catching serious software failure as it happens. This brought us onto looking at logging to the console so that an administrator can see what is going on in real time.

Our final examples combined both the console and file approaches together to give us a more complete logging solution. We showed how a single Logger can log to multiple destinations with different levels of log message. For example, we saw an application that logged all fatal errors to the console for immediate attention and all messages to a file for record keeping.

In the next chapter we will examine how to use a single instance of Tomcat for hosting multiple web sites.

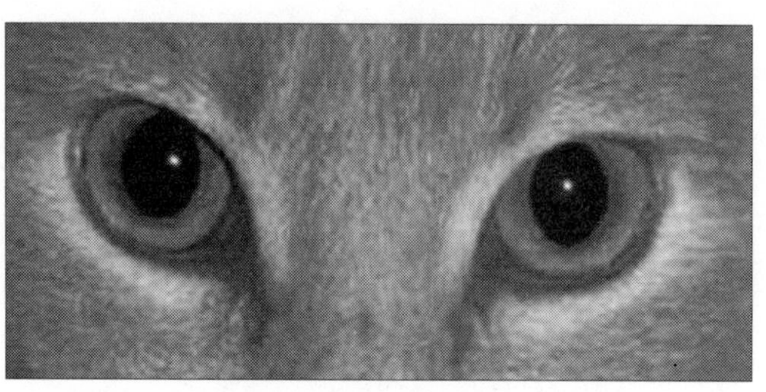

19

Shared Tomcat Hosting

With the introduction of the Tomcat JSP/servlet container from the Apache Software Foundation, host providers around the world have started providing world-class servlet/JSP support to their customers. Typically, these hosting services, whether in-house or outsourced, are based on shared hosting in which hundreds of sites could be running on a single computer sharing resources like the web server, the database server, the mail server, and various other services. Thus, all the services that are typically used in this scenario need to have in-built support for shared hosting.

This chapter looks at how Tomcat lends itself to be used in a shared hosting scenario. We will first look at the concept of virtual hosting that helps web servers (like Apache) to work. This is because Tomcat interacts with web servers quite intimately. We will then take a look at how we can make the Tomcat 3.x series of servlet containers work with virtual hosting. The Tomcat 4.x series incorporates a different set of configuration to work in a shared hosting scenario. This would be the next topic that we will look at. We finally look at various ways in which we can tune Tomcat to use its resources in an optimum way.

Virtual Hosting

In this chapter, a web site refers to the contents of a distinct Fully Qualified Domain Name (FQDN), which is served by a web server. Strictly, a FQDN consists of two parts – a host name, and a domain name. For example, the FQDN `www.wrox.com` consists of the host name `www` and the domain name `wrox.com`. The domain name `wrox.com` has other hosts like `p2p` and `mail`, whose FQDNs would be `p2p.wrox.com` and `mail.wrox.com`. However, since in this text the distinction between an FQDN and a domain name is not relevant, we will use the terms interchangeably.

As of June 2002, over 38 million web sites were contacted by Netcraft (source: http://www.netcraft.com/survey/) as part of their monthly web server survey. This shows the enormous number of web servers that provide their services on the Internet. A standard web server in a default configuration only allows one domain to be served from the machine. For a host provider to serve hundreds of domains from his location, this would mean setting up hundreds of computers for serving all the web sites. Certainly, this is not a scalable solution.

Also, IP addresses are an increasingly scarce resource. A web-hosting provider would get a limited number of IP addresses from its connectivity providers for hosting. Using one IP address for every web host would quickly eat up all the allocated IP addresses. To overcome these limitations, virtual hosting is used to make use of all our available resources, be it services, IP addresses, or other computing resources, in an optimal way.

We'll start off by looking at the Apache web server and how it implements web virtual hosting in two ways:

- **IP-based virtual hosting**
  Based on **multihoming hosts** (that is, machines with multiple Network Interface Cards (NIC), each with distinct IP addresses), every domain to be served is allocated one IP address. The web server listens to each of these network interfaces, and serves resources from the relevant domain based on the IP address that the request had arrived on.
- **Name-based virtual hosting**
  The web server listens on the IP addresses configured on the host, and serves resources from the relevant web site, based on the HTTP request headers from the web client.

IP-Based Virtual Hosting

In this form of virtual hosting, the machine is configured to have as many IP addresses as the number of hosts that it is to serve. So a machine that is to host 10 web sites would need 10 IP addresses configured. These additional IP addresses may either be configured by adding physical network interfaces (NIC) to the machine, or, as is more common, by adding aliased network interfaces to the computer.

Normally when you add a NIC card to your machine, you configure it with a single IP address, which you henceforth use in various services. However, it is possible to configure the same NIC card with more than one IP address. Adding these additional IP addresses involves using operating system-specific commands for first creating a virtual interface and then configuring it with a virtual IP address. This process normally involves using a physical NIC and adding virtual interfaces on top of it, a process also commonly known as aliasing.

For example, on Linux you can use the `ifconfig` command to add a virtual interface and configure it with an IP address at the same time. If you already have an Ethernet interface named `eth0` configured, you can add an aliased interface called `eth0:1` (in Linux, virtual Ethernet interfaces are named in the syntax `<physical-interface-name>:<virtual-interface-index>`), using the command:

```
ifconfig eth0:1 <virtual-IP> netmask <virtual-IP-netmask>
```

Implementing IP-Based Virtual Hosting in Apache

Adding IP-based virtual hosts in Apache is trivial. All you have to do is add a `<VirtualHost>` block to Apache's `httpd.conf` file for each corresponding web site, and a few associated parameters. Let's look at a sample configuration:

```
<VirtualHost 192.168.1.200>
    ServerName www.somedomain.com
    DocumentRoot /opt/sites/www.somedomain.com/web
    ServerAdmin support@somedomain.com
    ErrorLog /opt/sites/www.somedomain.com/log/error
    TransferLog /opt/sites/www.somedomain.com/log/access
</VirtualHost>

<VirtualHost 192.168.1.201>
    ServerName www.otherdomain.com
    DocumentRoot /opt/sites/www.otherdomain.com/web
    ServerAdmin support@otherdomain.com
    ErrorLog /opt/sites/www.otherdomain.com/log/error
    TransferLog /opt/sites/www.otherdomain.com/log/access
</VirtualHost>
```

Here, we have configured two IP-based virtual hosts `www.somedomain.com` and `www.otherdomain.com` running on the IP addresses `192.168.1.200` and `192.168.1.201` respectively.

Each of the virtual hosts is defined in a `<VirtualHost>` section:

- The `ServerName` directive sets the domain name to be served by this virtual host.
- The `DocumentRoot` directive points to the base directory to be used for serving pages for this domain.
- The `ServerAdmin` directive lists the e-mail address of the web server administration personnel.
- `TransferLog` and `ErrorLog` points to the log files to be used for web site access and web site error messages respectively.

The two IP addresses used in the `<VirtualHost>` directives should belong to network interfaces on the machine Apache would be running on. As you might have observed, each of the web sites has its own document root and its own log files for access and error logging. There are various other directives that you can put in these virtual host definitions to customize them. Leaving out these other directives would cause the virtual host to inherit their values from the global settings in the configuration file.

Some common mistakes to watch out for:

- Apache, in its default configuration, starts up and listens on all the configured network interfaces on the machine. If, for some reason, you have configured Apache to listen on only a restricted number of IP addresses on the machine using the `Listen` directive, you have to make sure that it listens on all the IP addresses of the various IP-based virtual hosts for all of them to work.

- You can't just use any combination of IP addresses and web host names. This is commonly done by configuring the client machine to use a DNS (Domain Name Service) server. The web client would query this DNS server for the IP address of the given host name, and then use the IP address returned by the DNS server to connect to the web server. The web server at the same time would be expecting requests for the host name at the IP address specified in the corresponding `NameVirtualHost` directive.

  Needless to say, if the IP address given in the `NameVirtualHost` directive doesn't match the one returned by the DNS server for the host name, the web client and the server won't be able to talk to each other.

- You could use the FQDN of the web site in place of the IP address in the `<VirtualHost>` directive. In this case, there should not be any problems in the DNS resolution of the host names in the machine. This is because when Apache starts up, it resolves each of the FQDNs in its `<VirtualHost>` directives to their IP addresses before offering the web service. Problems in resolving these addresses (when a DNS server could not be reached in time) during startup could cause Apache to abort prematurely.

Name-Based Virtual Hosting

While IP-based virtual hosts help in maximum usage of resources, they are still not feasible in places where hundreds of domains need to be hosted on the same machine. In such cases, either obtaining one IP address for each host or configuring many network interfaces on the same machine becomes a logistical nightmare. In these cases, name-based virtual hosting is used.

Name-based virtual hosting depends solely on an extension of the HTTP 1.0 protocol. In an HTTP 1.0 protocol, a web client or a browser merely had to make a TCP connection to port 80 of a web server and request a document using a relative location identifier, for the web resource to be fetched. For example, to access the document http://www.somedomain.com/help.txt, the browser had to look up the IP address of www.somedomain.com, make a TCP connection to port 80 of the IP address and could get the complete resource just by using the HTTP `GET` command:

```
$ telnet 192.168.1.200 80

Trying 192.168.1.200...
Connected to 192.168.1.200.
Escape character is '^]'.
GET /help.txt HTTP/1.0
```

Here is the response:

```
HTTP/1.1 200 OK
Date: Thu, 25 Jul 2002 08:24:58 GMT
Server: Apache/1.3.26 (Unix)  PHP/4.2.1 mod_ssl/2.8.9 OpenSSL/0.9.5a
Last-Modified: Wed, 16 May 2001 20:40:47 GMT
ETag: "1069e0-1a01-3b02e5cf"
Accept-Ranges: bytes
Content-Length: 6657
Connection: close
Content-Type: text/plain

[... rest of the the contents of help.txt]
```

However, this allowed only one web site to be accessed per IP address, otherwise, it would be impossible to discover the host for which the request was intended.

To tackle this problem, the `Host:` header as introduced in HTTP 1.1 is used to determine the web site from which the resource is requested.

With this new header, the HTTP headers exchanged between an HTTP/1.1-compliant web client and a server would look like this.

From the client:

```
GET /help.txt HTTP/1.0
Host: www.somedomain.com
```

and the response from the server:

```
HTTP/1.1 200 OK
Date: Thu, 25 Jul 2002 08:24:58 GMT
Server: Apache/1.3.26 (Unix)  PHP/4.2.1 mod_ssl/2.8.9 OpenSSL/0.9.5a
Last-Modified: Wed, 16 May 2001 20:40:47 GMT
ETag: "1069e0-1a01-3b02e5cf"
Accept-Ranges: bytes
Content-Length: 6657
Connection: close
Content-Type: text/plain

[... rest of the the contents of help.txt]
```

The additional `Host:` header in the client request helps the web server distinguish between all the domains that share the same IP address.

Implementing Name-Based Virtual Hosting in Apache

Implementing name-based virtual hosting in Apache is not much different from implementing IP-based virtual hosting. It only requires us to add the `NameVirtualHost` directive which tells the Apache server that the requests to the following IP address should be examined for the `Host:` HTTP header. Documents should be subsequently fetched depending on the value of this parameter and the related virtual host definition later on in the configuration.

A sample Apache name-based configuration would be like the following.

```
NameVirtualHost 192.168.1.200

<VirtualHost 192.168.1.200>
    ServerName www.somedomain.com
    DocumentRoot /opt/sites/www.somedomain.com/web
    ServerAdmin support@somedomain.com
    ErrorLog /opt/sites/www.somedomain.com/log/error
    TransferLog /opt/sites/www.somedomain.com/log/access
</VirtualHost>

<VirtualHost 192.168.1.200>
    ServerName www.otherdomain.com
```

```
        DocumentRoot /opt/sites/www.otherdomain.com/web
        ServerAdmin support@otherdomain.com
        ErrorLog /opt/sites/www.otherdomain.com/log/error
        TransferLog /opt/sites/www.otherdomain.com/log/access
    </VirtualHost>
```

In this configuration shown above, two web sites, `www.somedomain.com` and `www.otherdomain.com`, are being hosted on the same IP `192.168.1.200`. After a request comes to the IP address, Apache would use the `Host:` parameter and the `ServerName` parameter of each of the virtual host definitions to determine which definition this request should be sent to. The only setting that has to be done to use name-based virtual hosting, is to set up DNS settings for each of the FQDN to be hosted so that the client can resolve the IP addresses correctly. Compare this to IP-based virtual hosting where each of the IP addresses also had to be configured on the network interfaces of the machine.

Some common mistakes in name-based virtual hosting:

- If a web request has been made to an IP address listed against `NameVirtualHost`, and the applicable virtual host could not be determined, Apache sends the request to the *first* virtual host block in the Apache configuration for that IP address. The request is *not* sent to the default document root of the whole server. Therefore, the first `<VirtualHost>` section for every `NameVirtualHost` IP address should be a domain where unresolved web requests could also be handled.
- Since SSL connections are not on HTTP, headers like `Host:` cannot be extracted in advance. Therefore, it is not possible to have multiple SSL servers running on the same IP address. For this reason, each SSL-enabled web site needs to be configured on a unique IP address.
- Older web clients and many web access software libraries still use the old HTTP 1.0 protocol. Since they don't send the `Host:` header to the web server, name-based virtual hosting would not work properly with them. However, these incompatible clients are really rare by now, one wouldn't miss much by excluding them from your prospective client list. Prominent browsers like Netscape 2.0+, IE 3.0+, Lynx 1995+ all support the `Host:` header.

Virtual Hosting with Tomcat

Now that we know how to make Apache work with virtual hosts, we take a look at the main focus of this chapter – virtual host support in Tomcat. Before we go on, let's decide what we expect from Tomcat in a shared hosting environment.

Tomcat could work either in a standalone mode, in which it packs in both an HTTP server and the JSP/servlet container, or in a cooperative manner with a web server like Apache. If you are unsure about this topic, Chapters 11-13 provide details on setting up Tomcat with Apache in various different ways.

Now when we expect Tomcat to provide virtual hosting support, we mean the following – given that two or more web hosts are served from the same machine, when a request comes for a particular resource on one of these hosts, Tomcat should be able to successfully disambiguate the host for which the request had been received and fetch the required resource from the host document base.

For Tomcat working in a standalone mode, the request in question can target static pages, as well as JSP and servlets. When working along with another web server like Apache, the web server itself handles the virtual hosts and processing of subsequent static pages. Therefore the only thing that needs to be seen is whether Tomcat could handle the servlets and JSPs while distinguishing the various hosts involved.

The versions of Tomcat covered in this section include Tomcat version 3.3 – the latest stable version of Tomcat implementing Servlet 2.2 and JSP 1.1 specifications, as well as Tomcat version 4.0.4 – the latest stable version of Tomcat implementing Servlet 2.3 and JSP 1.2 specifications.

Example Configuration

For the purpose of assigning IP addresses to private networks, the Internet Assigned Numbers Authority (IANA) has assigned three blocks of IP addresses, as specified in the specification document RFC 1918 (http://www.rfc-editor.org/rfc/rfc1918.txt). These IP address blocks are:

- 10.0.0.0 - 10.255.255.255
- 172.16.0.0 - 172.31.255.255
- 192.168.0.0 - 192.168.255.255

In the following sections, we will explain how to configure Tomcat to serve two virtual hosts – `europa.dom` and `callisto.dom` running on the same machine with the common IP address `10.0.0.1` as an example of name-based virtual hosting. Our private network uses the IP range block `10.0.0.0-10.0.0.255`, that is, every IP address in our network is of the form `10.xxx.xxx.xxx`, with the exclusion of `10.0.0.0` and `10.0.0.255`, which have special meaning in networks. Every IP address in our network is also allocated a host name in the domain named `.dom`.

As is likely in a production scenario, both these domains would be hosted on a directory outside the Tomcat base directory. The hosting scheme that we would be using is as follows.

Each of the domains would have their own document area in `/home/sites/<domain-name>/`. Web applications or WAR files would be deployed in a subdirectory named `webapps/` under it and static HTML pages and scripts, if we want them to be kept separately from the web applications, would be deployed in a subdirectory named `web/` under it.

As a web application example for the domain `europa.dom`, a web application called `shop` would be deployed under `/home/sites/europa.dom/webapps/shop` or alternatively the `shop.war` web application archive could be deployed under `/home/sites/europa.dom/webapps/`. If Apache is supposed to serve static pages and scripts, they have to be deployed using `/home/sites/europa.dom/web/` as the document root. If Tomcat itself is to be used to serve static pages in a default context, an additional default web application called `ROOT` is to be deployed as `/home/sites/europa.dom/webapps/ROOT/`, and all static content are to be served from this directory itself.

Why should we have the web applications kept separated from the static pages? This is because in many cases of a shared hosting scenario, the hosting requirement of the clients would include Tomcat support, as an additional feature to their regular web needs. For most of their static site content, the separate web directory would suffice, and Apache would handle them without any problems. For those clients who want to add web applications, they can simply drop their WAR files in the `webapps/` directory without mixing them up with the static content.

Also, for performance reasons, Tomcat is often configured to extract the WAR file to a directory with a similar name. For a web administrator, the WAR directories would create confusion with those directories created for serving static content. Thus keeping these two entities (static files and web applications) separate would keep the directory structure clean and more maintainable:

```
/home/sites/
            europa.dom/
                       web/
                       webapps/

            callisto.dom/
                         web/
                         webapps/
```

Also, a sample JSP file, appropriately named `test.jsp`, would be placed in the document base of the main web application of each of these domains. For example, the content of `/home/sites/europa.dom/webapps/ROOT/test.jsp` is as follows:

```
<html>
  <head>
    <title>Welcome to Europa!</title>
  </head>
  <body>
    <%
      out.println("You are currently viewing the contents of "
                  +"the Europa web server");
    %>
  </body>
</html>
```

Remember to change the names for the `callisto.dom` domain. Note that we have not used the more flexible `request.getServerName()` method. The reason is that if the virtual host setting is not configured correctly, Tomcat (which provides the server environment to the JSP file) would send incorrect host information to the internal JSP handler. The resulting server name displayed on our browsers could confuse us while configuring for virtual hosting. Why didn't we then just write the server name in HTML itself? This is to check whether the whole setup is able to serve JSP (and hence servlets) properly. An incorrectly set up virtual hosting scenario, could for example cause the external web server itself to serve the JSP file, and since it cannot interpret the JSP source, it would show us the unparsed contents of the JSP file itself.

Feel free to change these setup details to suit your own server hosting policy. Just remember to change the settings as given below accordingly.

Virtual Hosting with Tomcat 3.3

The task of configuring virtual host support in Tomcat 3.3 consists of two steps – adding virtual host supporting web application definitions, which is sufficient if Tomcat is being run as a standalone server, and adding suitable directives in the Apache configuration (`$APACHE_HOME/conf/httpd.conf`), if Tomcat is being run as an external servlet engine. Let's look first at the scenario in which Tomcat is used as a standalone server, serving static pages, as well as JSPs and servlets.

Tomcat Components

To understand the relationship between the various components of Tomcat when Tomcat is being used as a standalone server, let us take a look at the following diagram:

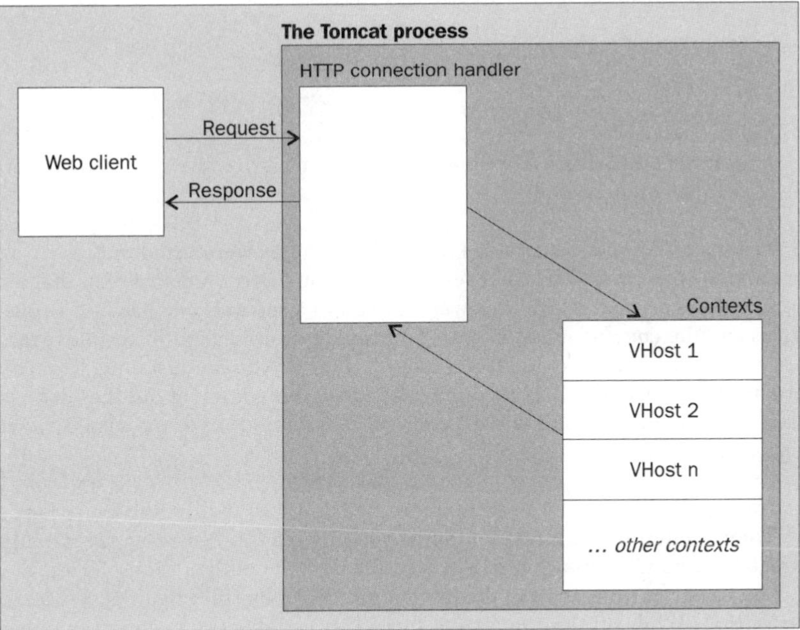

The web client in this case directly sends the HTTP request to the Tomcat process listening at port 8080. The HTTP connector handles the web client interaction. Tomcat then takes a look at the `Host:` header present in the HTTP request. If one is present, it tries to look up a virtual host with a name matching the one requested. If such a virtual host is found, the context parameter of the virtual host is taken and merged with the context parameters of the default configuration and the file served accordingly. The resultant output is sent back to the web client using the HTTP connector again.

If no context with the given virtual host is found, Tomcat tries to match the context path to the contexts that do not belong to any virtual hosts. If one is found, that context is used to send back the results. If no such context is found either, the default (with context path empty) context is used to send back the result, in which case the context path is matched to a physical directory or filename, failing which an HTTP 404 error is generated and send back to the client.

Tomcat 3.3 As a Standalone Server

To add a virtual host, we first need to add a virtual host context file. Before we look at that, let's take a brief look at how Tomcat looks at context files. A **context file** is a configuration file listing the various web applications deployed on this server, and their corresponding context paths.

The global configuration file for Tomcat – `$TOMCAT_HOME/conf/server.xml`, specifies files to be read by Tomcat to add contexts. The particular configuration directive that is of interest to us is the `<ContextXmlReader>` directive.

In the default Tomcat installation, you would find two such directives as follows:

```
[…]
        <!-- Backward compat: read the Context declarations from server.xml-->
        <ContextXmlReader config="conf/server.xml" />

        <!-- Separated Context -->
        <ContextXmlReader config="conf/apps.xml" />
[…]
```

Each of the `<ContextXmlReader>` directives informs Tomcat that the specified files are to be scanned for context lists and the contexts loaded.

In the initial versions of Tomcat (version 3.1.x), all the contexts were listed in the `$TOMCAT_HOME/conf/server.xml` file itself. However, it was soon discovered that it would be far more manageable if the context definitions were moved to a separate file itself, to avoid mixing up any global directives and the context-specific ones. To provide drop-in support for older setups, Tomcat 3.3 still reads in the `server.xml` file again for context listings. If you are installing Tomcat for the first time, or upgrading an older setup, it is recommended that you comment out the first `<ContextXmlReader>` element and add all your context definitions to the `apps-*.xml` files in the conf directory of `$TOMCAT_HOME`.

The second `<ContextXmlReader>` element instructs Tomcat to read in the `conf/apps.xml`. Interestingly, Tomcat interprets this instruction to not only read in `conf/apps.xml` file, if present, but also any file matching `conf/apps-*.xml`. In fact, the default configuration of Tomcat uses this feature by not having an `apps.xml` file at all in the `conf/` directory, but files like `apps-admin.xml` and `apps-example.xml`. While all the contents of these files could easily been put in one single `apps.xml` file, it helps us keep context definitions of different web applications and of related web applications together.

We start our configuration process by creating a subdirectory under the `conf/` directory of `$TOMCAT_HOME` where we would keep all our virtual host configurations.

```
$ mkdir conf/vhosts
```

We instruct Tomcat to read in context listings from files in this directory. For this let's add the following directive in `conf/server.xml` just after the other `<ContextXmlReader>` directories:

```
        <!-- virtual host definitions -->
        <ContextXmlReader config="conf/vhosts/vhost.xml" />
```

This instructs Tomcat to read in the files of the form `conf/vhosts/vhost-<domain_name>.xml` for context listings.

Now, we have to actually create the context listing files for the various virtual hosts. Let's take a look at the context listing of `europa.dom` as contained in `conf/vhosts/vhost-europa.xml`.

```
<?xml version="1.0" encoding="ISO-8859-1"?>
<Server>
  <Host name="europa.dom" >
```

```
    <Context path=""
             docBase="/home/sites/europa.dom/webapps/ROOT" >
      <LogSetter name="tc_log_europa_root"
                 path="/home/sites/europa.dom/logs/tc_root.log" />
    </Context>
    <Context path="/admin"
             docBase="/home/sites/europa.dom/webapps/admin" >
      <LogSetter name="tc_log_europa_admin"
                 path="/home/sites/europa.dom/logs/tc_admin.log" />
    </Context>
  </Host>
</Server>
```

This defines two contexts for the virtual host `europa.dom`. One of them is the default context (that is with empty context path) whose `docbase` is set to the `ROOT` web application for the domain. The other context is mapped to `/admin` that would use the `admin` web application for the domain. We could add as many `<Context>` elements for the virtual host as we would need. Each of the contexts has been given its own log file.

Note that the root element in the virtual host context file is different from that in normal context files like that in the default `conf/apps-admin.xml` or `conf/apps-example.xml` context files.

Normal context files define contexts in a `<webapps></webapps>` root element. For virtual hosts, the difference is that the `<Context>` directives are put in their respective `<Host>` parent elements, which in turn have to be inside the `<Server>` root element. While you can include as many `<Host>` elements inside the same `<Server>` element as you want, with each of them containing all the contexts applicable to the virtual host, it is certainly not a scalable model when the number of hosts can be very large.

In our scheme, each of the virtual host has a separate context file. While the context file of `europa.dom` was displayed a while before, let's take a look at the context file for `callisto.dom`.

```
<?xml version="1.0" encoding="ISO-8859-1"?>
<Server>
  <Host name="callisto.dom" >
    <Context path=""
             docBase="/home/sites/callisto.dom/webapps/ROOT" >
      <LogSetter name="tc_log_callisto_root"
                 path="/home/sites/callisto.dom/logs/tc_root.log" />
    </Context>
    <Context path="/admin"
             docBase="/home/sites/callisto.dom/webapps/admin" >
      <LogSetter name="tc_log_callisto_admin"
                 path="/home/sites/callisto.dom/logs/tc_admin.log" />
    </Context>
  </Host>
</Server>
```

Next we use the test file as was mentioned earlier, and after modifying it suitably for both the domains, we deploy it in the respective `ROOT` web application.

Finally, we restart Tomcat to let it read in the new settings.

```
$ $TOMCAT_HOME/bin/tomcat.sh shutdown
$ $TOMCAT_HOME/bin/tomcat.sh startup
```

Examine the Tomcat logs to see if there are any error messages. If you spot any, go back and recheck the settings.

Now check the working of virtual hosts by viewing the respective URLs of `callisto.dom` and `europa.dom`:

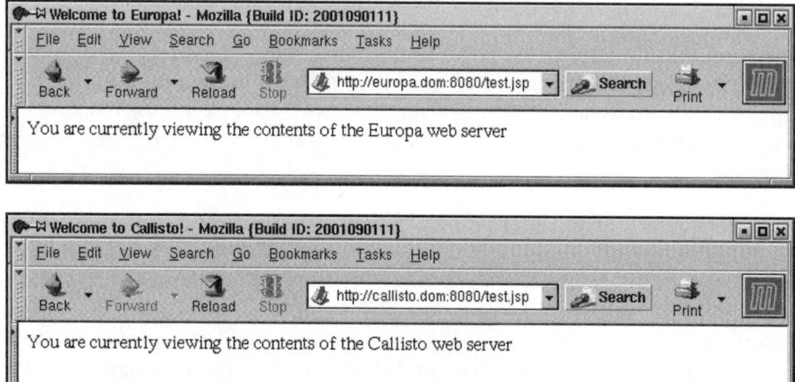

Tomcat 3.3 with Apache

When Tomcat is used as an out-of-process servlet container along with Apache, there are two sets of configuration that need to be done, one in Tomcat and the other in Apache.

For Tomcat, the configuration as shown in the last section remains more or less the same, The only difference is that, because the HTTP connector is not being used, we can disable it in the `server.xml` configuration file.

At Apache's end, as has been shown in the previous chapters, an adapter for Tomcat has to be used. Here, we will use the `mod_jk` adapter using the AJP 1.3 protocol for communicating with Tomcat. The AJP protocol was covered in Chapter 11 and `mod_jk` was covered in Chapter 13.

A diagrammatic representation of how the components are involved is shown next. One can compare it with the previous diagram to see the functional differences.

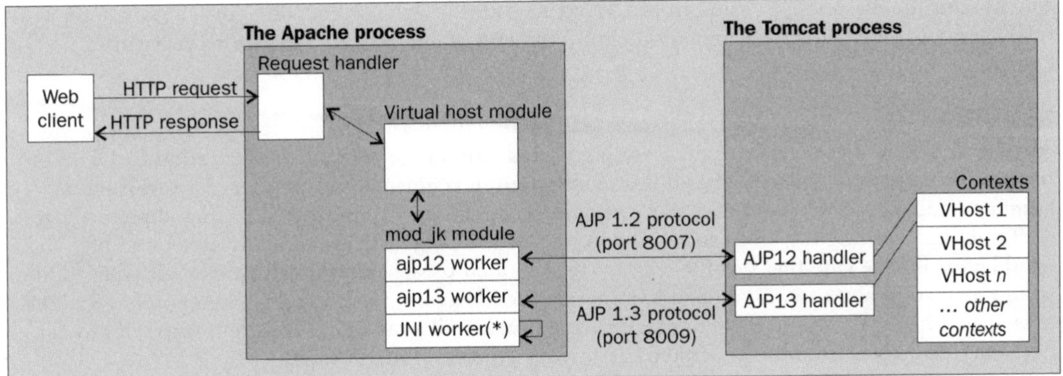

Here, Apache receives the HTTP request from the client. It then looks up the appropriate virtual host entry using the `Host:` parameter in the request. In the virtual host entry, we ask `mod_jk` to forward all appropriate servlet and JSP requests to the appropriate worker. The worker could be either one using the AJP 1.2 protocol or the AJP 1.3 protocol, or a JNI interface could be used to communicate with a Tomcat process started within the Apache adapter.

While it is possible for all the types of workers to be simultaneously used, it is more common to have a single kind of worker being used throughout the installation. If the worker is an `ajp1.2`, it opens a TCP-based AJP 1.2 protocol connection to the Tomcat server which receives the request via its AJP 1.2 connector. Tomcat then examines the request to see whether any of its virtual host definitions match the request. This is similar to the matching process in the standalone Tomcat server. The servlet response is then sent back through the AJP 1.2 connector to the `mod_jk` module. This in turn instructs Apache to send the reply back to the web client.

Configuring Apache

Assuming that `mod_jk` has been appropriately set up in Apache to communicate with Tomcat as explained in Chapter 13, we take a look at adding virtual host support to this configuration.

As explained in the *Apache Name-Based Virtual Hosting* section earlier, for every virtual host definition we need to add a `<VirtualHost>` section in Apache (in fact the Tomcat `<Host>` configuration definition is very similar to this concept). Now, along with the rest of the virtual host contents, we add some `mod_jk` mount statements connecting certain resources to Tomcat.

One time-saving way to get the appropriate virtual host configuration is to ask Tomcat to generate it for us.

All we have to do is run the Tomcat startup script asking it to not interfere with any running Tomcat processes but to simply generate the `mod_jk` configuration file. This requires the `<ApacheConfig>` directive to be present in the `$TOMCAT_HOME/conf/server.xml` file. In the default configuration, this directive is present in the file. It enables the Tomcat module that creates the appropriate `mod_jk` configuration file. However, unlike earlier versions of Tomcat, this file is not generated on every startup. To generate the file, we run the following command in the Tomcat root:

```
$ $CATALINA_HOME/bin/startup.sh jkconf
```

This creates the file mod_jk.conf in the $TOMCAT_HOME/conf/auto/ directory. Take a look at all the relevant virtual host directives and add them to the end of our existing Apache httpd.conf configuration file.

Notice that we are not including the generated file directly in our Apache configuration using the Apache Include directive, but rather adding it manually in the Apache configuration file. This is because the generated Apache virtual host configuration is normally barebones. As a web server administrator you are likely to add many additional directives like those for logging, directory/file ACL's, URL rewriting rules and so on. If you make the change to the originally generated file, you would have to take care that this file was not regenerated by accident, in which case all your additions would be lost. In any case, if you had to generate the file again, for example, when you have added a new virtual host, you would have to make your additions all over again. It is therefore safer to copy the necessary directives from the generated file to your Apache configuration.

The part of the newly generated configuration file that is of interest to us is given below. We have added the DocumentRoot directives for each of the virtual hosts to suit our hosting scheme:

```
NameVirtualHost *
<VirtualHost *>
    ServerName europa.dom
    DocumentRoot /home/sites/europa.dom/web

    JkMount /admin ajp13
    JkMount /admin/* ajp13
</VirtualHost>

<VirtualHost *>
    ServerName callisto.dom
    DocumentRoot /home/sites/callisto.dom/web

    JkMount /admin ajp13
    JkMount /admin/* ajp13
</VirtualHost>
```

When compared to the Apache virtual host directives shown at the beginning of this chapter, the only major difference that we see is the new JkMount directives.

After adding these directives to the Apache httpd.conf file, we restart Apache and try to access the previously used test URL. However, this time we don't send the request to port 8080 of the Tomcat web server but the standard HTTP port 80 on which Apache should be listening.

However, on accessing http://europa.dom/test.jsp we get a HTTP 404 error. What are we doing wrong this time? We will discuss this in the next section.

Request Sharing Between Tomcat 3.3 and Apache

The default auto-generated mod_jk.conf file only sends non-empty context path requests to Tomcat. Therefore, while we have defined two contexts for the virtual hosts – one as the default with an empty context path and one with an explicit context path (/admin) – only the requests for the context /admin are passed on to Tomcat:

As can be seen in the <VirtualHost> directive above, JkMount is only performed on the /admin context path.

What is happening is that mod_jk is not listening for requests on the default context, and those requests are being handled by Apache itself. Since the document root of Apache is different from that of the default context, Apache doesn't find the file and returns an error. Even if the document root of Apache and the default context are the same, it still wouldn't have solved our problem, because Apache doesn't understand JSP – Tomcat does. So Apache would end up displaying the contents of the JSP file instead of parsing and interpreting it as required.

What we need is a way to pass the requests made to the default context to Tomcat. Fortunately, Tomcat allows us to do this using a small addition to the <ApacheConfig> directive in server.xml. We simply change the value of the noRoot attribute to false from its default value of true. This would pass ALL the requests made to the default context, to the default context of the virtual host in Tomcat. After making the changes, we execute the command for generating the mod_jk.conf file again:

```
$ $TOMCAT_HOME/bin/startup.sh jkconf
```

We examine the <VirtualHost> directives in the newly created mod_jk.conf file again. We find that two new mount points have been added. Also, the DocumentRoot of the virtual host has been changed to the web application document base of the default context. Keeping the previous document root intact, we add the new JkMount directives in each of the <VirtualHost> sections of the existing httpd.conf file. These additions are of the form:

```
<VirtualHost *>
[...]
    JkMount / ajp13
    JkMount /* ajp13

[...]
</VirtualHost>
```

Now we are able to see the expected contents of http://europa.dom/test.jsp. However, is our present configuration what we want? We put a sample HTML file in our <VirtualHost> document root (/home/sites/europa.dom/web) and try to access it through the browser. We get a HTTP 404 error now, and if we carefully observe the message, we would find out that Tomcat and not Apache is generating the error this time.

What is happening now is that Tomcat has taken over all the references of the root URL including static files. This is not what we want, right? We want Tomcat to handle only servlets and JSPs.

To allow this, we add the attribute forwardAll with the value false to the same <ApacheConfig> directive in the $TOMCAT_HOME/conf/server.xml file. This attribute if not given, normally defaults to true. We regenerate the mod_jk.conf file again.

```
$ $TOMCAT_HOME/bin/startup.sh jkconf
```

We examine the generated file, and we find that the configuration has changed dramatically this time:

```
<VirtualHost *>
    ServerName europa.dom

    #################### europa.dom:/ ####################

    DocumentRoot "/home/sites/europa.dom/webapps/ROOT"
    <Directory "/home/sites/europa.dom/webapps/ROOT">
        Options Indexes FollowSymLinks
        DirectoryIndex index.jsp index.html index.htm
    </Directory>

    # Deny direct access to WEB-INF and META-INF
    #
    <Location "/WEB-INF/*">
        AllowOverride None
        deny from all
    </Location>

    <Location "/META-INF/*">
        AllowOverride None
        deny from all
    </Location>

    JkMount /servlet  ajp13
    JkMount /servlet/*  ajp13
    JkMount /*.jsp ajp13

    #################### europa.dom:/admin ####################

    # Static files
    Alias /admin "/home/sites/europa.dom/webapps/admin"

    <Directory "/home/sites/europa.dom/webapps/admin">
        Options Indexes FollowSymLinks
        DirectoryIndex index.jsp index.html index.htm
    </Directory>


    # Deny direct access to WEB-INF and META-INF
    #
    <Location "/admin/WEB-INF/*">
        AllowOverride None
        deny from all
    </Location>

    <Location "/admin/META-INF/*">
        AllowOverride None
        deny from all
    </Location>

    JkMount /admin/servlet  ajp13
    JkMount /admin/servlet/*  ajp13
    JkMount /admin/*.jsp ajp13
</VirtualHost>
```

What has happened is that now, instead of blindly sending all root references to Tomcat, `mod_jk` is now sending much more specific URLs. In fact, servlets in the root context would be served only either when they are prefixed with the `/servlet/` path, or they are aliased to various mappings in the `web.xml` web application descriptor of the default context.

We replace the previous contents of the `<VirtualHost>` definitions with the new ones, including the `DocumentRoot` directive this time. If we restart the Apache server, and try to access the test JSP file we see that it works. We try to access the file that we created earlier in the static HTML document root, for example, in `/home/sites/europa.dom/web` and try to access it. It still fails with a `HTTP 404` message. Only this time we see that Apache and not Tomcat returns the error. This is natural because the document root of the `<VirtualHost>` has been changed to that of the default Tomcat context.

This brings to our attention an important constraint while deploying Tomcat in this configuration. If we want a Tomcat default context in the web application, we *have* to have the `DocumentRoot` of the `<VirtualHost>` directive to point to the docbase of the default context. Otherwise default context documents would simply not be accessible.

Having covered extensively the use of virtual hosts in Tomcat 3.x, we now turn towards the latest version: Tomcat 4.x.

Virtual Hosting with Tomcat 4.x

Virtual host configuration in Tomcat 4.x is different from that in Tomcat 3.x in a number of ways. Mostly, this has been because Tomcat 4.x was rewritten from scratch and the whole architecture of the various components of Tomcat has changed.

One common factor between the two configurations is that the configuration in Apache for transferring requests for servlets and JSP pages to the Tomcat process has more or less remained the same while using the `mod_jk` adapter. In addition, Tomcat 4.x can also use `mod_webapp`, which we will see later.

We first take a look at configuring Tomcat 4.x as a standalone server implementing virtual hosts.

Tomcat 4.x As a Standalone Server

Virtual host definitions in Tomcat 4.x have to be provided in the server configuration file, `server.xml` itself. Once these additions have been done, we simply need to restart Tomcat to use the virtual host definitions.

Editing server.xml

The default sample `server.xml` file of the Tomcat 4.x build contains two services – one for the standalone server, and one for the server that cooperates with an Apache web server using the WARP protocol. We can remove the definition for the second service and reuse that of the first service.

The top-level `<Service>` element for the standalone server would look like the following:

```
<Server port="8005" shutdown="SHUTDOWN" debug="0">
  <Service name="Tomcat-Standalone">

  </Service>
</Server>
```

The rest of the configuration would go inside this `<Service>` container element. We then add the Connectors to be used for this service. Since this is a standalone server, we only need the HTTP/1.1 connector to communicate with the outside world.

We add the following Connector definition inside the `<Service>` element.

```
<Connector className="org.apache.catalina.connector.http.HttpConnector"
           port="8080"
           minProcessors="5"
           maxProcessors="75"
           enableLookups="true"
           acceptCount="10"
           debug="0"
           connectionTimeout="60000"/>
```

This sets up Tomcat to listen to port 8080 for incoming web requests.

We now add the `<Engine>` element to the `<Service>` by adding the following lines just after the `<Connector>` element and inside the `<Service>` element:

```
<Engine name="Standalone" defaultHost="europa.dom" debug="0">

</Engine>
```

This specifies an engine for the service that processes incoming requests from the connectors. After any request has been received by the connector and passed on to the engine, the engine would then take a look at the HTTP headers, especially the `Host:` tag, and determine which of the virtual host definitions that it handles would receive the request. If none of the virtual host seems to match the request headers, the engine passes on the request to a default host. The name of the default virtual host is specified in the attribute `defaultHost`. The value of this attribute must match a `<Host>` definition in the engine.

For our purposes, we see that the virtual host definition of `europa.dom` is served by default when a web request is made using the IP address (instead of a host name).

We next add the virtual host definition of `europa.dom` to the engine. We add the following content inside the `<Engine>` element:

```
<Host name="europa.dom" debug="0"
      appBase="/home/sites/europa.dom/webapps"
      unpackWARs="true">
</Host>
```

This defines a virtual host entry for `europa.dom` in Tomcat. We further add some logging functionality to this virtual host by placing the following content within the `<Host>` element:

```
<Valve className="org.apache.catalina.valves.AccessLogValve"
       directory="/home/sites/europa.dom/logs"
       prefix="europa_access."
       suffix=".log"
       pattern="common"/>

 <Logger className="org.apache.catalina.logger.FileLogger"
         directory="/home/sites/europa.dom/logs"
         prefix="europa_catalina."
         suffix=".log"
         timestamp="true"/>
```

This defines two logging services for this virtual host. The `<Logger>` element is covered in Chapter 5.

We now add the contexts to serve for this virtual host, inside the `<Host>` element.

```
<Context path="" docBase="ROOT" debug="0"/>
<Context path="/shop" docBase="shop" debug="0" />
```

We have added two contexts here. The first one is the default context with an empty context path. This context either has to be defined explicitly or provided automatically by Tomcat (that is, without you defining it here) if you have a web application called `ROOT` in the `appBase` of the virtual host.

As an example of how new web applications other than the default one have to be added to the site, we have also added the web application called `shop` which uses the `/shop` context path.

One nice thing about context definitions in Tomcat 4.x is that it provides automatic contexts in case you haven't defined them in the host definition. To provide this functionality, Tomcat looks at directories inside the `appBase` directory. If these directories follow the web application structure, specifically if they contain a `WEB-INF/web.xml` file in them, Tomcat automatically provides contexts with context paths equal to the name of the directory under `appBase`.

> *Remember that the default parameters of these contexts are picked up from* `$CATALINA_HOME/conf/web.xml`.

If you need to override some global parameters to these contexts, you need to place them within the `<Context></Context>` elements. Examples would be, logging for this context in a separate file, context parameters, resource definitions, and so on.

This completes the virtual host definition for `europa.dom`. For the virtual host `callisto.dom`, we add another virtual host entry similar to that of `europa.dom`:

We save this file as `$CATALINA_HOME/conf/server.xml` and restart the Tomcat service.

We first check the test JSP file in the `europa.dom` virtual host using the URL http://europa.dom:8080/test.jsp:

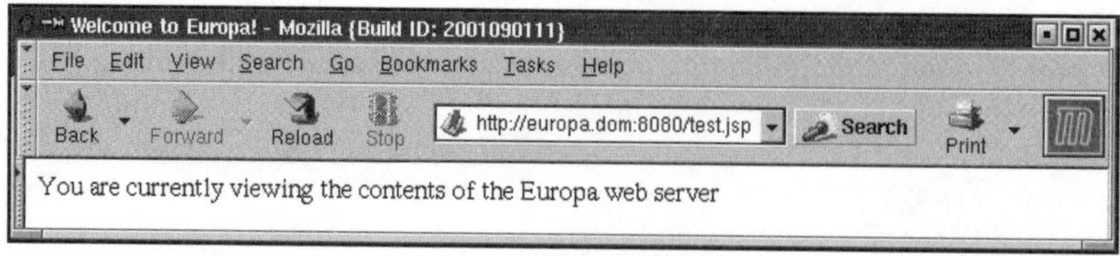

We then check out the callisto.dom using the URL http://callisto.dom:8080/test.jsp:

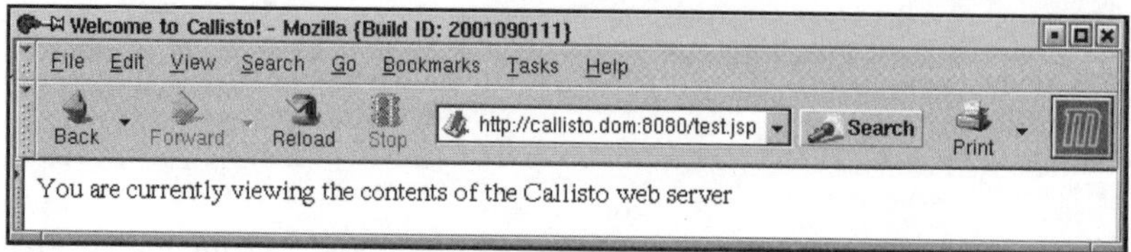

We then check whether the default host setting of the <Engine> element is working properly. For this we use a host name other than the ones specified explicitly as <Host> definitions. Let's try accessing using the IP address 10.0.0.1:

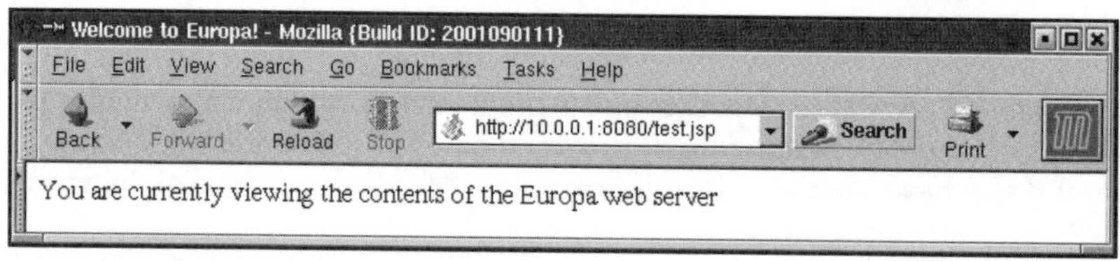

As we can see, Tomcat serves the contents of the europa.dom virtual host, as defined in the default virtual host entry of the engine.

Now that we have Tomcat 4.0 working as a standalone server for the virtual hosts, let's make it work along with Apache.

Tomcat 4.0 with Apache

As we saw in the Tomcat 3.3 Apache configuration section, Apache communicates with Tomcat using connectors like mod_jk. In Tomcat 4.x, support for another kind of adapter called mod_webapp has also been added. While we will concentrate on using mod_jk in this section, as it is considered to be more stable than the new mod_webapp, we will touch mod_webapp briefly at the end.

We can use the same mod_jk connector in both versions of Tomcat (it's the same at the Apache end after all). However, if you rely on Tomcat to automatically generate the mod_jk.conf file, the procedure for Tomcat 4.x is a bit different to the one in Tomcat 3.3 and will be explained shortly.

Tomcat 4.0 with the AJP 1.3 Connector

To use Tomcat along with the AJP connectors of Apache, we need to modify the previously used server.xml file.

First of all we change the name of the <Service> element to reflect the fact that Tomcat is now working along with Apache. While this is not strictly necessary, it helps in distinguishing between multiple configuration files of Tomcat lying in your machine:

```
[...]
  <Service name="Tomcat-Apache-mod_jk">
 [...]
```

We then replace the HTTP/1.1 <Connector> definition with the given AJP1.3 <Connector> definition instead.

The HTTP connector could be left in place if you still want Tomcat to handle web requests directly at port 8080.

```
<Connector className="org.apache.ajp.tomcat4.Ajp13Connector"
            port="8009"
            minProcessors="5"
            maxProcessors="75"
            acceptCount="10"
            debug="0"/>
```

That is all we have to do to configure Tomcat to communicate with the Apache mod_jk adapter. However, to make our configuration of Apache easier, we can ask Tomcat to auto-generate the required Apache configuration files.

Auto Generating mod_jk.conf

To auto-generate the Apache configuration files, we have to add appropriate <ApacheConfig> listeners at various points in the server.xml file.

We start by generating the global mod_jk configuration, which is done by adding the following just after the <Service> opening element in the server.xml file:

```
<Listener className="org.apache.ajp.tomcat4.config.ApacheConfig"
          modJk="/usr/local/apache/libexec/mod_jk.so"
          jkDebug="info"
          workersConfig="/usr/local/tomcat/conf/jk/workers.properties"
          jkLog="/usr/local/tomcat/logs/mod_jk.log"
          noRoot="false"
          forwardAll="false" />
```

You would notice the familiar noRoot and forwardAll attributes from the <ApacheConfig> element of Tomcat 3.3. They have similar functions here:

- The modJk attribute contains the path to the mod_jk connector module for Apache. This path would be used in the auto-generated output to inform Apache where to load the module from.
- jkDebug attribute indicates the level of logging which could be one of debug, info, error, or emerg. Not setting this attribute would cause logging to be disabled.
- workersConfig contains the path to the worker.properties file that needs to be mentioned in the generated file for the connector to find the workers to send the request to. jkLog contains the path to the file to be used for logging.

To generate the <VirtualHost> sections we add the following just after the opening element of all the <Host> entries.

```
        <Listener className="org.apache.ajp.tomcat4.config.ApacheConfig"
                  append="true"  />
```

The final server.xml file should look like this:

```
<Server port="8005" shutdown="SHUTDOWN" debug="0">
  <Service name="Tomcat-Apache-modjk">
     <Listener className="org.apache.ajp.tomcat4.config.ApacheConfig"
               modJk="/usr/local/apache/libexec/mod_jk.so"
               jkDebug="info"
         workersConfig="/usr/local/tomcat/build/conf/jk/workers.properties"
               jkLog="/usr/local/tomcat/logs/mod_jk.log"
               noRoot="false"
               forwardAll="false" />

    <Connector className="org.apache.ajp.tomcat4.Ajp13Connector"
               port="8009"
               minProcessors="5"
               maxProcessors="75"
               acceptCount="10"
               debug="0"/>

    <Engine name="Standalone" defaultHost="europa.dom" debug="0">

      <!-- Virtual host definition for europa.dom -->
      <Host name="europa.dom" debug="0"
            appBase="/home/sites/europa.dom/webapps"
            unpackWARs="true">
        <Listener className="org.apache.ajp.tomcat4.config.ApacheConfig"
                  append="true" />
        <Valve className="org.apache.catalina.valves.AccessLogValve"
               directory="/home/sites/europa.dom/logs"
               prefix="europa_access."
               suffix=".log"
               pattern="common"/>

        <Logger className="org.apache.catalina.logger.FileLogger"
                directory="/home/sites/europa.dom/logs"
                prefix="europa_catalina."
                suffix=".log"
                timestamp="true"/>
        <Context path="" docBase="ROOT" debug="0"/>

        <Context path="/shop" docBase="shop" debug="0" />

      </Host>

      <!-- Virtual host definition for callisto.dom -->
      <Host name="callisto.dom"
            debug="0"
```

```
            appBase="/home/sites/callisto.dom/webapps"
            unpackWARs="true">
      <Listener className="org.apache.ajp.tomcat4.config.ApacheConfig"
                append="true"  />

      <Valve className="org.apache.catalina.valves.AccessLogValve"
             directory="/home/sites/callisto.dom/logs"
             prefix="callisto_access."
             suffix=".log"
             pattern="common"/>

      <Logger className="org.apache.catalina.logger.FileLogger"
              directory="/home/sites/callisto.dom/logs"
              prefix="callisto_catalina." suffix=".log"
              timestamp="true"/>
      <Context path="" docBase="ROOT" debug="0"/>

      <Context path="/shop" docBase="shop" debug="0" />

    </Host>
  </Engine>
 </Service>
</Server>
```

Restart Tomcat to get the auto-generated `mod_jk.conf` file. It will be in `$CATALINA_HOME/conf/auto`.

While we can use the auto-generated files directly in our Apache configuration with the `Include` directive, we should remember that this time Tomcat generates these files *every time* it starts. So any changes made to this file will be lost. In cases where you would like to make any custom changes to the virtual host definitions, for example, adding the Apache ACL to certain file locations, we should instead write this configuration file by hand. This is in contrast to Tomcat 3.3, which generates the file only when asked to do so. Of course, in Tomcat 4.0.x, once you have got the generated `mod_jk.conf`, you can always remove the `ApacheConfig` `<Listener>` elements from the `server.xml` file. This way when Tomcat restarts it won't regenerate the file.

In either case, the final `mod_jk.conf` file should look like the following:

```
<IfModule !mod_jk.c>
  LoadModule jk_module /usr/local/apache/libexec/mod_jk.so
</IfModule>

JkWorkersFile "/usr/local/tomcat/build/conf/jk/workers.properties"
JkLogFile "/usr/local/tomcat/build/logs/mod_jk.log"

JkLogLevel emerg

NameVirtualHost *

<VirtualHost *>
    ServerName europa.dom
```

```
    DocumentRoot "/home/sites/europa.dom/webapps/ROOT"
    <Directory "/home/sites/europa.dom/webapps/ROOT">
        Options Indexes FollowSymLinks
        DirectoryIndex index.jsp index.html index.htm
    </Directory>

    <Location "/WEB-INF/*">
        AllowOverride None
        deny from all
    </Location>

    <Location "/META-INF/*">
        AllowOverride None
        deny from all
    </Location>

    JkMount /servlet  ajp13
    JkMount /servlet/*  ajp13
    JkMount /*.jsp ajp13
    JkMount /shop  ajp13
    JkMount /shop/*  ajp13

    Alias /shop "/home/sites/europa.dom/webapps/shop"

    <Directory "/home/sites/europa.dom/webapps/shop">
        Options Indexes FollowSymLinks
        DirectoryIndex index.jsp index.html index.htm
    </Directory>

    <Location "/shop/WEB-INF/*">
        AllowOverride None
        deny from all
    </Location>

    <Location "/shop/META-INF/*">
        AllowOverride None
        deny from all
    </Location>

    JkMount /shop/servlet  ajp13
    JkMount /shop/servlet/*  ajp13
    JkMount /shop/*.jsp ajp13
</VirtualHost>

<VirtualHost *>
    ServerName callisto.dom

    DocumentRoot "/home/sites/callisto.dom/webapps/ROOT"
    <Directory "/home/sites/callisto.dom/webapps/ROOT">
        Options Indexes FollowSymLinks
        DirectoryIndex index.jsp index.html index.htm
    </Directory>

    <Location "/WEB-INF/*">
```

```
        AllowOverride None
        deny from all
    </Location>

    <Location "/META-INF/*">
        AllowOverride None
        deny from all
    </Location>

    JkMount /servlet  ajp13
    JkMount /servlet/*  ajp13
    JkMount /*.jsp ajp13

    Alias /shop "/home/sites/callisto.dom/webapps/shop"

    <Directory "/home/sites/callisto.dom/webapps/shop">
        Options Indexes FollowSymLinks
        DirectoryIndex index.jsp index.html index.htm
    </Directory>

    <Location "/shop/WEB-INF/*">
        AllowOverride None
        deny from all
    </Location>

    <Location "/shop/META-INF/*">
        AllowOverride None
        deny from all
    </Location>

    JkMount /shop/servlet  ajp13
    JkMount /shop/servlet/*  ajp13
    JkMount /shop/*.jsp ajp13
</VirtualHost>
```

Restart Tomcat and Apache and check the test files for the virtual domains again.

Tomcat 4.0 with mod_webapp

Setting up the new Apache-Tomcat mod_webapp connector is not much different from setting up the mod_jk connector, with the important difference that Tomcat does not have a module like `<ApacheConfig>` for automatic generation of mod_webapp Apache configuration files. Even though Tomcat's automatic generation of `mod_jk.conf` is convenient, commercial shared hosting providers won't rely on it too much, because of the myriad different directives that they would like to put in the `<VirtualHost>` entry. They would rather have their own automated scripts to generate the `mod_jk.conf` files with their additions. Given that, the syntax for writing a mod_jk configuration and a mod_webapp configuration is not much different

If you want a comparison between the two connectors, see Chapter 11.

Configuring Apache

To configure Apache for mod_webapp, instead of the mod_jk-specific commands in the Apache configuration file, we add the mod_webapp directives. Instead of the LoadModule and AddModule directives of mod_jk, we add:

```
LoadModule webapp_module libexec/mod_webapp.so
AddModule mod_webapp.c
```

Also, replace the other global Jk* directives with:

```
WebAppConnection tomcat_warp warp localhost:8008
```

This defines a WARP connection with the name tomcat_warp for communicating with the Tomcat server on the same host at port 8008. We now replace all the JkMount directives with WebAppDeploy directives. WebAppDeploy directives are of the form:

```
WebAppDeploy <webappname> <warpconnection> <contextpath>
```

Thus the new Apache configuration file, which we would name as mod_webapp.conf, would look like this:

```
LoadModule webapp_module libexec/mod_webapp.so
AddModule mod_webapp.c

WebAppConnection tomcat_warp  warp  localhost:8008

NameVirtualHost *

<VirtualHost *>
    ServerName europa.dom

    WebAppDeploy ROOT tomcat_warp /
    WebAppDeploy shop tomcat_warp /shop

    DocumentRoot "/home/sites/europa.dom/webapps/ROOT"

    <Directory "/home/sites/europa.dom/webapps/ROOT">
        Options Indexes FollowSymLinks
        DirectoryIndex index.jsp index.html index.htm
    </Directory>

    <Location "/WEB-INF/*">
        AllowOverride None
        deny from all
    </Location>

    <Location "/META-INF/*">
        AllowOverride None
        deny from all
    </Location>

    Alias /shop "/home/sites/europa.dom/webapps/shop"
```

```
    <Directory "/home/sites/europa.dom/webapps/shop">
        Options Indexes FollowSymLinks
        DirectoryIndex index.jsp index.html index.htm
    </Directory>

    <Location "/shop/WEB-INF/*">
        AllowOverride None
        deny from all
    </Location>

    <Location "/shop/META-INF/*">
        AllowOverride None
        deny from all
    </Location>

</VirtualHost>

<VirtualHost *>
    ServerName callisto.dom

    WebAppDeploy ROOT tomcat_warp /
    WebAppDeploy shop tomcat_warp /shop

    DocumentRoot "/home/sites/callisto.dom/webapps/ROOT"

    <Directory "/home/sites/callisto.dom/webapps/ROOT">
        Options Indexes FollowSymLinks
        DirectoryIndex index.jsp index.html index.htm
    </Directory>

    <Location "/WEB-INF/*">
        AllowOverride None
        deny from all
    </Location>

    <Location "/META-INF/*">
        AllowOverride None
        deny from all
    </Location>

    Alias /shop "/home/sites/callisto.dom/webapps/shop"

    <Directory "/home/sites/callisto.dom/webapps/shop">
        Options Indexes FollowSymLinks
        DirectoryIndex index.jsp index.html index.htm
    </Directory>

    <Location "/shop/WEB-INF/*">
        AllowOverride None
        deny from all
    </Location>

    <Location "/shop/META-INF/*">
```

```
        AllowOverride None
        deny from all
    </Location>

</VirtualHost>
```

Note how the default context is sent to the ROOT webapp. Another point to be noted is that in this configuration, Tomcat would serve even the static files of the web application. Also, when Tomcat serves the default context of the virtual host through WARP protocol, the <Directory> directives are ignored, and hence the <Directory> directives given above are strictly redundant. However, the <Location> directives are still processed by Apache. These are in a way redundant too. Without these <Location> directives, any requests of files in META-INF and WEB-INF directories would be passed by mod_webapp to Tomcat, which according to the Servlet API specification would reject such requests. Having the <Location> ACL directives in the Apache configuration actually stops such requests before they are passed to Tomcat.

This configuration file should be added to the Apache configuration using the Include directive, replacing the previous mod_jk configuration.

Configuring Tomcat 4.x

For configuring Tomcat to receive requests only through the WARP protocol of mod_webapp, we need to modify the server.xml file. In the last used server.xml, we have to replace the AJP <Connector> elements with WARP <Connector> ones. Also, since <ApacheConfig> can't handle WARP-based configurations, we remove all the <Listener> elements previously used to auto-generate Apache configuration files. The final server.xml file would look like this.

```
<Server port="8005" shutdown="SHUTDOWN" debug="0">
  <Service name="Tomcat-Apache-warp">

    <Connector className="org.apache.catalina.connector.warp.WarpConnector"
               port="8008" minProcessors="5" maxProcessors="75"
               acceptCount="10" debug="0"/>

    <Engine className="org.apache.catalina.connector.warp.WarpEngine"
            name="Apache" defaultHost="europa.dom" debug="0">

      <!-- Virtual host definition for europa.dom -->
      <Host name="europa.dom" debug="0"
            appBase="/home/sites/europa.dom/webapps"
            unpackWARs="true">
        <Valve className="org.apache.catalina.valves.AccessLogValve"
               directory="/home/sites/europa.dom/logs"
               prefix="europa_access."
               suffix=".log"
               pattern="common"/>

        <Logger className="org.apache.catalina.logger.FileLogger"
                directory="/home/sites/europa.dom/logs"
                prefix="europa_catalina."
                suffix=".log"
                timestamp="true"/>
```

```
        <Context path="" docBase="ROOT" debug="0"/>

        <Context path="/shop" docBase="shop" debug="0" />

      </Host>

      <!-- Virtual host definition for callisto.dom -->
      <Host name="callisto.dom" debug="0"
            appBase="/home/sites/callisto.dom/webapps"
            unpackWARs="true">

        <Valve className="org.apache.catalina.valves.AccessLogValve"
               directory="/home/sites/callisto.dom/logs"
               prefix="callisto_access."
               suffix=".log"
               pattern="common"/>

        <Logger className="org.apache.catalina.logger.FileLogger"
                directory="/home/sites/callisto.dom/logs"
                prefix="callisto_catalina."
                suffix=".log"
                timestamp="true"/>

        <Context path="" docBase="ROOT" debug="0"/>

        <Context path="/shop" docBase="shop" debug="0" />

      </Host>
    </Engine>
  </Service>
</Server>
```

We should now restart Apache and Tomcat and check the functioning of the two virtual hosts.

Fine-Tuning Shared Hosting

While we have discussed standard configuration of shared hosting with Tomcat, every host provider has several other specific requirements for providing Tomcat-based services to multiple clients. We now discuss two common configuration enhancements of Tomcat:

- Separate JVM for each virtual host
- Setting memory resource limits for each Tomcat JVM

Separate JVM for Each Virtual Host

In the entire previous configuration, we discussed how multiple hosts could be served from the same Tomcat process. While this would suffice for many providers, there would be others who would rightly raise the issue of security between the virtual hosts.

Since all the virtual hosts lie in the same request processing engine, trusted contexts in these virtual hosts (which can access Tomcat internal objects, load/unload other webapps and so on, like the default manager web application) would have access to the common Tomcat internal classes and can hence encroach on each other's territory.

This would be a logistical nightmare. One possible solution would be to set up one <Engine> per virtual host in the same server.xml file. Since each <Service> container element in the file could have only one child <Engine> element, this would mean adding one service per virtual host with the accompanying engine. However, since every service has its own set of connectors, this would also mean setting up different connectors listening on different ports for each engine. Therefore for each virtual host, mod_jk or mod_webapp in the Apache configuration would have to forward to a different worker.

While this removes the problem of sharing information between the virtual hosts, it still causes a bit of discomfort over how a relaxed security policy in Tomcat can give one domain enough privileges to bring down the whole Tomcat process.

The more secure, albeit more resource-intensive solution to such possible security problems is to have one Tomcat process per virtual host. Luckily, Tomcat 4.x has support for running multiple Tomcat processes using the same Tomcat binary installation.

Tomcat depends on two environment variables to find its internal classes. These are used to find the configuration-specific files. These variables are $CATALINA_HOME and $CATALINA_BASE.

- $CATALINA_HOME is needed for any Tomcat 4.x build to function properly. Tomcat uses this variable to find out its internal classes and libraries.
- $CATALINA_BASE is used by Tomcat to find the location of the configuration-specific files and directories like configuration files, the scratch directory where JSP pages are compiled, log files, and the various web applications. In case $CATALINA_BASE is not set, it defaults to the value of $CATALINA_HOME.

Therefore, for having separate Tomcat processes, all we have to do is set the value of $CATALINA_BASE to a different area of the disk for each virtual host with its own server.xml file. This server.xml file would have only one virtual host definition, different connector port numbers, and different directories for logs, scratch areas, and so on.

As an example, for the two virtual domains that we would be serving, we can store their respective configurations in two different directories under /home/sites/<domain-name>/catalina. So in our case, $CATALINA_HOME could be equal to /usr/local/tomcat/build. For europa.dom, $CATALINA_BASE could be /home/sites/europa.dom/catalina and for callisto.dom, $CATALINA_BASE could be set to /home/sites/callisto.dom/catalina.

The server.xml file of europa.dom located at /home/sites/callisto.dom/catalina/conf/server.xml should then be modified thus:

- Changing the attribute port of the <Server> root element that is used to shut down the Tomcat process. Let's keep it 8105.
- Changing the AJP connector port to 8109
- Ensuring that only the virtual host definition of europa.dom is present, and the default host of the <Engine> is set to this domain.

For the `server.xml` file of `callisto.dom` located at `/home/sites/callisto.dom/catalina/conf/server.xml`, the changes should be:

- Changing the `<Server>` port to `8205`
- Changing the AJP connector port to `8209`
- Ensuring that only the virtual host definition of `callisto.dom` is present, and the default host of the `<Engine>` element is set to this domain

Normally, the `worker.properties` file in Tomcat contains definitions for an AJP 1.2 and an AJP 1.3 worker, both working on the same host, and normally these definitions are sufficient because there is only one AJP worker running on the machine. In default configurations, only the AJP 1.3 worker is used. The `worker.properties` file could normally be kept anywhere, but should we keep it in `$CATALINA_HOME/conf/jk`. The Apache `modjk` directive `JkWorkersFile` should contain the path to this file.

However, in this case, we are running two different Tomcat instances each with an AJP 1.3 worker listening on a unique port. Therefore, we need to inform our Apache connector using the `worker.properties` file, that we would be connecting to two different workers running on different ports.

The AJP worker properties file is changed to look as shown below. In the `worker.list` parameter, we have mentioned that we would be connecting to two different workers. One named `ajp_europa`, we would use to pass requests to the Tomcat instance running the `europa.dom` domain. The other worker that we need to connect to is named `ajp_callisto`, and we would use this to connect to the Tomcat instance serving the `callisto.dom` domain:

```
worker.list=ajp_europa, ajp_callisto

worker.ajp_europa.port=8109
worker.ajp_europa.host=localhost
worker.ajp_europa.type=ajp13
worker.ajp_europa.lbfactor=1

worker.ajp_callisto.port=8209
worker.ajp_callisto.host=localhost
worker.ajp_callisto.type=ajp13
worker.ajp_callisto.lbfactor=1
```

We then proceed to configure each of these worker connections. The type of both these workers is AJP 1.3. We therefore set `worker.`*`workername`*`.type` of each of these workers to be the same. The different ports to connect to for each of these workers is stated using the `worker.`*`workername`*`.port`. For each of our workers, we set the port to the one mentioned in the AJP `<Connector>` element of the corresponding Tomcat instance configuration.

For example, the Tomcat instance serving the `europa.dom` domain has its AJP1.3 connector listening on port 8109. Therefore `worker.ajp_europa.port` is set to `8109`. The `worker.workername.host` parameter of both these workers is set to `localhost` because Tomcat is running on the same machine as Apache. This parameter is useful when you want to run Tomcat in a physically different machine than Apache. The `worker.workername.lbfactor` parameter is not useful here, but comes in handy when you want `mod_jk` to load-balance connections to a Tomcat instance over two or more AJP workers:

The Apache mod_jk.conf file is now changed to reflect the new worker names. All references of the worker name ajp13 in the definition of the VirtualHost section for the europa.dom domain are changed to ajp_europa. Similarly, all the references of the worker name ajp13 in the definition of the VirtualHost section for the callisto.dom domain are changed to ajp_callisto.

All that is required now is to start the two instances of Tomcat with the $CATALINA_BASE set to the catalina subdirectory of the domains. For this we write a shell script to start all the Tomcat instances as required. We create this shell script with the name start_sites.sh in $CATALINA_HOME and make it executable:

```
#!/bin/bash

SITE_ROOT="/home/sites"
SITES=`ls ${SITE_ROOT}`

for x in ${SITES}
do
        CATALINA_BASE="${SITE_ROOT}/${x}/catalina"
        echo "Starting server: ${x} . Using CATALINA_BASE=${CATALINA_BASE}"

        CATALINA_BASE=${CATALINA_BASE}
        bin/startup.sh
done
```

Similarly we create a shell script for shutting down all the servers. This shell script is created with the name shut_sites.sh in $CATALINA_HOME and also made executable.

```
#!/bin/bash

SITE_ROOT="/home/sites"
SITES=`ls ${SITE_ROOT}`

for x in ${SITES}
do
        CATALINA_BASE="${SITE_ROOT}/${x}/catalina"
        echo "Shutting server: ${x} . Using CATALINA_BASE=${CATALINA_BASE}"

        CATALINA_BASE=${CATALINA_BASE}
        bin/shutdown.sh
done
```

Now we stop all the instances of Apache and Tomcat in the system. We start the Tomcat instances using the start_sites.sh script and follow it by starting the Apache daemon.

These startup and shutdown scripts could be now used in a system initialization script like the rc init scripts kept in /etc/init.d on Linux systems.

Thus we now have independent Tomcat processes for each of the virtual sites.

Setting Memory Limits To the Tomcat JVM

Whether we have all the virtual hosts running under the same Tomcat process or we allocate separate Tomcat processes for each of them, we are still at risk of a resource problem.

The problem is that a Java VM on starting up allocates a fixed amount of memory for dynamic allocation. With a number of JVMs running, this number might either be too high choking the virtual hosts that need more memory, or it might be too low, causing sub-optimal performance for the various hosts.

Depending on the number and the type of virtual hosts that you are running, you might want to tweak this setting to your advantage. This setting of memory, more specifically heap memory (which is used while allocating all dynamic data structures), is done by sending a command-line parameter to the Java executable while the Tomcat process is started.

The options that can be set are:

- Initial Java heap size – Using parameter (`-Xms`)
- Maximum Java heap size – Using parameter (`-Xmx`)
- Java thread stack size – Using parameter (`-Xss`)

For example to set an initial heap size of 20 Mb (or 20 * 1024 * 1024 =20971520), you should pass the parameter `-Xms20971520` to the JVM (or the more succinct `-Xms20m`).

Factors Determining Memory Requirements

The nature of applications being run on the JVM determines the optimum heap sizes. Heavy multithreaded servers like Tomcat, which have a tendency to allocate/deallocate objects a lot, are quite sensitive to heap size because a lot of memory can be held up at times waiting to be garbage-collected. Increasing the heap size in such scenarios could help a lot.

On the other hand, very large heap sizes should be avoided by keeping `-Xmx` low. If other apps overload the machine, the heap could start using the swap space (space allocated on the hard disk as an extension of RAM, when all the memory in RAM has been used up. This is also known as **virtual memory**), thus reducing the performance of the system significantly. While a reasonable amount of swap usage is common for production servers, serious cases of continuous swapping commonly known as thrashing could slow down the machine to a crawl.

The JVM normally starts with as little memory as possible as specified in `-Xms`, and then slowly increases memory needs as required by the application to the limit specified in `-Xmx`. If you have enough memory, you can set `-Xms` to the same value as `-Xmx`. This could lead to faster startup time for the Java application. Always keep `-Xms` to a reasonable size to make applications more responsive.

The default value for `-Xms` and `-Xmx`, which differs from platform to platform, is normally too small for server applications. Also, the heap resizing from `-Xms` to `-Xmx` happening slowly over time, causes the server to slowly pick up performance. To reduce this startup latency you can set both these limits to be the same. However, if your needs are minimal, you would lose the advantage of the JVM automatically choosing the optimum heap size (between `-Xms` and `-Xmx`) for your application.

If you are adding processors to your SMP (Symmetric MultiProcessing) machine be sure to increase memory, because unlike memory allocations, which can be parallelized over the SMP, the garbage collection could not be, and therefore it could soon turn out to be the bottleneck in your application.

Heavy database-oriented applications consume a lot of memory because of result sets, temporary tables resulting from `JOIN` statements, and so on.

In the end, your optimum heap sizes could only be determined by your specific needs like:

- How many Tomcat instances would you be running?
- What kind of traffic do you expect on the site?
- Does your web application use a lot of data transactions involving heavily filled up databases?
- How much RAM are you willing to put on the machine?
- How many processors does your machine have?

Setting Memory Limits in Tomcat

The parameter that you want to pass to the JVM can be set in the environment variable `JAVA_OPTS`. Let's modify our earlier multiple Tomcat process starting script to send these options to the JVM, so that each of the virtual hosts is restricted to these limits.

The modified script would look like the following. Here we are setting the minimum and the maximum heap limits of each Tomcat instance to 20 MB and 50 MB respectively:

```
#!/bin/bash

JVM_OPTIONS="-Xms20m -Xmx50m"
SITE_ROOT="/home/sites"
SITES=`ls ${SITE_ROOT}`

for x in ${SITES}
do
        CATALINA_BASE="${SITE_ROOT}/${x}/catalina"
        echo "Starting server: ${x} . Using CATALINA_BASE=${CATALINA_BASE}"

        CATALINA_BASE=${CATALINA_BASE}
        JAVA_OPTS="${JVM_OPTIONS}"
        bin/startup.sh
done
```

You can modify the values in `JVM_OPTIONS` as you think fit for your hosting requirements.

Summary

In this chapter we went through various topics related to using Tomcat-based sites in a shared hosting scenario. We initially took a look at the concept of shared hosting, and the various types of shared hosting that are possible. We then looked briefly at how Apache needs to be configured to support virtual hosting.

For configuring Tomcat to work with virtual hosting, we examined two currently popular versions of Tomcat – version 3.3 which supports the older Servlet 2.2/JSP 1.1 specifications, and version 4.x which supports the new Servlet 2.3/JSP 1.2 specifications. In both these versions, we configured Tomcat to work both as a standalone web server, and as a servlet/JSP engine for Apache. Apache could be configured to use the `mod_jk` connector to communicate with Tomcat, while in Tomcat 4.x; we also have the option of using the `mod_webapp` connector. We then examined some commonly required performance and security enhancements for using virtual hosts with Tomcat.

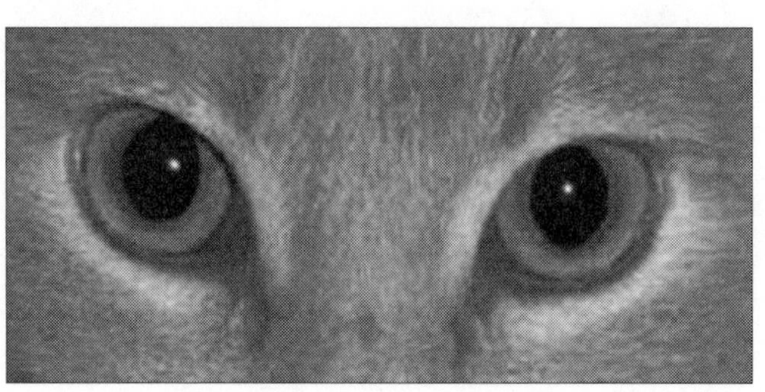

20

Server Load Testing

By now, we've learned how to install, configure, and secure a distributed Tomcat environment. The saddest moment for a system administrator is to endure the hard work of installing, configuring, and tweaking an installation only to have it subverted as the application server buckles under a production load. Server load testing is an often neglected, but highly valuable, way to save us this anguish.

Server load testing is the process of simulating client requests so that a server can experience large amounts of activity in a controlled environment. The purpose of load testing is to understand the scalability and performance limits of a server before it is exposed to a heavy production load.

This chapter will give us an understanding of server load testing, and by the end of it we will:

- Understand the elements of scalability
- Know how to load test with the Jakarta JMeter framework
- Have the ability to interpret the results of these load tests to drive the architectural decisions we make at deployment time
- Be able to compare server load testing and application load testing

Elements of Scalability

We hear a lot about scalability in the information technology field. So what is scalability? And, what are the various factors that affect it?

Scalability is the ability of a system to handle an increased load without severely degrading its performance or reliability. Web site scalability is defined by the difference in performance between a site handling a small number of clients and a site handling a larger number of clients, as well as the ability to maintain the same level of performance by simply adding resources to the installation.

There are many factors that affect scalability of a web application, including server hardware configuration, networking equipment and bandwidth, server operating system, volume and quantity of back-end data, and so on. In this section, we will focus on some of the factors that are within our control, as administrators of a Tomcat installation. The load testing sections will provide an opportunity to explore these factors in your own environment.

Software Configuration

In setting up and configuring Tomcat, there are several decisions you need to make that will affect the scalability of your installation. We will discuss some of the major decision areas here, but this is by no means an exhaustive list.

JVM Settings

We've heard a surprising number of stories about frustrated system administrators who have gone through development and testing of an application in a new servlet container or application server without problems, subsequently facing embarrassing outages at production time due to their application server running out of memory.

The JVM sets memory usage for itself, the limits of which are configurable via command-line switches to the Java Runtime Environment. There are two very important switches to remember as we set up a new Tomcat instance:

Argument	Description
`-Xms<size>`	The initial heap size for the JVM
`-Xmx<size>`	The maximum heap size for the JVM

If these parameters are not explicitly set, the JVM will use its defaults. The defaults are dependent on the version of the JVM in use.

Initial heap size is the less frequently needed setting. It specifies the amount of RAM to allocate to the Java heap – the location where object instances are stored – at the time the JVM starts up. In a memory-intensive, heavily loaded application, initial heap size can be important; if the JVM starts up with a very small heap size and it is quickly pounded by many requests that require large object instantiations, it will struggle to keep up with the memory allocation needs, and potentially may not recover in some situations.

The more frequently used parameter is the maximum heap size. It specifies the upper limit of RAM that the JVM will allocate to the heap. In a data-intensive application with long-lived objects, small memory usage may quickly build up. If the memory required to run an application exceeds the maximum heap size configured, the JVM will fail with a `java.lang.OutOfMemory` error. This offers us protection from memory usage issues at a system-wide level, but it is also our responsibility to be very careful in making decisions with respect to maximum heap size. In any new application server setup, JVM maximum heap size is a crucial parameter to keep an eye on.

> **It is advisable to modify the JVM defaults for maximum heap size, since they are insufficient to sustain even moderately sized web sites.**

This topic is covered in more detail in Chapter 3.

Connector Choice and Configuration

As discussed in Chapters 11-13, there are three supported connectors for Tomcat 4.0 and, from the various criteria used to decide on using them, performance is one that should not be ignored. Before deciding on a connector, we should perform load tests against each of them to properly compare their performance.

Regardless of which connector we choose, we must be aware of several of the parameters, defined in Tomcat's `server.xml`, that may affect our server's performance. Each connector type, by way of the `<Connector>` element, allows the configuration of the following performance-critical attributes. For an exhaustive discussion of these elements, see Chapters 11-13.

enableLookups

The default value for this attribute is `true`. It looks up each incoming IP address and attempts to resolve it to a host name. While this can come in handy while viewing log files, it puts an extra load on the server as well as the network, and should therefore be used with caution.

minProcessors

A processor is a thread that handles requests for a connector on a given port. Setting `minProcessors` too high can result in a large number of unnecessary threads, which will put an extra burden on the JVM. Setting it too low can cause delays in responses which come in soon after the server starts, as the server will have to spawn a separate thread for incoming requests if it is already servicing the number of clients equal to this setting.

During load tests, we can monitor thread counts via operating system-specific tools, such as `ps` in most Unix versions. If we see this number rapidly increasing and eventually reaching a plateau, the number of threads reached at the plateau makes a good general `minProcessors` setting. The default setting for `minProcessors` is 5.

maxProcessors

This setting imposes a limit on the number of processors (threads) the server will start, regardless of the server load. If the server receives more simultaneous requests for a given connection than this setting is configured for, the requests will block until a thread is freed to handle them. If this number is set too high, heavily loaded sites run the risk of a performance slowdown as the JVM struggles to manage the large number of threads and network connections that will be created.

Again, with `maxProcessors`, we can monitor thread counts during load testing to get an idea of what our setting should be. If we see the thread count reach near what the `maxProcessors` setting is configured at, followed by a server performance slow-down, we should probably then increase this setting and repeat the experiment. The default setting for `maxProcessors` is 20.

acceptCount

Closely related to the previous two attributes, acceptCount specifies how many connections the server will accept, while waiting for a free connection processor. Incoming connections over and above this limit will be refused. While it might be tempting to increase this to a very high number, setting it too high could result in your system running out of free file descriptors, which can cause processes – or under extreme circumstance, operating systems – to crash or become unstable. The default setting for this attribute is 10.

The settings we choose for these attributes will be largely dependent on the types of applications we are deploying and the nature of the requests that will be serviced. For example, a site that rapidly receives a large number of requests that can be serviced very quickly could get by with a lower maxProcessors setting, but might initially benefit from increasing minProcessors to a number greater than the default of 5. Applications with slower back-end response times might require maxProcessors, and even acceptCount, to be increased beyond their defaults.

Session Configuration

Tomcat's default session manager is very fast, as it stores its data in memory. However, there is an obvious trade-off between the speed and memory consumption on the server. The primary tool we have to manage this trade-off is the <session-timeout> subelement of the <session-config> element in the server.xml file. We must weigh our memory concerns against the needs of the application and its users. For example, an application requiring a great deal of complex data entry might have a requirement that its sessions stay active for at least an hour. It may be necessary to increase the maximum heap size of the JVM to accommodate a higher <session-timeout> setting.

In extreme cases, where sessions need to be active for hours at a time, such as a data entry application or a point-of-sale system, it might be worthwhile to consider using Tomcat's persistent manager implementation. It allows inactive sessions to be paged to a persistent store – such as the filesystem or a JDBC-accessible data source – until they are needed again. Reactivation of the sessions will be sluggish in terms of performance, but the memory trade-off might prove to be worth the cost.

Deployment Architecture

For a system as simple as Tomcat, it's surprising how many different architectural configurations we can create with it. The simplest, a single stand alone Tomcat server using the HTTP connector, might be appropriate for very small installations. However, as load increases and applications become more resource-intensive, deployment architecture can make or break an application's performance.

Questions to ask at this stage are:

- **Is one JVM enough?**
  It's possible under certain conditions for the JVM itself to become a bottleneck, even if a single server is sufficient. Our experience has shown that the JVM isn't optimized for dealing with huge amounts of memory, so breaking it into multiple processes on the same system may help.
- **Is one physical server enough?**
  If application performance is constrained by the limits of the operating system or server hardware, it might be necessary to load balance two or more application servers.
- **Is the Tomcat web server sufficient?**
  While Tomcat has an HTTP connector, it isn't optimized as an HTTP server. Bringing Apache or other supported web servers into the picture would increase performance as these products are designed for handling only HTTP requests.

- **Is one web server enough?**
  It's possible to load balance multiple web servers, even leaving a single Tomcat instance behind all of them.

Asking these questions before and during load testing will give us a targeted set of goals, which will help us to systematically narrow down or validate our architectural choices.

Application Code

No matter how hard we try or how smart we are, a well-configured server is no match for inefficient application code deployed within it. If a developer chooses, for example, to create synchronized static variables and reference them in every request or to open database connections and never close them, there is no amount of server configuration wizardry that will save us from the trouble that lies ahead.

The best weapon we can have in such a situation is a clear understanding of the unadulterated performance of our server. Human nature dictates that, when the going gets bad, the developer gets defensive. How many times have we heard, "It worked fine on my PC, it must be the server that's slowing it down?" Regardless of what the reality is, in such cases, the onus is always on the server administrator to identify the bottleneck. Thorough pre-application load testing and analysis will not only allow us to cast off undeserved blame but also to more quickly identify application performance bottlenecks as and when they crop up.

Load Testing with JMeter

Now it's time to get down to the actual business of load testing. We've considered some of the variables that might affect our system's scalability, and we're ready to start testing the system's limits. The first thing we're going to need, unless we've got an adequate number of people with web browsers and a lot of spare time, is some software to help us simulate a heavy load.

There are numerous options available, including open source software, commercial packages – some affordable, some extremely expensive – and the often erroneously-chosen option of writing our own load tester. In our case, as we focus on the Apache Jakarta collection of software, we need not look very far. Tomcat's sister project, JMeter, fits the bill quite nicely.

Though JMeter is capable of load testing FTP, JDBC datasources, and even Java objects, we will focus this discussion on load testing HTTP servers and applications.

Installing and Running JMeter

At the time of writing, JMeter's home page is located at http://jakarta.apache.org/jmeter/. From here, you can download the latest JMeter distribution as either a gzip or ZIP archive. This archive includes both source and binaries; installation is as simple as unpacking the archive.

After unpacking JMeter, you'll notice that the directory structure within is both intuitive and familiar, as there is a welcome amount of consistency between the directory structures of all Jakarta projects. Initially getting started is as simple as entering the `bin` directory and running either `jmeter.bat` (on Windows) or the `jmeter` shell script (on Linux or Unix).

Making and Understanding Test Plans

Having started JMeter, we find ourselves staring at JMeter's Swing interface pictured below:

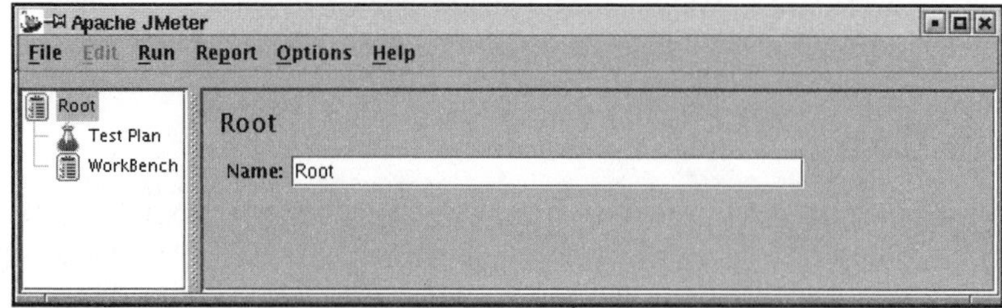

JMeter's user interface consists of a tree in the left-hand pane, representing the list of items and actions we can add as we go along, and a right-hand pane that provides configuration forms and output windows for items we add to the left-hand pane.

At the heart of any JMeter session is the **test plan**, which is a list of actions that we want JMeter to perform. The test plan is a top-level node in the test tree. Elements are added to the test plan by right-clicking on its node and selecting Add from the popup menu.

Let's get started with the simplest possible test plan for testing an HTTP server before getting into more advanced options in the sections to come. The first element in every test plan is a **thread group**. The similarity of the name thread group to the `ThreadGroup` concept in Java development is not a coincidence. A thread group is a collection of elements, having its own set of Java threads and a separate configuration.

By right-clicking the Test Plan node in the left-hand pane and selecting Add, we see that a thread group is the only available element directly under a test plan. After adding the thread group, you can click its icon in the left-hand pane to expose the thread group configuration pane. As promised, we'll keep it simple for now and leave the default configuration values, but we'll take time to understand the options available to us:

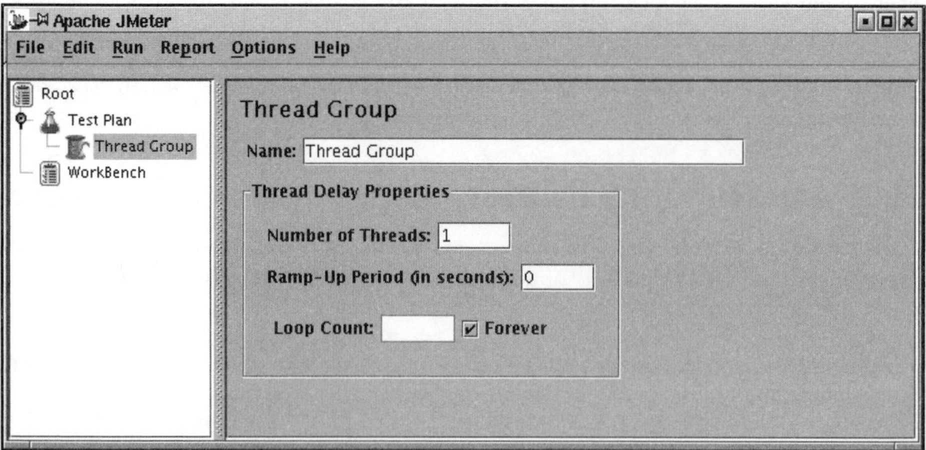

The following configuration parameters are available:

- **Name**
  The name doesn't need to be changed in a simple test plan, but if we were to have multiple thread groups, it would be advantageous to choose a more descriptive name that reflects its purpose.
- **Number of Threads**
  This is how many threads we would like the thread group to spawn to carry out its work. If we wanted to simulate a heavy load, we would want to increase this number to simulate simultaneous users.
- **Ramp-Up Period (in seconds)**
  JMeter will start with one thread and will add threads evenly over the course of the specified period until the Number of Threads configured above has been reached.
- **Loop Count**
  This is how many times we want to execute the elements of this thread group. The default is Forever, which means the elements of the test plan will execute until we tell them to stop.

Now that we have a thread group, we're ready to actually start doing something with it. Right-clicking on the Thread Group icon will produce the same popup menu as before, only the Add menu will have many more options to choose from. Let's now select Generative Controller and then HTTP Request. This is shown in the screenshot below:

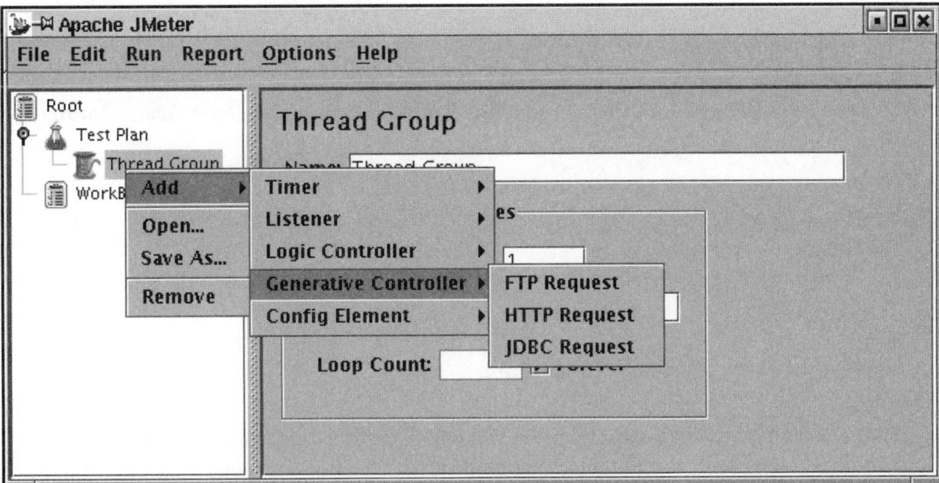

Generative controllers are so named, because they **generate** requests to a server. Clicking on the freshly added HTTP Request icon will expose its configuration panel to the right. This is a much busier screen than the thread group configuration one as shown:

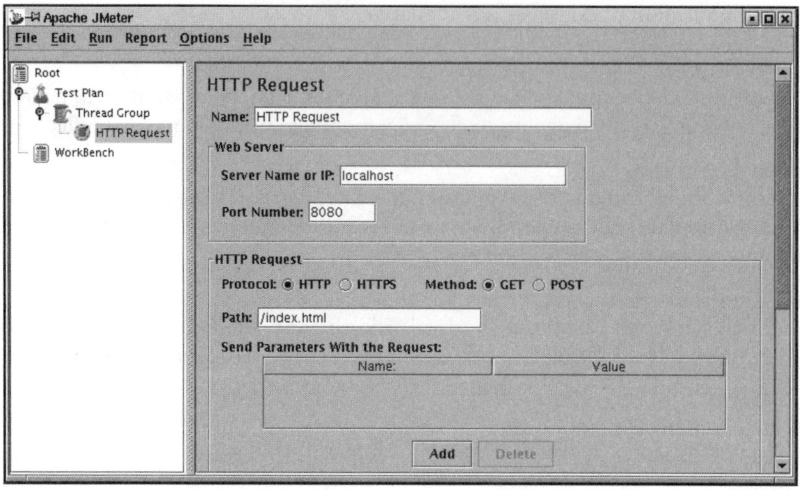

Here's a rundown of the configuration options available:

- **Name**
  This is the same as in the thread group configuration.
- **Server Name or IP**
  A resolvable hostname or IP address of the server we want to test.
- **Port Number**
  The port number of the HTTP server. The standard is 80 unless specifically configured differently.
- **Protocol**
  HTTP or HTTPS.
- **Method**
  Sets whether the test should send a `GET` or a `POST` request, which depends on what the page we are requesting is expecting.
- **Path**
  The URI of the page we are going to test.
- **Parameters**
  If we're testing a dynamic application, the page might expect some parameters to be submitted along with the request. For example, if we're testing shopping cart functionality of an online store, we might send a model number for the product to add to our shopping cart.
- **Filename**
  Some web applications accept file uploads via HTTP `POST`. This is to specify which file we would like to upload with the request.
- **Parameter Name**
  The file will be uploaded as a key/value pair. This is the name of the key that the web application will use to reference the file in the request.
- **MIME Type**
  The type of the file we are uploading. For example, an HTML file would have a MIME type `text/html` and an Adobe Acrobat file would be `application/pdf`.

- **Retrieve All Images and Java Applets**
  If this is set, when a request is made for a web page, the page will be parsed and all embedded images and applets will be downloaded as part of the request. If we were to test a graphics-intensive site for performance, this would more accurately reflect the end-user experience, as the bulk of the response time would be apportioned to the downloading of images.

Again, we'll keep this simple by filling in only the bare minimum number of fields for our first test. Assuming we have a Tomcat installation on the same machine from which we are running JMeter, we can set the Server Name to localhost, Port to 8080 (the default HTTP connector port for Tomcat), and the Path to `/index.html`. If we were to run JMeter on a different physical machine from the server, we would simply need to set the Server Name to the appropriate host or IP of the server we wanted to load test. All other parameters can remain unchanged for now. When we're done, our configuration should look like the previous screenshot.

We have now done enough to start pounding our Tomcat installation with requests for its index page. We can start the test by selecting Start from the JMeter's Run menu. However, the example isn't very practical so far, since there's no way to capture or view the results of our test. Let's continue with one more test element before running our first test.

JMeter was designed to internally separate the execution of a test plan from the collection and analysis of the test plan's results. For those that are interested, this is accomplished internally by use of the Observer or, as it is sometimes called, Event Listener design pattern. This is reflected in the JMeter UI by its use of the listener terminology. Controllers are responsible for doing things and listeners are responsible for reacting to those actions. Thus, if we want access to the results of a test plan, we must use one of the JMeter listeners.

To finish off our simple test plan, let's add one now. Again, right-click on the Thread Group icon, select Add and then Listener. From the several built-in listeners, select View Results Tree.

Selecting the View Results Tree icon in the left-hand pane will expose its output window on the right. There is no configuration required for this listener. When running a test with a view results tree listener, we can watch each response as it is received from the server. Selecting the response from the upper part of the right-hand pane, we will see the actual data returned in the bottom part of that pane.

Before starting the test, we should save our work. Right-click on the Test Plan icon in the left-hand pane and choose Save As from the popup menu. For consistency, use the default `.jmx` extension when saving your test plan.

We are now ready to run our first test.

Now, click the View Results Tree icon, and choose Start from the Run menu on the menu bar. You should now see the Root node in the upper-right pane change to a folder icon as test results start to trickle in. Double-click that node to open it, revealing the individual test results contained within. Selecting any of the results will change the bottom pane to show you the data received in the response, as well as the load time (in milliseconds), the HTTP response code, and the HTTP response message.

The following figure shows our completed test plan with the view results tree listener activated:

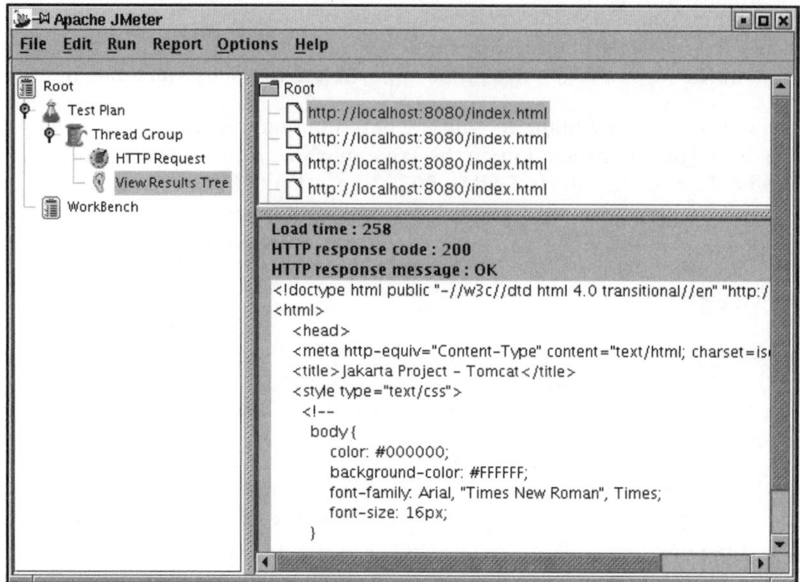

Since we didn't tell the thread group not to loop forever, JMeter will continue making requests until we either close the JMeter application or choose Stop from the Run menu on the menu bar.

JMeter Features

We now know how to load test a web server and how to view the results of the test. We can get some idea of how well our Tomcat server is responding to the test, in terms of load time and stability. If we were content to manually click through each result in the View Results Tree window, visually inspecting the full page returned, this might be enough. Fortunately, JMeter provides many more features to aid us in capturing and analyzing load data. There are five major feature types in JMeter:

- Timer
- Listener
- Logic controller
- Generative controller
- Config element

We will present HTTP-related highlights of these feature groups in the sections to follow.

Timer

In the configuration presented in the previous example, JMeter will spawn one thread and start making requests as fast as it and the server being tested can keep up. In real-world cases, it might not make sense to so relentlessly pound the server with a constant onslaught of requests. Only in exceptional cases will a server be faced with a large number of simultaneous requests with no delay in between them.

To spare our server the full brunt of this load, not to mention making the load more representative of the real world, we can add a timer to our thread group. This will introduce some intelligent logic, which regulates the frequency and speed of each thread's requests. There are three types of timers currently included with JMeter – two random timers and one constant timer.

The constant timer, as one might guess, inserts a configurable and constant delay between each request for a given thread. The delay interval is specified in terms of milliseconds and its default is 300.

The two random timers are Gaussian random timer and uniform random timer. These timers both simulate real-world traffic more accurately by inserting randomly calculated delays between the requests for each thread. The uniform random timer appends a truly random delay to a configurable constant delay, while the Gaussian random timer uses a statistical calculation to generate a pseudo-random delay. Each random timer takes a configurable constant time to which its random calculation will be appended.

To add a timer, right-click a thread group, select Timer from the Add menu, and choose the timer we want. Timers added to a thread group will affect the entire thread group to which they are added, but will not affect peer thread groups. Adding multiple timers to a thread group will have an additive effect on the delay between requests.

Listener

As discussed previously, listeners are JMeter's way to monitor and react to the results of the requests it sends. The previous example used the view results tree listener to show the data returned from the server as well as the response time, the HTTP response code, and the HTTP response message. As we saw previously, a listener is added by right-clicking on a thread group, and selecting the desired listener from the Listener submenu under the Add menu.

The listener only listens the activity from the thread group it is added to. So, if we have two thread groups added to our test plan, thread group A and thread group B, a listener added to thread group B will be oblivious to anything that happens in the scope of thread group A. The following is a list of the listeners currently provided by default with JMeter:

Listener	Description
Modification controller	With the help of response-based modifier child elements, this listener can modify request content, based on programmatic factors, such as parsed HTML output.
Assertion results	Views the output of the Assertion elements of a thread group.
File reporter	Writes the URLs sampled and their associated response times to a file for further analysis or posterity.
View results	Provides a real-time view of test results.
View results tree	Same as View Results, but organizes the results into a tree.
View graph tree	Real-time collection of graphs, organized by the URL or resource sampled.

Table continued on following page

Listener	Description
Thread group	Simply a container for additional elements that may have separate threading or looping behaviors.
Graphfull results	A cumulative graph of the response times of each request made.
Graph results	A simple graph view, plotting individual data points, mean response time, and standard deviation of response time for all requests in its parent thread group.
Spline visualizer	A graph view of all data points made during a test plan run. Will show the results as an interpolated curve.

Each listener can be grouped into one of a few categories:

- Visualization listeners
- Data listeners
- Other listeners

Visualization Listeners

View graph tree, **graphfull results**, **graph results**, and **spline visualizer** all create graphical, real-time depictions of the test results. Graph results, pictured below, is the simplest and most popular of these, plotting mean response time in blue, standard deviation in red, and each individual data point in black (which are kind of hard to see in black and white, but the standard deviation is the upper line, the average response time is the lower line, and the data points are the dots):

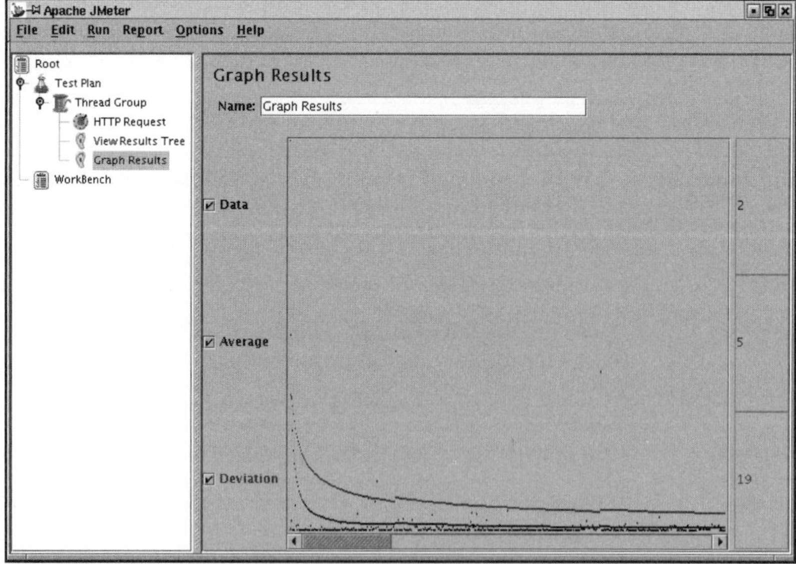

The standard deviation is about 19 seconds and the mean response time was 5 seconds. Mean and deviation are explained later in the *Interpreting Test Results* section.

Data Listeners

File reporter, **view results**, and **view results tree** concern themselves with capturing the raw data, response time, and return codes returned from the server. While view results and view results tree are useful as status checkers while running tests, file reporter is perhaps the most important of the listeners. File reporters perform the simple task of logging response time to a file, as well as capturing optional data such as which resource was requested and parameters sent with the request. This is an important tool, because it allows you to keep your data for posterity as well as to import the data into other more sophisticated tools for more detailed analysis (we'll talk about some of these tools later):

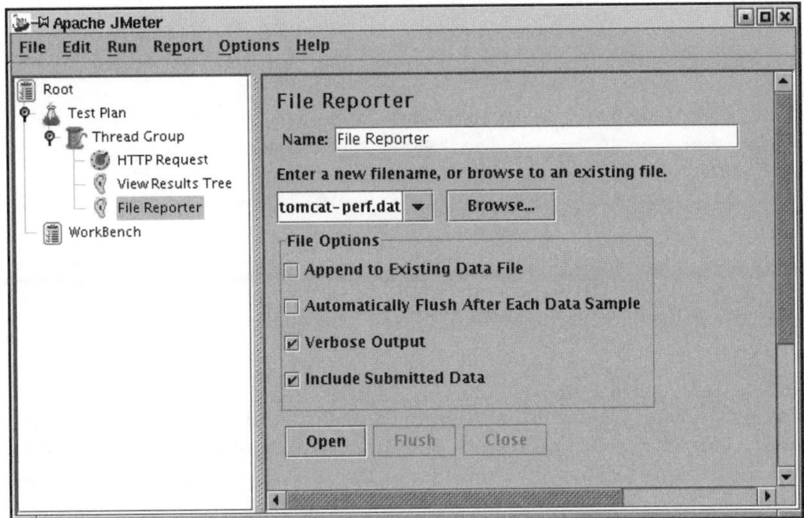

File Reporter offers the following configuration options:

- **Name**
  Descriptive name for the File Reporter element as it will appear in the test plan.
- **Filename**
  The path to the output file to be created by the file reporter.
- **Append to Existing Data File**
  If checked, the file reporter will append to existing data in the file. If not checked, the file will be overwritten each time it is opened.
- **Automatically Flush After Each Data Sample**
  If checked, responses will be written to the file as they come in. If left unchecked, the Flush button at the bottom of the screen must be clicked to write any pending data to the file.
- **Verbose Output**
  This will include the resource requested (such as the URL) as a column in the output data if checked.
- **Include Submitted Data**
  Will include any parameters submitted with the request as a column in the output data.

At the bottom of the File Reporter configuration screen are three buttons: Open, Flush, and Close. Before starting a test run, we must click the Open button to open the file for writing. If we have left the Automatically Flush After Each Data Sample option unchecked, we will need to press the Flush button whenever we want the response data to be finally written to our output file. After running a test, we must click the Close button to release JMeter's hold on the output file.

Using the above configuration and an HTTP request with one parameter, the following text-based data file was created:

```
# Sample data created by null

#       URL                                      Milliseconds  Data

http://test.wrox.com:80/tomcat_load?NAME=Scott 2060,NAME=Scott
http://test.wrox.com:80/tomcat_load?NAME=Scott 2280,NAME=Scott
http://test.wrox.com:80/tomcat_load?NAME=Scott 2440,NAME=Scott
http://test.wrox.com:80/tomcat_load?NAME=Scott 2610,NAME=Scott
```

The first entry is the URL that we tested, the number is the response time in milliseconds, and the third item is the data we sent to the URL. This data could be easily imported into another tool, such as OpenOffice, Microsoft Excel, SAS, or Minitab for detailed analysis.

Other Listeners

The three remaining default JMeter listeners perform distinct and unrelated tasks. These three listeners are: **modification controller**, **assertion results**, and **thread group**. We already know about thread groups. Its presence on the Listeners menu allows us to nest thread groups within thread groups.

The modification controller is a container element for a special type of listener, whose job it is to modify requests before they are sent. Requests whose samples we want to modify can be added as subelements under a modification controller. Additionally, we will need to add a response-based modifier to the modification controller, which will actually do the real modification work. JMeter comes with one such modifier, the HTTP HTML link parser. This modifier can be used to change the behavior of subsequent requests using the parsed output of prior requests. For example, with an HTTP HTML link parser, we could change the URLs we are going to sample based on the links on the first page we get back from the server.

To use the HTTP HTML link parser, we must first add an HTTP request generative controller to our test plan that downloads an initial page containing the links to be parsed and used in successive requests.

So, for example, if we have a site that has a portal page containing links to each of the site's sub-pages, our first step would be to create an initial HTTP request generative controller that downloads this page. Then, in the same thread group, we can add a modification controller from the Logic Controller menu. Under this element, we should add an HTTP HTML link parser from the Response Based Modifiers menu and another HTTP request generative controller. The HTTP HTML link parser requires no additional configuration.

Under the new HTTP request generative controller, we can set the Path attribute to .*, which will instruct the HTTP HTML link parser to insert all links parsed as successive Path settings for HTTP requests made using this element. The Path can be any valid Perl5-style regular expression.

So, for example, if the first HTTP request we make is to the default Tomcat 4.0 index page, we could set the path for the HTTP request generative controller inside the modification controller to be `/examples/.*`, which would match any parsed link from that page under the `/examples/` path on the Tomcat server. Using the Tomcat index page as an example, a view of the finished element tree is pictured below:

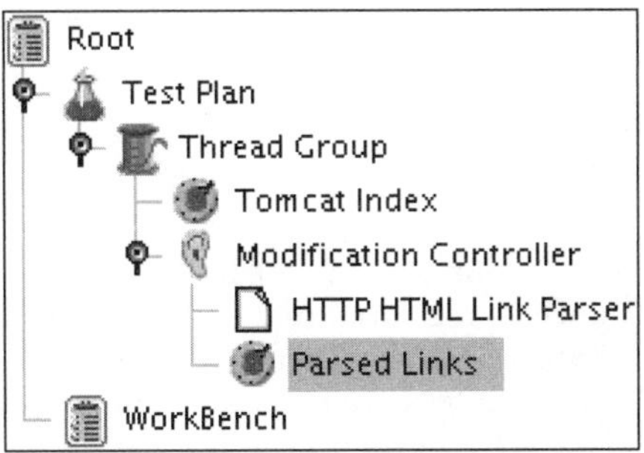

In this scenario, we first added an HTTP request generative controller named Tomcat Index, pointing to the / page of our Tomcat server. We then added a modification controller containing an HTTP HTML link parser and a new HTTP request generative controller, which we called Parsed Links. As the Path attribute of the Parsed Links HTTP request generative controller, we specified /examples/.*. Under Server Name, we specify the name of the Tomcat server.

When executed, this test plan will first download the Tomcat index page and parse it. It will also parse all the links on the same host that match the regular expression `/examples/.*`, which the Parsed Links HTTP request generative controller will then cycle through.

If we also wanted to parse links to other hosts, we could also use the same regular expressions in the Server Name field of the Parsed Links HTTP request generative controller. And, similarly, if we wanted to dynamically parse form options from a `<select>` element of a form, we could use regular expressions in the Name: column of Send Parameters With Request.

The last kind of listener available is the **assertion results listener**. Assertion results allow us to view the results of Assertion elements that have been added to generative controllers. We will take a more detailed look at both assertion and assertion results in the section on generative controllers, later in this chapter.

Logic Controller

A logic controller's primary purpose is to manage the execution flow of a test plan. They are containers for other executable Test Plan elements. Logic controllers that are added to a thread group – or even as a sub-node of another logic controller – will be treated by their parent execution context as a single node to be executed. Elements added beneath logic controller nodes will be executed according to the rules of the specific logic controller to which they are added.

Like thread groups, logic controllers create a separate visibility space for listeners, timers, and other elements, which are context-specific. We can think of logic controllers as the closest approximation JMeter test plans have with the `while`, `for`, and `function` constructs of typical programming languages.

We'll proceed with a discussion of the built-in logic controllers that currently ship with JMeter:

- Interleave controller
- Simple controller
- Loop controller
- Modification controller
- Once only controller

Interleave Controller

The **interleave controller** will execute one of its sub-elements each time its parent container loops. It will execute them in the order in which they are listed in the configuration tree. For example, if we were to create an interleave controller with four elements under a thread group set to loop 14 times, JMeter would execute the entire set of interleave controller sub-elements three times, and would then execute only the first two sub-elements a fourth time (4 + 4 + 4 +2 == 14):

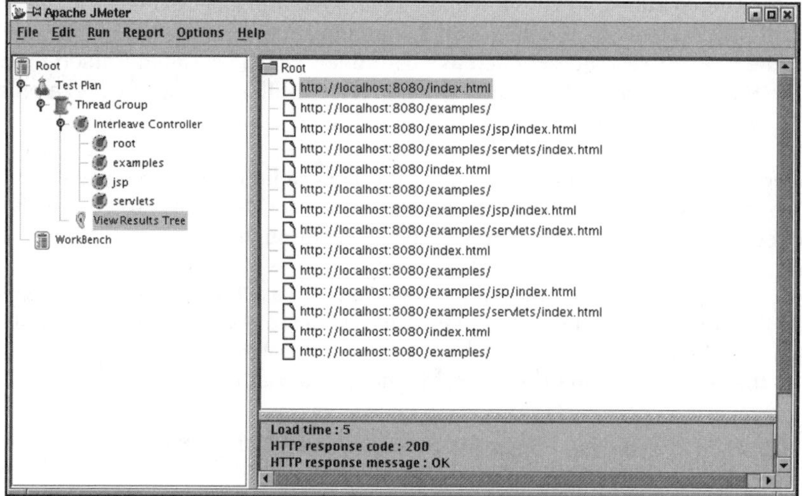

Interleave controllers are good for testing a sequential process where each request depends on the previous request having been run for successful completion. An obvious example is an online shopping application, where a user would search for an item, add it to their shopping cart, enter credit card details, and finalize the order.

Simple Controller

The **simple controller** is simply a container for other elements; it provides no special behavior. We can use the simple controller to logically organize test elements in much the same way as we use folders on a filesystem to logically separate their contents. If we were to load test a site with a non-trivial amount of functionality, it would make sense to use Simple Controller elements to separate the tested functionality into related modules to keep the test plan more maintainable. This will enhance maintainability of the test plan in the same way that dividing large software projects into modules and functions enhances maintainability of the software.

Loop Controller

The **loop controller** will loop through all of its sub-elements as many times as specified in the loop controller's configuration panel. Therefore, any elements under the loop controller will execute this number of times, multiplied by the number of times the parent thread is set to loop. If we were to configure a loop controller to loop 4 times under a thread group which loops 4 times, each sub-element of the loop controller will be executed 16 times.

Modification Controller

The **modification controller** is both a logic controller and a listener. For details about modification controllers, refer to the *Other Listeners* section.

Once Only Controller

Not surprisingly, the **once only controller** executes its child elements only once during the run of a load test. This controller can be used to execute an initial login, create an application entity on which other tests depend (for example, creating an order in a sales application so we can manipulate it with other requests), or to perform any other operation that needs to happen only once.

Generative Controller

As mentioned in our first JMeter example, generative controllers generate requests to be sent to a server. There are three types of in-built generative controller: **HTTP request**, **FTP request**, and **JDBC request**. FTP request and JDBC request, which load test FTP and database servers respectively, are beyond the scope of this chapter. We covered the basic parameters of HTTP request earlier. We'll now briefly cover some of the elements that are not generative controllers but have a strong relationship with HTTP request generative controller and can be added as nodes below HTTP Request elements by right-clicking an HTTP Request element and selecting Add from the pop-up menu.

HTTP Header Manager

In some cases, application testing will require specific HTTP headers to be set to get a valid reflection of true application performance. For example, if an application performs different actions depending on the browser type making the request, it is necessary to set the `User-Agent` header when making test requests. We use the HTTP header manager to explicitly set header keys and values to be sent as part of each request. If added as a node under an HTTP Request element, the custom headers will only be sent for the request under which they are added. These headers will be sent with every request in the same branch if they are set at the thread group level.

The configuration of HTTP header manager is simple and very similar to configuring the Name/Value parameters in an HTTP Request element.

HTTP Authorization Manager

The **HTTP authorization manager** handles requests that require HTTP authentication. Like the HTTP header managers, they can be added either directly underneath an HTTP Request element or to an entire branch of a tree. Their configuration parameters are simple, accepting a base URL from which it will attempt to send authentication credentials, plus the obligatory username and password.

HTTP Cookie Manager

Most modern web applications use cookies in some shape or form. Therefore, in most cases, we will need to add an HTTP Cookie Manager element to our test plan. Like HTTP authorization managers and HTTP header managers, HTTP cookie managers can accept a hard-coded list of cookies that should be sent for every request. In this way, we can simulate a browser that has previously visited a site. Additionally, HTTP cookie managers can mimic a browser's ability to receive, store, and resend cookies. So, for example, if a cookie is dynamically assigned to each visitor, the HTTP cookie manager will receive it and resend it with every appropriate subsequent request.

HTTP cookie managers can also be added to either a thread group or directly to an HTTP Request element, depending on the scope of its intended influence.

Assertion

Even if our application is giving us sub-second responses, we have no cause to celebrate if its output is invalid. An **assertion** gives us a way to validate the actual data returned as a result of each request so that we can be sure that the server is both responsive **and** reliable. Assertions are created as sub-elements of generative controllers, such as the HTTP request generative controller. An assertion is a declaration of some truth we wish to test against.

In our JMeter testing, we could declare, for example, that the resulting output should contain the word `Hello`. When this assertion exists, the response of the HTTP request to which it is added will be checked for the existence of `Hello` and will throw an assertion failure if the string is not present. Now, let's take a look at a simple example of assertion.

Given the simple HTML file below, we will build an assertion that validates its output during load testing.

```
<html>
  <body>
    Hello, World!
  </body>
</html>
```

Assuming we've already deployed the file to an accessible HTTP server, the first step is to build an HTTP request generative controller into our test plan that will access the file's URL. After creating the HTTP request generative controller, we can now right-click on the HTTP Request icon, and choose Assertions | Assertion from the Add menu. Clicking on the new Assertion icon will display a panel like the one below:

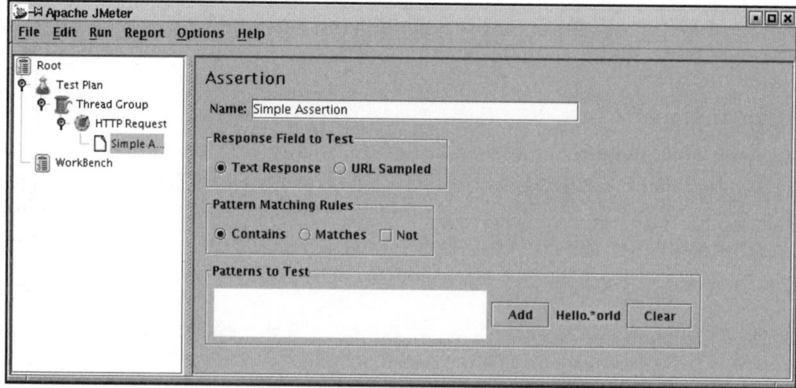

In the screenshot opposite, we have changed the Name field to Simple Assertion and entered one pattern in the textbox, adding it to the assertion by clicking the Add button. JMeter assertions accept Perl5-style regular expressions, so the assertion we've added will match occurrences of the string `Hello`, followed by any number of characters, followed by the string `orld`. `Hello, World` is a matching occurrence of this regular expression, so the assertion should pass. Of course, this kind of pattern matching is overkill for our small, static example, but in larger, dynamic pages, they can be a great help.

In this example, we're selecting the Contains option so that the page contains the pattern we've added. If we wanted to check the entire web page, we could use the Matches option, which would check that the page returned directly matches the pattern(s) we add.

Now that we've added an assertion, we will need to add an **assertion results listener** to view the successes and failures of our assertion. To do this, we can go to the HTTP request generative controller's parent thread group, and simply add the listener from the popup menu. Assertion results listeners require no configuration. They will display all assertion results for any assertion in their thread group. If the assertion passes, it will print the string identifying the resource request – in this case the URL. If there is a failure, it will print an indented failure message directly below the resource identifier, stating the pattern match that failed.

Configuration Element

The **configuration element**'s job is to modify requests in some way. It offers a pluggable way to add request modification logic from various types of default values to automatic building of requests. While there are currently ten types of configuration elements, we will focus our attention on the HTTP-specific elements. We have already covered HTTP authorization managers, HTTP cookie managers, and HTTP header managers in this section, so we will turn our attention to the remaining two HTTP-specific configuration elements.

As we went through the first JMeter example, it became quickly evident that creating anything more than a trivial HTTP test plan would get tedious very quickly. The manual interface, though user-friendly, requires us to enter some of the same data repeatedly. Computer-savvy people – especially server administrators – never like to have to do things manually. That's why JMeter provides both the HTTP Request Defaults and HTTP Proxy Server configuration elements. As we will see, each solves this problem in its own unique way.

HTTP Request Defaults

In most cases, each test plan will be created for a single server environment or online application. Because of this, we'll find ourselves typing the same server name, port, path, or parameters into each new HTTP request generative controller we add to the test plan. **HTTP request defaults** eliminate this duplication of work by allowing us to specify defaults for many of the HTTP Request element's configuration parameters. After adding the defaults, we can leave these fields blank in any HTTP Request element in the same thread group. Fields left blank in the HTTP Request element will default to the values listed in the corresponding HTTP Request Defaults element.

For example, if we were load testing an application that follows the Model View Controller design pattern, with all traffic flowing through a single HTTP servlet, we may have a common base URL for every request like the one listed below:

http://loadtest.wrox.com/servlet/Router

This servlet will provide access to different functionality in the application via a request parameter such as the following:

http://loadtest.wrox.com/servlet/Router?action=addToCart
http://loadtest.wrox.com/servlet/Router?action=checkOut

The server name, port, protocol, and path are common to all HTTP requests that access this application, with only the request parameters varying. In such a case, we could add an HTTP Request Defaults element as illustrated below:

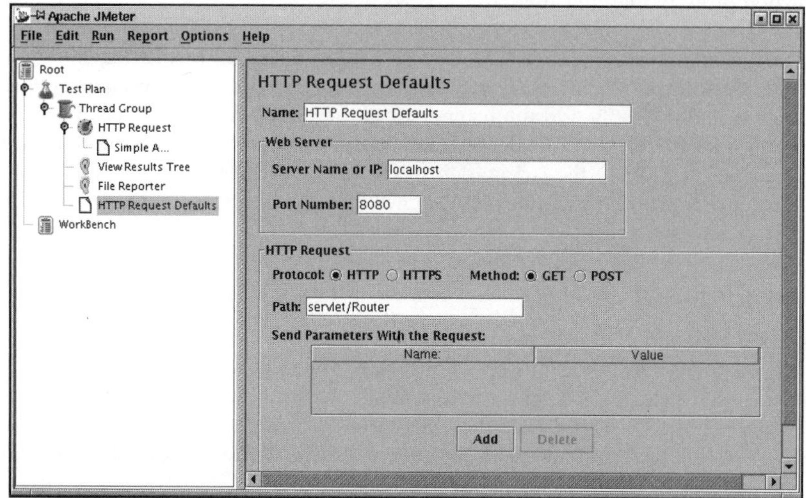

We have set default values for the Server Name, Port Number, Protocol, and Path. Any requests that are in the same thread group will inherit these settings unless they are explicitly overridden in their own configurations. To access any addToCart and checkOut features of our imaginary application, we would need to add HTTP Request elements, leaving all configuration options blank except for the addition of the `action` parameter and corresponding values. In a large load test scenario with potentially tens of HTTP requests, this will really save us time as well as giving our fingers a break from typing.

HTTP Proxy Server

JMeter also provides the **HTTP proxy server** that enables JMeter to watch a user's browser activity and auto-generate HTTP Request elements based on the requests made from the web browser. Also good for large load tests with numerous HTTP requests, the JMeter HTTP proxy server implements a simple proxy for HTTP requests. As depicted in the diagram oppsite, all requests that are made during the browsing session – along with their parameters – are captured and converted into JMeter HTTP Request elements:

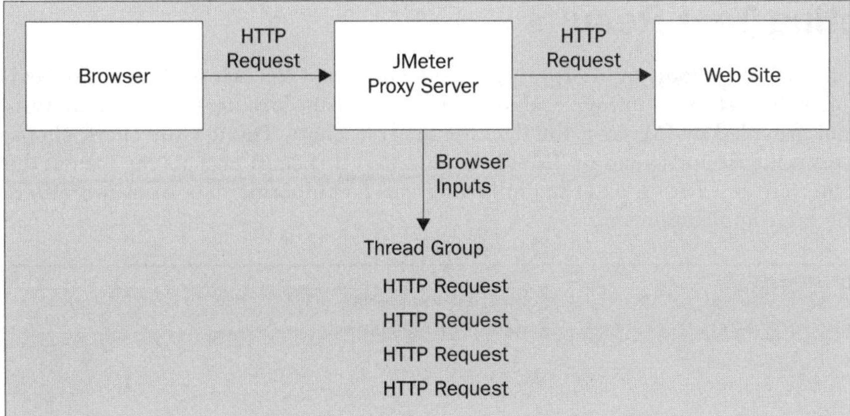

Generating a large number of HTTP Request elements for our test plan is as simple as reconfiguring our browser's HTTP proxy setting and clicking through the features we want to load test.

To start using the HTTP proxy server, we must first add the element to the thread group or logic controller under which we want the resultant HTTP Request elements to be created. We can then open the HTTP proxy server's configuration screen. The port number defaults to 8080.

> **If we were running Tomcat on the same machine with its default port numbers, this default would conflict, so we need to change it to an unused port on the system.**

In the Patterns to Include and Patterns to Exclude textboxes, we can optionally add regular expressions that match the URLs for which we want to generate HTTP Request elements. All browser traffic will be proxied through the HTTP Proxy element. However, if any patterns are listed here, only those requests which match an include pattern or are not excluded by a pattern will be converted into HTTP Request elements.

In case you need help configuring the proxy option in your web browser:

- **Internet Explorer 5+**
  Bring up the Tools | Options | Internet Options control panel. Now select the Connections | Settings button for the appropriate network connection (dial-up vs. LAN). Select Use a proxy server. In the Address field, type `localhost` (or the host name of the computer running the JMeter HTTP proxy – it need not be the local machine), and in the Port field, type the port you chose when you configured the HTTP Proxy element.

- **Netscape 6/Mozilla**
  Bring up the preferences dialog by choosing Edit | Preferences. Expand the Advanced tree element in the left-hand pane. Select Proxies | Manual Proxy Configuration. Type `localhost` in the HTTP Proxy field, and the port that you configured for JMeter HTTP Proxy in the Port field. If you plan to access HTTPS requests, type the same values for SSL Proxy.

Interpreting Test Results

JMeter comes with few tools to interpret the results of a load test. Most of these are real-time views that update as the tests are running, and are not really meant for after-the-event analysis. The one analysis tool provided by JMeter is the data file analysis chart. To view the chart, choose Analyze Data File from the Report menu on JMeter's menu bar; this chart accepts the format that the file report listener creates. Let's look at the following chart, comparing data from two different servers running the same application:

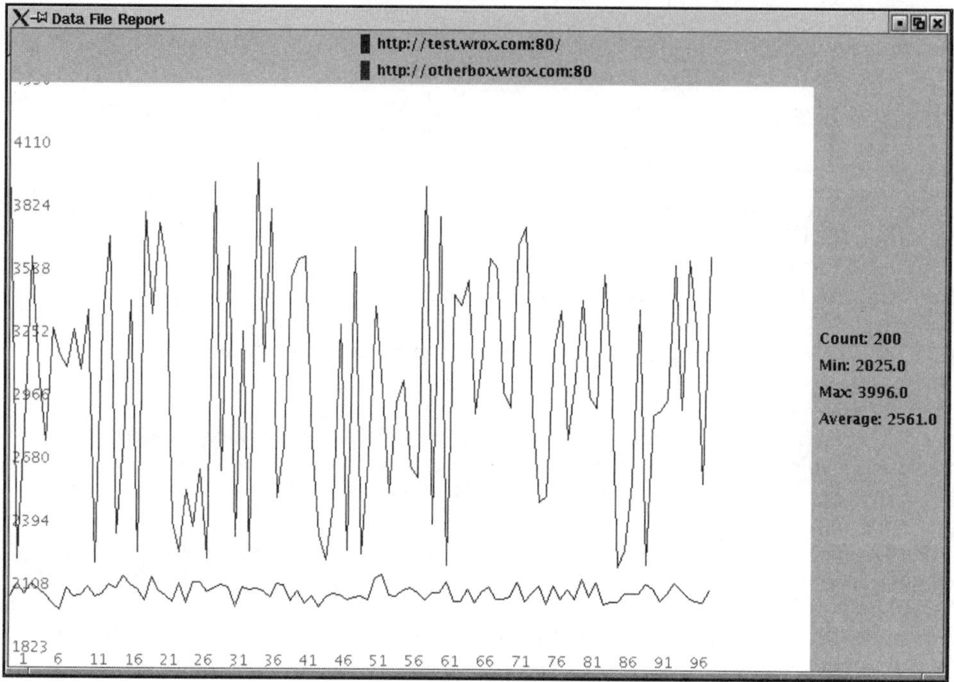

In this picture, the lower line represents the response data from a machine called `test.wrox.com` and the upper line represents response data from another machine called `otherbox.wrox.com`. The **combined** average response time across these two servers is 2561.0 milliseconds. We can tell by looking at the graph that the `test.wrox.com` server yields both faster and more predictable results, because the data points consistently fall underneath the data points for `otherbox.wrox.com`, and the spread of their distribution is much narrower. In situations such as this, this simple JMeter graphing functionality is sufficient to make a decision. Let's now turn our attention to a more realistic situation:

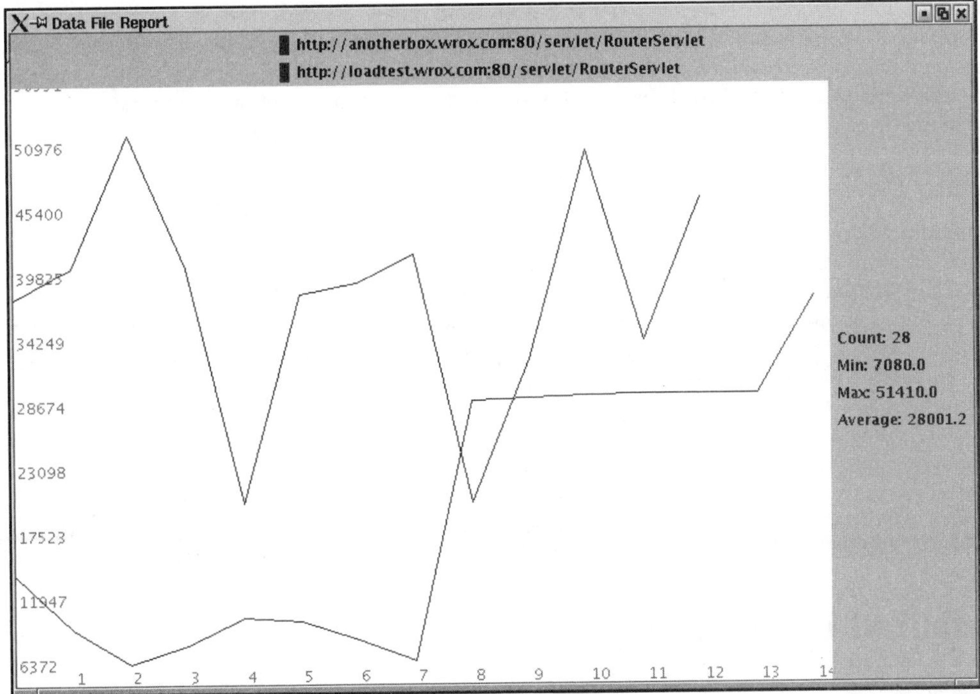

What does this tell us? What conclusions can we draw from this chart? We know that we have sampled two URLs for a total of 28 data points. The combined minimum response time across the two samples was about 7 seconds, the combined maximum was about 51 seconds, and the average was 28 seconds.

Which server performed better? Do we prefer the erratic performance of the top line or the steadily decreasing performance of the bottom line? How much worse might the bottom sample get with time?

The simple fact is that, at the time of this writing, **JMeter is not a reporting tool**. Given an obvious difference between two samples, we might be able to make out a difference in a simple graph such as this, but for real analysis, we're better off using a real analysis tool. Fortunately, JMeter's simple text output format lends itself to be imported into any of the popular tools.

So, now we've got a bunch of data imported into our favorite analysis tool. What are we looking for? The two simplest measures are mean and standard deviation.

Mean

The mean is the average response time for a sample. It gives us an indication of the central tendency of our server's performance. Using the samples from the second graph above, we find that the mean response time for the upper line is about 38 seconds, whereas the mean response time for the lower line is about 19 seconds. This would make the server represented by the lower line better in terms of performance.

But what about variation? If our server has a very good mean response time, but a huge amount of variation among the samples, we'll end up with the average user having a decent experience, and the occasional user or request having a really bad (or really good) experience. It's this kind of variation that drives an unpredictable and frustrating end-user experience. A good measure of variation is standard deviation.

Standard Deviation

Standard deviation is a measure of how widely values in a sample are dispersed from the mean value. Hence, a higher standard deviation indicates more variance in response time. In the second sample above, the standard deviation for the top line is about 9 seconds, and the standard deviation for the bottom line is about 11 seconds. Though the mean is lower in the bottom line sample, the variation is higher by about 2 seconds. We can use this data to help drive our decisions when load testing, especially while comparing two different configurations or architectures.

There are many ways to splice and dice performance data. Sometimes, mentally comparing two samples is enough. Other times, it might make sense to delve into more complex statistical tools, such as regression analysis, for predictive modeling of a process's performance. While a description of these statistical methods is beyond the scope of this book, there are many online and printed statistics resources to be had: http://www.prndata.com/statistics_sites.htm is a good place to start.

Distributed Load Testing

By now you might be getting the feeling that, while JMeter has a lot to offer, it's a little unrealistic to expect one JVM already running a Swing interface to adequately put an application server under heavy load; this simply won't give us an idea of how the application will perform if unleashed onto the Internet. After all, when we discussed the elements of server scalability, we said that a single JVM can only do so much and that sometimes it's necessary to split the load among numerous JVMs. Scalability applies not only to our application servers but also to our load testing software. Thankfully, the developers of JMeter had the same idea. JMeter can run in server mode, allowing the JMeter GUI client to connect and control it remotely. There are two major reasons we might want to explore this capability:

- **Scalability**
  A single JMeter instance isn't enough to simulate the heaviest of loads. Enough simultaneous threads running in JMeter will cause JMeter's performance to suffer, resulting in potentially inaccurate data from our tests. We may also be faced with the issue of JMeter's host machine running into physical CPU or memory limitations. To solve this problem, we can run multiple JMeter servers, each with a reasonable number of active threads, and remotely configure the test plans, start, and stop the servers. Keeping your JMeter agents in good health ensures that the server whose scalability is really in question is adequately challenged.

- **Server Proximity**
  As an extreme example, imagine trying to load test a server in the Eastern United States while sitting in India. It would be difficult to have any acceptable degree of confidence in the tests, since network latency and packet loss would play such a critical role in the process. In a case such as this, it's possible to install a JMeter server somewhere physically close to the server we wish to test, and then to control and collect results from it from our remote location.

The picture opposite illustrates the method in which JMeter interacts remotely between a JMeter client, a JMeter server, and a web server:

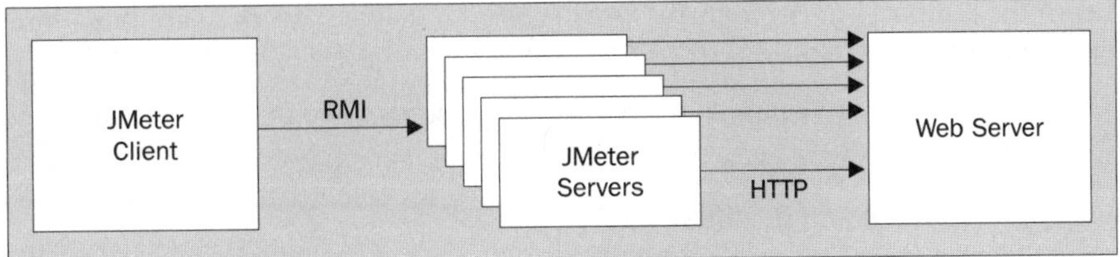

The following is a step-by-step guide to setting up and running tests using the JMeter server:

- Install the standard JMeter distribution on the intended JMeter server machine(s).
- JMeter uses Java's Remote Method Invocation (RMI) to communicate between the client and the server, so the `rmiregistry` program must be started next (make sure that the `ApacheJMeter.jar` file from the JMeter `bin` directory is in the classpath when you run `rmiregistry`).
- Start the JMeter server process by entering JMeter's `bin/` directory and executing either `jmeter-server.bat` or the `jmeter-server` shell script, depending on your host operating system.
- Optionally, repeat on multiple hosts.
- On the client machine, edit your `jmeter.properties` file (located in the `bin` directory of JMeter's installation directory).
- Uncomment and change the `remote_hosts` property to include a comma-separated list of the JMeter server machines. These can be either DNS-resolvable host names or IP addresses.
- Start the JMeter client by running the `jmeter-cl.bat` or `jmeter-cl` shell script.
- Load or create a new test plan.
- Two new options will be present in the Run menu: Remote Start and Remote Stop. In each of these options, any servers listed in the `remote_hosts` property will be available for stopping and starting.
- Proceed with the JMeter GUI as usual.

Server Load Testing vs. Application Load Testing

Server load testing and application load testing are closely linked. The performance of a server depends very much on the applications that run on it, and the performance of an application depends heavily on the server on which it runs. The most important thing, for a server administrator, is to be aware of the boundaries between server performance and application performance. This will enable us to more quickly understand performance issues as new applications are added to our server.

Preparing for Server Load Testing

To best prepare for server load testing, it's important to first establish our goals:

- Establish a baseline for server performance that we can use to compare with application performance

- Learn the limits of our deployment architecture, so that we can compare these limits against expected site usage
- Validate architectural decisions we've made, or compare two or more potential decisions that best fit our needs

Given these goals, we should do the following:

- Establish a controlled environment that won't be affected by external forces. For example, running the server load test against a physical server with many other processes running on it will potentially taint the results – we won't know if performance is being driven by our server or by some external force.
- Prepare installation and configuration for alternative architectures to test. If we were comparing load-balanced Tomcat with a single Tomcat server, we should already have prepared both server setups.
- Select requests to be made on the Tomcat server. We must choose the right mix of requests so as to thoroughly exercise the functionality of the server without taking the risk of skewing the results with performance-heavy application code. Since we're trying to test the server **on its own**, we should avoid overly complex processing or IO-intensive application logic in this initial baseline load test. We suggest a good mix of static resources, JSP pages, servlets, and code that manipulates user sessions.
- Prepare a test plan. If using JMeter, we can configure thread groups with various numbers of threads and then compare the effects of increased concurrent usage. For this, we can either use multiple thread groups or, preferably, perform multiple JMeter runs, reconfiguring each time.

After running these tests and capturing the data, we are ready to add an application to our system and see what the effect is.

Preparing for Application Load Testing

Preparing for application load testing is a little more involved than preparing for server load testing. But, fortunately for us, most of the responsibility lies with the application developer. Again, let's establish the goals of our application load test. We will present them by role:

Administrator:

- Understand application performance as it relates to isolated server performance. This gives us a rough idea of how an application might affect our server, as well as giving us an early warning that there is a problem with an application.
- Verify server stability with the addition of potentially error-prone or inefficient application code.

Programmer:

- Verify that the application performs well under heavy load
- Verify that the application returns reliable results under heavy load
- Verify that the server is up to the task of delivering what the application needs

Given these roles the administrator and programmer are responsible for the following:

Administrator:

- Establish a controlled environment that won't be affected by external forces
- Prepare analysis of pre-application server load testing for proper comparison

Programmer:

- Establish and communicate performance goals, according to the end-user or customer requirement.
- Develop test plans for critical application processes, including assertions for each request. It often helps to have business users, potentially the application's business stakeholder, to define these requests, as the application's developer might be tempted to only include tests that they know the application will pass.
- Optionally, enable application logging to further break down application performance into its various subcomponents.

If an application follows the Model View Controller design pattern, it is sometimes possible to create distinct Views for load and acceptance testing purposes. These Views can be customized for easy validation using assertions, while driven seamlessly by the same business logic that drives the application's standard HTML View. When presentation logic is complex and potentially error-prone, it's best to avoid this technique, but when most or all of the logic is performed before the View comes into play, this can be a helpful technique to minimize testing effort.

Handling the Data

Keep the resulting data and the test plan you created. There aren't many applications that go to production one time and never change. Even seemingly trivial changes can cause serious load issues. If an application developer were to, for example, accidentally swap two variable names in a `for` loop, the right combination of HTTP Request elements to an application can bring a server to its knees. It's important to continuously load test over time, as server performance can seriously degrade as new application code is added. We'd prefer not to let this situation sneak up on us; frequent load testing allows us to analyze the trends in our server's performance as they relate to external factors, such as the amount of site traffic and new application releases.

Summary

Load testing is an important but often overlooked activity of the system administrator. It can help us to make initial architectural decisions as well as to validate the decisions we've previously made. In this chapter, we examined the following topics:

- Scalability, the ability for a system to handle increased load without experiencing degraded performance or reliability, is driven by many factors. In a Tomcat installation, some of those factors are server hardware, software configuration, and deployment architecture.
- JMeter is a full-featured, open source load tester, which is part of the Jakarta project. We covered JMeter load testing techniques from the simple to the advanced.

- Server load testing and application load testing require different approaches. They are tightly coupled, and the most important job of the server administrator is to gauge how application code affects server performance, and to understand which factors contribute to performance issues.

Though we have focused our discussion on using JMeter for load testing, there are numerous tools available, both in the public domain and as commercial products. Two of the market leading commercial products are Segue's Silk Performer and Mercury Interactive's Load Runner. Both offer very advanced scripting features, allowing end users great flexibility in specifying load test behaviors. With this flexibility comes the price of increased complexity, but both companies offer comprehensive documentation as well as training programs on their products.

The open source world also has more to offer in terms of load testing tools. From the up and coming OpenLoad (http://openload.sourceforge.net/), to the more mature (but UI-less) Grinder (http://grinder.sourceforge.net/), there are numerous options available. A great resource for finding the latest in open source load testing tools is the FreshMeat.net open source software archive site (http://www.freshmeat.net/), which includes a category specifically for these kinds of tools under "Topic :: Software Development :: Testing :: Traffic Generation".

Additionally, there are many testing resources available on the Web. A great place to look for an ever-evolving list of sites is the Open Directory Software Testing list (http://www.dmoz.org/Computers/Programming/Software_Testing/), which is a directory of sites that focus on testing topics.

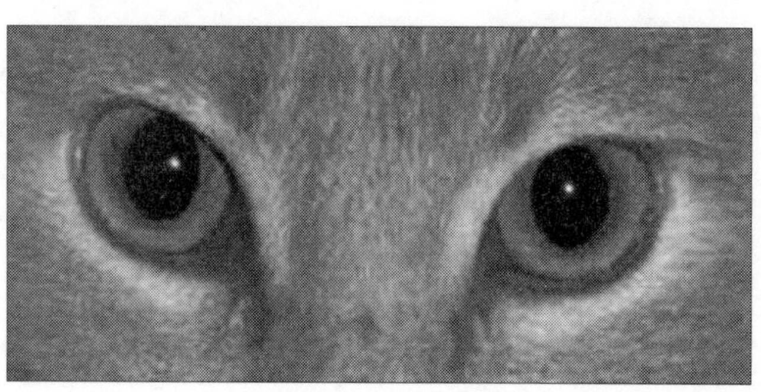

Axis

Apache Axis is the third generation Apache SOAP toolkit. As of this writing, the latest version that is available on the official Apache site is Beta 3. SOAP plays a vital role in the development of web services. Axis eases the generation of SOAP code for a web service.

The origins of Axis lie in the early development of Apache SOAP that began at IBM. The first version of the toolkit was called SOAP4J, the later version was named Apache SOAP version 2 in which SOAP 1.1 was used. The major problem with Apache SOAP v2 was that it did not have any support for WSDL. It also lacked flexibility; its RPC provider did not provide access to the headers in the SOAP envelope.

Because of these and several other issues the Apache SOAP project was stopped. However, it was resurrected and modified to incorporate both SOAP and the upcoming XML Protocol (XMLP) specification and is now known as Apache Axis.

Installing Axis

The Axis installation file may be downloaded from http://xml.apache.org/axis/. Extract the gzipped file to the desired folder. After extracting the files, we will need to configure Axis with Tomcat. Copy the newly created `AXIS_HOME/webapps/axis` folder to the `CATALINA_HOME/webapps` folder. We will configure our web applications in this folder. Now to configure the web application folder under Tomcat, add the following line under the `<Host>` element in the `CATALINA_HOME/conf/server.xml` file:

```
<Context path="/axis" docBase="axis" debug="0" reloadable="true"/>
```

Next, we need to add the .jar files in AXIS_HOME/lib directory to the CLASSPATH. Also we need to add the XML parser (xerces.jar) file in the CLASSPATH. This is done using the following command:

```
export CLASSPATH=$CLASSPATH:$CATALINA_HOME/common/lib/xerces.jar:
<AxisInstallation>/lib/axis.jar:<AxisInstallation>/lib/clutil.jar:
<AxisInstallation>/lib/jaxrpc.jar:
<AxisInstallation>/lib/log4j-core.jar: <AxisInstallation>/lib/commons-
logging.jar: <AxisInstallation>/lib/tt-bytecode.jar:
<AxisInstallation>/lib/wsdl4j.jar
```

Before running the above command, replace <AxisInstallation> with the appropriate directory name of the Axis installation.

To test the installation, start Tomcat and browse to http://localhost:8080/axis/. If the installation is correct, you will see the Axis home page in the browser as shown below:

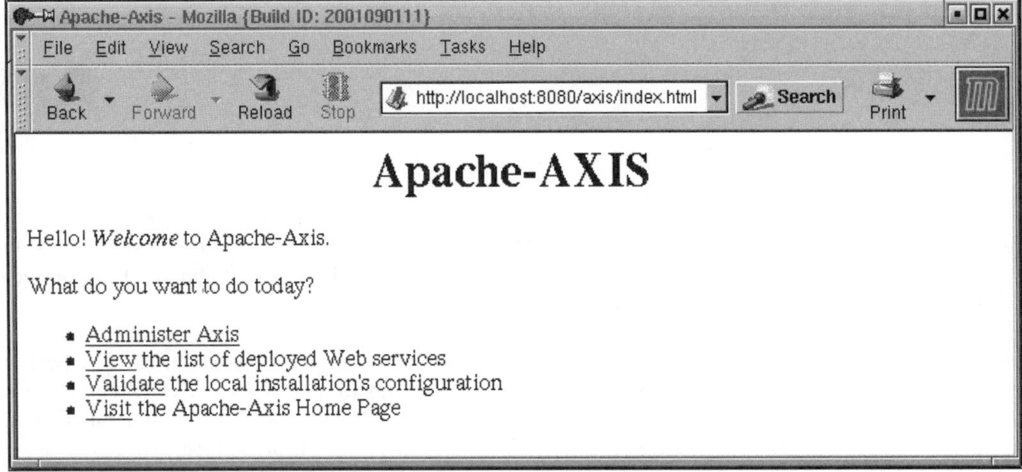

Now, follow the View link on this page; you will get the following page:

Implementing Axis

We will take a simple example to show how you can go about creating and deploying your own service, using Axis. Plus we will also take a look at creating a client application that uses our service.

Developing HelloService

We will create a simple web service that prints a greeting to the user. The web service will expose a method called `sayHello()` to the client. The method takes a `String` argument and returns a `String` message to the client. To create the web service, we will write a Java class called `HelloService` as shown below:

```
public class HelloService {
  public String sayHello(String arg) {
    return "Hello " + arg;
  }
}
```

This completes the development of the web service. We do not have to compile the above Java code.

Deploying HelloService

Axis provides two ways to deploy a service:

- Using a JWS file
- Passing WSDD file to `AdminClient`

The first approach is much simpler. The only thing we have to do is copy the web service source file to `CATALINA_HOME/webapps/axis` and rename it as a `.jws` file.

For our first web service we will choose the first way. Copy the `HelloService.java` file to the `CATALINA_HOME/webapps/axis` directory and rename it `HelloService.jws`.

When we invoke the service the `JWSHandler` sets the JWS filename and the service name in the `MessageContext`. The `JWSProcessor` then locates the JWS file and creates a temporary file with a `.java` extension. It then compiles this Java file. Finally `JWSProvider` is responsible for invoking this service. The `JWSProvider` also puts the response message into the `MessageContext` and sends it to the response flow service chain. This process is shown in the following diagram:

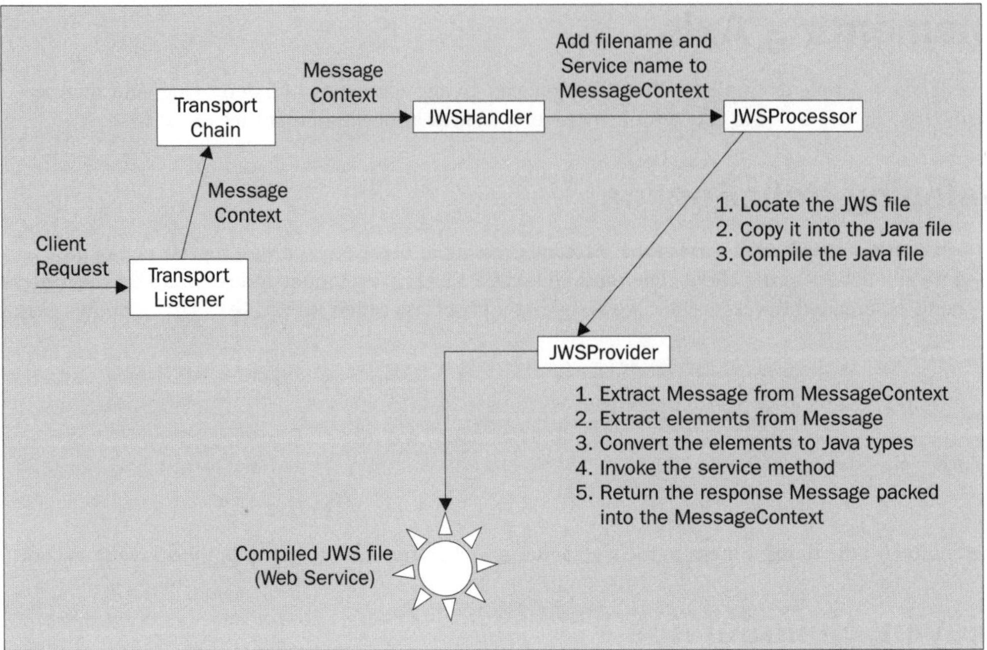

Writing a Client for HelloService

The client code that uses the `HelloService` is shown below:

```
import org.apache.axis.client.Call;
import org.apache.axis.client.Service;

import javax.xml.rpc.namespace.QName;

public class TestClient {
  public static void main(String[] args) {
    try {
      String endpoint = "http://localhost:8080/axis/HelloService.jws";

      Service service = new Service();
      Call call = (Call) service.createCall();

      call.setTargetEndpointAddress(new java.net.URL(endpoint));
      call.setOperationName("sayHello");

      String ret = (String) call.invoke(new Object[] {"John"});

      System.out.println(ret);
    } catch (Exception e) {
      System.err.println(e.toString());
    }
  }
}
```

This is a console-based application. In the `main()` method, we create an instance of the `Service` class and call its `createCall()` method to construct a SOAP call to the remote server. The `Service` class is used as the starting point for accessing SOAP web services. It is the Axis JAXRPC dynamic invocation interface implementation of the `Service` interface.

The `setTargetEndpointAddress()` method sets the URL for the web service to be called. The `setOperationName()` sets the method name to be called. The `invoke()` method calls the remote method and takes an array of type `Object` as a parameter. The array should be initialized with the list of parameters required by the remote method. In this case, the remote method requires only one single `String` parameter. The remote method returns a `String` message that is printed on the user console in the following statement.

Compile the above client program and run it using the `java` command. This will output as follows:

Hello John

The SOAP request generated by the client looks like this:

```
<?xml version="1.0" encoding="utf-8"?>
<SOAP-ENV:Envelope xmlns:xsd="http://www.w3.org/2001/XMLSchema"
                   xmlns:SOAP-ENV="http://schemas.xmlsoap.org/soap/envelope/"
                   xmlns:xsi="http://www.w3.org/2001/XMLSchema-instance">
  <SOAP-ENV:Body>
    <ns1:sayHello xmlns:ns1="">
      <testParam xsi:type="xsd:string">John</testParam>
    </ns1:sayHello>
  </SOAP-ENV:Body>
</SOAP-ENV:Envelope>
```

The client gets the response as a SOAP message. This is shown below:

```
<?xml version="1.0" encoding="UTF-8"?>
<SOAP-ENV:Envelope xmlns:xsd="http://www.w3.org/2001/XMLSchema"
                   xmlns:SOAP-ENV="http://schemas.xmlsoap.org/soap/envelope/"
                   xmlns:xsi="http://www.w3.org/2001/XMLSchema-instance">
  <SOAP-ENV:Body>
    <sayHelloResponse
         SOAP-ENV:encodingStyle="http://schemas.xmlsoap.org/soap/encoding/">
      <sayHelloResult xsi:type="xsd:string">Hello John!</sayHelloResult>
    </sayHelloResponse>
  </SOAP-ENV:Body>
</SOAP-ENV:Envelope>
```

To learn more about Axis see *Axis: The Next Generation of Java SOAP* from *Wrox Press (ISBN 1-86100-715-9)*. To learn more about Axis and other web services get *Professional Open Source Web Services* from *Wrox Press (ISBN 1-86100-746-9)* or go to http://xml.apache.org/axis/.

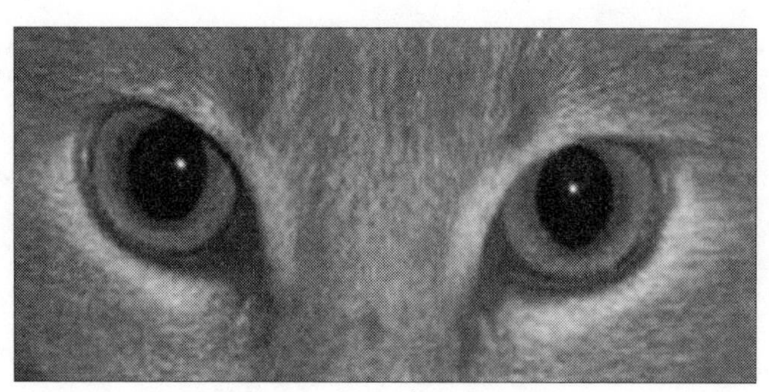

B

Apache SSL Setup

Since Digest authentication is so poorly implemented by browsers, the only alternative for the web server administrator looking to keep passwords secure is to find a way to encrypt passwords sent with Basic authentication. Fortunately this is easy if the server also supports the Secure Socket Layer (SSL), which may be one reason why Digest authentication has not made the progress it might have been expected to.

SSL-capable servers negotiate with clients and automatically encrypt resources requested through a secure URL. They also encrypt the HTTP requests for those resources, including authentication exchanges (the SSL dialog happens before the authentication dialog). Note that although SSL is often used with authentication, it does not in itself authenticate anything – it merely encrypts the network connection.

The upshot of this is that a directory protected with Basic authentication can use encrypted passwords if SSL is used. For example, if a directory is set up to be authenticated like so:

```
<Location /private>
  AuthName "Authorized Personnel Only"
  AuthType Basic
  AuthUserFile auth/personnel.auth
  require valid-user

  SSLEnable on
  SSLRequireSSL
</Location>
```

we can access this directory with our username and password encrypted by SSL by using an https URL like https://www.alpha-complex.com/private/authorized.html. The `SSLRequireSSL` directive forces clients to use SSL to connect, otherwise they are denied. If we wanted to be friendlier at this point we could use a redirection or alias to point unencrypted clients to another page.

For SSL to work we also need a few other things in place first, so this is the subject that we will discuss in this appendix.

SSL and Apache

SSL is an encrypted communications protocol for sending information securely across the Internet. It sits between Apache and the TCP/IP protocol and transparently handles encryption and decryption when a client makes a secure connection. Importantly, SSL is not a part of HTTP but a separate layer in its own right, so it will also work underneath protocol handlers in Apache 2.0.

SSL uses an encryption technique called **public key cryptography**, where the server end of the connection sends the client a public key for encrypting information, which only the server can decrypt with the **private key** it holds. The client uses the public key to encrypt and sends the server its own key, identifying it uniquely to the server and preventing onlookers at points between the two systems from mimicking either server or client (generally known as a man-in-the-middle attack).

In addition to being able to encrypt the connection, public key cryptography allows a client to authenticate the server with a trusted third party, known as a **Certificate Authority** (CA). The Certificate Authority is often an independent organization that has verified that the owner of the server is really who they claim to be.

Secure HTTP (that is, an https: URL) is usually distinguished from regular unencrypted HTTP by being served on a different port number, 443 instead of 80. Clients told to access a URL with Secure HTTP automatically connect to port 443 rather than 80, making it easy for the server to tell the difference and respond appropriately.

It's important to note that SSL does place an added strain on the server. Since every SSL page is encrypted, the server is performing more work and able to serve less content in the same period of time. Many sites solve this by using multiple servers and having insecure documents served from a separate server, thereby spreading the load. If an SSL server is needed, it's worth considering what sort of load is expected and budgeting CPU power appropriately.

There are several solutions for implementing SSL with Apache including the Apache-SSL project and the commercial StrongHold and Raven SSL implementations. However, in this section, we're going to look at implementing SSL with the `mod_ssl` module and the OpenSSL library. `mod_ssl` abstracts SSL functionality into a separate module, making it easy to upgrade it independently of Apache. It has also been made the standard SSL implementation in Apache 2.0. This has been made possible primarily because the patent on the RSA algorithm held by RSA Inc. has now expired and US laws on export encryption, which previously made integrating SSL into the standard Apache distribution impossible, have been relaxed.

In this section we'll look at building `mod_ssl` from source and installing it, as well as SSL configuration options and strategies. We also take a look at how SSL interoperates with other Apache features like virtual hosts and authentication and how we can sometimes use this to our advantage.

Downloading OpenSSL and ModSSL

In Apache 2.0, mod_ssl is part of the standard distribution, so if we're lucky we already have it built and ready to go. It is possible that we might want to build mod_ssl from source. If so, we can either use the Apache 2.0 source tree, as distributed in all Apache binary distributions or downloaded separately, or download mod_ssl for Apache 1.3 from http://www.modssl.org/, which is the mod_ssl home page for Apache 1.3 servers.

We may also need to build and install the OpenSSL libraries that provide the underlying encryption on which mod_ssl is based. This can be found at http://www.openssl.org/.

If building for Apache 1.3, note that mod_ssl requires patches to be applied to the original Apache sourcecode. The Apache 1.3 source must be patched with the correct version of mod_ssl. For this reason the mod_ssl package comes with the Apache version number built in, for example, mod_ssl-2.8.7-1.3.23. This translates as 'mod_ssl version 2.8.7 for Apache 1.3.23'. Thankfully Apache 2.0 removes the need to worry about these patches.

Also, the expiry of the RSA patent means that the RSAREF library is no longer required. This simplifies things enormously if we are building mod_ssl from source.

We can often make use of prebuilt packages too – these are available for both Apache 1.3 mod_ssl and OpenSSL for some platforms while packages for Linux systems are available from http://www.rpmfind.net/ and http://nonus.debian.org/, for example. Some distributions, notably Mandrake Linux version 8, provide a very full Apache installation including many additional third-party modules and SSL support out-of-the-box. Mandrake calls this package the 'Advanced Extranet Server'.

Building and Installing the OpenSSL Library

OpenSSL provides basic cryptographic support for mod_ssl and is also used by many applications other than Apache, like OpenSSH.

OpenSSH is a free implementation of the SSH protocol available for a wide variety of platforms.

It is quite likely, therefore, that we already have OpenSSL and do not need to install it. If we don't and can't install a binary package we can download the source from the URL noted above and install it ourselves.

After unpacking OpenSSL, change down into the top directory and run the config script:

```
# cd /usr/local/src/openssl-0.9.7
# ./config
```

This should automatically configure the library build for the target platform. If the config script guesses wrongly (probably because we're using a platform that it doesn't recognize) we can override it by using the Configure script instead, as we will see later.

While installing the libraries we can also set the installation paths. Historically, the default install location for both the OpenSSL libraries and their support files is /usr/local/ssl; we can change this by specifying arguments to the script:

```
# ./config --prefix=/usr/local/apache/libexec/ssl
  --openssldir=/usr/local/apache/ssl
```

It isn't actually necessary to install OpenSSL completely, as we can tell mod_ssl where to look for the OpenSSL libraries when we come to build it. However if we want to use them for other applications or we want to build them as dynamically linked libraries (DLLs), it is useful to install them permanently.

In addition, the following options, none of which have double minus prefixes, can be used to customize the library. By default OpenSSL builds everything that it can, but we may want to disable some features or alter the build options of others:

Option	Function
no-threads	Disable the use of threaded code in the library. Threaded code is more efficient but may cause problems on some platforms. The default is to let the config script figure it out; this option might need to be set for more obscure platforms. On Apache 1.3 (and Apache 2.0 using the prefork MPM) where the server is not threaded this option should be specified to improve performance, since thread optimization does not help in these cases.
no-asm	Do not use platform-specific assembly code to build the library. The OpenSSL package comes with fast assembly language routines for several different processor types and platforms, and the config script will pick one if it finds a suitable match. This option forces the build process to resort to slower C-based routines instead. Normally the config script will work this out automatically; use this option to override it.
no-dso	Do not build as a shared library but build as a statically linked library only. This is improved from earlier releases of mod_ssl, where dynamic libraries were sometimes hard to create. Note that mod_ssl can link against a static OpenSSL library and still be dynamically loaded into Apache. This may be useful for distributing mod_ssl to remote sites without installing libraries as well.
386	Relevant to x86 processor architectures only. The default assembly code provided for these processors requires a 486 or better. Specifying this option causes OpenSSL to be built with 386-compatible assembly code.
no-<cipher>	Disable a particular cipher from the library. The list of ciphers included (and which can be specified here) is: bf, cast, des, dh, dsa, hmac, md2, md5, mdc2, rc2, rc4, rc5, rsa, sha, for example: # ./config no-hmac
-D, -l, -L, -f, -K	Passes flags to the compiler or linker stages, for example: -L/usr/local/lib

`rsaref` is omitted from this list, as it is no longer relevant. For a short list of options use `./config --help`.

For example, to configure OpenSSL to build a shared library using threads, and exclude the `md2` and `rc2` ciphers, we would use:

```
# ./config --prefix=/usr/local/apache/libexec/ssl
  --openssldir=/usr/local/openssl-0.9.7 no-md2 no-rc2
```

Once the build process is configured, the library can be built and tested with:

```
# make (or make all)
# make test
```

If we are also installing the libraries, we can use:

```
# make install
```

Alternatively, we can do all three steps in one go with:

```
# make all test install > build.log
```

This creates and installs the OpenSSL libraries as statically linked libraries with a `.a` suffix.

Specifying the Platform and Compiler Explicitly

OpenSSL also comes with an alternative configuration script, `Configure`, that allows us to specify the target platform and compiler explicitly, rather than have the `config` script try to work it out itself. Running `Configure` on its own will produce a syntax usage line and a long list of possible target platforms and variations, like this:

```
# ./Configure

Usage: Configure [no-<cipher> ...] [-Dxxx] [-lxxx] [-Lxxx] [-fxxx] [-Kxxx]
[rsaref] [no-threads] [no-asm] [no-dso] [386] [--prefix=DIR] [--
openssldir=OPENSSLDIR] os/compiler[:flags]

pick os/compiler from:
BC-16                  BC-32 BS2000-OSD       CygWin32        FreeBSD
FreeBSD-alpha          FreeBSD-elf            MPE/iX-gcc      Mingw32
NetBSD-m68             NetBSD-sparc           NetBSD-x86      OS390-Unix
OpenBSD                OpenBSD-alpha          OpenBSD-mips    OpenBSD-x86
OpenUNIX-8             OpenUNIX-8-gcc         OpenUNIX-8-gcc-shared
OpenUNIX-8-pentium     OpenUNIX-8-pentium_pro OpenUNIX-8-shared
ReliantUNIX SINIX      SINIX-N                VC-MSDOS        VC-NT
VC-W31-16              VC-W31-32              VC-WIN16        VC-WIN32
aix-cc                 aix-gcc                aix43-cc        aix43-gcc
alpha-cc               alpha-cc-rpath         alpha-gcc       alpha164-cc
alphaold-cc            bsdi-elf-gcc           bsdi-gcc        cc
cray-t3e               cray-t90-cc            darwin-ppc-cc   dgux-R3-gcc
```

```
dgux-R4-gcc               dgux-R4-x86-gcc          dist             gcc
hpux-brokencc             hpux-brokengcc           hpux-cc          hpux-gcc
hpux-m68k-gcc             hpux-parisc-cc           hpux-parisc-cc-o4
hpux-parisc-gcc           hpux-parisc1_1-cc        hpux-parisc2-cc
hpux10-brokencc           hpux10-brokengcc         hpux10-cc        hpux10-gcc
hpux64-parisc-cc          hpux64-parisc2-cc        irix-cc          irix-gcc
irix-mips3-cc             irix-mips3-gcc           irix64-mips4-cc
irix64-mips4-gcc          linux-alpha+bwx-ccc      linux-alpha+bwx-gcc
linux-alpha-ccc           linux-alpha-gcc          linux-aout       linux-elf
linux-elf-arm             linux-ia64               linux-m68k       linux-mips
linux-mipsel              linux-ppc                linux-s390       linux-sparcv7
linux-sparcv8             linux-sparcv9            ncr-scde         newsos4-gcc
nextstep                  nextstep3.3              purify           qnx4
qnx6                      rhapsody-ppc-cc          sco3-gcc         sco5-cc
sco5-cc-pentium           sco5-gcc                 solaris-sparc-sc3
solaris-sparcv7-cc        solaris-sparcv7-gcc      solaris-sparcv8-cc
solaris-sparcv8-gcc       solaris-sparcv9-cc       solaris-sparcv9-gcc
solaris-sparcv9-gcc27     solaris-x86-cc           solaris-x86-gcc
solaris64-sparcv9-cc      sunos-gcc                ultrix-cc        ultrix-gcc
unixware-2.0              unixware-2.0-pentium     unixware-2.1
unixware-2.1-p6           unixware-2.1-pentium     unixware-7
unixware-7-gcc            unixware-7-pentium       unixware-7-pentium_pro
debug                     debug-ben                debug-ben-debug
debug-ben-strict          debug-bodo               debug-levitte-linux-elf
debug-linux-elf           debug-linux-elf-noefence
debug-rse                 debug-solaris-sparcv8-cc
debug-solaris-sparcv8-gcc debug-solaris-sparcv9-cc
debug-solaris-sparcv9-gcc debug-steve              debug-ulf
```

The possible options that can be given to `Configure` are identical to the `config` options above with the sole exception of the final OS/compiler option, which is obligatory and picked from the list above. For example, to build a debug version of OpenSSL on Linux we could use:

```
# ./Configure [options we supplied to config] debug-linux-elf
```

This should only be necessary if the `config` script guesses wrongly, or we need to add our own platform to the list if none of the existing ones work.

Building and Installing mod_ssl for Apache 2.0

Once the OpenSSL libraries have been built, we can build `mod_ssl`. How difficult this is depends on whether we are building for Apache 1.3 or Apache 2.0. Apache 2.0 contains `mod_ssl` anyway, so building it is simply a case of building Apache with SSL:

```
# ./configure --enable-ssl ...other options...
```

Or if we have OpenSSL in a different place then Apache expects (as set by `--openssldir`, above):

```
# ./configure --enable-ssl --with-ssl=/usr/local/openssl-0.9.7 ...other options...
```

This is all we should need to do; building and installing Apache will also install `mod_ssl`. We still need the OpenSSL libraries, however – see above.

Building and Installing mod_ssl for Apache 1.3

To function in Apache 1.3, mod_ssl needs to patch the Apache sourcecode to extend the Apache API, so we must use the configuration script supplied with mod_ssl rather than the one supplied with Apache. Handily, mod_ssl knows how to drive Apache's configuration script and will pass APACI options to it if we specify them to mod_ssl's configuration script.

The one-step way to build Apache 1.3 and mod_ssl is to give mod_ssl's configuration script something like the following:

```
# ./configure --with-apache=/usr/local/src/apache_1.3.23
  --with-ssl=/usr/local/openssl-0.9.7 --enable-module=ssl
# cd /usr/local/src/apache_1.3.23
# make
# make install
```

This creates a statically linked Apache with mod_ssl included into the binary. As well as passing the --enable-module to Apache's configuration script, this also invisibly passed --enable-rule=EAPI to activate the patches made to Apache's sourcecode.

Here we've assumed that we originally unpacked Apache and OpenSSL into directories under /usr/local/src and have already been into the OpenSSL directory and built the libraries there. Of course, in reality the sourcecode for the different packages can go anywhere, so long as we tell mod_ssl's configuration script where to find them.

We can supply any APACI options to this configuration script, and mod_ssl will pass them to Apache's own configuration script after it has patched the Apache sourcecode. For example, to specify Apache's install directory and target name and build most modules, with all built modules made into dynamically loadable modules (including mod_ssl), we could put:

```
# ./configure  --with-apache=/usr/local/src/apache_1.3.23
  --with-ssl=/usr/local/src/openssl-0.9.7 --prefix=/usr/local/apache1323
  --target=httpd139 --enable-module=ssl --enable-module=most --enable-shared=max
  ... other APACI options ...
```

Here --prefix, --target, --enable-module, and --enable-shared are all passed as options to Apache's configuration script.

Retaining Use of Apache 1.3's configure Script with mod_ssl

If mod_ssl is the only module that needs to be configured externally, it is easy to use the configure script supplied by mod_ssl and use it to pass APACI options to the Apache 1.3 configuration script. However, if we have several modules that need to use their own installation scripts then the process gets more complex – we cannot drive Apache's configuration from all of them at once.

As an alternative we can use mod_ssl's configuration script to make the EAPI patches to Apache only, then use Apache's configuration script to set up Apache as usual. We could also go on to another module and use its configuration script. Once Apache is built with EAPI included we can return to mod_ssl's sourcecode and build it as a loadable module by telling it to use apxs. The steps to do this are:

- Build OpenSSL
- Patch Apache's sourcecode
- Do other third-party module preparations
- Configure and build EAPI-patched Apache
- Build and install mod_ssl with apxs

Build OpenSSL

We first build the OpenSSL libraries, without installing them. In this case we're building for a site outside the United States, so we have to disable the IDEA cipher, which is patented in Europe:

```
# cd /usr/local/src/openssl-0.9.7
# ./config no-idea
# make
```

Patch Apache's Sourcecode

Next we need to patch the extended API that mod_ssl needs into Apache but without running Apache's configuration script:

```
# cd /usr/local/mod_ssl-2.8.7-1.3.23
# ./configure --with-apache=/usr/local/src/apache_1.3.23 --with-eapi-only
```

Prepare Third-Party Modules

We can now go to other modules with non-trivial installation procedures and carry out any necessary preparations. Note that some modules (mod_php being one) need to be built after the mod_ssl patches have been applied to work and need -DEAPI added to their compiler flags at the configuration stage. For this reason it is always a better idea to deal with the EAPI patches before handling other third-party modules.

Some modules, like mod_ssl, can also drive Apache's configuration from their own configuration scripts, so we could do the rest of the configuration here if we only had one other module to deal with. Otherwise, we go on to the next step.

Configure and Build EAPI-Patched Apache

As we're going to build mod_ssl later we must enable mod_so, either explicitly with --enable-module=so or implicitly by using --enable-shared. In this case, we're going to compile all modules as dynamic modules. We're also going to test this server before we use it in anger, so we give it a different installation root and target name to distinguish it from the existing installation.

To enable the EAPI interface required by mod_ssl, we need to enable the EAPI rule that was added to Apache's configuration options when we patched the source:

```
# cd /usr/local/src/apache_1.3.23
# ./configure --prefix=/usr/local/apache1323 --target=httpd139
  --sbindir=\$prefix/sbin --enable-module=all --enable-shared=max
  --enable-rule=EAPI
# make
# make install
```

If the source is patched correctly and the EAPI rule has been activated, we should see `-DEAPI` included in the list of flags passed to the compiler during the build process.

Build and Install mod_ssl with apxs

Now we can build `mod_ssl` using `apxs`:

```
# cd /usr/local/src/mod_ssl-2.8.7-1.3.23
# ./configure --with-ssl=/usr/local/src/openssl-0.9.7
  --with-apxs=/usr/local/apache1323/sbin/apxs
# make
# make install
```

This works because we previously built Apache with the EAPI patches in place, so we don't need to apply them again.

We need to adjust for the actual locations of OpenSSL and `apxs`, of course. We can also create some test certificates at this point prior to installing by instead using:

```
# make
# make certificate
# make install
```

This step, and certificates in general, are covered in more detail starting at Installing a Private Key later in this appendix.

Strangely, although the `makefile` generated by the configuration script uses `apxs` to install `libssl.so` (the filename under which `mod_ssl` is created), it does not add the necessary `LoadModule` and `AddModule` lines to the configuration file. We can fix this easily with:

```
# /usr/local/apache1323/sbin/apxs -i -a -n mod_ssl pkg.sslmod/libssl.so
```

This actually does the installation too, so the `make install` is redundant. If we already have the directives in `httpd.conf` for loading `mod_ssl` (from a previous installation perhaps), `make install` is just fine, as well as being shorter to type.

Once `mod_ssl` is installed and running in Apache, we can check to see if it is present by generating an information page with `mod_info`. If present, `mod_ssl` will announce itself on the Apache version line:

```
Apache/2.0.39 (Unix) mod_ssl/3.0a0 OpenSSL/0.9.6b
```

Basic SSL Configuration

To have Apache respond to SSL connections we also need to make sure it is listening to port 443, the default port for SSL. If we're also serving regular HTTP requests that means we need to listen to port 80 too, giving us:

```
Listen 80
Listen 443
```

To actually enable SSL we need to tell Apache how and when to use it by entering SSL directives into its configuration. `mod_ssl` provides a lot of directives, but the ones of crucial importance are:

```
# Switch on the SSL engine (for Apache 1.3 Apache-SSL use SSLEnable instead)
SSLEngine on
# Specify the server's private key
SSLCertificateKeyFile conf/ssl/www.alpha-complex.com.key
# Specify the certificate for the private key
SSLCertificateFile conf/ssl/www.alpha-complex.com.crt
```

This presumes that the server's private key and certificate is in a directory called `conf/ssl` under the sever root. Depending on our requirements we might easily prefer to have them somewhere else entirely. We'll talk more about these files and how to create them in a moment.

If we're loading SSL dynamically, these directives must be located after the `LoadModule` (plus `AddModule`, for Apache 1.3) directives for Apache to understand them. If we put the directives at the server level (that is, outside a virtual host container), then the entire server will be SSL-enabled, and ordinary HTTP connections will no longer work on any port. However, we can also put all three directives in an IP-based virtual host to enable SSL for one host only, in this case a host dedicated to port 443, the SSL port:

```
<VirtualHost 192.168.1.1:443>
  ServerName www.alpha-complex.com
  DocumentRoot /home/www/alpha-complex
  ... virtual host directives ...
  SSLEngine on
  SSLCertificateFile conf/ssl/www.alpha-complex.com.crt
  SSLCertificateKeyFile conf/ssl/www.alpha-complex.com.key
</VirtualHost>

<VirtualHost 192.168.1.1:*>
  ServerName www.alpha-complex.com
  DocumentRoot /home/www/alpha-complex
  ... virtual host directives ...
</VirtualHost>
```

We can also put the `SSLCertificateFile` and `SSLCertificateKeyFile` directives in the server-level configuration and leave just the `SSLEngine` directive in the virtual host. This allows us to reuse the same key and certificate for several virtual hosts, and each one that requires SSL just needs to have an `SSLEngine` directive in its virtual host container. Virtual hosts that do not use SSL pay no attention to the key and certificate directives, and aren't affected by them.

Returning to our original example, this configuration is all we need for Apache to support SSL. Apache will accept both unencrypted and encrypted connections for any page on the server. This is not what we ultimately want, but we can refine it to enforce use of SSL in specific areas, as well as define `SSLRandomFile` to improve the randomness of our encryption, as described later. `mod_ssl` also supports a range of other SSL directives that we can use to customize SSL in various ways. For example, a simple and obvious thing to do is enforce the use of SSL in a specific location, which we can do with:

```
<Directory /home/www/alpha-complex/secure/>
  SSLrequireSSL
</Directory>
```

This rejects ordinary HTTP connections that try to access resources in the secure section of the site; other parts of the site can still use SSL, but it is not enforced or required. Now we have the minimal configuration we require to secure all or part of the site. As a refinement, we can also automatically redirect clients to use SSL; we will see this later, too.

A worked example SSL configuration is distributed as standard with Apache. It is called `ssl.conf`, and contains a lot of additional helpful comments.

Installing a Private Key

The key and certificate files we've defined above don't exist yet. Ultimately we will want to use a private key with an officially signed certificate, so we can verify ourselves as being bona fide on the Internet. But for now we can create a temporary certificate and test that SSL works with it. It may well be that we got a test key and certificate when we installed Apache, but even so we may want to replace it, so this section is still relevant. Certificates normally expire after a certain amount of time, so if we have an official one (signed by a recognized Certificate Authority) we will need to replace it from time to time.

If we installed `mod_ssl` from source, or used `--enable-module=ssl` in Apache 2.0's configuration script, we can make use of an automated script to help us perform all the necessary key and certificate installation steps, including setting up `httpd.conf`. To do this, type:

```
# make certificate
```

This will carry out all the steps detailed below for us and is a very convenient way to set up Apache for SSL the first time. Otherwise, or if we are replacing a certificate, we can carry out the process manually.

OpenSSL provides a utility called `openssl`. If OpenSSL was fully installed this will be located under whatever directory was given to the OpenSSL configuration script (`/usr/local/ssl` by default). Otherwise, we can find it in the `apps` directory of the OpenSSL sourcecode. In this case we can copy it to Apache's `sbin` directory, for example:

```
# cp /usr/local/openssl-0.9.7/apps/openssl /usr/local/apache/sbin/
```

We can use this to create a DES3-encrypted private key for Apache to use with either of the following equivalent commands:

```
# openssl genrsa -des3 1024 > www.alpha-complex.com.key
# openssl genrsa -des3 -out www.alpha-complex.com.key 1024
```

We can actually call this key file anything we like, but we choose the domain name of the server because we can then create other keys for different virtual hosts and give each a name that identifies the host it is for. The `.key` suffix is also not obligatory, but it is the usual one for key files. In the process of setting up SSL, we'll also create `.csr` and `.crt` files, so sticking to the common extensions makes life simpler. Executing the command will generate some diagnostic information about the key being generated and then ask for a pass phrase:

```
Generating RSA private key, 1024 bit long modulus
................+++++
................+++++
e is 65537 (0x10001)
Enter PEM pass phrase:
Verifying password -Enter PEM pass phrase:
```

Since `mod_ssl` will ask us for this pass phrase every time we start up Apache, we can also create an unencrypted private key by leaving out the `-des3` option:

```
# openssl genrsa 1024 > www.alpha-complex.com.key
```

This is often done to allow servers to start automatically without an administrator present. This is especially useful when a machine needs to be rebooted remotely. Apache will accept this key quite happily, but we must make absolutely sure that the directory for keys and certificates – `/usr/local/apache/conf/ssl` in this example – and the files in it are all only readable by root:

```
# chmod 400 www.alpha-complex.com.key
```

If we fail to do this and a third party gets hold of the private key, they could use it to impersonate the server, and security would be fundamentally broken.

Creating a Certificate Request and Temporary Certificate

To validate the private key we need a certificate. To get an officially signed certificate, we need to generate a **Certificate Request** file, or CSR. To create our own temporary certificate we can simply sign our own request while we wait for an official one to be created for us. This certificate won't pass muster if a client checks it and finds it is not signed by a recognized certificate authority, but they may (depending on their configuration settings) choose to accept it anyway, either for just this session or until it expires.

The `openssl` utility can both create and sign certificate requests. To create the CSR we use something like:

```
# openssl req -new -key www.alpha-complex.com.key -out www.alpha-complex.com.csr
```

Note that for this and some other variants of the `openssl` command, we need a configuration file located in the directory specified when OpenSSL was built. If OpenSSL was not fully installed, install the configuration file by hand from `apps/openssl.cnf`.

The CSR generation process will ask us questions about our identity, which will be built into the request and used by the signing authority as part of the certificate we are issued in return. This information is collectively known as a Distinguished Name (DN). Since we'll use this CSR for both testing and the official certificate, it is important to get this information right:

```
You are about to be asked to enter information that will be incorporated
into your certificate request.
What you are about to enter is what is called a Distinguished Name or a DN.
There are quite a few fields but you can leave some blank
For some fields there will be a default value,
If you enter '.', the field will be left blank.
-----
Country Name (2 letter code) [AU]:AC
State or Province Name (full name) [Some-State]:SSL Sector
Locality Name (eg, city) []:Alpha Complex
Organization Name (eg, company) [Internet Widgits Pty Ltd]:The Computer
Organizational Unit Name (eg, section) []:CPU
Common Name (eg, YOUR name) []:www.alpha-complex.com
Email Address []:webmaster@alpha-complex.com
```

```
Please enter the following 'extra' attributes
to be sent with your certificate request
A challenge password []:
An optional company name []:
```

We must fill these in with the correct values for the server and server operator; any fields that do not apply may be let blank. The Common Name (CN) is the server's main domain name, www.alpha-complex.com in this case, regardless of the exhortation 'YOUR name' – this is true only for personal certificates. This is important, since browsers will generate a security warning if the certificate's CN does not match the URL that the client asked for.

The A challenge password and An optional company name attributes are usually left blank. These are used with certificate revocation, which is discussed later. For most applications a challenge password is not required.

Once the CSR has been generated, we can sign it ourselves to create a temporary certificate for the private key we generated earlier:

```
# openssl req -x509 -key www.alpha-complex.com.key -in \
  www.alpha-complex.com.csr -out www.alpha-complex.com.crt
```

This reads the CSR in, signs it with the key, and writes out the resulting certificate. This command is a good one to remember, since it encapsulates the process of certificate creation in one step; any kind of certificate can be created by using it.

Now we can install these two keys (if we didn't create them there in the first place) into the `conf/ssl` directory so Apache can see them. When we start Apache it should ask us for a pass phrase, if we encrypted the private key file, and start up with SSL. If we did encrypt the file and don't get the pass phrase prompt, it's a good indication that the SSL directives are missing from the configuration. We can check the configuration by using `mod_info`'s information page and test that SSL works by asking for the URL https://www.alpha-complex.com/.

In fact the server will respond to a secure HTTP connection on either port 80 or 443. However, clients will default to port 443.

Note that we cannot use a `telnet` client to test an SSL connection, since `telnet` has no idea about public key cryptography. We can use another variant of the `openssl` utility to test the connection instead:

```
# openssl s_client -connect localhost:443 -state
```

This will produce a longish printout of negotiations between `openssl` and Apache, which can be used for analyzing problems or debugging. For really extended output add the `-debug` option as well. Assuming the connection is established, we can get a page from the server with something like:

```
GET / HTTP/1.0
<return>
<return>
```

This should have the expected results, with a few additional SSL-related messages tagged on to the end.

Getting a Signed Certificate

Chances are that if we use a modern web browser to test the above URL, we'll get a warning message about the site using a certificate that hasn't been signed by a recognized authority, asking us if we want to accept it. That's fine for testing but a little unfriendly for visitors. To make this message go away we have to either spend some money and get the CSR signed by a recognized CA or add our own server certificate to the list of authorized certificates recognized by the browser. This second option is quite effective for corporations that provide secure services for selected clients. Note that this simply involves importing the server's certificate, which is a trivial process on most browsers. For the rest of us a signed certificate from a publicly recognized CA is required.

The two largest certificate authorities are Verisign and Thawte, with OpenSRS a smaller but notable competitor. Verisign certificates can be applied for online at http://www.verisign.com/products/site/index.html. Information and forms for requesting a certificate from Thawte can be found at http://www.thawte.com/certs/server/. Thawte also has Help pages for setting up SSL keys and certificates, including Apache-SSL and Apache+`mod_ssl`, at http://www.thawte.com/certs/server/keygen/.

Of the two, Thawte is significantly cheaper, despite that fact that it is now a wholly owned subsidiary of Verisign. Thawte also gets extra credit for supporting Apache early on (at one point they were the only source of certificates, since at that time Verisign was refusing to grant certificates for Apache servers), as well as having support pages dedicated to it. Thawte has continued to be a valuable supporter of Apache, even after Verisign acquired them.

Several other companies have grown to fill the CA space. Notably, OpenSRS has moved to make digital certificates more accessible by re-selling Entrust Certificates at wholesale prices to their sales agents. An OpenSRS certificate with strong encryption can be purchased for around 1/3rd the cost of a Verisign or Thawte certificate.

The key part of the online application process is sending the CSR, in this case www.alpha-complex.com.csr/, to the authority. It is important to send the right file – do not send the temporary certificate (extension `.crt`) and especially not the private key file. In general, the CSR is pasted into an HTML form as a complete file. Note that all parts of the file are required, and it must be sent as-is with no additions or missing characters.

Whichever the CA we choose, it will generally require the following information from us to prove our identity (a not-unreasonable requirement given that we are asking them to verify to other people that we are who we say we are):

- Proof of ownership of the organization name specified in the CSR. For companies this is usually a fax of the company registration certificate.
- Proof of the organization's ownership of the domain name specified in the CSR. For most web sites, a hard copy of the domain registration information retrieved from the WHOIS database.
- Proof that the person requesting the certificate is actually authorized to do so.

The exact requirements vary from company to company; consult the appropriate web site for more information. It is important to consider that the choice of CA can have an effect on how much a site is trusted and by whom. It is very easy for a site administrator to act as their own Certificate Authority, as mentioned above, but there is no external validation of that site's identity. This is probably fine if the site is only providing services to a small, known community that can externally verify the server and administrators' identity. If a site is providing e-commerce services, accepting personal information, or performing financial transactions, then external validation by using a commercial, well-known third-party CA provides the site with a credible outside check about the server's identity.

Several browsers come with a list of Certificate Authorities that they already know about and have some public keys for. For applications where the client does not know the server and needs to trust them, such as an e-commerce application, having a digital certificate signed by an already-known CA will make it easier for the client to verify the server's identity.

Summary

SSL can be used to carry out secure communications across the network. SSL uses the concept of public key cryptography, where the server gives the client a public key to encrypt information, but only the server can unencrypt the data using its private key. In addition, the client can request a certificate from the server to confirm that the server is actually who it says it is, and that it can be trusted.

It is important not to confuse authentication with SSL, and just because a connection is secure, it doesn't mean that the application on the other end is who it says it is. A server can only be insecure or secure, there is no in-between.

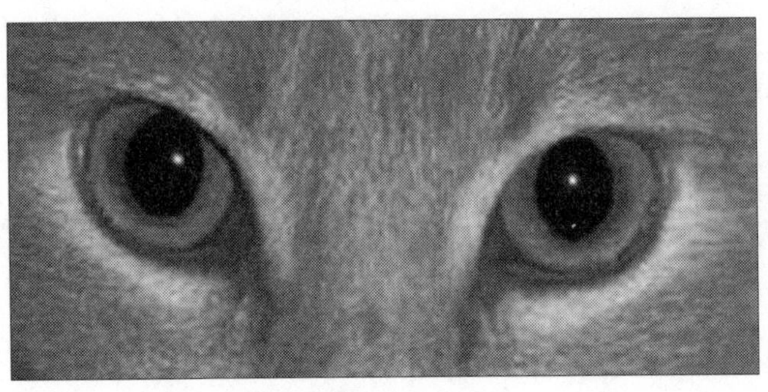

Index

A Guide to the Index

The index is arranged alphabetically in word-by-word order (so that, for example, New York would precede Newark). An unmodified page reference usually indicates general treatments of topics; sub-headings refer to particular aspects. An asterisk (*) indicates variant endings and (where used in the text) acronyms of three or more letters have been preferred to their expansions as main entries, on the grounds that they are easier to recall.

Symbols

A

B

C

D

E

I

K

L

M

N

O

P

R

S

T

U

V

W

X

Z

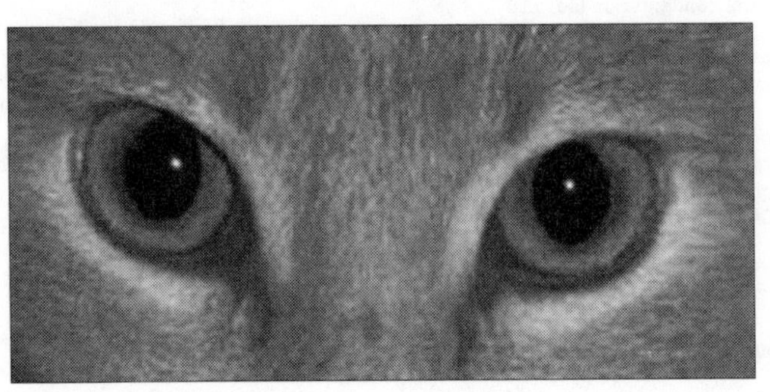

Registration Code : 77365U7E1K7F2SG02

Wrox writes books for you. Any suggestions, or ideas about how you want information given in your ideal book will be studied by our team. Your comments are always valued at Wrox.

Free phone in USA 800-USE-WROX
Fax (312) 893 8001

UK Tel.: (0121) 687 4100 Fax: (0121) 687 4101

Professional Apache Tomcat– Registration Card

Name ____________________
Address ____________________
____
____
____
City __________ State/Region __________
Country __________ Postcode/Zip __________
E-Mail ____________________
Occupation ____________________
How did you hear about this book?
❒ Book review (name) ____________
❒ Advertisement (name) ____________
❒ Recommendation ____________
❒ Catalog ____________
❒ Other ____________
Where did you buy this book?
❒ Bookstore (name) __________ City __________
❒ Computer store (name) ____________
❒ Mail order ____________
❒ Other ____________

What influenced you in the purchase of this book?
❒ Cover Design ❒ Contents ❒ Other (please specify):
____
How did you rate the overall content of this book?
❒ Excellent ❒ Good ❒ Average ❒ Poor
What did you find most useful about this book? ____________
____
____
What did you find least useful about this book? ____________
____
____
Please add any additional comments. ____________
____
____
What other subjects will you buy a computer book on soon?
____
What is the best computer book you have used this year?
____

Note: This information will only be used to keep you updated about new Wrox Press titles and will not be used for any other purpose or passed to any other third party.

Note: If you post the bounce back card below in the UK, please send it to:

Wrox Press Limited, Arden House, 1102 Warwick Road,
Acocks Green, Birmingham B27 6HB. UK.

Computer Book Publishers

NO POSTAGE
NECESSARY
IF MAILED
IN THE
UNITED STATES

BUSINESS REPLY MAIL

FIRST CLASS MAIL PERMIT#64 CHICAGO, IL

POSTAGE WILL BE PAID BY ADDRESSEE

WROX PRESS INC.
29 S. LA SALLE ST.
SUITE 520
CHICAGO IL 60603-USA